Running Money

Professional Portfolio Management

The McGraw-Hill/Irwin Series in Finance, Insurance, and Real Estate

Stephen A. Ross
Franco Modigliani Professor of Finance
and Economics
Sloan School of Management
Massachusetts Institute of Technology
Consulting Editor

FINANCIAL MANAGEMENT

Adair
Excel Applications for Corporate Finance
First Edition

Block, Hirt, and Danielsen
Foundations of Financial Management
Thirteenth Edition

Brealey, Myers, and Allen
Principles of Corporate Finance
Tenth Edition

Brealey, Myers, and Allen
Principles of Corporate Finance, Concise
Second Edition

Brealey, Myers, and Marcus
Fundamentals of Corporate Finance
Sixth Edition

Brooks
FinGame Online 5.0

Bruner
Case Studies in Finance: Managing for Corporate Value Creation
Sixth Edition

Chew
The New Corporate Finance: Where Theory Meets Practice
Third Edition

Cornett, Adair, and Nofsinger
Finance: Applications and Theory
First Edition

DeMello
Cases in Finance
Second Edition

Grinblatt (editor)
Stephen A. Ross, Mentor: Influence through Generations

Grinblatt and Titman
Financial Markets and Corporate Strategy
Second Edition

Higgins
Analysis for Financial Management
Ninth Edition

Kellison
Theory of Interest
Third Edition

Kester, Ruback, and Tufano
Case Problems in Finance
Twelfth Edition

Ross, Westerfield, and Jaffe
Corporate Finance
Ninth Edition

Ross, Westerfield, Jaffe, and Jordan
Corporate Finance: Core Principles and Applications
Second Edition

Ross, Westerfield, and Jordan
Essentials of Corporate Finance
Seventh Edition

Ross, Westerfield, and Jordan
Fundamentals of Corporate Finance
Ninth Edition

Shefrin
Behavioral Corporate Finance: Decisions That Create Value
First Edition

White
Financial Analysis with an Electronic Calculator
Sixth Edition

INVESTMENTS

Bodie, Kane, and Marcus
Essentials of Investments
Eighth Edition

Bodie, Kane, and Marcus
Investments
Eighth Edition

Hirschey and Nofsinger
Investments: Analysis and Behavior
Second Edition

Hirt and Block
Fundamentals of Investment Management
Ninth Edition

Jordan and Miller
Fundamentals of Investments: Valuation and Management
Fifth Edition

Stewart, Piros, and Heisler
Running Money: Professional Portfolio Management
First Edition

Sundaram and Das
Derivatives: Principles and Practice
First Edition

FINANCIAL INSTITUTIONS AND MARKETS

Rose and Hudgins
Bank Management and Financial Services
Eighth Edition

Rose and Marquis
Money and Capital Markets: Financial Institutions and Instruments in a Global Marketplace
Tenth Edition

Saunders and Cornett
Financial Institutions Management: A Risk Management Approach
Seventh Edition

Saunders and Cornett
Financial Markets and Institutions
Fourth Edition

INTERNATIONAL FINANCE

Eun and Resnick
International Financial Management
Fifth Edition

Kuemmerle
Case Studies in International Entrepreneurship: Managing and Financing Ventures in the Global Economy
First Edition

Robin
International Corporate Finance
First Edition

REAL ESTATE

Brueggeman and Fisher
Real Estate Finance and Investments
Fourteenth Edition

Ling and Archer
Real Estate Principles: A Value Approach
Third Edition

FINANCIAL PLANNING AND INSURANCE

Allen, Melone, Rosenbloom, and Mahoney
Retirement Plans: 401(k)s, IRAs, and Other Deferred Compensation Approaches
Tenth Edition

Altfest
Personal Financial Planning
First Edition

Harrington and Niehaus
Risk Management and Insurance
Second Edition

Kapoor, Dlabay, and Hughes
Focus on Personal Finance: An Active Approach to Help You Develop Successful Financial Skills
Third Edition

Kapoor, Dlabay, and Hughes
Personal Finance
Ninth Edition

Running Money

Professional Portfolio Management

Scott D. Stewart, PhD, CFA
Boston University

Christopher D. Piros, PhD, CFA
*Boston University
and Reykjavik University*

Jeffrey C. Heisler, PhD, CFA
Venus Capital Management, Inc.

The McGraw·Hill Companies

McGraw-Hill
Irwin

RUNNING MONEY: PROFESSIONAL PORTFOLIO MANAGEMENT
Published by McGraw-Hill/Irwin, a business unit of The McGraw-Hill Companies, Inc., 1221 Avenue of
the Americas, New York, NY, 10020. Copyright © 2011 by The McGraw-Hill Companies, Inc. All rights
reserved. No part of this publication may be reproduced or distributed in any form or by any means, or
stored in a database or retrieval system, without the prior written consent of The McGraw-Hill Companies,
Inc., including, but not limited to, in any network or other electronic storage or transmission, or broadcast
for distance learning.

Some ancillaries, including electronic and print components, may not be available to customers outside the
United States.

This book is printed on acid-free paper.

1 2 3 4 5 6 7 8 9 0 DOW/DOW 1 0 9 8 7 6 5 4 3 2 1 0

ISBN 978-0-07-353058-1
MHID 0-07-353058-1

Vice president and editor-in-chief: *Brent Gordon*
Publisher: *Douglas Reiner*
Executive editor: *Michele Janicek*
Director of development: *Ann Torbert*
Editorial coordinator: *Katherine Mau*
Vice president and director of marketing: *Robin J. Zwettler*
Marketing director: *Rhonda Seelinger*
Associate marketing manager: *Dean Karampelas*
Vice president of editing, design and production: *Sesha Bolisetty*
Senior project manager: *Susanne Riedell*
Senior production supervisor: *Kara Kudronowicz*
Design coordinator: *Joanne Mennemeier*
Media project manager: *Suresh Babu, Hurix Systems Pvt. Ltd.*
Cover image: *Ryan McVay/Getty Images*
Cover design: *Joanne Mennemeier*
Typeface: *10.5/12 Times New Roman*
Compositor: *Laserwords Private Limited*
Printer: *R. R. Donnelley*

Library of Congress Cataloging-in-Publication Data

Stewart, Scott Dudley, 1958-
    Running money: professional portfolio management/Scott Stewart, Christopher Piros,
    Jeffrey Heisler.—1st ed.
        p. cm. —(The McGraw-Hill/Irwin series in finance, insurance, and real estate)
    Includes index.
    ISBN-13: 978-0-07-353058-1 (alk. paper)
    ISBN-10: 0-07-353058-1 (alk. paper)
     1. Portfolio management. 2. Investments. I. Piros, Christopher Dixon. II. Heisler, Jeffrey,
    1959- III. Title.
    HG4529.5.S72 2011
    332.6—dc22   2009048233

To my wife, Pam, and our children John, Chris, Kate, and Anne.

—SDS

To my wife, Chris, and our sons Matt, Drew, and Daniel.

—CDP

To Kaisa and our boys Charles, Philip, Thomas, and Peter.

—JCH

About the Authors

Scott Stewart   *Boston University*

Scott Stewart is a research associate professor in the Finance and Economics Department at Boston University School of Management, and the faculty director of the Master of Science in Investment Management (MSIM) program. Dr. Stewart joined Boston University following a career in portfolio management running global equity, fixed-income, and asset allocation money, including 14 years at Fidelity Investments, where he was founder and equity group leader of the $45 billion Structured Investments Group. He managed the Fidelity Fifty® Fund, Fidelity Select Equity™ Portfolios, Fidelity Funds America, and the Perpetual America Fund and co-managed the Fidelity Freedom Funds®, earning recognition for superior investment performance from Micropal, *the Financial Review, The Wall Street Journal* and *Barron's*. He was also a senior advisor to equity research at Fidelity and earlier a portfolio manager at State Street Bank Asset Management Division (now State Street Global Advisors). His research interests include portfolio management techniques, the behavior of institutional investors, equity valuation, and the use of technology in investment management. He speaks at both academic and practitioner conferences and has published articles in *The Financial Analysts Journal, Journal of Portfolio Management,* and *The Financial Review.* Dr. Stewart actively manages money, consults, and teaches courses in investment research and portfolio management. He earned his MBA and PhD in finance at Cornell University and is a CFA charterholder.

Christopher Piros   *Boston University and Reykjavik University*

Christopher Piros is an independent investment professional with over twenty years of experience conducting research, developing strategy, and managing portfolios. As Director of Investment Strategy and Portfolio Management at Prudential Investments LLC he established and led PI's discretionary portfolio management activities from launch to over $15 billion. He and his team also formulated the investment strategy advice disseminated through the firm's wealth management platform. Earlier he was a senior vice president and global fixed-income portfolio manager at MFS Investment Management. Before assuming portfolio management responsibilities, he established and headed the firm's fixed-income quantitative analysis group. Prior to MFS he developed valuation and derivatives intensive strategies at Drexel Burnham Lambert's Quantitative Asset Management Group and was on the finance faculty of Duke University's Fuqua School of Business. He teaches in the MSIM programs at both Boston University and Reykjavik University and is on the advisory board of the program at BU. His research has been published in the *Journal of Finance.* Dr. Piros earned his PhD in Economics at Harvard University and is a CFA charterholder.

Jeffrey Heisler   *Venus Capital Management, Inc.*

Jeffrey Heisler is the chief risk officer and the chief compliance officer at Venus Capital Management, an investment advisor that specializes in relative value trading strategies in emerging markets. Previously he was a senior analyst for Gottex Fund Management, a leading fund of funds manager with AUM over $8 billion. Dr. Heisler was an assistant professor in the Finance and Economics Department at Boston University School of Management, and the founding faculty director of the Master of Science in Investment Management (MSIM) program. He remains active in the MSIM program as a member of the advisory board and an occasional teacher at both Boston University and Reykjavik University. His research on the behavior of individual and institutional investors has been published in both academic and practitioner journals. He earned his MBA at the University of Chicago and his PhD in finance at New York University. He is also a CFA charterholder.

Preface

The investment landscape is ever-changing. Today's innovative solution will be taken for granted tomorrow. In writing *Running Money: Professional Portfolio Management,* our goal was to expose students to what it is really like to run money professionally by providing the *tools*.

Broadly speaking, this book focuses on the business of investment decision making from the perspective of the portfolio manager—that is, from the perspective of the person responsible for delivering investment performance. It reflects our combined professional experience managing multibillion-dollar mandates within and across the major global and domestic asset classes, working with real clients, and solving real investment problems; it also reflects our experience teaching students. Before writing this text, we taught the Portfolio Management Course in the Master of Science in Investment Management (MSIM) programs at Boston University and Reykjavik University in Iceland. The MSIM curriculum encompasses and extends the CFA Body of Knowledge™ required of candidates for the CFA® designation. This text grew from these courses and was refined as we used early versions of the manuscript in class. Two draft chapters of this book have also been included in the CFA Institute's continuing education program for charterholders since 2007.

This book aims to build on earlier investment coursework with minimal repetition of standard results. Ideally the student should already have taken a broad investments course that introduces the analysis of equity, fixed income, and derivative securities. The material typically covered in these courses is reviewed only briefly here as needed. In contrast, new and more advanced tools are accorded thorough introduction and development. Prior experience with Microsoft Excel spreadsheets and functions will be helpful because various examples and exercises throughout the book use these tools. Familiarity with introductory quantitative methods is recommended as well.

We believe this book is most effectively used in conjunction with cases, projects, and real-time portfolios requiring hands-on application of the material. Indeed this is how we teach our courses, and the book was written with this format in mind. This approach is facilitated by customizable Excel spreadsheets that allow students to apply the basic tools immediately and then tailor them to the demands of specific problems.

It is certainly possible to cover all 16 chapters in a single-semester lecture course. In a course with substantial time devoted to cases or projects, however, the instructor may find it advantageous to cover the material more selectively. We feel strongly that Chapters 1, 2, and 14 should be included in every course—Chapters 1 and 2 because they set the stage for subsequent topics, and Chapter 14 because ethical standards are an increasingly important issue in the investment business. In addition to these three chapters, the instructor might consider creating courses around the following modules:

- The investment business: Chapters 3, 6, 13, and 16
  - These chapters provide a high-level perspective on the major components of the investment business: clients, asset allocation, the investment process, and performance. They are essential for those who need to understand the investment business but who will not be involved in day-to-day investment decision making.
- Managing client relationships: Chapters 13, 15, and 16
  - These chapters focus on clients: their needs, their expectations, their behavior, how they evaluate performance, and how to manage your relationships with them. Virtually

everyone involved in professional portfolio management needs to understand this material, but it is especially important for those who will interact directly with clients.

- Asset allocation: Chapters 3–5, 11, and 12
  - Asset allocation is a fundamental component of virtually every client's investment problem. Indeed widely cited studies indicate that it accounts for more than 90 percent of long-term performance. Chapters 3–5 start with careful development of basic asset allocation tools and progress to advanced topics including estimation of inputs, modeling horizon effects, simulation, portable alpha, and portfolio insurance. Chapter 11 brings in alternative asset classes. Chapter 12 addresses rebalancing and the impact of transaction costs and taxes. These chapters are essential for anyone whose responsibility encompasses portfolios intended to address clients' broad investment objectives.
- Security and asset class portfolio management: Chapters 6–12
  - Starting with an overview of the investment process (Chapter 6), these chapters focus on the job of managing a portfolio of securities within particular asset classes: equities (Chapters 7 and 8), fixed income (Chapter 9), international (Chapter 10), and alternatives (Chapters 11). Chapter 12 addresses rebalancing and the impact of transaction costs and taxes.

Of course these themes are not mutually exclusive. We encourage the instructor to review all the material and select the chapters and sections most pertinent to the course objectives.

Running Money: Professional Portfolio Management includes several features designed to reinforce understanding, connect the material to real-world situations, and enable students to apply the tools presented:

- **Excel spreadsheets:** Customizable Excel spreadsheets are available online. These spreadsheets allow students to apply the tools immediately. Students can use them as they are presented or tailor them to specific applications.
- **Excel outboxes:** Text boxes provide step-by-step instructions enabling students to build many of the Excel spreadsheets from scratch. Building the models themselves helps to ensure that the students really understand how they work.
- **War Story boxes:** Text boxes describe how an investment strategy or product worked— or did not work—in a real situation.
- **Theory in Practice boxes:** Text boxes link concepts to specific real-world examples, applications, or situations.
- **End-of-chapter problems:** End-of-chapter problems are designed to check and to reinforce understanding of key concepts. Some of these problems guide students through solving the cases. Others instruct students to expand the spreadsheets introduced in the Excel outboxes.
- **Real investment cases:** The appendix provides four canonical cases based on real situations involving a high net worth individual, a defined benefit pension plan, a defined contribution pension plan, and a small-cap equity fund. The cases are broken into four steps that can be completed as students proceed through the text. The material required to complete the first step, understanding the investor's needs and establishing the investment policy statement, is presented in Chapters 1 and 2. Step 2, determining the asset allocation, draws on Chapters 3–5. Step 3, implementing the investment strategy, draws on the material in Chapters 6–13. The final step, measuring success, brings together the issues pertaining to performance, ethics, and client relationships addressed in Chapters 13–16.

This book was conceived to share our investment management and university teaching experience. Writing it has been a lot like being a portfolio manager: always challenging, sometimes frustrating, but ultimately rewarding. We hope the book challenges you and whets your appetite for running money.

Supplements

The Online Learning Center (OLC) Web site, www.mhhe.com/sph1e, contains the Excel spreadsheets and additional supplementary content specific to this text. Sample exams, solutions, and PowerPoint presentations are available to the instructor in the password-protected instructor's center. As students read the text, they can go online to the student center to download the Excel spreadsheets, check answers to the end-of-chapter problems, and review the supplemental case material.

- **Case spreadsheets:** Excel spreadsheets give students additional material for analysis of the cases.
- **Solutions to end-of-chapter problems:** Detailed solutions to the end-of-chapter problems help students confirm their understanding.
- **Sample final exams:** Prepared by the authors, the sample exams offer multiple-choice and essay questions to fit any instructor's testing needs.
- **Solutions to sample final exams:** The authors offer detailed suggested solutions for the exams.
- **PowerPoint presentation:** Prepared by the authors, the PowerPoint presentation offers full-color slides for all 16 chapters to use in a classroom lecture setting. Organized to accompany each chapter, the slides include images, tables, and key points from the text.

Acknowledgments

This book would not have been possible without the academic training provided to us by many dedicated teachers. We'd especially like to thank our doctoral thesis advisors Stephen Figlewski, Benjamin Friedman, and Seymour Smidt for their gifts of time, encouragement, and thoughtful advice. We'd also like to recognize several professors who challenged and guided us in our academic careers: Fischer Black, David Connors, Nicholas Economides, Edwin Elton, Robert Jarrow, Jarl Kallberg, John Lintner, Terry Marsh, Robert Merton, William Silber, and L. Joseph Thomas.

The practical experience we received in the investment industry helped us make this book unique. We thank all our colleagues at Fidelity, Gottex, MFS, Prudential, State Street, and Venus for their support and good ideas over the years. Space does not permit listing all the individuals with whom we have shared the pursuit of superior investment performance for our clients. We would be remiss, however, if we did not acknowledge Steve Bryant, Ed Campbell, Ren Cheng, Jennifer Godfrey, Richard Hawkins, Timothy Heffernan, Cesar Hernandez, Dick Kazarian, Richard Leibovitch, Liliana Lopez, Robert Macdonald, Kevin Maloney, Vik Mehrotra, Les Nanberg, William Nemerever, Marcus Perl, Dan Scherman, Robin Stelmach, and Myra Wonisch Tucker.

We also want to thank those who helped with specific sections of the text, including providing data and suggestions to improve chapters, cases, and examples. These include Scott Bobek, Richard Hawkins, Ed Heilbron, Dick Kazarian, John O'Reilly, Marcus Perl, Jacques Perold, Bruce Phelps, Jonathan Shelon, and George Walper, as well as the MSIM students at Boston University and Reykjavik University who used drafts of this text.

Michele Janicek, Executive editor, and Katherine Mau, Editorial coordinator, provided invaluable guidance and encouragement throughout the project. We also wish to thank all of the other McGraw-Hill staff members who worked on the book.

We are grateful to the following individuals for their thoughtful reviews and suggestions for this text:

Honghui Chen
University of Central Florida

Ji Chen
University of Colorado-Denver

Douglas Kahl
The University of Akron

David Louton
Bryant University

Mbodja Mougoue
Wayne State University

Zhuoming Peng
Western Oregon University

Craig G. Rennie
University of Arkansas

Alex P. Tang
Morgan State University

Damir Tokic
University of Houston-Downtown

Barbara Wood
Texas Christian University

Finally, a special thank you to our families and friends for their support and patience during the long journey of writing this book; it would not have been possible without them.

Brief Contents

Table of Contents

Brief Contents

Table of Contents

Chapter 16
Managing Client Relations   499

Chapter 1

Introduction

1.1 Introduction

The investment business is an exciting industry for a career. The stakes are high and the competition is keen. Investment firms are paid management fees to invest other people's money, and their clients expect expert care and superior performance. Managing other people's money is a serious endeavor. Individuals entrust their life savings and their dreams for attractive homes, their children's educations, and comfortable retirements. Foundations and endowments hand over responsibility for the assets that support their missions. Corporations delegate management of the funds that will pay future pension benefits for their employees. Successful managers and their clients enjoy substantial financial rewards, but sustained poor performance can undermine client well-being and leave a manager searching for a new career.

Many bright and hardworking people are attracted to this challenging industry. Because their competitors work so hard, portfolio managers must always be at their best and continue to improve their skills and knowledge base. For most portfolio managers, investing is a highly stimulating vocation, requiring constant learning and self-improvement. Clients are demanding, especially when results are disappointing. Although this is considered a stressful job by many people, some professionals continue to manage money into their 80s or 90s.[1]

Portfolio management is becoming more sophisticated due to the ongoing advancement of theory and the growing complexity of practice, led by several trends:

- Advances in modern portfolio theory.
- More complex instruments.
- Increased demands for performance.

---

[1] Consider Charlie Munger, born in 1924, who is six years older than his investing partner, Warren Buffett.

EXHIBIT 1.1
Mutual Fund (including ETFs and UITs)* and Institutional Assets in the United States, in $ Billions.

Source: Investment Company Institute (ICI) and Plan Sponsor Network (PSN).

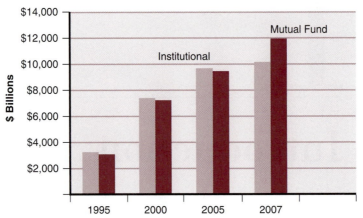

*Exchange Traded Funds (ETFs) and Unit Investment Trusts (UITs).

- Increased client sophistication.
- Rising retirement costs, and the growing trend toward individual responsibility for those costs.
- Dramatic growth in assets under management.

These trends parallel the growing use of mathematics in economics, the improvements in investment education of many savers, and the increasing competitiveness of the industry. Assets controlled by individual investors have grown rapidly. In 2005 half of all U.S. households owned stock. Of those who held stocks, 90 percent owned stock mutual funds while nearly 50 percent owned individual stocks. By 2007 the mutual fund industry had expanded to $12.0 trillion under management from $2.8 trillion in 1995; it managed over 8,700 funds and employed over 165,000 Americans.[2] The size of the institutional money management business has also grown. Exhibit 1.1 shows that pension plan, foundation, and endowment assets grew threefold between 1995 and 2007 to over $10 trillion.

Portfolio management is based on three key variables: the objective for the investment plan, the initial principal of the investment, and the cumulative total return on that principal. The investment plan, or strategy, is tailored to provide a pattern of expected returns consistent with meeting investment objectives within acceptable levels of risk. This investment strategy should be formed by first evaluating client requirements, including willingness and ability to take risk, cash flow needs, and any constraints, such as legal restrictions. Given the cash flow needs and acceptable expected risk and return outcomes, the allocation between broad asset classes is set in coordination with funding and spending policies. After investment vehicles are selected and the plan is implemented, performance should be analyzed to determine the strategy's success. Ongoing review and adjustment of the portfolio are required to ensure that it continues to meet client objectives.

This book presents effective portfolio management *practice,* not simply portfolio *theory.* The goal is to provide a primer for people who wish to run money professionally. The book includes the information a serious portfolio manager would learn over a 20-year career—grounded in academic rigor yet reflecting real business practice and presented in an efficient format. Importantly, this book presents tools to help manage a portfolio into the future; that is what a portfolio manager is paid to do. Although the book discusses the value of historical data, it guides the reader to think more about the

[2] Investment Company Institute Factbooks, 2002–2008.

2008 was a terrible year for the markets. The S&P 500 fell nearly 40 percent, high-yield bonds declined over 25 percent, and in December Bernie Madoff admitted to what he claimed was a $50 billion Ponzi scheme. Although these numbers are shocking, they are not unprecedented, and the reasons behind them are not new. Security values can change drastically, sometimes with surprising speed. Declining values can be a response to peaking long-term market cycles, short-term economic shocks, or the idiosyncratic risk of an individual security.

Market cycles can take months or years to develop and resolve. The dot-com bubble lasted from 1995 to 2001. The March 2000 peak was followed by a 65+ percent multiyear decline in the NASDAQ index as once lofty earnings growth forecasts failed to materialize. The S&P 500 dropped over 40 percent in 1973 and 1974 as the economy entered a period of stagflation following the boom of the 1960s and the shock of the OPEC oil embargo. Black Monday, October 19, 1987, saw global equity markets fall over 20 percent in a single day. The collapse of Enron destroyed more than $2 billion in employee retirement assets and more than $60 billion in equity market value. We are still calculating the dollar impact of the subprime mortgage crisis.

Each of these examples had a different cause and a different time horizon, but in each case the potential portfolio losses were significant. To assist investors, this book outlines the basic—and not so basic—principles of sound portfolio management. These techniques should prepare the investor to weather future market swings. The broad themes include

- Creating and following an investment plan to help maintain discipline. Investors often appear driven by fear and greed. The aim should be to avoid panicking when markets sell off suddenly (1974, 1987) and missing the potential recovery, or overallocating to hot sectors (the dot-com bubble) or stocks (Enron), and being hurt when the market reverts.
- Focusing on total return and not yield or cost.
- Establishing and following proper risk management discipline. Diversification and rebalancing of positions help avoid outsized exposure to particular systematic or idiosyncratic risks. Performance measurement and attribution provide insight into the risks and the sources of return for an investment strategy.
- Not investing in what you do not understand. In addition to surprisingly good performance that could not be explained, there were additional red flags, such as lack of transparency, in the Enron and Madoff cases.
- Behaving ethically and insisting that others do too.

Although attractive or even positive returns cannot be guaranteed, following the principles of sound portfolio management can improve the likelihood of achieving the investor's long-range goals.

implications for the future. Simply studying historical records and relationships is a sure way to disappoint clients.

This is not a cookbook or a collection of unrelated essays; the chapters tell a unified story. This book presents techniques that the reader may use to address real situations, not merely simplified, stylized problems, such as the simple case presented in the following Theory in Practice box. A working knowledge of investments, including derivatives, securities analysis, and fixed income, is assumed, as well as basic proficiency in Excel. Where necessary, the book presents careful development of new tools that typically are not covered in an MBA curriculum.

Jean is retired and single, with approximately $700,000 in assets. Jean earns a small amount of income from a part-time job, receives Social Security payments, and collects income from investments. Jean owns a home and has a modest lifestyle. Jean needs to decide how to invest her assets and set a realistic spending policy. What information is needed to advise Jean effectively? What needs to be done to determine the best course of action for Jean's assets?

The following exhibit lists key data to help answer these questions and frame the problem:

Assets	
Total equities	$ 415,000
Total bonds	125,000
Home	130,000
Income	
Assets	12,000
Other	11,000
Expenses	26,500

What would be the next steps in exploring the situation? What additional information about Jean and the financial situation would be nice to know?

1.2   What Is a Portfolio Manager?

Investment management firms employ many investment professionals. They include a CEO to manage the business, portfolio managers supported by research analysts, salespeople to attract and retain clients, and a chief investment officer to supervise the portfolio managers. Many more people work behind the scenes, such as risk officers and accounting professionals, to make sure the money is safe. A portfolio manager may be defined by three characteristics:

1. Responsible for delivering investment performance.
2. Full authority to make at least some investment decisions.
3. Accountable for investment results.

Investment decisions involve setting weights of asset classes, individual securities, or both to yield desired future investment performance. *Full authority* means control over these decisions. For example, portfolio managers do not need the approval of a committee or superior before directing allocation changes. In fact, on more than one occasion portfolio managers have resigned after their full discretion was restricted. A chief investment officer has authority not over security selection but over the portfolio manager's employment, making the chief investment officer a portfolio manager for the purposes of this book. A fund-of-funds manager retains control over the weights of the underlying fund managers and therefore is a portfolio manager. The typical mutual fund manager who issues orders for individual equity, fixed income, or derivative securities is the most visible form of portfolio manager.

A portfolio manager is held *accountable* for his or her performance whether or not it meets expectations. Portfolio managers typically have benchmarks, in the form of a market index or group of peers, and their performance results are compared with these benchmarks for client relationship, compensation, and career advancement purposes. Portfolio managers do not necessarily follow an active investment process. Managers of passive portfolios are portfolio managers because they are responsible and held accountable to their clients and firm for their portfolio returns. If performance does not meet client expectations, at some point the portfolio manager will be terminated. But if results exceed expectations, clients may increase the level of their commitment, thereby generating higher management fees for the portfolio manager's firm. Portfolio managers are accountable to their firm, which is seeking to maintain and expand revenues, and they receive bonuses (or perhaps pink slips) depending on performance.[3]

Analysts may be held accountable for their recommendations, in some cases with precise performance calculations. However, they do not set security weights in a portfolio and are not ultimately responsible for live performance. Portfolio managers may use analysts' recommendations in decision making, but the ultimate security selection is under their control. Although analysts are not portfolio managers based on the definition here, they can obviously benefit from understanding the job of the portfolio manager.

Risk officers are responsible for identifying, measuring, analyzing, and monitoring portfolio and firm risks. While they may have discretion to execute trades to bring portfolios into compliance, they are not portfolio managers. They do not bear the same responsibility and accountability for performance. In fact, it is recommended that portfolio management and risk functions be separated to avoid potential conflicts of interest.

1.3   What Investment Problems Do Portfolio Managers Solve?

Asset Allocation and Asset Class Portfolio Responsibilities

The job of a portfolio manager is to help clients meet their wealth accumulation and spending needs. Many clients expect to preserve the real value of their original principal and spend only the real return. Some have well-defined cash inflows and outflows. Virtually all clients want their portfolio managers to maximize the value of their savings and protect them from falling short of their needs.

The **asset allocation problem** requires portfolio managers to select the weights of asset classes, such as equities, bonds, and cash, through time to meet their clients' monetary needs. Asset allocation determines a large portion of the level and pattern of investment performance. The remainder is determined by the individual asset class vehicle(s) and their underlying holdings. The goals of asset allocation are to manage variability, provide for cash flow needs, and generate asset growth—in other words, risk and return, either absolute or relative to a target or benchmark. The client is diversified in most situations by holding investments in several reasonably uncorrelated assets. Derivative instruments may help with this process. Asset allocation may also be a source of excess performance, with the portfolio manager actively adjusting weights to take advantage of perceived market under- and overvaluation.

Many portfolio managers do not make asset allocation decisions. Instead, they are hired to run a pool of money in a single asset class, or style within an asset class. They may have a narrowly defined benchmark and limited latitude to select securities outside a prespecified universe—such as a small-cap value manager or a distressed high-yield bond manager. In most cases the strategy or style is independent of the client—the portfolio manager follows his or her investment process regardless of the client's broader wealth and spending needs. In fewer cases the portfolio is customized to the client's needs. For example, immunized fixed income portfolios involve

[3] Some investors feel someone is not a true investment professional until he or she has been fired by at least one client and therefore understands the seriousness and challenge of this responsibility.

customized duration matching. Equity completeness funds are customized to provide dynamic, specialized sector and style characteristics.

Representative Investment Problems

Client relationships are typically defined by formal documents with stated investment objectives that include return goals, income needs, and risk parameters. Objectives and related guidelines are determined by client type, individual situation, and preferences.

More and more individual investors are seeking the support of professional portfolio managers. Retail mutual funds began growing rapidly in the bull market of the 1980s. There are now more mutual funds than stocks on the New York Stock Exchange, and hundreds of exchange traded funds (ETFs), all directed by portfolio managers. In most cases these managers are charged with individual asset class management; the number of traditional balanced mandates requiring management of asset class weights has grown less rapidly. Currently popular horizon-based funds, which have grown to exceed $200 billion, are made up of multiple asset classes whose weights change through time in a prespecified fashion. Such funds require two levels of allocation—one determining the asset class weights and the other the fund or security weights within the individual asset classes.

The high net worth business has grown rapidly, with the level of service tied to client asset levels. Clients with more than $5 million in assets typically receive face-to-face advice on asset allocation and manager selection that is supplemented by other money-related services. Smaller clients receive a lower level of service through questionnaires and phone conversations.

A defined benefit (DB) plan represents a pool of money set aside by a company, government institution, or union to pay workers a stipend in retirement determined by a prespecified, wage-based formula. A DB plan is characterized by a schedule of forecast future cash flows whose shape is determined by the sponsor's employee demographics. The present value of this stream of payments, or liability, varies with interest rates. A portfolio manager's goal is to set both asset allocation and funding policies to meet these cash flow needs at the lowest possible cost and lowest risk of falling short of the required outflows. Plans frequently hire a pension consultant to help them with in-house asset allocation, or in some cases they hire an external DB asset allocation manager. Recent legislation requires corporations to include in their financial statements the effect of changes in liability relative to changes in the market value of the assets held to offset it. This motivates the need to closely manage the relationship between the assets and the liability, and many companies are replacing their DB plans with alternative forms of employee retirement programs to avoid the inherent risk.

The most popular replacement vehicle is the defined contribution (401(k) or DC) plan. The DC plan is a hybrid program, combining a company sponsor with individual users of the program. Individual employees decide how much to save and how to invest, and the company supports this effort with contribution matching and advisory support services. Portfolio managers are hired by the company to provide diversified multi-asset investment options, individual asset class product management, and customized asset allocation advice and vehicle selection.

Portfolio managers are responsible for underlying asset class portfolios on a stand-alone basis and within multi-asset class products. Seldom are they the same as the asset allocators because portfolio management tends to improve with specialization; for example, high-yield bonds trade differently than investment-grade bonds, both of which trade differently than emerging market bonds. In most cases there are both active and passive managers in the same asset class, though less liquid markets generally have fewer index funds. Asset classes with higher potential risk-adjusted active return (alpha) and less liquidity command higher fees and portfolio manager compensation. In these portfolios the managers are responsible for setting security weights, but they must also seek out available securities and be conscious of the ability to sell their positions.

1.4   Spectrum of Portfolio Managers

Financial advisors provide individual and institutional clients with asset allocation recommendations, manager search capabilities, manager monitoring, and performance analysis. Registered investment advisors (RIA) cater to high net worth investors and may also provide tax guidance, insurance strategy, estate planning, and expense management services. In some cases sophisticated RIAs may be defined as *money therapists,* helping clients process their feelings about wealth, charitable giving, and handling money within their families. High-end advisors typically charge a basis point fee that declines with increasing asset levels. *Family offices* may provide services beyond strict money management, even providing travel agent functions.

Pension consultants recommend investments and managers for institutional investors. They tend to be more rigorous in their process than managers of high net worth assets—for example, studying liability dynamics when proposing asset allocation and funding policies for a DB plan. Although RIAs may have earned the Certified Financial Planner® designation, which includes topics in estate planning and tax policy, many pension consultants will have earned the Chartered Financial Analyst® charter, a longer and more rigorous professional program. Many pension consulting firms have one or more liability actuaries on staff as well. Pension consultants speak in terms of benchmarks and portfolio risk, whereas advisors to smaller individual investors may not even focus on total return. Although they are sophisticated, there is still a need to manage relations with pension clients. They may need to be educated about asset liability management, introduced to new asset classes, or supported in periods of unhealthy funding status. Pension plans, foundations, and endowments have been known to blame (that is, fire) their investment consultants when overall results are subpar.

Fund-of-funds managers take investment advice a step further, taking full discretion of the assets, placing the assets with individual securities managers, and in many cases charging performance fees for doing so. Funds-of-funds became popular in the new millennium by providing simultaneous exposure to a diversified mix of hedge funds.

Over the last 10+ years traditional brokerage firms, or *wire houses,* have transitioned from a commission-based to a fee-based business, providing basic asset allocation services and in-house mutual fund products. They walk a fine line, balancing their clients' investment objectives with their own need to sell their employers' products. *Wrap accounts,* popularized in the mid-1990s, are offered by brokerage houses and are defined by their individual securities or mutual fund holdings. They offer separate accounting and flat basis point fee structures, including trading commissions. *Trust banks,* or trust departments of banks, are a smaller part of the business today but continue to manage pools of assets passed down between generations within trust vehicles. As banks have grown through consolidation, their trust management has become more centralized and standardized.

The mutual fund industry grew rapidly during the post-1981 equity and later bond bull markets. Individual investors returned to equity funds in droves during that period

EXHIBIT 1.2
Profile of Portfolio Managers by Rigor and Level of Specialization

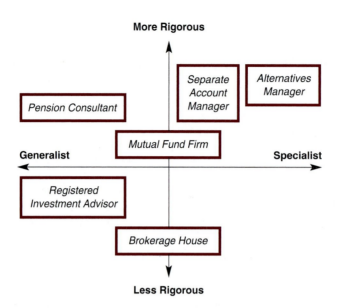

after withdrawing assets during the 1970s bear market. In the 1990s mutual fund firms sought to capture the growing DC market as companies began favoring 401(k) plans over traditional DB programs. Mutual fund companies competed with investment performance,[4] low-cost packages offering *record keeping* (asset collection, safekeeping, and reporting); cafeteria-style investment programs (individual mutual fund, balanced products, and brokerage); and by the late 1990s, full menus offering any investment option, including competitors' funds. Lifestyle and horizon-based products were introduced during that period, meeting the need for automatic diversification of the growing 401(k) balances. The percentage of U.S. households invested in mutual funds grew from less than 10 percent in 1980 to close to 45 percent by 2007. Over 45 million U.S. households currently own mutual funds in tax-deferred accounts.[5]

Separate account money managers tend to specialize in a few investment disciplines, though larger firms have diversified beyond their original disciplines or even asset classes. Their clients may be institutional investors, but smaller firms also have high net worth investors. Sometimes large firms specialize in an asset class attractive to individual investors, such as municipal bonds.[6] Institutional investors, frequently with the help of consultants, will select specialist managers to fill out their asset allocation profiles.

Alternative managers, including hedge funds and private equity funds, are perhaps more sophisticated than mutual funds and traditional separate account managers. They may manage short positions, trade derivatives, and use leverage. In addition, they have more control over client access to liquidity and can limit transparency. Alternative investment vehicles include commingled *limited partnerships* and separate accounts.

Portfolio managers may be categorized by investment process rigor and level of specialization, as shown in Exhibit 1.2.

---

[4] Interestingly, in the mid-1990s when Vanguard's passive fixed income performance and a competitor's active equity performance dominated the mutual fund business, Vanguard introduced the idea of offering a competitor's mutual funds, in this case equity funds, combined with its own bond funds in a single program. Before that event 401(k) plans tended to include only one management firm.

[5] Investment Company Institute, "Trends in Ownership of Mutual Funds in the United States, 2007."

[6] Appleton Partners, a $2 billion money manager, specializes in municipals for wealthy individuals as well as institutional investors.

1.5   Layout of This Book

Portfolio managers are charged with setting the weights of asset classes and individual securities. They need tools to help them balance the returns and risks of investing in these assets through time. In many cases, risk and return are measured relative to a benchmark; in others, absolute return is the objective. Some portfolio managers prefer to make decisions based on *fundamental* information while others prefer utilizing mathematical models. In the following chapters this book provides the basic tools for helping set investment weights for each of these scenarios. Several chapters use some mathematics to introduce the models; this approach is intended to help the reader develop the intuition needed to make effective decisions about asset and security selection. It also supports the development of the Excel-based tools designed to provide immediate, hands-on experience in applying key concepts.

Chapters 3–5 introduce and develop the tools for setting efficient asset allocations; Chapter 12 explains how to rebalance these weights through time. The techniques for setting weights of individual securities within an asset class are presented for equity and fixed income portfolios in Chapters 7–10. A discussion of alternative asset classes is the focus of Chapter 11. Chapter 6 reviews the key ingredients for any successful active or passive investment strategy involving asset allocation or security selection.

Portfolio managers must be aware of important incentives and responsibilities to meet their clients' needs. This book explains how the investment business works, including a review of business incentives that may motivate healthy or inappropriate behavior. This is the focus of Chapter 14.

The investment business would not exist without clients. Clients have money they want to grow. They have liquidity needs. They are willing to pay fees to portfolio managers who can help them meet these goals, but they will not hesitate to terminate a relationship if a manager fails to deliver. Success is often measured based on risk and return, but ultimately terminal wealth counts. Chapter 2 provides a detailed summary of investment objectives and guidelines for the majority of investors. Tools for analyzing investment results are presented in Chapter 13. To help portfolio managers understand how to land and keep their clients, Chapter 15 reviews investor and client behavior, and Chapter 16 discusses managing client relationships. Once you secure your first clients and begin running money professionally, you will want to do your best to keep them.

Problems

1. List the most popular names in the investment management business. What types of portfolio manager are they?
2. List one popular portfolio management firm for each type of portfolio manager shown in Exhibit 1.2.
3. Go online and find the top- and worst-performing mutual funds for the last 12 months. What approach do they follow for managing money?
4. List three common rules of thumb for investing for retirement. How valid do you think each one is?
5. Consider the Theory in Practice: A Simple Case box, and explore the following questions:
   a. Based on the limited information, does Jean appear to be a sophisticated investor?

b. How much risk (consider one definition) is Jean willing to assume financially and emotionally?

c. What is Jean's investment horizon?

d. How should your answers influence the recommended asset allocation and asset class selection?

e. Propose a mix of stocks, bonds, and cash for Jean. What's a reasonable spending policy? From where will the cash flow come?

Chapter  2

Client Objectives for Diversified Portfolios

Chapter Outline

2.1   Introduction

Portfolio management is about delivering investment performance that enhances clients' ability to achieve their underlying goals. Therefore, understanding clients and their situations is the first step in a successful investment process. What do the clients *need?* What do they *want?* What can they *tolerate?* And of course, what are their current financial situations?

This chapter focuses on understanding clients, assessing their circumstances, and translating that information into actionable blueprints for portfolios. These **investment policy statements (IPSs)** summarize the understanding between clients and their advisors. In a sense an IPS is like a contract: Everything that is expected of each party should be spelled out as clearly as possible in the IPS.

While investment returns are easily understood, investment risk means different things to different people. We therefore begin this chapter with a discussion of alternative notions of risk and some of the associated measures of risk. Section 2.3 outlines the steps of the portfolio management process and discusses details of the IPS. Section 2.4 focuses on institutional clients—specifically foundations, endowments, defined benefit (DB) pension plans, and defined contribution (DC) plans. Section 2.5 is devoted to managing money for individuals. A brief introduction to single asset class mandates is provided in Section 2.6 in preparation for the detailed discussion contained in Chapters 6 through 10.

2.2 Definitions of Risk

In basic terms, investing is about risk and return. Although various issues arise in the *ex post* measurement of return (see Chapter 13), there is little question about what we mean by *investment return*. In contrast, *risk* is much more difficult to define. But to paraphrase Justice Potter Stewart, we know it when we see it.[1]

Intuitively, risk refers to the possibility that a client's expectations and objectives might not be met. This general notion begs some important questions. What is the relevant horizon? Is it the likelihood of missing the objective or is it the potential magnitude of a shortfall? Perhaps it is some combination of likelihood and magnitude. How should we turn our concept of risk into a usable measure of risk? Is it appropriate to be concerned about interim results—that is, the path of wealth before the investment horizon is reached?

It should be clear that no simple, universal notion of risk is sufficient for all situations; risk can mean different things to different people at different times. Nonetheless, both effective communication with clients and management of investment strategies require one or more concrete, quantifiable notions of risk. Later chapters, especially Chapters 3, 5, and 13, explore the use of various risk measures in some detail. For present purposes, however, we need not worry about precise definitions and formulas.

Most notions of risk fall into one of two categories. The first is volatility. From this perspective, deviations—positive or negative—from the expected outcome constitute risk. As we will see in Chapter 3, volatility is generally associated with the statistical concept of standard deviation or, equivalently, variance. These measures have the advantage that there is an explicit and relatively simple relationship between the risks of individual assets and the risk of a portfolio of assets. Thus it is straightforward to incorporate volatility into the operational aspects of the portfolio management process: portfolio construction, monitoring, and evaluation.

However, most clients find it difficult to grasp the link between portfolio volatility and their ultimate goals because they do not view the possibility of achieving better-than-expected returns as risk. This is especially true for individual investors because they tend to associate risk with losing money rather than with uncertain returns and their ultimate goals pertain to consumption of goods and services rather than portfolio value. Institutional clients are generally more comfortable associating risk with volatility. This is partly because institutional clients are often investment professionals with a solid understanding of investment processes. In addition, business plans and actuarial studies typically provide an explicit link between their ultimate goals, such as funding certain activities, and portfolio performance objectives. Nonetheless, many institutional clients also find volatility to be an insufficient measure of risk.

Risk measures in the second category incorporate this view by focusing only on outcomes below some threshold return. These "downside risk" measures are especially useful when the distribution of potential asset returns does not resemble the familiar, symmetrical bell curve associated with the normal distribution. Unfortunately the intuitive appeal of downside risk measures comes at an analytical cost: There is no clear, reliable relationship between the downside risk of individual assets and the

---

[1] In the case of *Jacobellis v. Ohio* (1964), Stewart agreed that pornography was hard to define and wrote, "I shall not today attempt further to define the kinds of material I understand to be embraced within that shorthand description; and perhaps I could never succeed in intelligibly doing so. But I know it when I see it, and the motion picture involved in this case is not that."

corresponding downside risk of portfolios. Thus downside risk measures are more difficult to incorporate explicitly into the portfolio management process.[2]

Risk and return are inherently related to time. Throughout this book we will be careful in relating risk and return to the investment horizon. The level of expected return typically scales with the investment horizon. For example, if we expect to earn 5 percent per year, then we expect to earn 50 percent over 10 years.[3] Under special circumstances outlined in Chapter 3, the variance of return is also proportional to the investment horizon. However, downside risk measures are generally *not* proportional to the investment horizon. As shown in Chapter 5, when downside risk measures are incorporated, the investment horizon can have a significant impact on the portfolio strategy.

The nearby Excel Outbox illustrates simple risk measures over one- to five-year investment horizons. In this sample the portfolio return averages 10.7 percent per year with an annual standard deviation of 13 percent. Applying a common rule of thumb, the investor can expect the return to be within plus or minus one standard deviation of the mean roughly 66 percent of the time and within plus or minus two standard deviations 95 percent of the time. In this case these ranges correspond to −2.31 to 23.75 percent and −15.34 to 36.78 percent, respectively, for the one-year horizon. Confidence intervals of this type probably provide the best intuitive understanding of risk as measured by volatility.

Note that the multiperiod means and variances are roughly proportional to the investment horizon. The means are exactly proportional. The variances are not exactly proportional to the horizon because they were computed from a specific sample rather than from the theoretical distribution. Because the standard deviation is the square root of the variance, it increases roughly as the square root of the horizon. This relationship will play a recurring role in Chapters 3–5.

The Excel Outbox also shows three downside risk measures. The first is the probability of losing money. In this sample roughly 22 percent of the annual returns were negative. The frequency of losses drops by roughly half over two-year horizons and by roughly 90 percent over five-year horizons. Clearly risk as measured by the shortfall probability declines rapidly as the investment horizon increases. The second downside risk measure, average loss, reflects the average magnitude of any loss that occurs. Although losses occurred less frequently over longer horizons, the average loss was of similar magnitude (6–10 percent) regardless of the horizon. Thus the potential severity of cumulative losses is roughly the same at each horizon.

The third downside risk measure is the 95 percent confidence lower bound, associated with a concept known as **Value-at-Risk (VaR).** Here we are most worried about extremely poor returns and want a risk measure that summarizes worst-case outcomes. VaR is the threshold at which there is only a small probability, 5 percent here, of a lower return. Conversely there is a high probability, 95 percent in this example, of a higher return. The VaR threshold rises from −12.22 percent for one-year horizons to +10.1 percent over five-year horizons. Thus as with shortfall probability, VaR indicates declining risk over longer investment horizons.

[2] Chapters 3 and 5 show how to incorporate downside risk measures into asset allocation modeling. Chapter 11 revisits the issue in the context of so-called alternative asset classes. Chapter 13 discusses the application of various risk measures in performance evaluation. The appendix to Chapter 13 provides details on calculating risk measures from historical data.

[3] This is strictly true only if we measure returns in logarithmic terms. See Chapter 3 for the details of handling multiperiod returns.

Excel Outbox

The Excel spreadsheet "Chapter 02 Excel Outboxes.xls" contains a sample of 100 annual returns and corresponding cumulative returns for two-, three-, four-, and five-year periods. At the top of the worksheet is a table of simple risk measures to be calculated using built-in Excel functions.

	A	B	C	D	E	F	G
2							
3							
4				Simple Risk Measures			
5		1 year	2 years	3 years	4 years	5 years	
6							
7	Mean						
8	Variance						
9	Standard Deviation						
10	Probability of Loss						
11	Average Loss						
12	95% Confidence Lower Bound						

Enter the following formulas for the one-year horizon:

Measure	Cell	Formula to Enter
Mean	B7	= Average(B19:B118)
Variance	B8	= VARA(B19:B118)
Standard deviation	B9	= Sqrt(B8)
Probability of loss	B10	= Countif(B19:B118,"<0")/Count(B19:B118)
Average loss	B11	= Sumif(B19:B118,"<0")/Countif(B19:B118,"<0")
95% Confidence lower bound	B12	= Percentile(B19:B118,0.05)

Then copy cells B7:B12 to cells C7:F12 for the longer horizons. The completed table should look like this:

	A	B	C	D	E	F	G
2							
3							
4				Simple Risk Measures			
5		1 year	2 years	3 years	4 years	5 years	
6							
7	Mean	0.1072	0.2156	0.3280	0.4395	0.5496	
8	Variance	0.0170	0.0322	0.0477	0.0674	0.0807	
9	Standard Deviation	0.1303	0.1793	0.2185	0.2596	0.2842	
10	Probability of Loss	0.2200	0.1111	0.0714	0.0412	0.0208	
11	Average Loss	−0.0797	−0.0970	−0.0918	−0.0853	−0.0618	
12	95% Confidence Lower Bound	−0.1222	−0.0643	−0.0280	−0.0140	0.1010	

All the risk measures just discussed reflect uncertainty about absolute portfolio return. In many instances we may be interested in risk relative to a benchmark or liability. Mathematically this is straightforward: We can simply apply the same risk measures to the difference in returns between the portfolio and the benchmark. For example, the standard deviation of return differentials, called **tracking error,** indicates how closely a portfolio tracks the benchmark. Note that relative risk measures imply that the benchmark is riskless; thus these measures are predicated on the assumption that performance equal to the benchmark would satisfy the client's underlying objective.

Risk measures can also be designed to distinguish among systematic, unsystematic (that is, idiosyncratic), and total risk. This decomposition provides a useful connection between measures of absolute risk and relative risk. Because these measures arise most naturally in the context of performance measurement and evaluation, we will postpone discussion of these measures to Chapter 13.

Armed with this brief introduction to the issue of defining and measuring risk, we now turn to the main focus of this chapter: clients and their objectives.

2.3 The Portfolio Management Process and the Investment Policy Statement

What do we mean by *portfolio management?* Based on the popular press, one might simply equate it with trading securities in an attempt to beat the market. Certainly many of the best-known, highest-paid portfolio managers are lauded for their ability to pick securities within some well-defined universe, such as U.S. small-cap growth stocks. However, this is a narrow perspective that completely divorces portfolio management from the ultimate needs of the client. A more holistic perspective on portfolio management, reflected in the Chartered Financial Analyst (CFA®) curriculum for example, focuses on the need to address the client's complete financial picture. We adopt this broader perspective here.

The portfolio management process can be broken into eight key steps:

1. Evaluate client characteristics.
2. Assess market opportunities.
3. Define objectives and constraints.
4. Set overall investment strategy, including asset allocation.
5. Select investment managers and specific vehicles.
6. Implement strategy.
7. Measure and evaluate performance.
8. Monitor and adjust.

Evaluating client characteristics is particularly important with respect to individuals. Institutional clients are stewards of other people's money and can usually maintain dispassionate objectivity with respect to investment opportunities. Individual clients are rarely dispassionate: It is, after all, their money. Emotions, experiences, hopes and dreams, and biases all matter. Firms that cater to very high net worth clients take the time to understand their clients well and to tailor custom strategies. At the other end of the spectrum, mass-market firms typically assign clients to generic strategies based on a simple questionnaire.

Both the client and the portfolio manager need a realistic assessment of market opportunities. In the late 1990s many clients and advisors extrapolated historical data into a belief that U.S. stock returns of roughly 13 percent per annum would prevail into the indefinite future.[4] This belief led many to invest heavily in equities and sustain massive losses when the technology bubble burst. Of course the market recovered from its 2002 lows to reach new highs in October 2007. By the fall of 2008, however, equity investors had suffered a "lost decade" as the market relinquished all its gains

---

[4] The tendency to extrapolate the past, especially very recent experience, is discussed in Chapter 15.

since 1998. Setting realistic expectations is so important that we devote an entire chapter (Chapter 4) to this problem.

As will be discussed below, the plan for the account should be documented explicitly in an investment policy statement (IPS) summarizing the understanding between the client and the advisor. The central sections of the IPS define the risk and return objectives as well as important constraints on the portfolio. Once these components are defined, the next step is to determine the overall investment strategy, considering both the account parameters and the assessment of market opportunities. The result is typically referred to as a strategic asset allocation because the primary focus is on the long-term allocation among major asset classes. For clients with well-defined liabilities, such as DB pension plans, both the assets and the liabilities should be included in the analysis.

The next step is to select the investment managers and vehicles that will be used to fulfill the strategic asset allocation. For example, the large-cap growth allocation might be filled with an index fund, by hiring an active manager for a separate account, or by some combination of managers and funds. In principle, the asset allocation and fulfillment decisions should be made concurrently rather than sequentially. However, it is standard practice to set the asset allocation first, assuming generic performance within each asset class, and then select managers. Chapter 5 discusses a more sophisticated approach known as *portable alpha*.

Implementation of the strategy entails careful consideration of cash flows, liquidity, transaction costs, and taxes. All these factors affect how the portfolio should be managed through time in response to changing investment opportunities and client circumstances. Chapter 12 addresses these issues in detail.

The last two steps in the portfolio process embody feedback. First we need to measure and evaluate performance. Is the portfolio performing as expected? Is value added coming from the expected sources and in the expected magnitudes? Is the return more than commensurate with the risks taken? Performance analysis is the focus of Chapter 13. The final step is to monitor and adjust the portfolio to stay within guidelines, correct any observed weaknesses, and reflect changes in the environment.

The Investment Policy Statement

Suppose you were suddenly assigned to take over the accounts managed by a colleague who was not available to bring you up to speed. Where would you find the information necessary to make a seamless transition? The primary purpose of the investment policy statement (IPS) is to summarize key information about the client and the investment strategy so that any competent investment professional can readily implement the plan. The IPS also serves as the operating agreement between the client and the manager.

Exhibit 2.1 outlines the components of a typical IPS reflecting the standard espoused in the CFA® curriculum. The IPS starts with a brief description of the client; more detailed information about the client is deferred to the discussion of objectives and constraints. The stated purpose of the IPS is generally straightforward: to document the pertinent facts and the understanding between the parties. The duties component of the IPS usually sets forth the services the advisor will provide and, just as importantly, what related activities the advisor will not perform on behalf of the client. This section might also indicate that the advisor may rely on certain information and representations from the client.

The heart of the IPS begins with the objectives; this is where the client's ultimate goals are translated into concrete statements about portfolio risk and return. Return is

EXHIBIT 2.1
Components of the Investment Policy Statement

- Description of client
- Purpose of the IPS
- Duties of the parties
- Objectives and constraints
  - Objectives
    - Return
    - Risk
  - Constraints
    - Liquidity
    - Time horizons
    - Taxes
    - Legal and regulatory
    - Unique circumstances
- Asset allocation targets and ranges
- Guidelines for portfolio adjustment and rebalancing
- Schedule for portfolio and IPS reviews

typically addressed first. Goals that absolutely must be met can usually be translated into a required rate of return. For example, spending requirements and preservation of real purchasing power might require an endowment fund to earn at least a 4 percent long-term real return. Goals with some flexibility in magnitude or timing translate into a desired rather than required return target. Such targets are easier to meld with potentially conflicting risk considerations. Although income or cash flow may be important considerations in the final portfolio, modern practice dictates specifying return objectives in terms of total return. On the other hand, return targets may be expressed in real or nominal terms and may be pretax or after-tax, provided these characteristics are clearly identified for the reader. In some cases it is appropriate to define an objective relative to a benchmark rather than as an absolute return.

The risk objectives section of the IPS should address both the client's ability and willingness to bear risk. The *ability* to bear risk is mainly a function of whether potential adverse outcomes would jeopardize the client's most critical goals. Wealthy individuals and overfunded pension funds are considered to have an above average or high ability to bear risk. An individual's *willingness* to bear risk is determined primarily by psychological issues. Thus wealthy individuals might be unwilling to bear substantial risk even though they are able to do so. For institutional clients, willingness to bear risk reflects more cold-blooded business considerations. For example, the sponsor of an overfunded pension plan might eschew risk within the plan because severe losses might require large contributions that might jeopardize critical projects within its core business. If ability and willingness to bear risk conflict, the standard recommendation is for the advisor to educate the client but ultimately be guided primarily by willingness rather than ability to bear risk because the client must be comfortable with the risk taken.

The risk section should also discuss how the client perceives risk. Short-term volatility is almost always an important dimension of risk. As discussed in the previous section, however, clients often have other perceptions of risk more closely tied to their ultimate goals. For individuals these notions typically revolve around losing money or falling short of longer-term accumulation targets. For institutions risk is often relative—underperforming a benchmark, competitors, or projected liabilities.

There are five main categories of constraint in the standard IPS. Each provides specific information that must be incorporated into the investment strategy. These constraints are not truly separate from the risk and return objectives; in particular, the constraints almost always play a role in assessing the client's ability to bear risk:

- *Liquidity:* Any significant payment(s) that must be funded out of the portfolio should be recorded here. Liquidity needs over multiple time horizons may be addressed, but the primary focus is on near-term (less than one year) and recurring needs. High liquidity needs reduce the ability to bear risk because higher-risk assets should not be viewed as routinely available to meet liquidity demands.

- *Time horizons:* Most clients have multiple investment horizons corresponding to specific future events and goals. For individuals, these horizons often reflect life cycle stages. Longer horizons are deemed to imply a greater ability to bear risk. In general, each period or horizon documented here will be associated with a different asset allocation in the next section of the IPS.

- *Taxes:* The client's tax status affects both the selection of instruments, such as taxable versus tax-exempt bonds, and the appropriate strategy for handling potentially taxable events, such as capital gains or losses.

- *Legal and regulatory:* Institutional clients are often subject to external constraints imposed by legal and regulatory requirements. Trust and estate considerations could impose constraints on individuals that would also fall in this category.

- *Unique circumstances:* This category covers any special situations and concerns specific to the client. For example, a prohibition on so-called sin stocks would be listed here.[5]

Given the objectives and constraints, the next section of the IPS specifies the asset allocation strategy. This includes selection of appropriate asset classes and target portfolio weights for each of the significant timeframes discussed in the IPS, the allowable ranges around the targets, and the degree to which the advisor may exercise discretion in managing the allocations. The capital market assumptions—that is, the asset class risk and return estimates—underlying the recommended portfolio(s) are also documented in this section.

The next to last section lays out the plan for adjusting and rebalancing the portfolio through time. In essence this section describes the implementation steps of the portfolio management process. Taxes, transaction costs, and liquidity considerations are central to this discussion.

The final section, the schedule for portfolio and IPS reviews, addresses client communications. How often will the manager routinely meet with the client to review the portfolio? Annual or quarterly meetings are typical. Will the manager provide interim reports? What, if any, specific or specialized information does the client require? A schedule for routinely reviewing the IPS with the client should also be established so that it is updated to reflect any significant changes in the client's situation. This process is especially important for individual clients because many facets of life affect their investment needs.

Exhibit 2.2 contains a condensed version of a real IPS established for a small private endowment fund.[6] This IPS is a realistic example rather than a model. Although

---

[5] Sin stocks are shares of companies in businesses such as tobacco, alcohol, gambling, firearms, and even defense. Unique constraints may also reflect political considerations. South Africa during apartheid and Darfur today are two examples. Interestingly, as of December 2008 the Vice Fund (VICEX), which invests in sin stocks, had outperformed the socially responsible Vanguard FTSE Social Index (VFTSX) by roughly 8 percent per year over the preceding five years.

[6] The exhibit is based on the IPS and other information found on the camp's Web site. The names of the camp and foundation have been changed to protect their privacy.

EXHIBIT 2.2 **Sample Investment Policy Statement: Walnut Lodge Camp Endowment Fund**

Source: Excerpted and adapted from the IPS and other materials on the camp's Web site.

- Description of Client

   The endowment fund supports the mission of Walnut Lodge Camp. The camp provides a camping experience for children with disabilities and fosters independence and acceptance of others through social, recreational, and educational aspects of life.

- Purpose of the IPS

   The purpose of this investment policy statement (IPS) is to establish a clear understanding between the investor and the advisor of the investment goals and objectives and management policies applicable to the portfolio.

- Duties of the Parties

   The advisor shall be responsible for (1) designing, recommending, and implementing an appropriate asset allocation plan; (2) advising the investor about the selection of asset categories; (3) identifying specific assets within each asset category; (4) monitoring the performance of all selected assets; (5) recommending changes to any of the above; (6) periodically reviewing the suitability of the investments for the investor; (7) being available to meet with the investor at the investor's request; and (8) preparing and presenting appropriate reports.

   The investor shall be responsible for (1) oversight of the portfolio; (2) defining the investment objectives and policies of the portfolio; (3) directing the advisor to make changes in investment policy, and overseeing and approving or disapproving the advisor's recommendations regarding policy, guidelines, objectives, and specific investments on a timely basis; (4) providing the advisor with all relevant information about the investor's financial conditions and risk tolerances and notifying the advisor promptly of any changes to this information; and (5) ensuring the accuracy of all information provided to the advisor for creation and monitoring of this investment policy statement.

- Objectives

   The investor desires long-term investment growth sufficient to maintain inflation-adjusted support of the camp's mission.

   The investor's income stability, insurance coverage, liquidity, and net worth provide financial capacity to take increased risk. The investor indicates willingness to accept occasional declines in portfolio value in order to enhance growth potential. Taking both factors into account, the investor's risk tolerance may be characterized as moderate.

- Constraints
   - Liquidity: The investor will maintain adequate liquid reserves outside the portfolio.
   - Time horizon: Indefinite.
   - Taxes: The investor is tax-exempt.
   - Legal and regulatory: Subject to the Uniform Prudent Investor Act (UPIA).
   - Unique circumstances: Leverage, short sales, and direct investment in various types of securities are prohibited.

- Asset Allocation Targets

Fixed income		40 %
U.S. / global	20/20	
Equity		60 %
U.S. (large/small)	24/12	
International developed (large/small)	6/6	
Emerging markets (large/small)	3.6/2.4	
REITs		6

- Guidelines for Portfolio Adjustment and Rebalancing

   The advisor shall review the portfolio annually and rebalance the portfolio back to the recommended weights if the equity/fixed income weighting differs from the target by more than 5 percent.

- Schedule for Portfolio and IPS Reviews

   The advisor shall provide the investor with appropriate reports on a regular basis.

   The advisor and the investor should review this investment policy statement together every two years.

it is unusually complete, it could be enhanced in a couple of key areas. Most endowments have an explicit spending policy governing the flow of funding to the supported organization—in this case the camp. For example, university endowments might spend 3–5 percent of (average) assets per annum. Although it may also be documented elsewhere, an endowment's spending policy is mission critical and should be discussed in detail in the objectives section of the IPS.

In the absence of an explicit spending policy, characterizing this endowment's risk tolerance as "moderate" seems a bit conservative because the client is described as both willing and able to take risk. Hence the "moderate" characterization probably reflects a significant spending requirement that is not spelled out in the IPS.

Assigning qualitative labels such as "moderate," "average," or "above average" to describe a client's risk tolerance is fairly standard practice. In many instances such labels are used to steer mass-market clients into off-the-shelf investment solutions. However, the labels are not informative in isolation and certainly would not suffice in dealing with large institutional clients expecting a customized solution. Whenever possible, qualitative assessments of the client's risk tolerance should be associated with quantitative risk measures and parameters. For example, for an endowment fund "moderate" risk tolerance might correspond to less than a 5 percent chance of reduced spending based on a rolling three-year average of assets.

Finally, the reporting section of this IPS is vague. It should spell out a more specific schedule for meetings and reports. Quarterly reports and annual meetings are common.

2.4   Institutional Clients

Most institutional investors fall into one of three categories. **Foundations** and **endowments** provide funding for ongoing charitable, educational, and other socially worthwhile activities. **Pension plans** provide income and accumulated assets to support employees in retirement. **Financial institutions** such as insurance companies and banks invest in assets and issue liabilities in an effort to generate a profit for their owners.

Financial institutions tend to match their assets closely to their liabilities because their profitability and solvency depend on earning a return spread over their liability costs. Whatever their particular product line, they are essentially in the business of asset–liability management and maintain the requisite specialized investment expertise within their firms. Thus they are not prototypical clients for most portfolio managers.[7] We will therefore focus our attention on the institutions that typically hire outside managers for most of their investments: foundations, endowments, and pension plans.

Foundations and Endowments

Foundations and endowments are similar institutions. Broadly speaking, both types of institutions provide funding for activities that are deemed socially worthwhile. Foundations typically provide direct support for charitable activities or research grants aimed at finding solutions to significant problems, such as cancer or poverty. In general, foundations

[7] Financial institutions do hire outside subadvisors to manage individual asset class portfolios that they then package and distribute to investors as part of their product line. For example, a life insurance company might hire an outside manager to run a large-cap growth fund and embed the fund into a variable annuity. The variable annuity is essentially a mutual fund with some tax advantages (see Chapter 12). From the subadvisor's perspective, however, there is little difference between this assignment and managing other similar mutual funds. Individual fund mandates are discussed briefly in Section 2.6 and in depth in Chapters 6–10.

EXHIBIT 2.3
Largest U.S. Foundations: December 31, 2007

Source: Pensions & Investments.

Foundation	Assets ($ billions)
Bill and Melinda Gates	38.9
Ford	13.8
J. Paul Getty	10.1
Robert Wood Johnson	10.1
William and Flora Hewlett	9.3
W. K. Kellogg	8.4
Lilly Endowment	7.7
David and Lucile Packard	6.6
Andrew W. Mellon	6.5
Gordon and Betty Moore	6.4

EXHIBIT 2.4
Largest U.S. Endowments: December 31, 2007

Source: Pensions & Investments.

Endowment	Assets ($ billions)
Harvard University	34.6
Yale University	22.5
Stanford University	17.1
Princeton University	15.8
University of Texas System	15.6
MIT	10.0
Columbia University	7.2
University of Michigan	7.1
University of Pennsylvania	6.6
Texas A&M System and Foundations	6.6

disburse their gifts to many unaffiliated recipients. In contrast, endowments generally provide funding for a specific entity or a small group of closely affiliated entities.

Exhibits 2.3 and 2.4 show the 10 largest U.S foundations and endowments. The largest foundations bear the names of their founders or benefactors, so it is easy to identify the primary source of their assets. Four of the top 10 foundations were established relatively recently by the founders of giant technology companies: Gates (Microsoft), Hewlett (HP), Packard (HP), and Moore (Intel). The others reflect older but equally recognizable names in other industries. How these foundations spend their money is not so obvious. On the other hand, each of the 10 largest endowments bears the name of a college or university; in fact this is true of the 50 largest endowments. Clearly endowment money is devoted primarily to supporting higher education. The 10 largest foundations and the 10 largest endowments range from about $6 billion up to about $35–40 billion. As we will see later, the largest pension funds are much larger.

Some foundations are required to distribute all their assets over a finite horizon. More typically, however, foundations and endowments provide funding for their beneficiaries in perpetuity. Hence preserving the real, inflation-adjusted value of the assets is an important component of their investment objectives. With that in mind, we will consider the key components of the IPS:

Objectives

Returns: Foundations and endowments need long-term returns sufficient to cover spending, inflation, and expenses. A baseline for their required return is given by their long-term target spending or distribution rate (as a percentage of assets) plus expected inflation and expenses.

Most endowments have ongoing efforts to attract donations. These contributions may be viewed in one of two ways: as a funding source for current or planned future expenditures or as funding for growth in expenditures beyond the currently planned level. The former perspective may allow a reduction in the required return on portfolio assets because future spending is expected to be covered in part by then-current donations. The latter perspective implies that the portfolio must generate sufficient return to fund all currently expected future spending. As a result, expected future donations do not reduce the required portfolio return. Endowments tend to put more emphasis on the latter perspective. Unlike endowments and public charities, most private foundations do not rely on a steady stream of contributions.

Private foundations must distribute at least 5 percent of their assets per annum on average to maintain their tax-advantaged status. On average, endowments distribute at somewhat lower rates.[8] However, a higher spending rate may be required if the endowment provides a large portion of the endowed entity's operating budget.

Risk: Foundations and endowments are generally able to bear the relatively high risk commensurate with the objective of maintaining or increasing real portfolio value net of required spending. Their horizons are long, and their obligations are not contractual. Risk tolerance is mitigated, however, if spending is relatively high or if spending must be insulated against portfolio volatility.

While both foundations and endowments tend to smooth absolute spending levels, this is especially important for endowments because they typically provide significant portions of the operating budgets of their affiliated institutions. To stabilize spending, endowments often base current spending on a multiyear rolling average of assets rather than simply current assets. Alternatively, they may adopt a formula relating current spending to both recent spending and assets. For example, a simple geometric spending rule is given by

$$\text{Spending(t)} = \gamma\,\text{Spending(t}-1) + (1-\gamma)\,[\theta\,\text{Assets(t}-1)]$$

The parameter γ controls the relative weight on previous spending versus assets, while θ is the long-term spending rate as a fraction of assets. Higher values of γ and θ generally imply lower risk tolerance because asset volatility makes it difficult to sustain a high, stable level of spending.

Constraints

Liquidity: In general, foundations and endowments have limited needs beyond current spending. However, institutions that invest heavily in private equity and other vehicles that require commitments that will be drawn on at later dates must also ensure that sufficient liquidity will be available to meet these capital calls.[9]

Horizon: Usually infinite, but some foundations have finite lives.

Taxes: Endowments are tax-exempt. Private foundations pay either 1 percent or 2 percent tax depending on current versus historical average spending rate. Both are

---

[8] See *Pensions & Investments,* December 22, 2008, for spending rates in 2005–2007 by size of endowment.

[9] This became a major problem in 2008–2009 when some alternative investment vehicles (such as hedge funds) invoked anti-redemption clauses ("gates") and other vehicles issued capital calls, at least in part to replenish assets lost due to redemptions.

EXHIBIT 2.5   **Smoothing Real Spending: An Example**

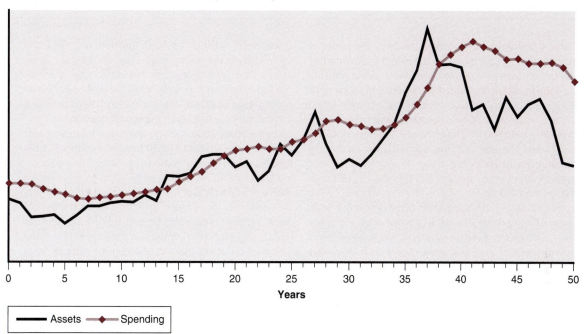

Years

— Assets   ◆ Spending

taxed on income from sources unrelated to their primary mission—so-called unrelated business income.

Legal and regulatory: Most states have adopted the Uniform Management of Institutional Funds Act (UMIFA). The primary consideration is the so-called prudent investor rule, which requires the same consideration of portfolio risk, return, and expenses as a prudent investor would exercise. IRS rules governing the use of tax-exempt funds also apply. Endowments must conform to donor restrictions on the use of donated funds.

Unique circumstances: Donation of securities or illiquid assets may result in concentrated positions. Some investments (such as sin stocks) may conflict with institutional objectives or guiding principles.

Exhibit 2.5 illustrates the smoothing induced by the simple geometric spending rule shown above. Due to the weight placed on previous spending, $\gamma = 0.8$ in this example, fluctuations in the level of assets are transmitted only partially to current spending. Over time, however, spending adjusts to the level of assets. If no weight were placed on the previous spending level ($\gamma = 0$), current spending would mirror the short-term volatility of the assets. On the other hand, divorcing spending from assets entirely ($\gamma = 1$) would be untenable. In the exhibit, assets peak in year 37 and fall sharply over the next 13 years due to a combination of poor investment performance and high spending. This suggests a mismatch between the spending and investment policies. Either the spending policy needs to be more responsive to assets (lower γ) or the portfolio needs to be less aggressive.[10]

[10] The portfolio returns in this example were randomly generated with a mean real return of 5 percent and a standard deviation of 15 percent. This is an aggressive, growth-oriented portfolio, roughly consistent with investing 100 percent in a domestic equity portfolio.

War Story   *Ivy-Covered Endowment Woes*

Harvard University's endowment has been the target of envy for many years. It is by far the largest endowment in the United States. Along with the Yale endowment (the second largest), it is credited with pioneering a cutting-edge approach to institutional asset management based on heavy use of so-called alternative asset classes and derivative instruments. The Harvard Management Company hired the best and the brightest and paid them handsomely. Returns were strong: 15.7 percent per year versus 9.2 percent for the S&P 500 over the 15 years ending in June 2008.

In the fall of 2008, however, the ivy-covered walls came crashing down. The Harvard endowment was more than 100 percent invested—that is, it was levered. It was heavily invested in illiquid asset classes such as private equity and hedge funds. It had large synthetic positions in various asset classes created with derivative contracts. Then came the collapse of Lehman Brothers and AIG. The

global credit markets ceased to function, and stock and commodity prices plummeted. The endowment faced a mounting liquidity crisis as it tried to raise the cash needed to cover margin calls. It sold what it could, but its cutting-edge approach left it with illiquid positions and commitments to fund even more such positions.

By February 2009 the university was projecting that the endowment would lose 30 percent, roughly $11 billion, for the fiscal year ending in June 2009—a staggering blow to a university that relies on its endowment for more than one-third of its operating budget. As a result, the university announced pay freezes and retrenchment in its ambitious capital expenditure program to build a new high-tech campus on the Boston side of the Charles River across from the Cambridge campus it has occupied for nearly 375 years.

Source: For a detailed account, see *Forbes,* "How Harvard's Investing Superstars Crashed," February 20, 2009.

Pension Plans

There are two main types of employer-sponsored pension plans in the United States: **defined benefit** (DB) plans and **defined contribution** (DC) plans. As of year-end 2007 these plans accounted for roughly 64 percent of the $17.6 trillion in U.S. retirement assets.[11]

The terms *defined benefit* and *defined contribution* describe the key distinction between these two plan types. In a defined benefit (DB) plan the employer is contractually obligated to make a stream of benefit payments to employees during their retirement. To fulfill these obligations the employer segregates assets in a pooled investment fund—the pension fund. Strictly speaking, the employer does not own the assets in the pension fund: They may only be used for the employee beneficiaries of the plan.[12] Nonetheless the employer bears the investment risk because it must cover any shortfall if the required benefit payments cannot be met from the fund. In addition, because employees receive benefits until they die, the employer bears the risk of unexpectedly long life spans. In contrast, with a defined contribution (DC) plan the employees bear both the investment risk and the longevity risk.

A DC plan is really a savings and investment platform that employees can use to fund their own retirement. There is no pooled pension fund. Instead employees make contributions to their own accounts and invest in the various investment vehicles on the platform. The employer runs the platform for the employees and may make

[11] Investment Company Institute, "Despite Choppy Markets, Workers Keep Saving," July 22, 2008.

[12] Some plan sponsors have been successful in recovering "excess" assets from overfunded DB plans. This usually involves terminating the existing plan and perhaps replacing it with a new plan. In the late 1980s the ability to tap excess assets in target firms' pension funds helped fuel leveraged buyouts. Not surprisingly, the law was subsequently changed to make it more difficult to extract surplus pension assets.

EXHIBIT 2.6
Participation in DB and DC Plans: % of U.S. Private Sector, Active Worker Participants

Source: EBRI.

	1979	2005
Defined benefit only	62	10
Defined contribution only	16	63
Both plan types	22	27

periodic contributions to each employee's account; that is the extent of the employer's obligations. In particular, no employee is promised a stream of benefits or is assured of accumulating sufficient assets at retirement. In addition, participants pay the investment fees and expenses in a DC plan, whereas the employer pays them for a DB plan.

As Exhibit 2.6 shows, there has been a strong trend away from DB plans and toward DC plans since the late 1970s. In 1979, 84 percent of U.S. private sector, active worker plan participants had a defined benefit plan. By 2005, 90 percent had a defined compensation plan, and 63 percent had *only* a DC plan. In fact by 2008 nearly half of private retirement assets were held in DC plans. This trend stems from two main factors. First, employers have been eager to shed the relatively high cost of DB plans and to transfer the investment and longevity risk of retirement funding to employees. Second, the growth of DC plans has helped meet the need for portable pensions as workers change jobs more frequently. Almost by definition, DB pension plans are not portable. Workers stop accruing additional benefits and may forfeit some or all accumulated benefits when they leave the firm. In contrast, DC plan assets can be rolled over into a new employer's DC plan or into an individual retirement account (IRA).

These forces have also given rise to a variant of the traditional DB plan: the **cash balance plan.** As in a traditional DB plan, the employee accrues benefit credits each year based on salary and years of service. The benefits are a liability of the employer. The difference is that these credits represent current cash value rather than future payments. The employee's account also earns an interest rate determined and periodically adjusted within the plan. Upon retiring, the employee can take the account balance as a lump sum or use it to purchase an annuity. Similarly, if the employee leaves the firm before retirement, the account balance can be rolled over to an IRA or a DC plan. Thus cash balance plans provide portability. As with a traditional DB plan, the employer bears the investment risk. The investment risk is more limited, however, because benefits grow more slowly than with a traditional, final average salary plan. As with a DC plan, employees bear the longevity risk if they elect the lump sum option. Many firms that have not abandoned the DB format altogether have found it advantageous to freeze their traditional DB plans—that is, stop accrual of additional benefits and establish cash balance plans for subsequent benefit accruals.

The breakdown of plan types across sectors is presented in Exhibit 2.7. Although the total assets held in DB and DC plans are roughly equal, the sector percentages differ markedly. Unions and the public sector favor DB plans. The corporate sector predominantly offers DC plans, which now account for 63 percent of corporate plan assets.[13]

As shown in Exhibit 2.8, the 10 largest DB plans alone held over $1.5 trillion in assets at the end of 2007. These plans are huge relative to the largest foundations and endowments. Eight of the 10 largest plans cover public sector employees. The only private sector plans on the list are those of a crippled industrial icon (GM) and a

---

[13] The tax-exempt institutions category consists of 403(b) plans.

EXHIBIT 2.7
Participation in DB and DC Plans: 2008

Source: Spectrem Group *Retirement Market Insights 2009.*

	($ billions)	%
DB	4,029	51.2
Corporate	1,584	20.1
Public	2,158	27.4
Union	287	3.6
DC	3,835	48.8
Corporate	2,731	34.7
Public	397	5.0
Union	95	1.2
Tax-exempt institutions	612	7.8
Total	7,864	100.0

EXHIBIT 2.8
Largest U.S. Retirement Plans: December 31, 2007

Source: *Pensions & Investments*/Watson Wyatt.

Fund	Assets ($ billions)
California Public Employees	254.6
Federal Retirement Thrift	223.3
California State Teachers	176.2
New York State Common	164.4
Florida State Board	142.5
General Motors	133.8
New York City Retirement	130.3
AT & T	117.5
Texas Teachers	114.9
New York State Teachers	106.0

former regulated monopoly (AT&T). In the case of GM, the ongoing cost of retirement benefits was one of the main factors that drove the firm into bankruptcy in 2009 and motivated transitioning some pension and retiree health care plan assets and liabilities to the United Auto Workers union.

The business of managing tax-exempt institutional assets is even more concentrated than the assets themselves. Exhibit 2.9 shows the assets managed by the largest institutional managers. At the end of 2007 these 10 firms managed nearly $5.3 trillion in U.S. tax-exempt, institutional assets—roughly triple the combined assets of the 10 largest pension funds, the 10 largest endowments, and the 10 largest foundations.

Defined Benefit Plans

Unlike foundations, endowments, and DC plans, defined benefit plans have explicit contractual liabilities. Virtually every aspect of managing the plan and the associated assets revolves around modeling, valuing, and funding these liabilities.

A DB plan's obligations are conceptually simple. Eligible employees are promised benefit payments in retirement linked to their salaries and years of service. For example, the annual benefit payment might be given by

$$(2\% \text{ of Final salary}) \times (\text{Years of service})$$

By this formula an employee retiring after 20 years with the firm and with a $50,000 final salary would receive $20,000 per year in retirement. However, translating this basic promise into a projection of the plan's overall liabilities is complex—so complex, in fact, that a whole industry is dedicated to **actuarial valuations** for DB plans.

Forecasting the stream of future benefit payments is complicated by several factors affecting how much each participant will be owed, when, and for how long. First,

EXHIBIT 2.9
Largest Managers of U.S. Tax-Exempt Institutional Assets: December 31, 2007

Source: *Pensions & Investments.*

Manager	U.S. Tax-Exempt Institutional Assets ($ billions)
State Street Global	900.0
Barclays Global	818.3
Fidelity Investments	662.0
BNY Mellon	529.6
Northern Trust Global	519.5
Legg Mason	470.7
TIAA–CREF	396.6
Vanguard	377.5
Capital Research	343.0
Prudential Financial	252.4

vesting provisions deny benefits to employees who do not complete a minimal number of service years. Some fraction of currently unvested employees will leave before becoming vested. Second, some employees who are, or will become, vested will leave before retirement. They will still be due benefits at retirement age but less than if they remained with the firm. Third, the life span of each participant is uncertain. Some will collect benefits for a long time, others for only a short time. Fourth, the wage used in the benefit calculation must be projected out to each participant's termination or retirement date. Fifth, many plans allow participants to choose among various payment options including lump sum distribution and various annuity structures. These elections affect the timing and ultimately the valuation of the liabilities.

Exhibit 2.10 illustrates projected benefit payments for a plan where employees will no longer accrue additional benefits but may still become vested in the future. The upper panel of the exhibit shows the yearly benefits from 2009 to 2067.[14] Each payment is broken into the portion due to inactive participants (already retired or departed employees) and the portion due to currently active participants. This plan is facing a rapid escalation of benefit payments as currently active employees retire over the next 15 years. Indeed the projected payments nearly double by 2025 before declining sharply as first the already inactive participants and then the currently active participants pass away.

The bottom panel of the exhibit shows the present value of the payments in the upper panel. In the absence of future contributions, setting aside these amounts now would exactly fund each future payment if the plan's assets earned the discount rate (6.1 percent here). Although the payments themselves rise rapidly until 2025, their present values peak in 2011.

To assess the funding status of a DB plan, it is common to consider only the first 30 years of projected payments because the discounted value of more distant payments has only a minor impact on the liability. In this example the liability would be the sum of the present values shown for 2009–2038. Exhibit 2.11 shows what happens to this liability measure as we roll forward in calendar time: It declines sharply. Why? As we roll our 30-year window forward, the nearest benefit payment (2009) drops out of the window and a more distant payment (2039) rolls into the window. If the payment stream were level, this would have no effect on the measured liability.[15] In this

---

[14] This example is based on the liabilities of a real plan shortly after it closed to new accruals. However, calendar time has been adjusted.

[15] Of course the near-term payment that drops out of the liability window still represents a current cash outflow.

EXHIBIT 2.10
DB Plan Benefit Payments

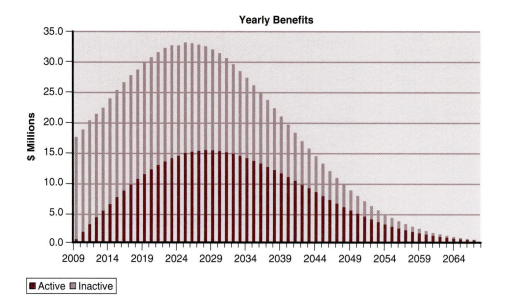

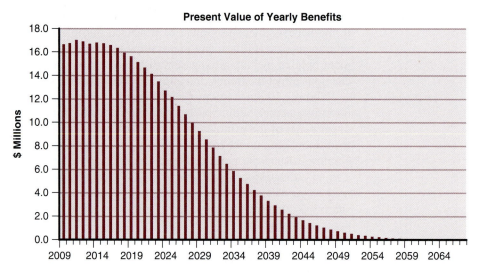

example, however, the measured liability drops quickly over time because the distant payments are much smaller than the near-term payments. Of course if the yearly benefit payments rise sharply as in Exhibit 2.10 but then plateau rather than declining, our rolling 30-year window measure of liabilities would escalate rapidly too.

The point of Exhibit 2.11 is to show that merely comparing plan assets to the usual liability measure can give a distorted view of the plan's true funding status and hence lead to inappropriate portfolio strategies or funding policies. Both the level of liabilities and the change in liabilities over time must be considered.

Given the huge assets involved and the importance of retirement funds to workers' welfare, it should not be surprising that pensions are subject to highly complex legal, regulatory, and accounting requirements. The legal foundation is the **Employee Retirement Income Security Act (ERISA)** of 1974. ERISA set minimum standards for private sector pension funds in several areas, including participation, vesting, benefit accrual, funding, and the accountability of plan fiduciaries. It also established the Pension Benefit Guarantee Corporation (PBGC), a self-financing, federally chartered

EXHIBIT 2.11
Example of DB Plan Liability Evolution over Time

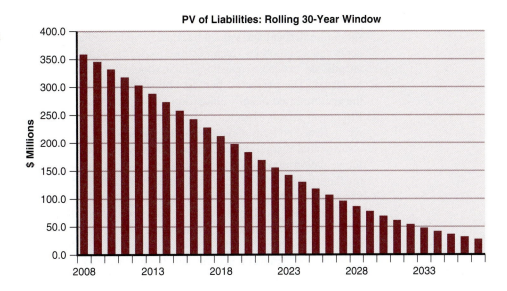

corporation that insures private sector defined benefit plans. Recent changes in DB plan funding requirements were established by the Pension Protection Act of 2006, the most comprehensive pension legislation since ERISA, whereas the accounting treatment of defined benefit plans was recently updated by Financial Accounting Standards Board Statement #158 (FASB 158).

Under ERISA anyone who exercises discretionary authority over a plan's management or assets, including anyone who provides investment advice to the plan, is considered a **fiduciary.** Acceptance of a fiduciary duty means that one must always act solely in the interest of the client and must put the client's interests ahead of one's own. In the case of a DB plan, the clients are the beneficiaries of the plan—not the sponsor firm, the trustees of the plan, or the administrators.

ERISA establishes a particularly high fiduciary standard. First, plan fiduciaries must act with the care, skill, prudence, and diligence of a prudent person *acting in a like capacity.* This is known as the **prudent expert rule**—a higher standard than the prudent investor rule applied under the UMIFA (discussed earlier). Second, fiduciary responsibilities under ERISA cannot be delegated to someone else. Third, a plan fiduciary may be personally liable for damages to the plan or fund.

The Pension Protection Act of 2006 established new rules in an effort to force full funding of private pension plans. Each year sponsors must now contribute at least enough to (1) cover the benefits earned that year and (2) make up any underfunding within seven years. To make full funding more attractive, the act extended tax deductibility of contributions to plans that are overfunded by up to 50 percent. For purposes of assessing funding status, the liabilities of the plan must be valued using a three-segment (< 5 years, 5–20 years, >20 years) yield curve reflecting a two-year average of investment-grade corporate bond yields from the top three qualities (AAA, AA, A). The act also defined rules for identifying plans deemed to be at risk. In general, a plan is considered at risk if it is less than 80 percent funded based on normal actuarial assumptions and less than 70 percent funded based on more conservative assumptions that increase the present value of liabilities. At-risk plans are subject to higher contribution requirements, limitations on benefit changes, higher PBGC insurance premiums, and potential penalties. Plans that are less than 60 percent funded are subject to even more stringent rules, including prohibitions of lump sum benefit distributions and payouts of deferred executive compensation and special executive pension plans.

Before the Pension Protection Act it was somewhat unclear how pension liabilities should be defined and valued because various regulatory bodies specify different concepts and assumptions. Technicalities aside, the various liability measures reflect different answers to two key questions. First, should the liabilities include expected future wage increases? The **projected benefit obligation (PBO)** includes these increases, whereas the **accumulated benefit obligation (ABO)** reflects only current wages. In addition, the PBO incorporates expected future vesting patterns, whereas the ABO reflects only currently vested benefits. Given generally rising wages, the PBO often exceeds the ABO by a substantial margin. Second, at what rates should the liability payments be discounted for valuation purposes? Although alternative definitions may be relevant for specific regulatory purposes, the Congress effectively answered these questions in the 2006 law. For assessing the funding status of ongoing plans, the PBO is the relevant liability measure. The ABO concept is still relevant because it reflects the obligation the sponsor could lock in by terminating the plan today. As already noted, the Pension Protection Act also specifies the yield curve to be used in valuing the liabilities.

In general, financial accounting standards shield a company's financial statements from fluctuations in the market value of assets and liabilities by focusing on historical costs and smoothing recognition of changing values. Unfortunately this practice can distort the firm's financial condition. In the case of pension obligations, FASB 158 overturned long-standing practice by requiring recognition of a plan's current funding status on the balance sheet as either a noncurrent asset (overfunded plans) or a noncurrent liability (underfunded plans). Changes in the funding status do not flow through the income statement. Instead these changes hit shareholders' equity directly. Thus in the wake of FASB 158 management and shareholders are apt to be more sensitive to fluctuations in a plan's asset–liability balance.

With this background, let us consider the objectives and constraints components of the DB plan investment policy statement:

Objectives

Returns: Defined benefit plans require a return sufficient to cover projected liabilities in conjunction with planned contributions. For fully funded plans this implies a required return approximately equal to a weighted average of the discount rates applied to each future payment in the PBO calculation. With the exception of plans with little or no ongoing benefit accruals, such as terminated plans, closed plans, and those with few active participants (nonretirees), this will primarily reflect the longest segments of the investment-grade yield curve mandated by the Pension Protection Act. Underfunded plans will need to balance the risk associated with a higher target return against the need for more substantial contributions.

In practice, liability projections often include only the first 30 years of future payments. Over time the near-term benefits will be paid and more distant obligations will be recognized as they roll into the 30-year measurement window. Payment of current benefits reduces assets and measured liabilities dollar-for-dollar. The reduction in measured liabilities is offset, however, by the recognition of obligations that were previously beyond the measurement window. Thus a plan that appears fully funded will tend to become underfunded unless it earns a return somewhat higher than the liability discount rate. The magnitude of this effect depends on the time profile of the benefit obligations. Overall growth/contraction or changing demographics of the workforce may cause the measured PBO to trend upward or downward as the 30-year measurement window rolls forward in calendar time (for an example, see Exhibit 2.11). Hence the target return should reflect the built-in growth (implying higher required return) or contraction (lower required return) in measured liabilities.

Risk: Because DB plans have explicit contractual liabilities, risk is relative. That is, risk should be assessed in terms of the plan's surplus/deficit of assets versus liabilities—that is, the funding status—rather than the asset portfolio alone.

The plan's ability to bear risk depends on four main factors: (1) the surplus, (2) the size of the plan relative to the sponsor's business, (3) the health of the sponsor, and (4) the demographics of the workforce. Relatively small, overfunded plans with healthy, profitable sponsors and young workforces can afford to take significant investment risk. Conversely, plans that are severely underfunded, are large relative to the sponsor's business, are sponsored by a struggling firm, or have large near-term obligations to retirees have limited capacity for investment risk.

In accordance with the ERISA fiduciary standards, the plan's willingness to bear risk must reflect only the interests of the beneficiaries—that is, the plan participants. In particular, additional investment risk should not be taken without the reasonable expectation that doing so will enhance the magnitude and security of the promised benefits.

Constraints

Liquidity: Needs depend on the magnitude of near-term (one to two years) benefit payments net of expected contributions. The greater the percentage of liabilities arising from retirees (the so-called retired lives component) and those near retirement, the greater the need for liquidity.

Horizon: Investment horizons depend on whether the plan is expected to terminate or remain a going concern. Terminating plans have short-term horizons corresponding to the expected termination date. Ongoing plans have at least two horizons. The first reflects the need to attain (or maintain) fully funded status within seven years as required by the 2006 law. The second reflects the presumption that both the sponsor and the plan have infinite lives. Additional horizons may need to be specified corresponding to significant changes in the nature of the liabilities, the status of the sponsor, and the legal and regulatory environment.

Because interest rates are a key driver of the value of the liability stream, the duration of the liabilities is also an important horizon for management of the plan. (See Chapter 9 for a discussion of duration, its interpretation as a time horizon, and its relationship to holding period returns.)

Taxes: Defined benefit plans are tax-exempt.

Legal and regulatory: Governed by ERISA and the Pension Protection Act of 2006; federal oversight by the Department of Labor, the PBGC, the IRS, and the FASB; must also comply with laws and regulations of other jurisdictions, such as states.

Unique circumstances: It is in the interest of the beneficiaries to limit the correlation between the two primary sources of funding for the plan: the investment portfolio and the profitability and solvency of the sponsor.

If the timing and magnitude of benefit payments were known with certainty, the liabilities of a defined benefit plan would resemble, and could be funded by, a portfolio of bonds. In practice the liabilities are not known, but a significant portion of the obligations, such as payments to retirees, are highly predictable. Therefore a customized fixed income portfolio matching the characteristics of the projected benefit payments approximates a riskless investment for the plan.[16] The plan's ability and willingness to

---

[16] Construction and management of structured fixed income portfolios are discussed in Chapter 9.

According to consulting firm Towers Perrin, the pension plans of the *Fortune* 100 companies were 125.8 percent funded at the end of 1999, the height of the technology bubble. By 2002 these same plans were only 81.9 percent funded. This drastic shift in pension plan status, along with a string of high-profile corporate bankruptcies, such as Enron, provided impetus for the stricter funding rules contained in the Pension Protection Act of 2006.

After five years of equity market appreciation, the outlook for U.S. pension plans looked brighter by the end of 2007. Mercer, another large consulting firm, estimated that the pension plans of the S&P 1500 companies were 104 percent funded. At that point it looked as if the more stringent funding requirements due to phase in starting in 2008 would not pose a significant problem.

Disaster struck in 2008. With typical equity allocations of around 60 percent, pension assets fell sharply as the stock market collapsed. Adding insult to injury, yields on investment-grade corporate bond indexes dropped sharply in December 2008—largely due to the removal from the index of bonds that were downgraded to junk status. The drop in rates translated into sharply higher liability valuations. As of year-end 2008 Mercer estimated the funding ratio for the S&P 1500 plans at only 75 percent. Several large firms, such as Motorola, froze their pension plans, and others were likely to pursue that course.

Under the provisions of the 2006 act, any plan that was less than 92 percent funded in 2008 would have had to be brought up to fully funded status immediately. Faced with sharply lower funding levels, a credit crisis, and a deepening recession, the government was forced to grant relief to struggling plan sponsors.

Source: See *The Wall Street Journal,* "Pension Plans Take Healthy Turn," January 23, 2007; *Dow Jones Newswires,* "Pensions See Record Deficit; More Frozen Plans Expected," January 7, 2009; *Dow Jones Newswires,* "Pensions Further Hammered by December Discount Rate Drop," January 12, 2009; and *WashingtonPost.com,* "House Passes Bill to Ease Pension Crunch for Retirees, Companies," December 11, 2008.

bear risk dictate the extent to which the actual portfolio can deviate from this benchmark in an effort to enhance return.

Defined Contribution Plans

As we have already noted, defined contribution plans are tax-deferred, retirement saving and investment platforms provided by employers for the benefit of employees. Employees of for-profit companies have 401(k) plans; tax-exempt institutions such as universities offer employees 403(b) plans; and public sector employees have 457 plans.[17] The plan labels come from the sections of federal tax code that authorize each type of plan. Exhibit 2.12 shows the assets held in various types of DC plans as of yearend 2007 and 2008. Although there remain some technical differences among the programs, the essentials are the same, and we will treat *DC plan* as synonymous with a 401(k) plan in the following discussion.

401(k) plans are hybrids. On one hand, as pension plans they are institutions subject to the fiduciary rigors of ERISA and the Pension Protection Act. To discharge their fiduciary obligations, sponsors and administrators must design and maintain a platform with investment options appropriate for the retirement needs of the organization's full spectrum of employees. For an investment advisor seeking "shelf space" on

[17] From the participant's perspective, 529 college savings plans are similar to DC retirement plans. The main difference, of course, is the purpose for which assets are accumulated and the correspondingly different saving and distribution timeframes. In addition, 529 plans are sponsored by states rather than employers.

EXHIBIT 2.12
Defined Contribution Assets

Source: Spectrem Group *Retirement Market Insights 2009*.

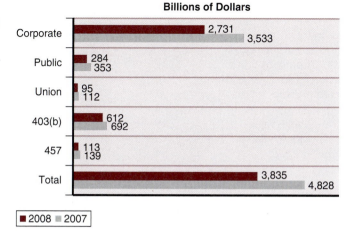

Billions of Dollars

	2008	2007
Corporate	2,731	3,533
Public	284	353
Union	95	112
403(b)	612	692
457	113	139
Total	3,835	4,828

■ 2008 ■ 2007

the platform or to administer the plan, this is an institutional sale not unlike pitching to a DB plan, endowment, or foundation. On the other hand, given the available options, the employees make the investment decisions that determine whether they accumulate sufficient assets at retirement. Thus successful DC plans need to address the needs and foibles of these ultimate clients.

Exhibit 2.13 shows the 10 largest managers of DC plan assets as of year-end 2007. Not surprisingly, 7 of the 10 were also on the list of the largest managers of U.S tax-exempt institutional assets (Exhibit 2.9). However, the ordering of the lists is somewhat different. State Street Global and Barclays Global, best known for managing huge indexed portfolios at low fees for institutional clients, topped the list for overall tax-exempt assets. In contrast, three of the four largest DC plan managers—Fidelity, Capital Research (better known as American Funds), and Vanguard—are best known for retail mutual funds. TIAA–CREF is a less familiar retail brand, but it was a pioneer of pooled retirement accounts and has recently expanded its presence in mutual funds. T. Rowe Price is also a large mutual fund firm. Three large insurance companies round out the list.

How do plan participants allocate their investments within 401(k) plans? Exhibit 2.14 shows that as of year-end 2008 the average account held roughly 42 percent in equity, 41 percent in fixed income, 14 percent in balanced funds containing both equity and bonds, and 3 percent in other asset classes. These allocations clearly reflect the equity

EXHIBIT 2.13
Largest Managers of Defined Contribution Plan Assets: December 31, 2007

Source: *Pensions & Investments.*

Manager	U.S. Tax-Exempt Institutional Assets ($ millions)
Fidelity Investments	548.3
TIAA–CREF	396.6
Capital Research	343.0
Vanguard	320.3
Barclays Global	221.2
State Street Global	205.9
T. Rowe Price	124.9
Prudential Financial	112.8
ING	87.4
AIG Investments	79.7

EXHIBIT 2.14
401(k) Average Asset Allocations (%)

Source: Spectrem Group.

	2007	2008
Equity	53	42
Diversified Equity	37	29
Company Stock	16	13
Balanced Asset Allocation	16	14
Fixed Income	27	41
Bonds	6	6
Stable Value	19	32
Money Market	2	3
Other	4	3

market crash of 2008. Accounting for the blended nature of balanced funds, this corresponds to roughly a 50–50 split between stocks and bonds, which is well below the approximately 65 percent equity allocation observed at the end of 2007.

A breakdown of equity holdings reveals that 13 percent were allocated to company stock. High company stock allocations have been a focus of concern with respect to 401(k) plans. The collapse of Enron highlighted the danger of investing DC plan assets in employer stock. When the firm failed, employees lost not only their jobs but a large portion of their retirement assets—assets that would have been protected if not invested in Enron stock. In response to this problem, the Pension Protection Act of 2006 stipulated that employees must be allowed to sell company stock within a 401(k) plan, even if the firm contributed the stock as part of a matching program.

Another area of concern was the allocations to money market and stable value funds. The Pension Protection Act also changed the rules for setting the default investment option for participants who do not select specific funds. Prior to the 2006 act, the default option was generally the plan's most conservative vehicle: a money market or stable value fund. Unfortunately, due to ignorance, inertia, or a belief that default options represent recommendations, people tend to stick with default choices. Thus it was believed that participants were being encouraged to select investments that were too conservative for their long-term retirement goals. The Pension Protection Act remedied this by allowing funds with "age-appropriate" asset class mixtures to be designated as default investment options.

The new rule opened the way for so-called **life cycle funds** to be used as default options in 401(k) plans. These funds, also called *target date funds,* are designed to become more conservative as the investor approaches retirement. Target risk funds, which have static asset allocations, were also permitted for default usage. According to EBRI data, 67 percent of all DC plans offered life cycle funds in 2007, compared with only 12 percent in 1996; and at the end of 2007 these funds represented 7.4 percent of the average account—almost half of the average allocation to balanced funds.

With or without life cycle funds, 401(k) participants have generally adopted the prescription for progressively more conservative portfolios as they approach retirement. Exhibit 2.15 shows the average allocations to equities, fixed income, and balanced funds by age cohort. Twenty-somethings hold the lowest fixed income allocation, the most balanced funds, and a heavy allocation to equities. Their relatively heavy allocation to balanced funds may reflect a greater propensity to adopt life cycle funds. Participants in their thirties had the highest allocations to equities. Those in their forties shifted slightly more into fixed income. The transition out of equities and into fixed income becomes pronounced as participants move into their fifties and then their

EXHIBIT 2.15
401(k) Allocations by Age Group: 2007

Source: EBRI.

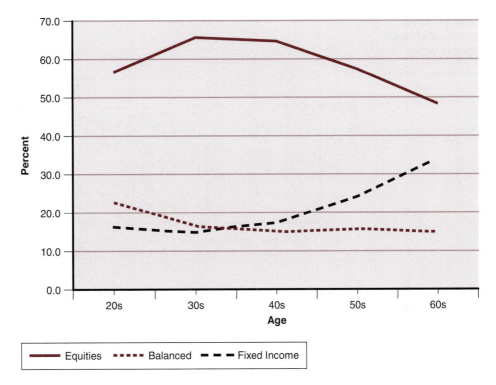

sixties. Interestingly, the average equity allocation is still almost 50 percent for those in their sixties—a sign that participants understand the risk of outliving their assets if they invest too conservatively.

2.5 Individual Investors

Working with institutional clients is mainly about the numbers—the dollars and cents. Individual investors recognize the importance of the numbers too, but psychology is usually just as important. For example, how clients obtained their wealth may be just as important as its magnitude. Their perception of risk may depend as much on whether they feel in control as on objective statistical measures of potential outcomes. Similarly, as we will discuss in Chapter 15, their attitude toward gains and losses may reflect a variety of situational biases and external influences. Thus understanding clients' "investment personalities" can be as important as understanding their financial situations.

Understanding the Client: Situational Profiling

The process of gathering and assessing information about individual clients is sometimes called **situational profiling.** In essence, the aim is to classify clients based on four factors: source of wealth, measure of wealth, stage of life, and personality. In this context *measure of wealth* refers not only to the absolute size of a portfolio but also to a client's perception of his or her wealth. In general, higher perceived wealth translates into higher risk tolerance. That is, for a given portfolio value, those that perceive themselves as wealthy tend to be willing to take more risk.

Exhibit 2.16 breaks down five major sources of wealth reported by so-called affluent investors—those with $1–5 million of investable assets. The largest proportion of these investors obtained their wealth primarily through participating in employer

EXHIBIT 2.16
**Sources of Affluent
Investor Wealth**

Source: Spectrem Group 2003
Affluent Investor Study.

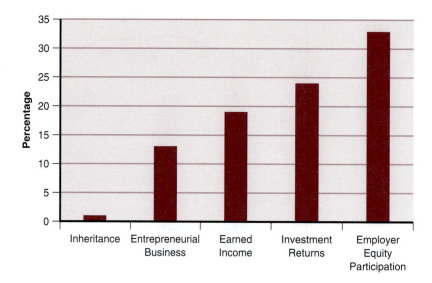

equity plans. On the other end of the spectrum, only a small fraction of respondents gained their wealth via inheritance. In between are those who appear to have contributed more directly to their own wealth in one of three ways: starting a business, saving earned income, or generating investment returns.

Each of these self-reported sources of wealth suggests something about the individual. Almost by definition, entrepreneurs like the feeling of controlling their own destiny and are comfortable taking risks within the sphere of their own expertise. They may be uncomfortable, however, with less familiar risks or situations beyond their control. In addition, their ability to take portfolio risk may be limited as long as their wealth remains tied up in their business. Individuals who acquired their wealth through meticulous saving of earned income may fear losing it, especially if their early investment experiences were poor. Those who acquired wealth primarily through investment returns may exhibit overconfidence in their own investment skills and, as a result, be inappropriately tolerant of risk. Concentrating wealth in any single security is inherently risky, so those who acquired their wealth via employer stock may have a high tolerance for risk. On the other hand, these employees might have been locked into a concentrated position by vesting, marketability, or tax considerations.[18]

Inherited wealth and family wealth create a variety of issues. Individuals who inherited the bulk of their wealth often fear failure and may be indecisive or highly risk averse. Fear of being exploited may make them suspicious of other people's motives. Situations in which individuals share in, but do not necessarily own or control, family wealth introduce further complications. Control of the assets is one potential issue, especially while the family members who generated or accumulated the wealth are still involved. Due to estate taxes (see Chapter 12), tax-efficient transfer of assets between generations is almost always a critical consideration. While setting up one or more **trusts** can help solve estate tax problems, these vehicles highlight the competing interests of present and future generations. Typically older beneficiaries want trusts to generate high, stable streams of income, whereas the interests of future or younger beneficiaries are served by greater focus on capital appreciation.

---

[18] See the discussion of the lock-in effect of unrealized capital gains in Chapter 12.

As people age they pass through life cycle stages that affect both their objectives and their financial resources. In the **accumulation phase** an individual has a long horizon and growing income, but financial net worth is typically small relative to liabilities and future needs. Due to their long horizon and earning potential, such individuals can take significant investment risk with funds not allocated to specific short-term goals (including a liquid emergency reserve). By the middle to late stages of their careers, most individuals are, or at least aim to be, earning more than enough to cover current expenses. In this **consolidation phase,** financial net worth is building. As individuals advance through this stage, their investment horizon begins to shorten, diminishing their ability to take risk.

For many individuals the **spending phase** of the life cycle corresponds to retirement. Others could retire but have not. In this phase individuals are financially independent, and expenses can be covered by investment income and assets. Although the investment horizon may still be fairly long, reliance on investment income and assets to cover expenses implies a diminished ability to accept risk. When individuals are confident that their assets exceed their lifetime needs, they enter the **gifting phase,** in which tax-efficient asset transfer and philanthropy become primary considerations.

In the mid-1980s Bailard, Biehl, and Kaiser developed a two-dimensional scheme for classifying individual investor personalities. One dimension, shown on the horizontal axis in Exhibit 2.17, reflects how the investor makes decisions. Some people are careful, analytical decision makers, whereas others rely on intuition and tend to be impetuous. The second dimension reflects the investor's general attitude toward uncertainty: cautious or confident. "Individualists" (upper left quadrant) are careful and confident. They do their homework, are confident in their abilities, and avoid extreme volatility. They are ideal clients, but they may choose to invest by themselves. Independent professionals often fall into this group. "Guardians" are cautious and careful; these investors have a strong desire for financial security and wealth preservation. They choose advisors carefully and remain loyal to those who do not surprise them. "Adventurers" are willing to "go for it" with concentrated bets. These volatile clients are strong-willed, entrepreneurial, and confident in their own ideas and intuition

EXHIBIT 2.17
Bailard, Biehl, and Kaiser Psychological Needs Model

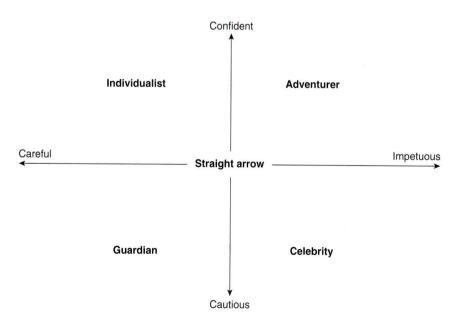

about investing. "Celebrities" do not want to miss out on what's "hot." Lacking their own investment ideas, they chase performance and easily fall prey to high-turnover, high-cost strategies that can undermine performance. "Straight arrows" are too well-balanced to fall into any of the other categories. At least hypothetically, they are the average investor.

The Individual's IPS: Objectives and Constraints

Once the situational profile is complete, the information must be distilled into the appropriate components of the investment policy statement. As before, we briefly outline the key considerations for the objectives and constraints portions of the IPS:

Objectives

Returns: Individual investors usually have multiple goals and multiple time horizons. Some of the goals, such as maintaining current standards of living and supporting loved ones, are critical, whereas others, like a second home or early retirement, reflect aspirations. Critical goals give rise to a required return target. Achieving this target must be feasible based on realistic investment opportunities and must not require excessive risk. A higher target return consistent with attaining at least some of the client's aspirations can be balanced against risk considerations. The return objective should clearly state whether the target reflects before-tax or after-tax and real or nominal performance.

If the client's critical goals are not consistent with risk-appropriate investment opportunities, the advisor must educate the client and assist in setting feasible goals.

Risk: Both the investor's ability and willingness to take risk must be addressed. The ability to take risk depends primarily on objective criteria such as the investor's wealth relative to his or her needs and the investment horizons corresponding to important goals and life cycle stages. Higher wealth and longer investment horizons indicate greater ability to take risk. Willingness to take risk is subjective. This is where the psychological aspects of situational profiling are brought to bear.

If the investor's ability and willingness to bear risk conflict, the advisor should educate the client in an attempt to resolve the conflict. If a conflict remains, the IPS should generally reflect the more conservative perspective. In particular, investors should not be induced to take more risk than they are willing to bear.

Constraints

Liquidity: Individuals need highly liquid assets sufficient to meet normal living expenses in the near term plus an emergency reserve equal to 3–12 months of living expenses depending on the stability and security of cash income. Additional liquid reserves may be needed for major, situation-specific events.

Horizon: Individuals usually have multiple investment horizons corresponding to life cycle stages and specific goals and events. The most important horizons, such as expected changes in financial obligations, resources, and retirement, usually necessitate breaking the investor's full horizon into subperiods and delineating a different investment strategy for each.

Taxes: Taxes are a major consideration for individuals. Most investors are subject to both federal and state income taxes. However, most also have the ability to shelter at least some of their investments via defined contribution (DC) plans and other tax-advantaged accounts. Depending on their level of wealth, individuals may also be subject to estate taxes. The individual's specific circumstances should be addressed here and reflected in the recommended investment strategy.

Legal and regulatory: The prudent investor rule requires the same consideration of portfolio risk, return, and expenses as a prudent investor would exercise. Tax laws pertaining to investment income, asset transfers, and use of tax-advantaged accounts are key considerations.

Unique circumstances: Individuals often have special circumstances such as concentrated positions in illiquid or restricted equities or ownership of a family business. External assets such as a beneficial interest in a trust not covered by the IPS would also be discussed here. Similarly, significant contingent obligations such as potential support of a chronically ill family member should be covered and its potential impact reflected in the assessment of the investor's ability to take risk.

Trends in the Wealth Management Business

Advising individual investors is, of course, a business. Therefore, advisory firms typically tailor their services and fees to attract certain types of clients. Because fees (that is, revenues) are a function of assets under management, this results in a stratification of the market based on the client's investable assets. In one such breakdown, Cerulli Associates found that the "affluent," those with $1–5 million to invest, were advised primarily by mutual fund companies and commercial banks. Those with $5–25 million, labeled "high net worth" investors, generally command the somewhat more customized and sophisticated services offered by brokerage firms and registered investment advisors (RIA). "Ultra high net worth" individuals with $25 million or more receive highly customized attention at private banks or establish so-called family offices of their own with investment professionals dedicated to handling their financial affairs.

In general, the trend among advisors has increasingly been to target the upper end of the "affluent" range and the lower end of the "high net worth" range. These investors face many of the same issues— taxes, estate planning, concentrated positions, and wealth preservation—that have always concerned their wealthier colleagues. The number of investors in this range, say $3–10 million, has grown rapidly—at least until the bear market of 2008.[19] In addition, technology, financial innovation, and collaborative arrangements with external service providers (accountants, lawyers, and actuaries) have made it cost-effective to offer more sophisticated, customized services at lower asset levels. Yet fees remain attractive for advisors in this market segment because fee schedule breakpoints often provide deep discounts only at higher asset levels.

Meanwhile clients have shifted their attitudes regarding advice over time. Before the 1990s the prevailing attitude was "do it *for* me."[20] In the 1990s there was a shift toward "do it myself." The growth of index funds and the strong tailwind provided by the technology bubble during this period probably emboldened investors to go it alone. After the tech bubble burst, however, things did not seem so easy. On the other hand, due in part to defined contribution plans, more and more investors had become used to making at least some of their own investment decisions. Thus it is not too surprising that since the start of the new millennium the prevailing attitude has shifted toward "do it *with* me."

In the late 1990s the VIP Forum identified several trends in the wealth management arena.[21] The first, increasing pressure for performance, may have been accentuated by the illusion of easy gains created by the then-expanding technology bubble. Nonetheless

[19] In their *Affluent Market Insights 2009,* the Spectrem Group reports the number of "affluent" ($500K+net worth) and "millionaire" ($1MM+net worth) households falling 28 percent and 27 percent respectively. Note that Spectrem and Cerulli use the term "affluent" differently.

[20] Tiburon Research, "Consumer Wealth, Target Markets, and Marketing Strategies," 2005.

[21] The VIP Forum, "Voice of the Millionaire, Volume I," 1998.

War Story *What Have You Done for Me Lately?*

The market turmoil of 2008 clearly impacted investor wealth. In its *Affluent Markets Insight 2009* the Spectrem Group reports that the largest number of investors indicate they lost 30–40 percent of their net worth from September 2008 through year-end. In addition, almost half of those with 5–10 years to retirement say they are being forced to delay their retirement.

It has also clearly affected investors' view of financial advisors. Only 36 percent of investors felt their advisors performed well during this crisis, compared to the 85

individuals would prefer the personalized service they expect from a smaller organization, they worry about the advisor's long-term solvency and fraud risk, in light of the Madoff scandal. While larger brand-name organizations are viewed as safer due to the assumed protection of a government bailout should they experience problems, they are viewed as responsible for the crisis and as a result unsuitable to manage the investors' assets.

Understandably, investors feel bad about losing money and especially bad about losing a lot. As dis-

Type of Advisor	View Positively	Neutral	View Negatively
Accounting firm	7%	60%	33%
Bank	8	30	61
Full service broker	7	49	45
Independent financial planner	11	57	32
Insurance company	5	40	56
Investment advisor	10	54	36
Mutual fund company	9	58	33
Private bank	11	43	46
Trust company	6	58	37

Source: Spectrem Group *Affluent Market Insights 2009.*

percent who were satisfied with their advisors in the spring of 2008. This more negative view extends to all financial services firms. This is particularly true for banks, viewed negatively by 61 percent of investors. Independent financial planners and private banks are viewed more positively, but only by 11 percent of investors.

These results would seem to suggest a potential shift toward self-directed assets or independent planners. However, there are conflicting concerns. While many

cussed in Chapter 15, investors may become angry in those situations and fire their portfolio manager(s) at the wrong time. As discussed in Chapter 16, it is important for investment professionals to manage expectations, communicate often, and express understanding in periods of poor performance. Recommending a diversified strategy, setting rebalancing rules with limited flexibility, and training eyes on both valuation and fundamentals will help keep these periods to a minimum.

there can be little doubt that performance was, is, and will remain the primary criterion in hiring and firing managers. The study also noted increasing pressure on fees and expenses as increasingly self-reliant clients gained easier access to relative performance data and lower-cost alternatives such as index funds and exchange traded funds (ETFs). This trend has been reinforced as institutional managers move "down market" and retail managers move "up market" to capture a share of the perceived sweet spot: high net wealth individuals. Interestingly, despite the unique needs of individual investors, such as taxes and life cycle considerations, half of the high net worth managers surveyed said they managed institutional and individual portfolios similarly.

The VIP Forum study also found that the traditional notion of investment management as a relationship business was breaking down. Clients were becoming less attached to individual advisors. Face-to-face contact was declining in importance. Clients were increasingly spreading their business among a network of advisors. This suggests that a fundamental shift in the client–advisor relationship occurred around the turn of the millennium. Indeed it suggests that the traditional advisory model no longer satisfies the increasingly complex needs of individual investors. More recently a large advisory firm suggested that today's clients are seeking a "trusted advisor and integrator," someone who focuses holistically on their needs, orients the business around those needs, provides thoughtful advice rather than products, and seamlessly integrates a collaborative network of experts into the relationship.[22]

It seems inevitable that the dramatic wealth destruction that began in late 2007 and accelerated in late 2008 will change the wealth management landscape. Fortunes have been lost. Dreams have been shattered. Many investors feel they have been ill served by their financial advisors, by the firms that employ them, and by the regulatory bodies that supervise them. For better or worse, the time is ripe for fundamental changes in the business.

2.6 Asset Class Portfolios

Up to this point we have retained the broad, holistic notion of portfolio management established in Section 2.3. The preceding two sections focused on assessing client characteristics and defining appropriate objectives and constraints for the overall investment strategy. The next step of the investment process entails determining the actual strategy—in particular the allocation across asset classes. Chapters 3–5 examine the asset allocation decision in detail.

Given the asset allocation decision, the assets devoted to each asset class are typically assigned to portfolio managers whose job is to manage a portfolio of individual securities that reflects the characteristics of the asset class. Some such managers may be asked to track an asset class–specific benchmark as closely as possible (passive management); others have a mandate to deviate from the benchmark in an effort to generate superior (risk-adjusted) returns (active management).

Part of the overall portfolio manager's job is to set guidelines for each asset class portfolio manager so that the combination of individual portfolios is consistent with the overall investment strategy. The guidelines should cover at least the following issues:

- Permissible investments:
  - Universe of securities and/or benchmark index.
  - Prohibited securities.
  - Policy regarding derivatives.
- Risk and return expectations:
  - Target excess return and associated measurement period.
  - Risk constraints:
    - Permissible tracking error.
    - Maximum underperformance.

It is in the interest of all parties—the client, the overall portfolio manager, and the asset class manager—to be as explicit as possible in setting the guidelines. Vague statements are open to interpretation, and silence may or may not confer consent. As an example, consider the bare-bones guidelines in Exhibit 2.18. If performance

[22] SEI, "The Transformation of Wealth Management—Part I," 2008.

EXHIBIT 2.18
Sample Bare-Bones
Guidelines

- XYZ hired to manage a large-cap growth equity portfolio.
- Seek to outperform the S&P 500 over a market cycle.
- Tracking error not to exceed 3 percent.
- Underperformance not to exceed 5 percent in any 12-month period.
- Also outperform the CPI.

is good, these guidelines may suffice. Following a period of disappointing performance, however, it is quite possible the parties will have different views on what
could, and should, have been done differently within the parameters of the mandate. Section 7.7 of Chapter 7 addresses developing better guidelines for an equity
mandate.

Given the guidelines, the asset class manager must design and implement an investment process to deliver the expected results. In practice, of course, the investment process must be in place before the manager would even be considered for the mandate.
Chapters 6–10 focus in detail on managing equity, fixed income, and international or
global portfolios.

Summary

Portfolio managers make decisions on behalf of their clients that impact the clients'
ability to attain their most fundamental objectives—financial and nonfinancial. Therefore understanding a client's needs, wants, attitudes, and circumstances is a crucial
step in establishing and maintaining a successful advisor–client relationship.

The process of assessing a client's unique investment problem culminates in
establishing an investment policy statement (IPS) that serves as the operating agreement between the advisor(s) and the client. Aside from outlining the duties of each
party, the IPS has three key components: (1) a detailed description of the client's
risk and return objectives, (2) a detailed description of constraints arising from the
client's liquidity, time horizon, and tax, legal and regulatory, and unique circumstances, and (3) a statement of the proposed investment strategy as embodied in target asset class weights. This chapter focused on defining objectives and constraints
for four major types of institutional clients—foundations, endowments, defined
benefit pension plans, and defined contribution or 401(k) plans—and for individuals. Tools for determining appropriate asset allocations are the focus of the next
three chapters.

After studying Chapter 2, students should be equipped to complete the "First Deliverable" assignment for the individual, defined benefit, and defined contribution cases
in the appendix. For the equity fund case, students should also study Section 7.7 of
Chapter 7.

The following problem is in the form of an investment case involving setting investment and distribution policy for a university endowment. A summary of the case is
provided here, followed by a list of questions and an investment proposal.

Investment Case
Investment Firm: JAKE Investment Management LLC
Client: Braeburn University

Background

Braeburn University has an endowment of $800 million as of the end of 2002. Historically the university has been 100 percent invested in equities, with a growth bias. The endowment pays out 3.5 percent each year, based on the three-year average market value. The university has an annual budget of $500 million.

	Fund	S&P500	Bonds
1999	33.2%	9.0%	−10.1%
2000	−22.4	−2.0	21.5
2001	−20.4	−17.3	3.6
2002	−27.9	−24.3	17.0

Issues

Endowments may generate income to support current financial needs. However, spending the money now leaves less for the future.

Spending a fixed dollar amount leads to a varying percentage and a tendency to spend a greater percentage when securities are cheaper. Spending a fixed percentage leads to a varying dollar amount, which makes it difficult to plan program funding.

Investing in low-volatility assets tends to yield low returns. Investing in high-return assets tends to lead to volatile asset values, income, and consequently funds available for program spending.

The Assignment

The trustees have been disappointed with the performance of the account, and you have been hired to review the plan. They request a review of endowment investment and spending policies and a proposal for asset allocation.

Problems

1. Identify the following, or state that it is missing in the attached JAKE investment report:
   - Objectives
     - Summary of problem
     - Objectives
     - Constraints and issues
   - Asset allocation and funding plan
     - Funding status
     - Asset allocation analysis
     - Recommendation
     - Summary: How to meet goals, objectives, and constraints

- Implementation/mechanics
  - Vehicles and selection process
  - Time line
  - Management issues
  - Ongoing communication
  - Measuring success
2. What problems are there with this analysis and recommendation?
   a. Arithmetic means are used to calculate inflation and 60/40 historical averages for use in the chart comparing asset and expense growth. How would the time requirement change if JAKE used lower geometric means?
   b. In the same analysis and chart, withdrawals are assumed to be zero. If 3.5% annual withdrawals are included, how would the time requirement change? What should JAKE recommend to Braeburn in that situation?
3. How could the analysis and recommendation be improved?

JAKE Investment Management LLC

Investment and Spending Policy Review
Client: Braeburn University
Date: January 2007

Summary of Situation

Braeburn University retains an endowment of $800 million, invested 100 percent in equities. The endowment provides a 3.5 percent payout (based on three-year average market value) to the school, whose annual expense budget is $500 million.

Objective

Identify the optimal investment allocation and spending policy.

- The key goal may be to grow the endowment enough to generate income equal to 10 percent of annual expenses.
  - The fund will grow in nominal returns.
  - Expenses will grow with inflation.
- Investment policy should also minimize the following:
  - Volatility of income.
  - The risk of missing the target asset level.

Observations

- The size of the endowment, while large in dollar terms, is small compared to the size of the school: 3.5 percent of the endowment represents not much more than 5 percent of the school's annual budget.
  - Large universities exhibit endowments ranging up to $20+ billion.

- Once the endowment grows to $1.4 billion, the 3.5 percent withdrawal will represent 10 percent of annual expenses.
- The 3.5 percent spending policy is conservative.
  - A lower spending rate will support higher endowment growth.
  - University spending rates commonly range up to 5.5 percent.
  - A 5 percent spending policy would represent 8 percent of current expenses.
- The full equity allocation with a growth bias may be designed for long-term appreciation but may be unnecessarily undiversified. The following chart, based on three-year annualized returns between 1973 and 2006, illustrates that three-year returns for a 100 percent equity portfolio vary from −50 percent to +150 percent, even when it is diversified among equity classes.

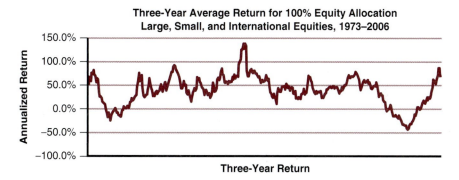

- Spending policy may be structured with a minimum spending need, with surplus funds available for flexible initiatives, thereby reducing the volatility of endowment funding for ongoing expenses.

Recommended Asset Allocation

Goal: Grow the endowment to meet 10 percent of annual expenses over a 5–10 year period.

- Inflation has averaged 4.75 percent between 1970 and 2006.
- 60/40 equity/bond mix has generated an arithmetic mean 10.7% annual return
- Will need 11 years at these rates, excluding any withdrawals. 10-year horizon requires a target 11% annual return.

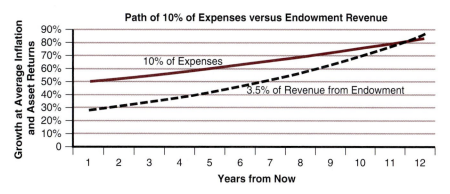

Risk: Limit the risk of losing more than 10 percent of the endowment over any three-year period.

Asset Allocation Optimization Guidelines

JAKE Investment Management has defined a multistep asset allocation optimization process:

1. Diversify among multiple asset classes.
2. Set a maximum weight of 25 percent in any class.
3. Maximize return.
4. Minimize the risk of significant negative returns.

Asset Allocation Optimization Technique

JAKE Investment Management uses a sophisticated asset allocation optimization process that defines risk as the variability of annual returns less than zero. It combines historical risk measurements with long-term return forecasts. The goal is to provide a high return with a low chance of significantly negative returns in a given year. The specific steps are listed here:

1. Partial moments optimization process:
   a. Maximize forecast return.
   b. Forecast based on James–Stein estimates.
   c. Correlations based on historical experience.
2. Incorporate the following:
   a. Investment-grade bonds, large and small caps, developed and emerging market equities, venture capital, private equity, hedge funds, commodities, and real estate.
   b. Constraints:
      i. No shorting.
      ii. Maximum 25 percent in any asset class.
3. The optimization results are listed here, including weights, return forecasts, and risk analysis:

Weights

	Percentage of Portfolio
Cash	7
Bonds	25
U.S. large cap	3
U.S. small cap	0
International equities: developed	0
International equities: emerging	15
Venture capital	0
Private equity	0
Hedge funds	25
Real estate	25
Commodities	0
Total	100

Expected Return

James-Stein Log Estimates: 9.3% versus 9.4% for benchmark

Historical Arithmetic Means: 11.3% versus 10.7% for benchmark

Risk Analysis versus 60/40 Benchmark Annual 1970 – 2006

Note: Calendar year returns for beta and standard deviations. Frequencies based on rolling 12-month periods.

| | Beta | Active Standard Deviation | Standard Deviation | % Frequency of Return | | | |
				<–5%	<–10%	<–25%	Minimum
Portfolio	0.56	9.8%	10.8%	4.9%	2.6%	0.0%	–24.7%
Benchmark	1.00	0.0%	13.0%	9.9%	3.3%	0.2%	–26.9%
Difference	(0.44)	9.8%	–2.2%	–4.9%	–0.7%	–0.2%	2.2%

Observations

1. The J/S Forecast return is similar to the benchmark but below the 10 percent revenue-funding target return. The historical arithmetic mean return is above the benchmark and the target. More than 10 years may be needed to meet the funding target level.
2. The overall risk is lower than the conservative 60/40 mix.
3. The historical frequency of a return < −10% in a given year is approximately 2.5 percent.

Historical Simulation

The proposed mix is stress tested back to 1970, as illustrated in the following chart:

Historical Record of Recommended Mix

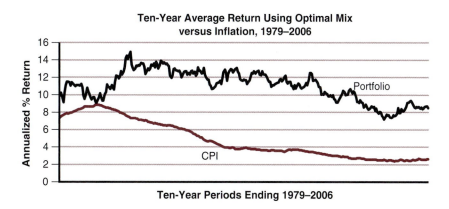

Ten-Year Average Return Using Optimal Mix versus Inflation, 1979–2006

The simulation suggests several conclusions:

- The portfolio clearly outpaces inflation over long periods.
- A lower portfolio return coincides with lower inflation.

Selection of Investment Vehicles for Asset Allocation

The key to effectively implementing the target asset allocation is to ensure that selected managers will actually deliver the basic asset class return, and in some cases deliver value added with limited downside risk. Our philosophy for manager selection includes identifying managers who can articulate a credible investment philosophy, have developed an investment process to apply that philosophy, and have built an infrastructure to deliver satisfactory investment results. Staff, experience, and ethical standards are all reviewed. This philosophy is consistent with Treynor (FAJ). A commitment to excellence is a key requirement. Performance track records are reviewed for consistency in delivery and with the investment philosophy. This is consistent with academic evidence (Stewart, JPM). We assign managers with the expectation for the relationship to last 5–10 years. Managers are also selected to complement each other, thereby providing diversification.

JAKE Investment Management offers low-cost passive equity and fixed income management through the use of ETFs, derivatives, or individual securities. Our professional staff is highly experienced, is supported by extensive resources, and has built a highly successful 10-year record for all disciplines.

1. *Large-cap U.S. equity and fixed income investments:*

   We propose two passive portfolios managed by JAKE versus the S&P 500 and Lehman Aggregate indexes. The opportunity for value added in these two disciplines is remote, especially net of monitoring costs and active management fees.

2. *Active cash manager:*

   We recommend selecting Cash Manager A or Cash Manager B to manage a high–quality, short-term fund. Both managers have passed our rigorous review process and have maintained a relationship with us for over five years. Recommended guidelines include average maturity of less than six months and quality of issues A or A1/P1 or higher. Both managers offer experienced professional staff with broad resources. Track records are excellent for both commingled and separate accounts. We recommend selecting the manager with the staff the client is most comfortable working with.

3. *Three actively managed asset classes:*
   - *Emerging markets*

     We believe fundamental and quantitative techniques may add value in emerging market investments net of fees and transaction costs. Our preference is for hybrid managers who use both types of techniques.

   - *Hedge funds*

     We believe it makes sense to utilize long/short strategies to deliver active returns from both buy and sell ideas. Our selection is biased toward firms that offer a philosophy that benefits from both sides of the asset valuation challenge. We seek a collection of both fundamental and quantitative managers who complement each other. Reasonable investment capacity limits must be taken seriously by hedge fund managers. We partner with Cambridge Associates in preparing our list of managers. Because manager liquidity is limited in the hedge fund world, it may take years before large allocations are fully invested.

- *Real estate*
  We believe that investment-grade real estate investments generate subpar returns unless the asset class is generally undervalued. Instead we seek development firms, "Brownfield" projects, and investments in developing markets, including Eastern Europe.

Time Line for Transition

Several issues are involved in implementing asset allocation changes. These include transaction costs, market valuation, and market timing. The first decision must involve market valuation. We conduct ongoing reviews of markets, identifying three ranges, as illustrated here:

$$\longleftarrow\joinrel\joinrel\joinrel\joinrel\joinrel\joinrel\joinrel\joinrel\joinrel\joinrel\joinrel\joinrel\joinrel\joinrel\joinrel\joinrel\longrightarrow$$

| Significant undervaluation | Fair valuation | Significant overvaluation |
| (25% or less of the time) | | (25% or less of the time) |

If target markets fall in the significantly undervalued zone, we will be quicker to move into that asset class. We may temporarily use derivatives if they are cost-effective. We will dollar average significant changes if valuations appear to be fair. Speed of change will also be influenced by liquidity levels, with less liquid markets associated with slower movements.

JAKE Asset Valuation

Process:
- Identify the appropriate valuation measure.
- Calculate the statistical distribution of the valuation measure.
- Classify significant levels one standard deviation above and below the mean.

Current market conditions:
- Large-cap U.S. equities: overvalued.
- Fixed income: fair.
- Real estate: fair except for U.S. investment grade, which is overvalued.
- Emerging markets: fair.
- Hedge funds: manager-specific.

Time Line

1. Liquidate U.S. equity position within 1 month.
2. Implement fixed income allocation over 3 months.
3. Fine-tune emerging market allocation over 3 months.
4. Implement real estate allocation over 12 months.
5. Implement hedge fund allocation over 12 months.

Fee Proposal

- Asset allocation advice and monitoring: 15 basis points annually on all assets.
- Passive equity and fixed income management: 5 basis points annually on invested assets.
- Manager searches: $50,000 per external manager hired.

Investment Firm–Client Relationship

The professional staff at JAKE Investment Management LLC is satisfied only when our clients are more than satisfied. Our goal is to deliver on stated investment objectives with which our clients are comfortable.

We are readily available to conduct analysis, meet with client personnel, and investigate problem issues. With Braeburn University, our goals are these:

1. Long-term (10-year) investment results to increase the endowment's contribution to university revenue to the 10 percent level.
2. Limited volatility over one- and three-year periods, limiting downside results to no more than 10 percent in any year.
3. Effective management of the optimal asset allocation and manager selection, based on market valuations and manager capabilities, in order to deliver goals 1 and 2.
4. Effective communication.

3

Asset Allocation: The Mean–Variance Framework

Chapter Outline

3.1 Introduction: Motivation of the Mean–Variance Approach to Asset Allocation

Asset allocation is the term used to describe the set of weights of broad classes of investments within a portfolio. For an individual investor, asset allocation can be represented by the proportional investment in bond mutual funds, stock mutual funds, and money market investments. For example, if an investor holds $1,500 in bond mutual funds, $3,000 in stock mutual funds, and $500 in money market funds, this asset allocation can be described as 30 percent bonds, 60 percent stocks, and 10 percent cash. This set of weights would provide an initial summary of the risk profile of the individual investor's investments, prior to completing a more detailed description of the funds owned or an even more detailed description of the individual securities held in the funds. Why does this allocation represent the risk profile? Certain investments reflect greater volatility, and investing in multiple asset classes tends to be less risky than placing 100 percent in any one investment.

Once an investor's goals and objectives have been defined, setting the asset allocation target is the first step in developing an investment program. These weights will define the overall behavior of the portfolio and should be set to match the risk and return targets for the investor. For example, an investor concerned about total return risk would tend to have a higher weight in money market funds than would a more risk-tolerant investor.

Asset allocation techniques represent tools that help professionals set the optimal mix between broad classes of investments. They are used to determine how much money should be placed in stocks versus bonds and so on. Different techniques may be used for short-term and long-term investment horizons, but they all have the same goal of setting proportional investments.

Asset allocation tools can help solve many investment problems, including those faced by individual investors, defined benefit pension (DB) plans, defined contribution (401(k)) plans, endowments, and foundations. Although the techniques may be similar in concept, there are important differences between the tools applied to different problems. For example, DB plans are characterized by a detailed cash flow stream listing projected payments to retirees. This stream reflects the liability that must be met in the long term through funding and investment. The asset allocation of a DB plan must optimize the match between plan assets and this liability. On the other hand, 401(k) plans do not reflect a single, well-defined liability. Individual investors must decide their asset allocations utilizing proxies for the liability, such as expected retirement expenses and future sources of income, as well as risk preferences.

Types of Asset Allocation

There are at least three types of asset allocation: **strategic, tactical, and dynamic.** Strategic allocation, as defined by Nobel Prize winner Bill Sharpe (1987), is set based on long-term goals. For example, if you need to set your asset allocation today for the next 30 years, you would be defining a strategic allocation. A fixed strategic allocation would be consistent with constant investment opportunities and risk tolerances. A fixed allocation may not be a good fit for an individual who plans to switch from saving to spending sometime in the future. In practice, strategic allocations are reviewed and revised at least every three to five years.

Tactical asset allocation responds to short-term changes in investment opportunities. Investors who frequently adjust their exposure to stocks, bonds, and cash are called *market timers* and set their allocations tactically. They seek to profit from short-term movements in the market, expect to change their asset weights in the near future, and may not worry much about the long-term implications of their average weights. Some active allocation managers may define a band around strategic weights, within which weights may be set in the short term but never deviate by so much so that tactical bets overwhelm the strategic allocation. For example, a long-term average target weight of 50 percent stocks with a ± 10 percent band yielding a 40–60 percent range would incorporate both strategic and tactical allocations.

Dynamic asset allocation is driven by changes in risk tolerance, typically induced by cumulative performance relative to investment goals or an approaching investment horizon. Portfolio insurance, popular in the mid-1980s, was a dynamic allocation strategy. It was designed to replicate the behavior of a put option by constantly adjusting the allocation to stocks based on the market level. This delta hedge was implemented using futures contracts and worked well until market liquidity collapsed in the 1987 crash. Other forms of dynamic allocation include constant proportion portfolio insurance, constant horizon portfolio insurance, and dynamic horizon asset allocation models.

Asset Classes

Asset allocation refers to setting the weights of asset classes. **Asset classes** are typically defined as groups of securities with similar characteristics. Statistically their constituents exhibit high correlations within each class, but low correlation

EXHIBIT 3.1   **Historical Correlations: Monthly Gross Returns, 35 Years Ending 12/31/2008**

	US Small Stk	S&P500	Int'l Stock	US High Yield	US Corp Bond	US Govt Bond	30-Day Tbill	US Inflation
US Small Stk	1.00	0.79	0.51	0.57	0.27	0.04	−0.02	−0.03
S&P500		1.00	0.59	0.57	0.36	0.14	0.03	−0.06
Int'l Stock			1.00	0.46	0.26	0.09	0.01	−0.06
US High Yield				1.00	0.62	0.34	0.05	−0.06
US Corp Bond					1.00	0.87	0.09	−0.16
US Govt Bond						1.00	0.14	−0.16
30-Day Tbill							1.00	0.44
US Inflation								1.00

EXHIBIT 3.2   **Historical Returns: Annualized Gross, Ending 12/31/2008**

	Last 50 Years	Last 35 Years	Last 10 Years	Last 5 Years
US Small Stk	12.5%	12.6%	3.0%	−0.9%
S&P500	10.0%	10.0%	−1.4%	−2.2%
Int'l Stock	N/A	9.8%	1.2%	2.1%
US High Yield	7.1%	8.2%	2.2%	−0.8%
US Corp Bond	6.8%	8.3%	4.9%	2.6%
US Govt Bond	6.9%	8.5%	6.3%	6.4%
30-Day Tbill	5.4%	5.9%	3.2%	2.9%
US Inflation	4.1%	4.4%	2.6%	2.8%

between the classes. As mentioned previously, stocks, bonds, and cash are the most common forms of asset classes; they may be expanded to include international stocks and bonds, real estate, venture capital, hedge funds, high-yield (junk) bonds, and commodities. The return correlations between the classes are frequently assumed to be stable and offer attractive diversification, on average. However, under some circumstances such as periods of market crises, correlation levels can shift quickly and eliminate diversification benefits.[1] This occurred in late 2008 when correlations among risky assets (such as equity classes and high-yield bonds) quickly approached 1. Long-term correlation estimates are reported in Exhibit 3.1, illustrating the high correlation between the domestic equity classes and relatively low correlation between equities and government bonds. Investment-grade corporate and lower-quality high-yield bonds exhibit somewhat stronger correlation with equities. Investment-grade corporate bonds are highly correlated with government bonds, but high-yield corporate bonds appear more closely related to equities. Inflation exhibits low correlation with investments, except for very short-maturity Treasury bills.

Exhibit 3.2 reports historical returns across several asset classes for multiple time horizons. Over the long term, small-cap stocks have generated the strongest performance at the cost of higher volatility, as shown in Exhibit 3.3. Corporate bonds earned returns similar to those of government bonds, though the latter are of longer duration

[1] This issue frequently arises in the context of global investing and is discussed in Chapter 10.

EXHIBIT 3.3   **Historical Standard Deviation: Annual Gross Returns, Ending 12/31/2008**

	Last 50 Years	Last 35 Years	Last 10 Years	Last 5 Years
US Small Stk	25.2%	23.0%	21.7%	21.4%
S&P500	17.6%	18.9%	21.2%	21.2%
Int'l Stock	N/A	23.2%	25.5%	28.1%
US High Yield	12.0%	13.6%	13.3%	15.5%
US Corp Bond	8.8%	9.2%	4.7%	3.5%
US Govt Bond	6.9%	6.5%	5.3%	4.8%
30-Day Tbill	2.8%	3.0%	1.8%	1.7%
US Inflation	3.0%	3.2%	1.1%	1.6%

and the results were impacted by the events of 2008. Net of inflation, the real return of fixed-income investments has been much lower than that of stocks over longer periods. The reliability of sample statistics will be discussed in detail in Chapter 4.

Asset allocation tools are motivated by economic theory and built using mathematics. They rely on assumptions about human behavior—most importantly that investors prefer higher returns and lower risk. There is a lot of flexibility in defining the parameters for the mathematics. For example, returns may be defined over different periods—one month, one year, or 30 years. Risk may be defined as short-term volatility, the chance of losing money, or the probability of meeting wealth goals. Combining investor objectives and preferences and the statistical behavior of asset classes within a mathematical model can provide a useful tool for setting optimal asset weights.

However, oversimplification of investor goals or the behavior of asset returns can yield the wrong solution. For example, an economic utility function may be easy to apply mathematically, but it may not effectively capture individual or corporate preferences. Investors look at more than the standard deviation of returns when they evaluate risk. Moreover, the characteristics and behavior of asset classes are not stable and may need to be described by more than mean return and return standard deviation. Finally, highly sophisticated approaches that more accurately fit reality may be difficult for the final user to understand, creating the opportunity for a mismatch between the investor's goals and the solution. The key to successfully using these tools is to balance sophistication with simplicity and apply healthy doses of intuition and skepticism.

The Mean–Variance Framework

The **mean–variance (M–V)** framework, originally developed by Nobel Prize winner Harry Markowitz (1952) and others, is a popular model for computing optimal asset allocations. The math is easy and fairly well describes reality. The model is fair in the sense that risk, return, and preferences can all be included in some form; in addition, specific allocations can be computed.

To apply this framework some assumptions about reality are required. Investors need to be risk averse and wealth maximizing; these assumptions reflect the real world. Another assumption is that either returns are normally distributed (or can be transformed to that distribution), or investors are interested only in mean and variance (or semivariance); this is only an approximation of reality. Statistical analyses indicate that historical returns exhibit fatter tails than are suggested by normal distributions. In other words, really bad and really good things happen more frequently than predicted by a bell-shaped curve. If you use a M–V model to set allocations, in practice it makes sense to examine setting allocations using risk and return data generated over different

War Story *Horizon Funds*

Dynamic allocation horizon funds were introduced in the mid-1990s as a better investment option for 401(k) investors than fixed allocation lifestyle funds. The first mutual fund product offered a linear path for the target allocation to equities, declining to a level close to zero as the fund's horizon (the investor's approximate retirement date) approached. On top of this structure was a tactical process that actively timed the equity allocation as market conditions allowed.

A linear allocation path was simple, easy to understand and describe, but inappropriate. The investor's perception of risk is not necessarily linear in time. Some portfolio managers recognized this and included nonlinear paths built on long-term downside risk targets. This technique is reviewed in Chapter 5. Many subsequently developed competing products avoided tactical allocation because the strategic levels were key to investment success, and these passive allocations were dynamic in their own right. Moreover, many funds included active security selection.

During the development of these products in the 1990s (and later enhancements in the mid-2000s), historical testing alone could have suggested that higher equity allocations would always yield better results. This was because stocks had experienced a 10+ -year bull market, and any increase in equities would have generated higher historical returns. Left to their own devices, inexperienced financial modelers could demonstrate that 100 percent equity allocations would always dominate any other mix. Taken to its logical conclusion, this model predicted that there was no need for diversification and asset allocation! Only the understanding that things sometimes do not work out as expected, suspected through intuition and observed through experience, would lead to more conservative allocations for retirement savers. Retirees would all have benefited from this in late 1998, 2000–2002, and 2008.

periods. It is also helpful to confirm your results with historical simulations that include worst-case scenarios. Chapter 7 addresses these issues in greater detail.

What can we do with the mean–variance framework? Given a model, we can estimate future market values of wealth. We can also calculate confidence intervals around these expectations. The probability of losing different levels of wealth over different periods can be estimated, given mean–variance assumptions. And a model user can calculate an optimal mix of investments reflecting an investor's trade-off preferences between risk and return. Risk may be defined as return variance, semivariance, the probability of losing money, or the risk relative to a liability. Moreover, varying time horizons may be included as well as wealth, return, risk, and borrowing constraints.

The following section provides the theoretical underpinnings of the mean–variance framework, followed by a section describing how to apply this theory in a computer program or spreadsheet. The theory begins by describing a world in which prices move randomly through time according to a lognormal probability distribution. Returns calculated from these prices move according to a normal distribution. Once expected returns, variances, and covariances of asset classes are estimated, we can calculate the expected returns and variances of portfolios reflecting different asset weights. For a given expected portfolio return, we can search for the weights associated with the portfolio offering the lowest overall variance; we call this the **minimum variance portfolio (MVP),** which we can use to plot the **efficient frontier.**

In this world individuals display a utility function, which converts expected returns and variances into a single value that is meaningful to them and can be communicated to others. This function trades off mean and variance with a sensitivity parameter defined as the **risk aversion coefficient.** Utility values can be compared for portfolios with different asset weights, and the individual can select the asset weights with the highest value. This is the optimal asset allocation. Because the utility function dislikes variance, this portfolio will be on the efficient frontier.

Theory in Practice
The Importance of Asset Allocation

Asset allocation policy is important. Brokerage firms, mutual fund companies, and financial pundits can all be found to state that 90 percent of portfolio returns are determined by asset allocation policy. What does this mean?

A research study by Brinson, Hood, and Beebower (1986) reported that, on average, over 90 percent of the variability in pension plan total returns could be explained by their asset allocation policies. The 90 percent is the *R*-square from regressing quarterly plan returns on the returns of asset class indexes. Security selection, market timing, trading costs, and style factors should explain the rest. For a given fund over a short period, a portfolio's asset allocation policy will determine, with high probability, much of the portfolio's return. Note, however, that this will not necessarily be the case for all funds in all periods because the result is only an average.

A study by Ibbotson and Kaplan (2000) demonstrated that asset allocation, on average, explained an even larger percentage (100 percent) of long-term (they used 5- and 10-year) portfolio total returns. Again, this will not be the case for all portfolios because the result is only an average. If an investor hires index managers, by definition asset allocation will determine future total returns. In contrast, if an investor hires highly concentrated managers, asset allocation may be overwhelmed, at least in the short run, by asset class manager performance. With diversified equity and fixed-income investments, for the long term, asset allocation is much more important than selecting the mix of asset class managers.

Ibottson and Kaplan also determined that relative performance between two multi-asset class funds is influenced by asset allocation as well. Relative returns are influenced less than total returns because asset class total returns have been removed to a large extent. The influence is determined by how different the asset allocation policies of the funds are. In the study's data set, asset allocation explained 40 percent of relative annual return variability, the remainder being explained by style, market timing, trading costs, and security selection. As a result, asset allocation policy is important in determining the performance of one portfolio versus another, but other factors are cumulatively more important.

What can we take from this? In general, the decision to place 0 percent or 50 percent in stocks is more important than which equity manager is hired. But the decision to place 50 percent or 55 percent in stocks is less important than which equity manager is hired.

One of the nice things about the mean–variance framework is that it can be customized to more closely reflect a real investment problem. For example, the risk aversion coefficient can be adjusted to make risk seem more unattractive, reflecting a conservative investor. With normality, variance can be converted into probabilities of high or low returns so we can compare portfolios by, for example, their chance of losing money over time. This is called *shortfall risk* and is a useful tool for setting investment policy for individuals and institutional investors. It is easy to add asset classes—there is no need to be limited to two or three. The relevant time frame can be changed by simply converting returns and variances into longer-period measures. Most investors do not wish to leverage their investments; this can be represented within the model with a **long-only constraint,** which requires all asset weights to be zero or positive. A liability, such as a pension plan's benefit payment stream, may be added to the model as a negative fixed-income asset class. Each of these features will be either discussed in the following theory section or developed in the subsequent application section.

The mean–variance framework is not fully customizable, however. For example, it is difficult to implement intraperiod cash flows (such as 401(k) contributions) within the model. Nonnormal distributions (those with fatter tails than reflected in the normal distribution) may not be included in the mean–variance model. In addition, changing investment opportunities (such as changing expected returns and variances through time) are difficult to include. In practice, optimal portfolios often

Investment advisors come in all shapes and sizes. Pension consultants in particular tend to be highly sophisticated—they need to be. Their clients are plan sponsors, responsible for investing the money set aside to pay benefits to their companies' employees after they retire. Pension assets are large—the largest 10 represented over $1.5 trillion as of December 2007. As a result, improper asset allocation will cost employers a lot of money.

Pension consultants provide advice on how to invest pension assets—selecting the professional managers, the asset classes, and the asset allocation. One asset allocation tool they use is the mean–variance model. They use this for educational purposes, such as explaining risk–return trade-offs to their clients. And they use it for advising on asset allocation policy—both for education and for proposing targets. For example, mean–variance modeling was relied on heavily for making the case in the mid-1980s to invest internationally.

Pension consultants know mean–variance modeling is a useful technique that must be applied with caution and supplemented with additional tools. For example, the decision to invest internationally was based on the expected benefit of both higher return and lower risk. Higher returns were not realized in the late 1980s and 1990s but were in the 2000s.

Sophisticated consultants frequently supplement the process with studies of historical data. They confirm the results of their mean–variance model with simulated confidence intervals. Less sophisticated consultants "apply an oversimplified 401(k) model, ignoring cash flow concerns. For pension consultants, this means they ignore the liability side of the equation, "paying it only lip service," in the opinion of one veteran investment professional, who goes on to say, "The good ones have a longer-term view of the problem and recognize the existence of the liability, but their approach may be static. For example, they'll say, 'Looking out three years, this is what your liability will be, so we should set asset allocation policy based on that.' Many don't recognize that you need to consider that your liability will change again in another three years," as well as the importance of setting today's allocation with future changes in the liability in mind. A review of Exhibits 2.10 and 2.11 confirms the importance of these observations.

reflect corner solutions with 0 percent weights for most assets or, in the extreme, 100 percent allocated to a single asset. Moreover, results may be highly sensitive to small changes in assumptions, making it difficult for the practitioner to set appropriate asset allocations. These issues can wait—there are more advanced techniques to handle them, and they will be addressed in Chapter 5. For now we will explore the theory behind mean–variance asset allocation.

3.2 Theory: Outline of the Mean–Variance Framework[2]

Utility Theory

More than 50 years ago Markowitz (1952) developed a simple framework, known as mean–variance (M–V) analysis, for analyzing the trade-off between risk and return for portfolios containing several assets. As will become apparent later, this framework has some important limitations. Nonetheless it is by far the most common approach to practical asset allocation decisions. This section provides a formal introduction to the M–V model.

In practice an investor can make investment decisions at various intervals over the course of their investment horizon. One simplifying assumption of the M–V model

---

[2] See Appendix 1 for a review of the basic statistical concepts and common probability distributions used in this section.

EXHIBIT 3.4
Risk Averse Utility

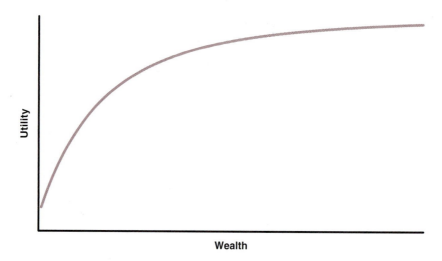

is that the investor will select the same portfolio in each of these subperiods, and, as a result, the investor's decision problem may be treated as if there were only a single period. The conditions required to validate this assumption will be discussed in Chapter 5.

In economics it is standard to assume that investors base their decisions on a **utility function** that maps wealth to their subjective assessments of the **utility,** the level of welfare or satisfaction, provided by this level of wealth. Because future wealth is uncertain, investors attempt to maximize the expected value of utility. Letting W denote wealth and $U()$ the investor's utility function, we can write this formally as

$$\max E[U(W)] \qquad (3.1)$$

where E represents taking the expected value of the expression in brackets. The utility function, illustrated in Exhibit 3.4, has two key properties. First, utility rises with wealth because more wealth is assumed to be preferred to less. The slope of the utility function reflects the investor's **marginal utility:** the change in utility due to a small change in wealth. Second, utility rises at a decreasing rate as wealth increases. That is, there are diminishing benefits to each increment of wealth, and marginal utility declines as wealth increases.[3]

A simple example will illustrate the relationship among wealth, risk, and expected utility.[4] Suppose an investor is offered a choice between two investments; one is riskless and the other entails risk. The riskless investment results in a wealth level denoted by $W2$ in Exhibit 3.5. The risky investment has two possible outcomes denoted by $W1$ and $W3$. The utility associated with each level of wealth is reflected by the height of the utility function at that point. The expected payoff on the risky investment is assumed to be $W2$—that is, the same as the certain outcome from the riskless investment. An investor who does not care about risk would be indifferent between these two investments because they provide the same expected wealth. Our risk-averse investor, however, evaluates the investments on the basis of expected utility.

---

[3] Consider the pleasure obtained from the first, second, third, or more cup of coffee in the morning. For most people, even something pleasurable becomes less pleasurable, and possibly even unpleasant, in excess.

[4] The following discussion is summarized in the Excel Outbox.

EXHIBIT 3.5
Expected Utility and
Risk Aversion

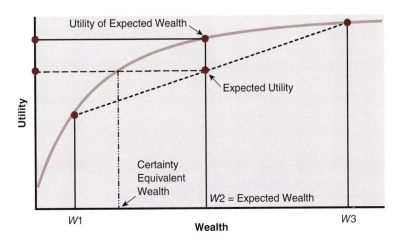

The expected utility of the riskless investment is simply the utility of $W2$ because the outcome is known with certainty. The expected utility of the risky investment is a weighted average of the utilities at $W1$ and $W3$. The upward-sloping dashed line in Exhibit 3.5 shows weighted averages corresponding to varying the probability of the two possible outcomes. Note that this line lies below the utility function except at the endpoints.[5] The point labeled "expected utility" lies on this line directly above the expected wealth level, $W2$, and has the same probability of outcomes. The vertical distance between this point and the point labeled "utility of expected wealth" is the penalty (in utility) that the investor assigns to the risk. Although the two investments give the same expected wealth ($W2$), the risk-averse investor prefers the riskless investment.

Continuing the example, we might ask what level of certain wealth the investor would view as equivalent to the risky investment. In the exhibit this is labeled as the "certainty equivalent wealth" (CEW). The utility of this wealth level is equal to the expected utility of the risky investment. The horizontal distance between the CEW and the expected level of wealth ($W2$) is a measure of the compensation—in expected wealth—that the investor requires for bearing the risk inherent in the risky investment. The risky investment is preferred to any level of certain wealth less than the CEW, while any level of certain wealth greater than the CEW is preferred to the risky investment.

The absolute level of utility is not relevant to the investor's decisions because more wealth is always better. The curvature of the utility function—the benefit of a gain versus the pain of a loss—is what matters. The curvature of the utility function reflects the investor's **risk aversion** or willingness to take risk. The most useful measure of risk aversion, known as the coefficient of **relative risk aversion (RRA)**, is defined by

$$\text{RRA} = -\frac{\%\text{ change in marginal utility}}{\%\text{ change in wealth}} \tag{3.2}$$

Because marginal utility declines as wealth increases, the negative sign in Equation (3.2) implies that RRA is (by convention) positive. In general the RRA depends on the

[5] The endpoints correspond to cases in which there is actually no uncertainty because one of the outcomes ($W1$ or $W3$) has zero probability while the other has probability 1.

level of wealth at which it is measured. The higher the RRA, the more risk averse the investor. In terms of Exhibits 3.4 and 3.5, the higher the RRA, the more pronounced the curvature of the utility function.

To obtain concrete results it is usually necessary to limit attention to a specific class of utility functions. One of the simplest and most useful utility functions for investment analysis is the so-called power utility or constant relative risk aversion (CRRA) utility function, defined by

$$U(W) = W^{\gamma}/\gamma \quad \gamma < 1 \tag{3.3}$$

As its name implies, the CRRA exhibits constant relative risk aversion equal to $(1 - \gamma)$. Typically γ is assumed to be negative.[6]

Excel Outbox *Utility Function*	To make Exhibit 3.5 more concrete, assume that you are offered either $50,000 ($W2$) for sure or a coin flip where you win $100,000 ($W3$) with heads or nothing ($W1$) with tails. Use the worksheet <Utility – Template> in spreadsheet Chapter 03 Excel Outboxes.xls. Assume your utility function displays constant relative risk aversion and takes the form W^{γ}/γ, where $\gamma = 0.5$—that is, $U(W) = 2\sqrt{W}$. In cell B1 enter 0.5. *Note:* $\gamma = 0.5$ implies a relatively high tolerance for risk. To capture more risk-averse preferences, γ is usually negative (as noted in the text). A $\gamma > 0$ is used here so that the utility function plots in the first quadrant where both wealth and utility are positive. There is nothing wrong with letting the utility function take negative values, as it does when $\gamma < 0$, because it is still increasing in wealth. However, positive values of utility are more intuitive.

	A	B	C	D	E	F	G
1	γ						
2							
3	Option		W	Probability	U(W)	E[U(W)]	CEW
4	Sure thing						
5	Coin Flip	Tails					
6		Heads					

Define the options:

- Sure thing: In cell C4 enter 50000, and in cell D4 enter 1. That is, the payoff is $50,000 with a probability of 100 percent.
- Coin flip: In cell C5 enter 0, and in cell C6 enter 100000. In cells D5 enter 0.5, and in cell D6 enter =(1 − D5). That is, there is a 50 percent chance of tails with a $0 payoff and a 50 percent chance of heads with a $100,000 payoff.

Calculate the utility of the options:

- U(W): In cell E4 enter =(C4^$B$1)/$B$1 and then copy E4 to E5:E6.
- The expected utility of the options is calculated as $\Sigma_i\, p_i\, U(W_i)$.
- Sure thing: In cell F4 enter =(D4*E4).
- Coin flip: In cell F5 enter =(D5*E5) + (D6*E6).

The sure thing has a utility of 447.21, and the coin flip has an expected utility of 316.23. As a result, the sure thing is preferred to the coin flip. This is the definition of risk aversion. Both options have an expected payoff of $50,000, but the lower-risk alternative is preferred.

---

[6] Logarithmic utility, $U(W) = \ln(W)$, is an important special case of CRRA utility. It is obtained as the limit of Equation (3.3) as γ goes to zero.

The question then becomes, What sure payoff would make you indifferent to the coin flip? That is, what level of wealth has a utility of 316.23?

- In cell G5 enter =($B$1*F5)^(1/$B$1). This is the inverse function of the utility function. The result is $25,000. That is, the coin flip would be preferred to a sure thing with a payoff below $25,000.

	A	B	C	D	E	F	G
1	γ	0.5					
2							
3	**Option**		**W**	**Probability**	**U(W)**	**E[U(W)]**	**CEW**
4	Sure thing		50,000	1.0	447.21	447.21	
5	Coin Flip	Tails	0	0.5	0.00	316.23	25,000
6		Heads	10,000	0.5	632.46		

Here are the inputs to the *X–Y* chart:

- In cell B9 enter =C4.
- In cell B10 enter =C5.
- In cell B12 enter =C6.
- In cell B13 enter =G5.
- In cell B11 enter =$D5*B10 + $D6*B12.
- In cell C9 enter =(B9^$B$1)/$B$1, and then copy C9 to cells C10 and C13 and cells C15:C36.
- In cell C11 enter = $D5*C10 + $D6*C12.

Note that the CEW for the coin flip lies on the utility function directly to the left of the E[U(W)] while the E[U(W)] lies directly below U(W) for the sure thing.

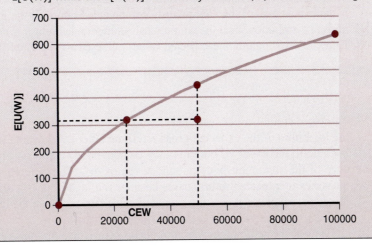

Return Behavior

The next step in developing the theory is to define the behavior of asset prices and returns. Suppose there are n assets (or asset classes) available to the investor and the investment horizon is T years. Let $P_i(t)$ denote the price of asset i, $i = 1, \ldots, n$, at time $t = 0, \ldots, T$. The time at which the investment decision is to be made is denoted by $t = 0$, whereas the end of the investment horizon is denoted by $t = T$. The prices of the assets at the beginning of the period are known. The prices during and at the end of the investment horizon are uncertain and are assumed to have a lognormal distribution. Specifically it is assumed that the prices at times t and $t - 1$ are related by

$$P_i(t) = P_i(t - 1) \exp[X_i(t)] \tag{3.4}$$

where $X_i(t)$ has a normal distribution with

$$\text{Mean} = \alpha_i$$
$$\text{Variance} = \sigma_i^2.$$

The random variables $X_i(t)$ and $X_i(s)$ are assumed to be uncorrelated unless $t = s$.

The *continuously compounded* return on asset i in the tth period is defined as the natural logarithm of the ratio of prices at the beginning and end of the period. Equation (3.4) gives the return as[7]

$$r_i(t) = \ln[P_i(t)/P_i(t - 1)] = X_i(t) \tag{3.5}$$

Because the continuously compounded return is equal to $X_i(t)$, it has a normal distribution with mean and variance given for Equation (3.4). Our assumptions also imply that asset returns may be contemporaneously correlated across assets, but they are not correlated across time periods. Combining this with the assumption that means and variances are constants, it follows that we are assuming investment opportunities are the same in every subperiod.

Before proceeding with the development of this model, we need to clarify the relationship between continuously compounded returns as defined in Equation (3.5) and another, perhaps more familiar, measure of return. The *gross return* is simply the ratio of prices at the beginning and end of the period. In our model the gross return on the ith asset is $\exp[X_i(t)]$. A comparison of Equations (3.4) and (3.5) shows that the continuously compounded return equals the logarithm of the gross return. Conversely, the gross return is the exponential of the continuously compounded return. If the gross return has a lognormal distribution, then the continuously compounded return is normal and vice versa. Under this assumption the expected values of these two measures of return are related by

$$\ln(E[\exp(X_i)]) = E[X_i] + \tfrac{1}{2}\text{var}(X_i) \tag{3.6}$$
$$= \alpha_i + \tfrac{1}{2}\sigma_i^2 \equiv \mu_i$$

To help distinguish between these two concepts of return, we have defined μ_i to be the logarithm of the expected gross return on asset i. According to Equation (3.6) this is equal to the expected continuously compounded return, α_i, plus one-half the variance of the continuously compounded return, σ_i^2. The difference between these two measures of expected return arises because the logarithm is a nonlinear function. So it matters whether we take the expected value first and then the logarithm or first take the logarithm and then the expected value.[8]

Each of the return concepts introduced here is useful, and each has advantages in certain applications. The advantage of gross returns is that the gross return of a portfolio is a simple weighted average of the gross returns of the underlying assets. This is not true for continuously compounded returns. The advantage of working with continuously compounded returns is that multiperiod returns are simply the sum of the returns in each

[7] See Appendix 1 for a review of compounding and multiperiod returns.

[8] Note that Equation (3.6) holds only when X_i has a normal distribution. However, a theorem known as Jensen's Inequality implies that the "log of the expected value" is greater than the "expectation of the log" for any probability distribution. This same theorem is responsible for the fact that the utility of expected wealth exceeds the expected utility of wealth in Exhibit 3.5.

period. This is not true for gross returns. Therefore in single-period models it is usually best to work with gross returns. In multiperiod contexts logarithmic returns are the natural choice. Because we want to relate the M–V framework to more general multiperiod problems, we will work primarily with continuously compounded returns. But we cannot forget about gross returns altogether, so we will be careful to specify "gross return" whenever that is the relevant concept.

Let $R_i(T)$ denote the cumulative continuously compounded return on asset i over the entire T-year investment horizon. Then

$$R_i(T) = \ln[P_i(T)/P_i(0)] \qquad (3.7)$$
$$= \Sigma_t \ln[P_i(t)/P_i(t-1)]$$
$$= \Sigma_t r_i(t).$$

So as indicated earlier, the cumulative (continuously compounded) return over the investment horizon is simply the sum of the (continuously compounded) returns in each of the underlying periods. Because the mean of a sum is equal to the sum of the means, the expected return over the T-year horizon is

$$\Sigma_t \alpha_i = \alpha_i T \qquad (3.8)$$

Return Variance

In general, the variance of a sum is *not* equal to the sum of the variances because the covariance between each pair of elements in the sum must be taken into account. In this case, however, all the covariances are zero. So the variance of the T-year return is

$$\Sigma_t \sigma_i^2 = \sigma_i^2 T \qquad (3.9)$$

The standard deviation is the square root of the variance and is therefore equal to $\sigma_i \sqrt{T}$. Note that the mean and variance of the continuously compounded return are proportional to the length of the investment horizon, T. The standard deviation, however, is proportional to the *square root* of the horizon. The relationship among risk, return, and investment horizon will be examined more fully later in this section.

Excel Outbox
Calculating
Returns

A spreadsheet provides an opportunity to explore these concepts. The monthly index level for the S&P 500 is given in cells C8:C1005 in reverse chronological order. Because these are index levels, there is no need to adjust for dividends and splits.

Use the worksheet <Returns – Template> in the spreadsheet Chapter 03 Excel Outboxes.xls.

The calculation of continuously compounded returns is given by $r(t) = \ln[P(t)/P(t-1)]$.

- In cell E8 enter = LN(C8/C9) and then copy cell E8 to cells E9:E1004.

As defined in the text, the gross return is given by = $P(t)/P(t-1)$. Note that the ending value, $P(t)$, equals $[P(t-1) + (P(t) - P(t-1))]$. To isolate the change in value, we need to calculate the net return, defined as $[(P(t)/P(t-1) - 1]$.

- In cell F8 enter = C8/C9 – 1, and then copy cell F8 to cells F9:F1004.

Summary statistics:
- In cell E1 enter = COUNT(E$8:E$1004) and then copy this to cells E2:E5.
- In cell E2 replace "COUNT" with "AVERAGE".
- In cell E3 replace "COUNT" with "STDEV".
- In cell E4 replace "COUNT" with "MAX".
- In cell E5 replace "COUNT" with "MIN".
- Copy cells E1:E5 to cells F1:F5.

(continued)

(continued)   Here are the results:

	A	B	C	D	E	F
1	S&P 500 Index - Monthly Data			Obs	997	997
2				Mean	0.73%	0.88%
3				S.D.	5.51%	5.54%
4				Max	35.46%	42.56%
5				Min	−35.28%	−29.73%
6						
7	OBS	DATE	SP500		r(t)	Gross-1
8	1	Jan-09	842.62		−6.95%	−6.71%
9	2	Dec-08	903.25		0.78%	0.78%

- There are 997 months in the sample.
- The monthly α = 0.73 percent. Notice that μ = 0.73 + ½ 5.51² = 0.88 percent, which is the estimated monthly mean of the net return (gross − 1) series. [*Note:* Strictly speaking we should compare μ to the *log* of the mean *gross* return. But LN(1 + x) ≈ x for small values of x. Here x is the monthly average net return, and (1 + x) is the monthly average gross return.]
- Notice that the total continuous compound return from the sample [=LN(C$8/C$1004)] is the same as the sum of the monthly continuous compound returns [=SUM(E8:E1004)].
- The monthly σ = 5.51 percent.
- The most noticeable difference is the maximum and minimum returns. For r(t), the maximum (35.46 percent) and minimum (−35.28 percent) one-month returns are nearly identical in absolute value, which is expected for a symmetric distribution such as the normal. This is not the case for the net return (gross − 1): The maximum one-month return (42.56 percent) is considerably higher than the absolute value of the minimum one-month return (−29.73 percent).

To examine the shape of the return distributions, construct frequency distributions:

	H	I	J	K
2		N	r	Gross-1
3	45.0%	0.0%	0.1%	0.3%
4	35.0%	0.0%	0.2%	0.0%
5	30.0%	0.0%	0.0%	0.1%
6	25.0%	0.0%	0.1%	0.0%
7	20.0%	0.5%	0.3%	0.3%
8	15.0%	4.2%	2.0%	2.2%
9	10.0%	17.3%	12.8%	14.0%
10	5.0%	33.3%	45.7%	44.3%
11	0.0%	29.8%	28.2%	28.5%
12	−5.0%	12.4%	7.7%	7.8%
13	−10.0%	2.4%	1.5%	1.4%
14	−15.0%	0.2%	0.6%	0.5%
15	−20.0%	0.0%	0.4%	0.4%
16	−25.0%	0.0%	0.2%	0.1%
17	−30.0%	0.0%	0.0%	0.0%
18	−35.0%	0.0%	0.1%	0.0%
19	−45.0%	0.0%	0.0%	0.0%
20		100.0%	100.0%	100.0%

- In cell I3 enter =NORMDIST($H3,$E$2,$E$3,TRUE)-NORMDIST($H4,$E$2,$E$3,TRUE) and then copy this to cells I4:I19. In cell I19 delete "-NORMDIST ($H19,$E$2, $E$3,TRUE)".

- In cells J3:J19 enter =FREQUENCY(E8:E1004,H3:H19)/$E$1 and then <SHIFT> <CTRL><ENTER> to enter this as a range array formula.
- In cells K3:K19 enter as an array =FREQUENCY(F8:F1004,H3:H19)/F$1.

Notice that while both the continuously compounded and net (gross − 1) return distributions follow the general shape of the normal curve, they both display positive skew (the empirical distributions are not symmetric) and kurtosis (there are more observations in the tails). The significance of these deviations from normality will be addressed in various contexts throughout the book.

Portfolio Return and Variance

Suppose an investor allocates a portfolio according to a set of weights, ω_i, that sum to unity (1). The gross return on the portfolio is then a weighted average of the gross returns on the individual assets. Unfortunately the logarithm of a sum is not equal to the sum of logarithms. So the continuously compounded portfolio return is not exactly a weighted average of the continuously compounded asset returns. However, it is approximately equal to that sum plus volatility adjustments. To avoid confusion with asset prices, let W (for wealth) denote the portfolio. The continuously compounded portfolio return is approximately[9]

$$R_W(\text{T}) = \Sigma_i \omega_i R_i(T) + \tfrac{1}{2}\Sigma_i \omega_i \sigma_i^2 T - \tfrac{1}{2}\sigma_W^2 T \qquad (3.10)$$

The first term in Equation (3.10) is the weighted average of the underlying asset returns. The second and third terms are volatility adjustments that adjust the level of the portfolio return for the difference in expected value between gross returns and continuously compounded returns. The second term adjusts each of the underlying asset returns upward by one-half its variance. Looking at Equation (3.6), we see that this adjusts the mean of each return upward to the log of its expected gross return. Together the first two terms capture a weighted average of underlying asset gross returns and are approximately equal to the log of the gross return on the portfolio. The third term then adjusts the mean of the portfolio return downward by one-half the variance of the portfolio return, $(\sigma_W^2 T)$, which will be defined in Equation (3.13). This adjustment is exactly analogous to the relationship shown in Equation (3.6) for individual asset returns except that instead of adding the variance term to the right side of Equation (3.6) we are subtracting it from the left side.

Next we need to obtain the mean and variance of the portfolio return. Using a standard result from probability, the expected value of a weighted average is the same as the weighted average of the expected values. Therefore, from Equation (3.10) the *expected portfolio return* is

$$\Sigma_i \omega_i \alpha_i T + \tfrac{1}{2}\Sigma_i \omega_i \sigma_i^2 T - \tfrac{1}{2}\sigma_W^2 T \equiv (\mu_W - \tfrac{1}{2}\sigma_W^2)T \qquad (3.11)$$

where we have defined

$$\mu_W \equiv \Sigma_i \omega_i(\alpha_i + \tfrac{1}{2}\sigma_i^2) = \Sigma_i \omega_i \mu_i \qquad (3.12)$$

The *variance of the portfolio return* is more complex because it must take into account not only each asset's own variance but also the covariance between each pair of assets. Applying a standard result for the variance of a weighted average gives

$$\sigma_W^2 T \equiv [\Sigma_i \Sigma_j \omega_i \omega_j \sigma_{ij}]T \qquad (3.13)$$

---

[9] This approximation is used extensively in Campbell and Viceira (2002). Given our assumption that gross asset returns are lognormal, Equation (3.10) holds exactly if portfolio weights are continuously rebalanced. With rebalancing at discrete intervals it is only an approximation.

where σ_{ij} denotes the covariance between the returns on assets i and j. For $i = j$ the covariance is equal to the variance of asset i. Note that μ_W is *linear* in the portfolio weights whereas the variance is *quadratic* because it involves squares and cross products of the weights.

Objective Function

Now we are ready to consider the growth of wealth, asset allocation, and the setting of asset weights. If the investor puts $1 of wealth into the portfolio at time $t = 0$, it will grow to

$$\exp[R_W(T)] \tag{3.14}$$

at the end of the investment horizon. Substituting this for wealth in the constant relative risk aversion utility function (Equation (3.3), it follows that an investor with CRRA utility will select portfolio weights to maximize

$$E\{(1/\gamma)\exp[\gamma\, R_W(T)]\} \tag{3.15}$$

Because $R_W(T)$ displays a normal distribution, the expression in brackets in Equation (3.15) has a lognormal distribution. The mean of this distribution is given by

$$(1/\gamma)\exp[\gamma(\mu_W T - \tfrac{1}{2}(1 - \gamma)\sigma_W^2 T)] \tag{3.16}$$

The exponent factor may be eliminated in the problem because maximizing Equation (3.16) is equivalent to maximizing

$$(\mu_W - \lambda\sigma_W^2)\,T = [\mu_W - \tfrac{1}{2}(1 - \gamma)\sigma_W^2\,]T \tag{3.17}$$

where, for simplicity, we have defined $\lambda \equiv \tfrac{1}{2}(1 - \gamma)$. This is the **objective function** for the basic M–V model. The goal is to maximize the expected utility of final wealth, but that has been translated to expected return less a weighted variance term. Also note that μ_W is actually the log of the expected gross return on the portfolio rather than the expected continuously compounded return. The difference between these two measures has been subsumed into the variance component of the objective function.[10] To see this, look back at Equation (3.11).

Constraints

The M–V model stipulates that the investor will trade off additional expected return against additional portfolio variance at a constant rate. Formally, the investor's decision problem is to select portfolio weights, ω_i, to maximize Equation (3.17) subject to the **budget constraint** that the portfolio weights sum to unity—that is, $\Sigma_i\,\omega_i = 1$. The risk aversion coefficient, λ, reflects the penalty the investor assigns to an increase in the portfolio variance.

It is often desirable to add additional **constraints** to the basic M–V model. For example, the investor may be prohibited from taking a short position in some or all

---

[10] We could regroup the terms in the objective as $[(\mu_W - \tfrac{1}{2}\sigma_W^2) + \tfrac{1}{2}\gamma\sigma_W^2]$ so that the "mean term" is the expected log return (see Equation (3.11). But there would no longer be a clear distinction between the "mean" and "variance" components of the objective because the portfolio variance would appear in both components. In addition, the mean component would no longer be linear in the portfolio weights.

of the available assets. This **long-only constraint** means that for each such asset the solution must satisfy $\omega_i \geq 0$. Similarly, the investor may want to limit the probability of earning a return below some threshold level. Under our assumptions, the continuously compounded return has a normal distribution. Therefore the probability of a return less than or equal to a threshold H is given by the cumulative normal distribution evaluated at H. Assuming the investor wants to limit this probably to at most K, the constraint would be given by

$$N(H,(\mu_W - \tfrac{1}{2}\sigma_W^2)\,T,\sigma_W^2 T) \leq K \qquad (3.18)$$

where N denotes the cumulative normal function. Equation (3.18) is usually referred to as a **shortfall constraint.** Bringing the pieces together, we can write the more general problem compactly as

Choose $\omega_i, i = 1, \ldots, n$ to

Maximize $\mu_W T - \lambda\sigma_W^2 T$

Subject to

Budget constraint: $\Sigma_i\,\omega_i = 1$

Long-only constraint: $\omega_i \geq 0$

Shortfall constraint: $N(H,(\mu_W - \tfrac{1}{2}\sigma_W^2)T,\sigma_W^2 T) \leq K$ for some H and K

This problem is easily solved by standard optimization packages such as the "Solver" add-in in Microsoft Excel.

Investment Horizon

It is often argued that stocks are less risky over long investment horizons and, as a result, that investors should allocate a higher proportion of their portfolios to stocks the longer their investment horizon. Although the advice is probably sound—most practitioners take it for granted—the arguments advanced to support it are often not well grounded. It is therefore useful to examine this issue more closely.

We have just derived the basic M–V model from first principles: expected utility of wealth maximization and careful treatment of investment opportunities. Under the assumption that (continuously compounded) asset returns have the same normal distribution in each subperiod and are uncorrelated over time, we showed that both the mean and variance of portfolio returns are proportional to the investment horizon T. The investor's objective function (Equation (3.17)) is likewise proportional to T. Because the horizon is just a scale factor in the objective function, it could simply be eliminated without changing the problem. The optimal portfolio allocation must therefore be the same for all horizons. Imposing constraints on the portfolio weights, such as the long-only constraint, does not change this conclusion. Therefore the basic M–V model does not support the notion that asset allocation should depend on the investment horizon.

In many applications of the M–V model, the objective function is recast in terms of the mean and variance of *return per period* rather than of cumulative return (wealth). For continuously compounded returns, return per period is simply the cumulative return divided by the investment horizon. Equations (3.11) and (3.13) give the mean return per period for the portfolio as

$$(1/T)(\mu_W - \tfrac{1}{2}\sigma_W^2)T = \mu_W - \tfrac{1}{2}\sigma_W^2 \qquad (3.19)$$

while the variance is

$$(1/T)^2(\sigma_W^2 T) = \sigma_W^2/T \qquad (3.20)$$

The expected return per period is constant, but the variance of the return per period declines as the investment horizon increases. From this perspective risk does appear to decline with longer horizons. Indeed it appears to drop quickly; for example, a two-year investment appears to be only half as risky as a one-year investment, and a 10-year investment looks only one-10th as risky. The secret is that the total risk is being spread across more and more periods. Total risk—that is, the variance of wealth—is actually rising but not fast enough to offset the effect of spreading the risk across more periods. Notice that total risk (variance) increases at a rate of T while the per-period risk decreases at a rate $1/T$ due to the $(1/T)^2$ scale factor.

If we replace the mean and variance of wealth with the mean and variance of return per period, the mean–variance objective function becomes[11]

$$\mu_W - \tfrac{1}{2}\left(1 - \frac{\gamma}{T}\right)\sigma_W^2 \qquad (3.21)$$

It should be clear that the optimal portfolio allocation *will* depend on the horizon if we maximize this objective instead of the original objective. But what is really going on here? Comparing Equation (3.21) with the right side of Equation (3.17) shows that the only difference is that the risk aversion parameter γ has been divided by the time horizon. Thus using the mean and variance of return per period in the M–V framework is equivalent to assuming that risk aversion is lower with a longer investment horizon. Given that assumption it should be no surprise that the investor selects a riskier portfolio over longer horizons—but this is not because the assets are less risky! It is not the risk that is declining; it is the investor's aversion to risk. Unfortunately that is not how the story is usually told. Instead Equation (3.20) is used—often in graphical form—as "proof" that risk declines sharply as the investment horizon is extended.

Focusing on return per period is an expedient way to make asset allocation depend on the time horizon. As we have shown, however, it gives a distorted view of the relationship between risk and horizon. In Chapter 5 we will relax the assumption that investment opportunities are the same in each period. Without that assumption some assets may indeed be more or less risky over longer horizons. Thus a more solid foundation can be built for the notion that risk, and asset allocation, depends on the investor's time horizon.

A link between asset allocation and investment horizon can be introduced within the M–V framework by adding a shortfall constraint. In doing so we are relaxing

---

[11] Note that we are being careful here to replace the mean of the continuously compounded return with the corresponding per-period value from Equation (3.19) rather than mechanically replacing $(\mu_W\,T)$ with μ_W.

our assumption that the utility function fully describes the investor's attitude toward wealth. In particular, the investor is assumed to have strong feelings about falling below some threshold level of wealth. The shortfall constraint in Equation (3.18) can be rewritten as

$$N\left(\frac{H - (\mu_W - \frac{1}{2}\sigma_W^2)T}{\sigma_W \sqrt{T}}\right) \leq K \qquad (3.22)$$

where the left side is the probability of (log) wealth less than or equal to H according to the standard normal distribution. Holding everything else constant, this probability declines as T increases. As a result, a portfolio that violates the constraint at a short horizon may satisfy it at a longer horizon. Consider the portfolio that the investor would select in the absence of the shortfall constraint. If it violates the constraint at short horizons, the investor will pick the best portfolio that does satisfy the constraint. Beyond some horizon, however, the constraint will no longer be binding, and extending the horizon beyond that point will not affect the investor's asset allocation.

While it is important to understand the conceptual foundations of the M–V framework, its strengths, weaknesses, and investment implications can be fully understood only by applying it. The next section explores the model with a series of progressively realistic applications.

3.3   Practice: Solution of Stylized Problems Using the Mean–Variance Framework

Asset allocation modeling is best learned through doing—that is, applying the M–V framework to live examples. Through this experience, the reader should understand the power and limitations of the model. For example, applying historical variance, covariance, and mean returns within a two–asset class model with few constraints can provide varying optimal mixes as the modeler varies the risk aversion coefficient. This simple application will illustrate the efficient frontier and the optimal weights for the investor.

As inputs are varied by estimating the mean–variance parameters over different periods, it will become clear that optimal mixes depend on the historical period chosen. The user will begin to understand that in the real world, results may be highly sensitive to forecasts. Moreover, as the number of assets and constraints are increased, optimal solutions may become unattainable, unstable, or corner solutions, dependent entirely on how the constraints are formulated. At this point the modeler will be interested in the alternative methods for exploring asset allocation examined in Chapter 5.

This section begins with the development of a two–asset class problem, such as stocks and bonds, where the investor seeks to diversify. There will be only two constraints: the long-only constraint and the budget constraint. The Excel Outboxes will illustrate how to build and solve the problem within an Excel spreadsheet. The template of the spreadsheet is provided online. It is your job to fill in the data and formulas.

Following the two–asset class example, we will extend the model to more asset classes, explore the importance of time horizons, consider including a shortfall constraint, and finish with a review of an asset–liability problem.

The Efficient Frontier

Consider an investor who seeks to determine the optimal balance between stocks and bonds. The first task is to create the M–V frontier, which is the set of portfolios with the lowest risk for a given level of return. From this set the efficient frontier, the portfolio with the highest return for a given level of risk, is identified. Once the investor identifies the efficient frontier, the goal is to identify the portfolio with the risk that best fits with their preferences.

The M-V frontier represents the portfolios available to and appealing to the investor. Given the assumptions about investor preferences, these portfolios have the lowest level of risk for a given return. If there are only two risky assets, we can easily identify this set of portfolios by examining a range of potential weights for one asset, then setting the weight of the second asset using the budget constraint, $\omega_1 + \omega_2 = 1$. However, this technique is not feasible with more than two assets. First, there are too many possible asset weight combinations to consider for the method to be efficient. Second, it is not clear which asset weight combinations best satisfy the assumptions of investor preferences. Here we will explore a more general approach that may be applied to $n > 2$ assets. We will present the problem in words and then translate it into equations, and finally illustrate it in the Excel Outboxes.

To trace the M–V frontier, the goal is to:

Minimize	the portfolio standard deviation
by choosing	the weights of the risky assets
subject to	a fully invested portfolio (the budget constraint) for a given level of return.

This translates into the program (where n = number of risky assets and W = portfolio):

Minimize	σ_W
by choosing	ω_i
subject to	$\Sigma_{i=1,n}\, \omega_i = 1$
	$\mu_W = \mu_{Target}$
where	$\mu_W = \Sigma_{i=1,n}\, \omega_i \mu_i$
	$\sigma_W = (\Sigma_{i=1,n}\, \Sigma_{j=1,n}\, \omega_i\, \omega_j\, \sigma_i\, \sigma_j\, \rho_{i,j})^{1/2}$

For the two risky assets Stocks (S) and Bonds (B), we have the following:

Minimize	σ_W
by choosing	ω_S and ω_B
subject to	$\omega_S + \omega_B = 1$
	$\mu_W = \mu_{Target}$
where	$\mu_W = \omega_S \mu_S + \omega_B \mu_B$
	$\sigma_W = (\omega_S^2 \sigma_S^2 + \omega_B^2 \sigma_B^2 + 2\omega_S \omega_B \sigma_S \sigma_B \rho_{S,B})^{1/2}$

EXHIBIT 3.6

Efficient Frontier, Two Asset Portfolios of Varying Weights

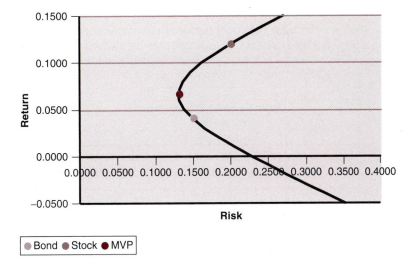

● Bond ● Stock ● MVP

This program can be solved using an optimization tool such as Excel's Solver (explained in the Appendix 2). The frontier may be plotted as a line, defined by the lowest level of risk for each level of return; this is illustrated in Exhibit 3.6. For diversifying assets, the plot is typically a curved line.[12] The frontier has essentially two regions defined by the portfolio's expected return:

Region one: $\mu_{\text{Target}} \geq \mu_{\text{MVP}}$

Region two: $\mu_{\text{Target}} < \mu_{\text{MVP}}$

Here μ_{MVP} is the return on the minimum variance portfolio (MVP), the portfolio with the lowest risk across all levels of return. In the graph, the MVP lies at the leftmost point of the curve.

There are several key observations regarding the frontier:

- The efficient frontier consists of the portfolios where $\mu_{\text{Target}} \geq \mu_{\text{MVP}}$.
- Rational investors will only hold a portfolio where $\mu_{\text{Target}} \geq \mu_{\text{MVP}}$. Portfolios where $\mu_{\text{Target}} < \mu_{\text{MVP}}$ would never be held by a rational investor because there is another portfolio that offers a higher return for the same level of risk. In other words, all attractive portfolios are included on the efficient frontier.
- The ability to sell short will improve the risk–return characteristics of the efficient frontier. This is because the portfolio can take more advantage of the diversifying assets.

Note that eliminating the ability to sell short requires the addition of the long-only constraint ($\omega_i \geq 0$) for those assets that cannot be sold short.

The spreadsheets described in the following Excel Outboxes explore the creation and selection of portfolios of just two risky assets, without the long-only requirement. The Efficient Frontier Excel Outbox describes how to identify the portfolios the investor could select—that is, the portfolios with the highest return for a given level of risk. The Optimal Portfolio Excel Outbox describes how to identify the particular portfolio the investor would select given his or her level of risk aversion. Templates are provided online.

---

[12] Some practitioners present the efficient frontier as a fat line composed of many points, reflecting portfolios offering similar risk–return profiles. The idea is to illustrate the fact that many portfolios, some with very different weights, may lead to similar risk and return values, as a warning to the user to avoid assuming false precision in practicing mean–variance techniques.

Excel Outbox
Efficient Frontier

We will construct an Excel spreadsheet to demonstrate the application of the above equations. Use the worksheet <EF - Template> in the spreadsheet Chapter 03 Excel Outboxes.xls.

Each construction step will be explained in the text. For background on how Solver optimizes the problem, see Appendix 2. The template appears as follows:

	A	B	C	D	E	F	G
1		**Mean-Variance Efficient Frontier**					
2		Two risky assets					
3		No riskless asset					
4		Short sales					
5							
6							
7							
8	**Program**	**Objective**	MIN	σ_ω		=	
9							
10							
11		**Variables**				Stock	Bond
12			ω				
13							
14		**Constraints**			Portfolio		
15			$\Sigma\omega$	=		=	
16			μ_ω	=		=	
17							
18							
19		**Where**					
20					μ_ω	=	
21					σ_ω	=	
22							
23	**Data**	**Statistics**				SP500	Tbond
24			μ				
25			α				
26			σ				
27							
28			ρ				
29			SP500				
30			Tbond				

Data

The first step is to select the two risky assets and enter their summary statistics into the Data range of the worksheet. In this example the assets are the Treasury bond (Tbond) and S&P 500 (SP500) indexes as the bond and stock respectively. The summary statistics are available on the "Data" worksheet in the spreadsheet. For example, the annual log return for the SP500 is located in cell I6 of the "Data" worksheet. To enter the annual equivalent in cell F25, click on cell F25, type " = ", click the "Data" tab, and then click cell I6. You should see =Data!I6 appear in the cell. Use the following table to enter the remaining summary statistics:

	C	F	G
23		SP500	Tbond
24	μ	= +F25+0.5*F26^2	= +G25+0.5*G26^2
25	α	=Data!I6	=Data!L6
26	σ	=Data!I7	=Data!L7
29	ρ	=Data!I11	=Data!I14
30			=Data!L14

Where

For formatting and presentation ease, the formulas for the portfolio return and standard deviation are entered into cells G20 and G21 respectively. The portfolio return formula is

$$\mu_W = \omega_S\mu_S + \omega_B\mu_B$$

and is entered into cell G20 as

$$=(F12*\$F\$24)+(G12*\$G\$24)$$

where cells F12 and G12 are the weights and cells \$F\$24 and \$G\$24 are the returns on the SP500 and TBonds respectively. The "\$" are used so we can copy this equation to other cells without changing the cell references. The portfolio standard deviation formula is

$$\sigma_W = (\omega_S^2\sigma_S^2 + \omega_B^2\sigma_B^2 + 2\omega_S\omega_B\sigma_S\sigma_B\rho_{S,B})^{\frac{1}{2}}$$

and is entered into cell G21 as follows:

$$=SQRT(F12^2*\$F\$26^2+G12^2*\$G\$26^2+2*F12*\$G\$12*F26*\$G\$26*\$G\$29)$$

Here cells \$F\$26, \$G\$26, and \$G\$29 reference the standard deviations and correlation of the SP500 and Tbond respectively.

Objective

Because the goal is to minimize the portfolio standard deviation, the objective cell simply references the standard deviation formula entered in cell G21:

$$=G21$$

Variables

The decision variables, entered in cells F12 and G12, are the portfolio weights for SP500 and Tbond. These are the solution, so there is no formula to enter. However, you cannot leave these cells empty because Solver needs a starting point. Start with an equal weighting for each asset by entering ½ in each cell:

$$0.5$$

Constraints

This program has two constraints: The portfolio has to be fully invested, and we are interested in solving the program for a particular level of return. A constraint has three elements: the calculated value, the inequality or equality condition, and the target value.

Budget Constraint

Weights represent the proportion of the total investment held in each asset:

$$\omega_i = \text{Investment in asset } i/\text{Total investment}$$

For example, if you had \$10,000 to invest and put \$6,000 in SP500 and \$4,000 in Tbond, the weights for the portfolio are

$$\omega_S = \$\text{Stocks}/(\$\text{Stocks} + \$\text{Bonds}) = \$6,000/\$10,000 = 0.60$$
$$\omega_B = \$\text{Bonds}/(\$\text{Stocks} + \$\text{Bonds}) = \$4,000/\$10,000 = 0.40$$

Notice that because all the money is invested in stocks and bonds,

$$\omega_S + \omega_B = (\$\text{Stocks} + \$\text{Bonds})/(\$\text{Stocks} + \$\text{Bonds}) = \$10,000/\$10,000 = 1.00$$

This is the budget, or full investment, constraint: $\omega_S + \omega_B = 1$. The sum of the weights, the calculated value, is entered into cell E15:

$$=SUM(F12:G12)$$

(continued)

(continued) The target value, or 1, is entered into cell G15:

$$1.0000$$

The inequality is entered when the program is entered into Solver.

Target Return
The target return constraint determines the level of return examined. The calculated value is the portfolio return for the given weights. This is the formula already entered into cell G20 and is referenced in cell E16, so enter this into E16:

$$= +G20$$

The target value, entered into cell G16, is the return of interest. This is the parameter that will change as we repeatedly solve for different points along the frontier. Start with a value of 6 percent:

$$= 0.06$$

The worksheet is now complete and should appear as follows:

	A	B	C	D	E	F	G
1		**Mean-Variance Efficient Frontier**					
2		Two risky assets					
3		No riskless asset					
4		Short sales					
5							
6							
7							
8	**Program**	**Objective**	MIN	σ_ω		=	0.1128
9							
10							
11		**Variables**				Stock	Bond
12			ω			0.5000	0.5000
13							
14		**Constraints**			Portfolio		
15			Σ_ω	=	1.0000	=	1.0000
16			μ_ω	=	0.0966	=	0.0600
17							
18							
19		**Where**					
20					μ_ω	=	0.0966
21					σ_ω	=	0.1128
22							
23	**Data**	**Statistics**				SP500	Tbond
24			μ			0.1384	0.0549
25			α			0.1184	0.0520
26			σ			0.1997	0.0761
27							
28			ρ				
29			SP500			1.0000	0.1712
30			Tbond				1.0000

We will calculate the efficient frontier by using Solver to minimize portfolio risk for a target expected return. The Solver window should include G8 as the objective to Min, and constraints should include the values in rows 15 and 16, as follows:

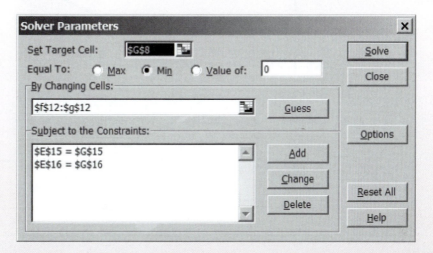

This optimization should be repeated for the range of return values listed in the worksheet in column I. Note that the MVP, or the minimum variance portfolio, is computed by deleting the return target constraint. Copy the weights, portfolio return, and risk into the columns to the right of column I.

The completed template is available online in the worksheet <EF-Completed> in the spreadsheet Chapter 03 Excel Outboxes - Completed.xls. The results are listed in the following table, and the M-V frontier is charted in Exhibit 3.7:

	I	J	K	L	M
7					
8	Target	ω		Portfolio	
9	μ	Stock	Bond	μ	σ
10	0.1500	1.1393	−0.1393	0.1500	0.2259
11	0.1200	0.7800	0.2200	0.1200	0.1595
12	0.1384	1.0000	0.0000	0.1384	0.1997
13	0.0900	0.4208	0.5792	0.0900	0.1013
14	0.0600	0.0616	0.9384	0.0561	0.0745
15	MVP	0.0788	0.9212	0.0572	0.0744
16	0.0549	0.0000	1.0000	0.0549	0.0761
17	0.0400	−0.1779	1.1779	0.0400	0.0906
18	0.0300	−0.2977	1.2977	0.0300	0.1062
19	0.0000	−0.6569	1.6569	0.0000	0.1656
20	−0.0300	−1.0162	2.0162	−0.0300	0.2325
21	Stock	1.0000	0.0000	0.1384	0.1997
22	Bond	0.0000	1.0000	0.0549	0.0761
23	MVP	0.0788	0.9212	0.0614	0.0744

(continued)

(concluded)

EXHIBIT 3.7

Efficient Frontier for Excel Outbox

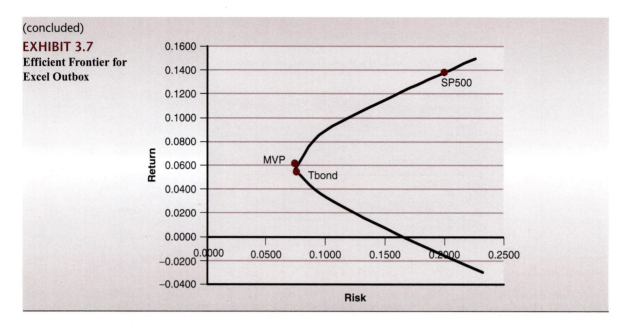

The Optimal Portfolio

Now that the most efficient portfolios available to the investor have been indentified the next question is, given the assumptions about investor preferences, which portfolio should the investor select? Stated as an optimization program, we wish to:

Maximize	the investor's utility given his or her level of risk aversion
by choosing	the weights of the risky assets
subject to	a fully invested portfolio.

This translates into the equations:

Maximize	$\mu_W - \lambda\sigma_W^2$
by choosing	ω_i
subject to	$\Sigma_{i=1,n}\,\omega_i = 1$
where	$\mu_W = \Sigma_{i=1,n}\,\omega_i\mu_i$
	$\sigma_W = (\Sigma_{i=1,n}\,\Sigma_{j=1,n}\,\omega_i\,\omega_j\,\sigma_i\,\sigma_j\,\rho_{i,j})^{\frac{1}{2}}$

Notice that the target return constraint has been removed. Instead of identifying the portfolios the investor could hold, the goal becomes to identify the portfolio the investor should hold given his or her assumed risk preferences. We can simplify these equations for the two risky assets Stocks (S) and Bonds (B):

Maximize	$\mu_W - \lambda\sigma_W^2$
by choosing	$\omega_S,\ \omega_B$
subject to	$\omega_S + \omega_B = 1$
where	$\mu_W = \omega_S\mu_S + \omega_B\mu_B$
	$\sigma_W = (\omega_S^2\sigma_S^2 + \omega_B^2\sigma_B^2 + 2\omega_S\omega_B\sigma_S\sigma_B\rho_{S,B})^{\frac{1}{2}}$

The optimization solution represents the asset weights of the portfolio offering the highest utility for the given level of risk aversion. The Optimal Portfolio Excel Outbox presents a template and provides steps for computing the optimal portfolio for a given level of risk aversion for two risky assets. The description covers the additions or changes made to the complete version of the previously presented "Efficient Frontier" program. The sections not covered can be completed using the instructions describing the <EF - Template> worksheet.

Excel Outbox
Optimal Portfolio

This box reviews a simple spreadsheet that calculates the optimal weights for a portfolio of two risky assets.

Use the worksheet <OP – Template> in the spreadsheet Chapter 03 Excel Outboxes.xls. The template should appear as follows:

	A	B	C	D	E	F	G
1		**Mean-Variance Optimal Portfolio**					
2		Two risky assets					
3		No riskless asset					
4		Short sales					
5							
6							
7							
8	**Program**	**Objective**	MAX	$E[\mu] - \lambda\sigma^2$			=
9			λ				
10							
11		**Variables**				Stock	Bond
12			ω				
13							
14		**Constraints**			Portfolio		
15			$\Sigma\omega$	=		=	
16							
17							
18		**Where**					
19					μ_ω	=	
20					σ_ω	=	
21							
22	**Data**	**Statistics**				SP500	Tbond
23			μ				
24			α				
25			σ				
26							
27			ρ				
28			SP500				
29			Tbond				
30							

The objective is to maximize utility. The utility function is entered into cell G8 as

$$=G19 - D9 * G20\verb|^|2$$

Note that the optimization should be set to maximize cell G8 Max. The assumed risk aversion coefficient is entered into cell D9. This is the parameter that will change as we solve for different portfolios along the frontier. Start with a value of 1.00:

$$=1$$

Constraint

Because we have already identified the portfolios that the investor could invest in, the target return constraint is no longer needed. Delete it from the Solver window, which should appear as follows:

(continued)

(concluded)

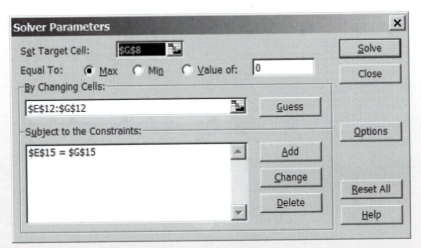

After we enter 0.5 for the weights and use the same formulas for the Where and Data sections as in the efficient frontier exercise, the worksheet is complete and should appear as follows:

	A	B	C	D	E	F	G
1		**Mean-Variance Optimal Portfolio**					
2		Two risky assets					
3		No riskless asset					
4		Short sales					
5							
6							
7							
8	**Program**	**Objective**	MAX	E [m] - $\lambda\sigma^2$		=	0.0839
9			λ		1		
10							
11		**Variables**				Stock	Bond
12			ω			0.5000	0.5000
13							
14		**Constraints**			Portfolio		
15			$\Sigma\omega$	=	1.0000	=	1.0000
16							
17							
18		**Where**					
19					μ_ω	=	0.0966
20					σ_ω	=	0.1128
21							
22	**Data**	**Statistics**				SP500	Tbond
23			μ			0.1384	0.0549
24			α			0.1184	0.0520
25			σ			0.1997	0.0761
26							
27			ρ				
28			SP500			1.0000	0.1712
29			Tbond				1.0000
30							

The solution is included online in worksheet <OP - Completed> in the spreadsheet Chapter 03 Excel Outboxes - Completed.xls. Once you verify your answers, you can compute optimal portfolios using different risk aversion parameters.

Investment Horizons

The optimization program can be modified to include the possibility of extending the investment horizon to a longer period. There are two important results concerning the investment horizon in the basic M–V framework:

1. If investors maximize total holding period utility and the asset return distributions are the same in each subperiod and uncorrelated over time, *the optimal portfolio allocation is the same for all investment horizons.*

2. If the program is recast in terms of the mean and variance of return per period, *risk appears to decline with longer horizons.* However, as we discussed in Section 3.2, this gives a distorted view of the relationship between risk and horizon.

If we include a variable investment horizon, we need to modify the program to include extended risk and return horizons, as illustrated here (the changes are shown in boldface):

Maximize	the investor's utility given her or his level of risk aversion
by choosing	the weights of the *n* risky assets
subject to	the budget constraint the long-only constraint
where	**the portfolio return is the weighted return over horizon T** **the portfolio variance is the weighted covariance over horizon T.**

The long-only constraint, requiring some weights ω_i to be greater than or equal to zero, will also be incorporated. This translates into the equations:

Maximize	$\mu_W - \lambda\sigma_W^2$
by choosing	ω_i
subject to	$\Sigma_{i=1,n}\,\omega_i = 1$
	$\boldsymbol{\omega_i \geq 0\ \forall\ \textbf{designated}\ i}$
where	$\boldsymbol{\mu_W = T\ \Sigma_{i=1,n}\ \omega_i\,\mu_i}$
	$\boldsymbol{\sigma_W = (T\ \Sigma_{i=1,n}\Sigma_{j=1,n}\omega_i\omega_j\sigma_i\sigma_j\rho_{i,j})^{1/2}}$

For this program the long-only constraint is applied only to designated assets—those that cannot be sold short (the symbol $\forall$ denotes "for all"). The program is solved for any investment horizon *T,* and the solution represents the asset weights of the optimal portfolio (the highest utility for the given risk aversion coefficient over the investment horizon). The key implications of this investment problem are:

- The portfolio return increases in proportion to the investment horizon; that is, the 30-year return = 30 × 1 - year return because it is a log-return.

- The portfolio standard deviation increases in proportion to the square root of the investment horizon; that is, the 30-year standard deviation = $\sqrt{30}$ × 1 - year standard deviation.

- The asset weights are the same for all investment horizons.

To illustrate how recasting the program into the mean and variance of return per period distorts the relationship between risk and horizon, we can calculate the annualized return

EXHIBIT 3.8 **Horizon Return Confidence Interval**

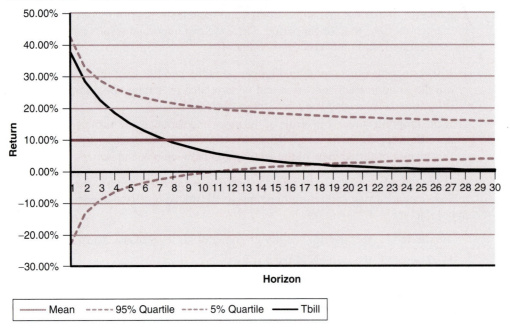

for each investment horizon along with statistical *confidence intervals.* For each horizon the per-period distribution of log return is given by[13]

$$\frac{R_W(T)}{T} \sim N\left(\mu_W(1) - .5\sigma_W^2(1)\mathrm{B}, \frac{\sigma_W(1)}{\sqrt{T}}\right) \qquad \textbf{(3.23)}$$

where $\mu_W(1)$ is the one-year portfolio return, $\sigma_W(1)$ is the one-year portfolio standard deviation, and T is the investment horizon. Exhibit 3.8 illustrates the 5th and 95th percentiles of this distribution for horizons out to 31 years. By definition, the per-period return will fall between these values with 90 percent confidence. The exhibit also shows the median (50th percentile) of the distribution, which, because the normal distribution is symmetric, is also the mean. Note that the mean return is the same at every horizon, but the 90 percent confidence interval narrows as the investment horizon increases. As a result, it appears that risk is declining with the horizon. As explained in the previous section, however, the standard deviation of final wealth increases with the horizon—but not fast enough to offset the effect of spreading the risk across more periods.

A simple example should clarify the situation. Suppose we start with $1 and our log return is either +1 percent per year or −1 percent per year for T years with equal probability. That is, the mean return per period is zero and the standard deviation of per-period return is 1 percent. After 1 year we have either $1.01 or $0.99, after 10 years either $1.11 or $0.91, and after 100 years either $2.71 or $0.37. The point is that ± 1 percent per period has a huge impact over a long horizon. So a narrower distribution of per-period returns at longer horizons does not indicate low or even declining risk.

On the other hand, the probability of exceeding a specified target return per period increases with the horizon if the target return is less than the expected return per period. Conversely, the probability of realizing a return less than the target declines.

---

[13] The mean and variance of the per-period log return were given in Equations (3.19) and (3.20).

For example, assuming the expected return on the portfolio exceeds the riskless rate, the probability of underperforming T-bills declines as the horizon increases. In Exhibit 3.8 this probability is virtually zero at 30 years. We will build on this idea soon when we introduce shortfall constraints. But first we need to allow for a broader set of asset classes.

	Excel Outbox									

Excel Outbox
Five-Asset
Efficient Frontier

The previous Excel Outboxes illustrated the application of mean–variance theory for two assets. This box expands the number of asset classes to five, including Treasury bills, corporate bonds, Treasury bonds, the S&P 500 index (large-cap stocks), and the S&P 600 index (small-cap stocks).

Use the worksheet <5AEF-Template> in the spreadsheet Chapter 03 Excel Outboxes. xls. The template should appear as follows:

	A	B	C	D	E	F	G	H	I
1		**Mean-Variance Efficient Frontier**							
2		Two risky assets							
3		No riskless asset							
4		Short sales							
5									
6									
7	Program	**Objective**	**MIN**	$\sigma\omega$			=		
8									
9									
10									
11		**Variables**			Corp	SP500	SP600	Tbill	Tbond
12			ω						
13									
14		**Constraints**					Portfolio		
15			$\Sigma\omega$	=				=	
16			$\mu\omega$	=				=	
17									
18		**Where**							
19							$\mu\omega$	=	
20							$\sigma\omega$	=	
21									
22	Date	**Statistics**			Corp	SP500	SP600	Tbill	Tbond
23		μ							
24		α							
25		σ							
26									
27		ρ							
28		Corp							
29		SP500							
30		SP600							
31		Tbill							
32		Tbond							
33									

Where

The changes presented here extend the formulas for portfolio return and standard deviation to work easily with more than two asset classes. Although the portfolio return formula could be entered directly as the sum of the weights times the return for each asset and the standard deviation formula as the sum of the weights times the covariance for

(continued)

(concluded)

each asset pairing, this is clumsy and becomes impractical for large portfolios. Instead we will use Excel matrix formulas. The portfolio return formula is entered into cell J19 as

$$=SUMPRODUCT(F11:J11,F23:J23)$$

where cells F11:J11 are the cell range containing the weights, and cells F23:J23 reference the cell range of the expected asset returns.

The portfolio standard deviation formula is entered into cell J20 as

$$=SQRT(MMULT(MMULT(F11:J11,Data!H17:L21),TRANSPOSE(F11:J11)))$$

where cells Data!H17:L21 reference the cell range of the variance covariance matrix on the "Data" worksheet. (*Note:* This is an array formula.) After entering the formula, type <CTRL><SHIFT><ENTER> rather than simply <ENTER>. The resulting formula will appear bracketed:

$$\{=SQRT(MMULT(MMULT(F11:J11,Data!H17:L21),TRANSPOSE(F11:J11)))\}$$

Otherwise the cell will display the error message #VALUE!
The completed worksheet should appear as follows:

	A	B	C	D	E	F	G	H	I
7	Program	Objective	MIN	σω		=	0.1062		
8									
9									
10		Variables			Corp	SP500	SP600	Tbill	Tbond
11			ω		0.2000	0.2000	0.2000	0.2000	0.2000
12									
13		Constraints					Portfolio		
14			Σω	=			1.0000	=	1.0000
15			μω	=			0.0995	=	0.0250
16			ω	>					0
17									
18		Where							
19							μω	=	0.0995
20							σω	=	0.1062
21									
22	Date	Statistics				Corp	SP500	SP600	Tbill	Tbond
23			μ			0.0591	0.1384	0.2090	0.0363	0.0549
24			α			0.0568	0.1184	0.1619	0.0363	0.0520
25			σ			0.0679	0.1997	0.3067	0.0093	0.0761
26									
27			ρ						
28			Corp		1.0000	0.2225	0.1784	0.0857	0.8364
29			SP500			1.0000	0.8585	−0.0161	0.1712
30			SP600				1.0000	−0.0256	0.1071
31			Tbill					1.0000	0.1071
32			Tbond						1.0000
33									

The completed worksheet is provided online in worksheet <5AEF − Completed> in the spreadsheet Chapter 03 Excel Outboxes - Completed.xls.

The Shortfall Constraint

Investors, particularly individuals, may have a different view of risk than that assumed by the standard utility function. They may especially dislike losses of any kind, or the likelihood of negative returns, in addition to disliking overall return volatility. One simple approach for incorporating this preference is to add the shortfall constraint introduced in Section 3.2. The shortfall constraint can be used to construct a portfolio that limits the probability of earning a return below some threshold level. The probability of a return less than or equal to a threshold H is given by the cumulative normal distribution evaluated at H. The constraint to limit this probability to be at most K would be given by

$$N(H,(\mu_W - \tfrac{1}{2}\sigma_W^2)\,T, \sigma_W^2\, T) \leq K \qquad (3.24)$$

where N denotes the cumulative normal function. The program for computing the optimal portfolio weights now becomes:

Maximize	the investor's utility given her or his level of risk aversion
by choosing	the weights of the n risky assets
subject to	the budget constraint
	the long-only constraint
	the probability of a return less than or equal to H being at most K
where	the portfolio return is the weighted return over horizon T
	the portfolio variance is the weighted covariance over horizon T.

This translates into the equations:

Maximize	$\mu_W - \lambda\,\sigma_W^2$
by choosing	ω_i
subject to	$\Sigma_{i=1,n}\,\omega_i = 1$
	$\omega_i \geq 0\ \forall$ designated i
	$N(H,(\mu_W - \tfrac{1}{2}s_W^2)\,T, \sigma_W^2\,T) \leq K$
where	$\mu_W = T\,\Sigma_{i=1,n}\,\omega_i\,\mu_i$
	$\sigma_W = (T\,\Sigma_{i=1,n}\,\Sigma_{j=1,n}\,\omega_i\,\omega_j\,\sigma_i\,\sigma_j\,\rho_{i,j})^{1/2}$

Just as in the previous case, the solution to the shortfall problem will provide the highest possible utility as long as the program's constraints are met. However, in this case the optimal portfolio offers an additional feature; the probability of earning a return below H will be no higher than K. The key implications of this problem are:

- The asset weights of the optimal portfolio change for the investment horizons where the shortfall constraint is binding. For example, the shorter the time horizon, the less risky the optimal portfolio. As a result, using the shortfall scenario is one way to make asset allocation depend on investment horizons.
- The asset weights are the same for the investment horizons where the shortfall constraint is not binding. If the optimal portfolio is the same with or without the shortfall constraint for a given horizon, then this will also be true at any *longer* horizon. The optimal portfolio is the same for all these horizons.

Asset–Liability Management

In many instances the investor's objective is to fund a set of cash liability payments. Defined benefit pension plans are a classic example of this type of problem. The pension plan promises future payments to its beneficiaries based on salary, years of service, and other aspects of their employment. Projecting and valuing the plan's liability are difficult tasks because the benefit formulas are complex and the final payments are contingent on future events pertaining to the plan sponsor and its employees. For large, well-established plans, however, a large portion of the future payments can be projected with a high degree of confidence because they are fully *vested*—that is, the beneficiaries have already earned the right to receive them. Therefore, at least to a first approximation, the plan's liability can be viewed as a known stream of future payments, and the main driver of its value will be the level of interest rates. In essence, the pension plan is short a long-term bond.

The portfolio now includes this liability. The liability is added to the portfolio with a negative weight because it is effectively a short position. The weight on the liability is *not* a choice variable; it is dictated by the value of the liability relative to the value of the plan's assets. In addition to the budget constraint that requires the asset weights to sum to 1, we now have the constraint that the liability weight is fixed. The program is:

Maximize	the investor's utility given their level of risk aversion
by choosing	the weights of the n risky assets
subject to	the budget constraint
	the long-only constraint
	the probability of a return less than or equal to H being at most K
where	the portfolio return is the weighted return over horizon T
	the portfolio variance is the weighted covariance over horizon T.

This translates into the equations:

Maximize	$\mu_W - \lambda \sigma_W^2$
by choosing	ω_i
subject to	$\sum_{i=1,n} \omega_i = 1$
	$\omega_i \geq 0 \ \forall$ designated i
	$\boldsymbol{\omega_L = -(\text{liabilities/assets})}$
	$N(H,(\mu_W - \tfrac{1}{2}\sigma_W^2)\,T, \sigma_W^2 T) \leq K$
where	$\mu_W = T\sum_{i=1,n} \omega_i \mu_i + \omega_L \mu_L$
	$\sigma_W = [T(\sum_{i=1,n}\sum_{j=1,n}\omega_i\omega_j\sigma_i\sigma_j\rho_{i,j} + 2\sum_{j=1,n}\omega_i\omega_L\sigma_i\sigma_L\rho_{i,L} + \omega_L^2\sigma_L^2)]^{\frac{1}{2}}$

The key implications of this problem are:

- When the liability is added into the problem, the optimal solution reflects lower stock weights and higher bond weights. The value of the liability is assumed to be impacted primarily by interest rates; therefore, its movements are highly correlated with the bond asset classes. Bonds act as hedging assets, and the optimal portfolio includes a heavier allocation to these asset classes than was the case in the absence of the liability.
- We need to be careful in interpreting risk and return. The return here is actually the percentage change in the ratio of the plan's *surplus* (Assets – Liability) to its assets, while risk is now the variance of these changes.

It is often useful to summarize uncertainty with a statement such as "wealth will be between X and Y with Z percent probability." In statistical parlance, the range from X to Y is a Z percent confidence interval.

In the model developed here, assuming we start with wealth of $1, the logarithm of wealth at the end of T periods has a normal distribution with mean (αT) and variance $(\sigma^2 T)$. According to the normal distribution, 90 percent of the outcomes lie within ± 1.645 standard deviations of the mean. Thus the 90 percent confidence interval for the logarithm of wealth is

$$[\alpha T - 1.645\sigma\sqrt{T}, \alpha T + 1.645\sigma\sqrt{T}]$$

To find the corresponding confidence interval for wealth, we simply convert from log wealth to wealth using the exponential function. So the 90 percent confidence interval for wealth is

$$[e^{(\alpha T - 1.645\sigma\sqrt{T})}, e^{(\alpha T + 1.645\sigma\sqrt{T})}]$$

To illustrate, letting $\alpha = .075$ and $\sigma = .20$, implying that $\mu = .095$, the 90 percent confidence intervals for wealth at various horizons are shown in the second and third columns of the following table. Note that while the lower confidence bound declines initially and then rises gradually, the upper confidence bound rises rapidly and at an accelerating rate. The confidence interval is *not* symmetric around mean wealth—the lower confidence bound is much closer to the mean than is the upper confidence bound. To put it differently, the distribution does not spread out evenly above and below the mean—it is highly skewed to the upside.

Horizon	Log Wealth	Wealth			
(T)	Mean	Mean	Lower Bound	Upper Bound	Probability of Loss
1	0.075	1.100	0.776	1.498	35.4%
5	0.375	1.608	0.697	3.036	20.1
10	0.750	2.586	0.748	5.991	11.8
30	2.250	17.288	1.565	57.504	2.0

The table also shows that the probability of loss declines rapidly as the horizon increases. Again, this reflects the strong upward skew in the lognormal distribution. Note that introducing positive serial correlation in the return distribution would lead to higher long-term variance estimates and correspondingly wider confidence levels. This is discussed in later chapters.

While the probability of loss over long periods may seem small, bad results are not impossible. Moreover, the path along the way may be volatile. In fact, the risk of experiencing a large drawdown before the horizon is quite large. Applying the same parameters of mean returns and standard deviation, there is a 34 percent probability of being down at least 25 percent and a 7 percent chance of being down by 50 percent at some point over a 30-year horizon.

	The Probability of Being Down 25% or 50%	
Horizon	25% Draw down	50% Draw down
1	8.8%	0.0%
5	27.8	3.2
10	32.2	5.9
20	33.8	7.2
30	34.0	7.4

Note that interim drawdowns can be difficult for investors to endure emotionally and can be a serious financial problem if they coincide with periods of negative cash flow. As a result, investment risk should not be taken lightly.

For short investment horizons it may not be possible to satisfy a shortfall constraint. In this situation the program may be modified to minimize the probability of a shortfall in place of maximizing utility:

Minimize	**the probability of a portfolio return below the threshold**
by choosing	the weights of the risky assets
subject to	the budget constraint
	the long-only constraint
where	the portfolio return is the weighted return over horizon T
	the portfolio variance is the weighted covariance over horizon T.

This translates into the equations:

Minimize	$N(H,(\mu_W - \tfrac{1}{2}\sigma_W^2)\,T, \sigma_W^2\,T)$
by choosing	ω_i
subject to	$\Sigma_{i=1,n}\,\omega_i = 1$
	$\omega_L = -(\text{liabilities/assets})$
	$\omega_i \geq 0 \;\forall\; \text{designated } i$
where	$\mu_W = T\,\Sigma_{i=1,n}\,\omega_i\mu_i + \omega_L\mu_L$

$$\sigma_W = [T(\Sigma_{i=1,n}\Sigma_{j=1,n}\omega_i\omega_j\sigma_i\sigma_j\rho_{i,j} + 2\Sigma_{j=1,n}\omega_i\omega_L\sigma_i\sigma_L\rho_{i,L} + \omega_L^2\sigma_L^2)]^{\tfrac{1}{2}}$$

In this version of the asset allocation problem we are no longer trading off risk with the expected return of our portfolio; instead we focus only on the probability of eroding the asset–liability ratio. As we saw earlier, different horizons will result in different allocations.

Practice Summary

This section has illustrated the application of the M–V framework in solving several important investment problems. In its simplest form, we can use the framework to calculate the most efficient mixes of assets and solve for the optimal mix of assets in terms of risk and return. We can expand the application to include multiple time horizons, shortfall constraints, and liability management. The Excel Outboxes showed how to apply the basic equations in a spreadsheet format. The end-of-chapter problems will test the reader's skill in applying the spreadsheet to answer further questions.

Summary

This chapter introduced the motivation, mathematics, and practice of mean–variance portfolio optimization. We discussed a lot of math, but it is important to derive the mechanics in order to fully understand the mean–variance tool—both its features and its shortcomings. The model is powerful. In its simplest form, it incorporates varying returns, investor preferences about return and risk, and many asset classes and may be used to compute optimal mixes of assets. With a little modification, it may be used to manage downside risk, varying time horizons, and asset–liability relationships.

However, there are issues with the model. It assumes that (log) returns are normally distributed with known, constant mean and variance. In the basic model, the resulting allocations are the same through time. And although shortfall risk may be managed, it is a direct derivation of the normal return distribution. Finally, results are tied to the specified return and risk estimates.

Fortunately, some of these assumptions can be relaxed. Unfortunately, the complexity of the problem grows dramatically when we do so. Techniques for developing inputs to the model—more accurate than simply relying on historical averages—are discussed in Chapter 4. Many of these are straightforward. Methods for solving more complex asset allocation problems are introduced in Chapter 5.

Problems

1. To illustrate how utility changes with changes in the inputs, use the spreadsheet created in Section 3.2 to examine what happens to the level of certainty equivalent wealth (CEW) as the parameter γ, the payoff $W3$, and the probability of heads change.

2. You have been invited to play a coin-flipping game. The coin is flipped until heads appears for the first time. The payoff is $P(n) = 2^n$ where n is the number of tails. For example, if heads is the result of the first flip, $n = 0$ and $P(n) = \$1$. The table shows the results for the first four potential flip sequences. How much would you be willing to pay to play this game?

Flip Sequence	N	P(n)
H	0	$1
T,H	1	$2
T,T,H	2	$4
T,T,T,H	3	$8
. . .		

3. Visit the Vanguard Web site and take the investor questionnaire (www.Vanguard .com and follow the "Go to the site" link for personal investors; then → Planning and education → Create your investment plan then complete the investor questionnaire). What key characteristics about you as an investor is the questionnaire trying to determine?

4. Use the two-asset spreadsheet to review the impact of correlation on the shape of the feasible and efficient frontiers and the optimal portfolio mix. The formula for the MVP is $W(S) = (\sigma(B)^2 - \sigma(S)\,\sigma(B)\,\rho(S,B))/(\sigma(S)^2 + \sigma(B)^2 - 2\,\sigma(S)\,\sigma(B)\,\rho(S,B))$.

5. Go to Yahoo and download the price series for 10 randomly selected stocks (mix the sectors you choose and so on). Calculate and plot the portfolio standard deviation for portfolios of 1 stock and 2, 5, and 10 stocks.

6. Using the <OP - Completed> worksheet in Chapter 03 Excel Outboxes.xls, set the risk aversion coefficient equal to 0 (zero), remove the long-only constraint, and reoptimize the portfolio. What happens?

7. Use the N risky asset spreadsheet template (the <5AEF - Completed> worksheet in Chapter 03 Excel Outboxes.xls) to save the optimization results for five risky assets with expected returns from -0.05 through 0.125.

   a. Solve the program for each target level of return and copy the weights into the results table for two scenarios: no short sale and short sales allowed.

   b. Chart your results. What is the difference between the two scenarios?

   c. Why would investors hold only portfolios where $\mu_{Target} \geq \mu_{MVP}$?

8. Create an optimization problem spreadsheet with the shortfall constraint. The template is provided in the <SF-Template> worksheet in the Chapter 03 Excel Outboxes.xls Chapter Questions.xls file.

	A	B	C	D	E	F	G	H	I	J
1		**Mean-Variance Optimal Portfolio**								
2		Five risky assets								
3		No riskless asset								
4		Short sales								
5		Shortfall constraint								
6		Horizons								
7	**Inputs**	Horizon T								
8										
9										
10	**Program**	**Objective**	MAX	$E[\mu] - \lambda\sigma^2$		=				
11			λ							
12										
13		**Variables**				Crop	SP500	SP600	Tbill	Tbond
14			ω							
15										
16		**Constraints**				Portfolio				
17			$\Sigma\omega$	=				=		
18			Prob(<0)	=				<=		
19										
20										
21		**Where**								
22							μ_ω	=		
23							σ_ω	=		

Constraint

Shortfall constraint: Assume the threshold is zero and the target is 5 percent. That is, limit the probability of a negative return to be less than or equal to 5 percent. To calculate the shortfall probability, enter the following in cell H18:

$$=NORMDIST(0, J22 - 0.5 \cdot J23\wedge 2, J23, TRUE)$$

The "TRUE" indicates the cumulative distribution. The target value, entered into cell J18, is 5 percent:

$$=0.05$$

In Solver, add the constraint H18 ≤ J18.
The completed worksheet should appear as follows:

	A	B	C	D	E	F	G	H	I	J
1		**Mean-Variance Optimal Portfolio**								
2		Five risky assets								
3		No riskless asset								
4		Short sales								
5		Shortfall constraint								
6		Horizons								
7										
8	**Inputs**	Horizon T					1			
9										
10	**Program**	**Objective**	MAX	$E[\mu] - \lambda\sigma^2$		=	0.0882			
11			λ	1						
12										
13		**Variables**				Crop	SP500	SP600	Tbill	Tbond
14			ω				0.2000	0.2000	0.2000	0.2000	0.2000
15										
16		**Constraints**						Portfolio		
17			$\Sigma\omega$	=				1.0000	=	1.0000
18			Prob(<0)	=				0.18831	<=	0.0500
19										
20										
21		**Where**								
22								μ_ω	=	0.0995
23								σ_ω	=	0.1062

For charting purposes the formulas for the portfolio return and standard deviation should be copied into cells to the right of the program range.

    a. Solve the program for 1-, 5-, 10-, 15-, 20-, 25-, and 30-year investment horizons using a 1.0 risk aversion parameter; then copy the weights into a results table.

    b. Explore the optimal asset weights for differing horizons where the shortfall constraint is met.

9. Using the shortfall constraint spreadsheet created in Problem 8, set the shortfall constraint = 0 ($K = 0$) and $T = 1$. What happens?

10. Create an optimization framework for an asset–liability problem. The template for the worksheet is provided in the <AL − Template> worksheet in the Chapter 03 Chapter Questions.xls file and should appear as follows:

	A	B	C	D	E	F	G	H	I	J	K
1		Mean-Variance *Asset Optimal* Portfolio									
2		Five risky assets									
3		No riskless asset									
4		Short sales									
5		Shortfall constraint									
6		Horizons									
7											
8	Inputs	Horizon T									
9											
10	Program	Objective	MAX	$E[\mu] - \lambda\sigma^2$			=				
11			λ	1							
12											
13		Variables				Crop	SP500	SP600	Tbill	Tbond	Liability
14			ω								
15											
16		Constraints					Portfolio				
17			$\Sigma\omega$	=				=			
18			Prob(<0)	=				<=			
19											
20											
21		Where									
22							μ_ω	=			
23							σ_ω	=			

Where

The portfolio now includes the liability. Therefore, the portfolio return and standard deviation formulas need to be updated. The portfolio return formula in cell J22 is now

$$=G8 \cdot SUMPRODUCT(F14:K14,F26:K26)$$

where F14:K14 is the cell range containing the weights and F26:K26 references the cell range of the expected asset returns in the worksheet.

    The portfolio standard deviation formula in cell J23 is now

$$\{=SQRT(G8 \cdot MMULT(MMULT(F14:K14,Data!H17:M22), TRANSPOSE(F14:K14)))\}$$

where Data!H17:M22 references the cell range of the variance–covariance matrix on the "Data" worksheet. Return statistics for the liability have been assumed.

Variables

The decision variables, entered in cells F14:K14, are the weights for the assets and liability. The asset weights are the solution, so there is no formula to enter. The liability is added to the portfolio with a negative weight because it is effectively a short position.

The weight on the liability is also not a choice variable: It is dictated by the value of the liability relative to the value of the plan's assets. For this example, assume that the assets just cover the liability. Therefore, enter -1 into cell K14:

$$=-1.0000$$

Constraint

Budget constraint: The budget constraint now requires the portfolio weights, inclusive of the liability, to sum to 0 rather than summing to 1 as they did in the case of assets only. The formula entered into cell H17 is the sum of the asset and liability weights:

$$=SUM(F14:K14)$$

The target value, entered into cell J17, is 1 plus the weight of the liability:

$$=1 + K14$$

The worksheet is now complete and should appear as follows:

	A	B	C	D	E	F	G	H	I	J	K
1		Mean-Variance *Asset Optimal* Portfolio									
2		Five risky assets									
3		No riskless asset									
4		Short sales									
5		Shortfall constraint									
6		Horizons									
7											
8	Inputs	Horizon T					1				
9											
10	Program	Objective	MAX	$E[\mu] - \lambda\sigma^2$		=	0.0406				
11			λ	1							
12											
13		Variables				Crop	SP500	SP600	Tbill	Tbond	Liability
14			ω			0.2000	0.2000	0.2000	0.2000	0.2000	−1.0000
15											
16		Constraints					Portfolio				
17			$\Sigma\omega$	=			0.0000	=	0.0000		
18			Prob(<0)	=			0.33603	<=	0.0500		
19											
20											
21		Where									
22							μ_ω	=	0.0527		
23							σ_ω	=	0.1102		

For collecting the data, the formulas for the portfolio return and standard deviation may be copied into the results template to the right of the program range.

    a. Solve the program for the 1-, 5-, 10-, 15-, 20-, 25-, and 30-year investment horizons; then copy the weights into the results table.

    b. How do the weights on stocks in this example compare with earlier examples? Explain why they may be different.

    c. What is the definition of *return* in this example?

11. Suppose the liability in Problem 10 was perfectly positively correlated with both the S&P 500 and S&P 600 and had a standard deviation of 0.06. That is, the liability had the following correlations:

Asset	Original	Modified
TBill	−0.016	−0.016
Corp	0.960	0.960
SP500	0.040	**1.000**
SP600	−0.017	**1.000**
TBond	0.895	0.895

Reoptimize the portfolio for each of the following initial portfolios:

	TBill	Corp	SP500	SP600	TBond
Allocation 1	0.2	0.2	0.2	0.2	0.2
Allocation 2	1.0	0.0	0.0	0.0	0.0
Allocation 3	0.0	1.0	0.0	0.0	0.0
Allocation 4	0.0	0.0	1.0	0.0	0.0
Allocation 5	0.0	0.0	0.0	1.0	0.0
Allocation 6	0.0	0.0	0.0	0.0	1.0

Appendix 1

Returns, Compounding, and Sample Statistics

A. Returns

The total holding period return (HPR) of an asset is defined as the dollars earned over the period, including price appreciation and distributions, divided by the dollars invested:

$$\text{HPR} = \{\text{Ending value} - \text{Beginning value} + \text{Distributions}\}/\text{Beginning value}$$

In general, the return of a position in asset i over the period from $t - 1$ to t is

$$h_i(t) = \{V_i(t) - V_i(t - 1) + D_i(t)\}/V_i(t - 1)$$

where $V_i(t)$ is the value of asset i at time t and $D_i(t)$ is any distributions made over the holding period. For a single unit of the asset, this can be expressed in terms of the asset price:

$$h_i(t) = \{P_i(t) - P_i(t - 1) + D_i(t)\}/P_i(t - 1)$$

This definition assumes that the distributions occur at the end of the holding period, ignoring the possibility that the distribution was received earlier in the period and reinvested. The gross return in period t is simply $(1 + h_i(t))$.

Suppose we have a sequence of returns, $h_i(s)$, $s = 1, n$. The gross return over the multiperiod horizon is the product of the gross returns. That is,

$$(1 + h_i(1))(1 + h_i(2))\ldots(1 + h_i(n))$$

The logarithmic return in period s is $r_i(s) = \ln(1 + h_i(s))$.

B. Continuous Compounding

Logarithmic returns implicitly reflect continuous compounding—that is, subdivision of the return period into finer and finer increments. The general compounding formula is

$$V_i(t) = V_i(0)(1 + r_i/t)^{T/t}$$

where $V_i(0)$ = the initial value of asset i, r_i = the rate of return on asset i, T = the holding period, and t = the number of compounding periods within the holding period (T). This formula reflects earning a return of (r_i/t) in each of (T/t) subperiods. As the number of compounding periods goes to infinity, the formula converges to

$$V(t) = V(0)\exp(r_iT)$$

where exp = 2.718. To calculate the continuously compounded rate of return on asset i per period over the holding period from 0 to T, rearrange this equation:

$$r_i = \ln(V_i(T)/V_i(0))/T$$

C. Sample Statistics[14]

Given a sample of log returns, $r_i(t)$, $t = 1,T$, we can calculate sample statistics to estimate risk and return parameters.

Mean Return

The mean is calculated as the average return of the sample:

$$\alpha_i = (1/T)\Sigma_t r_i(t)$$

Variance and Standard Deviation

The variance of a random variable is measured as the average squared deviation from the mean:

$$\sigma_i^2 = (1/(T-1))\Sigma_t(r_i(t) - \alpha_i)^2$$

In computing the sample variance it is standard to divide by $(T-1)$ rather than T because one degree of freedom was used in computing the mean. The standard deviation is simply the square root of the variance:

$$\sigma_i = \sqrt{\sigma_i^2}$$

The variance of a sequence of returns may be calculated from the variance of the single-period return under the assumption of independent and identically distributed random variables. A common application is annualizing standard deviations calculated from monthly returns. For continuously compounded returns (that is, logarithmic returns), the formula for variance over the period 1 through T based on the one-period variance is

$$\sigma_{1,T}^2 = T\,\sigma_1^2$$

For a sample of *gross* returns, the corresponding formula is

$$S_{1,T}^2 = (S_1^2 + M_1^2)^T - M_1^{2T}$$

---

[14] With returns, *r*, defined as logarithmic returns, the notation here corresponds to the parameter definitions established in Section 3.2 and summarized in Appendix III. For example, the expected log return is denoted by α. Of course sample statistics can be computed for any data series.

where M is the mean and S is the standard deviation.[15] This formula is exact if gross returns are lognormal. Otherwise it is a useful approximation.

Covariance

The basic measure of association is covariance. The sample covariance subtracts the sample mean from each series and averages the product of corresponding deviations:

$$\sigma_{i,j} = (1/T)\Sigma_t (r_i,(t) - \alpha_i)(r_j(t) - \alpha_j)$$

This measure captures both the volatility of the variables and their directional relationship.

Correlation

The pure measure of association is correlation. It is pure in the sense that it removes the variation of return to express the association only in terms of the direction:

$$\rho_{i,j} = \sigma_{i,j}/(\sigma_i\sigma_j)$$

By construction the correlation coefficient lies between -1 and 1.

D. Application in Excel

Sample Statistics and Excel Formulas

Statistic	Equation	Excel Formula
Return	$\alpha_i = (1/T) \Sigma_t r_i(t)$	=AVERAGE(Cell(i,1):Cell(i,T))
Variance	$\sigma_i^2 = (1/(T - 1))\Sigma_t (r_{i,t} - \alpha_i)^2$	=VAR(Cell(i,1):Cell(i,T))
Standard deviation	$\sigma_i^2 = (1/(T - 1))\Sigma_t (r_{i,t} - \alpha_i)^2$	=STDEV(Cell(i,1):Cell(i,T))
Covariance	$\sigma_{ij} = (1/T) \Sigma_t (r_{i,t} - \alpha_i)(r_{j,t} - \alpha_j)$	=COVAR(Cell(i,1): Cell(i,T),Cell(j,1):Cell(j,T))
Correlation	$\rho_{ij} = \sigma_{ij}/(\sigma_i \sigma_j)$	=CORREL(Cell(i,1): Cell(i,T),Cell(j,1):Cell(j,T))

Here Cell(i,t) represents the cell reference for the return of asset i at time t.

For illustration, the Chapter 03 Excel Outboxes spreadsheet contains historical data. The "Data" worksheet provides monthly returns, from January 1926 through December 1993, for the following assets:

Asset	Abbreviation	Range
Treasury bills	TBill	C25:C840
Corporate bonds	Corp	D25:D840
Large stocks (S&P 500)	SP500	E25:E840
Small stocks	SP600	F25:F840
Treasury bonds	TBond	G25:G840

Two series are provided for each asset: the HPR and the logarithmic HPR (lnHPR), where

$$\text{lnHPR} = \ln(1 + \text{HPR})$$

[15] We use M and S here to distinguish them from the corresponding measures for log returns. Note that in our standard notation, $\mu = $ log of the mean gross return $= \ln(M)$.

The mean returns, standard deviations, correlation table, and covariance matrix, or summary statistics, are entered in the range A1:M22. The working version should look like this:

Summary Statistics

OBS	DATE	Arithmetic					Logarithmic					Liability
		Corp	SP500	SP600	TBill	TBond	Corp	SP500	SP600	Tbill	Tbond	
Monthly	α	0.0043	0.0099	0.0141	0.0028	0.0038	0.0047	0.0099	0.0135	0.0030	0.0043	
	σ	0.0196	0.0576	0.0885	0.0027	0.0220	0.0196	0.0576	0.0885	0.0027	0.0220	
Annual	α	0.0514	0.1188	0.1688	0.0342	0.0458	0.0568	0.1184	0.1619	0.0363	0.0520	0.045
	σ	0.0679	0.1997	0.3067	0.0093	0.0761	0.0679	0.1997	0.3067	0.0093	0.0761	0.060
CORRELATIONS	ρ											
1	Corp	1.0000	0.2262	0.1851	0.0964	0.8380	1.0000	0.2225	0.1784	0.0857	0.8364	0.000
2	SP500		1.0000	0.8461	-0.0259	0.1723	0.2225	1.0000	0.8585	-0.0161	0.1712	0.200
3	SP600			1.0000	-0.0436	0.1019	0.1784	0.8585	1.0000	-0.0256	0.1071	0.075
4	TBill				1.0000	0.1112	0.0857	-0.0161	-0.0256	1.0000	0.1003	0.990
5	TBond					1.0000	0.8364	0.1712	0.1071	0.1003	1.0000	0.900
	Liability						0.000	0.200	0.075	0.075	0.900	1.000
COVARIANCE	Ω											
1	Corp						0.005	0.003	0.004	0.000	0.004	0.000
2	SP500						0.003	0.040	0.053	0.000	0.003	0.002
3	SP600						0.004	0.053	0.094	0.000	0.002	0.001
4	TBill						0.000	0.000	0.000	0.000	0.000	0.001
5	TBond						0.004	0.003	0.002	0.000	0.006	0.004
	Liability						0.000	0.003	0.002	0.000	0.005	0.005

Appendix 2

Optimization

Optimization models have five key elements:

1. Objective: the measure to optimize.
2. Decision variables: what is changed to optimize the objective.
3. Constraints: limitations on the decision variables.
4. Parameters: constants in the formulas.
5. Assumptions.

The optimization process finds the set of decision variable values, from all the possible sets of values satisfying the constraints, that optimize (maximize or minimize) the objective.

Parameters and Assumptions

Parameters are the constant coefficients of the model. They enter into the calculation of the objective function and/or the constraints. Although *you* may change these values, they are held constant in the optimization. Often you will have several cases or variations of the same problem to solve, and the parameter values will change in each problem variation.

Decision Variables

Decision variables usually measure the amounts of resources to be allocated to some purpose or the level of some activity. In finance, this resource is typically money and is expressed as a weight, ω_i, indicating the percentage invested in asset i relative to the total amount invested:

$$\omega_i = \text{Investment in asset } i/\text{Total investment}$$

For example, if you invest \$6,000 in stocks (S) and \$4,000 in bonds (B), the weights for this simple two-asset portfolio are

$$\omega_S = \$ \text{ Stocks}/(\$ \text{ Stocks} + \$ \text{ Bonds}) = \$6,000/\$10,000 = 60\%$$
$$\omega_B = \$ \text{ Bonds}/(\$ \text{ Stocks} + \$ \text{ Bonds}) = \$4,000/\$10,000 = 40\%$$

Notice that because the money is fully invested in stocks and bonds,

$$\omega_S + \omega_B = (\$ \text{ Stocks} + \$ \text{ Bonds})/(\$ \text{ Stocks} + \$ \text{ Bonds}) = \$10,000/\$10,000 = 100\%$$

Objective

The objective, expressed as a function that depends on the decision variables, has two elements: how the objective is measured and what you are seeking to do. For example, if the objective is to minimize the risk of the portfolio, the measure would be the portfolio standard deviation formula and the goal would be to minimize.

Constraints

Constraints reflect limits on the decision variables. In most models constraints play a key role in determining what values are allowed for the decision variables, and, as a result, what values the objective can attain.

To define a constraint, you specify a formula involving the decision variables. Then you impose a condition ($<=$, $=$ or $>=$) and limit on the formula's value.

Variable Constraints

Constraints can be used to limit the following:

- The value of the decision variables in aggregate. For example, the requirement that the asset weights total to 1 is called the budget, or full investment, constraint and is expressed as $\omega_S + \omega_B = 1$.
- The value of specific decision variables. For example, the investor may be prohibited from taking a short position in some or all of the available assets, the long-only constraint. For these assets the weights have to be positive, or for each asset i, $\omega_i \geq 0$.
- The expected behavior of the portfolio. For example, if the investor dislikes losses (the likelihood of negative returns) rather than volatility (the total variation in return), a shortfall constraint can be included in the optimization program. A shortfall constraint can be used to construct a portfolio that limits the expected probability of earning a return below some threshold level.

Solution

A solution, or set of decision variable values, that satisfies all the constraints is called a *feasible solution.* Most optimization algorithms start with a feasible solution and then find another feasible solution by changing the decision variables. If the new feasible solution increases (decreases) the value of the objective function when maximizing (minimizing), the new feasible solution is kept and the process repeated until changing the decision variables does not improve the objective. An *optimal solution* is a feasible solution where the objective function reaches a maximum (or minimum) value.

The *global optimal solution* (if there is one) is the feasible solution with the best objective function value among all feasible solutions. A *local optimal solution* is a feasible solution with the best objective function "in the vicinity"—that is, there are no other nearby feasible solutions with better objective function values.

Optimization Failure

Optimization programs like Solver are designed to find optimal solutions, ideally global; but this is not always possible. In some cases *the program is not properly specified:*

- If the program is *underconstrained,* the objective is unbounded. In theory, the optimizer would continue to run forever because changing the decision weights would continue to improve the objective. In practice, the optimizer will stop running after a set time limit or number of iterations and report that the program did not converge. The decision variables reported are the last feasible solution the optimizer reached before stopping. These variables *do not* represent an optimal solution. Problem 6 at the end of the chapter was an example of an underconstrained program.
- If the program is *overconstrained,* no set of decision weights satisfies all the constraints. Problem 9 at the end of the chapter was an example of an over-constrained program.

    In other cases, *the inputs are not well defined:*

- Quadratic optimization requires that the objective function be convex. For portfolio optimization, this means that the portfolio variance is positive—that is, $\sigma_P^2 = \Sigma_{i=1,N}\Sigma_{j=1,N}\omega_i\omega_j\sigma_{i,j} \geq 0$. See Problem 11 at the end of the chapter for an example.

    Or *the solution space is not well defined:*

- If there are many local optimal solutions, it will not be clear that the solution produced by the optimizer is global. A simple way to check is to start the optimizer from different locations in the solution space—that is, change the initial values of the decision variables before solving. See Problem 11 at the end of the chapter for an example.

    In many cases, though, it may be enough to find a good solution—one that is better than the solution you are using now and offers insights into the problem at hand.

Linear Programming

A linear program (LP) is an optimization in which both the objective function and the constraints are linear. The specific assumptions include:

1. The objective and constraints are linear.
2. Proportionality: Output = Constant x input.
3. Additivity: Total output = Σ_i Output(i).
4. Divisibility: The decision variables take real rather than integer values.
5. Certainty: The problem can be modeled.

Issues involving the constraints include whether they are *binding*. Also imbedded in the solution is specialized information called *shadow prices*.

Quadratic Programming

A quadratic program (QP) involves optimization of a quadratic objective function subject to linear constraints. The mean–variance problem is a quadratic problem.

Excel Solver

Solver is a numerical optimization program included with Excel. To start Solver, from the toolbar select <u>T</u>ools then Sol<u>v</u>er. . . .[16] The Solver menu appears as follows:

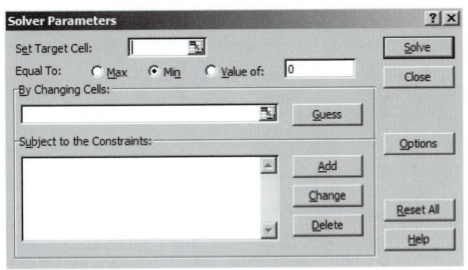

The Solver menu parallels the optimization program:

Optimization	Solver
Objective	Set Target Cell:
	Equal To:
Decision variables	By Changing Cells:
Constraints	Subject to the Constraints:

The <u>O</u>ptions button allows you to control certain aspects of the solution process, load or save problem definitions, and define parameters for both linear and nonlinear problems. Solver has default settings that are appropriate for most problems. Select <u>H</u>elp from the <u>O</u>ptions menu for a description of the optimization parameters and their settings.

<u>R</u>eports provides a detailed summary of the solutions that are available on the Solver results screen. Select <u>H</u>elp from the Solver Results menu for a description of the reports available and their content.

---

[16] If Sol<u>v</u>er. . . does not appear as an option on the Tools menu, select Add-<u>I</u>ns. . . and then check the box for Solver Add-in. If Solver Add-in does not appear as an option, it needs to be copied from the Excel install disk.

To illustrate the use of Solver, let's solve the two risky assets program. The goal of the program was to identify a portfolio along the frontier by finding the portfolio weights that minimized the portfolio standard deviation for a given level of return. This translates into Solver as follows:

Optimization	Solver			
Objective	Set target cell:	$G$8		
	Equal to:	MIN		
Variables	By changing cells:	$F$12:$G$12		
Constraints	Subject to the constraints:	$E$15	=	$G$15
		$E$16	=	$G$16

To fill in the menu, follow these steps:

Enter cell $G$8 in the Set Target Cell: field.

Click Min for Equal To:.

Enter the cells $F$12:$G$12 in the By Changing Cells: field.

To enter constraints, click the Add button. The **Add Constraint** menu should appear:

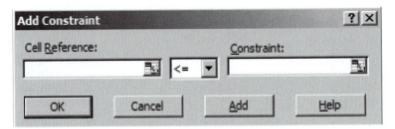

To add the full investment constraint, enter $E$15 in the Cell Reference: field, select = as the relation, and enter $G$15 in the Constraint: field. If desired, these steps can be repeated to add the target return and no short position constraints.

When complete, the menu should appear as follows:

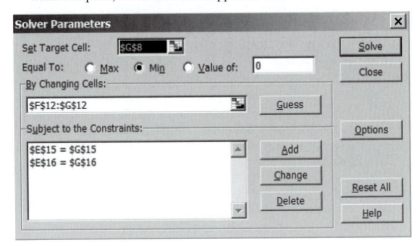

Click <u>S</u>olve. You should now see a Solver Results menu:

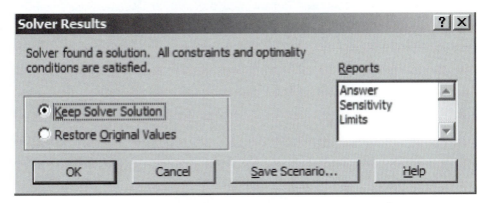

Solver has found a solution that satisfies the constraints. Select <u>K</u>eep Solver Solution and click OK. The worksheet should appear as:

	A	B	C	D	E	F	G
1		**Mean-Variance Efficient Frontier**					
2		Two risky assets					
3		No riskless asset					
4		Short sales					
5							
6							
7							
8	**Program**	**Objective**	MIN	σ_ω		=	0.0745
9							
10		**Variables**				Stock	Bond
11			ω			0.0616	0.9384
12							
13							
14		**Constraints**			Portfolio		
15			Σ_ω	=	1.0000	=	1.0000
16			μ_ω	=	0.0600	=	0.0600
17							
18							
19		**Where**					
20					μ_ω	=	0.0600
21					σ_ω	=	0.0745

The solution, in cells F12 and G12, states that the portfolio allocated 6.16 percent in stocks and 93.84 percent in bonds has an expected return of 6 percent. These weights can be copied to the results table and represent one point along the frontier. To solve for additional points at different target return levels, change the value in cell G16 and resolve. Repeating this process for each target return produces a reasonably complete frontier.

Appendix 3

Notation

Investment

$P_i(t)$	Price of asset i at time t
W	Wealth
B	Bond
S	Stock
n	Number of assets
T	Investment horizon
U	Utility function or utility
t	Time
ω_i	Weight of asset i
λ	Coefficient of risk aversion ($= \frac{1}{2}(1 - \gamma)$)
γ	Risk aversion parameter
$E[\,]$	Expected value
R_i	Cumulative return for asset i ($= \Sigma_{t=1,T}\, r_i(t)$)
$r_i(t)$	Log return for asset i at time t
H	Shortfall constraint threshold return level
K	Shortfall constraint probability level
L	Liability
$X_i(t)$	Random variable for asset i at time t ($\sim N(\alpha_i, \sigma_i^2)$)
$\ln$	Natural logarithm function
$\exp$	2.718, base for natural logarithm

Statistical

N	Cumulative normal distribution
α_i	Expected continuously compounded return for asset i
μ_i	Log of expected gross return for asset i ($= (\alpha_i + \frac{1}{2}\sigma_i^2)$)
σ_i^2	Variance of (log) return for asset i
σ_i	Standard deviation of return for asset i
$\sigma_{i,j}$	Covariance of return between asset i and asset j
$\rho_{i,j}$	Correlation of return between asset i and asset j ($= \sigma_{i,j}/(\sigma_i \sigma_j)$)

Chapter 4

Asset Allocation Inputs

Chapter Outline

4.1   Sensitivity of the Mean–Variance Model to Inputs

The previous chapter developed the machinery of the M–V model and illustrated its application through a series of examples and problems. In this chapter we address the issue of estimating the inputs—expected returns, variances, and covariances—required to make the model operational.

The M–V framework is the workhorse of practical asset allocation. Almost everyone uses it, yet virtually nobody is entirely happy doing so. Without doubt, the primary cause of dissatisfaction is the model's sensitivity to its inputs. Small changes in the inputs—especially the expected returns—can cause substantial changes in the "optimal" portfolio.[1] Frequently a small change is sufficient to drive the optimal portfolio from one corner solution to another. That is, a small change causes some assets to drop out of the optimal portfolio altogether and other assets, which had been absent before, to suddenly emerge with substantial weight in the new portfolio. This problem becomes more acute as the number of asset classes increases. The same problem arises in a different form if we allow short positions—that is, if we do not impose a long-only constraint. In this case the optimal portfolio will almost always include all available asset classes, with some held long and some sold short. But small changes in the inputs may cause abrupt shifts from being long a particular asset to being short that asset (or vice versa) even though the improvement in the M–V objective function is negligible.

Why are the results so sensitive? A simple example will help provide some intuition. Suppose there are three asset classes and two of them have identical parameters: the same expected return, the same variance, and the same covariance with the third asset class. Furthermore, assume these two asset classes are perfectly correlated. It should be

---

[1] A classic demonstration and discussion of this sensitivity can be found in Michaud (1989). Michaud (1998) provides extensive analysis of the statistical properties of the M–V efficient frontier when the inputs are subject to estimation error.

clear that we really need only one of these two asset classes. If we include both of them in the portfolio, their combined weight can be split arbitrarily between them without affecting either the risk or the expected return of the portfolio. Suppose we increase the expected return on one of these assets by a tiny amount. Suddenly we are no longer indifferent between them. We want to go long the one with the higher expected return and, if possible, short the one with the lower expected return. Thus the optimal portfolio is extremely sensitive to the expected returns on these two asset classes.

This example may seem a bit contrived, but it actually captures the essence of the problem. As we add asset classes to the M–V model, it becomes increasingly likely that there are combinations of the available assets that are highly correlated.[2] The M–V optimizer will tend to go long one of these combinations and, if allowed, short another. Small changes in expected returns will cause the optimizer to switch from one combination to the other. In the process, the weights on particular assets in the overall portfolio may be unstable or take extreme values. The optimizer does not see this as a problem because it does not attach any significance to whether a particular asset is held long, sold short, or omitted from the portfolio. We, the investors, do care about the weights on particular asset classes because they correspond to the way investment opportunities are traditionally defined. We want to make an allocation to, say, a small-capitalization value manager—not a bundle of long and short positions in several asset classes that look like a small-capitalization value manager in risk–return terms. Because the optimizer does not understand the distinction, we are often forced to impose constraints in an effort to get results that make sense.

Of course the real problem is that we do not know the true values of the necessary model inputs: the expected returns, variances, and covariances. If we knew these values, we could be confident that the optimizer was giving us accurate advice. Without that certainty, we are left with the task of trying to estimate the parameters and dealing with the consequences of the optimizer's sensitivity to the inputs.

The next section discusses estimation of M–V inputs when investment opportunities are assumed to be constant through time. Section 4.3 relaxes the assumption that investment opportunities are constant.

There is a vast amount of academic research on estimation techniques that have been or could be applied to generate inputs for asset allocation analysis. Of necessity, this chapter only introduces some of the important issues and concepts. It is not intended as a rigorous or exhaustive treatment of statistical techniques.

4.2 Constant Investment Opportunities

Using Sample Moments

The most straightforward approach to estimating expected returns, variances, and covariances is to use what statisticians call **sample moments** to estimate the corresponding **population moments.** This is a fancy way of saying that we use the familiar sample

---

[2] This reflects the fact that asset returns tend to be dominated by a few common risk factors. As the number of assets increases there will tend to be various combinations with similar exposure to the common risk factors and for which diversification has nearly eliminated asset-specific risks. These combinations will be highly correlated and have similar overall risk. Mathematically, the problem arises because the covariance matrix of returns is (or becomes) "ill-conditioned." In especially perverse cases, it may even be possible to construct a portfolio with a negative variance: See Problem 11 of Chapter 3 for an example.

mean, sample variance, and sample covariances from a historical sample of returns to estimate the corresponding unknown parameters.

This approach is so common and simple to apply that it is easy to overlook the fact that it rests on a very strong assumption. Given a historical sample, we can always calculate the usual sample statistics in Excel or some other software package. But unless the parameters we are trying to estimate are truly constants—like the number Pi in mathematics—we may not be estimating what we really want, which are the risk and return characteristics that will govern the *future*. For now we will accept the assumption that investment opportunities do not change over time. In Section 4.3 this assumption will be relaxed.

In developing the M–V model we found it useful to work with continuously compounded returns (see Equation (3.5) of Chapter 3) because the continuously compounded return over a period of *T* years is simply the sum of the returns in each of the subperiods. This is true regardless of how we choose to define a period—a year, a quarter, or a month. This is especially convenient here because we want to examine whether sampling the data more frequently, such as quarterly instead of annually, gives more precise estimates of the underlying parameters.

Assume that returns are normally distributed with a constant mean α and a constant variance σ^2 per unit of time and that returns are uncorrelated across periods. This is the model set forth in Chapter 3. Our current focus is on estimating the parameters α and σ^2.[3]

Suppose we have data covering *T* years with *M* observations drawn at intervals of *h* years such that $T = hM$. Letting $r_h(i)$ denote the *i*th observation when the period length is *h*, the sample mean return is

$$\bar{r}_h = \frac{1}{M}\sum_i r_h(i) \tag{4.1}$$

and the sample variance is given by

$$S^2 = \frac{1}{M-1}\sum_i (r_h(i) - \bar{r}_h)^2 \tag{4.2}$$

Applying standard results for the mean and variance of a sum of random variables, the expected value of the sample mean is (αh) and its variance is $[(\sigma^2 h)/M]$. Because we want an estimate of the expected return per unit of time, α, our estimate is given by annualizing the sample mean—that is, multiplying by $(1/h)$. This gives an estimator with the correct expected value. The variance of this estimate is $(1/h)^2$ times the variance of the sample mean itself. That is, the variance of the estimate is

$$\frac{\sigma^2 h}{h^2 M} = \frac{\sigma^2}{hM} = \frac{\sigma^2}{T} \tag{4.3}$$

Equation (4.3) embodies an important result. Note that the variance of our estimate depends on the total length of the sample, *T*, but does not depend on how often we sample within that overall period. So chopping the sample period into shorter subperiods does not improve the precision of the estimate of the mean return. Monthly

---

[3] Recall that a different, but closely related, concept of mean return appears in the M–V objective function. Under our assumptions, this measure, the logarithm of the expected gross return, is given by $\mu = \alpha + \frac{1}{2}\sigma^2$. Therefore, it is a function of the two fundamental parameters.

EXHIBIT 4.1
95% Confidence Intervals for Expected Return

Length of Sample (Years)	Lower Bound	Upper Bound
10	0.70 %	19.30 %
25	4.12	15.88
50	5.84	14.16
75	6.61	13.39
100	7.06	12.94
400	8.53	11.47
900	9.02	10.98

data are no better than quarterly or annual data. Indeed we might as well admit that we have only one observation: the return for the whole *T*-year period! The only way to get a more precise estimate is to have a longer sample—that is, increase *T*.

To get a feel for how precise our expected return estimate might be, suppose our estimate of the annual mean is 10 percent and the (true) annual standard deviation of returns is 15 percent. Exhibit 4.1 gives the 95 percent confidence interval for the expected return for various sample periods. As we can see from the table, the implications are dire. In order to have confidence that our estimate is off by no more than ± 1 percent, we need 900 years of data! For more realistic sample periods of 100 years or less the estimate is little better than a guess.

When we consider estimating the variance of returns, the situation improves considerably. Under the assumption that returns are normally distributed, the expected value of the annualized sample variance (Equation (4.2) multiplied by $(1/h)$) is σ^2, and its variance is[4]

$$\frac{2\sigma^4}{M-1} \tag{4.4}$$

The precision of the estimate improves as the number of observations, *M*, increases. For estimating the variance, 10 years of monthly observations are as good as 120 years of annual observations. In either case we have 120 observations. Similarly, for a given sample period *T*, the precision of the estimate improves as the period is chopped into shorter subperiods—that is, as *M* increases and *h* decreases while we hold $T = (M\,h)$ constant.

Exhibit 4.2 presents 95 percent confidence intervals for the sample standard deviation. The sample standard deviation is, of course, simply the square root of the sample variance. It has the advantage of having the same dimension (percent) as the expected return. The exhibit presents results for 3-, 5-, and 10-year sample periods with quarterly, monthly, weekly, and daily sampling frequencies. As in Exhibit 4.1, the true standard deviation is 15 percent. It is apparent from Exhibit 4.2 that sampling more frequently has a dramatic impact on the precision of the estimate. Even with only three years of data we can be 95 percent confident of being within ± 1 percent of the true value if we use daily data. With 10 years of data the same level of precision can be achieved with weekly observations. Obviously this is a drastic improvement over the 900 years required to achieve such accuracy for the sample mean.[5]

---

[4] This follows from the fact that the random variable defined by $[(M-1)\,S^2/\sigma^2]$ has a chi-square distribution with $(M-1)$ degrees of freedom. See Mood, Graybill, and Boes (1974), p. 245.

[5] It should be clear that the results in Exhibits 4.1 and 4.2 depend on the standard deviation of returns. For example, if the standard deviation were 10 percent instead of 15 percent it would take "only" 400 years to have 95 percent confidence that our estimate of expected return is within ± 1 percent.

EXHIBIT 4.2
95% Confidence
Intervals for the
Sample Standard
Deviation

Sample Period (Yrs)	Frequency	Lower Bound	Upper Bound
3	Quarterly	8.83	21.17
3	Monthly	11.50	18.49
3	Weekly	13.33	16.67
3	Daily	14.24	15.76
5	Quarterly	10.27	19.72
5	Monthly	12.30	17.70
5	Weekly	13.71	16.29
5	Daily	14.41	15.59
10	Quarterly	11.68	18.31
10	Monthly	13.10	16.90
10	Weekly	14.09	15.91
10	Daily	14.79	15.42

Clearly risk measures such as the variance and standard deviation can be esti-mated much more precisely than expected returns. It is therefore common practice to treat risk estimates as if they are measured very precisely even though substan-tial estimation error may still be present. For example, one often encounters a graph purporting to show changes in an asset's risk over time based on a moving window of, say, 36 monthly returns. Implicit in this type of presentation is the assumption that each point in the chart reflects the true risk at that point in time. As illustrated in Exhibit 4.2, however, estimates based on 36 monthly observations are subject to substantial error. In our example, the 95 percent confidence interval covers a range of 7 percent (11.50–18.49 percent) around the true value of 15 per-cent. From a statistical perspective, fluctuations within that range are just noise. We should therefore be wary of ascribing too much practical significance to such variations.

Notwithstanding the error inherent in the usual risk measures, it should be clear that getting decent expected return estimates must be of even greater concern for most asset allocation applications. As a result, in the remainder of this chapter we will focus primarily on this task.[6]

James–Stein Estimation

Given a historical sample of returns, is there a better estimate of the expected return than the sample mean? If we are focused on estimating the expected return for only a single asset class and we have no a priori knowledge of the true value, the answer is that no estimate based solely on the data is more reliable than the sample mean for *all* possible values of the (unknown) true mean. However, if we are interested in estimating

---

[6] There is a substantial literature on more sophisticated approaches to risk estimation. One strand of research deals with the structure of risk across assets. We will touch on this when we discuss using risk models to impose cross-sectional structure on expected return estimates. A second strand of research dealing with the time series properties of variances is generally associated with the term *autoregres-sive conditional heteroscedasticity* (ARCH). These models tend to be most relevant for analyzing high-frequency data and for situations, such as option pricing, in which volatility estimation is critically important for valuation. Kritzman (1991) provides a brief introduction to ARCH.

expected returns for three or more asset classes, it turns out that we can do better than using the individual sample means. This somewhat surprising result is called *Stein's paradox.*[7]

Stein estimators are based on the idea of "shrinking" the individual sample means toward a common value referred to as the *grand mean*. Why might this improve our estimates? Suppose we have calculated the sample mean return for N asset classes. Some of these will probably overestimate their corresponding (unknown) true values, and some will underestimate the corresponding true expected returns. We do not know for certain which are overestimates and which are underestimates. However, the highest estimates are more likely to be the overestimates, and the lowest values are more likely to be the underestimates. Therefore, adjusting the estimates toward a common central value is likely to improve their accuracy.

One version of the James–Stein estimator for the expected return on the ith asset class is given by[8]

$$\bar{r}_i - \phi_i(\bar{r}_i - \bar{r}^*) \tag{4.5}$$

$$\phi_i \equiv \text{Min}\left[1, \left(\frac{\sigma_i^2/T}{\sum(\bar{r}_i - \bar{r}^*)^2/(N-3)}\right)\right]$$

where $\bar{r}_i$ is the sample mean for the ith asset class, $\bar{r}^*$ is the average of the sample means across the N asset classes, and σ_i^2 is the variance of asset i. Note that ϕ_i is always between zero and 1. The James–Stein estimate of asset i's expected return is its sample mean minus a fraction of the amount by which its sample mean exceeds the grand mean. The parameter ϕ_i shrinks the sample mean toward the grand mean.

In the definition of ϕ_i the term in brackets is essentially a ratio of variances. The numerator is the variance of asset i's sample mean. A higher variance implies that we should have less confidence that the sample mean is a good estimate of the true expected return. As a result, the shrinkage parameter increases as this variance increases. The denominator is a measure of the dispersion of all the sample means around the grand mean. If all the sample means are tightly clustered around the grand mean, we have greater confidence in the implicit assumption that the true expected returns are similar across the asset classes. Conversely, if the sample means are widely dispersed, we should put less weight on this assumption and impose less shrinkage toward the grand mean. Therefore, the shrinkage parameter declines as the dispersion of sample means increases.

Exhibit 4.3 applies the James–Stein estimator to eight major asset classes over the 24-year period from 1985 through 2008. The first five classes are equities, and the last three are fixed-income classes. The annualized sample means range from a high of 10.10 percent for the Russell 2000 Value index to a low of 5.81 percent for the Russell 2000 Growth index. Interestingly, the three fixed-income asset classes had average returns that fell within the range of equity returns—that is, they were not systematically lower than the equity returns. However, the fixed-income returns did

---

[7] See Efron and Morris (1977) for an excellent exposition of Stein's paradox and applications of Stein estimators.

[8] This version of the James–Stein estimator assumes sampling errors are independent across the asset classes. Jorion (1986) provides a more general version allowing for correlated errors.

EXHIBIT 4.3   James–Stein Estimation: Monthly Data 1985–2008

	Annualized Sample Moments		James–Stein Estimation		
	Mean (α)	Standard Deviation	Volatility Ratio	Shrinkage Parameter	James–Stein Estimate (α)
Russell 1000 Value	10.03%	14.67%	3.012	1.000	8.22%
Russell 1000 Growth	8.42	18.21	4.639	1.000	8.22
Russell 2000 Value	10.10	17.15	4.115	1.000	8.22
Russell 2000 Growth	5.81	23.89	7.987	1.000	8.22
MSCI EAFE	8.91	17.63	4.351	1.000	8.22
Barclays High Yield	7.39	8.61	1.037	1.000	8.22
Barclays Aggregate Bond	7.83	4.34	0.264	0.264	7.93
Citigroup Hedged Non-U.S. Government	7.27	3.25	0.148	0.148	7.41
Grand mean	8.22				
Standard deviation of sample means	1.46				

have substantially lower volatility. For each of the equity classes, the James–Stein estimator shrinks the sample mean all the way to the grand mean of 8.22 percent because in each case the volatility ratio is much greater than 1. According to the James–Stein estimator, the sample means are so imprecise, relative to the dispersion of sample means across asset classes, that they provide no basis for assigning different expected returns to the five equity asset classes.[9] In particular, the relatively low sample mean for the Russell 2000 Growth index is brought up to equality with the other equity classes.

The impact on the three fixed-income asset classes is mixed. The James–Stein adjustments are modest for the Barclays Aggregate and the Citigroup Hedged Non-U.S. Government indexes because their low volatilities imply that the sample means are relatively reliable estimates. After shrinkage, the expected returns for these fixed-income classes are below the expected return on equities. On the other hand, the sample mean for the Barclays High Yield is too imprecise and too similar to those of the equity classes to allow for differentiation. Therefore, the James–Stein estimate for high-yield bonds is the same as for the equity classes.

The James–Stein estimator may be viewed as belonging to a class of estimators referred to as *Bayesian.* Bayesian techniques combine "prior" information with new information to generate a more refined estimate. In the case of the James–Stein estimator, the prior information is the assumption that expected returns should be similar (indeed identical) across asset classes. The James–Stein estimator adjusts this initial judgment based on the new information contained in the sample means. The extent of the adjustment is determined by the volatility ratio embedded in the shrinkage parameter ϕ.

[9] Note that it is the mean of the log return, α, that is equalized here. To get our M–V model inputs, we need to convert to the log of the expected gross return, $\mu = \alpha + \frac{1}{2}\sigma^2$. Due to the volatility adjustment, these are not equalized.

Excel Outbox *James–Stein* *Estimator*	This outbox provides the opportunity to work with James–Stein estimators by recreating Exhibit 4.3. Use the worksheet <JS – Template> in the spreadsheet Chapter 04 Excel Outboxes.xls. The spreadsheet provides the data on tab <LN Asset Class Returns>. The template should appear as follows:

	A	B	C	D	E	F	G	H	I
1	James-Stein Estimator								
2									
3	Grand Average				Beg:				
4	σ^2 of Sample Means				End:				
5	Dispersion measure				Length:				
6	# assets								
7	Years								
8									
9									
10									
11		Russell 1000 Value TR	Russell 1000 Growth TR	Russell 2000 Value TR	Russell 2000 Growth TR	MSCI EAFE TR	Barclays Hi-Yld TR	Barclays Aggregate Bond TR	Citigroup US$ Hedged Non-US$ Gvt TR
12	Annualized Mean								
13	Annualized s								
14	Annualized s^2								
15									
16	Volatility Ratio								
17	Shrink Factor								
18									
19	J-S Estimator (α)								
20	J-S Estimator (μ)								

Note: The spreadsheet has been rotated, relative to the table in the text, to conform to the columnar data.

This spreadsheet allows us to dynamically set the sample period. This is done in cells E3:E5 using the OFFSET and MATCH functions:

- In cell E3 enter the beginning date of the sample period using the format MM/YYYY (it must be $\geq$ January 1985).
- In cell E4 enter the ending date of the sample period using the format MM/YYYY (it must be $\leq$ December 2008).
- In cell E5 enter =COUNT(OFFSET('LN Asset Class Returns'!$A$1,MATCH($E$3,'LN Asset Class Returns'!$A$2:$A$289,0),0):OFFSET('LN Asset Class Returns'!$A$1,MATCH($E$4,'LN Asset Class Returns'!$A$2:$A$289,0),0)).

The function in cell E5 counts the number of months between the beginning and ending dates.

- =MATCH(lookup_value,lookup_array,[match_type]). This function looks for an exact match (match_type=0) for the beginning date (lookup_value=$E$3) within the dates of the sample period (lookup_array='LN Asset Class Returns'!$A$2:$A$289) and then returns the number indicating its position within the array.
- =OFFSET(reference,rows,cols). This function returns the cell reference that is "rows" rows and "cols" columns from the reference cell. A positive (negative) value moves to the right (left) and down (up) from the reference cell.

The spreadsheet should now show the following:

	A	B	C	D	E	F	G	H	I
1	James–Stein Estimator								
2									
3	Grand Average			Beg:	Jan-85				
4	σ^2 of sample means			End:	Dec-08				
5	Dispersion measure			Length:	288				
6	# assets								
7	Years								

The asset class summary statistics are calculated in cells B12:I14. The annualized mean return is given by the monthly average scaled to 12 months:

$$\bar{r}_h = \frac{1}{M}\sum_i r_h(i)$$

- Copy the formula in cell E5 to cell B12, and then replace "COUNT" with "12*AVERAGE".

The annualized variance is calculated similarly:

$$S^2 = \frac{1}{M-1}\sum_i (r_h(i) - \bar{r}_h)^2$$

- Copy the formula in cell B12 to cell B13, and then replace "12*AVERAGE" with "SQRT(12)*STDEV".
- In cell B14 enter =B13^2.
- Copy cells B12:B14 to cells C12:I14. *Note:* Use Paste Special Formula to avoid overwriting the table formatting.

The global summary statistics are calculated in cells B3:B5:

- The global mean $(\bar{r}^*)$ is calculated as the average of the asset class means. In cell B3 enter =AVERAGE(B12:I12).
- The dispersion of sample means is calculated as $\sum (\bar{r}_i - \bar{r}^*)^2/(N-3)$. Use the Excel VAR function and then adjust to get $(N-3)$ instead of $(N-1)$ in the denominator.
- In cell B4 enter =VAR(B12:I12).
- In cell B5 enter =B4*($B$6-1)/($B$6-3).
- In cell B6 enter =count(B12:I12).
- In cell B7 enter E5/12.

The James–Stein estimators are calculated in cells B16:I20:

- Volatility ratio: In cell B16 enter =(B14)/($B$7*$B$5).
- Shrink factor (ϕ_i): In cell B17 enter =MIN(1,B16).
- In cell B19 enter =B12 − B17*(B12-$B$3).
- In cell B20 enter =B19 + 0.5*B14.
- Copy cells B16:B20 to cells C16:I20 using Paste Special Formula to avoid overwriting the table formatting.

The finished worksheet is provided online as worksheet <JS – Complete> in the spreadsheet Chapter 04 Excel Outboxes-Completed.xls.

Linking Returns to the Economy

The preceding two methods used only historical return data to estimate parameters. Both of those methods—sample moments and James–Stein estimation—implicitly assume that we have no other useful information on which to base our estimates. If we use each asset's unadjusted sample mean as our estimate of its expected return, then, at least in principle, we must be willing to accept *any* value as a reasonable estimate as long as it happened sometime in the past. The James–Stein approach imposes the assumption that expected returns should be similar across assets; however, it says nothing about what constitutes a reasonable level for asset returns. We now consider how some basic economic reasoning can anchor return expectations for broad asset classes. In particular, the focus is on estimating the return on the domestic stock market.

We start by recognizing a simple fact: The stock market represents ownership of the productive capital in the economy. Ultimately the aggregate stock market must be driven by the return earned on capital invested in the real economy. To understand the implications of this fact, we draw on some results from the neoclassical theory of economic growth.[10]

The assumption that investment opportunities are constant implies that we should focus on what economists often call the *steady state* behavior of the economy. According to the neoclassical theory of optimal economic growth, the long-run growth rate of real output equals the growth rate of the labor force plus the rate of labor productivity growth. To keep the mix of capital and labor constant, capital must also grow at this rate. In addition, the share of output paid to each factor of production is constant. Finally, assuming consumers dislike postponing consumption, the long-run rate of return on capital exceeds the growth rate of output. This implies that the required growth of equity capital can be financed out of retained earnings with the excess paid out as dividends. Therefore, it is reasonable to assume that no new shares are issued and that a constant fraction of earnings is paid out as dividends. To be consistent with the notion of constant investment opportunities, we must also assume that the mix of debt and equity financing is constant.

Now consider what this tells us about equity returns. Let S_t denote the level of the stock market at time t, E_t denote the level of earnings at time t,[11] and M_t the price–earnings multiple prevailing at time t. The level of the market can be written as

$$S_t = E_t * M_t \tag{4.6}$$

Multiplying and dividing Equation (4.6) by the gross domestic product, GDP_t, and defining K_t as the ratio of earnings to GDP gives

$$S_t = GDP_t * K_t * M_t \tag{4.7}$$

Note that K_t is the share of profits in the economy.

Using Equation (4.7), we can express the rate of capital appreciation over a T-year horizon as follows:

$$(1/T)\ln\left(\frac{S_T}{S_0}\right) = (1/T)\ln\left(\frac{GDP_T}{GDP_0}\right) + (1/T)\ln\left(\frac{K_T}{K_0}\right) + (1/T)\ln\left(\frac{M_T}{M_0}\right) \tag{4.8}$$

---

[10] Chapter 3 of Dornbusch, Fischer, and Startz (2001) offers a readable exposition of the basic neoclassical growth model. In what follows, we implicitly assume that productivity growth arises from what Dornbusch et al. refer to as "labor-augmenting" technical change. Readers with a strong mathematics background may want to consult Chapter 16 of Intriligator (1971) for a discussion of optimal growth.

[11] Note that E represents earnings here. In other parts of the book, it is the expected value operator.

EXHIBIT 4.4
Decomposition of
S&P 500 Returns:
Log Returns
1946–2007

	Annual Return/Growth Rate	Standard Deviation
S&P 500 return	10.82%	15.31%
Real GDP growth	3.01	2.97
Inflation	3.94	3.29
EPS/GDP	−0.12	17.62
PE ratio	0.32	23.80
Dividend yield	3.67	1.49
Total	10.82	

The first term on the right side of this equation is the growth rate of GDP. The second term is the rate at which the share of profits in the economy expands or contracts. Similarly the third term is the rate at which the price–earnings multiple expands or contracts.

According to the neoclassical growth model, the share of output paid to capital approaches a constant in the long run. Assuming a constant debt-to-equity ratio, this implies that K_t, the share of profits in the economy, also tends toward a constant value. As a result, over sufficiently long horizons—that is, as T gets large—the middle term in Equation (4.8) must be very small. Now consider changes in the price–earnings ratio. The long-run price–earnings ratio cannot be negative because investors would not pay a positive price for negative earnings (losses) and would not part with positive earnings at a negative price. Similarly, the price–earnings ratio is effectively bounded above by the unwillingness of investors to pay an arbitrarily high price for a dollar of earnings. Therefore, over sufficiently long horizons the last term in Equation (4.8) must also be very small. Putting these results together, we see that the long-term rate of capital appreciation on the stock market cannot deviate "too much" from the growth rate of nominal GDP. Under our assumption that no new shares are issued, this rate of capital appreciation will correspond to the growth of retained earnings.

It may seem that we have gotten nowhere because we have simply replaced the problem of estimating the capital appreciation component of stock market returns with the problem of estimating the nominal growth rate of the economy. However, economic growth in large industrialized economies is far more stable than the stock market. Therefore, estimates based on historical averages are far more reliable. In addition, economic theory provides substantial guidance for estimating the secular behavior of real growth and inflation.

Exhibit 4.4 decomposes the post–World War II return on the S&P 500 into five parts: real GDP growth, inflation, reported earnings per share (EPS) relative to GDP, expansion of the price–earnings (PE) ratio, and the dividend yield. Because we are working with logarithmic returns, the components are additive. The exhibit also shows the annual standard deviation of each component. Of the 10.82 percent annual return on the market, only 0.20 percent is attributable to the combined impact of the PE and EPS/GDP ratios. These two components are highly volatile, but their movements tend to offset each other because the same variable—earnings—is the numerator of one ratio and the denominator of the other. On net, the capital appreciation component of return during this period was close to the growth of nominal GDP.

The correspondence between market appreciation and nominal economic growth is not always this close. If we extend our sample backward to include the depression of the 1930s, the gap between earnings growth and nominal economic growth widens substantially. Similarly, if we end the sample in 1999—the peak of the late-1990s technology bubble—the combined impact of the two ratios is close to +1 percent per year. In contrast, including the dramatic collapse of earnings and stock prices in 2008 (extending the sample by just one year) shifts the postwar impact of these ratios to -0.60 percent per year. Thus these components of return *can* be significant even over long horizons. In general, however, this should not be our *expectation*. Indeed the analysis just outlined is most useful when these components have had a large impact on historical returns because it allows us to strip out aspects of the historical period that are unlikely to be repeated and to adjust other components in light of changing circumstances. For example, one might believe that 3.0 percent is a reasonable estimate of future real economic growth—say 1 percent labor force growth plus 2 percent productivity increases—but that average inflation is likely to be closer to 2.5 percent than the 3.94 percent postwar average. Then the market would be expected to appreciate at 5.5 percent instead of the 7.15 percent historical average.

What about the dividend yield? Here we face an interesting dilemma. For a given estimate of the rate of capital appreciation, our estimate of the market's total return increases or decreases one-for-one with our estimate of the dividend yield. In theory, however, the long-run return on the market should not depend on the dividend yield. Why? In the long run the marginal unit of productive capital must earn just enough to cover the cost of capital—that is, the required return. Firms will be indifferent between reinvesting an extra dollar of earnings and paying out an extra dollar of dividends. Of course if they pay out too much (too little) in dividends, they will have to issue (buy back) shares to keep equity capital growing at the same rate as the economy. Thus the same required return on equities can be consistent with a variety of dividend policies. A higher (lower) dividend payout ratio will be offset by slower (faster) capital appreciation as higher (lower) share issuance substitutes dollar-for-dollar versus retention of earnings.[12] The composition of return—dividend yield versus capital appreciation—would differ, but the total would be the same.

At this stage we are left with essentially two choices. We could fully specify an economic growth model, estimate all its parameters, and determine the long-run real return on equity capital. Adding an assumption regarding dividend policy would then determine the dividend yield and price appreciation components of return. This is an elegant, but labor-intensive, approach. Alternatively we can simply make a reasonable assumption about the dividend yield and combine it with the insights gained from Equation (4.8). We will illustrate this second, more pragmatic, approach.

What is a reasonable estimate of the dividend yield? The historical average is one obvious candidate. Over the 62-year period 1946–2007 the dividend return averaged 3.67 percent with a standard deviation of 1.49 percent. Assuming a normal distribution and recalling our earlier results for the variance of a sample mean (Equation (4.3)), this implies we could be 95 percent confident that the true value of the expected dividend return lies between 3.30 percent and 4.04 percent. We might pick, say, 3.50 percent as our estimate of dividend return and combine it with a 5.5 percent rate of price appreciation to arrive at an estimate of 9.00 percent total (log) return on the market.

Recent history suggests a much lower dividend return. Over the 15 years 1994–2008 the dividend return on the S&P 500 averaged only about 1.9 percent. If we are adamant in assuming that investment opportunities never change, we can dismiss this estimate as much less reliable than one based on the longer sample. However, if we are willing to admit that the assumption of an unchanging world is only a convenient approximation, it is worthwhile examining what more recent evidence may be capturing.

---

[12] Equation (4.8) still holds if shares are being issued or repurchased. However, we must interpret the left side of the equation (S) as the aggregate value of shares outstanding rather than the value per share.

Simple arithmetic shows that the dividend yield (dividends divided by price) is equal to the dividend payout ratio (dividends divided by earnings) divided by the PE ratio. A lower dividend yield must reflect a lower payout ratio, a higher PE ratio, or a combination of both. During the 1994–2008 period, both of these components put downward pressure on the dividend yield. In part this was due to the rapid growth and increased importance of the information technology sector. In general, technology companies retained and reinvested their earnings, and the market accorded their stocks relatively high PE ratios in anticipation of continued rapid growth. Indeed in the late 1990s belief in the so-called new economy was so strong that even "vaporware" firms with no real products, much less current earnings or dividends, had substantial market capitalization. The effect, of course, was to increase the market's PE ratio and reduce the market's payout ratio. A combination of tax policies and accounting standards reinforced and broadened this effect by taxing dividends more heavily than capital gains and by encouraging firms to compensate their employees—especially the highest-paid employees—with stock options rather than increased salary and bonus payments. Faced with these incentives, it is not surprising that corporate decision makers substituted share repurchases for dividend growth and, more generally, pursued policies designed to generate short-term price appreciation. The result, again, was a lower dividend yield.

The relationship among the PE ratio, payout ratio, and dividend yield provides a convenient way to estimate the dividend yield. In the postwar period, the average payout ratio for the S&P 500 has been roughly 0.5 with roughly 90 percent of the observations falling between 0.33 and 0.64. The average PE ratio in the postwar period has been about 16. Assuming a payout ratio of one-half and a long-term PE ratio of 16 implies a dividend yield of 3.13 percent (= 0.5/16): somewhat below the postwar average dividend return but well above the more recent experience. If we believe the payout ratio will remain in the lower end of the postwar experience, at say 0.40, then with a PE ratio of 16 our dividend yield estimate would be 2.50 percent. This same estimate would be consistent with a 0.50 payout ratio if, as argued by Siegel (2002), greater economic stability, lower transaction costs, and favorable tax treatment of dividends justify an average PE ratio of 20 in the future. On the other hand, if the crash of 2008 causes a permanent shift toward income-oriented investments, the average PE ratio could be 12 and the payout ratio 0.6. That would imply a 5 percent dividend yield on the market.

The crash of 2008 is not the only reason the market's dividend yield may be moving back toward its longer-term average. U.S. tax policy and accounting standard changes during the Bush administration tend to mitigate the incentive to favor capital gains over dividends. In particular, most U.S. investors now face the same tax rate on dividends as on long-term capital gains, and firms must now recognize employee stock options as an expense. In addition, the technology sector is growing more slowly and, as befits a more mature industry, beginning to pay its share of dividends. Finally, as the baby boom generation enters retirement, it is reasonable to expect that the steady income provided by dividends will be more highly valued by investors.

As a final note on the present framework, it is worthwhile to observe that Equation (4.8) holds over any horizon. As a result, it can generate forecasts over any desired investment horizon. Suppose we had done the decomposition outlined in Exhibit 4.4 at the end of 1999. As already noted, the combined impact of the PE and EPS/GDP ratios added almost 1 percent per year over the period 1946–1999. The cumulative impact was therefore to raise the level of the market by roughly 40 percent relative to what would have been justified by postwar economic growth. We might have projected that the cumulative impact would be eliminated over, say, the next four years. In formulating a long-term estimate of expected return we would have stripped out the 1 percent as we discussed. In generating an estimate for the next four years we would have taken out another 10 percent per year (= 40%/4) to reflect the anticipated correction. Starting from the 1946–1999 average return of 12.18 percent this would have given an estimate for 1999–2003 of only 1.18 percent per year. In fact the S&P 500 *lost* 5.49 percent per year over the subsequent four years. So the adjustment would not have gone far enough, but it would have provided much better guidance than the historical average.

Allowing short-term and long-term expectations to differ is, of course, not consistent with the assumption that investment opportunities are constant. Adjusting the components of expected return in light of changing market conditions is a pragmatic approach to dealing with the evolution of investment opportunities. A more formal approach is discussed in Section 4.3. For now we return to the problem of estimating expected returns under the assumption that they are constant over time.

Implied Views

Given a set of inputs, an M–V optimizer is apt to generate portfolios that do not adhere to the user's notion of what constitutes a reasonable portfolio. As discussed in Section 4.1, this reflects the fact that the model attaches no significance to specific asset classes and is perfectly willing to adopt odd or extreme combinations to achieve an incremental risk–return improvement. Ultimately the problem can be traced to the model's sensitivity to the inputs. Small changes that the investor might consider immaterial induce large changes in the optimized portfolio. The method of implied views addresses this problem by letting the model determine expected returns so that a user-specified benchmark portfolio is on the efficient frontier with no constraints imposed on portfolio weights. Thus the user is assured that at least this one "reasonable" portfolio will be among the portfolios deemed optimal by the model. In essence, this approach makes sure the expected returns are consistent with the risk structure—that is, the variances and covariances—across asset classes. The hope is that this will curtail the optimizer's erratic tendencies.

Suppose we want to make sure a specific portfolio is on the (unconstrained) M–V efficient frontier. That is, we want it to have the highest possible expected return for a given variance. It turns out that this will be true if, and only if, the expected returns on all available asset classes satisfy

$$\mu_i = \mu_0 + \beta_i \left(\mu_p - \mu_0 \right) \tag{4.9}$$

where μ_i is the expected return on the ith asset class, μ_p is the expected return on our benchmark portfolio, μ_0 is the expected return on a portfolio that is uncorrelated with the benchmark portfolio, and β_i is the covariance of asset class i with the benchmark portfolio divided by the variance of the benchmark. The betas can be estimated by using the assumed portfolio weights to create a historical data series for the benchmark and calculating its variance and its covariance with each asset class. Alternatively, as is done in the accompanying Excel Outbox, the variance–covariance matrix of asset class returns can be used to calculate betas.

Note that Equation (4.9) uses μ rather than α to denote expected returns. Consistent with the notation adopted in Chapter 3, μ is the logarithm of the expected gross return. Recall that the mean component of the M–V model reflects this measure of expected return. So the implied views we "back out" of the model will also reflect this concept. To estimate the underlying expected log return, α, for each asset we simply subtract half its estimated variance because under our assumptions $\alpha = \mu - \frac{1}{2}\sigma^2$.

EXHIBIT 4.5   Implied Views

	Benchmark Portfolio Weight	Beta versus Benchmark	Target Log of Expected Gross Return (μ)	Implied Means	
				Expected Log Return (α)	Log of Expected Gross Return (μ)
Russell 1000 Value	0.20	1.382		7.62%	8.70%
Russell 1000 Growth	0.20	1.740	9.88%	8.22	9.88
Russell 2000 Value	0.04	1.457		7.48	8.95
Russell 2000 Growth	0.04	2.056		8.06	10.92
MSCI EAFE	0.12	1.375		7.12	8.68
Barclays High Yield	0.05	0.593		5.73	6.11
Barclays Aggregate	0.27	0.133	4.59	4.50	4.59
Citigroup Hedged Non-U.S. Government	0.08	0.056		4.29	4.34
Benchmark portfolio					7.44
Zero-beta portfolio					4.16

Equation (4.9) is the Black (1972) "zero-beta" version of the familiar capital asset pricing model (CAPM) with our benchmark portfolio playing the role of the "market" portfolio.[13] Although it may be useful to select the benchmark based on market value weights (a proxy for the market), this is not necessary. The portfolio must simply be one that is deemed a reasonable solution for a representative investor. In general, however, it should include all available asset classes in some positive proportion.

To generate expected returns for each asset class, we must specify values for μ_p and μ_0. These two parameters dictate the absolute magnitude of expected returns as well as the compensation for the systematic risk reflected by the betas. If we have estimates of expected returns for two of the asset classes, we can use Equation (4.9) to find values for μ_p and μ_0 that are consistent with these estimates. We might use, for example, estimates derived from one of the previous methods to set values for these parameters.

The implied views approach is illustrated in Exhibit 4.5 using the same asset classes and sample period as we used previously for James–Stein estimation. The benchmark portfolio weights were chosen to reflect reasonable holdings for a U.S. investor. In particular, the portfolio reflects the tendency of U.S. investors to overemphasize U.S. assets relative to the share of these assets in a market capitalization–weighted global index. Targets for the log of expected gross returns (μ) were set for the Russell 1000 Growth index and the Barclays Aggregate bond index at 9.88 percent and 4.59 percent respectively. Using the standard deviation shown in Exhibit 4.3, the target for the Russell 1000 Growth corresponds to an expected log return (α) equal to the James–Stein estimate in Exhibit 4.3. The last column of the exhibit gives the means required to make the benchmark portfolio mean–variance efficient. As noted earlier, these are logs of expected gross return (μ). By construction, the means for the Russell 1000 Growth and Barclays Aggregate indexes are equal to the targets. The next to last column shows the corresponding values for expected log return (α).

The impact of risk adjustment becomes apparent if we compare the results for the Russell 2000 Value index and the Russell 2000 Growth index with our earlier estimates

---

[13] See any standard investments textbook for a discussion of the CAPM. If there is a riskless asset, then the expected return on the zero-beta portfolio must be equal to the riskless rate.

of expected log return. Recall that the Russell 2000 Value index had a much higher sample mean than the Russell 2000 Growth index: 10.10 percent versus 5.81 percent. The James–Stein estimator shrank both of these estimates to the grand mean of 8.22 percent because the disparity was most likely due to sampling error. The implied views method indicates that the expected log return on the Russell 2000 Value index needs to be 0.58 percent lower (7.48 percent versus 8.06 percent) than the expected log return on the Russell 2000 Growth index to induce investors to hold them in equal proportions. In terms of the log of expected gross returns (μ), the difference is even more pronounced. The required difference in μ is 1.97 percent.

The expected returns for the fixed-income asset classes, including high-yield bonds, are well below those of the equity classes. This should not be surprising because we anchored the expected return (μ) on the Barclays Aggregate at 4.59 percent. However, it also reflects the fact that all the fixed-income classes have much lower risk (as measured by beta) than the equity classes. The betas reflect the lower absolute volatility of the fixed-income classes as well as their relatively low correlation with the benchmark portfolio.

Excel Outbox
Implied Views

This outbox provides the opportunity to work with implied views by recreating Exhibit 4.5. Use the worksheet <Implied – Template> in the spreadsheet Chapter 04 Excel Outboxes.xls. The spreadsheet provides the data on tab <LN Asset Class Returns>. The template should appear as follows:

	A	B	C	D	E	F	G	H	I
1	**Implied Views**								
2									
3	Beg:								
4	End:								
5	Length:								
6									
7		Russell 1000 Value TR	Russell 1000 Growth TR	Russell 2000 Value TR	Russell 2000 Growth TR	MSCI EAFE TR	Barclays Hi-Yld TR	Barclays Aggregate Bond TR	Citigroup US$ Hedged Non-US$ Gvt TR
8	Annualized Mean								
9	Annualized σ								
10	Annualized σ^2								
11	**Variance/Covariance Matrix**								
12	Russell 1000 Value TR								
13	Russell 1000 Growth TR								
14	Russell 2000 Value TR								
15	Russell 2000 Growth TR								
16	MSCI EAFE TR								
17	Barclays Hi-Yld TR								
18	Barclays Aggregate Bond TR								
19	Citigroup US$ Hedged Non-US$ Gvt TR								
20									
21	Equilibrium Weight								
22	Target Expected Log Return (α)								
23	Target Log of Expected Gross Return (μ)								
24									
25	Covariance w/Equilbrium Portfolio								
26	Beta wrt Equilbrium Portfolio								
27									
28	Implied Means Expected Log Return (α)								
29	Implied Means Log of Expected Gross Return (μ)								
30									
31	Variance of Equilibrium Porfolio								
32	Risk Premium								
33	Expected Return on 0-Beta Portfolio								
34	Expected Return on Equilibrium Portfolio								

Note: The spreadsheet has been rotated, relative to the table in the text, to conform to the columnar data.

This spreadsheet allows us to dynamically set the sample period. This is done in cells B3:B5 using the OFFSET and MATCH functions:

- In cell B3 enter the beginning date of the sample period using the format MM/YYYY (it must be ≥ January 1985).
- In cell B4 enter the ending date of the sample period using the format MM/YYYY (it must be ≤ December 2008).
- In cell B5 enter =COUNT(OFFSET('LN Asset Class Returns'!$A$1,MATCH($B$3,'LN Asset Class Returns'!$A$2:$A$289,0),0):OFFSET('LN Asset Class Returns'!$A$1,MATCH ($B$4,'LN Asset Class Returns'!$A$2:$A$289,0),0)).

The function in cell B5 counts the number of months between the beginning and ending dates:

- =MATCH(lookup_value,lookup_array,[match_type]). This function looks for an exact match (match_type=0) for the beginning date (lookup_value=$B$3) within the dates of the sample period (lookup_array='LN Asset Class Returns'!$A$2:$A$289) and then returns the number indicating its position within the array.
- =OFFSET(reference,rows,cols). This function returns the cell reference that is "rows" rows and "cols" columns from the reference cell. A positive (negative) value moves to the right (left) and down (up) from the reference cell.

The asset class summary statistics are calculated in cells B8:I10. The annualized mean return is given by the monthly average scaled to 12 months:
- Copy the formula in cell B5 to cell B8, and then replace "COUNT" with "12*AVERAGE".

The annualized standard deviation is calculated in a similar manner:
- Copy the formula in cell B8 to cell B9, and then replace "12*AVERAGE" with "SQRT(12)*STDEV".
- In cell B10 enter =B9^2 to get the variance.
- Copy cells B8:B10 to cells C8:I10. *Note:* Use Paste Special Formula to avoid overwriting the table formatting.

Here's how to calculate the variance–covariance matrix. *Note:* Be careful to distinguish "$B$1" from "B$1":

- In cell B12 enter =12*COVAR(OFFSET('LN Asset Class Returns'!$B$1,MATCH($B$3,'LN Asset Class Returns'!$A$2:$A$289,0),0):OFFSET('LN Asset Class Returns'!$B$1,MATCH ($B$4,'LN Asset Class Returns'!$A$2:$A$289,0),0),OFFSET('LN Asset Class Returns'!B $1,MATCH($B$3,'LN Asset Class Returns'!$A$2:$A$289,0),0):OFFSET('LN Asset Class Returns'!B$1,MATCH($B$4,'LN Asset Class Returns'!$A$2:$A$289,0),0)).
- Copy cell B12 to cells B13:B19.
- Change "$B$1" to "$C$1" (highlighted in the previous equation) in cell B13.
- Change "$B$1" to "$D$1" (highlighted in the previous equation) in cell B14.
- Change "$B$1" to "$E$1" (highlighted in the previous equation) in cell B15.
- Change "$B$1" to "$F$1" (highlighted in the previous equation) in cell B16.
- Change "$B$1" to "$G$1" (highlighted in the previous equation) in cell B17.
- Change "$B$1" to "$H$1" (highlighted in the previous equation) in cell B18.
- Change "$B$1" to "$I$1" (highlighted in the previous equation) in cell B19.
- Copy cells B12:B19 to cells C12:I19.

Here's how to calculate the implied views:

- In cells B21:I21 enter the equilibrium portfolio weights. Start with the values in Exhibit 4.5; these can be changed to explore other portfolios.
- In cell B31 enter =MMULT(B21:I21,MMULT(B12:I19,TRANSPOSE(B21:I21))). Note that this is a range array formula and requires the use of <CTRL><SHIFT> when entering.

(continued)

(concluded)

- In cell C22 enter 0.0822, and in cell H22 enter 0.05. These are the values in the exhibit; other assets can be selected with corresponding changes to cells B32 and B33.
- In cell B23 enter =IF(ISNUMBER(B22),B22 + 0.5*B10,"") and then copy to cells C23:I23.
- In cells B25:I25 enter =MMULT(B21:I21,B12:I19). Note that this is a range array formula and requires the use of <CTRL><SHIFT> when entering.
- In cell B26 enter =B25/$B$31 and then copy to cells C26:I26.
- In cell B32 enter =(C23−H23)/(C26−H26).
- In cell B33 enter =C23 − C26*B32.
- In cell B34 enter =B32 + B33.
- In cell B28 enter =B29 − 0.5*B10 and then copy to cells C28:I28.
- In cell B29 enter =$B$33 + B26*$B$32 and then copy to cells C29:I29.

The finished worksheet is provided online as worksheet <Implied – Complete> in the spreadsheet Chapter 04 Excel Outboxes-Completed.xls. The outcome when other assets are used to define the target expected gross returns is explored in the end-of-chapter problems.

Cross-Sectional Risk Models

As we have noted, the implied views method is equivalent to generating expected returns based on the zero-beta version of the CAPM. As a result, it can be interpreted as reflecting an equilibrium in which only systematic risk is compensated with additional expected return because risk unrelated to the market can be diversified away. From a more pragmatic perspective, it is simply a way to ensure a degree of consistency between expected returns and risk across asset classes. This section explores the use of cross-sectional risk models in more depth. In the process we will gain a better understanding of why the M–V model is so sensitive to its inputs.

Consider a universe of M assets. By assumption, the variances and covariances of the asset returns are constant. Each asset's return can be written as a combination of (at most) M risk components or factors. That is, the return on the ith asset can be written as

$$r_i = \sum_{j=1}^{M} a_{i,j} f_j \qquad (4.10)$$

where f_j is the jth risk factor and $a_{i,j}$ is asset i's sensitivity or "exposure" to this factor. The factors can always be constructed so that they are uncorrelated. In practice it is often useful to work with correlated factors, but for exposition it is convenient to assume that they are uncorrelated.

One method of constructing uncorrelated risk factors allows us to rank them in terms of their contribution to the *total variation* of asset returns, defined as the sum of the variances across the M assets. The first factor is most important, the second factor is next, and so on. Exhibit 4.6 summarizes the results of applying this method—known as *principal components*[14]—to the eight asset classes examined in earlier sections.

[14] A related procedure known as *factor analysis* attempts to find $K < M$ common risk factors such that the residual or unexplained risks for each asset are uncorrelated. Factor analysis yields correlated factors but uncorrelated residuals. Principal components yield uncorrelated factors, but if we focus on only the first K factors then, strictly speaking, the residual risks are correlated across assets because they correspond to the omitted factors. The advantage of principal components is that we can unambiguously measure the importance of each factor.

EXHIBIT 4.6

Factor Contributions to Risk (%)

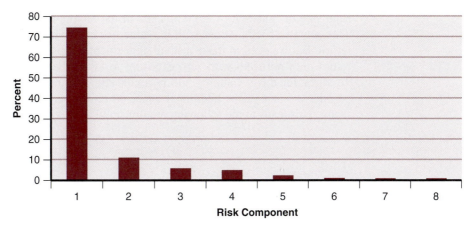

The first risk component accounts for roughly 74 percent of the variation, the second component 11 percent, and the third component 6 percent. Together these three components account for 91 percent. In contrast, the three least important components combined account for only 1.9 percent.

These results are typical. A few risk factors can almost always account for a large portion of the variation in asset returns. Indeed four or five factors are often enough even when the number of assets is very large. This implies that the risk characteristics of any specific asset can be replicated almost exactly by a combination of the other assets. To see this, suppose five risk factors account for all but a negligible portion of returns. In terms of Equation (4.10) this means that only the first five terms are important. To replicate the return on, say, asset M we need to form a portfolio that has the same exposure to each of the first five factors as asset M. A portfolio's exposure to each factor is simply a weighted average of each constituent asset's exposure to that factor. To match asset M's exposure to the first five factors, the portfolio weights, ω_i, must satisfy five linear equations of the form

$$\sum_{i=1}^{M-1} a_{i,j}\omega_i = a_{M,j} \qquad (4.11)$$

If there are many assets, many portfolios will satisfy these conditions. We can choose the one that minimizes the error arising from the fact that we did not match asset M's exposures to the negligible factors. After we have matched exposures to the important factors and minimized the error from the negligible factors, the portfolio will almost exactly replicate the return of asset M. Of course the same argument holds for replicating any of the other assets.

What does this imply about the behavior of the M–V model? A lot as it turns out. If multiple portfolios have nearly identical risk exposures, a mean–variance optimizer will find them even if they are not at all apparent to the user. The optimizer will exploit any apparent opportunity to marginally improve expected return without taking on more risk even if doing so entails violent shifts in the allocation to specific assets; and thus we will see optimized portfolios that are very sensitive to the inputs—especially the expected returns.

It should be clear that two portfolios with the same risk exposures should have the same expected return. How can we enforce this condition? A moment's reflection suggests a simple solution: Just set the expected return on the *i*th asset equal to the right side of Equation (4.10) with each of the factors replaced by its expected value. Then any two combinations with the same risk exposures will have the same expected return. But we need to make a small adjustment to this idea. In general, the expected return on a portfolio with zero exposure to all of the risk factors will not be zero. To allow for this we simply add in a constant and interpret the other terms as risk premiums—that is, the additional expected return per unit of exposure to each risk factor. This leads to the following relationship:

$$\mu_i = \mu_0 + \sum_{j=1}^{M} a_{i,j}\phi_j \qquad\qquad \textbf{(4.12)}$$

The constant term in this equation is analogous to the return on the zero-beta portfolio in Equation (4.9). It will be equal to the riskless rate if a riskless asset exists. The ϕ_j are the risk premiums earned for bearing factor risk. Some or perhaps most of these risk premiums may be zero. Typically only the most important factors will be assigned a nonzero risk premium because exposure to less important factors can be made negligible by diversification. This is the essence of the well-known arbitrage pricing theory (APT).

Note that, as was the case in Equation (4.9) for the implied views method, we have written Equation (4.12) in terms of the log of expected gross return (μ) rather than the expected log return (α). At first blush it seems we could specify the model either way. However, the logic of the model dictates that all portfolios with the same risk exposures have the same expected return. That is, Equation (4.12) should hold for portfolios as well as individual assets. This requires that the expected return on a portfolio be equal to a weighted average of the underlying asset expected returns. As discussed in Chapter 3, this is not true in terms of expected log returns (α), but it is approximately true in terms of the log of expected gross returns (μ).[15] Therefore, we employ the latter concept of mean return in Equation (4.12).

Up to this point we have not needed to identify the risk factors. In principle, it is not necessary to do so. In practice, however, the factors need to be identified to give the model economic content. Purely statistical or mathematical procedures such as principal components (or factor analysis) yield abstract factors that have ideal properties, such as being uncorrelated (or creating uncorrelated residuals); but they do not necessarily correspond to the economic and financial variables that form the basis of investment analysis. Without that correspondence we cannot judge whether the model is capturing economically relevant risks and assigning appropriate risk premiums.

Because our focus is on using a factor model to generate expected returns, a detailed discussion of how such models are constructed would take us too far afield. In general, there are three steps. First, a set of observable variables is selected as the factors. These are usually macroeconomic variables or fundamental characteristics of a firm such as its size, price-to-book value ratio, industry classification, etc. Second, historical returns for a large universe (hundreds if not thousands) of securities are regressed on the factor variables to estimate their factor exposures. Third, portfolios are formed that each have unit exposure to one of the factors and zero exposure to all the other factors. The average return on the portfolio minus the riskless interest rate is the risk premium for the corresponding factor. Once the model is estimated, it can be applied to virtually any asset or asset class. Of course the model will work best for assets that have

---

[15] See the development of Equations (3.11) and (3.12) in Chapter 3.

characteristics similar to the universe used to estimate the model. For example, if the model is based only on equities we cannot expect it to work well for bonds.

Exhibit 4.7 applies a customized version of a commercial factor model to the eight asset classes considered throughout this chapter. Note that there are 10 factors but only eight asset classes. This seems strange because we know that only eight factors are needed to completely capture the returns on these asset classes. The mystery is resolved by the fact that the 10 factors underlying Exhibit 4.7 are not the idealized factors in Exhibit 4.6. The factors used in Exhibit 4.7 were chosen for their economic meaning and for their ability to summarize a large universe of (mostly U.S. equity) securities. Even with 10 factors, the model does not completely capture the risk of these eight asset classes. This is one of the penalties of requiring that the factors correspond to understandable economic and financial variables.

The factors in this model fall into three categories: bond market factors, equity market factors, and macroeconomic factors. The first two factors reflect the returns on short-term and long-term government bonds. As might be expected, these factors are most relevant for the bond asset classes. The third factor, the return on long-term corporate bonds minus the return on government bonds, can be interpreted as reflecting investor confidence. The exposures to this factor show that, all else the same, when corporate bonds outperform government bonds, equities also do well. The four equity market factors segment the market on the basis of size (market capitalization) and style (Value/Growth). Due to the way these factors are constructed, the exposures for the large-capitalization (Russell 1000) Value and Growth indexes show a clean breakdown by capitalization and style, but the small-capitalization (Russell 2000) indexes do not. Not surprisingly, these factors have little impact on the bond asset classes. Among the macroeconomic factors, only economic growth has an important impact on most of the asset classes. As would be expected, faster growth raises equity returns—especially small-capitalization growth stocks—and hurts the Barclays Aggregate index of investment-grade U.S. bonds. The currency factor affects only the MSCI EAFE index of non-U.S. equities. The Citigroup Non-U.S. Government bond index does not have a significant currency exposure because the return selected is currency-hedged.

The last row of the exhibit gives the risk premium—that is, the extra return per unit of factor exposure—associated with each factor, whereas the last column gives the total risk premium for each asset class. Note that the risk premiums for exposure to the growth style and for foreign currency exposure are negative and of significant size. As a consequence, the risk premiums for the Russell 1000 Growth and MSCI EAFE indexes are quite low relative to the other equity classes. Why? Large-capitalization growth stocks did poorly and the U.S. dollar was quite strong during most of the sample period. The model simply reflects the data; it is up to the user to evaluate the results. In this case we would probably want to make some adjustments to the factor risk premiums before applying Equation (4.12) to generate expected returns for the asset classes.

It bears emphasizing that the usefulness of the factor model in the current context derives from the ability to impose cross-sectional consistency between the risk structure of asset returns and the expected returns. It does *not,* in general, provide reliable estimates of expected returns directly from a sample of returns data. Although the risk exposures are presumed to be estimated reliably, the raw factor risk premiums are apt to be distorted by sample-specific outcomes. This should not be surprising because the raw factor risk premiums are essentially sample means. They each reflect the average performance of a hypothetical portfolio with unit exposure to one of the factors and zero exposure to the other factors. Whatever would have happened to these portfolios

EXHIBIT 4.7 Factor Model Exposures and Risk Premiums

	Factor Exposures										
	Bond Market Factors			Equity Market Factors				Macroeconomic Factors			
	Short-Term Government Bond Return	Long-Term Government Bond Return	Corporate versus Government Bond Return Differential	Large Capitalization	Small Capitalization	Growth Style	Value Style	Inflation	Economic Growth	Currency versus U.S. Dollar	Risk Premium (Annual %, Log)
Russell 1000 Value	0.00	−0.02	1.33	0.80	0.00	0.00	1.00	0.18	1.34	0.00	6.45
Russell 1000 Growth	0.00	0.09	2.35	1.20	0.00	1.00	0.00	0.03	3.16	0.00	1.75
Russell 2000 Value	−0.46	0.24	1.85	0.56	0.76	−0.59	0.30	−0.05	1.20	0.04	8.84
Russell 2000 Growth	0.26	0.35	3.40	1.05	1.12	0.84	0.05	−0.37	4.13	−0.05	8.84
MSCI EAFE	−0.66	0.16	1.71	0.83	0.27	−0.71	−0.64	−0.06	2.05	0.67	2.27
Barclays High Yield	−0.86	0.52	1.93	0.11	0.09	0.03	0.07	−0.12	0.89	0.01	2.04
Barclays Aggregate	0.51	0.42	0.22	−0.01	0.01	0.01	0.01	0.02	−0.13	0.00	2.37
Citigroup Hedged Non-U.S. Government	0.22	0.21	0.10	−0.03	0.00	−0.07	−0.02	0.00	0.05	−0.02	1.34
Factor premium (annual, log)	1.93	3.10	0.59	2.56	3.91	−3.94	3.20	0.25	0.30	−3.68	

during the sample period—good or bad—shows up as the corresponding risk premiums. The upshot is that we should expect to adjust the risk premiums to bring them into line with our assessment of the future. Once we have done so, the factor model translates them into an internally consistent set of expected returns for the individual assets.

Combining Estimates: Mixed Estimation

The estimation methods just outlined use somewhat different information or use the same information in somewhat different ways. Obviously we can simply pick our favorite approach or pick the method that seems most appropriate for a given situation. However, because more information usually leads to better estimates, it might be advantageous to combine estimates in some way. We outline next a methodology called *mixed estimation* that combines two sets of estimates.

Consider the simplest case: combining two estimates of the expected return on a single asset.[16] Denote the two estimates as $\tilde{\mu}_1$ and $\tilde{\mu}_2$. Each is assumed to be equal to the true expected return, μ, plus an error, e_i, and the two errors are assumed to be uncorrelated. Formally,

$$\tilde{\mu} = \mu + e_i \qquad i = 1,2 \tag{4.13}$$

Denote the variances of the errors by v_i. If, for example, the estimates are sample means from two different periods, their variances would be given by Equation (4.3). Mixed estimation combines these two estimates by creating a weighted average with greater weight on the more precise estimate—that is, the estimate with the smaller variance. Specifically, the mixed estimator in this case is

$$\tilde{\mu}_{mx} = \left(\frac{v_2}{v_1 + v_2}\right)\tilde{\mu}_1 + \left(\frac{v_1}{v_1 + v_2}\right)\tilde{\mu}_2 \tag{4.14}$$

Under our assumptions, this estimate always has a smaller variance than either of the original estimates. In fact, it has the smallest variance of any weighted average of the two estimates. For example, if the two original estimates have the same variance, the mixed estimator is a simple average of those estimates, and its variance is half as large.

It does not matter whether we apply the mixed estimation technique to the log of expected gross returns (μ in our notation) or to expected log returns (α). To see this, recall that under our assumptions $\mu = \alpha + \frac{1}{2}\sigma^2$. So these two measures of mean return differ by a constant. Examination of Equation (4.14) shows that adding the same constant to each of the estimates $\tilde{\mu}_1$ and $\tilde{\mu}_2$ has the effect of adding that same constant to the mixed estimate $\tilde{\mu}_{mx}$. Thus we can apply the mixed estimation technique to either measure of expected return and then add or subtract half of the variance to get the mixed estimator for the other concept of expected return. This remains true when we consider multiple assets simultaneously.

Consider the case in which we have an equilibrium (implied view) estimate and an active view. The active view is that small-capitalization growth stocks (Russell 2000 Growth index) will do 2 percent better (12.92 percent versus 10.92 percent) than the implied view from Exhibit 4.5. The critical question becomes which view we consider

---

[16] The more general case involving multiple assets and correlated errors requires basic matrix operations and is covered in the chapter appendix.

EXHIBIT 4.8

Mixed Estimation versus Ratio of Error Variances

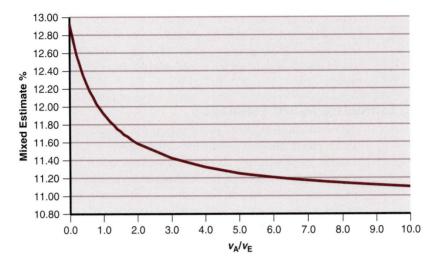

more accurate. Perhaps the active view is likely to have a tighter error distribution because this view incorporates the analyst's expectations based on current information. Conversely, if the analyst provides only a point estimate, the active view might not consider various alternative scenarios, resulting in a higher error variance relative to the implied view estimate.

Exhibit 4.8 plots $\tilde{\mu}_{mx}$ for different ratios, v_A/v_E, of the error variances. At one extreme, the active view is considered perfectly accurate ($v_A = 0$), with the result that $\tilde{\mu}_{mx}$ is set equal to the active view. If the error variances are considered the same ($v_A/v_E = 1$), $\tilde{\mu}_{mx}$ is 11.92 percent: the average of the equilibrium and the active view. Note that the mixed estimator declines at a decreasing rate as our relative confidence in the active view diminishes. Even if the active view is considered 10 times less reliable ($v_A/v_E = 10$), the mixed estimate will be 11.10 percent. Only if we have no confidence in the active view ($v_A = \infty$) will $\tilde{\mu}_{mx}$ equal the equilibrium estimate.

Note that Equation (4.14) can be rewritten as

$$\tilde{\mu}_{mx} = \tilde{\mu}_1 - \left(\frac{v_1}{v_1 + v_2} \right)(\tilde{\mu}_1 - \tilde{\mu}_2)$$

Comparing this to Equation (4.5) shows that the mixed estimator and the James–Stein estimator have the same form. Each shrinks an estimate based on new information ($\tilde{\mu}_1$ here) toward a prior estimate ($\tilde{\mu}_2$ here), with the shrinkage parameter determined by relative confidence in the two estimates. In the example here, the equilibrium estimate would probably be interpreted as the prior and the analyst's active view as the new information. However, these are arbitrary designations because the roles of $\tilde{\mu}_1$ and $\tilde{\mu}_2$ are completely symmetric in Equation (4.14).

4.3   Time-Varying Investment Opportunities

In developing the M–V model in Chapter 3 we assumed that investment opportunities are the same in every period. So far that assumption has been maintained as we discussed estimating the model's inputs. Now we will allow for the fact that investment opportunities seem to vary over time. In doing so we will lay the foundation for understanding the common perception that stocks are less risky over longer investment horizons. We will also develop some results that will be useful for Chapter 5's discussion of more advanced approaches to asset allocation.

One might well ask whether admitting that investment opportunities change over time does not just make the estimation problem worse. After all, if it can take hundreds of years of data to get a good estimate of a *constant* expected return, how can we possibly get a good estimate of a *changing* expected return? The answer, of course, is that we cannot—unless we bring in information other than the history of returns. This information comes in essentially two forms. First, some structure can be imposed on how investment opportunities are assumed to change over time. That is, we can impose a model of how the data may have been generated. Second, other variables can be introduced to help explain how investment opportunities change from period to period. Of course this requires a model, so it is really an extension of the first idea.

Once we introduce a model of return dynamics and additional variables that help predict returns, we must distinguish between **conditional** and **unconditional** means and variances. Investors are most interested in estimating the conditional mean and variance because these represent estimates of *future* risk and return based on currently available information.

A simple example illustrates these concepts. It is often asserted that U.S. stock returns are subject to an election cycle driven by the incumbent party's desire to generate a strong market going into the next election. If this is true, stock returns should, on average, be higher during the later years of a presidential term than in the early years. In Exhibit 4.9 the years 1926–2003 are evenly divided into two groups corresponding to the first and second halves of presidential terms. The first two lines of the exhibit give the mean and standard deviation of log returns *conditional* on being in the first half or second half of the term respectively. Clearly the second half of the presidential term has been more favorable for stock investors because the mean return is much higher and the volatility is lower compared to the first half of the term. The last row of the exhibit gives the mean and standard deviation of returns for all years without regard to the election cycle. These are the *unconditional* mean and standard deviation. These statistics reflect averaging out the information contained in the conditional mean and standard deviation.

To understand the relationship between conditional and unconditional parameters, it is useful to formalize the model. Suppose there are two random variables, X and Y, and knowing the value of Y helps predict the value of X. Y is assumed to take only two values, high and low, denoted by Y_H and Y_L. The mean and variance of X "conditional on knowing Y" are given by

$$E[X|Y] = \alpha_{X|Y} = \begin{cases} \alpha_H \text{ if } Y = Y_H \\ \alpha_L \text{ if } Y = Y_L \end{cases} \tag{4.15}$$

$$\text{var}[X|Y] = \sigma^2_{X|Y} = \begin{cases} \sigma^2_H \text{ if } Y = Y_H \\ \sigma^2_L \text{ if } Y = Y_L \end{cases} \tag{4.16}$$

EXHIBIT 4.9
Election Cycle for S&P 500: Log Returns 1926–2003

	Mean	Standard Deviation
First half of presidential terms	5.45%	20.86%
Second half of presidential terms	14.38	16.70
All years	9.92	19.42

The notation X/Y is read as "X given Y." These are the conditional mean and conditional variance of X. Note that each is a function of Y. In the election cycle example, the stock market return would be X, and Y would indicate the halves of the presidential term.

To find the *unconditional* mean of X we can simply take a weighted average of the conditional mean with weights reflecting the probability that Y takes each of its possible values. Assume Y takes its high value with probability p and its low value with probability $(1 - p)$. Then the unconditional mean of X is

$$E[X] = p\alpha_H + (1 - p)\alpha_L \qquad \textbf{(4.17)}$$

The right side of Equation (4.17) is the expected value of the conditional mean where the expectation is taken with respect to the probability distribution for Y. This can be written more generally as

$$E[X] = E[E[X|Y]] \qquad \textbf{(4.18)}$$

Equation (4.18) formalizes the notion that the unconditional mean "averages out" the information about X that is contained in the variable Y.

The relationship between the unconditional *variance* of X and the conditional parameters is more complex. There are really two sources of X's volatility. The first is random deviations around its conditional mean—the uncertainly that is left after we know the value of Y. Of course that is what the conditional variance captures. One component of the unconditional variance is the expected value of the conditional variance. This is analogous to Equation (4.18) for the mean. The second source of X's volatility is uncertainty about the conditional mean itself. Hence the second component of the unconditional variance is the variance of the conditional mean. Putting these two components together, we can write the general relationship as

$$\text{var}(X) = E[\text{var}[X|Y]] + \text{var}[E[X|Y]] \qquad \textbf{(4.19)}$$

Applying this to our simple model yields

$$\text{var}[X]=(p\sigma_H^2+(1-p)\sigma_L^2)+(p(\alpha_H - E(X))^2 + (1-p)(\alpha_L - E(X))^2) \quad \textbf{(4.20)}$$
$$=(p\sigma_H^2 + (1-p)\sigma_L^2) + p(1-p)(\alpha_H - \alpha_L)^2$$

The second line of this equation follows from Equation (4.17) after some simplification.

Let's illustrate these relationships by returning to the election cycle. Let Y_H correspond to the second half of the presidential term and Y_L correspond to the first half. What is the probability that $Y = Y_H$ for a randomly selected year? It is one-half. So $p = \frac{1}{2}$. Using Equation (4.17) and the conditional means shown in Exhibit 4.9, we find that the unconditional mean is $[\frac{1}{2}(5.45 + 14.38)] = 9.92$. Now consider the unconditional variance. Applying Equation (4.20) gives

Expected conditional variance	$.5(16.70)^2 + .5(20.86)^2$	$= 357.01$
Variance of conditional mean	$.5(14.38 - 9.92)^2 + .5(5.45 - 9.92)^2$	$= 19.94$
Unconditional variance		$= 376.95$

Taking the square root of the variance, we find that the unconditional standard deviation is 19.42 percent. If there were no uncertainty with respect to the conditional mean, the unconditional standard deviation would only be 18.89 percent ($=\sqrt{357.01}$). As a result, variation in the conditional mean return accounts for 0.53 percent of the unconditional volatility.

In this type of model, investment opportunities are characterized by a discrete set of alternative values (two in this example) indexed by the random variable Y. Each value of Y defines a distinct **regime.** Once we identify which historic periods belong to each regime, the conditional expected returns and variances can be estimated as constant parameters using the data from each regime.

Although the regime-switching framework is often used explicitly, it is probably even more commonly used implicitly. Every time we select one or more subperiods of data rather than all available data, we are implicitly assuming that the excluded data belong to another regime. Often this entails including the most recent data on the presumption that it is reflective of current conditions and excluding earlier data on the presumption that it is no longer representative.

Note that the unconditional mean and standard deviation calculated using Equations (4.17) and (4.20) are equal to the sample mean and standard deviation obtained directly from the data using all years (see Exhibit 4.9). Of course they reflect the same conditional means and standard deviations because we used the sample results for each regime as if they were the true values. But if our sample contained "too many" observations of one regime and "not enough" of the other, the sample mean and standard deviation using all years together would not match the unconditional parameters even if the conditional parameters were exactly correct. The point is that if your sample is not representative of the true probabilities, your estimates based on sample statistics will be distorted. In most cases, of course, we do not know the true probability of the regimes, and we are forced to assume that the frequency of each regime in the data adequately reflects the true probabilities. This is often a reasonable assumption but can be quite problematic if we are trying to take account of extremely low-probability events, such as a market crash. The likelihood of such events may be wildly overstated if they occur even once in a short sample and understated if they do not occur in the sample at all.

The distinction between conditional and unconditional means and variances has important implications for investment decisions. Conditional parameters change over time; unconditional parameters do not. Intuition suggests that we should adjust our asset allocation in response to changing investment opportunities. If we do not, we are throwing away valuable information—information that is reflected in conditional but not unconditional means and variances. The impact of changing investment opportunities on the optimal portfolio will be examined in detail in Chapter 5.

In our election cycle example, variation in the conditional expected return accounted for only a small portion of the unconditional variance. This might suggest that the distinction between conditional and unconditional variances can be ignored. It is therefore worth emphasizing that risk should be associated with the *conditional* variance. To illustrate this point clearly, consider a Treasury bill. Because T-bill rates vary over time, the unconditional variance of the T-bill return is positive. This is what we are estimating if we calculate the variance of T-bill returns from historical data. However, once we know today's T-bill rate, the conditional variance of the return is zero over a horizon matching the maturity; that is, the T-bill is riskless. Tying this back to our model and Equation (4.19), in this case *all* of the unconditional variance comes from uncertainty with respect to the conditional mean—the T-bill rate.

Let's now consider a model in which investment opportunities vary continuously with market conditions rather than taking only a few discrete values. Assume that the return on an asset is generated according to

$$r_{t+1} \equiv p_{t+1} - p_t = \alpha + \theta(\alpha t - p_t) + \varepsilon_t \qquad \textbf{(4.21)}$$

where p_t is the natural logarithm of the asset's price at time t, ε_{t+1} is normally distributed with mean zero and variance σ^2, and $0 \leq \theta < 1$. There are three components to the return. The first component is the constant long-term trend rate α. The second is a linear **mean reversion** term whereby the asset's price is pulled toward the trend $(\alpha\ t)$ at the constant rate θ.[17] The third component is the random term ε. If $\theta = 0$ the model reduces to the constant investment opportunities model examined in Chapter 3.

It is convenient to define a new variable, y_t, as the deviation of the asset price from trend. That is, $y_t = (p_t - \alpha t)$. Equation (4.21) can then be rewritten as

$$r_{t+1} = \alpha - \theta\ y_t + \varepsilon_{t+1} \qquad \textbf{(4.22)}$$

Conditional on the value of y_t the first two terms in Equation (4.22) are constant. Using this fact, it is straightforward to show that the conditional mean and variance of the return are given by

$$E(r_{t+1}|y_t) = \alpha - \theta\ y_t$$
$$\text{var}(r_{t+1}|y_t) = \sigma^2 \qquad \textbf{(4.23)}$$

The first line of Equation (4.23) indicates that when the asset's price is above trend $(y_t > 0)$, the expected return is below the long-term trend return α. Conversely, when the price is below trend, the expected return over the next period is greater than the long-term trend return. The second line in Equation (4.23) shows that the conditional variance of the return is constant.

To derive the unconditional mean and variance of the return we need the (unconditional) mean and variance of y_t. Using the definitions of y_t and r_{t+1}, Equation (4.22) can be rewritten as

$$y_{t+1} = (1 - \theta)\ y_t + \varepsilon_{t+1} \qquad \textbf{(4.24)}$$

This is a well-known time series model called a first-order autoregressive (AR1) model. It has mean zero and variance equal to $(\sigma^2/(1 - (1 - \theta)^2))$.[18] Using this fact, we take

[17] Time, t, enters Equation (4.21) as both a subscript and as a variable in its own right. The expression $(\alpha\ t)$ reflects multiplying the variable t by the constant parameter α.

[18] The important special case in which $\theta = 0$ must be treated with care. In this case y_{t+1} is equal to its lagged value plus a random shock. This type of process, known as a "random walk," has no tendency to revert toward a central value. Its unconditional mean is therefore undefined, and its unconditional variance is infinite. However, because $(y_{t+1} - y_t) = \varepsilon_{t+1}$ has mean zero and variance σ^2, we could work with these "first differences" rather than the level of the process. But it is easier to work directly with the asset return as given in Equation (4.21). If $\theta = 0$ the asset return is given by $r_{t+1} \equiv p_{t+1} - p_t = \alpha + e_{t+1}$. If $\alpha = 0$ this implies that the (log) asset price is itself a random walk. With $\alpha \neq 0$ the asset price is said to follow a "random walk with drift." Either way the unconditional variance of the *price* is infinite, but the unconditional mean and variance of the *return*—that is, the first difference of the (log) price—are well-defined and finite. In particular, the mean is α and the variance is σ^2. In addition, the conditional mean and variance are the same as the unconditional values.

the expected value of the conditional mean in Equation (4.23) to get the unconditional mean of the asset's return:

$$E(r_{t+1}) = \alpha \qquad (4.25)$$

From Equation (4.23) the variance of the conditional mean is given by

$$\text{var}[E(r_{t+1}|y_t)] = \theta^2 \, \text{var}(y) = \left(\frac{\theta^2}{1 - (1 - \theta)^2}\right)\sigma^2 \qquad (4.26)$$

As in Equation (4.19), combining the expected value of the conditional variance (the second line of Equation (4.23)) with the variance of the conditional mean (Equation (4.26)) gives the unconditional variance:[19]

$$\text{var}(r_{t+1}) = \left(\frac{2\theta}{1 - (1 - \theta)^2}\right)\sigma^2 \qquad (4.27)$$

The unconditional expected return and variance are constant. As a result, if we ignore the price–return dynamics embodied in Equation (4.21), we are again back in the constant-opportunities world that gave rise to the M–V model in Chapter 3. All the estimation techniques and issues discussed in the preceding sections of this chapter apply to estimating the unconditional parameters of the current model. The use of long-run economic relationships is of particular note in this context. If the current model is applied to the broadly defined stock market, then, as discussed in Section 4.2, the long-term mean return α must be consistent with the growth rate of the economy and a stable relationship between asset prices and economic fundamentals.

As in our regime-switching model, the conditional expected return in this model changes over time. Unlike that model, however, in this model the conditional expected return depends on the degree by which the market is above or below its long-run trend. This creates a (negative) correlation between the *current* return and *future* investment opportunities. Chapter 5 examines the impact this has on the optimal portfolio policy.

Up to this point investment opportunities have been considered only over a one-period horizon. Although the assumed price–return dynamics show up in the single-period expected return, there is no impact on the single-period conditional variance—that is, risk. As we will now demonstrate, however, this is not the case over multiperiod horizons.

Recall that the continuously compounded return over an *M*-period horizon starting at time t is simply

$$R_{t,M} = p_{t+M} - p_t = \sum_{i=1}^{M}(p_{t+i} - p_{t+i-1}) \qquad (4.28)$$

It is straightforward but tedious to evaluate the summation on the right side of this equation by repeated application of Equation (4.21) with appropriate adjustment of subscripts. Doing so yields

$$R_{t,M} = \alpha M + [(1 - \theta)^M - 1]y_t + \sum_{i=1}^{M}(1 - \theta)^{i-1}\varepsilon_{t+i} \qquad (4.29)$$

---

[19] Equations (4.26) and (4.27) cannot be evaluated directly if $\theta = 0$. Instead we must carefully take the limit as θ goes to zero. Doing so shows that the variance of the conditional mean goes to zero and the unconditional variance of the return goes to σ^2.

EXHIBIT 4.10
Models of S&P 500:
Annual Log Returns
1946–2003

| | | Election Cycle | | | |
		First Half	Second Half	Mean Reversion Parameter	Residual Standard Deviation
	Trend				
Trend only	10.96%				15.65%
Mean reversion	10.84			.137	15.10
Mean reversion and election cycle		5.95%	15.75%	.126	14.39

The first two terms on the right side of Equation (4.29) are known at time t, and each ε has zero mean. So the conditional expected return over the M-period horizon is

$$E[R_{t,M}|y_t] = \alpha M + [(1 - \theta)^M - 1]y_t \qquad (4.30)$$

The first term on the right side of Equation (4.30) is the long-term trend rate of return. The second component is the expected impact of mean reversion over the M-period horizon. Because θ is assumed to be positive but less than 1, this term is positive if the price at time t is below trend ($y_t < 0$) and negative if the price is currently above trend ($y_t > 0$). All the uncertainty is embodied in the last component of Equation (4.29). Using a standard result for the sum of a geometric series, the conditional variance of the M-period return is

$$\text{var}[R_{t,M}|y_t] = \left[\frac{1 - (1 - \theta)^M}{\theta}\right]\sigma^2 < M\sigma^2 \qquad (4.31)$$

The inequality on the right side of this equation indicates that for $0 < \theta < 1$ the conditional variance is less than proportional to the horizon.[20] Therefore, while total variance increases with the horizon, variance per unit of time decreases. In this sense, the asset really is less risky over longer horizons!

Let's apply this model to U.S. stock returns. Exhibit 4.10 shows parameters estimated from annual S&P 500 returns for the period 1946–2003. Three versions of the model are considered. The first version includes only the trend and therefore reflects constant investment opportunities. The second version introduces the mean reversion term. This is the model as specified in Equation (4.21). The third version generalizes the model by replacing the constant trend with the election cycle. The last column shows that the residual standard deviation declines as each element is added to the model, indicating that with the addition of each element the model captures more of the observed variation in return. The residual standard deviation for each model is the estimated conditional standard deviation based on that model. The mean reversion parameters indicate that roughly 13 percent of the deviation from trend is expected to be corrected per year; that is, if the market price is 1 percent above trend, the (conditional) expected return is 0.13 percent (13 basis points) lower.

The model that combines mean reversion and the election cycle does reasonably well in capturing the broad dynamics of five-year S&P 500 returns in the postwar period. The solid line in Exhibit 4.11 shows the actual annualized return over the subsequent five years. The dashed line shows the expected return over the same period

---

[20] In the constant-opportunities model of Chapter 3, the variance of the M-period return was shown to be proportional to the horizon; that is, the variance is $M\sigma^2$. To get this result from the formula in Equation (4.31) we must take the limit as θ goes to zero.

EXHIBIT 4.11   **Detrended Five-Year Returns**

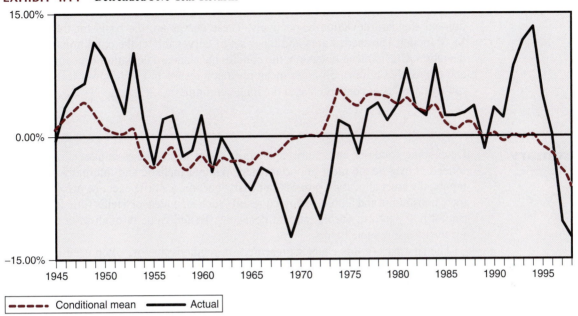

based on the model. Each series was detrended by removing the estimated election cycle. Although the actual return is much more volatile than the expected return, in general, the expected return correctly predicts whether the subsequent return will be above or below the election cycle trend. We should note, however, that the differences between the expected returns and the actual returns are not random. As a result, the model does not fully capture the market dynamics.

Exhibit 4.12 illustrates the impact of mean reversion on risk over longer investment horizons. The unconditional variance of the log of future wealth is proportional to

EXHIBIT 4.12   **Risk versus Horizon**

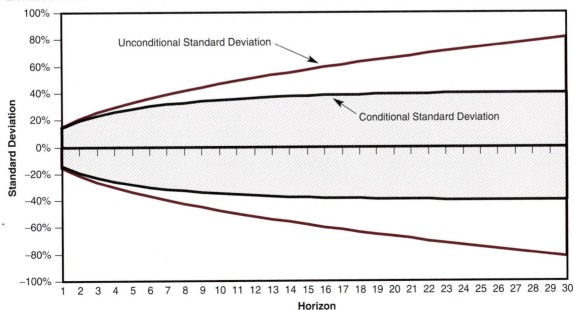

the investment horizon, so the unconditional standard deviation is proportional to the square root of the horizon. The upper and lower curves indicate ± 1 times the unconditional standard deviation respectively. These curves are the basis for the standard M–V model. The shaded area and inner set of curves reflect the conditional standard deviation. Due to mean reversion, the conditional standard deviation rises more slowly and approaches a limit. Stronger mean reversion results in both a lower level of long-run risk and faster convergence to the long-run limit.

Summary

Developing good risk and return inputs is a crucial step in the asset allocation process. Indeed, it may be the most important step. Without realistic and internally consistent inputs, the asset allocation process can easily become a sterile exercise involving arbitrary constraints and a predetermined result. Such an endeavor yields little insight and cannot really inform our investment decisions. To add value through asset allocation, we must have reliable inputs.

The first part of this chapter presented six methods that are often used in estimating the inputs for the M–V model developed in Chapter 3. Throughout that discussion investment opportunities, and therefore the relevant risk and return parameters, were assumed to be constant. The most common approach is to use sample moments calculated from historical return data. This works well for estimating variances and covariances because subdividing a given sample period into many subperiods substantially improves the accuracy of the estimates. As a result, good estimates of these risk parameters can be obtained even from relatively short samples. Unfortunately the same cannot be said of the sample mean. The accuracy of this estimator does not improve if we sample more frequently. Therefore, a very long sample may be required to obtain an accurate estimate of the expected return.

Because the sample mean can be so unreliable, it is often useful to incorporate additional information into our expected return estimates. One way to incorporate additional information is to use so-called Bayesian estimators such as the James–Stein estimator. Bayesian estimators combine prior information, or a prior estimate, with the sample data to yield a more reliable estimate. In the case of the James–Stein estimator, the prior information is simply the assumption that expected returns should be similar across asset classes. Based on this assumption, the James–Stein estimator adjusts sample means toward a common value. This gives more reliable estimates because it shrinks the most extreme sample means, those most likely to have been affected by sampling error, toward a central value.

Economic and financial theory can also anchor our estimates. This approach is especially useful in establishing a realistic level of returns for major asset classes. Using basic results from the neoclassical theory of economic growth, we showed that the long-term rate of price appreciation in the stock market should be closely tied to the growth rate of nominal GDP. Combining this insight with reasonable assumptions for the dividend payout and PE ratios provides an estimate of the expected stock market return that is grounded in economic fundamentals.

Because our objective is not forecasting per se, but rather making good portfolio decisions, it is important that our expected return estimates be internally consistent across asset classes and consistent with the estimated risk structure. The implied views method imposes this consistency by letting the M–V model tell us what expected returns would be required to make a specified benchmark allocation optimal for a representative investor. This is equivalent to assuming that the zero-beta version of the well-known capital asset pricing model (CAPM) holds with the specified portfolio playing the role of the market. Thus the implied views method can be interpreted as imposing the CAPM equilibrium. Alternatively, it can be viewed as simply a pragmatic way to ensure that at least one reasonable portfolio, the specified benchmark, is mean–variance efficient.

Multifactor risk models provide another method of imposing cross-sectional consistency among the asset classes. In practice, the variance–covariance structure of asset class returns, and hence portfolio returns, can be decomposed into only a few important dimensions or risk factors. This implies that there may be many portfolios with virtually the same exposure to each of the important risk factors. Consistency between risk and return implies that all such portfolios must have the same expected return. This leads to a linear relationship between expected return and exposure to the common risk factors. Specifying the risk premium earned for exposure to each risk factor and then applying this equation can generate internally consistent expected returns for various asset classes.

The last method considered in this chapter, mixed estimation, is actually a way to combine estimates. The blended estimate is a weighted average of the underlying estimates with greater weight given to the more reliable estimate. In one common application of this technique, an equilibrium expected return is blended with an analyst's subjective view. In this application, the equilibrium can be viewed as prior information that is being combined with new information coming from the analyst's view. As with the James–Stein estimator, mixed estimation can be interpreted as a Bayesian technique.

In the second part of the chapter we explicitly dropped the assumption that investment opportunities are constant through time. When investment opportunities are changing over time we must distinguish between conditional and unconditional notions of risk and return. At any date, the conditional parameters take into account any variables that help predict returns in the coming period while unconditional parameters treat this information as unknown. Because it would be foolish to ignore information, we want to base our investment decisions on conditional rather than unconditional risk and return parameters.

Two simple models were used to illustrate changing investment opportunities. In the regimes model, conditional investment parameters can take only a small, discrete set of possible values. As an example, we modeled the popular notion that the U.S. stock market is subject to an election cycle by allowing for two regimes corresponding to the first and second halves of the presidential term. In the simple mean reversion model, the expected return on the stock market takes on a continuum of values depending on the level of the market relative to its long-term trend. In this model, the single-period conditional variance of the market is constant, but over multiperiod horizons the variance per period actually declines. This model provides a foundation for the conventional wisdom that stocks are less risky over longer horizons. In Chapter 5 we will build on this foundation when we examine the impact of changing investment opportunities on asset allocation decisions.

Problems

1. Use the data in the <LN Intl Returns> worksheet of the spreadsheet Chapter 04 Questions.xls and the Excel spreadsheet developed in the James–Stein estimator outbox to
   a. Calculate estimates for the countries listed.
   b. Repeat estimating the James–Stein estimators to get JS estimates excluding Argentina and Brazil. [In cells B3, B4, and B6, change the range from B12:Y12 to D12:Y12.]
   c. Compare the data, statistics, and results for Argentina and Brazil with those of the other countries. What is different about these two countries? What do you know about them that might explain this difference? Assuming you need to include these two countries, what might you do to ensure that they do not skew the JS results for the other markets?
   d. Using Excel's chart wizard, create a chart that shows the JS estimate of alphas with and without Argentina and Brazil for each market along with its sample mean.

2. Using the data in Problem 1, apply the implied views method to compute expected returns (μ) for the 24 equity markets using an equally weighted target portfolio and setting the expected returns for the United States and Mexico equal to their James–Stein estimates.

3. Using annual data for S&P 500 returns from 1926 through the most recent calendar year-end, update the election cycle regime model in Exhibit 4.9.

4. Using annual data for S&P 500 returns from 1946 through the most recent calendar year-end and ordinary least squares regression, update the "trend only" and "mean reversion" model estimates in Exhibit 4.10. Use Equations (4.27) and (4.31) to compute the unconditional and conditional variances of return over 1-, 10-, and 20-year horizons (do not annualize). Convert these to standard deviations.

5. Use the worksheet <ME – 1 asset> in the spreadsheet Chapter 04 Chapter Questions.xls to show that α translates to μ in mixed views estimation.

6. Use the worksheet <ME – 2 active> in spreadsheet Chapter 04 Chapter Questions.xls to expand the mixed estimation technique to include two active views. In particular, add the view that the Barclays Aggregate Bond Index return will be 1.5 percent lower than the equilibrium—that is, 3.09 percent.

7. Using the Excel spreadsheet developed for the implied views method, set the target expected log return (α) for the Russell 1000 Value index and the Citigroup U.S.$-hedged Non-U.S.$ Government index to 7.62 percent and 4.29 percent respectively. Compare the implied expected returns for the other asset classes with those in Exhibit 4.5. Are they same? Why or why not?

Appendix

Mixed Estimation with Multiple Assets[21]

Mixed estimation is frequently used to blend a set of active views with equilibrium expected returns from the implied views approach.[22] Consider the case in which we have estimates for eight assets. If the estimation errors are uncorrelated across assets, we can simply apply Equation (4.14) in the text to each asset separately. However, if

[21] This appendix uses basic matrix operations: addition, multiplication, transposes, and inverses. A brief review of these tools can be found in virtually any econometrics textbook.

[22] This methodology was developed in Black and Litterman (1992).

the estimation errors are correlated across assets, the mixed estimator can be improved by incorporating the error correlation. To handle this case we need to generalize Equations (4.13) and (4.14) using matrices.

Let $\tilde{\mu}_1$ and $\tilde{\mu}_2$ denote (column) vectors containing expected return estimates for M and K assets respectively where $K \leq M$. Allowing $K < M$ implies that $\tilde{\mu}_2$ may contain estimates for only a subset of the assets. As before, each of the estimates in these two vectors is assumed to equal the corresponding true expected return plus an error. The two sets of estimates are assumed to be uncorrelated, but within each set the errors may be correlated across assets. Formally,

$$\tilde{\mu}_i = X_i \underline{\mu} + \underline{e}_i \quad i = 1,2 \qquad \text{(A4.1)}$$

where X_i is a matrix associating each expected return estimate with the corresponding true value contained in the vector $\underline{\mu}$ and $\underline{e}_i$ is a vector of estimation errors with variance–covariance matrix Ω_i. The vector $\underline{\mu}$ has M rows, so the matrix X must have M columns. Matrices X and Ω have the same number of rows (either K or M) as the estimate vector on the left side of the equation, and Ω is a nonsingular square matrix. With this notation, the mixed estimator is

$$\tilde{\underline{\mu}}_{mx} = \left[X_1^T \Omega_1^{-1} X_1 + X_2^T \Omega_2^{-1} X_2\right]^{-1} \left[X_1^T \Omega_1^{-1} \tilde{\mu}_1 + X_2^T \Omega_2^{-1} \tilde{\mu}_2\right] \qquad \text{(A4.2)}$$

A superscript T denotes the transpose of the matrix, and as usual, a superscript -1 denotes the inverse of the matrix. Despite its complexity, Equation (A4.2) essentially says that the mixed estimator for each expected return is a weighted average of the original estimates. In general, the combined estimate for each asset will depend on the original estimates for all the assets because the estimation errors are correlated.

| *Excel Outbox* *Mixed Estimation* | Consider the more general case of the example from Section 4.2, combining the implied views from Exhibit 4.5 with a single active view. The active view will remain that small-capitalization growth stocks will do 2 percent better than the equilibrium. Use the worksheet <ME – 8 assets> in the spreadsheet Chapter 04 Excel Outboxes.xls. |

Inputs

The implied view, $\tilde{\mu}_1$, is a column vector (8 × 1):

- In cells B21:B28 enter the values for $\underline{\mu}$ from Exhibit 4.5.

  The active view, $\tilde{\mu}_2$, is a single number (1 × 1):

- In cell I21 enter =B24 + 0.02.

  The result should appear as follows:

	A	B		F	G	H	I
20	Asset	μ_1	20	Asset			μ_2
21	Russell 1000 Value TR	8.70%	21	Russell 2000 Growth TR			12.92%
22	Russell 1000 Growth TR	9.88%					
23	Russell 2000 Value TR	8.95%					
24	Russell 2000 Growth TR	10.92%					
25	MSCI EAFE TR	8.68%					
26	Barclays Hi-Yld TR	6.11%					
27	Barclays Aggregate Bond TR	4.59%					
28	Citigroup US$ Hedged Non-US$ Gvt TR	4.34%					

(continued)

(continued)

The variance–covariance matrix (8 × 8), Ω_1, is estimated from the historical return series. This was done in developing the implied views spreadsheet, so link to that matrix:

- In cell B31 enter ='Implied − Complete'!B12.
- Copy cell B31 to C31:I31 and then copy cells B31:I31 to cells B32:I38.

The result should appear as follows:*

	A	B	C	D	E	F	G	H	I
30	Asset				Ω_1				
31	Russell 1000 Value TR	2.14%	2.19%	2.07%	2.48%	1.56%	0.74%	0.12%	0.03%
32	Russell 1000 Growth TR	2.19%	3.30%	2.26%	3.67%	1.95%	0.86%	0.12%	0.02%
33	Russell 2000 Value TR	2.07%	2.26%	2.93%	3.55%	1.61%	0.94%	0.06%	−0.01%
34	Russell 2000 Growth TR	2.48%	3.67%	3.55%	5.69%	2.37%	1.19%	0.02%	−0.04%
35	MSCI EAFE TR	1.56%	1.95%	1.61%	2.37%	3.10%	0.72%	0.10%	0.09%
36	Barclays Hi-Yld TR	0.74%	0.86%	0.94%	1.19%	0.72%	0.74%	0.11%	0.03%
37	Barclays Aggregate Bond TR	0.12%	0.12%	0.06%	0.02%	0.10%	0.11%	0.19%	0.09%
38	Citigroup US$ Hedged Non-US$ Gvt TR	0.03%	0.02%	−0.01%	−0.04%	0.09%	0.03%	0.09%	0.11%

X_1 (8 × 8) is an identity matrix:

- In cells B41:I48, enter 1 on the diagonal and 0 elsewhere.

The result should appear as follows:

	A	B	C	D	E	F	G	H	I
40	Asset				X_1				
41	Russell 1000 Value TR	1	0	0	0	0	0	0	0
42	Russell 1000 Growth TR	0	1	0	0	0	0	0	0
43	Russell 2000 Value TR	0	0	1	0	0	0	0	0
44	Russell 2000 Growth TR	0	0	0	1	0	0	0	0
45	MSCI EAFE TR	0	0	0	0	1	0	0	0
46	Barclays Hi-Yld TR	0	0	0	0	0	1	0	0
47	Barclays Aggregate Bond TR	0	0	0	0	0	0	1	0
48	Citigroup US$ Hedged Non-US$ Gvt TR	0	0	0	0	0	0	0	1

Because there is only one active view, Ω_2 (1 × 1) collapses to a scalar that is proportional to the historical variance of the Russell 2000 Growth:

- In cell B51 enter =E34.

X_2 (1 × 8) is a row vector:

- In cells B54:I54, enter 1 in the column of the asset with the active view and 0 elsewhere.

The result should appear as follows:

	A	B	C	D	E	F	G	H	I
50	Asset	Ω_2							
51	Russell 2000 Growth TR	5.69%							
52									
53	Asset				X_2				
54	Russell 2000 Growth TR	0	0	0	1	0	0	0	0

*The percent signs shown in the variance-covariance matrix reflect Excel formatting rather than actual units . For example, stated as a decimal the variance of the Russell 1000 Value index is .0214. Using Excel's percentage formatting to eliminate leading zeros, this appears as 2.14%.

Mixed Estimation

The mixed estimation, $\tilde{\underline{\mu}}_{mx}$, is a column vector (8 × 1). As indicated in the appendix, the formula for the mixed estimation is

$$\tilde{\underline{\mu}}_{mx} = \left[X_1^T\Omega_1^{-1}X_1 + X_2^T\Omega_2^{-1}X_2\right]^{-1}\left[X_1^T\Omega_1^{-1}\tilde{\underline{\mu}}_1 + X_2^T\Omega_2^{-1}\tilde{\underline{\mu}}_2\right]$$

To keep the formulas manageable, the spreadsheet breaks the formula into three parts:

$$\underset{(8\times1)}{\underline{\mu}_{mx}} = \underset{(8\times8)}{[A]^{-1}} \qquad\qquad\qquad\qquad \underset{(8\times1)}{B}$$

$$\underset{(8\times1)}{\underline{\mu}_{mx}} = \underset{(8\times8)}{X_1^T}\underset{(8\times8)}{\Omega_1^{-1}}\underset{(8\times8)}{X_1} + \underset{(8\times1)}{X_2^T}\underset{(1\times1)}{\Omega_2^{-1}}\underset{(1\times8)}{X_2} \quad \underset{(8\times8)}{X_1^T}\underset{(8\times8)}{\Omega_1^{-1}}\underset{(8\times1)}{\tilde{\mu}_1} + \underset{(8\times1)}{X_2^T}\underset{(1\times1)}{\Omega_2^{-1}}\underset{(1\times1)}{\tilde{\mu}_2}$$

The numbers in parentheses indicate the number of rows and columns for each element.

Part A:

- Highlight cells C11:J18 and enter
  =MMULT(TRANSPOSE($B41:$I$48),MMULT(MINVERSE($B$31:$I$38),$B$41:$I$48))
  +MMULT(TRANSPOSE($B$54:$I$54),MMULT(MINVERSE($B$51),$B$54:$I$54)).
- Press <CTRL><SHIFT><ENTER>.

	A	C	D	E	F	G	H	I	J
10	Asset					A			
11	Russell 1000 Value TR	388.32	−244.54	−295.36	182.55	−29.93	15.38	−17.97	−8.81
12	Russell 1000 Growth TR	−244.54	281.19	202.84	−195.44	−5.61	−16.66	−67.03	46.77
13	Russell 2000 Value TR	−295.36	202.84	386.66	−234.51	16.35	−77.10	3.73	17.03
14	Russell 2000 Growth TR	182.55	−195.44	−234.51	232.91	−14.11	5.19	58.88	−9.41
15	MSCI EAFE TR	−29.93	−5.61	16.35	−14.11	58.60	−20.51	28.44	−58.30
16	Barclays Hi-Yld TR	15.38	−16.66	−77.10	5.19	−20.51	269.92	−149.54	50.73
17	Barclays Aggregate Bond TR	−17.97	−67.03	3.73	58.88	28.44	−149.54	1036.60	−813.50
18	Citigroup US$ Hedged Non-US$ Gvt TR	−8.81	46.77	17.03	−9.41	−58.30	50.73	−813.50	1660.01

Part B:

- Highlight cells K11:K18 and enter
  =(MMULT(TRANSPOSE($B$41:$I$48),MMULT(MINVERSE($B$31:$I$38),$B$21:$B$28))+MMULT(TRANSPOSE($B$54:$I$54),MMULT(MINVERSE($B$51),$I$21))).
- Press <CTRL><SHIFT><ENTER>.

	A	K
10	Asset	B
11	Russell 1000 Value TR	0.26
12	Russell 1000 Growth TR	0.76
13	Russell 2000 Value TR	0.95
14	Russell 2000 Growth TR	2.76
15	MSCI EAFE TR	−0.63
16	Barclays Hi-Yld TR	3.39
17	Barclays Aggregate Bond TR	4.25
18	Citigroup US$ Hedged Non-US$ Gvt TR	37.03

$\tilde{\underline{\mu}}_{mx}$:

- Highlight cells B11:B18 and enter
  =MMULT(MINVERSE($C$11:$J$18),$K$11:$K$18).
- Press <CTRL><SHIFT><ENTER>.

(continued)

(concluded)

	A	B
10	Asset	μ_{mx}
11	Russell 1000 Value TR	9.14%
12	Russell 1000 Growth TR	10.52%
13	Russell 2000 Value TR	9.57%
14	Russell 2000 Growth TR	11.92%
15	MSCI EAFE TR	9.09%
16	Barclays Hi-Yld TR	6.31%
17	Barclays Aggregate Bond TR	4.60%
18	Citigroup US$ Hedged Non-US$ Gvt TR	4.33%

The expected return on the Russell 2000 Growth index increases 1 percent and is the average of the implied and active views. This is exactly what would be expected based on Equation (4.14) because the two estimates for this asset class were assumed to have the same variance. The expected returns for the other equity asset classes also increase because they are highly correlated with the Russell 2000 Growth index. In essence, the mixed estimation equation is indicating that, absent conflicting information, it would be inconsistent to raise our estimate for one equity class without raising our estimates for other correlated classes. Similarly, the estimate for high-yield bonds increases. However, it does not increase as much as the equity asset classes due to the lower correlation with the Russell 2000 Growth index and lower volatility. Finally, the Barclays Aggregate bond index and the Citigroup Hedged Non-U.S. Government bond index are essentially uncorrelated with the Russell 2000 Growth index, and therefore their expected returns are virtually unchanged.

	Implied Views	Active View	Mixed Estimate	Impact
Russell 1000 Value	8.70%		9.14%	0.44%
Russell 1000 Growth	9.88%		10.52%	0.64%
Russell 2000 Value	8.95%		9.57%	0.62%
Russell 2000 Growth	10.92%	12.92%	11.92%	1.00%
MSCI EAFE	8.68%		9.09%	0.41%
Barclays High Yield	6.11%		6.31%	0.20%
Barclays Aggregate Bond	4.59%		4.60%	0.01%
Citi Hedged Non-US Gov	4.34%		4.33%	−0.01%

Chapter  5

Advanced Topics in Asset Allocation

Chapter Outline

5.1   Introduction

The basic mean–variance (M–V) framework was developed in Chapter 3 in a multi-period context with careful treatment of investment opportunities and investor preferences. Although this was not the simplest approach to the M–V model, it provided a foundation from which we can now generalize and extend our discussion of asset allocation to more advanced issues and methods.

In deriving the M–V model we made several key assumptions. First, investment opportunities are the same in each period. Second, logarithmic returns have a normal distribution. Third, the investor's risk–return preferences are independent of investment horizon and are completely described by constant relative risk aversion (CRRA) with respect to final wealth. Fourth, there are no cash flows into or out of the portfolio before the end of the investment horizon. Given these assumptions, the investor holds the same portfolio in each period and selects that portfolio by maximizing the M–V objective function. Relaxing any of these assumptions will, in general, cause the investor to adopt an investment strategy that differs from the M–V prescription.

Because one of the most important implications of relaxing these assumptions is that the investment strategy becomes dependent on the investment horizon, the introduction of horizon effects into asset allocation is a major theme of this chapter. Another focus is the impact of *stochastically* changing investment opportunities.

One virtue of the M–V model is that it purports to provide a universal, yet simple, framework for deriving optimal asset allocation decisions. In this chapter we introduce a more general framework called *dynamic programming* (*DP*), which can, at least in principle, handle any asset allocation scenario we might encounter. In other words, it is "the right thing to do" and ought to be the framework of choice for asset allocation decisions. In practice, however, only stylized and relatively simple problems can be handled with DP. Even with today's vast computing power, direct application of DP remains primarily in the realm of theory and research; it is not yet a mainstay of the practitioner's toolbox. We introduce it here for two purposes. First, because it is "the right thing to do," a qualitative understanding of DP can help improve our pragmatic approaches. Second, we will apply it to obtain insight into the impact of changing investment opportunities and illustrate its practical application to a simplified problem.

The chapter is organized as follows. In Section 5.2 we incorporate horizon effects into the M–V model by allowing either the investor's preferences or the investment opportunities to depend on the investment horizon. These are pragmatic approaches designed to capture important horizon effects without losing the relative simplicity and tractability of the M–V model. These models do not allow for the fact that in making *current* investment decisions we should take into account possible *future* investment decisions. That is what DP allows us to do. After describing DP in general terms, Section 5.3 presents two applications. The first retains the M–V objective function but derives the optimal horizon-dependent portfolio policy using DP. In this first application the portfolio policy is not allowed to depend on the realization of uncertain events, such as the evolution of the investor's wealth. In the second application we demonstrate the full DP methodology in the context of stochastically changing investment opportunities. In this case the optimal policy is shown to depend on the level of the asset price (the market) in addition to the investor's wealth and investment horizon.

From our relatively simple applications of DP the reader should appreciate why it is difficult to apply this methodology to the larger-scale, more complex situations encountered in practice. In Section 5.4 we move from "the right thing to do" to a more pragmatic approach: simulation. Given a random number generator, we can simulate almost anything: We can deal with complex scenarios involving many assets, cash flows, unusual probability distributions, probabilistic constraints, and alternative performance criteria. Simulation is a powerful tool that can help us evaluate various investment strategies in realistic environments. This allows us to eliminate bad strategies and focus on better ones. In general, however, we cannot truly optimize in the sense of finding the best strategy for a given problem. We can merely pick the best among strategies that we prespecify. We will apply the simulation approach to examine the impact of required cash flows out of the portfolio, nonnormally distributed asset returns, and specialized objective functions. In addition, we will discuss how a simulation-based method known as *resampling* can make the M–V model more robust.

Section 5.5 discusses issues that arise from the fact that asset allocation decisions are usually made as if we are going to invest in generic asset class indexes, but the money is in fact entrusted to managers who attempt to enhance returns by deviating from these benchmarks. The most obvious impact of this practice is that the overall portfolio may not have the intended or expected characteristics. A less obvious, but perhaps even more significant, implication is that the amount of money entrusted to managers should depend on their ability to add value—their *alpha*—rather than the role of their generic asset class in the overall portfolio. The notion of separating the allocation of assets among managers from the allocation to asset classes is usually referred to as *portable alpha.*

The final section of this chapter considers portfolio insurance (PI) strategies. The name *portfolio insurance* derives from the fact that these strategies are designed to protect the portfolio from losses while capturing most, but not all, of the potential upside performance. Two types of PI strategies are discussed: option-based PI and constant proportional portfolio insurance (CPPI).

5.2   Horizon Effects in the M–V Framework

In Chapter 3 we briefly discussed two ways to introduce horizon effects into the standard M–V model. The first involved restating the objective function in terms of risk and return *per period.* This approach takes advantage of the fact that, given the underlying assumptions, the variance of per-period return over a *T*-period horizon is proportional to $(1/T)$ whereas the expected return per period does not depend on the horizon. Although this approach is often rationalized by the notion that assets are less risky at longer horizons, we showed that it actually reflects an assumption that *risk aversion* is horizon-dependent. The second approach involved introducing a shortfall constraint.

In this section we revisit the notion of horizon-dependent risk aversion and then consider horizon effects within the M–V model when risk and return really do vary with the investment horizon. Shortfall constraints are examined again in Section 5.3 in the context of DP.

Horizon-Dependent Risk Aversion

The objective function for the basic M–V model is given by

$$(\mu_W - \lambda \, \sigma_W^2) \, T \qquad\qquad (5.1)$$

where μ_W is the log of the expected (gross) return on the portfolio, σ_W^2 is the variance of the portfolio return, and $\lambda \equiv \frac{1}{2}(1 - \gamma)$ is the investor's risk aversion. In the formal derivation of the model, $(1 - \gamma)$ was the investor's underlying coefficient of relative risk aversion. Here we simply treat γ as a parameter.

In Chapter 3 we showed that replacing the mean and variance of portfolio return with the mean and variance of *per-period* return is equivalent to redefining risk aversion as $\lambda \equiv \frac{1}{2} (1 - \gamma/T)$. For negative values of γ, risk aversion declines as the investment horizon increases. Moving from a single-period horizon to an extremely long horizon, the investor's risk aversion declines by a factor of $(1/(1 - \gamma))$. Roughly speaking, we might expect the investor to increase the risk of their portfolio by a factor of $(1 - \gamma)$. This is a reasonably good approximation; indeed it is a good rule of thumb for how much an investor will allocate to equities (risky assets) versus bonds (safe assets). So if $\gamma = -2$ the investor will roughly triple the risk and the equity allocation as they move from a single-period horizon to an extremely long horizon.

Although this formulation of the model allows risk aversion, and therefore asset allocation, to depend on the investment horizon, it does not provide much flexibility. The long-run level of risk aversion is fixed at one-half, and the time profile is completely determined by $(1/T)$. As the only parameter, γ controls the ratio of long-horizon to short-horizon risk aversion. We can generalize the framework by introducing an additional parameter, ψ, equal to the long-horizon level of risk aversion and a function, $f(T)$, controlling the time profile. Risk aversion then becomes

$$\lambda(T) = \psi(1 - \gamma f(T)) \tag{5.2}$$

If we set $f(1) = 1$ and require that $f(T)$ go to zero at very long horizons, then risk aversion still declines by a factor of $(1/(1 - \gamma))$. In principle, any function satisfying these conditions could be used. However, we would like to link $f(T)$ to aspects of the investment problem that are not already captured by the basic M–V model with constant risk aversion. As an example, we will consider incorporating shortfall risk into $f(T)$.

As discussed in Chapter 3, the basic M–V model may not fully capture the investor's attitude toward risk. In particular, the investor may be concerned with the likelihood of losing money, or more generally, failing to achieve a threshold rate of return over the investment horizon. If so, the investor's attitude toward portfolio variance may depend on this shortfall probability. This can be modeled fairly simply as follows. Let $PS(T)$ denote the probability of shortfall for a standardized portfolio, such as an all-equity portfolio, over a T-period horizon. Then the ratio $[PS(T)/PS(1)]$ reflects the risk of a shortfall over a T-period horizon relative to a single-period horizon. This can be incorporated into risk aversion by setting

$$f(T) = \left(\frac{PS(T)}{PS(1)}\right)^{\phi} \tag{5.3}$$

where ϕ is a positive parameter that controls the sensitivity of $f(T)$ to changes in the probability ratio. Note that $f(1) = 1$. Given the assumption that logarithmic portfolio returns have a normal distribution, both $PS(T)$ and $f(T)$ decline toward zero as T increases provided the standardized portfolio has an expected return greater than the threshold return. Because γ is presumed to be negative in Equation (5.2), risk aversion declines as T increases.

Exhibit 5.1 illustrates the horizon profile of risk aversion for three choices of the function $f(T)$. The black line reflects the common practice of using per-period risk and return in the M–V objective—that is, $f(T) = 1/T$. The solid line, labeled "shortfall probability ratio," reflects Equation (5.3) with $\phi = 1$, and the dashed line, labeled "accelerated shortfall probability," reflects a value of ϕ greater than 1. In evaluating

EXHIBIT 5.1

Horizon Profiles of Risk Aversion

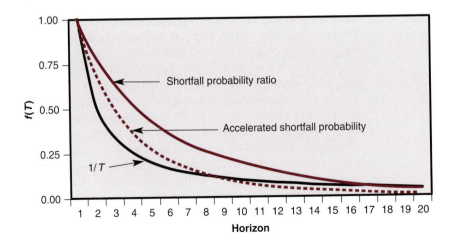

the shortfall probabilities the standard deviation was assumed to be twice the expected return. This is broadly consistent with a diversified equity portfolio. The threshold return for assessing a shortfall was set at zero—that is, avoiding a loss. We can see that the shortfall probability ratio declines more slowly than $(1/T)$. Thus for an investor who is concerned with the probability of losing money, the common practice of focusing on per-period returns (setting $f(T) = 1/T$) overstates the rate at which this risk declines as the horizon extends. As illustrated by the accelerated shortfall probability curve, the function given by Equation (5.3) allows us to adjust the speed at which risk aversion declines while retaining the underlying link to shortfall risk. As a result, we can exercise judgment in customizing the horizon profile without sacrificing the discipline of deriving it from underlying investment considerations.

It was suggested earlier that changes in risk aversion will result in roughly proportionate changes in the combined allocation to riskier asset classes (such as equities). Exhibit 5.2 illustrates this relationship. The solid curve reflects **risk tolerance** defined as the reciprocal of risk aversion (that is, $1/\lambda$), normalized to unity at a 20-year horizon. The dashed line is the allocation to equity assets using the eight asset classes considered in Chapter 4. Short sales were not allowed. The correspondence between the two curves is obvious. In fact the curves are virtually identical except for a proportional shift in level. Thus as a practical matter, the horizon profile of risk tolerance translates directly into the horizon profile of the asset allocation.

The upshot of Exhibit 5.1 and 5.2 is that Equations (5.1) through (5.3) provide a simple, flexible framework for incorporating views on how investment horizon ought to impact asset allocation while retaining a solid link to underlying investment considerations. If, based on experience or intuition, we have an idea about how much and how fast the equity allocation should increase with horizon, we can translate this into a corresponding profile for risk tolerance or aversion (look again at Exhibit 5.2). We can then select parameters γ, ψ, and ϕ in Equations (5.2) and (5.3) to match this profile as closely as possible. Of course the allocations generated from this profile are unlikely to match our intuition exactly. This is precisely the point. Linking risk aversion to relative shortfall risk, or some other investment criteria, imposes structure and consistency on the relationship between horizon and allocation. Given this structure, the M–V model can inform us rather than simply reproduce our preconceived notions; that is, the model can add value.

EXHIBIT 5.2
Stock Allocation versus Risk Tolerance

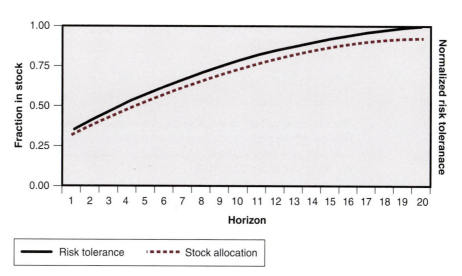

	A	B	C	D	E	F	G	H	I
1	Horizon Dependent Risk Aversion								
2									
3	Assumptions						Shortfall Constraint		
4	Long-term Risk Aversion						H		
5	Long-term Horizon (N)						μ		
6	Ratio: ST/LT Risk Aversion						σ		
7	Ratio: 1YR/10YR Risk Aversion						PS(1)		
8									
9	Program								
10	Objective	Min							
11	φ								
12	γ								
13	ψ								

Excel Outbox / *Horizon-Dependent Risk Aversion*

To explore horizon-dependent risk aversion, use the worksheet <HD RRA–Template> in the Chapter 05 Horizon Excel Outboxes.xls spreadsheet. The template should appear as follows:

Assumptions: Assume the long-term (LT) horizon is 30 periods with a LT risk aversion parameter of 1.25. The ratio of LT to short-term (ST) risk aversion is assumed to be 5 with risk aversion increasing by a factor of 3 from the 10-year horizon to the 1-year horizon.

- In cell D4 enter 1.25.
- In cell D5 enter 30.
- In cell D6 enter 5.
- In cell D7 enter 3.5

Shortfall constraint: The shortfall threshold will be to avoid a loss, and the standard deviation will be set to twice the mean return. The probability of shortfall for one period is denoted as PS(1).

- In cell G4 enter 0.
- In cell G5 enter 0.075.
- In cell G6 enter =2*G5.
- In cell G7 enter =NORMDIST(G$4,G$5,G$6,TRUE).

Program: Risk aversion is given by $\lambda(T) = \psi(1 - \gamma f(T))$, where $f(T)$ takes the form given in Equation (5.3):

$$f(T) = \left(\frac{PS(T)}{PS(1)}\right)^{\phi}$$

The objective will be to set φ so the risk aversion profile has the desired 1-year/10-year ratio by minimizing the squared difference between the desired 1-year/10-year risk aversion ratio and the calculated 1-year/10-year risk aversion ratio. The parameters γ and ψ are set by the properties that $f(1) = 1$ and $f(T) \approx 0$.

- In cell D10 enter = (I46/I37-D7)^2 [Note: "I" is a letter here, not a numeral.]
- When $f(T) = 0$, $\lambda = \psi(1 - \gamma(0))$; that is, $\lambda = \psi = $ LT risk aversion. In cell D13 enter =D4.
- When $f(1) = 1$, $\lambda = \psi(1 - \gamma)$. Substituting $\psi = $ LT risk aversion and simplifying, $\gamma = 1 - $ (ST risk aversion/LT risk aversion). In cell D12 enter =1-D6.

In the Solver menu,

- Set target cell: $D$10.
- Equal to: min.
- By changing cells: $D$11. In cell D11 enter 1 as a starting value.
- Subject to the constraints: $D$11 > =0.

	A	B	C	D	E	F	G	H	I
15					f(T)			λ	
16	t	T	PS(T)	1/T	φ = 1	φ = opt	λ = ψ(1−γ(1/T))	λ = ψ(1−γX)	λ = ψ(1−γXᵠ)

The risk aversion profile is calculated in cells A17:I46:

- In cell A17 enter 0. In cell A18 enter =A17 + 1, then copy to cells A19:A46.
- In cell B17 enter =$D$5-A17.
- In cell C17 enter =NORMDIST(G$4*B17,G$5*B17,G$6*SQRT(B17),TRUE).
- In cell D17 enter =1/B17.
- In cell E17 enter =IF($D$5 >=B17,C17/$G$7,0).
- In cell F17 enter =E17^$D$11.
- In cell G17 enter =$D$13*(1-$D$12*D17).
- In cell H17 enter =$D$13*(1-$D$12*E17).
- In cell I17 enter =$D$13*(1-$D$12*F17).
- Copy cells B17:I17 to cells B18:I46.

Now optimize using the Solver.
The charts should show that *f(T)* and λ are decreasing functions of the horizon:

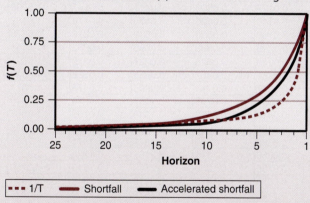

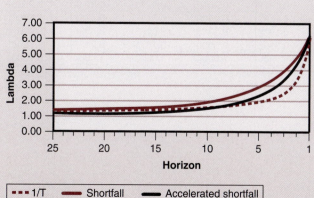

(continued)

(concluded)   The completed template should appear as follows:

	A	B	C	D	E	F	G	H	I
1	**Horizon Dependent Risk Aversion**								
2									
3	**Assumptions**					**Shortfall Constraint**			
4	Long-term Risk Aversion			1.25		H	0.00%		
5	Long-term Horizon (N)			30		μ	7.50%		
6	Ratio: ST/LT Risk Aversion			5		σ	15.00%		
7	Ratio: 1YR/10YR Risk Aversion			3.5		PS(1)	0.3085		
8									
9	**Program**								
10	Objective Min			0.0000					
11	ϕ			1.3215					
12	γ			−4.00					
13	ψ			1.250					
14									
15						f(T)			λ
16	t	T	PS(T)	1/T	$\phi = 1$	ϕ = opt	$\lambda=\psi(1-\gamma(1/T))$	$\lambda=\psi(1-\gamma X)$	$\lambda=\psi(1-\gamma X^{\phi})$
17	0	30	0.0031	0.0333	0.0100	0.0023	1.4167	1.3000	1.2614
18	1	29	0.0035	0.0345	0.0115	0.0027	1.4224	1.3074	1.2637
19	2	28	0.0041	0.0357	0.0132	0.0033	1.4286	1.3160	1.2664
20	3	27	0.0047	0.0370	0.0152	0.0040	1.4352	1.3260	1.2698
21	4	26	0.0054	0.0385	0.0175	0.0048	1.4423	1.3374	1.2738
22	5	25	0.0062	0.0400	0.0201	0.0057	1.4500	1.3506	1.2787
23	6	24	0.0072	0.0417	0.0232	0.0069	1.4583	1.3659	1.2846
24	7	23	0.0082	0.0435	0.0267	0.0083	1.4674	1.3836	1.2917
25	8	22	0.0095	0.0455	0.0308	0.0101	1.4773	1.4041	1.3003
26	9	21	0.0110	0.0476	0.0356	0.0122	1.4881	1.4278	1.3108
27	10	20	0.0127	0.0500	0.0411	0.0147	1.5000	1.4554	1.3236
28	11	19	0.0146	0.0526	0.0475	0.0178	1.5132	1.4874	1.3391
29	12	18	0.0169	0.0556	0.0549	0.0216	1.5278	1.5246	1.3580
30	13	17	0.0196	0.0588	0.0636	0.0262	1.5441	1.5680	1.3811
31	14	16	0.0228	0.0625	0.0737	0.0319	1.5625	1.6187	1.4094
32	15	15	0.0264	0.0667	0.0856	0.0388	1.5833	1.6779	1.4441
33	16	14	0.0307	0.0714	0.0995	0.0473	1.6071	1.7473	1.4867
34	17	13	0.0357	0.0769	0.1157	0.0579	1.6346	1.8287	1.5393
35	18	12	0.0416	0.0833	0.1349	0.0709	1.6667	1.9247	1.6043
36	19	11	0.0486	0.0909	0.1576	0.0870	1.7045	2.0380	1.6850
37	20	10	0.0569	0.1000	0.1845	0.1071	1.7500	2.1725	1.7857
38	21	9	0.0668	0.1111	0.2165	0.1324	1.8056	2.3326	1.9120
39	22	8	0.0786	0.1250	0.2549	0.1643	1.8750	2.5246	2.0713
40	23	7	0.0929	0.1429	0.3012	0.2048	1.9643	2.7561	2.2740
41	24	6	0.1103	0.1667	0.3576	0.2569	2.0833	3.0380	2.5346
42	25	5	0.1318	0.2000	0.4271	0.3249	2.2500	3.3855	2.8744
43	26	4	0.1587	0.2500	0.5142	0.4152	2.5000	3.8211	3.3261
44	27	3	0.1932	0.3333	0.6263	0.5388	2.9167	4.3815	3.9441
45	28	2	0.2398	0.5000	0.7771	0.7165	3.7500	5.1353	4.8326
46	29	1	0.3085	1.0000	1.0000	1.0000	6.2500	6.2500	6.2500

Excel Outbox
Optimization
with Horizon-
Dependent Risk
Aversion

To explore the impact of horizon-dependent risk aversion on asset allocation, use the worksheet <HD RRA Optimal–Template> in the Chapter 05 Horizon Excel Outboxes.xls spreadsheet. Note that this program builds on the basic optimization from Chapter 3. As such, the spreadsheet can be built either from scratch using the template or by modifying the basic asset allocation spreadsheet. The template should appear as follows:

	A	B	C	D	E	F	G	H	I	J	K
7											
8	**Program**	**Objective**	Max	$E[\mu]-\lambda\sigma^2$						=	
9			λ								
10			T								
11											
12		**Variables**		R1000V	R1000G	R2000V	R2000G	EAFE	HY	Agg	Citi Gvt
13			ω								
14											
15		Constraints									
16			$\Sigma\omega$							=	
17											
18											
19		Where									
20			μ_ω								
21			$\sigma_\omega{}^2$								
22											
23	**Data**	**Statistics**									
24				R1000V	R1000G	R2000V	R2000G	EAFE	HY	Agg	Citi Gvt
25			μ	0.1005	0.1175	0.1019	0.1295	0.0975	0.0639	0.0510	0.0486
26			Ω	0.0212	0.0219	0.0196	0.0242	0.0137	0.0054	0.0012	0.0006
27				0.0219	0.0346	0.0219	0.0380	0.0181	0.0068	0.0012	0.0004
28				0.0196	0.0219	0.0278	0.0351	0.0138	0.0072	0.0005	0.0001
29				0.0242	0.0380	0.0351	0.0596	0.0216	0.0097	0.0001	−0.0001
30				0.0137	0.0181	0.0138	0.0216	0.0302	0.0046	0.0008	0.0013
31				0.0054	0.0068	0.0072	0.0097	0.0046	0.0056	0.0010	0.0005
32				0.0012	0.0012	0.0005	0.0001	0.0008	0.0010	0.0020	0.0009
33				0.0006	0.0004	0.0001	−0.0001	0.0013	0.0005	0.0009	0.0011

Objective: The objective remains to maximize utility where risk aversion is now a function of the horizon.

- In cell K8 enter =K20-D9*K21.
- The risk aversion is drawn from the <HD RRA> worksheet. In cell D9 enter =VLOOKUP(D10,B37:C66,2,FALSE).

The horizon is an input. The procedure will be to optimize starting with the 1-period problem, $T=1$, and working back to the 30-period problem. Note that this model does not require that we work backward through time. Instead the spreadsheet was developed to simplify creation of the spreadsheet for the recursive shortfall model, introduced in the next section, which does require working backward through time.

- In cell D10 enter 1.

Variables: The decision variables are the weights of the eight assets.

- In cells D13:K13 enter 0.125 to seed the optimization.

Constraints: The portfolio will have full-investment and no-short-sale constraints.

- In cell I16 enter =SUM(D13:K13).
- In cell K16 enter 1.

(continued)

(concluded)

- The no-short-sale constraint will be entered in the Solver menu.

  Where: The portfolio return and variance are defined as follows:

- In cell K20 enter =MMULT(D13:K13,TRANSPOSE(D$25:K$25)).
- In cell K21 enter =MMULT(D13:K13,MMULT(D$26:K$33,TRANSPOSE(D13:K13))).

  Note: These are range array formulas and require <CTRL><SHIFT><ENTER> when they are entered.
  Data: Sample summary statistics are provided in the template.
  Results: The weights are translated into the portfolio summary statistics.

- In cell C37 enter =VLOOKUP(B37,'HD RRA'!$B$17:$I$46,8,FALSE).
- In cell L37 enter =M37-C37*N37.
- In cell M37 enter =MMULT(D37:K37,TRANSPOSE(D$25:K$25)).
- In cell N37 enter =MMULT(D37:K37,MMULT(D$26:K$33,TRANSPOSE(D37:K37))).
- In cell O37 enter =SUM(D37:K37).
- In cell P37 enter =NORMDIST(0,(M37-0.5*N37)*B37,SQRT(N37*B37),TRUE).
- In cell Q37 enter =SUM(D37:H37).

Copy row 37 down to row 66.
In the Solver menu,

- Set target cell: $K$8.
- Equal to: max.
- By changing cells: $D$13:K13.
- Subject to these constraints:

I16 = K16.
D13:K13 >=0.

Solve to calculate the optimal weights for $T = 1$, and then copy the solution to D66:K66. Repeat for $T = 2, 30$, copying the results to the appropriate row. *Note:* Due to the input sensitivity of MV, your results may vary.

	A	B	C	D	E	F	G	H	I	J	K	L	M	N	O	P	Q
35	Results	T	λ					ω				$E[\mu]-\lambda\sigma^2$	μ_ω	σ_ω^2	$\Sigma\omega$	Pr(<H)	$\Sigma\omega$(equity)
36				R1000V	R1000G	R2000V	R2000G	EAFE	HY	Agg	Citi Gvt						
37		30	1.2614	0.3556	0.3496	0.0185	0.0881	0.1882	0.0000	0.0000	0.0000	0.0789	0.1085	0.0234	1.0000	0.0003	1.0000
38		29	1.2637	0.3554	0.3489	0.0216	0.0854	0.1886	0.0000	0.0000	0.0000	0.0788	0.1084	0.0234	1.0000	0.0003	1.0000
39		28	1.2664	0.3516	0.3507	0.0287	0.0792	0.1898	0.0000	0.0000	0.0000	0.0788	0.1082	0.0233	1.0000	0.0004	1.0000
40		27	1.2698	0.3526	0.3484	0.0324	0.0758	0.1908	0.0000	0.0000	0.0000	0.0787	0.1081	0.0231	1.0000	0.0005	1.0000
41		26	1.2738	0.3465	0.3521	0.0420	0.0676	0.1918	0.0000	0.0000	0.0000	0.0786	0.1079	0.0230	1.0000	0.0006	1.0000
42		25	1.2787	0.3476	0.3492	0.0456	0.0642	0.1934	0.0000	0.0000	0.0000	0.0785	0.1078	0.0229	1.0000	0.0007	0.9906
43		24	1.2846	0.3427	0.3472	0.0477	0.0611	0.1918	0.0000	0.0094	0.0000	0.0784	0.1072	0.0225	1.0000	0.0009	0.9785
44		23	1.2917	0.3354	0.3441	0.0508	0.0589	0.1892	0.0000	0.0215	0.0000	0.0782	0.1065	0.0219	1.0000	0.0010	0.9654
45		22	1.3003	0.3284	0.3401	0.0528	0.0569	0.1871	0.0000	0.0346	0.0000	0.0780	0.1057	0.0214	1.0000	0.0011	0.9505
46		21	1.3108	0.3216	0.3349	0.0541	0.0553	0.1846	0.0000	0.0495	0.0000	0.0777	0.1049	0.0207	1.0000	0.0013	0.9334
47		20	1.3236	0.3151	0.3280	0.0541	0.0545	0.1817	0.0000	0.0666	0.0000	0.0774	0.1039	0.0200	1.0000	0.0015	0.9142
48		19	1.3391	0.3086	0.3195	0.0532	0.0545	0.1784	0.0000	0.0858	0.0000	0.0770	0.1028	0.0192	1.0000	0.0017	0.8925
49		18	1.3580	0.3012	0.3099	0.0531	0.0535	0.1748	0.0040	0.1035	0.0000	0.0766	0.1016	0.0184	1.0000	0.0019	0.8678
50		17	1.3811	0.2933	0.3007	0.0503	0.0532	0.1702	0.0078	0.1245	0.0000	0.0761	0.1003	0.0175	1.0000	0.0022	0.8408
51		16	1.4094	0.2840	0.2901	0.0491	0.0520	0.1656	0.0129	0.1462	0.0000	0.0755	0.0988	0.0166	1.0000	0.0024	0.8117
52		15	1.4441	0.2734	0.2781	0.0490	0.0502	0.1609	0.0186	0.1697	0.0000	0.0748	0.0972	0.0155	1.0000	0.0027	0.7795
53		14	1.4867	0.2624	0.2662	0.0467	0.0490	0.1552	0.0244	0.1962	0.0000	0.0739	0.0954	0.0145	1.0000	0.0030	0.7450
54		13	1.5393	0.2504	0.2529	0.0454	0.0472	0.1491	0.0308	0.2243	0.0000	0.0730	0.0936	0.0134	1.0000	0.0034	0.7076
55		12	1.6043	0.2376	0.2379	0.0436	0.0457	0.1428	0.0379	0.2545	0.0000	0.0719	0.0915	0.0122	1.0000	0.0037	0.6678
56		11	1.6850	0.2264	0.2204	0.0390	0.0459	0.1360	0.0461	0.2860	0.0001	0.0707	0.0894	0.0111	1.0000	0.0042	0.6257
57		10	1.7857	0.2112	0.2069	0.0383	0.0432	0.1262	0.0491	0.2778	0.0473	0.0693	0.0869	0.0099	1.0000	0.0046	0.5820
58		9	1.9120	0.1955	0.1928	0.0375	0.0404	0.1158	0.0517	0.2660	0.1003	0.0677	0.0844	0.0087	1.0000	0.0051	0.5368
59		8	2.0713	0.1791	0.1783	0.0369	0.0374	0.1051	0.0544	0.2538	0.1550	0.0660	0.0818	0.0076	1.0000	0.0057	0.4905
60		7	2.2740	0.1623	0.1636	0.0362	0.0343	0.0941	0.0572	0.2414	0.2109	0.0642	0.0791	0.0065	1.0000	0.0065	0.4437
61		6	2.5346	0.1450	0.1489	0.0359	0.0308	0.0831	0.0602	0.2289	0.2673	0.0623	0.0763	0.0055	1.0000	0.0077	0.3971
62		5	2.8744	0.1265	0.1352	0.0371	0.0265	0.0718	0.0617	0.2151	0.3261	0.0602	0.0736	0.0046	1.0000	0.0097	0.3500
63		4	3.3261	0.1094	0.1202	0.0364	0.0234	0.0606	0.0644	0.2023	0.3834	0.0580	0.0708	0.0038	1.0000	0.0132	0.3028
64		3	3.9441	0.0924	0.1051	0.0357	0.0202	0.0494	0.0671	0.1896	0.4406	0.0556	0.0681	0.0032	1.0000	0.0201	0.2551
65		2	4.8326	0.0751	0.0899	0.0351	0.0170	0.0380	0.0698	0.1766	0.4984	0.0530	0.0653	0.0025	1.0000	0.0364	0.2032
66		1	6.2500	0.0563	0.0733	0.0343	0.0136	0.0257	0.0728	0.1626	0.5614	0.0497	0.0623	0.0020	1.0000	0.0856	
67		0															

Horizon-Dependent Risk and Return

In Section 4.3 of Chapter 4 we introduced the distinction between conditional and unconditional means and variances. The main difference is that conditional means and variances change over time as new information that is useful in predicting future returns becomes available. Unconditional means and variances are long-run parameters that do not change as information arrives. For investment purposes we want to use all available information to refine our risk–return estimates. Therefore we should focus on conditional rather than unconditional parameters.

There are a variety of ways to model changes in conditional means and variances over time. The previous chapter illustrated a regime-switching model and a simple mean reversion model. In this section we generalize the mean reversion model to encompass multiple asset classes and additional variables that help predict future returns.

In the simple mean reversion model, logarithmic returns were assumed to follow a simple time series process that can be written as the two-variable system

$$r_{t+1} = \alpha - \theta y_t + \varepsilon_{t+1}$$

$$y_{t+1} = (1 - \theta)y_t + \varepsilon_{t+1}$$
(5.4)

where r_{t+1} is the return on the asset over the coming period, y_t is a variable that captures the predictable component of returns, α and θ are constants, and ε_{t+1} is the normally distributed random component of the return. This is an example of a multivariate process known as a **vector autoregression** of order one (VAR1).

Equation (5.4) has a very special structure. There is only one asset return (r_{t+1}), only one explanatory variable (y_t), and only one source of uncertainty (ε_{t+1}). Because there is only one source of uncertainty, r_{t+1} and y_{t+1} are perfectly correlated. In addition, notice that while y_t appears on the right side of each equation, r_t does not appear on the right side of either equation. Thus the past return, r_t, conveys no information that is not already captured by y_t. This should not be surprising because they are perfectly correlated.

In the next section we will take advantage of the special structure of Equation (5.4) to keep our DP application as simple as possible. For present purposes, however, we want to generalize the model to allow multiple assets and multiple explanatory variables that are not all perfectly correlated.

A more general VAR1 model can be written as

$$x_{t+1} = \Theta_0 + \Theta_1 x_t + \varepsilon_{t+1}$$
(5.5)

where x_{t+1} is a vector of asset returns and explanatory variables, Θ_0 is a constant vector, Θ_1 is a square matrix, and ε_{t+1} is now a vector of normally distributed random elements with zero means. To restate Equation (5.4) in this matrix notation, we would define

$$x_t = \begin{pmatrix} r_t \\ y_t \end{pmatrix} \qquad \Theta_0 = \begin{pmatrix} \alpha \\ 0 \end{pmatrix} \qquad \Theta_1 = \begin{pmatrix} 0 & -\theta \\ 0 & (1-\theta) \end{pmatrix}$$

Examination of Equation (5.5) shows that the vector x_t embodies all the useful information that is available at time t. This information is referred to as the "state of the world," and the variables in x_t are called *state variables*. As we will see, this simple model can generate interesting and complex patterns of risk and return. For now we will focus on conditional risk—standard deviations and correlations—leaving the impact of state-dependent expected returns until our application of DP.

Exhibits 5.3 through 5.6 reflect a VAR1 system estimated by Campbell and Viceira (2005) using quarterly data. The model is described in Appendix 1. There are three assets (stocks, constant-maturity five-year bonds, and T-bills) and three additional state variables (the nominal T-bill rate, the log dividend yield on stocks, and the yield spread between five-year zero-coupon bonds and T-bills). The original system was developed in terms of real return differentials among the assets. However, because the system presented in Equation (5.5) is linear, it can be transformed so we can study the risk structure of both real and nominal (logarithmic) returns for each asset.

The distinction between real and nominal returns raises two issues. First, we need to distinguish between the "real return on nominal assets" and "assets that pay a real return." Almost all financial assets are "nominal" in that their prices, cash flows, and returns are not explicitly linked to, or adjusted for, inflation. The real return on these assets is simply the return after subtracting inflation. There are, however, a few financial assets whose returns are explicitly linked to, or adjusted for, inflation. The most important of these are inflation-protected bonds such as Treasury Inflation-Protected Securities (TIPS) in the United States. TIPS offer near certainty with respect to their real return if held to maturity. In real terms they may be viewed as a riskless asset. In nominal terms, however, they are risky because their nominal return depends on realized inflation. The situation is reversed for nominal Treasury bonds: They are riskless (if held to maturity) in nominal terms but risky in real terms.

The second issue regarding real versus nominal returns relates to our investment objective. Should we focus on risk and return in real or nominal terms? The answer depends on the nature of the investor's implicit and explicit liabilities. In most instances the investor is implicitly trying to fund a stream of future real expenditures. This is usually the dominant consideration for individual investors. On the other hand, most explicit liabilities are defined in nominal terms. This would tend to be the dominant consideration for a defined benefit (DB) pension fund with a high ratio of retirees to current workers. Of course this depends on the nature of the promise made to the beneficiaries. In most instances the explicit promise is in nominal terms. However, some plans have cost-of-living adjustments. Alternatively, the sponsor firm may believe it has an implicit obligation to protect the retirees' standard of living. In that case the DB plan would focus on real rather than nominal returns.

Exhibits 5.3 through 5.6 show the risk characteristics of asset returns over horizons out to 120 quarters (30 years). Keep in mind that no model fully captures reality; nor is the system presented unique. Rather, it is presented as an example of a structure that can provide insights into how investment opportunities change through time based on currently available information. A different structure or different variables would demonstrate different return dynamics. Before examining the exhibits it is useful to review what we should expect to see. If all elements of the matrix Θ_1 were zero, we would be back in the world of constant investment opportunities. As shown in Chapter 3, the variance of multiperiod returns would be proportional to the horizon and the correlation among assets would be the same at all horizons. That is, if we graph variance per period or correlation versus horizon we would get a flat line. Because the square root of a constant is also constant, the same is true if we graph standard deviations instead of variances. Deviations from this pattern arise from the propagation of *shocks* (the ε) through the state variables (x) to subsequent values of the state variables through the matrix Θ_1. Over a T-period horizon there will be T sets of shocks ($\varepsilon_{t+i}, i = 1, \ldots, T$) that will each affect all subsequent values of x. As a result, the variances, standard deviations, and correlations of multiperiod returns reflect a complex interaction between the variance–covariance matrix of the shocks and the coefficient matrix Θ_1.

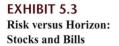

EXHIBIT 5.3
Risk versus Horizon:
Stocks and Bills

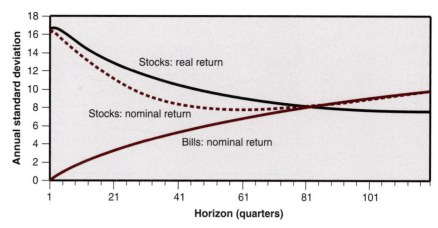

Exhibit 5.3 graphs the annualized standard deviations of real stock returns, nominal stock returns, and nominal T-bill returns. The volatility of real stock returns declines by roughly half and is still falling at 120 quarters. The volatility of nominal stock returns falls even faster initially but begins to rise for horizons beyond about 60 quarters. Stocks are clearly less risky, in terms of annualized volatility, over long horizons—especially in real terms. For T-bills the volatility of nominal returns is zero over a single period but increases sharply as the horizon extends. This reflects the fact that the nominal T-bill yield tracks inflation. According to the estimated model, shocks to inflation remain embedded in the level of future inflation for many periods. Therefore, inflation risk increases rapidly with longer horizons. Interestingly, the model indicates that at horizons beyond about 80 quarters the volatility of nominal returns is roughly equal for stocks and T-bills.

Are stocks a good hedge against inflation? According to this model, real stock returns are more volatile than nominal stock returns over short to intermediate horizons. For this to be true, the correlation between real stock returns and inflation must be strongly negative. That is, higher inflation tends to coincide with lower real stock returns. Thus stocks are not highly effective inflation hedges over short horizons. Over very long horizons, however, the model indicates that real stock returns are more stable than nominal stock returns, implying that stocks are a better inflation hedge over very long horizons.

The volatilities of real bond returns, nominal bond returns, and real T-bill returns are shown in Exhibit 5.4. As with stock returns, real bond returns tend to exhibit negative correlation over time: On average high returns are followed by low returns and vice versa. Thus the volatility of real bond returns is lower at longer horizons. The volatility of nominal bond returns drops sharply at short horizons because the contemporaneous correlation between the real bond return and inflation is strongly negative. Beyond four quarters, however, the real bond return is positively correlated with inflation, and the volatility of nominal bond returns rises rapidly once the volatility of inflation exceeds the volatility of the real bond return.

It is interesting to note that at long horizons, like 30 years, both stocks and bonds seem to be good inflation hedges because their real returns are much more stable than their nominal returns. Indeed the differential is more pronounced for bonds than for stocks. This would not be surprising if we were dealing with inflation-protected bonds. However, these are nominally denominated bonds. We can resolve the apparent mystery by noting that these bonds have a constant five-year maturity. In effect, over horizons substantially longer than five years these are floating-rate bonds. The income component of return will tend to rise and fall with inflation and hence tend to stabilize the real return.

EXHIBIT 5.4
Risk versus Horizon:
Bonds and Bills

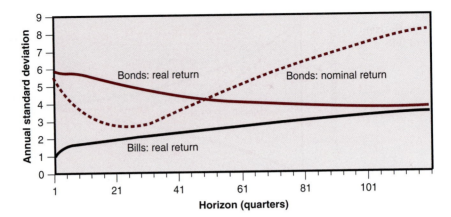

Next consider the correlation of asset returns at various horizons. Exhibit 5.5 shows the pairwise correlation of nominal returns. Clearly the common inflation component leads to strong positive correlation among all three asset classes at long horizons. Indeed the inflation component accounts for virtually all the correlation between stocks and the fixed-income instruments at long horizons because the correlation of their real returns is low. In nominal terms, bonds and bills are nearly perfectly correlated at long horizons because at sufficiently long horizons both are floating-rate instruments. Because nominal bill returns respond to inflation much more quickly than bond and stock returns, we get negative correlations at short horizons—very strongly so for bonds and bills.

The pattern of correlations among real returns shown in Exhibit 5.6 is difficult to interpret. The correlation between stocks and bonds starts low, rises to a high level at intermediate horizons, and then declines again at long horizons. Campbell and Viceira (2004) explain this pattern in terms of the impact of the nominal short rate at short to intermediate horizons and the impact of the dividend yield at long horizons. The other correlations are driven primarily by the dynamics of the nominal short rate.

It should be clear that investment decisions based on the risk structure illustrated in Exhibits 5.3 through 5.6 will be horizon-dependent and potentially quite different from decisions based on the assumption of constant investment opportunities. Both equities and constant-maturity bonds appear less risky over long horizons in real terms, but the impact is much larger for stocks. Hence we should expect to hold more stocks at long horizons. T-bills provide diversification and low risk only at short horizons. Beyond that they are probably dominated by bonds and stocks; this is especially true if we have a nominal rather than real return objective.

EXHIBIT 5.5
Correlation of
Nominal Returns

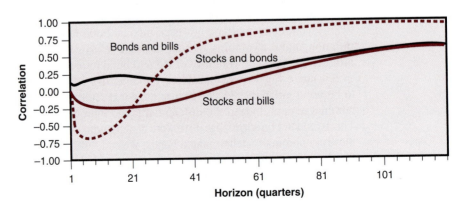

EXHIBIT 5.6
Correlation of Real
Returns

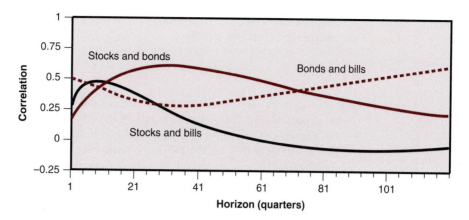

The constant-maturity bonds in the model discussed here may be viewed as a proxy for holding a fixed-income mutual fund. These funds are usually managed against a benchmark index that has a reasonably stable average maturity. The risk characteristics of a buy-and-hold portfolio of individual bonds would be quite different. For example, setting aside the risk of default, a zero-coupon bond held to maturity is riskless—in nominal terms if it is an ordinary bond, in real terms if it is inflation-protected. Similarly, coupon bonds are riskless, to a first approximation, over a horizon equal to their duration. The key point is that the role of bonds in an asset allocation depends on the nature of the bonds and how the bond portfolio will be managed. Depending on our horizon and whether our objectives are real or nominal, bonds may be quite safe or very risky.

5.3   Dynamic Programming

In the previous section we allowed asset allocation decisions to depend on the horizon either because risk preferences are affected by horizon or because the risk–return characteristics of available investments are horizon-specific. It was implicitly assumed, however, that the same portfolio would be chosen in each remaining period. That is, we did not allow our current strategy to reflect the decisions we would expect to make in the future under various scenarios. In effect, we assumed that the future will look like today even though we know it will not. We will now introduce a powerful framework, known as **dynamic programming (DP),** that allows us to incorporate future opportunities and decisions into our investment strategy. This is important because recognizing that we may, and probably will, change allocations in the future can help us make better decisions today.

The General Framework

Suppose the investor's objective is to maximize the satisfaction derived from a sequence of consumption expenditures $C_{t,T}$ from time t (now) to the horizon T and the wealth left at the end of the investment horizon, W_T. As in the previous section, we will denote the state of the world, including the investment opportunities, by x_t. The state of the world may include information that is specific to the investor's own history. The investor's problem is to choose a *portfolio policy function* $\omega(W_t, x_t, t)$ and a *consumption policy function* $c(W_t, x_t, t)$ to maximize the objective subject to relevant constraints. We need to emphasize that the optimal portfolio (the set of asset weights) and consumption policies are *functions* defining the optimal decisions for all possible combinations of time, wealth, and states of the world.

The first step in the DP framework is to define a **value function** $V(W_t, x_t, t)$ equal to the maximized objective at time t:

$$V(W_t, x_t, t) \equiv \max_{\omega, c} \; E_t \left[U(C_{t,T}, W_T) \right] \qquad (5.6)$$

The subscript on the expectations operator, E, indicates that $V(\cdot)$ reflects the conditional expectation of the objective based on information known at time t. It is a function of the state of the world at time t, wealth at time t, and time.

The key insight that makes DP work is that we can solve the problem by recursively working backward, period by period from the end of the investment horizon to the present. The objective at each step is to maximize the expected value of the next period's value function. When we have determined the optimal investment policy, consumption policy, and value functions at some time S we step back to time $S - 1$ to solve the problem

$$V(W_{S-1}, x_{S-1}, S - 1) \equiv \max_{\omega, c} \; E_{S-1} \left[V(W_S, x_S, S) \right] \qquad (5.7)$$

The process continues in this fashion until we reach the current period, often denoted as $t = 0$. Then (and only then) can we determine the best policies for the coming period.

In principle DP ought to be the framework of choice for asset allocation decisions; but it is difficult to apply to realistic problems. At each step we must determine policy functions encompassing all possible combinations of wealth, state variables, and time; this is a complex task even for relatively simple problems. For more complex problems we can use various approximation techniques. However, direct application of DP remains primarily in the realm of theory and research. It is not, yet, a mainstay of the practitioner's toolbox—but it can still help us make better asset allocation decisions. A qualitative understanding of DP can help us improve our pragmatic approaches to realistic asset allocation problems. And simple applications can show us the impact of relaxing the assumptions underlying the standard M–V model. In fact DP techniques are applied here to solve dynamic problems important for horizon-based investing.

In the rest of this section we present two DP applications. The first applies the logic of DP within the M–V framework to incorporate a shortfall constraint. We did this in Chapter 3 under the implicit assumption that we must hold the same portfolio in every period. Here we explicitly allow for the fact that we can choose a different portfolio depending on the time remaining to our horizon—that is, we allow the portfolio policy to be horizon-dependent. In this application, however, we do not allow the policy to depend on the state of the world or the investor's current wealth. So while we use the logic of DP to improve our model, it is not a full-blown application of DP. The second example incorporates the simple mean reversion model of the stock market studied in Chapter 4 into the asset allocation problem. This full-blown application of DP focuses on how stochastic investment opportunities affect the portfolio policy—but it is much more difficult to solve.

Mean–Variance with Recursive Shortfall Constraints

In this subsection we generalize the M–V model by allowing the impact of shortfall risk to induce different optimal portfolios depending on the remaining investment horizon. This demonstrates another practical method of building in horizon effects. It also illustrates the technique of DP in a simple model and serves as a transition to the full-blown DP application in which the optimal policy depends not only on horizon but also on the state of the world.

We generalize the notation of Chapter 3 slightly but retain the assumption made there that investment opportunities are lognormal and **independently and identically distributed (i.i.d.).**[1]

Let

$$\alpha(t,T) \equiv \sum_{i=0}^{T-t-1} \alpha(t+i) = \alpha(t) + \alpha(t+1,T) \qquad (5.8)$$

denote the expected log return on our portfolio over the remaining horizon as of time t. Because we are working with log returns, this is simply the sum of the expected log returns in each remaining period. Of course each expected return depends on the portfolio we select in that period. That is why we must work backward, determining our future investment policies before we can decide what to do today. The right side of Equation (5.8) shows that we can break the expected return over the remaining horizon into two parts: the expected return over the next period, $\alpha(t)$, and the expected return over all the subsequent periods. This recursive separation will be useful below.

Similarly, let

$$v(t,T) \equiv \sum_{i=0}^{T-t-1} \sigma^2(t+i) = \sigma^2(t) + v(t+1,T) \qquad (5.9)$$

denote the variance of our portfolio's log return over the remaining horizon. As with the mean, the variance is the sum of the variances in each future period and depends on our future portfolio decisions.[2] The right side of Equation (5.9) shows that we can separate the variance over the remaining horizon into two parts: the variance in the next period and the variance over all subsequent periods combined.

We will also need the log of the expected gross return. As before, we denote this with the Greek letter μ. For the remaining horizon, we can define

$$\mu(t,T) \equiv \alpha(t,T) + \tfrac{1}{2} v(t,T) = \mu(t) + \mu(t+1,T) \qquad (5.10)$$

The last equality follows from Equations (5.8) and (5.9).

We can now rewrite expected utility (Equation (3.16)) as

$$(1/\gamma) \ \exp\left[\gamma\big(\mu(t,T) - \tfrac{1}{2}(1-\gamma)\,v(t,T)\big)\right] \qquad (5.11)$$

In terms of the general DP framework, Equation (5.11) becomes the value function for this model once we substitute the values of $\mu(t,T)$ and $v(t,T)$ implied by the optimal portfolio policy. Using Equations (5.9) and (5.10), we can factor this into two

[1] Note that investment opportunities were not independently and identically distributed in the VAR1 model studied in Section (5.2). There the correlation of returns through time gave rise to the horizon dependence of risk.

[2] If we allowed asset returns to be correlated across periods, Equation (5.9) would also involve these correlations. Given our assumption that returns are i.i.d., however, all such terms disappear, leaving just the sum of each period's portfolio variance.

parts—one reflecting today's decisions embodied in $\mu(t)$ and $\sigma^2(t)$ and one reflecting future decisions embodied in $\mu(t + 1,T)$ and $v(t + 1,T)$.

$$(1/\gamma)\,\exp\left[\gamma\big(\mu(t) - \tfrac{1}{2}\,(1 - \gamma)\,\sigma^2(t)\big)\right] * \qquad \textbf{(5.12)}$$
$$\exp\left[\gamma\big(\mu(t + 1,T) - \tfrac{1}{2}\,(1 - \gamma)\,v(t + 1,T)\big)\right]$$

Because investment opportunities are i.i.d. and we are not allowing future portfolio policies to be state-dependent, the second exponential term of the objective function is not affected by, and in turn does not affect, today's investment decisions. So the objective in each period is to maximize the first term. This is equivalent to maximizing the single-period M–V objective $[\mu(t) - 1/2\,(1 - \gamma)\,\sigma^2(t)]$.

The recursive aspect of the problem enters when we incorporate the shortfall constraint. Equation (3.18) can be rewritten as

$$N(H,(\mu(t,T) - 1/2\,v(t,T)),v(t,T)) \leq K \qquad \textbf{(5.13)}$$

H is the threshold level of log return [= 0 if the test is losing money] between today, t, and the horizon, T. K is the acceptable shortfall probability (such as 5 percent). At time t the shortfall probability will depend on the portfolio policies to be followed in the remaining periods. The more conservative we will be later, the more aggressive we can be today. Therefore, at any given date the optimal policy will be at least as aggressive (and usually more) as it would be if we were forced to maintain the same policy over all remaining periods.

To solve this problem, we start at time $T - 1$—that is, with one period to go. Given the values of $\mu(T - 1)$ and $\sigma^2(T - 1)$ implied by the optimal policy at that time, we step back to time $T - 2$ and repeat the optimization. Then we step back to $T - 3$, $T - 4$, ... until we reach the current time t.

In general, it will turn out that the shortfall constraint is binding for horizons less than or equal to some number of periods n_b and nonbinding for all longer horizons. As a result, the optimal portfolio is constant for horizons longer than n_b.

EXHIBIT 5.7 **Recursive Shortfall**

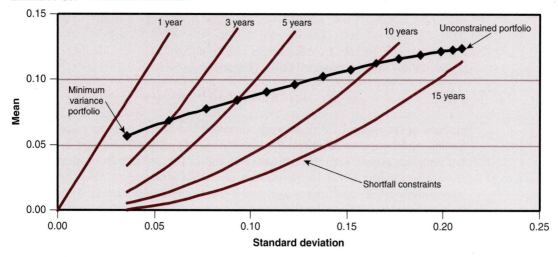

Exhibit 5.7 illustrates the solution process. Because investment opportunities are the same in each period, the efficient frontier—that is, the highest expected return for a given level of standard deviation—is also the same in each period. This is shown as the black upward-sloping curve in the exhibit. The other curves represent the shortfall constraints for various remaining investment horizons. For a given horizon, risk–return combinations below and to the right of the curve do not satisfy the shortfall constraint and are not feasible for that horizon.

The shortfall constraint moves down and to the right as the horizon increases; higher-risk portfolios become feasible as the horizon increases. Because each shortfall constraint depends on the portfolios that will be chosen at each shorter horizon, we must work backward from the last period (that is, with one period remaining) to the present.

At each date we want to select a portfolio that lies on the efficient frontier. (Why?) We also want to satisfy the relevant shortfall constraint. In general, the optimal portfolio for a given horizon will lie at the intersection of the efficient frontier and the shortfall constraint.

The exhibit shows a case in which it is not possible to satisfy the shortfall constraint for very short horizons: The minimum variance portfolio lies below and to the right of the shortfall constraint for the one-year horizon. One approach would be to specify a higher shortfall probability. Alternatively, we could assume that the minimum variance portfolio (MVP) is selected for horizons where the shortfall constraint cannot be satisfied. Given this choice for the one-year horizon, the shortfall constraint cannot be satisfied for the two-year horizon either. Knowing that the MVP will be selected in the last two periods, we see that the shortfall constraint *can* be satisfied for the three-year horizon, allowing us to move up the efficient frontier to the next point shown. With four years remaining we move up to the next point shown and so on until, with 15 years remaining, we reach the point labeled "unconstrained portfolio," and the shortfall constraint becomes nonbinding. Given the investor's risk aversion, this is the portfolio the investor would choose in the absence of the shortfall constraint. Because the shortfall constraint will not be binding, this same portfolio will be selected at all longer horizons.

Working backward from the shortest investment horizon, the optimal investment policy walks *up* the efficient frontier, getting more aggressive as the horizon extends. The reverse occurs when the investor actually implements the policy. Starting with a long horizon, the investor walks *down* the efficient frontier, adopting more conservative positions as the remaining horizon gets shorter.

It is instructive to consider what would happen if we allowed future investment decisions to depend on the investor's wealth at that future time. Then the outcome of today's investment decisions would affect future decisions. Favorable outcomes—that is, high wealth—would reduce the probability of a shortfall over the remaining horizon and hence allow more aggressive policies in the future. Unfavorable outcomes would require even more conservative portfolios in the future to limit the risk of shortfall. As a result, the impact of current decisions on future decisions would have to be considered in making today's decisions, and it would no longer be optimal to select portfolios on the M–V efficient frontier. Because points above the efficient frontier would not be feasible, the investor's optimal portfolio at each date would lie below the frontier; that is, it would be inefficient from a single-period M–V perspective.

Theory in Practice
Designing a Target Horizon Fund

Whose shortfall is it? If we are managing money for one investor, it is clear whose wealth should be incorporated into portfolio decisions. In the case of a mutual fund, however, it is not so clear. Shareholders' experiences in the fund, such as whether they experience shortfalls, will depend on when they bought into the fund. Each investor's *history* in the fund is unique, but all current shareholders share the same *future* if they hold the fund to the horizon date. At least one large investment firm has incorporated this fact into the recursive shortfall framework outlined here to develop its horizon-based retirement mutual funds. At each point in time, the shortfall constraint is based on protecting against losses over the remaining horizon. In effect, the strategy always adopts the perspective of a new investor looking to protect his or her initial investment.

Excel Outbox
Recursive Asset
Allocation

A simple recursive dynamic programming asset allocation is examined using the worksheet <Recursive PS–Template> in the Chapter 05 Excel Outboxes.xls spreadsheet. The template should appear as follows:

	A	B	C	D	E	F	G	H	I	J	K
7											
8	**Program**	**Objective**	Max	$E[\mu]-\lambda\sigma^2$						=	
9			λ								
10			T								
11											
12		**Variables**		R1000V	R1000G	R2000V	R2000G	EAFE	HY	Agg	Citi Gvt
13			ω								
14											
15		Constraints									
16			$\Sigma\omega$							=	
17			$Pr(\leq H)$							$\leq$	
18											
19		Where									
20			Current	μ_ω							
21				σ_ω^2							
22			Cumulative	μ_ω							
23				σ_ω^2							
24											
25	**Data**	**Statistics**			R1000V	R1000G	R2000V	R2000G	EAFE	HY	Agg	Citi Gvt
26											
27			μ	0.1005	0.1175	0.1019	0.1295	0.0975	0.0639	0.0510	0.0486
28			Ω	0.0212	0.0219	0.0196	0.0242	0.0137	0.0054	0.0012	0.0006
29				0.0219	0.0346	0.0219	0.0380	0.0181	0.0068	0.0012	0.0004
30				0.0196	0.0219	0.0278	0.0351	0.0138	0.0072	0.0005	0.0001
31				0.0242	0.0380	0.0351	0.0596	0.0216	0.0097	0.0001	-0.0001
32				0.0137	0.0181	0.0138	0.0216	0.0302	0.0046	0.0008	0.0013
33				0.0054	0.0068	0.0072	0.0097	0.0046	0.0056	0.0010	0.0005
34				0.0012	0.0012	0.0005	0.0001	0.0008	0.0010	0.0020	0.0009
35				0.0006	0.0004	0.0001	-0.0001	0.0013	0.0005	0.0009	0.0011
36											

Objective: The objective remains to maximize utility.

- In cell K8 enter = K20-D9*K21.
- The risk aversion is given as 1.25. In cell D9 enter 1.25.

- The horizon is an input. The procedure will be to optimize starting with the 1-period problem, $T = 1$, and working back to the 30-period problem. In cell D10 enter 1.

  Variables: The decision variables are the weights of the eight assets.

- In cells D13:K13 enter 0.125 to seed the optimization.

  Constraints: The portfolio will be subject to full-investment, no-short-sale, and shortfall constraints.

- In cell I16 enter =SUM(D13:K13).
- In cell K16 enter 1.
- The 100 percent investment and no-short-sale constraints will be entered in the Solver menu. Add I16 = K16 and D13:K13>=0 as constraints.
- In cell I17 enter =NORMDIST(0,(K20 + K22-0.5*(K21 + K23)),SQRT(K21 + K23),TRUE).
- In cell K17 enter 0.01.

Note: Solve for the minimum variance portfolio (MVP) before adding the shortfall constraint to the Solver program.

Where: The current period portfolio return and variance are defined as follows:

- In cell K20 enter =MMULT(D13:K13,TRANSPOSE(D$27:K$27)).
- In cell K21 enter =MMULT(D13:K13,MMULT(D$28:K$35,TRANSPOSE(D13:K13))).

Note: These are range array formulas and require <CTRL><SHIFT><ENTER> when they are entered.

The cumulative return and risk for future periods are pulled from the results of prior optimizations:

- In cell K22 enter =VLOOKUP($D$10-1,$B$39:$O$69,13,FALSE).
- In cell K23 enter =VLOOKUP($D$10-1,$B$39:$O$69,14,FALSE).

Data: The summary statistics are the same as those displayed in <HD RRA Optimal> and are provided.

Results: The weights are translated into the portfolio summary statistics.

- In cell K39 enter =L39-$D$9*M39.
- In cell L39 enter =MMULT(C39:J39,TRANSPOSE(D$27:K$27)).
- In cell M39 enter =MMULT(C39:J39,MMULT(D$28:K$35,TRANSPOSE(C39:J39))).
- In cell N39 enter =N40 + L39.
- In cell O39 enter =O40 + M39.
- In cell P39 enter =SUM(C39:J39).
- In cell Q39 enter =NORMDIST(0,N39-0.5*O39,SQRT(O39),TRUE).
- In cell R39 enter =SUM(C39:G39).
- Copy cells K39:R39 to cells K40:R68.

	A	B	C	D	E	F	G	H	I	J	K	L	M	N	O	P	Q	R
37	Results		T				ω				$E[\mu]-\lambda\sigma^2$	Current		Cumulative		$\Sigma\omega$	Pr(<H)	$\Sigma\omega$(equity)
38			R1000V	R1000G	R2000V	R2000G	EAFE	HY	Agg	Citi Gvt		μ_ω	σ_ω^2	μ_ω	σ_ω^2			

First define the MVP. In the Solver menu

- Set target cell: K21.
- Equal to: min.
- Copy weights to C68:J68.

Solve to calculate the optimal weights for $T = 2$ through 30, copying the results to the appropriate row.

(continued)

(concluded)

- Enter 2 in cell D10.

  In the Solver menus

- Set target cell: $K$8.
- Equal to: max.
- Add constraint: $I$17≤ $K$17.

After running the Solver, note whether a solution was found satisfying all the constraints. If so, accept the solution and paste the results from row 13 to row 67. If not, copy the MVP from row 68 to row 67. Repeat with the value 3 in cell D10 and continue running the Solver, checking for a valid solution, and pasting the results (or the MVP), up to $T = 30$ in cell D10. The completed table should appear as follows:

| | | | | | | | ω | | | $E[\mu]-\lambda\sigma^2$ | Current | | Cumulative | | $\Sigma\omega$ | Pr(<H) | $\Sigma\omega$(equity) |
Results	T	R1000V	R1000G	R2000V	R2000G	EAFE	HY	Agg	Citi Gvt		μ_ω	σ_ω^2	μ_ω	σ_ω^2			
	30	0.3556	0.3496	0.0185	0.0881	0.1882	0.0000	0.0000	0.0000	0.0792	0.1085	0.0234	3.0000	0.5775	1.0000	0.0002	1.0000
	29	0.3556	0.3496	0.0185	0.0881	0.1882	0.0000	0.0000	0.0000	0.0792	0.1085	0.0234	2.8915	0.5541	1.0000	0.0002	1.0000
	28	0.3556	0.3496	0.0185	0.0881	0.1882	0.0000	0.0000	0.0000	0.0792	0.1085	0.0234	2.7831	0.5306	1.0000	0.0003	1.0000
	27	0.3556	0.3496	0.0185	0.0881	0.1882	0.0000	0.0000	0.0000	0.0792	0.1085	0.0234	2.6746	0.5072	1.0000	0.0003	1.0000
	26	0.3556	0.3496	0.0185	0.0881	0.1882	0.0000	0.0000	0.0000	0.0792	0.1085	0.0234	2.5661	0.4837	1.0000	0.0004	1.0000
	25	0.3556	0.3496	0.0185	0.0881	0.1882	0.0000	0.0000	0.0000	0.0792	0.1085	0.0234	2.4577	0.4603	1.0000	0.0005	1.0000
	24	0.3556	0.3496	0.0185	0.0881	0.1882	0.0000	0.0000	0.0000	0.0792	0.1085	0.0234	2.3492	0.4369	1.0000	0.0006	1.0000
	23	0.3556	0.3496	0.0185	0.0881	0.1882	0.0000	0.0000	0.0000	0.0792	0.1085	0.0234	2.2407	0.4134	1.0000	0.0008	1.0000
	22	0.3556	0.3496	0.0185	0.0881	0.1882	0.0000	0.0000	0.0000	0.0792	0.1085	0.0234	2.1323	0.3900	1.0000	0.0010	1.0000
	21	0.3556	0.3496	0.0185	0.0881	0.1882	0.0000	0.0000	0.0000	0.0792	0.1085	0.0234	2.0238	0.3666	1.0000	0.0012	1.0000
	20	0.3556	0.3496	0.0185	0.0881	0.1882	0.0000	0.0000	0.0000	0.0792	0.1085	0.0234	1.9153	0.3431	1.0000	0.0015	1.0000
	19	0.3556	0.3496	0.0185	0.0881	0.1882	0.0000	0.0000	0.0000	0.0792	0.1085	0.0234	1.8069	0.3197	1.0000	0.0018	1.0000
	18	0.3556	0.3496	0.0185	0.0881	0.1882	0.0000	0.0000	0.0000	0.0792	0.1085	0.0234	1.6984	0.2963	1.0000	0.0022	1.0000
	17	0.3556	0.3496	0.0185	0.0881	0.1882	0.0000	0.0000	0.0000	0.0792	0.1085	0.0234	1.5899	0.2728	1.0000	0.0027	1.0000
	16	0.3556	0.3496	0.0185	0.0881	0.1882	0.0000	0.0000	0.0000	0.0792	0.1085	0.0234	1.4815	0.2494	1.0000	0.0033	1.0000
	15	0.3556	0.3496	0.0185	0.0881	0.1882	0.0000	0.0000	0.0000	0.0792	0.1085	0.0234	1.3730	0.2260	1.0000	0.0040	1.0000
	14	0.3556	0.3496	0.0185	0.0881	0.1882	0.0000	0.0000	0.0000	0.0792	0.1085	0.0234	1.2646	0.2025	1.0000	0.0049	1.0000
	13	0.3556	0.3496	0.0185	0.0881	0.1882	0.0000	0.0000	0.0000	0.0792	0.1085	0.0234	1.1561	0.1791	1.0000	0.0059	1.0000
	12	0.3556	0.3496	0.0185	0.0881	0.1882	0.0000	0.0000	0.0000	0.0792	0.1085	0.0234	1.0476	0.1556	1.0000	0.0070	1.0000
	11	0.3556	0.3496	0.0185	0.0881	0.1882	0.0000	0.0000	0.0000	0.0792	0.1085	0.0234	0.9392	0.1322	1.0000	0.0082	1.0000
	10	0.3556	0.3496	0.0185	0.0881	0.1882	0.0000	0.0000	0.0000	0.0792	0.1085	0.0234	0.8307	0.1088	1.0000	0.0093	1.0000
	9	0.3389	0.3486	0.0510	0.0593	0.1913	0.0000	0.0108	0.0000	0.0791	0.1071	0.0224	0.7222	0.0853	1.0000	0.0100	0.9892
	8	0.3043	0.3071	0.0465	0.0566	0.1738	0.0092	0.1025	0.0000	0.0786	0.1015	0.0183	0.6151	0.0629	1.0000	0.0100	0.8883
	7	0.2698	0.2623	0.0401	0.0538	0.1559	0.0270	0.1911	0.0000	0.0774	0.0957	0.0146	0.5136	0.0446	1.0000	0.0100	0.7819
	6	0.2246	0.2248	0.0423	0.0433	0.1366	0.0458	0.2827	0.0000	0.0756	0.0896	0.0112	0.4180	0.0300	1.0000	0.0100	0.6715
	5	0.1893	0.1923	0.0336	0.0356	0.1077	0.0639	0.2191	0.1584	0.0729	0.0831	0.0082	0.3284	0.0188	1.0000	0.0100	0.5586
	4	0.1401	0.1530	0.0417	0.0268	0.0828	0.0586	0.2245	0.2726	0.0694	0.0763	0.0055	0.2453	0.0106	1.0000	0.0100	0.4443
	3	0.0913	0.1009	0.0335	0.0213	0.0476	0.0678	0.1892	0.4485	0.0638	0.0676	0.0030	0.1690	0.0051	1.0000	0.0100	0.2945
	2	0.0000	0.0000	0.0099	0.0000	0.0000	0.0832	0.1115	0.7955	0.0494	0.0507	0.0010	0.1014	0.0021	1.0000	0.0137	0.0099
	1	0.0000	0.0000	0.0099	0.0000	0.0000	0.0832	0.1115	0.7955	0.0494	0.0507	0.0010	0.0507	0.0010	1.0000	0.0595	0.0099
	0												0.0000	0.0000			

Note that the Solver may generate slightly different asset weights than those displayed here.

The Impact of Mean Reversion

Up to this point our discussion of portfolio strategy has not dealt directly with changing investment opportunities. We now address this important issue head-on.

It is probably obvious that over time we will want to shift toward asset classes that become more attractive and away from asset classes that become less attractive. Merely responding to current opportunities period by period is a **myopic** (near-sighted) **strategy** and, in general, is not the best we can do. The fundamental question is how we should incorporate uncertain future investment opportunities into our portfolio today. Appendix 2 extends our formal model to incorporate changing opportunities and applies DP to obtain the explicit solution. Before we examine the resulting portfolio policy, it is useful to develop some intuition about the problem.

Some Intuition about Changing Investment Opportunities

Let us assume that in each period there are only four possibilities: Realized investment returns are either high or low, and subsequent expected returns are either high or low. The situation is summarized in Exhibit 5.8. In quadrant I we realize a high return on

EXHIBIT 5.8
Current Return
versus Future
Opportunities

		Realized Return	
		High	Low
Future Expected Return	High	I	III
	Low	II	IV

our portfolio, and future expected returns are also high. If we end up here, our wealth will be relatively high and we will be able to reinvest it on attractive terms. Quadrant II has a high realized return but a low expected future return. Here our wealth will be high, but future opportunities are relatively poor. In quadrants III and IV our realized returns are low, so our wealth will also be relatively low. Our future opportunities will either be attractive (III) or unattractive (IV).

We can influence the likelihood of ending up in each of these quadrants by our current portfolio choice. Suppose we choose a portfolio that makes us likely to end up in either quadrant II or quadrant III. Then we will tend to have a lot of wealth to reinvest when opportunities are relatively unattractive, and little wealth to reinvest when opportunities are relatively attractive. Over time such a strategy tends to generate a relatively smooth accumulation of wealth because high (low) returns tend to be followed by low (high) returns. A strategy with a high probability of ending up in quadrants I and IV has the opposite effect. In this case high (low) returns tend to be followed by high (low) returns. Thus over time wealth is relatively volatile. Extreme levels of wealth at the investment horizon are much more likely under this strategy.

Which type of strategy should we follow? This depends on our risk aversion. Relatively risk-averse investors will tend to prefer hedging against adverse changes in investment opportunities by selecting a portfolio that is likely to lead to quadrants II and III. Relatively risk-tolerant investors will prefer to "speculate" on having a lot of wealth to reinvest when future opportunities are particularly attractive (quadrant I). Of course they risk having both little wealth and poor opportunities (quadrant IV). If some investors hedge and others speculate in response to changing investment opportunities, it should not be surprising that for investors whose level of risk aversion lies between these groups, it is best to do neither. That is, they follow the myopic strategy.

Portfolio Choice with Mean Reversion[3]

Armed with this intuition about how changing investment opportunities will affect the portfolio strategy, we can now extend the formal analysis we began in Chapter 3. A couple of simplifying assumptions help to keep things tractable. First, there are only two assets available: stocks and a riskless asset earning a logarithmic return r_f. Second, the only constraint on the investor's strategy is that portfolio weights sum to unity. That is, the investor may be long or short either asset in any amount, but all available funds (including short sale proceeds) must be invested.

The process generating stock returns is given by Equation (5.4). This is the simple mean reversion model studied in Chapter 4. Changes in investment opportunities are reflected in the state variable y_t. Positive (negative) values of y_t imply that the market price is above (below) its long-term trend and the expected return on the market is below (above) the trend return α.

---

[3] Our model is a discrete-time version of the slightly more general continuous-time model analyzed in Kim and Omberg (1996). The continuous-time model was used to generate Exhibits 5.9 through 5.11.

Using the constant relative risk aversion (CRRA) utility function given in Equation (3.3), Appendix 2 shows that the value function (as defined in Equation (5.6)) for this model takes the form

$$V(W_{t+1}, y_{t+1}, t+1) = \left(\frac{A_{t+1}}{\gamma} \right) W_{t+1}^{\gamma} \exp(\gamma\, B_{t+1}(y_{t+1})) \qquad (5.14)$$

where A_{t+1} does not depend on wealth (W_{t+1}) or the state variable (y_{t+1}) and B_{t+1} is a quadratic function of the state variable. At the horizon date T, $A_T = 1$ and $B_T = 0$ so that the value function is simply the underlying CRRA utility function of wealth. If investment opportunities are constant ($\theta = 0$ in Equation (5.4)), then B_{t+1} is identically zero for all t, and the current model reduces to the M–V model developed in Chapter 3.

The optimal portfolio policy takes the form

$$\omega(y_t, t) = m(y_t, t) - \gamma\, h(y_t, t) \qquad (5.15)$$

where $\omega(y_t, t)$ is the fraction of wealth invested in stocks. $m(y_t, t)$ is the myopic portfolio reflecting period-by-period optimization ignoring the relationship between current and future investment opportunities. $h(y_t, t)$ is the hedging component that reflects adjusting the portfolio to hedge against adverse changes in investment opportunities. In this model $h(y_t, t)$ is always nonnegative. Therefore, whether an investor holds more or less stock than the myopic portfolio depends only on the investor's risk aversion. Those with logarithmic utility ($\gamma = 0$) do not hedge. Those who are more risk averse ($\gamma < 0$) hedge by holding more stock. Those who are less risk averse ($0 < \gamma < 1$) actually speculate on future opportunities by holding less stock today. It may seem strange that mean reversion induces more risk-averse investors to hold more stock than they would otherwise and less risk-averse investors to do the opposite, but that is what is implied by the intuition we have just developed.

Before examining the optimal portfolio policy in more detail, it is useful to extend the model to include a minimum wealth target, W^*, at the horizon. Suppose the investor's objective exhibits constant relative risk aversion with respect to wealth above this minimum level ($W_T - W^*$). The previous results still hold if we replace wealth at time t, W_t, with "excess wealth" defined as $[W_t - W^*\exp(-r_f(T-t))]$. The optimal portfolio policy now calls for investing enough in the riskless asset to guarantee reaching the minimum wealth level at the horizon $[W^*\exp(-r_f(T-t))]$, investing a fraction $\omega(y_t, t)$ of excess wealth in stocks, and investing the remainder of excess wealth in the riskless asset. The total amounts invested in each of the assets are

$$\$\$ \text{ in stocks} = \omega(y_t, t)\left[W_t - W^* \exp(-r_f(T-t)) \right] \qquad (5.16)$$

$$\$\$ \text{ in riskless} = W_t - \omega(y_t, t)\left[W_t - W^* \exp(-r_f(T-t)) \right]$$

As we will discuss in Section 5.6, if ω is a constant greater than 1, this strategy is known as *constant proportional portfolio insurance* (CPPI). Of course in the present model ω is not constant unless investment opportunities are also constant ($\theta = 0$).

Exhibits 5.9 through 5.11 illustrate the behavior of the optimal fraction invested in stocks for the three types of investors: more risk averse ($\gamma < 0$), logarithmic ($\gamma = 0$), and less risk averse ($0 < \gamma < 1$). As one would expect, the fraction invested in stocks increases as risk aversion declines and vice versa. That is, more risk-tolerant investors have a higher baseline demand for stocks. To highlight the impact of mean reversion

EXHIBIT 5.9
Mean Reversion
Model: Impact of
Risk Premium

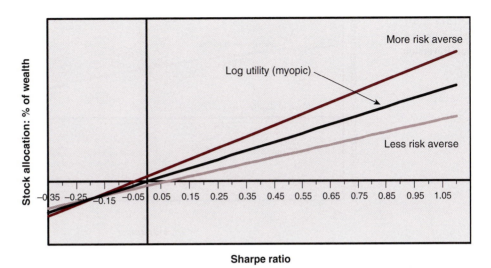

on the hedging component of the portfolio policy, the exhibits reflect rescaling so that the three investors have a common level of myopic demand for stocks.

Exhibit 5.9 shows that the fraction invested in stocks increases linearly as the so-called Sharpe ratio for stocks increases. The **Sharpe ratio** is the extra expected return per unit of risk we get for investing in stocks rather than in the riskless asset. In this model the Sharpe ratio increases linearly as the state variable, y_t, decreases. So the upward-sloping linear relationships shown in the exhibit reflect a linear relationship between the portfolio weight and y_t.

As we have discussed, both the myopic and hedging components increase as stocks become more attractive. Interestingly, more risk-averse investors are more responsive to changes in the attractiveness of stocks than less risk-averse investors. Thus if the market is mean-reverting, more risk-averse investors should be more aggressive market timers! This is due to the incentive to hedge.

The incentive to hedge arises from the consequences of changing investment opportunities for our ability to accumulate wealth over time. Given the assumed mean-reverting behavior of the stock market, an unexpectedly high stock market return in the current period leads to lower expected returns in the future and vice versa. The more we invest in stocks today, the more likely it is that we will have accumulated a lot of wealth when future returns on the market are expected to be poor. Similarly, our wealth will tend to be low when future market returns look great. Movements in wealth and investment opportunities tend to offset each other over time. By increasing our position in stocks, relative to the myopic allocation, we can hedge against adverse changes in investment opportunities and achieve a more stable accumulation of wealth over time. On the other hand, investing less in the market today increases the chances that we will have a lot of wealth to invest when future returns look better, and relatively little wealth to invest when future returns are likely to be poor. This implies a higher likelihood of both very high and very low wealth at the horizon. What should we do? That depends on how much we value greater stability versus the potential of greater upside. More risk-averse investors put a higher value on stability and hence increase their stock holdings relative to the myopic policy in order to hedge. Less risk-averse investors put a higher value on potential upside and therefore speculate on better future opportunities by reducing their current position in stocks relative to the myopic policy.

EXHIBIT 5.10
Horizon Impact of Mean Reversion

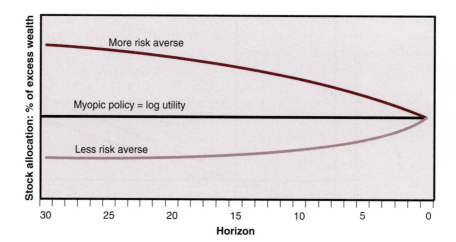

As shown in Exhibit 5.9, both types of investors tend to deviate proportionately more from the myopic strategy as the Sharpe ratio increases.[4]

Exhibits 5.10 and 5.11 show the impact of investment horizon on the optimal stock allocation. The expected return on the market is held constant at its long-run level—that is, $y_t = 0$. The minimum wealth level, W^*, is slightly less than current wealth. Note that the remaining investment horizon $(T - t)$ declines from left to right in the exhibits. Exhibit 5.10 shows the fraction of excess wealth invested in the stock market. The myopic policy puts the same fraction of excess wealth into stocks at all horizons. The longer the horizon, the greater the potential benefit of hedging future changes in investment opportunities. As a result, deviations from the myopic policy are larger at longer horizons. Because hedging demand is positive for the most risk-averse investors and negative for the least risk-averse investors, total stock allocations—including both the myopic and hedging components—should be more (less) similar at long (short) horizons.

Exhibit 5.11 reexpresses Exhibit 5.10 showing the stock allocation as a fraction of wealth rather than excess wealth. All three investors decrease their allocation to stocks as the horizon declines. This is due to the impact of the minimum wealth level W^*. As

---

[4] The lines cross at a negative Sharpe ratio. Below that level, less risk-averse investors appear to hedge while more risk-averse investors speculate. This seemingly perverse behavior is explained in Kim and Omberg (1996).

EXHIBIT 5.11
Horizon Impact of Mean Reversion: Stocks as a Fraction of Wealth

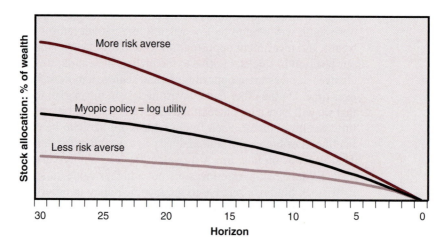

the horizon declines, the present value of the minimum wealth level increases. All else the same, this implies that excess wealth declines with the horizon, requiring a reduction in stock allocation. For the more risk-averse investor, this reinforces the decreasing incentive to hedge and results in a substantial reduction in equity allocation at shorter horizons. For the less risk-averse investor, there are opposing forces. This investor puts a bigger fraction of excess wealth into stocks at shorter horizons (see Exhibit 5.10), but excess wealth declines as the horizon gets shorter. The net effect depends on the level of excess wealth. If excess wealth is large, the investor may actually increase the stock allocation. If, as assumed in Exhibit 5.11, excess wealth is small, the investor decreases the stock allocation as the horizon gets shorter.

Before leaving this model, we should emphasize that virtually all real investors are likely to fall into the more risk-averse category. That is, they will want to dampen the volatility of their wealth by hedging against adverse changes in investment opportunities. In conjunction with mean-reverting stock prices, this implies holding more stock at long horizons but scaling back those allocations sharply as the investment horizon shortens.

Note that each of our DP applications—recursive shortfall and mean reversion models—leads to a portfolio policy that depends explicitly on the investor's horizon. Thus each enables us to go beyond the vague notion that the portfolio ought to depend on the horizon to an understanding of why and how. Moreover, at least in the case of the recursive shortfall model, we get a tractable extension of the M–V framework that is easy to apply in practice.

5.4   Simulation

Dynamic programming is hard work even for relatively simple, stylized problems. Seemingly minor changes to a problem can, and often do, make it intractable. So although it is the "right" thing to do, DP is not practical in most instances.

Whereas DP is rigorous and subtle, simulation is basically brute force. Given a random number generator and a powerful computer, we can simulate almost anything. This makes simulation almost ideal for analyzing complex, realistic problems. Does the investor have to fund a stream of payments under various scenarios? No problem: If you can define the scenarios you can simulate them. Do asset returns come from a distribution other than the normal? If so, the portfolio will almost always have some other distribution that cannot be described in terms of the underlying asset return distributions. No problem: Define the distribution for each asset and simulate the portfolio. Do you need to satisfy probabilistic constraints, such as the likelihood of exhausting net worth before death? No problem: Capture those statistics in the simulation.

Simulation is not, however, a panacea. As with any computer-based application, there is the issue of "garbage in, garbage out." It is easy to generate reams of useless, confusing, and misleading simulation results. Indeed the ease with which a complex model can be built almost invites us to "let it rip and think about it later." This issue becomes more important when we recognize that simulation can help us assess the implications of a particular strategy given our assumptions, but it can consider only strategies that have been preselected. Unlike DP, it cannot truly optimize in the sense of finding the best strategy for a given problem. It can only help us eliminate strategies with bad characteristics and select the best among the strategies we prespecify. In addition, using simulation to select the best strategy can be slow and cumbersome. Worse, the results may be unreliable because we may blindly ask the software to handle a problem with nasty mathematical properties.

The remainder of this section will focus on two applications of simulation. The first uses simulation to examine the impact of required expenditures, alternative probability distributions, and alternative performance objectives. The second is an innovation in applying the M–V framework known as *resampling*.

The Impact of Required Expenditures and Alternative Probability Distributions

So far we have retained the assumptions that the investor does not need to consider cash flows into or out of the portfolio before the horizon date and that logarithmic asset returns have a normal distribution. Except in a few special cases, such as spending being a constant fraction of current wealth, relaxing either of these assumptions would have been difficult to handle with DP. In contrast, we can incorporate these changes into a simulation quite easily.

Exhibit 5.12 shows seven variations of the same asset allocation problem. There are four asset classes: investment-grade bonds, high-yield bonds, large-cap value stocks, and small-cap growth stocks. The implied views method was used to generate expected returns consistent with the M–V allocation shown in case 1 of the exhibit. Chapter 3 showed that this is the optimal strategy if log returns are normally distributed and there are no required cash flows. With required cash flows or alternative probability distributions, the truly optimal strategy might depend on the remaining horizon or some other factor. Cases 2 through 7 consider different return distributions with a required annual expenditure equal to 10 percent of the investor's initial wealth. In each of these cases, the objective is to maximize the expected value of a CRRA utility function of final wealth, the investment horizon is 10 years, and the portfolio weights are assumed to be the same in each period.

In cases 2 and 3 logarithmic returns on all four asset classes have a normal distribution. With no required cash flows (case 2) the portfolio is the same as for the M–V objective. This is reassuring because case 2 reflects the same assumptions we used in Chapter 3 to derive the M–V framework. Due to sampling error, however, simulation will not always exactly match results derived by other methods. Comparing the simulation against another method is a good way to assess the severity of any bias in the simulation procedure before applying it to new problems. Thus cases 1 and 2 serve as our check on the simulation model.

Case 3 adds the required annual expenditure. If the investor earned nothing on the portfolio, this would exhaust the investor's wealth over the 10-year horizon. Clearly the investor cannot afford to lose money. Comparing cases 2 and 3 shows that this spending requirement has a substantial impact on the portfolio. Instead of a 60/40 percent

EXHIBIT 5.12   **Impact of Cash Flows and Alternative Probability Distributions**

				Portfolio Weights			
Case	Objective	Distribution of Log Stock Return	Spending % of Initial Wealth	Investment-Grade	High-Yield	Large Value	Small Growth
1	M–V			30%	10%	45%	15%
2	CRRA	Normal		30	10	45	15
3	CRRA	Normal	10	75	22	0	3
4	CRRA	Logistic		27	9	49	15
5	CRRA	Logistic	10	74	16	1	9
6	CRRA	Weibull		33	10	38	19
7	CRRA	Weibull	10	64	24	8	4

split between stocks and bonds, the investor puts 97 percent in bonds and only 3 percent in stocks. Suppose the requirement was to spend 10 percent of the *current* wealth in each period rather than a fixed amount. It turns out that such a spending plan has no effect on the portfolio; the investor would choose the same portfolio as in case 2. Why? If spending is proportional to wealth, then only wealth matters, and the best portfolio from a wealth perspective is not affected by a proportional spending requirement. The point, of course, is that the impact of spending requirements depends on their nature.

The M–V framework is often criticized because empirically logarithmic asset returns—especially stock returns—are not normally distributed. Instead they have **fat tails** in the sense that there is a higher probability of extreme returns than the normal distribution would imply. For example, goodness-of-fit tests applied to monthly log returns for the Russell 2000 Growth index suggest that two alternative distributions—the Logistic and the Weibull—fit the data better than the normal does. Exhibit 5.13 shows how these distributions differ from a normal distribution with the same mean and standard deviation. Like the normal, the logistic distribution is symmetric around the mean. But it is much more concentrated around the mean. In the exhibit the peak in the curve labeled "logistic" occurs at the common mean of the three distributions. As we move away from the mean in either direction, the probability assigned by the logistic declines much more rapidly than the normal. For a range of intermediate values in either direction, the logistic assigns lower probability than the normal; but as we move to more extreme returns, the logistic once again assigns higher probability than the normal. Thus the logistic has fat tails. The pattern is broadly similar for the Weibull distribution, but this distribution is not symmetric. The probability of extremely low returns is much greater than the probability of correspondingly high returns. On the other hand, the biggest concentration of probability, the peak in the curve, is above the mean. So relative to the normal, the Weibull implies that returns are more likely to be either somewhat better than the mean or very bad. Modestly poor performance is much less likely according to the Weibull distribution.

Cases 4–7 in Exhibit 5.12 show the impact of using these alternative distributions for stock returns. Bond returns are still assumed to be (log) normal. By construction the means, variances, and correlations are the same as before, so from a M–V perspective nothing has changed. Comparing case 4 to case 2 indicates that using the logistic distribution instead of the normal distribution shifts the allocation slightly in favor of stocks, but overall there is little impact. With required cash flows (case 5 versus case 3)

EXHIBIT 5.13
Deviations from
Normal Distribution

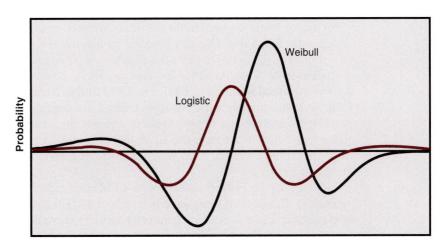

the impact is a little more pronounced, but again it is not dramatic. Even though the logistic distribution has fat tails, it is symmetric; so there is a higher probability of both very good and very bad returns. In addition, the probability of achieving returns near the mean is much higher. Overall the benefits appear to outweigh the negatives, making stocks slightly more attractive.

Cases 6 and 7 use the Weibull distribution for stock returns. This distribution is not uniquely determined by its mean and variance. To emphasize the impact of **skewness** on the portfolio, we chose the parameters to make the distribution as negatively skewed as possible consistent with the targeted mean and variance. Comparing case 6 to case 2 indicates that introducing negative skewness along with fat tails reduces the overall allocation to stocks slightly, but the allocation to small-cap growth increases. On the other hand, the allocation to stocks increases when there is a spending requirement (case 7 versus case 3). In this instance, however, most of the additional allocation goes into large-cap value at the expense of investment-grade bonds. Apparently the rightward shift of probability in the center of the distribution (see Exhibit 5.13) more than compensates this investor for the fat lower tail. Perhaps there is an element of rolling the dice because, as just noted, without the need to fund the required spending stream, the investor would not shift into stocks.

The key result from this simple example is that, on the whole, fat tails do not seem to be as big a problem as is often suggested. Fat tails in conjunction with negative skewness have somewhat more impact, and the shape of the distribution can interact with other aspects of the problem, like size and timing of cash flows. But it appears that means, variances, and correlations are much more important than the precise shape of the distribution. This useful result suggests the M–V framework can produce reasonable results despite the violation of a key assumption.

Specialized Objectives

Why does the shape of the distribution have so little impact on the portfolio? First, the differences among the three distributions are modest. Each has most of the probability in the middle and a single mode (highest-frequency point). Further, by construction, each has the same mean and standard deviation. Despite the presence of fat tails and skewness, the distributions are similar. Second, the constant relative risk aversion utility function is not very sensitive to modest changes in the shape of the distribution. Small changes in wealth cause only small changes in how much we value another dollar of wealth. Similarly, small changes in the probability of each wealth level cause only small changes in how we assess risk.

To induce larger changes in the portfolio, we need to magnify the impact of small changes in probability. This can be done by making the objective sensitive to specific events—like losing money. To illustrate this idea, let us consider something analogous to M–V optimization but replace the variance with a risk measure called the **lower partial moment (LPM)**. The LPM differs from the variance in two ways. First, we take squared deviations from a threshold return rather than squared deviations from the expected return. Second, whereas the variance reflects returns both above and below the mean, the LPM includes only returns below the threshold. Both the variance and the LPM weight the squared deviations by the corresponding probabilities.

Exhibit 5.14 shows the results of mean–LPM optimization using the same assets and probability distributions considered in Exhibit 5.12. The threshold return is zero—that is, breakeven. The risk aversion parameter was chosen so that the optimal portfolio in the (log) normal case is similar to the mean–variance result shown in Exhibit 5.12. The

EXHIBIT 5.14   Mean–Lower Partial Moment Optimization

	Distribution of Log Equity Returns		
	Normal	**Logistic**	**Weibull**
Optimal Portfolio Weights (%)			
Barclays Aggregate	31.00	60.00	35.00
High-yield	7.00	14.00	20.00
Large-cap value	43.00	8.00	28.00
Small-cap growth	19.00	18.00	17.00
Probability of loss (%)			
Normal portfolio	23.40	33.10	19.90
Logistic portfolio	17.40	21.10	16.40
Weibull portfolio	21.00	30.30	18.90
Square root of lower partial moment (%)			
Normal portfolio	3.69	8.10	4.57
Logistic portfolio	1.88	4.58	2.17
Weibull portfolio	2.82	5.83	3.40

first section of the exhibit reports the optimal portfolio for each of the three distributions. Compared with the normal case, the optimal portfolio for each of the fat-tailed distributions has substantially less total equity. The shift is especially pronounced for the logistic distribution: only 26 percent equity versus 62 percent with normally distributed returns.

The bottom two sections of the exhibit show two risk statistics—probability of loss and the square root of LPM—for each portfolio under each of the three distributional assumptions. The portfolios are labeled according to the distribution under which each is optimal; for example, the logistic portfolio is the optimal portfolio assuming equity returns are logistic. The exhibit shows that this portfolio has a 16.4 percent probability of loss, and the square root of the LPM is 2.17 if equity returns actually have a Weibull distribution instead of a logistic distribution. Note that the optimal portfolio for each distributional assumption does not necessarily have the lowest risk, as measured by the square root of the LPM, for that distribution because the optimizer seeks the best risk–return trade-off, not the lowest absolute risk.

For each portfolio the logistic distribution generates the highest probability of loss and the highest lower partial moment. From either of these perspectives the logistic distribution presents the most risk. It is therefore not surprising that the optimal portfolio based on this distribution is the most conservative. The Weibull distribution gives the lowest probability of loss for each portfolio. If we were concerned with only the likelihood of losing money and not the magnitude of the loss, this distribution would be the most favorable. However, the LPM of each portfolio is higher under the Weibull distribution than under the normal distribution. Therefore, taking account of both the magnitude and likelihood of losses, the Weibull appears less attractive than the normal, and the optimal portfolio based on this distribution is correspondingly more conservative.

The upshot of this analysis is that the shape of the distribution does matter. However, the impact is likely to be small unless we adopt a risk measure that is designed to be sensitive to small changes in the probability of specific events. In that case the results will be sensitive to our choice of risk measure, such as shortfall probability versus LPM, as well as the shape of the probability distribution.

Resampled Mean–Variance

In Chapter 4 we demonstrated that even for very long data samples there remains substantial uncertainty about the true mean return on an asset. Indeed Exhibit 4.1 gave an example in which it takes 900 years of data to be 95 percent confident that the sample mean is within 1 percent of the true mean return. This is problematic for the M–V framework because small changes in the inputs—especially the expected returns—can cause substantial changes in the optimal portfolio. Frequently a small change is sufficient to drive the optimal portfolio from one corner solution to another. This is the Achilles heel of the M–V framework.

Of course we do not have to rely solely on sample statistics. The fact remains, however, that any set of estimates is likely to be subject to significant estimation error. This means many sets of estimates are statistically equivalent in the sense that we cannot say that one set is better than another. Michaud (1998) pioneered a method called **resampling** to use this fact in conjunction with simulation to improve the results obtained from M–V analysis.[5]

Here is the general idea. Given initial estimates of means, standard deviations, and correlations for various asset classes, simulate a large number of alternative samples (such as 100 samples of 60 monthly returns) and calculate the sample statistics from each sample. These samples are statistically equivalent because they are drawn from the same underlying distribution. The next step is the key insight: Use each of these sets of sample statistics as inputs for M–V analysis and then average the resulting portfolio weights for each asset. Because the portfolio weights must sum to 1 in each M–V optimization, the averages will also sum to 1. Hence the portfolio budget constraint will be satisfied. More generally, any linear equality constraint that is satisfied by each optimization will also be satisfied by the averages.[6] This is not true for other statistics such as the median.

If each sample were sufficiently large, then each sample statistic would be virtually identical to the original estimate used to generate the samples. Because the estimates would all be the same, the M–V portfolios would also be the same, and resampling would be equivalent to using the original set of estimates. With typical sample sizes, however, there will be substantial variation among the sets of estimates and hence among the M–V results. Due to sampling error each asset will appear attractive in some samples and receive a high weight. In other samples the same asset will appear unattractive and receive a low weight. Averaging the portfolio weight for each asset across the samples eliminates both extremes and makes the final portfolio much less sensitive to the original estimates.

Exhibit 5.15 summarizes the results of drawing 100 samples of 60 monthly returns and using the sample statistics from each as inputs for M–V optimization with short sales prohibited. The implied views method was used to obtain initial estimates consistent with the portfolio labeled as the true portfolio in the exhibit. The remainder of the exhibit describes the distribution of outcomes for each asset class's portfolio weight. In general, the average of each portfolio weight is close to the correct value. Only the average weights for the Russell 1000 Value and Russell 2000 Value are off by more

---

[5] The basic idea can be implemented in various ways. Software packages incorporating versions of resampling are available from, for example, New Frontier Advisors and Ibbotson Associates.

[6] Because it averages case-by-case results, resampling does not impose inequality constraints properly on the final portfolio. Piros (2008) develops a more sophisticated method that imposes inequality constraints correctly without sacrificing the linear–quadratic structure of the M–V framework.

EXHIBIT 5.15   **Distribution of Portfolios from Statistically Equivalent Inputs**

	Russell 1000 Value	Russell 1000 Growth	Russell 2000 Value	Russell 2000 Growth	MSCI EAFE	Barclays Aggregate Bond	Barclays High Yield	Citigroup Hedged International Bonds
True portfolio	0.200	0.200	0.040	0.040	0.120	0.270	0.050	0.080
Summary statistics of sample portfolios								
Average	0.166	0.200	0.060	0.047	0.125	0.269	0.050	0.082
Maximum	0.350	0.362	0.196	0.175	0.169	0.411	0.187	0.318
75th percentile	0.249	0.274	0.112	0.083	0.138	0.330	0.083	0.136
Median	0.176	0.211	0.048	0.038	0.128	0.286	0.038	0.065
25th percentile	0.071	0.138	0.000	0.000	0.116	0.210	0.000	0.000
Minimum	0.000	0.020	0.000	0.000	0.046	0.000	0.000	0.000

than a percentage point. The range of outcomes is quite large for every asset class, and four of the asset classes receive no weight in at least 25 percent of the samples.

5.5   Asset Allocation with Active Managers

It is standard practice to approach asset allocation decisions as if the portfolio will be invested in generic asset classes, such as index funds. Once the asset allocation is set, however, the money is typically entrusted to managers who try to enhance returns by deviating from benchmarks. This practice means that the overall portfolio may not have the intended characteristics. A less obvious, but perhaps even more significant, implication is that the amount of money entrusted to such managers should depend on their ability to add value (their *alphas*) rather than the role of their generic asset classes in the overall portfolio. Separating the allocation of assets among managers from the allocation to asset classes is often referred to as **portable alpha.**

The standard approach of allocating assets to managers based on their asset classes directs assets to the most attractive asset classes even if that shifts funds away from the managers who add the most value within their asset classes—that is, those with the highest alphas. The presumption is that one must choose between high asset class returns and high value added; but this need not be the case. Portable alpha strategies can capture both the most attractive asset classes and the value added by the best managers regardless of their asset classes.

Exhibit 5.16 demonstrates how this works. To keep things simple, there are only two asset classes: stocks and bonds. Each comes in three flavors: passive, active, and market-neutral overlay. A market-neutral overlay is an alpha generation strategy that, by construction, is uncorrelated with the underlying asset class. As a result, active management can be viewed as a combination of the passive portfolio plus the market-neutral overlay. The top section of Exhibit 5.16 summarizes the investment parameters: expected returns, volatilities, and correlations. The parameters for the active portfolios are derived from the parameters assumed for the passive and overlay strategies. These parameter assumptions are somewhat arbitrary and are meant only for illustration. In particular, the relative performance of the overlay managers has been exaggerated to highlight the impact of portable alpha.

EXHIBIT 5.16   Asset Allocation with Portable Alpha

Investment Opportunities

	Expected Return	Standard Deviation	Correlations			
			Passive Stocks	Passive Bonds	Stock Overlay	Bond Overlay
Passive stocks	10.0	15.00	1.00	0.50		
Passive bonds	6.0	5.00	0.50	1.00		
Stock overlay	2.5	5.00			1.00	0.50
Bond overlay	5.0	5.00			0.50	1.00
Active stocks	12.5	15.81	.95	.47	.32	.16
Active bonds	11.0	7.07	.35	.71	.35	.71
Riskless rate	5.0					

Optimal Allocations

		Expected Return	Sharpe Ratio	Allocation to Active Managers		Net Asset Class Exposure		
				Stocks	Bonds	Stocks	Bonds	Cash
1	Passive only	8.80	.34			70	30	
2	Active only	11.94	.61	63	37	63	37	
3	Separate manager and asset class	13.41	.74	100		63	27	10
4	Separate and levered	15.00	.88	141		59		41

Implementation with Separation of Manager and Asset Class Allocations

		Cash Allocation to Active Managers	Derivative Positions		Borrowing
			Bond Index Total Return Swaps	Stock Index Total Return Swaps	
3	Separate manager and asset class	100% of fund assets to bond manager	Pay index return; receive LIBOR; 73% of assets	Receive index return; pay LIBOR; 63% of assets	None required
4	Separate and levered	141% of fund assets to bond manager	Pay index return; receive LIBOR; 141% of assets	Receive index return; pay LIBOR; 59% of assets	Borrow amount equal to 41% of fund assets

Passive stocks have a Sharpe ratio of 0.33 percent, and passive bonds have a Sharpe ratio of only 0.20 percent. On a risk–return basis, therefore, stocks are the more attractive asset class and all but the most risk-averse investors will want to have a heavy weighting in stocks. Consider a 70/30 mix of passive stocks and bonds that has an expected return of 8.8 percent and a standard deviation of 11.32 percent. This portfolio provides a base case against which to compare actively managed portfolios with the same level of risk.

By construction, the overlay portfolios capture the skill of the active stock and bond managers. On average the bond manager is able to outperform the passive benchmark by 5.0 percent with a 5.0 percent tracking error, whereas the stock manager achieves only 2.5 percent additional return with the same tracking error. The bond manager has an information ratio of 1.0 (5.0/5.0), whereas the stock manager's information ratio is 0.5 (2.5/5.0). All else equal, given the higher return per unit of risk *relative to the benchmark,* one would clearly prefer to invest with the active bond manager.

What is the best allocation consistent with a portfolio volatility of 11.32 percent? The middle section of the exhibit summarizes four cases. The passive only case is the base case with a 70/30 mix of passive stocks and bonds. The active only case takes account of manager skill but requires the allocation between asset classes to be the same as the allocation between active managers. The third case allows separation of manager and asset class decisions but does not allow the overall fund to be levered. The final case allows the fund to be levered. The exhibit shows the expected return, Sharpe ratio, allocation to active managers, and net asset class exposure. In each case the net asset class exposures sum to 100 percent.

Allocating to active managers increases the expected return sharply compared to the base case: to 11.94 percent from 8.80 percent. However, the allocation between stock and bonds changes little. Only 7 percent of the assets are shifted toward the superior manager. This is because the superior manager happens to manage the less attractive asset class.

If we drop the restriction that asset class exposure must coincide with the allocation of assets between managers, an additional boost to performance can be achieved: a 13.41 percent expected return against the 11.94 percent of the active only case. This is achieved by allocating 100 percent of the portfolio to the active bond manager and adjusting the asset class exposure to a 63/27/10 percent mix of stocks, bonds, and cash. The asset class exposure adjustment is made using derivatives; the details of the implementation are discussed below.

Leverage allows a final performance boost. A 15 percent expected return is obtained by allocating 141 percent to the active bond manager and adjusting the asset class exposure to a 59/0/41 percent mix of stocks, bonds, and cash. Even though the portfolio has no *net* exposure to bonds as an asset class, the bond manager contributes 7.05 percent (1.41 × 5) of the expected return through the market-neutral overlay.[7]

As this example demonstrates, the ability to separate asset class exposures from the allocation of funds among managers can substantially increase performance. As the relative attractiveness of various asset classes changes over time, there is no need to forgo the value added by the most skilled managers just because their asset classes are out of favor.

Before addressing the question of implementation, it is interesting to consider creating a stock fund using the active bond manager that, in this case, outperforms the active stock manager. The fund is constructed by giving all the assets to the active bond manager and then adjusting the asset class exposure to a 100/0/0 percent mix of stocks, bonds, and cash using derivatives. The expected return of 15 percent is 2.5 percent greater than that of the active stock manager (12.5 percent) with the same volatility and the same beta.

Implementation of a portable alpha portfolio can be broken into three components: (1) allocation of cash to active managers, (2) derivative positions to adjust the net asset

---

[7] In practice, the obtainable performance boost is likely to be much smaller because strategies with very high potential alphas tend to entail high transaction costs.

class exposures, and (3) borrowing. In the absence of leverage, no explicit borrowing is required. To illustrate implementation of this type of strategy, we will assume that the only derivatives used are index total return swaps. In practice other derivatives, like futures, may be more cost-efficient in some instances. The bottom portion of Exhibit 5.16 summarizes the three components of the portfolio for cases 3 and 4.

In the absence of leverage (case 3), the active bond manager receives 100 percent of the assets. The net exposure to the bond market is reduced to 27 percent by entering a total return swap in which the portfolio pays the return of the bond index and receives interest at the London Interbank Offer Rate (**LIBOR**). The notional amount of this swap is equal to 73 percent of the portfolio's assets. Exposure to stocks is created using a swap in which the portfolio receives the total return of the stock index and pays LIBOR. The notional amount of this swap is equal to 63 percent of the portfolio's assets. Because the portfolio receives LIBOR on one swap and pays LIBOR on the other, we simply net the notional amounts to determine the net amount implicitly invested at LIBOR. In this case it is 10 percent ($= 73 - 63$) of the portfolio assets. This results in a 63/27/10 percent mix of net exposures to stocks, bonds, and cash while capturing the alpha of the active bond manager for 100 percent of the portfolio.

When leverage is allowed (case 4) the portfolio borrows an amount equal to 41 percent of net assets and allocates 141 percent of the portfolio assets to the active bond manager. As before, the net exposure to bonds is adjusted by paying the bond index return and receiving LIBOR on a total return swap. In this case all of the bond exposure is offset. Exposure to stocks is again created by receiving the stock index return and paying LIBOR on a swap. In this case the notional amount of the stock index swap is 59 percent of net assets. Netting the LIBOR legs of the swaps and the borrowing (assumed to be at LIBOR) shows that the fund implicitly invests 41 percent ($= 141 - 59 - 41$) at LIBOR. As shown in the exhibit, a 59/0/41 percent mix of net exposures to stocks, bonds, and cash has been created while capturing the alpha of the active bond manager for 141 percent of the fund's net assets.

5.6   Portfolio Insurance

In the 1980s a dynamic strategy was developed that purported to protect an investor's stock portfolio from losses while capturing most of the potential upside. The essence of the strategy was to replicate a put option on the portfolio by buying and selling stocks or, equivalently, stock index futures. This so-called **portfolio insurance** strategy seemed to work well until October 19, 1987. As the U.S. stock market began to fall that Monday, the portfolio insurance strategy forced its adherents to sell stocks to reduce potential exposure to further market declines. But these sales helped push the market lower and forced the portfolio insurers to sell even more, creating a negative feedback loop. By the end of the day the S&P 500 index was down more than 20 percent. In hindsight the problem was obvious: In order for anyone to buy insurance, someone else must be willing to sell it. Those who thought they had insurance on their portfolios neglected the fact that no one had really agreed to sell it to them. When they insisted on selling stocks to implement the strategy, there were no buyers.

Although the original portfolio insurance strategy involved explicit replication of a protective put option, the underlying idea is more general. Consider a buy-and-hold strategy in which a portfolio of stocks is purchased at the beginning of the period and sold at the end of the period. The ending value of that strategy would vary linearly with the market value of the underlying stocks. This is illustrated by the straight

EXHIBIT 5.17
Payoff Profile for
Portfolio Insurance

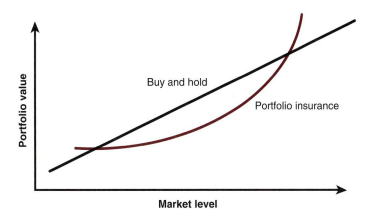

line in Exhibit 5.17. Suppose instead that the manager shifts money between stocks and a riskless asset based on market moves, buying stock whenever the market rallies (borrowing if necessary) and selling stock whenever the market declines. Because the manager tends to buy at high prices and sell at low prices, money is lost each time the market reverses direction. Hence this strategy will do worse than the buy-and-hold strategy if the market is trendless but volatile. On the other hand it will outperform the buy-and-hold strategy if the market trends strongly in either direction. So the final value of this strategy resembles the upwardly curved line in the exhibit. This "buy high, sell low" behavior and its profit profile may be taken as the generic definition of buying portfolio insurance. Sellers of portfolio insurance do the opposite.

Option-Based Portfolio Insurance

Classic option-based portfolio insurance is conceptually straightforward. For simplicity, assume that the investor buys one share of stock and a European put option on that share with strike price K and expiration at time T. By definition, a *European put option* gives the owner the right to sell the stock at the expiration date (and only then) for the exercise price if it is advantageous to do so. At expiration the put will be worth $\max[K - S_T, 0]$ where S_T is the stock price at time T. The combined position, the stock plus the put, will be worth $(S_T + \max[K - S_T, 0]) = \max[K, S_T]$. So the investor is guaranteed that the portfolio will be worth at least K as of the expiration date regardless of the stock price. It can be shown that the exercise price, K, can be set equal to the initial cost of the stock plus the put; therefore the initial value of the portfolio is insured.

The dynamic aspect of classic portfolio insurance arises if the put option is created synthetically by trading in the stock. The key to replicating an option is the amount by which its value changes when the price of the stock changes by a small amount. This is known as the option's *delta* and can be obtained from various option pricing models such as the well-known Black–Scholes formula. By convention, delta is usually stated as a positive number even though the value of a put option declines as the stock price increases. Under this convention, delta always lies between 0 and 1. It is small at very high stock prices because there is little chance the put will be worth exercising and, therefore, little change in the price in response to stock price changes; that is, delta equals 0. At very low stock prices the put is very likely to be exercised, and hence its price moves one-for-one (inversely) with the stock price; that is, delta equals 1. To replicate a put on one share of stock, we short delta shares of stock. As the stock price increases (decreases) delta declines (increases), so we have to buy back (sell) some shares. This is what makes the strategy dynamic.

Constant Proportional Portfolio Insurance

Although the notion of buying a put option to protect a portfolio is simple, the option replication process is based on complex option pricing formulas. A much simpler strategy is known as **constant proportional portfolio insurance (CPPI).**

Suppose an investor has current wealth W_t and wants to ensure that it will be at least W^* at a horizon date T. If there is a riskless asset earning a rate r_f, the investor can be assured of meeting this goal by investing $[W^* \exp(-r_f(T-t))]$ in the riskless asset. This is often referred to as the *floor,* and the amount by which current wealth exceeds the floor is referred to as the *cushion.* As long as the cushion is positive the investor can meet the objective. CPPI entails investing a multiple, ω, of the cushion in the stock portfolio and lending or borrowing at the riskless rate. CPPI can be summarized as

$$\text{\$\$ in stocks} = \omega\left[W_t - W^* \exp(-r_f(T-t))\right] \qquad (5.17)$$

$$\text{\$\$ in riskless} = W_t - \omega\left[W_t - W^* \exp(-r_f(T-t))\right]$$

This is exactly the form of the optimal policy in our dynamic programming model with mean reversion (see Equation (5.16)). The difference is that here the multiplier, ω, is required to be constant and greater than 1.

Note that the target investment in stocks increases or decreases more than one for one with increases or decreases in wealth. Hence the investor buys more stock as the market rises and sells stock as it declines. Thus, CPPI meets our generic definition of a portfolio insurance strategy.

Who Should Buy Portfolio Insurance?

As noted earlier, one pitfall encountered by portfolio insurance enthusiasts has been the need to ensure that other investors are willing to sell it. A question therefore naturally arises: Who should buy portfolio insurance and who should sell it? There are essentially two answers—one based on market views and one based on risk preferences.

In terms of market views, note that portfolio insurance is not really about market direction; it is about volatility and trending behavior. Investors who believe the market will move by a lot (in one direction or the other) will be inclined to buy portfolio insurance. Investors who believe the market will be range-bound will want to sell portfolio insurance. The former tend to be momentum players who extrapolate market moves. The latter tend to be contrarians who "sell into strength" and "buy on dips."

It might seem that buyers of portfolio insurance would tend to be more risk averse than sellers of portfolio insurance. This could be true, but Leland (1980) showed that it is not the *level* of risk aversion that matters—it is how risk aversion changes with wealth. Investors whose risk aversion increases faster than average as their wealth declines want to buy insurance. Those whose risk aversion changes more slowly than average are the sellers of insurance.

Summary

This chapter concludes our discussion of the asset allocation decision. Chapter 3 developed and applied the M–V framework. Chapter 4 provided tools for generating reasonable risk–return estimates and introduced the notion that investment opportunities may change over time. This chapter focused on the implications of relaxing some key assumptions underlying the basic M–V model. In particular, we examined the impact of changing investment opportunities, asymmetric or fat-tailed return distributions, estimation risk, and specialized objectives and constraints. In each case the investor is typically induced to deviate systematically from the portfolio policy prescribed by the basic M–V model.

When we relax the assumptions that formally justify the M–V framework we face a dilemma. In principle we should derive the optimal portfolio and spending policies using dynamic programming (DP). We applied this rigorous technique in our analysis of changing investment opportunities. But direct application of dynamic programming is limited to relatively simple problems, so we must seek more pragmatic approaches for realistic asset allocation problems. One approach is to augment the basic M–V framework with additional assumptions or constraints. For example, horizon effects can be introduced into the M–V model in a variety of ways. Two methods utilizing the probability of shortfall were considered here: one involving shortfall-dependent risk aversion and one based on recursive application of a shortfall constraint. Alternatively, the risk and return inputs can be made horizon-dependent. In this regard, a relatively simple vector autoregressive (VAR) model of asset returns generates substantially different risk parameters over various investment horizons.

When it is important to incorporate significant complexity into our analysis, the method of choice is simulation. A random number generator lets us simulate almost anything: many assets, cash flows, unusual probability distributions, probabilistic constraints, and alternative performance criteria. Simulation can help us eliminate bad strategies and focus on better ones. In general, however, it does not let us optimize in the sense of finding the best strategy for a given problem—we can only pick the best among strategies that we prespecify.

It is standard practice to make asset allocation decisions as if the portfolio will be invested in generic asset classes. After the asset allocation is set, however, the money is often entrusted to asset class managers who try to enhance returns, and thus the overall portfolio may not have the intended characteristics. The amount of money entrusted to these managers should depend on their respective abilities to add value rather than on the roles of the generic asset classes in the overall portfolio. Portable alpha strategies let us separate the allocation of assets among managers from the allocation to asset classes, enhancing overall performance.

No investor likes to lose money, and investment strategies that purport to insure against losses, but capture potential gains, are always in demand. Two such strategies were outlined in this chapter: option-based portfolio insurance and constant proportional portfolio insurance. Each involves dynamically shifting assets between a risky asset (or portfolio) and a riskless asset. Both strategies require buying the risky asset as its price rises and selling it as its price declines. The losses generated by this trading pattern—buying high and selling low—are the implicit cost of the insurance. But in order for some investors to buy portfolio insurance other investors must be willing to sell the insurance by taking the other side of each trade. There is no guarantee of finding a willing counterparty when needed, so portfolio insurance strategies may be more risky than they appear.

Problems * After studying Chapters 1-5, students should be equipped to complete the "2nd Deliverable" assignment for each of the cases at the end of the book.

1. Financial advisors generally recommend that their clients allocate more to higher risk–return asset classes (like equities) if their investment horizons are long.

   a. Is this advice consistent with the basic M–V model?

   b. Does adding a shortfall constraint to the M–V model make a difference? If so, how? If not, why not?

   c. Assuming investment opportunities change over time, what type of asset return behavior would justify this advice within the M–V framework?

2. Describe the following risk measures and explain why they might lead to different investment decisions:

   a. Variance.

   b. Shortfall probability.

   c. Lower partial moment.

3. Pacific Investment Management Company (PIMCO) is known for its expertise in managing fixed-income assets. The firm offers an equity mutual fund that actually holds bonds rather than stocks; the value added (alpha) over the benchmark (the S&P 500) comes from actively managing the bonds. Explain how this might be done.

4. Many investment professionals advise their clients to maintain a static strategic asset allocation. What implicit assumption(s) underlie this advice? Might it make sense to tactically shift allocations even if you do not believe you have superior forecasting skills? Why or why not?

5. Assume that stock returns tend to be mean-averting for long periods; that is, high (low) returns tend to be followed by high (low) returns. Would this tend to make investors want to hold more or less stock than they would otherwise? Why?

6. Your boss has asked you to evaluate a portfolio strategy that purports to capture all of the upside and none of the downside of the market. The key is a complex rule for buying and selling shares. You decide to simulate the strategy and discover that it lags the market on the upside and loses a small amount on average when the market declines. What's more, when you test the strategy with historical data it suffers sharp losses in a few volatile periods. How would you describe the essence of the trading rule to your boss? How would you explain your simulated results?

7. Describe and compare the following three methods of incorporating shortfall risk into the M–V model:

   a. Apply a shortfall constraint over the full investment horizon. Choose one portfolio to be held (with rebalancing each period) for the entire investment horizon.

   b. Apply a shortfall constraint recursively, allowing a different portfolio in each period over the investment horizon.

   c. Make risk aversion horizon-dependent by explicitly linking it to shortfall probability.

   Which method gives the user the most control over the horizon profile of the asset allocation? If being able to customize the horizon profile is important, why not allow it to be arbitrary?

8. Assume an asset's logarithmic returns are independently and identically distributed (i.i.d.) through time with 20 percent annual standard deviation.

   a. Compute the standard deviation of wealth over a 30-year horizon.

   b. Compute the standard deviation of the per-period return over a 30-year horizon.

    c. What, if anything, do your answers imply about whether this asset is more or less risky over longer horizons?

9. Use the spreadsheet <HD RRA> to examine the effects of changing these assumptions on the risk aversion profile:

    a. LT risk aversion.

    b. LT horizon.

    c. ST/LT ratio.

    d. 1-year/10-year ratio.

    e. The threshold return (H).

    f. Mean return.

10. Use the worksheet <Equity Allocation–Template> in the Chapter 05 Excel Outboxes.xls spreadsheet to compare the equity allocation across horizons for the horizon-dependent and recursive asset allocations.

	A	B	C	D
1	**Comparison of Equity Allocations**			
2				
3	**Horizon**	**Tolerance**	**HD RAA**	**Recursive**
4	30			
5	29			
6	:			
29	5			
30	4			
31	3			
32	2			
33	1			

11. Use the worksheet <DP Mean Reversion> in the file Chapter 05 Excel Outboxes.xls to graph and compare the horizon profiles of

    a. the myopic component of the stock allocation

    b. the hedging component of the stock allocation

    c. the optimal stock allocation

    when the market is 10 percent above trend ($y = 0.10$), 10 percent below trend ($y = -0.10$), and on trend ($y = 0.00$). Do deviations from trend affect the optimal portfolio uniformly at all horizons? If not, characterize the relationship.

12. Use the worksheet <DP Mean Reversion> in the file Chapter 05 Excel Outboxes.xls to compute the (30-year/1-year) and (30-year/10-year) ratios of optimal stock allocations.

    a. Using these ratios to approximate the corresponding risk aversion ratios in the horizon-dependent risk aversion model, fit the HD RRA model.

    b. Copy the horizon-dependent risk aversions from part (a) into the <HD RRA> Optimal spreadsheet and find the optimal portfolios for 1-, 5-, 10-, 15-, 20-, 25-, and 30-year horizons.

    c. Using Excel's chart wizard to create an *XY* graph, plot the HD RRA model's total equity allocation at these horizons versus the corresponding equity allocations from the DP mean reversion model. How well did the HD RRA model capture the horizon implications of the mean reversion?

13. Follow the steps here to trace how expected asset returns respond over time to a one-standard-deviation shock to each of the state variables in the VAR1 model given in Appendix 1. The system has been normalized so that the one-period, conditional standard deviation of each variable equals 1 and its long-term mean is

zero. Therefore, the responses represent deviations from the long-term mean. For example, a value of 0.20 indicates the variable is 0.2 standard deviations above its long-term mean.

Step 1: Enter the normalized coefficient matrix (Θ_1) into an Excel spreadsheet (put zeros in place of the blanks so that the Excel function MMULT will work properly).

Step 2: Create a column vector ε of shocks—one for each of the six state variables.

Step 3: Assign a value of 1 to one of the shocks and set the others to zero.

Step 4: Set the values of the state variables at time $t = 1$ equal to the corresponding shocks. That is, set the (column) vector x_1 equal to ε.

Step 5: Use the Excel function MMULT to multiply the matrix Θ_1 times the (column) vector x_1. The result is the vector of state variables at time $t = 2$, $x_2 = \Theta_1 x_1$. Repeat this process to determine the state variables at times $t = 3, \ldots, 20$.

Step 6: Use the Excel chart wizard to create a line graph of the results for the first three variables: the real bill return, the real excess return on stocks, and the real excess return on bonds.

Step 7: Change which variable is shocked and examine the graph again.

Appendix **1**

The Estimated VAR1 Model

The general form of the VAR1 model is

$$x_{t+1} = \Theta_0 + \Theta_1 x_t + \varepsilon_{t+1}$$

where x_{t+1} is a vector of asset returns and explanatory variables, Θ_0 is a constant vector, Θ_1 is a square matrix, and ε_{t+1} is a vector of normally distributed random elements with zero means and variance–covariance matrix Ω.

If, as usual, we work with logarithmic asset returns, then multiperiod returns are simply the sum of single-period returns. Thus T-period returns are elements of the vector

$$\sum_{1}^{T} x_{t+i}.$$

It can be shown that the conditional mean of this vector is linear in the state variables x_t with parameters that depend on the horizon T, while the variance–covariance matrix depends on the horizon but does not depend on the state variables.[8]

The VAR1 model underlying Exhibits 5.3 through 5.6 is summarized in the following table. The top section shows the coefficients of the state variables (Θ_1) after normalizing the variables so that the residual in each equation has unit standard deviation. To reduce the clutter of numbers, the table shows all the coefficients only for the equations describing the asset returns. For the equations explaining the other three variables, only the coefficient on that variable's own lagged value is shown. The bottom section of the exhibit shows the variance–covariance matrix of the residuals—that is, the random or unexpected component of each variable. Because we normalized the residual standard deviations to equal 1, this is also the correlation matrix for the residuals.

---

[8] See Campbell and Viceira (2004) for the relevant equations and their derivation.

Estimated VAR1 Model

	Real Bill Return	Real Stock Excess Return	Real Bond Excess Return	Nominal Bill Yield	Dividend Yield	Yield Spread
			Normalized Coefficient Matrix (Θ_1)			
Real bill return	**0.403**	0.013	0.001	0.115	−0.019	0.121
Real stock excess return	0.074	**0.027**	0.127	−0.066	**0.056**	−0.003
Real bond excess return	−0.023	−0.170	**−0.069**	0.035	−0.012	0.200
Nominal bill yield				**0.954**		
Dividend yield					**0.961**	
Yield spread						**0.760**
			Residual Variance–Covariance/Correlation Matrix			
Real bill return	1.000	0.221	0.357	**−0.349**	−0.223	0.143
Real stock excess return		1.000	0.119	−0.101	**−0.983**	0.015
Real bond excess return			1.000	**−0.755**	−0.141	0.147
Nominal bill yield				1.000	0.132	−0.754
Dividend yield					1.000	−0.042
Yield spread						1.000

In general, it is not possible to deduce the behavior of a complex system simply by examining the individual coefficients. However, the coefficient on each variable's own lagged value (the boldface values on the diagonal in the top section of the exhibit) is usually worth some attention. In the exhibit, this coefficient is positive for five of the six variables. For these variables, a high value in the current period tends to predict a high value in the next period. This effect is especially strong for the nominal bill yield and the dividend yield because the coefficient on the lagged value is nearly 1 in these two equations. These variables appear to be highly persistent in the sense that random shocks to these variables today will affect their value for many periods into the future. To the extent that these variables impact asset returns, they will be important drivers of longer-run risk characteristics.

According to the model, a high real excess return on stocks today predicts a slightly higher real excess return on stocks in the next period. Based solely on this parameter we might expect real stock returns to be positively correlated through time—mean-averting—and hence more volatile over long horizons. However, Exhibit 5.3 shows that the full system implies just the opposite. In contrast, a high real excess return on bonds today predicts a lower value next period. Based solely on this single parameter we might expect real bond returns to be negatively correlated through time and hence relatively stable over longer horizons. As shown in Exhibit 5.4, this is confirmed by the full system.

Although all the model parameters are potentially important, those that are especially helpful in describing the risk behavior of asset returns over various horizons are highlighted in boldface. A higher dividend yield today predicts a higher real excess stock return next period but a lower real excess return on bonds. A higher nominal bill yield today predicts a higher real excess bond return next period. The residual correlation matrix indicates that shocks to the dividend yield are almost perfectly negatively correlated with shocks to real excess stock returns. This reflects the fact that an unexpected increase (decrease) in stock prices implies a higher (lower) return but a decrease (increase) in the dividend yield. Looking again at the residual correlation matrix, we can see that shocks to the nominal bill yield have a strong negative correlation with real bill returns and real excess bond returns. Thus a sudden increase (decrease) in the nominal bill yield tends to be accompanied by unexpectedly low (high) real returns on these assets.

DP Solution of the Mean Reversion Model

In this appendix we outline the dynamic programming solution of the mean reversion model discussed in Section 5.3. To keep the exposition brief, we focus on the logic of the DP solution and omit the messy algebraic details.

A couple of simplifying assumptions help to keep the model tractable. First, there are only two assets available: stocks and a riskless asset earning a logarithmic return r_f. Second, the only constraint on the investor's strategy is that portfolio weights sum to unity. That is, the investor may be long or short either asset in any amount, but all available funds (including short sale proceeds) must be invested. Given this assumption the optimal investment strategy will vary smoothly with changes in investment opportunities.[9]

The process generating stock returns is given by

$$r_{t+1} = \alpha - \theta y_t + \varepsilon_{t+1} \qquad (A5.1)$$
$$y_{t+1} = (1 - \theta)y_t + \varepsilon_{t+1}$$

This is the simple mean reversion model studied in Chapter 4. Changes in investment opportunities are reflected in the state variable y_t. Positive (negative) values of y_t imply that the market price is above (below) its long-term trend and hence the expected return on the market is below (above) the trend return α. As in the M–V model of Chapter 3, it is useful to work with the logarithm of the expected gross return, denoted by μ, rather than the expected logarithmic return α. Recall that $\mu = \alpha + \frac{1}{2}\sigma^2$.

If a fraction ω_t is invested in stocks at time t, then the logarithmic return on the portfolio over the period from t to $t + 1$ can be written as (see Equation (3.10))

$$r_{p,t+1} = r_f + \omega_t \left(\mu - r_f - \theta y_t + \varepsilon_{t+1}\right) - 1/2 \, \omega_t^2 \sigma^2 \qquad (A5.2)$$

The portfolio expected return and variance are

$$E_t(r_{p,t+1}) = r_f + \omega_t \left(\mu - r_f - \theta y_t\right) - 1/2 \, \omega_t^2 \sigma^2 = \mu_{p,t} - 1/2 \, \sigma_{p,t}^2 \qquad (A5.3)$$
$$\sigma_{p,t}^2 = \omega_t^2 \sigma^2$$

where $\mu_{p,t}$ is the log of the expected gross return on the portfolio as defined in Equation (3.12).

As in the derivation of the M–V model in Chapter 3, the investor is assumed to have a constant relative risk aversion (CRRA) utility function with respect to final wealth, W_T, given by

$$U(W_T) = W_T^\gamma / \gamma \quad \gamma < 1 \qquad (A5.4)$$

---

[9] If we imposed realistic inequality constraints, such as no short sales, no borrowing, or differential rates for borrowing and lending, then changes in investment opportunities would have a discontinuous impact on the investment policy whenever the constraints were binding. This in turn would make it much more difficult to evaluate the joint probably distribution governing future investment opportunities and portfolio outcomes.

Let us hypothesize that the value function (as defined in Equation (5.6)) for this model takes the form

$$V(W_{t+1}, y_{t+1}, t+1) = \left(\frac{A_{t+1}}{\gamma}\right) W_{t+1}^{\gamma} \exp(\gamma B_{t+1}(y_{t+1})) \qquad \text{(A5.5)}$$

where A_{t+1} does not depend on wealth (W_{t+1}) or the state variable (y_{t+1}) and B_{t+1} is a quadratic function of the state variable. We will confirm below that Equation (A5.5) is correct. Note that at the final horizon, T, the value function must converge to the investor's underlying CRRA utility function with respect to terminal wealth. Equation (A5.5) satisfies this so-called boundary condition with $A_T = 1$ and $B_T = 0$.

Accepting, for now, that the value function at time $t + 1$ is given by Equation (A5.5), dynamic programming requires us to step back from time $t + 1$ to time t by evaluating the expectation of $V(W_{t+1}, y_{t+1}, t+1)$ conditional on information available at time t and then maximizing that expectation to find the optimal portfolio policy at time t. The optimized expected value then becomes the value function at time t (see Equation (5.7)).

Recognizing that $W_{t+1} = W_t \exp(r_{p,t+1})$ and that both W_t and A_{t+1} are known at time t, the problem is to evaluate

$$E_t[\exp(\gamma\,(r_{p,t+1} + B_{t+1}(y_{t+1})))] \qquad \text{(A5.6)}$$

Examining Equations (A5.1) and (A5.2) shows that $r_{p,t+1}$ depends on our choice of ω_t but y_{t+1} does not. Note that the term in brackets is not really additive in $r_{p,t+1}$ and $B_{t+1}(y_{t+1})$ because the exponential function is nonlinear. It could, however, be broken into the product of two exponential functions—one involving only $r_{p,t+1}$ and one involving only $B_{t+1}(y_{t+1})$. If we could take the expected value of these components separately, then the future investment opportunities embodied in $B_{t+1}(y_{t+1})$ would not affect current decisions. For this to be valid, however, $r_{p,t+1}$ and $B_{t+1}(y_{t+1})$ must be statistically independent random variables. However, Equations (A5.1) and (A5.2) show that both depend on the same underlying random variable ε_{t+1}. So they are not independent random variables, and the correlation between them will be reflected in the optimal investment policy.

Substituting from Equations (A5.1) and (A5.2), rearranging, and using the fact that ε_{t+1} has a standard normal distribution, we can evaluate the expectation in Equation (A5.6) to yield an equation that is proportional to

$$\exp\left\{\gamma\left[\left(\mu_{p,t} - \tfrac{1}{2}(1-\gamma)\sigma_{p,t}^2\right) + \gamma\,H_t(\omega_t, y_t)\right]\right\} \qquad \text{(A5.7)}$$

where H_t is a quadratic function of the portfolio weight and a linear function of the state variable y_t.[10] Maximizing this equation is equivalent to maximizing the expression in square brackets. There are two components. The first component is our familiar M–V objective reflecting the mean and variance of the portfolio over the next period. The second component, embodied in H, reflects the interaction of today's portfolio decision with future investment opportunities. Each of these components is quadratic in the portfolio weight and linear in y_t. Hence the objective function can be viewed as the sum of two mean–variance subproblems. Each of these subproblems contributes a

---

[10] The function *H* in this model is not related to the threshold return level, also denoted by *H,* in the recursive shortfall model.

piece to the optimal portfolio. Each piece (and hence the sum of the two pieces) is a linear function of the state variable y_t. The optimal portfolio weight can be written as

$$\omega(y_t,t) \;=\; m(y_t,t) \;-\; \gamma\, h(y_t,t) \qquad\qquad \textbf{(A5.8)}$$

$m(y_t,t)$ is the myopic portfolio. It reflects period-by-period optimization ignoring the relationship between current and future investment opportunities. In the second term, $h(y_t,t)$ is the hedging demand. It reflects adjusting the portfolio to hedge against adverse changes in investment opportunities. In this model, $h(y_t,t)$ is always nonnegative. Hence whether an investor holds more or less stock than the myopic portfolio depends only on the investor's risk aversion parameter γ.

We must now confirm that Equation (A5.5) is indeed the correct form for the value function. Given the assumed value function at time $t+1$, the value function at time t is proportional to the optimized value of Equation (A5.7). As noted, the expression in square brackets in Equation (A5.7) is a quadratic function of the portfolio weight. The optimal portfolio weight ω turned out to be linear in the state variable y_t. Substituting this linear relationship into Equation (A5.7), we see that the expression in square brackets becomes a quadratic function of the state variable. Comparing Equations (A5.7) and (A5.5) shows that the value function at time t takes the form given in Equation (A5.5) for some quadratic function $B_t(y_t)$. Thus if Equation (A5.5) is correct for some arbitrary date $t+1$ it is also correct at time t. We know it holds at the final horizon T; therefore it holds at all dates.

We now provide the key components of the explicit solution. The function A_t does not affect the portfolio policy and hence will be ignored here. The function B_t takes the form

$$B_t(y_t) \;=\; b_{0,t} \;+\; b_{1,t}\, y_t \;+\; b_{2,t}\, y_t^2 \qquad\qquad \textbf{(A5.9)}$$

while the optimal portfolio policy takes the form

$$\omega(y_t,t) \;=\; w_{0,t} \;+\; w_{1,t}\, y_t \qquad\qquad \textbf{(A5.10)}$$

The intercept $b_{0,t}$ does not affect the portfolio policy and can be ignored except to note that the boundary condition requires $b_{0,T}=0$. The values of $w_{0,t}$, $w_{1,t}$, $b_{1,t}$, and $b_{2,t}$ must be determined recursively starting from the final date T, where $b_{1,T}=b_{2,T}=0$, and working backward in time.

Given values of these parameters at time t, the portfolio policy parameters at time $t-1$ are

$$w_{0,t-1} \;=\; \frac{(\mu - r_f + \gamma\Phi_t\, b_{1,t})}{\Psi_t}$$

$$\textbf{(A5.11)}$$

$$w_{1,t-1} \;=\; \frac{(2b_{2,t}\,\gamma(1-\theta)\Phi_t - \theta)}{\Psi_t}$$

And the value function parameters are

$$b_{1,t-1} \;=\; b_{1,t}\,(1-\theta)[1 + 2\Phi_t\,\gamma\, b_{2,t}] + w_{0,t-1}\, w_{1,t-1}\Psi_t$$

$$\textbf{(A5.12)}$$

$$b_{2,t-1} \;=\; b_{2,t}\,(1-\theta)^2 + 2\gamma\Phi_t(1-\theta)^2 b_{2,t}^2 + \tfrac{1}{2}\,\Psi_t\, w_{1,t-1}^2$$

Where

$$\Psi_t \;=\; \sigma^2 - \gamma\Phi_t \qquad\qquad\qquad\qquad \Phi_t \;=\; \frac{\sigma^2}{1 - 2\gamma\sigma^2 b_{2,t}}$$

The myopic and hedging components of the portfolio policy are

$$m(y_{t-1}, t-1) = \frac{\mu - r_f - \theta\, y_{t-1}}{\sigma^2(1-\gamma)}$$

$$h(y_{t-1}, t-1) = \frac{(\sigma^2 - \Phi_t)(\mu - r_f - \theta y_{t-1})}{\sigma^2(1-\gamma)\,\Psi_t} - \frac{\Phi_t b_{1,t} + 2\Phi_t b_{2,t}(1-\theta)\, y_{t-1}}{\Psi_t}$$

Excel Outbox *Asset Allocation* *with Mean* *Reversion*	A simple recursive dynamic programming asset allocation with mean reversion is examined using the worksheet \<DP Mean Reversion–Template\> in the Chapter 05 Excel Outboxes.xls spreadsheet. The template should appear as follows:

	A	B	C	D	E	F	G	H	I	J	K	L	M
1	Asset Allocation with Mean Reversion												
2													
3	μ	0.10											
4	r_f	0.05											
5	σ^2	0.04											
6	γ	−5.00											
7	y	0.00											
8	θ	0.13											
9													
10	t	T–t	w_0	w_1	b1	b2	Ψ	Φ		m(y,t)	h(y,t)	ω(y,t)	ω(y,t)
11	30	0			0.000	0.000							
12	29	1											

Because the DP is solved recursively, we start in row 11 where $t = 30$ and $T - t = 0$. Note that t denotes the passage of calendar time, T is a fixed future horizon date, and $T - t$ is the remaining time to the horizon date. The recursion works backward from the horizon date $t = T = 30$ to the present, $t = 0$. As noted, $B_T = 0$, so cells E11 and F11 are seeded with 0.

The values for Ψ and Φ, Equation (A5.12), are calculated in columns G and H.

- Ψ: In cell G11 enter =\$B\$5-\$B\$6*\$H11, then copy to G12.
- Φ: In cell H11 enter =\$B\$5/(1-2*\$B\$6*\$B\$5*\$F11), then copy to H12.

The values for w_0 and w_1, Equation (A5.11), and b_1 and b_2, Equation (A5.12), are calculated in columns C:F.

- w_0: In cell C12 enter =(\$B\$3-\$B\$4 + \$B\$6*\$H11*\$E11)/\$G11.
- w_1: In cell D12 enter =(2*\$F11*\$B\$6*(1 − \$B\$8)*\$H11-\$B\$8)/\$G11.
- b_1: In cell E12 enter =\$E11*(1-\$B\$8)*(1 + 2*\$H11*\$B\$6*\$F11) + \$C12*\$D12*\$G11.
- b_2: In cell F12 enter =\$F11*((1-\$B\$8)^2)*(1 + 2*\$B\$6*\$H11*\$F11) + 0.5*\$G11*(\$D12^2).

The myopic and hedging components of the portfolio policy are calculated in columns J and K.

- Myopic: In cell J12 enter =(\$B\$3-\$B\$4-\$B\$8*\$B\$7)/(\$B\$5*(1-\$B\$6)).
- Hedging: In cell K12 enter =((\$B\$5-\$H11)*(\$B\$3-\$B\$4-\$B\$8*\$B\$7))/(\$B\$5*(1-\$B\$6)*\$G11)-((\$H11*\$E11 + (2*\$H11*\$F11*(1-\$B\$8)*\$B\$7))/\$G11.

The optimal portfolio policy, Equation (A5.8), is calculated in column L.

- In cell L12 enter =J12-\$B\$6*K12.

The optimal portfolio policy is confirmed using Equation (A5.10).

- In cell M12 enter =\$C12 + \$D12*\$B\$7.
- To complete the table, copy cells C12:M12 to cells C13:M41.

The results show that the allocation to equities declines as the investment horizon shortens and the hedging component declines to zero.

(continued)

(concluded)

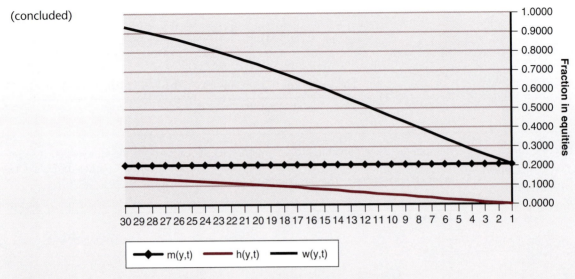

The completed table should appear as follows:

	A	B	C	D	E	F	G	H	I	J	K	L	M
1	Asset Allocation with Mean Reversion												
2													
3	μ	0.10											
4	r_f	0.05											
5	σ^2	0.04											
6	γ	−5.00											
7	y	0.00											
8	θ	0.13											
9													
10	t	T-t	w_0	w_1	b1	b2	Ψ	Φ		m(y,t)	h(y,t)	ω(y,t)	ω(y,t)
11	30	0			0.0000	0.0000	0.2400	0.0400					
12	29	1	0.2083	−0.5250	−0.0263	0.0331	0.2374	0.0395		0.2083	0.0000	0.2083	0.2083
13	28	2	0.2325	−0.5788	−0.0546	0.0647	0.2350	0.0390		0.2083	0.0048	0.2325	0.2325
14	27	3	0.2581	−0.6301	−0.0847	0.0948	0.2327	0.0385		0.2083	0.0100	0.2581	0.2581
15	26	4	0.2850	−0.6788	−0.1164	0.1234	0.2306	0.0381		0.2083	0.0153	0.2850	0.2850
16	25	5	0.3130	−0.7247	−0.1492	0.1504	0.2287	0.0377		0.2083	0.0209	0.3130	0.3130
17	24	6	0.3418	−0.7679	−0.1830	0.1758	0.2269	0.0374		0.2083	0.0267	0.3418	0.3418
18	23	7	0.3712	−0.8085	−0.2175	0.1996	0.2252	0.0370		0.2083	0.0326	0.3712	0.3712
19	22	8	0.4009	−0.8464	−0.2525	0.2219	0.2237	0.0367		0.2083	0.0385	0.4009	0.4009
20	21	9	0.4309	−0.8817	−0.2877	0.2426	0.2223	0.0365		0.2083	0.0445	0.4309	0.4309
21	20	10	0.4608	−0.9146	−0.3229	0.2619	0.2210	0.0362		0.2083	0.0505	0.4608	0.4608
22	19	11	0.4907	−0.9450	−0.3579	0.2798	0.2199	0.0360		0.2083	0.0565	0.4907	0.4907
23	18	12	0.5202	−0.9732	−0.3926	0.2963	0.2188	0.0358		0.2083	0.0624	0.5202	0.5202
24	17	13	0.5494	−0.9991	−0.4269	0.3116	0.2178	0.0356		0.2083	0.0682	0.5494	0.5494
25	16	14	0.5780	−1.0230	−0.4606	0.3256	0.2170	0.0354		0.2083	0.0739	0.5780	0.5780
26	15	15	0.6061	−1.0450	−0.4936	0.3385	0.2161	0.0352		0.2083	0.0796	0.6061	0.6061
27	14	16	0.6336	−1.0652	−0.5258	0.3504	0.2154	0.0351		0.2083	0.0850	0.6336	0.6336
28	13	17	0.6603	−1.0837	−0.5572	0.3612	0.2147	0.0349		0.2083	0.0904	0.6603	0.6603
29	12	18	0.6862	−1.1005	−0.5877	0.3712	0.2141	0.0348		0.2083	0.0956	0.6862	0.6862
30	11	19	0.7114	−1.1160	−0.6173	0.3802	0.2136	0.0347		0.2083	0.1006	0.7114	0.7114
31	10	20	0.7358	−1.1300	−0.6459	0.3885	0.2131	0.0346		0.2083	0.1055	0.7358	0.7358
32	9	21	0.7593	−1.1429	−0.6735	0.3960	0.2127	0.0345		0.2083	0.1102	0.7593	0.7593
33	8	22	0.7819	−1.1545	−0.7001	0.4029	0.2122	0.0344		0.2083	0.1147	0.7819	0.7819
34	7	23	0.8037	−1.1651	−0.7257	0.4091	0.2119	0.0344		0.2083	0.1191	0.8037	0.8037
35	6	24	0.8247	−1.1748	−0.7504	0.4148	0.2115	0.0343		0.2083	0.1233	0.8247	0.8247
36	5	25	0.8448	−1.1835	−0.7740	0.4199	0.2112	0.0342		0.2083	0.1273	0.8448	0.8448
37	4	26	0.8642	−1.1915	−0.7967	0.4246	0.2110	0.0342		0.2083	0.1312	0.8642	0.8642
38	3	27	0.8827	−1.1987	−0.8184	0.4288	0.2107	0.0341		0.2083	0.1349	0.8827	0.8827
39	2	28	0.9004	−1.2052	−0.8393	0.4326	0.2105	0.0341		0.2083	0.1384	0.9004	0.9004
40	1	29	0.9173	−1.2111	−0.8592	0.4361	0.2103	0.0341		0.2083	0.1418	0.9173	0.9173
41	0	30	0.9335	−1.2165	−0.8782	0.4392	0.2101	0.0340		0.2083	0.1450	0.9335	0.9335

Chapter 6

The Investment Management Process

Chapter Outline

6.1   Introduction

It is hard to determine whether your investment strategy has been successful if you cannot articulate your investment process. You may have superior performance relative to a prespecified benchmark, but you will not know if this performance is the result of skill or simply an unintended bias. Prospective customers will find it difficult to determine whether your strategy fits their needs if you cannot clearly explain how and why it works. In addition, it will be difficult to improve your process if you cannot define the key individual components of your approach.

This chapter discusses investment management techniques used for developing and implementing asset allocations based on the techniques introduced in Chapters 3 through 5. The chapter describes in detail a five-step process for developing successful investment strategies and explains how investors can ensure that quality is controlled throughout the process. Portfolio managers can follow this checklist to define, develop, and articulate their own investment strategies. Investors can use the process as a checklist when reviewing managers for selection. The five-step process also applies to passive investment strategies. Although they are not designed to produce added returns, passive strategies must be implemented intelligently—or they will *lose* value.

The following pages explore the concept of active management and describe both the philosophy and the application of several strategies. Portfolio construction techniques are reserved for a later chapter, so the featured portfolios are simple in structure. The chapter begins with a discussion of the efficient market hypothesis.

6.2   The Efficient Market Hypothesis (EMH)[1]

Investment strategies are generally categorized as active or passive. Active strategies assume that investment professionals can generate returns in excess of those created by passive strategies. This additional value justifies taking active risk and paying fees for active portfolio management. A natural question is whether we should expect positive alpha and if so under what market conditions. The **efficient market hypothesis (EMH)** provides a framework for answering these questions.

Definition of the EMH

The EMH states that security prices reflect all available information. The process through which securities reflect information is market competition. Any information, either data or the means of analyzing data, which investors find that helps predict future security prices will be used by investors today. These expected future prices translate into supply and demand for the security based on investors' asset allocation techniques, confidence levels, and capital bases. The result is that prices move to a new equilibrium level where investors can expect to earn a return commensurate with the risk taken. On average, informed investors are expected to profit, increasing their influence in the price-setting process, while uninformed investors are expected to lose, decreasing their influence in the price-setting process. This leads to a market where prices react immediately to new information due to the behavior of informed traders and where profitable strategies are exploited to the point where the inefficiency is removed. If the arrival of new information is unpredictable, then security price changes will also be unpredictable.

The EMH makes two key assumptions.[2] First, there are a large number of profit-maximizing participants who independently analyze and value securities. Second, these participants rapidly, and without bias, adjust their expectations to reflect new information.

Implications of the EMH

The implications of the EMH are these:

- To earn excess profits, an investor has to either obtain and trade on information before the market, or have and trade on information the market doesn't have, in the form of either proprietary data or a proprietary way of analyzing the data. This means holding a view at odds with current expectations.
- Market efficiency is *not* all or nothing. Different markets can display different degrees of efficiency, and the efficiency of a particular market can vary over time.

The EMH does *not* imply that no investor earns a profit; uninformed investors can get lucky, and some informed investors can profit from new information or insight. What it does imply is that, on average, investors should expect to earn the appropriate risk-adjusted return.

The EMH has been extensively tested and the literature is too vast to review in detail here, so only a brief outline of key findings is provided.[3] Because the potential

---

[1] This section is not intended to be an exhaustive discussion of the EMH, but rather an outline of its key concepts and implications for portfolio management.

[2] The implications of relaxing these assumptions are explored in the end-of-chapter problems.

[3] Malkeil (2003) provides a broad review of empirical studies, concluding that markets are more efficient than many studies claim and that, by and large, strategy profits do not exceed transaction costs.

set of information that can be traded is so broad, for practical purposes all tests examine only a subset of information. The result is the familiar taxonomy of weak-form, semistrong-form, and strong-form efficiency.[4]

Weak-form efficiency states that prices reflect all market trading information: past stock prices, volume, and short interest. Early tests examined technical analysis, simple filter rules (essentially attempting to find significant serial correlation), and charting rules, and could not reject the EMH.[5] However, later studies found evidence of significant short-term momentum and long-term reversal in stock prices.

Semistrong-form efficiency states that prices reflect all publicly available information: market trading data, financial statement information, opinions of management, and fundamental data about the economy and industries. These are tests of fundamental analysis and contrarian rules. **Contrarian rules** are simple trading strategies that use various price ratios, such as sorting stocks based on the price/earnings (P/E) ratio then forming a long portfolio of low P/E stocks and a short portfolio of high P/E stocks.[6] These strategies confirmed the mean reversion of returns over long horizons and were found to generate returns in excess of those predicted by CAPM. These strategies are referred to as **anomalies.**

One proposed explanation for this apparent inefficiency is that analysts extrapolate past performance too far into the future, resulting in the short-term overpricing of firms with good performance and underpricing of firms with poor performance, causing short-term price momentum. In the long term, when the forecast error is recognized, prices correct and reverse. Consistent with this view, it has been found that the stock of firms with low predicted growth outperforms the stock of firms with high predicted growth. Chapter 15 discusses the impact of human psychology and investor behavior on market pricing.

However, tests of the EMH hypothesize that the mean return to the active strategy is equal on a risk-adjusted basis to the expected return of a comparable passive strategy. Therefore, all tests of market efficiency are *joint tests* of both efficiency and the expectations model. If the expected risk-adjusted return model is incorrect, then results suggesting inefficiency are ambiguous. This provides alternative views—that the CAPM (or other risk model) is an incomplete model of systematic risk, or the apparent predictability of returns is due to changes in the risk premium.[7]

A third alternative is that these excess returns represent a liquidity premium. Amihud and Mendelson (1986) show that investors demand a risk premium to hold less liquid stocks. Smaller and less analyzed stocks tend to be less liquid. Liquidity can be particularly relevant when the strategy involves leverage. If incremental returns to active management are small, the level of assets matters if the cost of research is fixed.[8] Smaller firms can overcome this hurdle by using leverage. However, leverage

---

[4] It should also be noted that, by necessity, tests are conducted on the data available. While other markets have been examined, for the most part, this has meant focusing on the equity markets, for which a relatively long and detailed database is available.

[5] Kendall's (1953) early test was the motivation behind development of the EMH.

[6] Chapter 8 describes an example of a strategy buying low P/E and shorting high P/E stocks.

[7] Fama and French propose a three-factor model that includes return premiums linked to the P/B ratio, market capitalization, and market return, suggesting that the identified anomalies might be proxies for unidentified systematic risks. However, this is an ex post fix, adding to the model factors that cannot be explained by the original model. In addition, Daniel and Titman (1995) were unable to confirm that market capitalization and the P/B ratio were risk premiums. Barra and Northfield offer multifactor models that extend beyond price-based ratios.

[8] For example, a $10 billion fund would be willing to spend up $10 million to earn 0.1 percent in incremental return. However, a $100 million fund would be willing to spend only $100,000.

creates the tail risk of "picking up nickels in front of a steamroller." Periods of liquid, low-volatility markets may produce numerous funds with apparent positive alpha until a liquidity event results in large losses.[9]

There is less debate about **strong-form efficiency**—prices reflecting all information. Several studies have found that corporate insiders can trade profitably on their own company's stock. Grossman and Stiglitz (1980) argue that strong-form efficiency is logically inconsistent. Investors will spend time and resources to uncover new information only if they expect to profit from that information. In a strong-form efficient market, no investor benefits from information generation, so no information is generated.

These results confirm there is strong evidence that markets display short-term momentum with long-term reversion. The active view is that this pattern represents an exploitable market inefficiency. The passive view is that tests are inconclusive or cannot generate returns in excess of transaction costs. Three other issues imply this debate is likely to continue:

- Small excess returns are difficult to discern statistically from noise in market data. It would take a data series longer than we have to resolve with any precision whether skill truly exists.[10]

- Publicly reported return data can be biased. Selection (an investor is unlikely to publish the details of a positive alpha strategy, as opposed to academic research where a negative result is happily reported), survival, and self-reporting biases can skew test results. Although attempts have been made to estimate the size of these biases, their true impact is unknown.

- Even if we observe excess returns, tests are usually framed as a rejection of excess returns at a certain confidence level. This means that we should expect some tests to reject the hypothesis of zero excess returns simply by luck.[11]

The implications of the EMH for professional portfolio management are perhaps best illustrated by a familiar joke concerning a student walking on campus with two finance professors. The student sees a $20 bill on the ground and stops to pick up the bill. The professors merely chuckle to themselves and continue walking. After retrieving the bill and catching up to the professors, the student asks why they did not stop. The professors state, "If there was a $20 bill on the ground, someone would have clearly picked it up by now."

The EMH is not dogmatic. Although the markets are competitive, there are still profits to be made. There will be $20 bills to pick up. Perhaps the greatest value of the EMH is the healthy skepticism it suggests when you evaluate your and others' claims of a successful strategy. The EMH provides the benchmark for evaluating active strategies. The onus is on the analyst to reject the hypothesis of no alpha, identify the source of the inefficiency, and show that the inefficiency provides the basis for a consistent executable trading rule generating profits in excess of transaction costs. The $20 bills will not be everywhere, and we should not expect them to appear consistently in the

[9] See Lo (2007).

[10] This issue was explored in Chapter 4.

[11] The classic example is coin flipping (Problem 2 in Chapter 3); the likelihood of flipping 10 tails in a row is 1/2,048. According to the Bureau of Labor Statistics, 221,000 people held positions as financial analysts in 2006. That translates into potentially 108 lucky all-star analysts. Coincidentally, the WSJ selects 100 "Top Gun" stock pickers and earnings forecasters across 50 industry groups each year. Given the number of PMs, it is hard to know which track records represent true skill.

same place. It will not be long before others realize this. However, if you are convinced they are there, pick them up!

Even in an efficient market there is a role for analysis and portfolio management. Markets need analysts seeking profit opportunities to ensure that prices reflect available information. Investors need portfolio managers providing portfolio diversification to reduce idiosyncratic risk and to create a systematic risk profile appropriate for each investor. This risk profile includes the investor's risk aversion, risk capacity, and human capital risk. Portfolio construction can also incorporate tax considerations.

6.3 General Discussion of Investment Strategies

There are many approaches to investment management, including both passive and active strategies. Passive disciplines provide market exposure at low cost. Passive strategies include equity indexes that seek to mimic the S&P 500 Equity index (consider the multibillion-dollar Schwab S&P 500 Index Fund), the Barclays Capital (previously called Lehman) Aggregate Bond index (consider the multibillion-dollar Fidelity U.S. Bond Index Fund), or a fixed 60/40 mix in stock and bond indexes (consider the multibillion-dollar Vanguard Balanced Index Fund). Passive management techniques, including full replication and sampling strategies, are reviewed in Chapter 7.

Active strategies are meant to outperform passive strategies. Examples of active strategies include an equity fund that seeks to outperform the S&P 500 utilizing a fundamental stock-picking process or a balanced fund that implements dynamic allocations to stocks and bonds incorporating an active **market timing** discipline. Investment newsletters, Wall Street strategists, or mutual fund companies may offer market timing strategies. Their approach is to forecast short-term returns and balance them with forecast short-term risk. These forecasts may be generated quantitatively or qualitatively. As these forecasts change, so do the optimal allocations. Allocations may be determined using an M–V model with varying mean returns, standard deviations, and correlations. The manager implements the change in the underlying fund to reflect the model changes, using either cash (the individual stocks and bonds) or derivative instruments (futures contracts).

Chapter 7 will also introduce several active equity strategies, including sector rotation, style investing, and fundamental stock selection. In addition to fundamental stock-picking strategies where individual analysts study company financials and prospects, many managers use quantitative techniques for picking stocks. One of the first quantitative strategies, introduced in the 1970s by Wells Fargo, was an equity portfolio with an allocation bias toward stocks with unusually high dividend yields. The expectation was that high-yielding stocks would outperform the market averages. This bias was called a **tilt.** More advanced tilt strategies involved timing these biases, changing the portfolio tilt through time to capture short-term trends in the stock market.

Many active investment managers use derivatives within their strategies, either looking to profit from perceived mispricings or simply as a way to implement their strategies. Volatility estimates are imbedded within an option price, and managers may believe these volatility estimates are too high or low. Call-writing strategies are a bet that the income generated from selling options will dominate the impact from those options being exercised in the money.

Each of these investment strategies may be motivated by a good idea. However, a good idea is not enough to make an investment strategy successful. Strategies need to include many important ingredients to ensure a high probability of success. Even after a strategy is successfully introduced, its design cannot remain static. If the discipline does not constantly adjust to the environment, including competitive pressures, it probably will not succeed in the long term.

6.4 The Five Key Elements of the Investment Process

Introduction

Key elements of an investment process may be separated into five parts. These include the *philosophy of the strategy,* which is the basic idea behind the strategy. A portfolio manager should be able to explain why his or her investment strategy makes sense, at least in theory. Even though an investor may have a great idea, that idea must be converted into something observable, such as a data source. This is called **signal creation.** Once the signal is created, an investor needs to determine the action necessary to benefit from the signal. **Signal capture** includes specifying the investment instruments that may be used to transform the investment manager's desired action into a portfolio position. The investment manager also needs to consider *implementation issues.* When should trading be done? Is there enough liquidity? Finally, the manager should create a *feedback* process, studying the results of the strategy and using this analysis to improve the delivery of the first four steps of the process.

Philosophy of the Strategy

Few investors will want to contribute their assets to a fund if the manager cannot articulate why the fund's strategy should work. Defining a basic mechanism can be an effective way to begin the process of defining a strategy. Consider Archimedes, who explained the basic mechanism of a lever in 260 BC. A lever allows the user to multiply mechanical force and thus move objects larger than would be possible with the force applied directly. The basic mechanism is the co-movement of the fulcrum and lever: Pushing down on one side is converted into pushing up on the other side. The control mechanism is the length of the lever: The amount of work for a given force increases with the distance from the fulcrum. Archimedes used math to describe the exact relationships among force, work, and the relative distances from the fulcrum.

Some investment strategies can be described by mathematics. These include hedging strategies utilizing derivatives or passive disciplines. Most descriptions can benefit from the use of mathematics but rely to a greater extent on economic concepts, which depend on human behavior and cannot be fully defined by mathematics. All investment strategies must be supported by economic logic. For example, everyone knows that prices tend to rise with an increase in quantity demanded. Americans drive more in the summer, leading to upward pressure on gasoline prices. Gasoline suppliers know this and prepare to increase their production for the summer season. So the key to forecasting gas prices is to anticipate the level of increased demand relative to the level of increased supply; it is not sufficient to simply expect that demand will increase in the summer. For an active investment strategy, the manager needs to explain why valuations may be incorrect, and why the manager can see what others cannot. An investor needs to review this logic and decide whether it makes sense and whether the manager truly has the skill to successfully manage the strategy.

A portfolio manager should ask, "*Why* should it work?" A manager should also be prepared to explain *when* it should work and when it should not. Even good ideas do not work all the time. Consider exploring the market environments when the strategy works well; search for the times when it will not. Explore what happens after the strategy has worked well for a long period or worked particularly well over a short one. Also investigate whether the strategy's performance tends to reverse.

War Story   *The Danger of Not Articulating the Investment Philosophy*

Regression analysis, neural networks, and genetic algorithms were all popular techniques in the early 1990s for exploring statistical relationships between economic variables and future investment returns. Unfortunately they can be misused, identifying statistically significant correlations in historical data that do not reflect true causal relationships and therefore are unlikely to continue in the future. If we are not careful, we may rely too much on these techniques and reject the need to apply intelligent logic before developing investment strategy.

Consider one prospective strategy that initially sounded good but turned out to be a bust. The idea was to capture the **style bets** (active exposures to things like earnings growth, dividend yield, and price/book ratios) of a diversified set of active equity managers and take those same bets in another, separate portfolio. The expectation was that these bets were a residual of individual security selections made in the underlying portfolios, and they would reflect a bottoms-up consensus about which key market factors should perform well in the future. By collecting portfolio holdings of a group of astute managers in the past and estimating the relationship between these biases and subsequent performance, a mechanical strategy could be implemented that appeared to make the correct historical directional

bets on the factors. The idea was further tested by simulating a stand-alone equity portfolio incorporating intended historical biases. The strategy seemed to perform well in the past.

Unfortunately at least three things were wrong with this strategy design. There was no initial articulation of the strategy philosophy. The designers simply assumed the consensus bets made sense. They should have asked themselves why the individual stock bets should lead to logical consensus market factor bets. There was also no comparison of the bets in the separate portfolio and the original portfolios. Even if the individual stock bets made sense, they might destroy value at the factor level. In fact, an analysis done prior to implementation revealed that the bets in the stand-alone portfolio had the opposite sign of the original portfolios, which actually lost value from their style biases. The statistical procedure used to model the strategy reversed the sign of the bets to add value in the past. In addition, the simulation did not validate the strategy because it was both designed and tested using the same sample. The estimated relationships were the product of **data mining,** not careful thought. The implementation was done mechanically, without reflection. The philosophy behind the basic mechanism was faulty. Overall this was a bad idea—but an important lesson!

Signal Creation

A state treasurer in New England once said, "I don't understand this investment business. Why don't you simply buy energy stocks when energy prices are going up and sell the stocks when energy prices are declining?" Good idea. Of course everyone else has the same idea, forcing energy company stock prices to move simultaneously with oil, gas, or coal prices. As a result, an investor cannot reliably capture value using the published signal of rising energy prices. The signal is generally available too late to make any money from investing in energy stocks.

What is a signal? An investment signal is a fact that you can observe early enough to implement an investment bet. While most applicable for active management, signals can be used within a passive strategy, such as by signaling a rebalance trade. A signal can be numerical, like an earnings number. It can be subjective, such as the level of confidence expressed by company management during a conference call with analysts. The investment signal provides a basis from which to develop an investment decision-making process. If the signal is positive, you invest one way. If the signal is negative, you invest another way. If the signal is indeterminate, you assume a neutral position. A simple example is summarized in Exhibit 6.1. The term *significantly* points out the need to screen out noise. Only when a signal is clearly outside of a prespecified range should it be acted upon.

War Story · *The Danger of Not Thinking through the Investment Signal*

Tactical asset allocation (TAA) strategies involve timing the markets. The goal is to identify which asset class will outperform in the future and then overweight that asset class in your portfolio. One popular approach is to develop an econometric model based on market variables including trailing returns, dividend yields, and interest rates, as well as macroeconomic data including inflation, production levels, and GDP changes.

Consider one strategy that applied a probabilistic approach. The idea was not to forecast future returns but instead to estimate the probability of one asset class outperforming another. A *probit* statistical model can be used to estimate such a probability. When forecast probability differences were statistically significant, the manager would purchase futures contracts in the asset class expected to outperform and sell futures contracts in other asset classes. The original model was fitted using historical market data and historical economic data released by the federal government. The government frequently releases economic data with a lag. It takes time to tabulate and distribute the information collected from industries and other sources. When estimating an econometric model using historical economic data, the modeler should be careful to include an accurate measure of the time lag expected when the model is implemented. For example, recognize that the fourth quarter productivity number will be available not on December 31st but more likely four weeks later. There is a general

understanding of this issue in the investment business, including the recognition that this time lag may have been longer in the past.

What is less understood is that government economic data are subject to several revisions even after they are released. For example, current productivity figures are revised up to five weeks after initial release. Historical databases may store only the final revision. If you model and test your strategy using these data, you are effectively assuming that you knew the revised numbers before they were released. Think about this: If someone knew how economic data would be revised beforehand, they should be able to make money. Accurate testing requires building and testing the model with the originally released data.

Unfortunately the probabilistic TAA strategy just described was built using historical, revised data and implemented in real time with first release data. Initially the strategy seemed to work, but after a few quarters it stopped adding value. During a follow-up analysis of the strategy, it was observed that forecasts rerun with the historical database months later differed from the original forecasts run months earlier. The original forecasts that were run with first release data lost money when implemented using the model. The rerun forecasts, utilizing subsequently revised data, would have added value had the revisions been known in advance. But run live, they were useless.

Statistical techniques, such as standardizing based on historical variability, may be applicable here. Note that the level of portfolio turnover may be controlled by adjusting the required significance level of the signal; a higher significance level will make fewer signals significant and result in fewer trades.

Two key issues regarding investment signals affect the success of a strategy. First, the techniques for identifying the signal must be explored. Is the signal readily observable or do you need to dig for it? Can others observe the signal? Does the strategy's success rely on capturing the signal earlier than the competition or interpreting it more expertly? Second, the time lags between when the signal is available, when it is identified, and when it can be acted upon must be considered. Portfolio managers should think this through carefully because not all good ideas work in practice. A good signal is timely and clear so that it can serve as a basis for effective decisions.

EXHIBIT 6.1
The Investment Process: Signal-Based Decision Making

Signal direction	Investment action
Significantly positive	Go long
Significantly negative	Go short
Indeterminant	Be neutral

EXHIBIT 6.2
Issues to Explore When Designing a Paper Portfolio

1. Active bet to capture signal.
2. Exploration of signal significance required and associated turnover.
3. Securities utilized to convert bet into investment portfolio.
4. Weighting of securities.
5. Risk considerations:
   a. Diversification of active bets.
   b. Unintended bets.

Capturing the Signal

Once the signal is identified, to make money the signal must be converted into an investment position—or in other words, captured within a *paper portfolio,* which is a list of security positions that have not yet been traded. These securities could be individual stocks and bonds, indexes, or commodities. This is the portfolio that would be used for testing a strategy back in time. A **model portfolio** is a good example of a paper portfolio that is used as a target for creating a trade list. Model portfolios can change continuously but will not necessarily be tracked perfectly due to trading costs.

An accurate paper portfolio is based on the actual securities that are available in the marketplace. As a result, the portfolio manager must decide which *investment vehicles* will be used to capture the signal. Cash instruments like individual stocks are effective for capturing the output of a fundamental stock selection process. Derivatives, such as futures contracts, are effective for capturing market timing signals. Structured derivatives, such as OTC warrants that pay off when credit spreads move in a certain direction, are useful for capturing nonstandard investment signals. Securities, even if they are listed, do not necessarily trade actively. The portfolio manager needs to consider the volume of these issues and whether they can realistically invest at least a small level of assets.

Portfolio managers must also decide how to construct portfolios. They can select buy-rated stocks, but they still need to decide how to weight the stocks. Are they equally weighted or weighted based on market capitalization? Is there a benchmark on which managers need to focus? To maximize value added adjusted for risk taking, a manager should consider risk control. How diversified should the portfolio be? Is there a way to diversify the process with multiple signals? To capture the signal, the portfolio may be exposed to secondary, unintended bets that will not add value but will add noise. Is there a way to effectively control that risk without neutralizing the intended bet? These issues are summarized in Exhibit 6.2 and illustrated in the Theory in Practice box.

Implementation Issues

A paper portfolio is not a live portfolio. A trade list needs to be executed before the paper portfolio is converted into a live portfolio. Paper performance is not live performance, and live performance is what matters—it is the gain or loss of money in your pocket. The difference between paper performance and live performance is the result of transaction costs, trading restrictions, and portfolio management procedures.

Transaction costs will be reviewed in detail in Chapter 12, but it is important to introduce the issue within this chapter's discussion of strategy implementation. **Transaction costs** for stocks, many derivatives, and some bonds include commissions charged by a broker. For example, retail stock trades at discount brokers may be executed for $9.95 or less, regardless of the number of shares. Other brokers, including institutional brokers, charge a per-share fee such as 3 cents a share, and they may provide some support in developing and applying an execution strategy.

In the mid-1980s there was a growing need for consistent value added over equity benchmarks. It was difficult to outperform the S&P 500, and institutional investors, such as pension plans and endowments, were seeking better control over their active manager exposure. They had been disappointed that their managers might outperform for a period of time but then experience a performance reversal that erased the previous value added. The increasing importance of benchmarking at the overall plan level made it important to understand benchmark risk at the manager level.

One simple way to manage the benchmark risk of an equity portfolio is to restrict the difference in sector weights between an active portfolio and the index. This is a one-dimensional problem and can be easily solved. Simply invest the index proportion in energy, technology, and financial stocks, and actively select the individual names in weights reflecting their attractiveness. Risk from sector differences is eliminated. A manager could do this using a simple spreadsheet, a calculator, or even paper and pencil.

Unfortunately there typically remains a lot of benchmark risk in a sector-neutral portfolio. A portfolio's market cap exposure, tendency toward growth or value, and overall beta are not controlled in a simple sector-neutral or even industry-neutral portfolio. Importantly, nonsector differences will overwhelm sector differences in many market environments. This will be discussed in Chapter 7 with an illustration of the time series pattern of growth and value stocks, showing the sometimes dramatic swings in returns between growth and value biases. As a result, a manager seeking to isolate risk from stock selection needs to consider managing style risk in addition to controlling sector or industry risk.

There are additional costs beyond commissions. In fact, execution of over-the-counter securities, like NASDAQ stocks, Treasuries, and structured notes, do not include commissions, yet there certainly are transaction costs. The **market maker,** such as an NYSE specialist, who maintains an inventory in the security investors wish to buy or sell, needs to be paid to hold that inventory. This is reflected in the **bid–ask spread.** An investor can buy a security from a market maker at the ask price and sell it at the bid price. For securities that trade actively, the bid–ask spread could be just a few basis points. For a less actively traded municipal bond, the spread will be percentage points. Current bid and ask prices are typically quoted for a small volume of shares; for listed common stock, the prices could be quoted for hundreds or thousands of shares. As the size of the trade grows, the bid–ask spread tends to widen because market makers need to be paid to take on (or go short) a larger position, along with the associated risk that the position will move against them. The change in transaction costs due to trade volume is called **market impact.** Market impact is also described as the price paid for immediate execution compared to patiently waiting for other investors to submit orders. Lower volume and higher risk are associated with larger market impact.

Because transaction costs rise with increasing order volume, liquidity and capacity are important considerations for developing an investment strategy. **Liquidity** reflects the ease of trading a particular security or set of securities in different trade sizes. For example, small-cap stocks are less liquid than large-cap stocks because they tend to trade less frequently and in smaller daily volumes. Increasing the size of your orders leads to increasingly higher spreads, and at some point the trade simply cannot be executed at the intended size. The lower the liquidity level of the securities in which you plan to invest, the higher the transaction costs the strategy will experience. On paper this will require a higher expected value added from a strategy that uses less liquid securities.

The fundamental research process involves careful study of individual companies, seeking to identify securities that reflect low valuations and attractive growth opportunities. As part of the process, much effort is expended on sector analysis: What is going on in the sector? Is this a good place to be? What are the best stocks in that sector?

Consider the strategy discussed in the War Story: The Danger of Not Articulating the Investment Philosophy box. The strategy sought to capture signals from active portfolio managers to take style bets. Now consider a second strategy proposing active sector rotation. The idea was to rank sectors by their attractiveness based on fundamental analyst research observations and take active positions in the most attractive stocks within the most attractive sectors.

This was a complicated strategy with lots of moving parts. Before implementing the strategy with live money, a rigorous back test was conducted. This included setting individual stock weights to evaluate the validity of the philosophy, calculation of the signal, and monitoring of signal capture within the paper portfolio. A key observation led to the strategy being discarded. The stability of the signal was poor. Recommended sector position changes were frequent, leading to portfolio turnover levels in excess of 400 percent per annum. Attempts to reduce the level of turnover destroyed the value added. Transaction costs were not the binding problem; it was the lack of liquidity in the underlying securities. The stocks did not trade enough to make the strategy worthwhile. Although it could work at low asset levels (less than $50 million), the proposed management fees would not have covered management costs.

As the dollars in a strategy increase, the proportional level of transaction costs increases. As the level of assets under management (AUM) increases, at some point, no matter how much value added the strategy generates on paper, it will not be able to generate value in the live portfolio because transaction costs, per dollar, have risen too high. **Capacity** is the asset level of a strategy that, if exceeded, would lead to an unacceptably low level of realized value added. The feasibility of an investment strategy is also influenced by the trading required to implement it. Higher turnover leads to higher drag from transaction costs and a lower level of capacity.

The relationships among liquidity, transaction costs, required value added before trading costs, and capacity are summarized in Exhibit 6.3 and illustrated in the War Story: Considering Capacity before Going Live box. Many investors believe that less liquid and more volatile securities offer an opportunity for higher returns. This may or may not be the case, but it is necessary to earn a higher level of value added before trading costs from a strategy relying on trading less liquid securities.

Once transaction costs, liquidity, and capacity are reviewed, management procedures need to be defined to ensure effective implementation of the investment strategy. These operational procedures include steps for constructing the portfolio, setting trading rules, defining monitoring tools, and assigning personnel responsibilities. There are many ways to manage money, but in all cases clear procedures should be defined. Portfolio construction may be mechanical—prepared by a computer program or an expert spreadsheet run by the portfolio manager or trained assistant. Construction may

EXHIBIT 6.3
Implementation: Liquidity, Value Added, and Capacity

Liquidity	Security characteristics	Transaction costs	Required value added	Capacity
Low	Low volume, high risk	High	High	Low
High	High volume, low risk	Low	Low	High

be qualitative—built stock by stock with paper and pencil. Trading may be triggered using mechanical rules (such as when the current weight becomes significantly different from the target weight) or tied to market conditions (perhaps adjusted for changing bid–ask spreads and the trader's feel for the market).

Effective procedures define steps, assign responsibilities, and allow transparency and oversight. Cash may flow into and out of the portfolio. Who should be responsible for monitoring the cash level? Who should invest it? What level of highly liquid securities should be maintained in the portfolio to accommodate withdrawals? Steps should be defined to ensure that managers understand the overall process and that daily functioning does not break down.

Specific responsibilities should also be assigned. Who is responsible for overall performance? How are responsibilities delegated? How are portfolio positions monitored? How often are reports distributed and to whom? The War Story: Procedures, Portfolio Insurance, and the 1987 Crash box illustrates the importance of following well-defined procedures.

Feedback/Review Process

The only way to know *if* a strategy is working is to evaluate its performance relative to an appropriate benchmark. The only way to know *where* it is working is to calculate performance at each step in the process.

The three key sources for performance measurement are at the signal, signal capture, and implementation stages. As the strategy design moves from the signal to the signal capture and implementation stages, it experiences noise and a drag on performance. Studying the noise and drag will help managers better understand their strategies and identify where to focus resources for lowering risk, reducing costs, and improving performance. The signal stage is typically easy to calculate. It requires simply updating the data used to simulate the original strategy philosophy. If a manager does not follow a structured approach, it is acceptable to list the manager's themes and track the performance of bets on those themes. Consider a manager betting that energy prices will rise. Look at the changes in oil, natural gas, and coal prices. What kind of performance would an investor earn on an equally weighted portfolio of these commodities? Analyst stock recommendations are a popular signal. Equal-weighting or value-weighting all the buy, sell, and hold recommendations, by sector, and then comparing their performance to sector indexes is a good way to validate whether there is any value in the raw material. More advanced techniques for extracting the pure stock selection return, net of industry and style, provide information to more effectively evaluate pure stock picking and more accurately reflect what value is available to be captured within a portfolio diversified across sectors and styles.

The signal capture stage includes a paper portfolio, with all securities having target weights designed to reflect the value opportunity in the signal. Performance of this portfolio reflects ideal results, prior to the reality of transaction costs. This analysis may be complicated: The paper portfolio may already reflect the impact of liquidity and capacity in its design. If more granularity is desired, two paper portfolios can be created—one of them a very raw portfolio excluding consideration of trading realities.

Obviously results of the live portfolio are the most important: That is what managers earn for their clients. However, all three returns are important for evaluating the performance of the strategy. They help answer questions about the value in the signal, the ability to capture the signal, and the costs involved in implementing the strategy. Did the portfolio outperform due to betting the right way on the signal, or was it

War Story   *Procedures, Portfolio Insurance, and the 1987 Crash*

A popular investment strategy in the mid-1980s was called portfolio insurance. As discussed in Chapter 5, this strategy was developed to provide a floor on stock returns and was based on option valuation theory. Investors could pay a premium to limit the downside and still preserve much of the upside in their equity portfolios. The discipline appealed strongly to institutional investors who were concerned about stock market valuations following the strong bull market that began in 1982. They turned out to be correct. Other investors, assuming portfolio insurance would work as advertised, adopted these strategies to support a decision to increase their overall exposure to the equity markets. They turned out to be wrong.

At the time, for institutional investors, portfolio insurance consisted of separate overlay accounts that were run by specialized managers, providing optionlike protection. *Overlay* means the clients could continue running their equity portfolios without interference from the insurance accounts. These insurance portfolios would be managed with a down payment of 5–10 percent of the underlying assets, using equity index futures contracts to replicate the behavior of a theoretical put option by trading the futures dynamically as market levels changed. As long as the aggregate level of insurers and market movements were small relative to the dollar volume of the futures exchanges, there would be sufficient liquidity to implement all these overlay portfolios.

Dynamic replication of a put option involves selling futures as the market declines and buying them as the market appreciates. Ideally futures are traded simultaneously with the market movements. Due to trading costs, however, futures were typically traded only after the market moved a minimum amount. This led to less efficient option replication but saved costs when markets reversed—a reasonable trade-off. However, the trading rules were based on a thorough analysis of well-behaved markets over the long term.

As noted, the stock market trended upward during the mid-1980s with only short-lived declines. Traders at some portfolio insurance money management firms began to notice that following a short-term decline in the market, the market tended to rebound. If they held off selling after the decline and buying after the subsequent rebound, they observed that they could save costs and improve the performance of the accounts. As a result, some firms abandoned their cautious trading rules in favor of less frequent trading and began "letting it ride."

On October 19, 1987, stocks began to decline. True dynamic replication required portfolio insurance managers to sell futures—fast. Stocks continued to decline, and the number of sellers began to grow. This prompted continued declines, increasing costs for insurance managers who followed their trading rules. Liquidity levels declined as well, increasing bid–ask spreads and market impact costs. While more expensive than anticipated, these accounts were softening the decline. However, a number of managers held off trading, expecting the markets to rebound. Ultimately the market declined so much that they were forced to trade but at much lower levels. They had changed their trading rules, and their clients paid for it.

Portfolio insurance turned out to be a public relations failure. There were several reasons for this. Many buyers of the insurance did not understand the strategy. Portfolio insurance is designed to prevent losses of principal only at the expiration of the insurance, not all the time—unlike a stop-loss order, which sells out completely at a certain market level. Many buyers thought portfolio insurance would operate like a stop-loss order. Transaction costs were also much higher than anticipated, leading to greater than expected loss of principal at expiration. Managers did not anticipate that the strategy would suffer its biggest challenge when it was needed most. With the steep market decline, replication costs increased to a higher level than expected as liquidity declined along with market levels. This was an error in designing strategy implementation. The designers of the investment strategy did not effectively explore market liquidity and transaction costs and appropriately define product capacity.

Holding off on trading, though not widely publicized, was an even worse implementation mistake because it was a breakdown in procedure. The decision to delay trading was based on observed market behavior and conflicted with the basic premise of the strategy, which was to get the client out of the market as the market declined.

Portfolio insurance is still a great idea, and its costs are more predictable with the use of options instead of dynamically traded futures. However, it still faces a serious capacity challenge: Who wants to take the other side of that trade? This was discussed in Chapter 5.

War Story   *A Structured Active Small-Cap Equity Product*

In the late 1980s many institutional investors recognized the higher value added that could be generated from small-cap portfolios benchmarked versus the Russell 2000 index, as opposed to large-cap portfolios benchmarked versus the S&P 500 index. As a result, many investors hired passive managers for their large-cap mandates and active managers for their small-cap allocations. However, the total allocation to small-cap U.S. equities was relatively small, and investors were not always able to fund several managers to assure diversification and broad exposure to the asset class.

One management firm that housed a large investment research staff decided to develop an actively managed small-cap strategy that would match the Russell 2000 index market capitalization, style, and sector exposures. The analysis was completed studying the raw value added delivered by fundamental analysts within a small-cap universe, and a track record for a paper portfolio was easily constructed using historical records of recommended stocks. Performance was reviewed favorably, with active returns of 1,000 basis points per annum before transaction costs were included.

The next step in the strategy's development was to explore these costs to try to forecast future active returns.

Fortunately, a thorough, thoughtful analysis was conducted, including examining the bid–ask spreads and volume of the individual securities. It turned out that despite broad diversification and the lower weighting of smaller, less liquid names, the paper portfolio included many stocks with weights that could not be realistically achieved.

A new simulation was run that limited the individual weights of stocks at each rebalance period based on their then-current trading volume. The new simulation also demonstrated strong value added but approximately 3 percent less annually than the naïve construction process. Less than 20 percent of the portfolio was impacted, indicating that the least liquid stocks provided the greatest value added—but only on paper. The portfolio managers would have seen this when they first tried to invest the stocks, but it was better to identify the issue before signing up clients. Moreover, by adjusting the strategy early on, lower transaction costs (forecast using portfolio bid–ask spread analysis) were incorporated in the strategy design. The adjustment also significantly increased the capacity of the strategy.

---

serendipity that the paper portfolio was structured with unintended biases that just happened to pay off? Exhibit 6.4 summarizes these observations, and the *War Story:* A Structured Active Small-Cap Equity Product box illustrates their importance.

6.5   The Importance of Quality Control

During both product development and live portfolio management, quality is important to future success. Sloppy simulations, overconfidence, and a lack of understanding of probabilities can all lead to failed strategy design. Poor risk management, high transaction costs, and failing to understand where active return comes from are all sources of failure in live management. Although only key ideas are outlined here, there is a more thorough discussion in Chapter 12.

Quality control is imperative for developing effective investment strategies. Each of the five steps just reviewed takes thoughtfulness and attention to detail to ensure a successful strategy. One common mistake made in creating a new strategy is data mining,

EXHIBIT 6.4
Feedback:
Performance at Each
Step

1. Performance of raw material: signal stage.
2. Performance of paper portfolio: signal capture stage.
Difference = performance impact from capturing signal.
3. Performance of live portfolio: implementation stage.
Difference = performance impact from implementing strategy.

which can come in several forms. The simplest includes running a simulated strategy multiple times over the same sample period, adjusting the strategy slightly each time, to produce the best possible simulated record. This exercise does not provide high statistical confidence that the final strategy is repeatable; it merely illustrates the best of many possible scenarios, all explored over a given period. The data mining manager is almost guaranteed to be disappointed in the future.

Other forms of data mining include testing an idea you learned somewhere else to ensure that it works. Simply testing a strategy that you know is successful proves only that you understand the strategy. Testing a paper portfolio that captures a signal developed based on data mining does not validate the overall strategy—just the strategy's ability to capture the signal. Data mining issues are explored further in Chapter 12.

A statement often made in the investment community is "I never saw a simulation that didn't look good." This tends to be true because disappointing simulations are never publicized. This can be extended to the concept of **survivor bias** for live management. Managers who perform poorly get fired and may leave the business. The poor results are forgotten, leading to future overconfidence by investors. These managers no longer appear on their clients' quarterly analyses or consultants' recommended lists; or if they go out of business, they may disappear from the selection and research databases entirely.

Another familiar comment is "They had five live strategies and one or two worked really well the first few years." Is this a good measure of success? Not really. Even if the strategy involves no skill, there is a reasonably high expectation that at least two of five strategies will work better than average. To illustrate, define "working well" as three or more flips of heads out of five coin tosses. This may represent a single investment strategy outperforming in at least three of five annual periods. The probability of three or more heads in five tosses is 50 percent. However, the probability of three or more heads in at least two of five series is 81.25 percent.[12]

Managers can also benefit from studying and understanding their performance, even if it is already good. From where did the value added come from? Was it from the primary active bets or secondary bets? Was it from a bias in the portfolio? In the 1970s and 1980s value-style equity managers performed well relative to the S&P 500. However, when their management process was examined, it was found that most, if not all, of the outperformance could be replicated with a simple price/book value screen. Beware any manager who says, "No, I didn't consider looking at a custom index."

Another helpful recommendation is to slice and dice the strategy's simulated and live performance. For an equity portfolio, this means examining the batting average of all stocks, individually and within sectors, cap sizes, and style groupings. If there is value added in most groups, there is a higher probability there will be value added in the future for the whole portfolio discipline.

The following recommendations are helpful ways to ensure good quality in product development and portfolio management. First, assume it should not work. As outlined in Section 6.2, there has been extensive research on efficient markets, theorizing and testing the idea that virtually all information is reflected in security prices almost instantaneously, making it difficult if not impossible to truly add value from active management. The strategy designer should always assume markets are efficient and seek to explain thoroughly why this particular strategy is different.

---

[12] This is computed by subtracting from 100 percent the probability of all five series yielding two or fewer heads and the probability of four of five yielding two or fewer heads, which is $1.0 - 1/32 - 5/32 = 0.8125$. This assumes the five series of coin tosses are independent of each other. In reality, investment strategies may be correlated. This will change the probabilities, but the likelihood of two or more series realizing three or more heads remains reasonably high.

6.6   A Sample Investment Strategy: The SRY Model

To illustrate the five key steps for developing a successful investment strategy, consider the significant relative yield (SRY) model, a tactical asset allocation strategy that seeks to actively trade between U.S. equities and U.S. bonds. The strategy focuses on only two asset classes—the S&P 500 index and investment grade bonds—and is based on a simple valuation criterion. This section will develop a case for the strategy and present simulated results. The general idea for this discipline is not new, so there is an element of data mining, and statistical significance levels should be taken with several grains of salt.

The SRY model is related to the VAR forecast model introduced in Chapter 5 in that it uses yields on stocks and bonds and recognizes the existence of autocorrelation. Unlike the VAR model, however, this approach does not focus on forecasts of bond and stock earnings yields; it simply uses observable earnings and bond yields as current measures of market valuation.

The SRY is a variation of the "Fed model" but does not assume that yields are equal when the markets are in equilibrium. The Fed model, described in investment industry lore as a tool utilized by the Federal Reserve, proposes that bond and stock yields should be in parity, and suggests that stocks are overvalued whenever bond yields exceed equity yields. The SRY model does not assume a constant target ratio. Instead it is based on the observation that markets move in cycles and tend to reverse after reaching extreme levels. As described here, a trade signal occurs only if the current yields are significantly different, in a statistical sense, from recent historical levels.

The Fed model provides helpful theoretical support for the SRY model. It proposes that there should be a relationship between bond coupon and stock earnings yields because they represent yields on competing assets. The Fed model presents the yields as simple measures of comparative valuation—what is currently being earned on investments. It also suggests that current stock prices reflect the present value of future earnings, which are affected by changing discount rates and future earnings expectations.

Philosophy of the Strategy

Stocks and bonds are natural alternatives for an investor. Stocks offer opportunities for growth in cash flows and the associated price appreciation. Bonds offer opportunities for stable interest payments and price appreciation when interest rates decline. Historically, stocks are more volatile and bonds offer lower returns. There are distinct periods when bonds outperform stocks and vice versa. Stocks move in cycles, in part associated with the business cycle. Bond prices also move in cycles, but unlike stocks, they tend to underperform stocks in periods of economic growth, especially when the economy is rebounding from a weak period. If investors could identify these periods in advance, they could position their investments to reflect this forecast and earn a higher return than a fixed blend of the two assets. Exhibit 6.5 charts the ratio of the annual return on the S&P 500 relative to the return on the Barclays Aggregate Bond Index through time. The cycles represent an opportunity for investors to earn significant returns—but only if they can forecast this relative movement in advance.

One potential source of this pattern is the observed tendency for individuals to extrapolate current trends.[13] When companies' profits are growing, investors will bid

---

[13] This behavior is discussed in Chapter 15.

EXHIBIT 6.5
Stock Returns versus Bond Returns: 12-Month Relative Returns (S&P 500 Index Return/ Barclays Aggregate Bond Index Return)

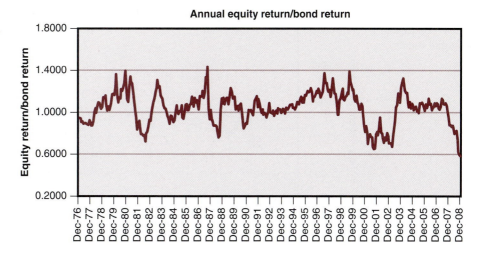

EXHIBIT 6.6
Cycle of Asset Price Levels

1. Growth in prospects over extended period.
2. Extrapolation of trend farther into future.
3. Extended appreciation and high current valuation.
4. Results failing to meet high expectations.
5. Price reversal.

up the price of their stock. At some point a company's results do not meet increased expectations, leading to selling and swift downward price adjustments. Price reversals tend to be most vicious following large, rapid price increases driven by increases in investor confidence. This extended appreciation happens in the overall stock market as well and can be identified by viewing measures of market valuation. By comparing current prices and current cash flows, such as earnings, investors can observe the level of expectations reflected in current prices. High valuations calculated with current cash flows indicate expectations of high future growth in cash flows. The basic mechanism, summarized in Exhibit 6.6, is that markets move, sometimes to extremes, based on investors inappropriately extrapolating trends over extended periods. Market valuations may be used to identify these extremes, which more often than not are not justified.

Consider Exhibit 6.7, which charts the ratio of two simple valuation metrics: equity earnings yield and bond yield. In this case earnings yield is the inverse of the trailing 12-month P/E ratio for the S&P 500. The bond yield is the yield-to-worst for the Barclays Aggregate.[14] High levels of the ratio reflect periods where stocks are highly valued relative to bonds. Mathematically this occurs because high valuations (paying a high price for current earnings) are associated with low earnings yields (the inverse of the P/E ratio), which are in the denominator.

Note one key observation: When the relative valuations reach an unusually high level, they tend to subsequently reverse. This is consistent with strong growth in expectations, followed at some point by an economic reality that cannot support these high expectations and associated valuations.

[14] Yield-to-worst is the lowest potential yield received on the bond without default. This accounts for call, repayment, or sinking fund provisions.

EXHIBIT 6.7
Relative Valuation of Stocks and Bonds

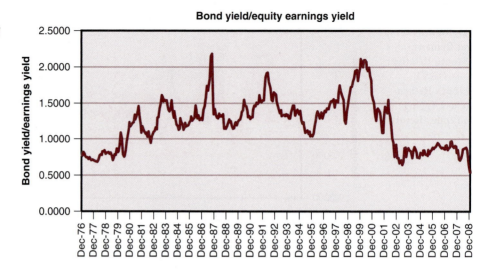

To summarize, the philosophy of the SRY strategy is that in more periods than not, unusually high valuations are associated with subsequent disappointments in performance. High levels may not guarantee that prices will reverse, but they suggest that any price reversal, when it does come, will be significant. If this is true, biasing the portfolio toward stocks or bonds when their relative values are unusually low should add value over a static mix of bonds and stocks.

Signal Creation

The data inputs used for this tactical asset allocation—trailing earnings, current stock prices, stated bond coupons, and current bond prices—are all readily available in virtually real time, even as far back as 1976. Although high-powered, widely connected computers were not common in 1976, investors could monitor market levels with Quotron and Telerate terminals, calculate relative earnings and bond yields with calculators, and then trade if necessary. This signal clearly meets the requirement of being easily observed early enough for an investor to act.

Although this relative yield measure is not sophisticated, it represents fair measures of valuation and may be all an investor needs to actively manage a stock/bond mix. Note that the manager does not need to dig for this measure, and it is readily available to all market participants. As a result, the investment strategy's success relies on insightful use of the information, not special access to it.

The brief discussion earlier in this chapter proposed that only unusually high or low values should suggest a trade. Consider a rule that signals a trade when the current yield ratio is significantly higher or lower than past values. The rule involves a two standard deviation band around the three-year moving average computed using monthly relative yield observations. The signal is defined formally in Exhibit 6.8.

EXHIBIT 6.8
Tactical Asset Allocation Signal

Signal	Allocation
Current > mean + 2 std dev	100% bonds
Current < mean − 2 std dev	100% stocks
Otherwise	50% bonds/ 50% stocks

EXHIBIT 6.9
Relative Yield and Signal Band

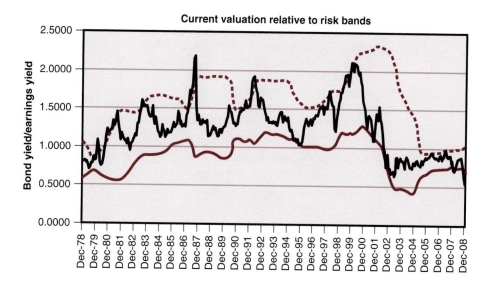

The signal is displayed through time in Exhibit 6.9. The dashed upper (lower) line represents the three-year average relative yield plus (minus) two standard deviations. A trade is indicated when the current level, illustrated by the solid line, breaks through the upper or lower band. If the current relative value exceeds the upper band, equities are considered overvalued relative to bonds and the portfolio is allocated to 100 percent bonds. If the current relative value falls below the lower band, the portfolio is allocated to 100 percent stocks. When the current relative yield is between the bands, the portfolio is allocated to 50 percent bonds and 50 percent stocks, which is a passive alternative.

By simulating this tactical asset allocation strategy over the period December 1978[15] through December 2008 using monthly observations, the process will indicate 33 allocation changes out of a possible 362, with an average active allocation lasting 2.8 months.

Capturing the Signal

A clear signal that may be easily calculated in real time must be captured in a paper portfolio. The vehicles used to express the signal are the S&P 500 index and the Barclays Aggregate Bond index. Today there are several alternatives from which to select in order to invest in these indexes. Currently derivatives, such as **index ETF**s, are readily available for either asset class. ETFs (exchange traded funds) are investment vehicles that seek to track a published index. Underlying assets are invested in a fund designed to track an index, and shares are offered representing ownership of these assets. But like stocks, these shares are also listed on exchanges and may be traded during the day. Performance of these shares closely tracks that of the published indexes. This is true because ETF shares can be redeemed for a basket of securities in the underlying fund, which tends to enforce parity between ETF shares and a portfolio designed to track the target index. As a result, it is not necessary to trade 500 individual stocks and scores of individual bonds in order to act on a change in the signal. All that is required are two trades: one in the S&P 500 Depository Receipt (commonly called a *spider*), ticker SPY, and one in the iShares Barclays Capital Aggregate Bond, ticker AGG.

---

[15] The first three years of data were used to calculate standard deviations.

Excel Outbox
The SRY Model

The spreadsheet Chapter 06 Excel Outboxes.xls illustrates the process for generating the trade signals for the SRY model. The <Data> worksheet contains the necessary return and yield data for the SPY and AGG. The trade signals and performance statistics are entered in the worksheet <Rule − Template>. The performance of the model is summarized in the <Summary> worksheet.

The return, growth of a dollar (GOAD), and yield for the equity and bond indexes are calculated in columns B:G. The relative performance, reported in Exhibit 6.5, of the stock and bond indexes is calculated in column H. The worksheet should appear as follows:

- In cell B6 enter =Data!B6.
- In cell C6 enter =C5*(1 + B6).
- In cell D6 enter =1/Data!G6.
- In cell E6 enter =Data!J6.
- In cell F6 enter =F5*(1 + E6).
- In cell G6 enter =Data!K6.
- Copy cells B6:G6 to cells B7:G401.
- Because the relative performance is calculated on an annual basis, in cell H18 enter =(C18/C6)/(F18/F6) and then copy cell H18 to cells H19:H401.

	A	B	C	D	E	F	G	H
1								
2								
3			S&P 500			Barclays Aggregate		
4		Return	GOAD	Yield	Return	GOAD	Yield	Equity/Bond Return
5			1.000			1.000		
6	Jan-76							
7	Feb-76							

The signal is calculated in columns J:O. Because the signal is based on the three-year moving average of the yield ratio, the formulas for the mean, the standard deviation, the bands, and the signal are first entered in row 41 (Dec-78). The bands are set as a multiple of the three-year rolling standard deviation. The size of the band is controlled in cells M5 and N5. These have been seeded with the value 2 but can be changed to explore other rules. The signal is as follows:

	1	If yield ratio > $\mu + X\sigma$	R(SRY) = R(SPY)
Signal =	0	Otherwise	R(SRY) = W R(SPY) + (1-W) R(AGG)
	−1	If yield ratio < $\mu - X\sigma$	R(SRY) = R(AGG)

The template should appear as follows:

	J	K	L	M	N	O
1						
2						
3						
4	Yield Ratio	3-year μ	3-year σ	$\mu - X\sigma$	$\mu + X\sigma$	Signal
5				2	2	
6						

- In cell J6 enter =G6/D6 then copy to cells J7:J403.
- In cell K41 enter =AVERAGE(J6:J41).
- In cell L41 enter =STDEV(J6:J41).
- In cell M41 enter =K41-$M$5*L41.
- In cell N41 enter =K41+$N$5*L41.

- In cell O41 enter =IF(J41>N41,1,IF(J41<M41,−1,0)).
- Copy cells J41:O41 to cells J42:O401.

	A	Q	R	S	T	U	V	W	X	Y	Z	AA	AB
1													
2													
3		Active		Passive		Passive			12-month return		Difference	Turnover	BA
4		Return	GOAD	Return	GOAD	Return	GOAD		Active	Passive			
5				50.0%		59.3%							
6	Jan-76												
7	Feb-76												

The performance statistics of the SRY model (active) and the benchmark (passive) are evaluated in columns Q:AB. The stock allocation of the passive strategy is set in cell S5 and seeded with a value of 50 percent, but it can be changed to explore other strategies. The template should appear as follows:

- In cell Q42 enter =IF(O41=0,$S$5*B42+(1−$S$5)*E42,IF(O41=1,E42,IF(O41= −1, B42))).
- In cell R42 enter =(1 + Q42)*R41.
- In cell S42 enter =$S$5*B42 + (1 − $S$5)*E42.
- In cell T42 enter =(1 + S42)*T41.
- In cell X53 enter =R53/R41 − 1.
- In cell Y53 enter =T53/T41 − 1.
- In cell Z53 enter =X53 − Y53.
- Turnover indicates when trades are executed. The sum of the column divided by 2 measures the total of round-trip trades executed. In cell AA42 enter =IF(O42 = O41,0,1).
- The batting average (BA) indicates whether the active strategy outperforms or underperforms the passive strategy. In cell AB53 enter =IF(Z53 < 0, −1,0).
- Copy the values down to row 401.

EXHIBIT 6.10
Sample Market Characteristics: Stock (SPY) and Bond (AGG) ETFs

	Product Inception	Dollar Volume	Discount/ Premium	Manager
SPY	2/18/1993	7,221,805,632	−0.09%	State Street
AGG	9/26/2003	22,060,940	0.28	Barclays

Note: Data were collected on January 24, 2006.

Implementation Issues

The paper portfolio now needs to be converted to an actual portfolio. To ensure effective implementation and perhaps check the feasibility of the strategy, transaction costs, liquidity, and capacity must all be evaluated. Although trading and transaction costs will be discussed in Chapter 12, a brief explanation of these costs is provided here. Recall that the strategy moves 50 percent of assets every time a trade signal is generated. For a $100 million portfolio, $50 million in both stocks and bonds is traded. The first step is to collect some basic information about the underlying instruments proposed for the live portfolio and evaluate their liquidity, transaction costs, and fees. These characteristics for the two ETFs are shown in Exhibit 6.10.

The SPY ETF trades over $7 billion in volume a day within nine basis points of the base fund. This suggests that the ETF should be easy to trade and that performance

EXHIBIT 6.11

Representative
Bid–Ask Spread and
Market Impact Data:
Stock (SPY) and
Bond (AGG) ETFs,
INET Electronic
Market

	$ Size (in Thousands) of Potential Trade	Bid–Ask Spread	One-Way Trade Impact
SPY			
Best	$ 202	0.01%	0.004%
Second best	9,158	0.02	0.012
Third best	14,710	0.04	0.020
Total	$24,070	0.03%	0.017%
AGG			
Best	$ 1,480	0.31%	0.154%
Second best	1,460	0.33	0.164
Third best	101	0.87	0.436
Total	$ 3,040	0.34%	0.168%

Note: Data were collected on January 24, 2006.

should be within basis points of the index. The bond ETF presents a greater problem. Daily dollar volume is only $22 million, and the 28 basis point premium suggests a higher tracking error than the equity ETF. If the signal needs to be implemented in one day and the trade can represent no more than 20 percent of daily volume (an investment industry rule of thumb), the capacity of the strategy is limited to $8.8 million if only the AGG ETF is used.[16] Fortunately bonds tend to be highly correlated with one another, and the U.S. Treasury market is one of the most liquid markets in the world, including the Treasury futures market where $115 billion is traded in 10-year note futures on a given day. Therefore futures contracts and other ETFs are available as investment vehicles to supplement the AGG. This increased capacity comes at the cost of greater potential tracking error given the less than perfect correlation between the AGG and other bond index alternatives. See Chapter 9 for a thorough discussion of bond portfolio management.

In addition to feasibility and capacity issues, it is also important to review the level of transaction costs. Exhibit 6.11 illustrates the bid–ask spread and market impact costs involved in utilizing the two ETFs. The data are based on Instinet's electronic crossing network (ECN) exchange named INET, which provides automated, intraday order matching for investors. Because this market is only one of many avenues to trade securities[17] the volume levels are a fraction of what can be traded, but the ladder of bid–ask quotes provides a range of costs at which one may expect to trade the ETFs at higher levels and provides an upper bound for implementing the strategy.

Trading small quantities of SPY generates a round-trip bid–ask spread cost close to one basis point. Increasing the order quantity leads to two and four basis point spreads, reflecting a growing market impact. A one-way trade would incur half the spread cost. The bond ETF is more expensive to trade, both in small quantities and as the order size increases. These results confirm that an effective implementation of the tactical strategy will require instruments other than the bond ETF.

[16] The largest bond transaction is limited to $4.4 million (= 0.20 × $20 million daily volume). Because each trade creates a 50 percent bond reallocation, the total strategy capacity would be $8.8 million. If the strategy involved only trading the stock ETFs, the strategy capacity would be $2.9 billion. This value is an underestimate because there are futures contracts, baskets of stocks, and other ETFs available as investment vehicles to supplement the SPY.

[17] In 2005 [0] INET trading represented approximately 13 percent of U.S. exchange trading.

EXHIBIT 6.12
Representative
Transaction Cost
Data: SPY ETF
Sample $10 Million
Trade (Price $125)

	Alternative Brokerage Commissions		
	$10/Trade	**1 Cent per Share**	**5 Cents per Share**
Bid–ask spread	0.010%	0.010%	0.010%
Market impact	0.030	0.030	0.030
SEC tax	0.002	0.002	0.002
Brokerage commission	0.000	0.008	0.040
Total	0.042%	0.050%	0.082%

Two other issues need to be explored: brokerage commissions and fees. A broker needs to be paid to execute an equity trade, including ETFs. Mutual funds withhold a management fee from the income on the fund; ETFs do this too. If the tactical strategy is utilized with the SPY and AGG ETFs, there will be a drag on performance from both commissions and management fees. Management fees will total 0.11 percent for the equity ETF and 0.20 percent for the bond ETF.

For its matching services, INET charges 0.3 cents a share; this would be embedded within any additional brokerage charge. The SEC taxes sell orders at the rate of 0.004 percent. Online retail brokers charge $5–15 per trade, regardless of share size. Institutional brokers, typically used by professional investment managers, charge per-share rates of 1 to 5 cents a share. Note that some institutions may trade directly with INET or another crossing network to avoid direct brokerage charges. As a result, to trade $10 million in SPYs, the total cost would be between four and eight basis points, depending on commission rates. These costs are illustrated in Exhibit 6.12.

The implementation issues may be summarized as follows:

1. ETFs may be appropriate for small asset levels, but realistically another method for capturing the return on the bond index will need to be developed.

2. Tracking error will be modest using the ETFs but needs to be explored, especially for the bond index.

3. Overall capacity for the strategy will be small if bond ETFs are used. Capacity will be very large if Treasury bonds or futures are used.

4. Transaction costs may be modest but need to be included in performance expectations. 100 percent annual turnover will generate a nontrivial drag on performance.

5. There will be some additional implementation effects on performance because trades will not be executed exactly at the close of trading (the pricing time used to develop the strategy). Brokers can provide execution prices guaranteed at the close, but at an additional commission charge.

Implementation concerns also involve setting management procedures, including defining processes, assigning responsibilities, developing monitoring systems, and setting oversight policies. Procedural implementation may be defined as the following:

1. Portfolio holdings review.
2. Signal production.
3. Order notification and transmission.
4. Order execution.
5. Order confirmation.
6. Performance monitoring.
7. Reporting and review.

The first step involves a personal review of the portfolio to ensure that it makes sense. Is it fully invested? Are the right securities at the right weights in the portfolio? Expert systems can support this function, but typically it is the final responsibility of the portfolio manager—the one whose neck is on the line for performance and any violations of portfolio restrictions.

The second step, signal production, is typically the responsibility of an analyst or a portfolio manager. Again, an expert system would be helpful in the SRY strategy to calculate yields and standard deviations in real time, updating the user and alerting him if values cross the upper or lower band. In practice, this process could be supplemented with fundamental analysts researching the stock and bond markets and the economy. The timing of the trading process, including contingencies, must also be considered. Should the signal be monitored in real time? What if the markets move dramatically toward the end of the day with just a few minutes before the market closes? What if the markets move overnight? What if the markets need to move only a small amount before a big trade is required? Some of these issues are reviewed in Chapter 12.

Order notification may begin with the output from an expert system that calculates recommended trades, prior to review by the portfolio manager or a trusted assistant before the order is communicated to the trader. In many cases a personal review and committee approval are required before a recommended tactical allocation change is converted to an order. Orders may be communicated electronically or over a recorded phone line for execution. Orders are similarly communicated to a broker. In smaller investment shops the analyst, portfolio manager, and trader may be the same person. Separating these duties requires formal communication but can provide a needed paper trail, improve effectiveness through specialization, and help avoid conflicts of interest (discussed in Chapter 14). Subsequent confirmation that the execution matches the order and a review of transaction costs early in the process avoids the compounding of trade errors and provides early feedback on changing market conditions. *Beware:* Trade errors never seem to help performance. The market invariably goes in the wrong direction when a sell is confused with a buy or an extra zero is placed by mistake in a share order.

Good performance is the portfolio manager's goal, and it is her or his job to deliver it. Constantly monitoring results, including attribution, can help the manager identify problems early. Regular portfolio reviews, including performance, should be prepared for senior management and clients. Performance measurement and attribution will be reviewed in detail in Chapter 13 and client reviews in Chapter 16.

Feedback/Review Process

A portfolio manager should review the validity of a strategy both before and after it is implemented. For the SRY strategy, it is important to prepare a back test and study its behavior, including portfolio changes, turnover, and performance. Back test results for the strategy are summarized in Exhibit 6.13. Performance is based on a fully invested portfolio with month-end signal creation and reallocation using published index returns.

The strategy successfully generated a higher net return than the 50/50 benchmark, yielding a 10.8 percent annualized gross return compared to 10.0 percent for the benchmark. The strategy generated slightly under 55 percent annual turnover, and the portfolio reflected an average equity allocation of 42.8 percent, well below the benchmark weight of 50 percent.

Does the back test suggest the strategy was successful? An assessment requires additional analysis. In particular, the performance needs to be evaluated for risk and adjusted for transaction costs and fees.

EXHIBIT 6.13
Simulation Results:
Tactical Asset
Allocation Strategy

TAA Strategy versus 50/50 Allocation Summary Statistics		
	TAA	**50/50**
Annualized gross return	10.78%	10.01%
Standard deviation	9.81%	9.66%
Sharpe ratio	1.10	1.04
% of 12-month underperforming	34.96%	
Annual turnover	55.00%	
Average equity allocation	42.80%	

1. Consider the standard deviation of returns. The active portfolio generated only a slightly higher level, 9.8 percent compared to the benchmark of 9.7 percent, resulting in a higher Sharpe ratio for the active strategy.

2. In addition, the strategy underperformed the benchmark in about 35 percent of the monthly observations—a decent batting average.

3. The higher return of the strategy is not simply due to a bias toward riskier, higher-returning equities. In fact, adjusting the passive strategy to reflect the average bond and equity allocations reduces the return of the passive strategy by 21 basis points per annum.

4. Transaction costs will certainly reduce active returns. Applying a 10 basis point cost to 55 percent turnover reduces compounded active return by 5 basis points—not enough to eliminate the active return or the superior Sharpe ratio.[18]

5. Management fees for the active portfolio will be higher than the 50/50 benchmark if the strategy is implemented with ETFs. On a weighted basis, this represents a 15.5 basis point management fee (= ½ × 11 basis points + ½ × 20 basis points). Of course the portfolio manager would seek to charge an additional fee for the active management. Perhaps the manager could charge a 10 basis point management fee, which would preserve moderate active return. However, due to the high level of potential capacity and the low level of resources necessary to manage this simple strategy, the product should still be profitable: $1 billion under management would generate $1 million in revenue and leave plenty of profits for a few employees. In practice, the firm could trade futures contracts and reduce the fee impact from the use of ETFs.

[18] Note that performance-based fees also lower the realized standard deviation of returns. In this example, all fees are independent of performance, based on either assets or turnover.

Excel Outbox

The summary table and charts are created using the <Summary–Template> worksheet in the Chapter 06 Excel Outboxes spreadsheet. The template should appear as follows:

	A	B	C	D	E	F	G	H
2		TAA Strategy v. 50/50 Allocation					Gross	
3		Summary Statistics					ETF	
4				TAA	50/50		Trade	
5	Annualized Gross Return						Net	
6	Standard Deviation						Fee	
7	Sharpe Ratio						Net-Net	
8	% of 12-month underperforming							
9	Annual Turnover							
10	Average Equity Allocation							

(continued)

(concluded)

The summary performance statistics are calculated in cells D5:E7:

- In cell D5 enter =Rule!$R401^(12/COUNT(Rule!$Q42:$Q401))−1.
- In cell D6 enter =(((STDEV(Rule!Q42:Q401)^2 + (1 + AVERAGE(Rule!Q42:Q401))^2))^12 − (1 + AVERAGE(Rule!Q42:Q401))^24)^0.5.
- In cell D7 enter =D5/D6.
- In cell E5 enter =Rule!$T$401^(12/COUNT(Rule!$S$42:$S$401)) − 1.
- In cell E6 enter =(((STDEV(Rule!S42:S401)^2 + (1 + AVERAGE(Rule!S42:S401))^2))^12 − (1 + AVERAGE(Rule!S42:S401))^24)^0.5.
- In cell E7 enter =E5/E6.

The trade statistics are calculated in cells E8:E11:

- The number of 12-month periods in which the passive strategy outperforms the active strategy equals the absolute value of the "BA" calculated in column AB. In cell E8 enter =ABS(AVERAGE(Rule!AB$42:AB$401)).
- The annual turnover is calculated as the scaled ratio of actual trades relative to potential round-trip trades. In cell E9 enter =12*SUM(Rule!AA42:AA401)/COUNT(Rule!AA42:AA401)/2.
- The average equity exposure for the active strategy is important for reviewing performance. In cell E10 enter =1 − (AVERAGE(Rule!O41:O401) + 0.5).

The net active returns are calculated in cells H2:H7:

- In cell H2 enter =D5 − E5.
- In cell H3 enter =0.5*0.0011 + 0.5*0.002.
- In cell H4 enter =E9*0.001.
- In cell H5 enter =H2 − H3 − H4.
- In cell H6 enter =0.001.
- In cell H7 enter =H5 − H6.

The success of a strategy can also be evaluated visually. Exhibit 6.14 illustrates the performance of the tactical strategy relative to the benchmark over the full period.

The time series shows the strategy consistently outperforming on a cumulative basis but suffering in February 2008, when the portfolio allocates to equities following a decline in equity prices and an increase in government bond prices. On a rolling three-year basis, stocks look cheap but continued to underperform bonds through 2008.

What other analysis should be done to further evaluate the validity of this strategy? Here are a few suggestions:

1. As mentioned earlier, implementation of the bond component needs to be further refined. Additional transaction costs and liquidity issues may be relevant for enhancing the strategy.

2. Transaction costs and liquidity parameters are presented based on current market conditions. Although the S&P 500 index and investment-grade bonds have always been highly liquid, equity index futures didn't exist before 1982, and program trades, with higher costs, would need to be tested before that date.

3. The strategy needs to be stress tested and its historical performance sliced and diced. The pattern of one-, three-, and five-year returns should be examined, including studying maximum and minimum returns. Performance during periods of recession and expansion, high and low inflation, and high and low volatility should be examined and the relationship between performance and economic environments explored. These analytical techniques are described in detail in Chapter 7.

EXHIBIT 6.14
Simulation Results: Tactical Asset Allocation Strategy

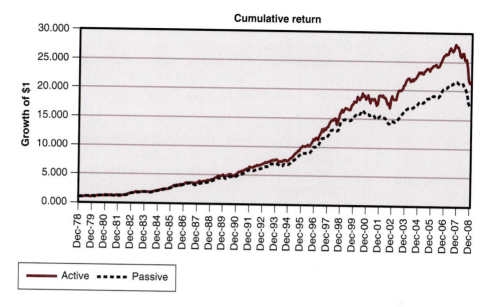

4. Consistency of performance should be further explored. The length of periods of very strong and weak performance, and the level of performance following these periods, need to be studied. This information can help the manager understand the frequency distribution of active and total performance under different conditions. Managing client expectations is one of the most important things a manager can do; fully articulating and teaching clients to understand return patterns can help maintain a book of business through periods of tough performance. As will be discussed in Chapter 16, the chapter on portfolio construction, this is especially important for TAA strategies that take only one bet at a time, and in many periods, no bet at all.

5. The pattern of allocations should be evaluated relative to economic environments. Special thought should be given to how future economic environments may differ from the past. For example, the high inflation rates of the 1970s and the subsequent declining interest rates of the 1980s may not happen again because today's Federal Reserve actively seeks to prevent such swings. The U.S. economy is more highly connected to foreign economies and more focused on services than it was in the past. Productivity is also much higher, and the markets may adjust more quickly as a result. Real-time financial market information is more readily available. The portfolio manager should also consider whether other investors are implementing the same strategy and competing for active returns.

6. What are the probabilities of success or failure? How often is the strategy right when valuations are at relative extremes? How bad can it get, and for how long, even if valuations suggest markets should reverse? These are just some things portfolio managers should consider as they ponder the appropriateness of their investment strategies.

Once a strategy goes live, special attention should be paid to overall short-term performance behavior, but the manager should not place too much emphasis on the sign and level of active return. Short-term variability, costs, and trading activity should be compared to the back test results of the proposed strategy and flagged for unusual differences. Higher-than-expected costs can quickly kill any strategy. All strategies can benefit from a little luck. It makes sense for managers to choose to start their track records when they feel their strategies have the highest chance of being successful in the short term.

Summary

This chapter is intended to help aspiring portfolio managers think about developing, implementing, and reviewing investment strategies. The discussion may be applied to any strategy—passive or active, single or multi-asset. The chapter described in detail five key elements to be considered for developing a successful investment strategy and illustrated these elements using the SRY model—a simple, valuation-based tactical asset allocation strategy.

The first element is the philosophy of the strategy—an explicit statement of why the strategy should work. The chapter concentrated on active disciplines, but passive strategies should also have a philosophy, even if it is simply the distinct investment belief that active management does not reliably deliver risk-adjusted value added. The second component is the creation of an investment signal that can be computed and displayed. In the SRY model the signal was the current ratio of stock and bond valuations relative to the historic average. The third element involves converting the investment signal into a paper portfolio. The fourth component is the transformation of the paper portfolio into a live, invested portfolio; and the fifth and final element is the review and adjustment of the strategy. An important ingredient in each element for the success of the strategy is quality control—that is, thoughtfulness and attention to detail.

Problems

1. Does your university or college offer a student-managed investment fund? If so, identify the five key elements of the fund. How could the strategy be improved?

2. Find an investment strategy on the Internet. Which of the five key elements are described? Which are missing? List two questions you would want to ask the manager.

3. Long Term Capital Management (LTCM), a hedge fund managed by prominent professionals, collapsed in 1998. Which of the five steps did it fail to perform successfully?

4. Find two investment products: a retail mutual fund and an institutional portfolio. Compare and contrast the two strategies' success at articulating the five key elements of effective strategy design.

5. Use the spreadsheet developed for the SRY model to answer the following questions:

   a. Which set of parameters would you select to optimize back test results if the SRY model was back tested from January 1976 through December 2005?

Back Test	Equity Allocation	Band Width (X)	Gross Annualized Return	Standard Deviation	Sharpe Ratio
1	50%	1			
2	50%	2			
3	40%	1			
4	40%	2			
5	60%	1			
6	60%	2			

   b. What is the expected active return?

    c. How does the selected strategy perform relative to the passive strategy from January 2006 through December 2008?

    d. What was the realized active return?

6. Repeat Problem 5 using the EAFE index.

7. What other parameter changes could be made to the strategy? How would you guard against data mining in this process?

Chapter  7

Introduction to Equity Portfolio Investing: The Investor's View

7.1   Introduction

So far our discussion of the portfolio management process has considered broad asset classes. The discussion of the M–V framework addressed the big picture, seeking to match overall asset class weightings to the individual's or institution's return objectives, risk preferences, time horizons, and investment constraints. That is, the focus has been to determine the overall allocation to equities, not the allocation to individual equity securities.

Stock portfolio managers focus on equity securities. There are two main types of equity: common and preferred. **Preferred stock** generally has a defined dividend that must be paid before dividends are paid to common stockholders; as a result, the price behaves much like a bond, especially if the dividend is secure. **Common stock** is more volatile; it represents an ownership share in the company, which can mean big payoffs if the company performs well or losses if the company does poorly. Company performance is typically measured by the level and growth of earnings and cash flow. As opinions about the company's prospects change, the stock price changes as investors trade on these changing opinions. The goal of a stock picker is to find a company whose fortunes may improve but whose stock price does not yet reflect those prospects, then buy and hold this stock until the stock performs or conditions change.

While stock pickers come in all shapes and sizes, there is more to equity management than stock picking. Equity managers may follow passive or active strategies, and each of them may follow a unique investing style. This chapter is devoted to the portfolio management process from the perspective of the investor who hires an equity manager; Chapter 8 will focus on the construction of equity portfolios. This chapter also introduces the equity side of the investment business and reviews in detail alternative approaches for developing the ideal allocation between different styles of equity managers. We end by discussing the manager selection process, offering proposals for forming investment guidelines for equity portfolios and a review of investment client objectives and expectations. This chapter is a broad overview of equity management, introducing many concepts and terms specific to equity portfolios. Several of the introductory discussions are general; these topics will be revisited in greater depth in later chapters.

7.2   Equity Strategies

Equity portfolio management may be divided into two categories: active and passive. A passive strategy is designed to provide exposure to an equity class with performance that is virtually identical to the equity class index. The performance objective of the portfolio manager may be to track the index return to within a few basis points, sometimes on a daily basis.

Active strategies seek to provide an attractive risk–return trade-off. This is done by investing the portfolio differently than the index and trading the portfolio through time. Although not always met, performance goals typically range from 25 to several hundred basis points over an index and may include three- to five-year performance horizons together with tolerance levels for underperformance over shorter periods.

Passive Strategies

One of the most popular passive equity strategies is an S&P 500 **full replication index fund.** The manager purchases all 500 stocks, or constituents, in the index in exactly the same weights as the index. The goal is to track the performance of the index as closely as possible with the return difference measured in basis points. Return differences result from cash allocations, contribution and redemption activity, changes in the index constituents, share rounding, and transaction costs. *Sampled* index funds purchase a diversified subset of the index constituents and are common for managing portfolios that replicate the performance of larger indexes such as the Wilshire 5000, an index designed to reflect the entire U.S. equity market. This approach to index fund management requires a sophisticated sampling approach to manage tracking risk. Management fees for index funds tend to be significantly lower than for actively managed funds because they are relatively easy to manage and there are numerous competitors, with management fees for S&P 500 index funds typically the lowest among index funds. Management fees for more specialized index funds, such as a single foreign country fund or an emerging market portfolio, are higher.

Structured Active Strategies

One approach to active equity management is similar to index management but includes modest active bets relative to the benchmark. This style may be called *index plus,* **structured active,** or *risk-controlled* active management. A more active equity approach, but still invested with the goal of managing risk relative to the benchmark, may be called **style neutral** or *core equity* investing. This strategy may actively allocate its assets among different sectors but tends to maintain the same overall exposure to value stocks or growth stocks as its benchmark. Style or **sector rotation** strategies offer higher turnover in hopes of being in the right style or industry at the right time. For example, these investors may rapidly move money from energy stocks to retail stocks to tech stocks. These strategies also tend to exhibit highly concentrated positions and high *active risk.*

Active risk equals the variability of portfolio returns relative to a benchmark index or peer group. It is frequently defined as the expected standard deviation of active returns; but as with asset allocation risk, it may also be reflected in downside probabilities and the chance of tail events. Based on work by Sharpe (1967), Rosenberg (1973), Fama and French (1992), and others, equity risk is viewed as being influenced by many factors. The CAPM model assumes there is a single market risk factor, and the level of risk is determined by a portfolio's beta relative to the market benchmark. Multifactor risk models recognize there are many potential risk factors, including value, growth, and industry exposures, each with its own variability and correlation. Any remaining risk may be considered specific risk, unique to a particular security, and may be diversified to a large extent. However, specific events can lead to large stock price moves, suggesting that individual active stock weights, in addition to market, style, and industry exposures, can be a large source of active performance.

Excel Outbox
Active Risk

Active strategies seek to outperform an index or peer group by taking bets relative to that benchmark; the risk of performing differently is called *active risk.* For passive managers, the term used is *tracking risk.* The level of risk is determined by the differences in style (including market capitalization or size) exposures, sector or industry exposures, and individual stock weights. As a result, the level of active risk depends on the benchmark—indexes with style characteristics more similar to the portfolio will generate lower active risk. Index fund active risk is typically less than 10 basis points for domestic equity indexes; for structured active strategies it represents less than 3 percent, while for fully active strategies it may be over 7 percent, even versus custom indexes. Stewart (1998) demonstrates that the average active risk over the period 1981–1996 of domestic active equity managers relative to the S&P 500 was 7 percent, and 10.5 percent for international managers relative to the EAFE index.

Active risk is typically defined as the standard deviation of differences in annual returns. The formula (see Appendix 1, Section C of Chapter 3) for the standard deviation of a sample of independent **gross** returns is

$$S_{1,T}^2 = (S_1^2 + M_1^2)^T - M_1^{2T}$$

where M is the mean and S is the standard deviation. We use M and S here to distinguish them from the corresponding measures for log returns. This formula is exact if gross returns are lognormal. Otherwise, it is a useful approximation.

The template provided in the spreadsheet Chapter 7 Excel Outboxes.xls should appear as:

	A	B	C	D	E	F
1	Active Risk Calculations					
2						
3				Monthly M		
4				Monthly S		
5				Annualized Active Risk		
6						
7			--------------Gross Returns-------------------			
8	Period	Equity Fund	S&P500	Russell 2000 Value	Active Return vs. S&P500	Active Return vs. Russell 2000 Value
9	1	0.0116	0.0166	0.0095		
10	2	−0.0183	0.0039	−0.0268		

(continued)

(concluded)

Active risk is measured as the standard deviation of the return difference between the portfolio and the benchmark:

- In cell E9 enter =B9-C9, then copy to cells E10:E68
- In cell E3 enter =AVERAGE(E9:E68)
- In cell E4 enter =STDEV(E9:E68)
- In Cell E5 enter =(((E4 ^2 + (1 + E3)^ 2)) ^12 − (1 + E3) ^24)^0.5.

The results should appear as:

	A	B	C	D	E	F
1	Active Risk Calculations					
2						
3				Monthly M	1.09%	
4				Monthly S	3.81%	
5				Annualized Active Risk	14.91%	
6						
7			---------------Gross Returns------------------			
	Period	Equity Fund	S&P500	Russell 2000 Value	Active Return vs. S&P500	Active Return vs. Russell 2000 Value
8						
9	1	1.16%	1.66%	0.95%	−0.50%	
10	2	−1.83%	0.39%	−2.68%	−2.22%	

The annualized active risk of the equity fund is 14.91 percent, indicating a very active strategy relative to the target S&P 500 index. This spreadsheet will be used for end-of-chapter Problem 3.

Some fund managers specialize in particular market sectors or offer highly customized portfolios; a sector-focused manager may specialize in energy, utilities, or technology stocks and may go short as well as long in these positions. Some investors conduct significant analysis on their collection of portfolio managers and seek another, compensating manager to offset any biases in the portfolio. **Completeness fund** managers study the client's current and past equity investments, identifying over- or underexposure to risks within the portfolio and filling them dynamically with a portfolio tailored to that particular client. The fund may be offered in either active or passive forms and either long-only or long/short structures.

Active Strategies

Different investors seek diverse investment approaches in various amounts. Different styles of management perform well in different periods. As a result, there are many different approaches to active equity portfolio management. Stock picking based on company fundamentals is the most traditional approach to equity management. Research analysts screen for the stocks of companies with particular characteristics—for example, low P/E multiples or high earnings growth rates. Then they review the financial statements of the companies that pass the screen, determining whether the stock prices are attractive. **Value-style** managers look for companies whose underlying value is judged to be higher than their current market price. Graham and Dodd's *Securities Analysis,* a book on value-style investing published in the mid-1930s, formalized this investment philosophy. *Growth-style* managers seek the stocks of companies that offer the opportunity for expanding revenue or earnings growth. In the 1960s, and 1920s, it was thought by some investors that valuation was not important for security selection because growth stocks would tend to "grow into their multiples" through never-ending earnings and price appreciation. Many tech stock investors in the late 1990s subscribed to this philosophy.

GARP (growth at a reasonable price) managers seek the best of both worlds, trading off growth prospects and valuation, and seeking to avoid paying too much for attractive earnings growth opportunities. These managers tend to hold large-cap stocks with long-term records of stable earnings growth. These stocks generally do well when overall market earnings growth slows. *Deep value* managers tend to have absolute valuation rules, such as requiring a stock to have a ratio of market capitalization to book value no higher than 1.0. *Book value* is the value of the company on its balance sheet. The characteristics sought by deep value managers tend to be extreme, and the portfolios may have large cash positions, especially when the market is highly valued overall. *Relative value* managers seek multiples that are lower than a benchmark, for example, the S&P 500, or set of comparable securities. The characteristics, and as a result performance, of relative value managers are less extreme than those of deep value managers. Value stocks in general tend to do well when the economy and average company profits have begun to recover from a period of weakness. *Earnings momentum* managers seek the stocks of companies that may experience accelerating growth in the near future, hoping to find them before other investors recognize the potential, and then sell them as other investors become aware and bid up the price. Interestingly, deep value managers and earnings momentum managers may peruse the same data in pursuit of stock ideas. *Investor's Business Daily* lists stocks at their 52-week highs, of interest to momentum managers, and stocks at their 52-week lows, of interest to value managers. *Core equity* managers select securities from all areas. Their portfolios are diversified across sectors and styles and offer characteristics similar to broad market indexes. They tend to be style neutral versus the broad market, and their investment process may include risk control techniques, though they tend to be more active and less quantitative than structured equity strategies. Quantitative techniques generally look to minimize exposure across a number of systematic risk factors. Small-cap and overseas equity managers may follow one of these disciplines, but focus on their specialized universes of stocks.

7.3   Selecting the Equity Mix

Equity Return Behavior

Over the long term, equities have provided higher returns than bonds or money market investments. The historical record also suggests that small-cap and international stocks behave differently from large-cap domestic stocks and that value and growth stocks follow different performance cycles. As a result, the desire for diversification suggests either investment in a single portfolio that provides exposure across the equity market or multiple investments in different styles.

The correlation between stock indexes composed of different universes of stocks measures the diversification potential of different equity styles. To illustrate the composition of style indexes, consider the Russell 3000 index, which is composed of the largest 3,000 American companies ranked by market capitalization adjusted for float. The Russell 3000 is divided into two indexes based on size: the Russell 1000 index, which tracks the largest 1,000, and Russell 2000 index, the smallest 2,000. These three indexes are further divided into style indexes based on characteristics such as price/book value ratios, where high book/price stocks tend to represent value stocks and

EXHIBIT 7.1
Russell Equity Style Indexes

Size	Style		
	Value	Core	Growth
Large	Russell 1000 Value	Russell 1000	Russell 1000 Growth
Core	Russell 3000 Value	Russell 3000	Russell 3000 Growth
Small	Russell 2000 Value	Russell 2000	Russell 2000 Growth

lower book/price stocks tend to be growth stocks. The different size and style indexes are summarized in Exhibit 7.1.

The Russell 1000 index may be further decomposed into the largest 200 and the next 800 as a measure of large-cap and mid-cap equities. Long-term historical estimates based on monthly gross returns for three market capitalization ranges, two styles, and the EAFE international index are listed in Exhibit 7.2. The estimates illustrate the high correlation between U.S. equities of the same style and relatively low correlation between foreign and U.S. equities. Statistically the index constituents exhibit high correlations within the style categories yet offer lower correlation within the size groups. However, note that these correlations are all higher than the correlations between assets shown in Chapter 3's Exhibit 3.1 because correlations tend to be higher between subasset classes (small-cap versus large-cap U.S. equities) than between asset classes (U.S. equities versus U.S. fixed-income). The correlation between international and U.S. equity returns is lower than the correlations between U.S. style and capitalization groups. When allocation decisions are made, such as the use of M–V optimization, the correlations between these indexes are frequently assumed to be stable and less than 1, offering attractive diversification. However, under some circumstances correlation levels can shift quickly, reducing or even eliminating expected diversification benefits. To illustrate, over the last 30 years the 12-month rolling correlation between U.S. (S&P 500) and international (EAFE) stock returns has varied from 0.96 to −0.43.

Mid-cap and small-cap stocks seem to be the most highly correlated. Large-cap stocks have been more highly correlated with international stocks than smaller-cap stocks. This makes sense because many constituents of the large-cap indexes are multinationals, exposed to foreign competition and currency variability.

In addition to correlations, it is interesting to review the historical performance of equity styles. Exhibit 7.3 reports annualized historical gross returns for the equity style and size groups.

As shown in Chapter 3's Exhibit 3.3, over the long term, smaller stocks have yielded the strongest historical performance. However, when the universe is divided by style,

EXHIBIT 7.2
Historical Correlations: Gross Monthly Russell Equity Index Returns, 1986–2008

	Large Growth	Large Value	Mid Growth	Mid Value	Small Growth	Small Value	International
Large Growth	1.000						
Large Value	0.812	1.000					
Mid Growth	0.880	0.710	1.000				
Mid Value	0.751	0.902	0.768	1.000			
Small Growth	0.771	0.630	0.945	0.738	1.000		
Small Value	0.659	0.742	0.781	0.897	0.858	1.000	
International	0.590	0.592	0.595	0.579	0.557	0.528	1.000

EXHIBIT 7.3
Annualized Historical
Gross Returns:
Russell Equity
Indexes, Ending
12/31/2008

	Last 5 Years	Last 10 Years	Last 20 Years
Large Growth	−3.6%	−5.1%	7.5%
Large Value	−1.4	0.1	8.6
Mid Growth	−2.3	−0.2	8.2
Mid Value	0.3	4.4	10.2
Small Growth	−2.4	−0.8	5.2
Small Value	0.3	6.1	10.0
International	2.1	1.2	3.5

EXHIBIT 7.4
Historical Standard
Deviation: Gross
Annual Returns
Ending 12/31/2008

	Last 5 Years	Last 10 Years	Last 20 Years
Large Growth	19.5%	26.3%	23.6%
Large Value	22.5	18.9	18.2
Mid Growth	25.4	28.9	24.1
Mid Value	25.3	20.2	19.4
Small Growth	22.0	27.5	23.8
Small Value	22.2	21.2	20.5
International	28.1	25.5	21.2

mid-cap value, followed closely by small-cap value, had the highest returns over the last 20 years. Small-cap growth has exhibited the weakest domestic equity style index returns over the period. The relative underperformance of international stocks can be seen in the 20-year period, reversing over the last five years. Note that small changes in period length and ending date can change the conclusion regarding relative performance. The late 1990s were a period of strong returns for large-cap growth stocks. If performance was compared through December 1999, growth would seem to dominate value, and large-cap returns would exceed small-cap returns. Dollar returns of international stocks experienced a rebound in 2003 and 2004 as the euro and yen appreciated. As a result, tactical decisions regarding when to invest in a particular style can be as important as the long-term strategic allocation.

Volatility measures of the indexes are shown in Exhibit 7.4. Small-cap and mid-cap returns have exhibited the highest volatility, especially in the growth category. Also, shorter-term volatility exceeds the longer-term average due to the late-1990s technology bubble and correction and the 2008 market decline.[1] The relationship among short-term risk measures tends to change—for example, small-cap and mid-cap growth were the most volatile return series for the five years ending in December 2003.

7.4   Alternative Equity Mixes

Different size and style equity groups offer different risk–return characteristics. As a result, there are several ways to gain exposure to equities. Broad-based equity index funds incorporate large numbers of stocks and typically set weights based on market capitalization.[2] With these investments there is no need to decide how to mix different groups of size and style; the weights adjust automatically based on market valuations.

[1] Large-cap growth stocks tend to hold up in recessionary environments.
[2] Note that the Dow Jones Industrial Average is composed of only 30 stocks, and uses share price, adjusted for splits and dividends, to set the index weights.

EXHIBIT 7.5
Market Valuations:
Percentages of Equity
Market—U.S. Equity
Indexes

Small-Caps	Mid-Caps	Large-Caps
8%	8–22%	74–83%

Note: Based on 2004 valuations.

Some mutual funds offer a portfolio reflecting the Wilshire 5000 index, which now includes over 6,000 U.S.-headquartered publicly traded issues. Institutional investors may seek a similar investment using commingled pools or separate accounts offered by investment management firms. A Wilshire 5000 portfolio makes it easy to gain full exposure to the U.S. equity market.

However, simply weighting styles by market capitalization, as reflected in a single market index portfolio, may be a problem if you want to tilt the portfolio, such as by overweighting small-cap or value stocks. The percentages of equity market value for small-cap, mid-cap, and large-cap stocks are shown in Exhibit 7.5. Because definitions vary, mid-cap and large-cap weights are presented as ranges. The S&P 500 currently represents over 80 percent of the U.S. equity market, though this will vary through time as relative valuations change.

Optimal Mean–Variance Allocations

Using the return data in Exhibit 7.3, we can see that a higher-than-market weighting in mid-cap stocks would have yielded higher performance over the last 20 years than a market-weighted portfolio. Although this higher return would be attractive, this weighting would also have yielded a more volatile portfolio. Rather than focusing on return, we can apply the asset allocation techniques presented in Chapters 3 and 4 to the equity allocation problem to find the optimal mix of equity styles based on risk and return assumptions.

Consider applying the M–V model with no borrowing and no short positions. The allocation will be across five equity groups: large-cap value, large-cap growth, small-cap value, small-cap growth, and international equities.[3] Given the low correlation between U.S. and international stocks and the higher return and lower volatility of value stocks, we might expect an optimal portfolio that is heavily weighted toward value stocks with a potential allocation to international stocks for diversification. Exhibit 7.7 displays the results of the M–V optimization run using the Excel spreadsheet developed in Chapter 3.

As we expected, the optimal portfolio weights are concentrated in large-cap and small-cap value stocks; however, these weights are sensitive to the mean–variance parameters. For example, if we adjust the risk aversion parameter to a value of 2.0, the optimal portfolio favors large-cap stocks: 62.2 percent in large-cap value stocks and 37.8 percent in small-cap value stocks. Alternative portfolio weightings are compared in Exhibit 7.8. A proportionately weighted portfolio reflects rough market weights: The 20 percent small-cap weight includes mid-cap stocks, and while foreign stocks represent approximately 50 percent of the global market, international stocks are assigned a 10 percent allocation to reflect the lower overseas allocation of U.S. investors with domestic liabilities. All weights for this portfolio are rounded to the nearest 5 percent.

[3] Historical summary statistics from January 1979 through February 2003 were used for the expected risk, return, and correlation measures. An end-of-chapter problem suggests updating these results with current market data.

Theory in Practice   *Style and the Economic Cycle*

When setting long-term strategic allocations between different equity styles, investors may want to consider where they are in the economic cycle. Consider value investors, who seek out stocks that are inexpensive relative to company book values—that is, stocks with relatively high B/P ratios. Stocks with high growth expectations tend to have low B/P multiples. As a result, value stocks and growth stocks perform almost in mirror image of each other. Historically value stocks tended to outperform the market when the economy was improving, whereas growth stocks outperformed when the economy was deteriorating. This was because investors sought out large companies with solid earnings prospects (large-cap growth stocks) when the economy showed signs of weakness. As a result, stocks with high long-term growth prospects were bid up while more economically sensitive stocks were bid down. When the economy began to stabilize, value stocks, especially depressed small-cap value stocks, rebounded. This pattern is illustrated in Exhibit 7.6, which compares GDP growth with active growth and value returns, measured by the return difference between the S&P Value and Growth indexes and the S&P 500, over rolling three-year periods. In the late 1990s this behavior changed, with the growing dominance of high-tech growth stocks relative to more traditional, stable growth stocks such as pharmaceuticals. Large drug companies, in particular, were suffering from political pressure regarding fair drug pricing at the time.

EXHIBIT 7.6
Growth, Value, and GDP Changes

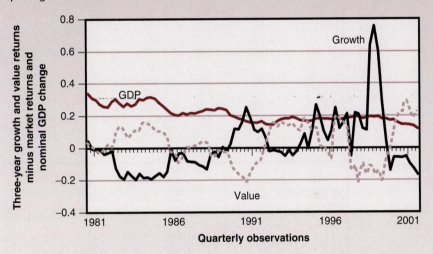

The late 1990s are easy to identify—the growth index is almost off the chart. As the economy showed evidence of declining in early 2000, the growth index collapsed as technology earnings forecasts weakened and sentiment reversed. This led to a change in the relationship between economic measures and the growth–value relationship for the next three years, at least for large-cap stocks. Stocks of industrial companies suffered deeply during the recession, but they had been relegated to the small-cap value indexes during the tech run-up, and rebounded sharply in 2003 once the economy bottomed. This behavior was more in line with the traditional relationship between value stock performance and economic growth.

The optimized portfolios ($\lambda = 1.0$, $\lambda = 2.0$) significantly dominate the equally weighted (Eq-Wtd) and capitalization-weighted (Prop-Wtd) portfolios. With $\lambda = 1.0$, the optimized portfolio has an expected return (log of the expected gross return) of 14.5 percent with a standard deviation of 15.6 percent and a 12-month shortfall probability of 19.7 percent. This compares to the capitalization-weighted portfolio return of

EXHIBIT 7.7
Mean–Variance
Model: Equity Asset
Classes

Mean/Variance Efficient Portfolio: No Borrowing, No Shorting							
Program T:			1				
MAX		$E[\mu] - \lambda * E[\sigma^2]$			=	0.1206	
		$\lambda =$		1			
	LGGR	LGVAL	SMGR	SMVAL	INTL Net	Portfolio	
ω	0.000	0.347	0.000	0.653	0.000	1.0000	=	1
μ						0.1449	
σ						0.1560	
Prob(<0)						0.1974	

Summary Statistics					
	LGGR	LGVAL	SMGR	SMVAL	INTL Net
μ	0.1275	0.1381	0.1158	0.1485	0.1099
α	0.1099	0.1273	0.0851	0.1340	0.0860
σ	0.1873	0.1469	0.2478	0.1705	0.1726
ρ					
LGGR	1.000	0.826	0.851	0.729	0.549
LGVAL	0.826	1.000	0.712	0.823	0.538
SMGR	0.851	0.712	1.000	0.872	0.508
SMVAL	0.729	0.823	0.872	1.000	0.491
INTL Net	0.549	0.538	0.508	0.491	1.000
Ω					
LGGR	0.035	0.023	0.039	0.023	0.018
LGVAL	0.023	0.022	0.026	0.021	0.014
SMGR	0.039	0.026	0.061	0.037	0.022
SMVAL	0.023	0.021	0.037	0.029	0.014
INTL Net	0.018	0.014	0.022	0.014	0.030

EXHIBIT 7.8
Mean–Variance
Alternative
Portfolios: Equity
Asset Classes

	Weights					μ	σ	Prob(<0)	SR
	LGGR	LGVAL	SMGR	SMVAL	INTL Net				
Eq–Wtd	0.200	0.200	0.200	0.200	0.200	12.6%	16.1%	24.1%	0.782
Prop–Wtd	0.350	0.350	0.100	0.100	0.100	12.9%	15.8%	23.0%	0.819
Tilt	0.300	0.400	0.050	0.150	0.100	13.2%	15.3%	21.6%	0.862
λ = 1	0.000	0.347	0.000	0.653	0.000	14.5%	15.6%	19.7%	0.929
λ = 2	0.000	0.622	0.000	0.378	0.000	14.2%	14.9%	19.0%	0.954
Min Var.	0.000	0.632	0.000	0.041	0.327	12.6%	13.8%	19.8%	0.918
Max Ret.	0.000	0.000	0.000	1.000	0.000	14.8%	17.0%	21.6%	0.871

12.9 percent with a standard deviation of 15.8 percent and shortfall probability of 23.0 percent. The descriptive statistics for the minimum variance (Min Var.) and maximum return (Max Ret.) portfolios are also reported, as well as characteristics for a portfolio with a 5 percent tilt (Tilt) toward large-cap and small-cap value stocks relative to the capitalization-weighted portfolio. As expected, the MVP also allocates to international stocks to gain the diversification benefit.

As discussed extensively in Chapter 4, statistical measures of returns depend on the period chosen, and different values of the measures used for expected risk and return lead to different optimal allocations. For example, international stocks were much stronger in the 1970s than in the period just illustrated, which was selected because small-cap index returns are not readily available before 1979. Expanding the estimation period to include the 1970s would likely result in larger allocations to international stocks for the optimized portfolios. In addition, the economic environment

EXHIBIT 7.9
Equity Asset Class Log Return Expectations (α): Historical versus JS, 1/79–2/03

	Historical	JS
Large Growth	11.0%	10.8%
Large Value	12.7	10.9
Small Growth	8.3	10.8
Small Value	13.4	10.8
International	8.6	10.8

Note: As with Exhibits 7.7 and 7.8, these estimates are calculated from the period January 1979–February 2003.

EXHIBIT 7.10
Optimal Equity Mix (Maximized Risk–Return Trade-Off) Using James–Stein Returns

	Weights								
	LGGR	LGVAL	SMGR	SMVAL	INTL Net	μ	σ	Prob(<0)	SR
Eq–Wtd	0.200	0.200	0.200	0.200	0.200	12.6%	16.1%	24.1%	0.782
Prop–Wtd	0.350	0.350	0.100	0.100	0.100	12.4%	15.8%	24.0%	0.786
Tilt	0.300	0.400	0.050	0.150	0.100	12.3%	15.3%	23.2%	0.807
$\lambda = 1$	0.000	0.404	0.089	0.115	0.392	12.3%	14.4%	21.6%	0.857
$\lambda = 2$	0.000	0.504	0.000	0.134	0.362	12.1%	13.8%	20.9%	0.878
Min Var.	0.000	0.632	0.000	0.041	0.327	12.1%	13.8%	20.9%	0.877
Max Ret.	0.000	1.000	0.000	0.000	0.000	11.9%	14.7%	23.0%	0.812

over the last few years has been favorable for value stocks, perhaps generating higher historical returns than might be expected in the future. Lastly, the outperformance of small-cap stocks over large-cap stocks was lower in the late 1990s than over longer periods, though this spread has widened in the last few years.

To reduce estimation error we can model expected returns using the James–Stein (JS) method, reported in Exhibit 7.9.[4] The JS estimates of expected returns are virtually identical to the historical grand mean across the asset classes. This results from the high variability of returns; suggesting any observed differences among average returns are likely due to noise. Given a much longer sample, historical means would be more reliable, and the JS method would place more weight on them.

As expected, using the JS expected returns in the M–V model yields a much higher allocation to international stocks. A summary of the portfolio characteristics using the JS estimates is presented in Exhibit 7.10. International stocks are diversifying, and this benefit becomes sufficiently attractive to increase the allocation from zero to over 35 percent when their expected return is increased. The optimal allocation to large growth stocks remains at zero given their relatively high volatility and correlation with other domestic equity classes. This does not mean that in practice an investor may want to ignore growth stocks or an active growth manager. There are periods when large-cap growth stocks are very attractive, as discussed in the Theory in Practice box.

Also note that the optimal allocation to small-cap growth stocks changes between the optimized portfolios (that is, with $\lambda = 1.0$ and $\lambda = 2.0$), even though the risk–return profile is similar. This illustrates the lack of stability in the M–V approach when expected returns are similar across assets. Actually implementing such an approach through time with regular parameter updates could lead to high turnover and volatile performance. One way to mitigate this issue is to start with capitalization weights and then adjust these weights on the margin to increase the expected utility of the portfolio.

---

[4] Note that one may assume that means change through time, perhaps motivating an investor to actively forecast short-term returns and use a mixed estimation approach to implement these forecasts.

This section has summarized an approach for exploring the appropriate mix of equity subasset classes within an investor's equity allocation. As discussed in Chapter 5, there are a number of shortcomings to simply utilizing M–V approaches, even if the user studies the influence of different statistical assumptions. Nonparametric techniques such as frequency analysis and more sophisticated return distributions such as those used in Monte Carlo techniques are also helpful in setting the target equity mix. For more information, see the Theory in Practice box.

Stress Testing Allocations

To this point we have used optimization techniques to set portfolio allocations. These allocations were optimal in terms of M–V trade-offs, downside risk targets, or managing risk dynamically. Descriptive statistics illustrating the risk profile of the portfolio could be generated.

Although these can be effective tools, there are other ways to understand the potential behavior of an optimized portfolio. One method is to *stress test* the portfolio by studying its behavior back through time. Historical testing indicates how the portfolio might perform in times of recession, inflation, or crisis. It is also a good technique for identifying the worst-case return (maximum drawdown) over a day, month, year, or longer period. Some of the most informative calculations include the worst 1 percent of months, the months with returns below a specified level, and the longest period with a negative return. In addition, because historical returns are non-normally distributed, the stress test estimates the historical skewness and kurtosis of the portfolio, providing additional information about the potential performance of the portfolio.

Stress testing also includes *scenario analysis,* the examination of particular events—typically to examine return behavior during crises. Events to consider include market cycles such as the dot-com bubble or the 1973–1974 stagflation; market shocks such as Black Monday, 9/11/2001, or the 1978–1979 oil shocks; and company-specific shocks such as Enron or LTCM. The performance over these events for various portfolio allocations gives investors a better understanding of their target mix and allows fine-tuning of the mix to better meet their objectives.

Stress testing is similar to another commonly used technique: *back testing.* Both use historical return series to explore the behavior of a strategy back through time. However, when done correctly, back testing avoids data mining by building the strategy utilizing one time period and testing it over another. Stress testing uses only one period, searching for extreme events instead of simply reviewing summary statistics. We should be careful with both methods, making sure not to simply fit the proposed strategy to historical results. Although a portfolio or strategy may look good in the past, unless the future replicates the past, it will likely disappoint.

For equity investing across market capitalization and style, stress testing involves collecting historical returns for equity indexes and computing weighted average returns for each period. By linking these blended returns over different periods, we can compute multiperiod total portfolio returns over different investment horizons. Exhibit 7.11 illustrates the results of stress testing different equity mixes. The maximum and minimum returns over 1-month, 3-month, 12-month, and 36-month periods are presented along with performance for several scenarios.

As you might expect, the mix created to generate the maximum return over the 1979–2003 period also generated some of the largest negative returns, but not in all cases. Interestingly, the minimum variance portfolio generated the highest 36-month return, suggesting that stress testing can identify the possibility of unexpected results for the future.

EXHIBIT 7.11 **Stress Test Results: Alternative Equity Mixes**

	Equal and Proportional Weights			Historically Based Optimization			
	Eq-Wtd	Prop-Wtd	Tilt	$\lambda = 1$	$\lambda = 2$	Min Var.	Max Ret.
Annual return	12.0%	12.4%	12.7%	14.2%	14.0%	12.4%	14.3%
Worst month	−23.7	−22.7	−22.3	−25.5	−23.2	−18.5	−28.3
Best month	12.0	12.4	12.2	11.8	11.8	11.2	12.2
Worst 3 months	−29.0	−29.2	−28.6	−30.5	−29.0	−23.2	−32.5
Best 3 months	22.5	24.6	24.4	26.7	26.9	19.0	28.9
Worst 12 months	−25.7	−27.3	−23.2	−23.9	−20.4	−19.7	−28.4
Best 12 months	69.1	66.4	65.1	79.4	71.5	56.1	89.6
Worst 36 months	−35.6	−35.9	−30.1	−11.6	−5.6	−23.6	−18.8
Best 36 months	140.1	135.4	136.4	130.4	127.4	176.5	151.4
3rd Q 1981	−13.8	−12.5	−12.0	−12.4	−11.5	−10.7	−13.6
Oct. 1987	−13.9	−9.1	−9.8	−17.2	−13.4	−13.2	−21.8
Year 1990	−14.9	−12.7	−12.6	−15.7	−14.0	−12.6	−17.9
3rd Q 1998	−23.7	−22.7	−22.3	−25.5	−23.2	−18.5	−28.3
Sept. 2001	−20.2	−21.0	−19.4	−12.7	−13.8	−15.4	−11.4
Year 2002	−10.9	−9.7	−9.3	−9.6	−8.6	−8.2	−11.0

Note: Time period January 1979 through February 2003.

7.5 The Equity Management Business

Equity Fund Structures

There are many forms of equity portfolios. They may be classified by the legal structure of the fund, the type of security held, the general investment strategy, or the specific investment style. The legal structure most widely recognized by the investing public is the **mutual fund** (see Exhibit 7.12). A mutual fund is a company that is registered with the Securities and Exchange Commission, retains officers and a board of directors, and hires an investment management firm to invest its pooled assets. In many cases the mutual fund is formed by the investment management company, which in turn selects the board of directors to oversee the fund and then hires itself to manage the fund. In other cases a distribution company forms the mutual fund and hires investment managers to invest the assets. **Open-ended mutual funds** allow investors to contribute to or redeem from the fund daily, or more frequently for some funds, based on the net asset value (NAV). The NAV is the price per share of the fund based on the value of the underlying assets divided by the number of shares outstanding. Each day, before 4:00 P.M. ET, investors may ask to buy or redeem shares at the upcoming closing share NAV, calculated using the closing prices of the underlying securities. As the astute reader may recall, this 4:00 P.M. closing time was abused in the early 2000s by investors seeking to take advantage of fund pricing, thereby diluting share values for passive investors; this episode is discussed in more detail in Chapter 13. Shares in **closed end funds** are traded between investors on stock exchanges, and are not regularly bought or redeemed directly with the fund.

Mutual funds may be sold directly or through advisors, which include brokers, insurance salespeople, and financial planners. Mutual funds are commonly used within IRAs, 401(k) plans, and 529 plans. Management fees and other expenses are charged directly to the fund. Some funds charge a transaction fee, called a _load,_ to invest or

EXHIBIT 7.12
Mutual Fund
Structure

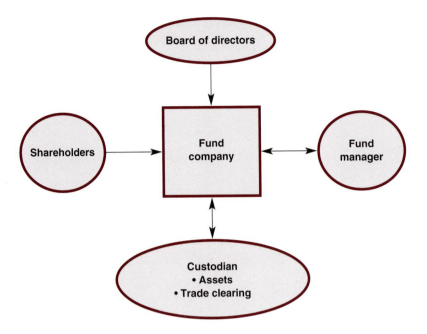

redeem, which is frequently shared between a financial advisor and the investment management company.

To help ensure their protection, the assets of the fund reside with a third-party custodian bank, whereas the buy and sell decisions for investing the assets are assigned to the investment manager. Some funds allow for transaction fees paid by investors moving into or out of the fund. This fee is then contributed to the fund to cover transaction costs for investing the assets.

Mutual funds are efficient for management firms but cannot be customized for individual investors. Although a fund has multiple clients and can have multiple share classes with different fee structures, the portfolio manager manages only one portfolio. As a result, investment policy, fees, and tax implications are all shared equally by shareholders of the same share class. The advantage to mutual fund investors is that they receive professional management for investing small balances at a reasonable fee.

Commingled pools are similar to mutual funds in that they combine individual investments into a single pool managed by a PM, but they are reserved for qualified pension or profit-sharing plans. Qualified plans are tax-free vehicles sponsored by an employer and registered with the federal tax and labor authorities. Corporate DB and DC pension plans are two examples of qualified plans. Commingled pools are offered to institutional investors by banks. Fees are typically charged outside the fund, which is paid directly based on an invoice rather than through the sale of assets. Large investors usually pay their managers as a percentage of assets using a basis point schedule that declines as assets increase. *Common trusts* and *limited partnerships* are also commingled vehicles, but these are available to nonqualified investors such as individuals and may be offered by nonbank companies. There are specific legal restrictions to these vehicles, including wealth requirements that investors must satisfy before they can invest. Limited partnerships are common vehicles for equity hedge funds.

Some investors may want custom management of their assets or want their assets segregated from other investors. In this case investors may choose a *separate account.* Like a mutual fund, the assets of a separate account may reside in a third-party bank or a brokerage custodial account, but they are composed of only one client's money rather than the pooled assets of multiple investors. Large pension plans, high net worth investors, and corporations select separate accounts for several reasons. They may need individualized management of their accounts for investment, legal, or tax purposes. For example, a religious organization may have guidelines for investing its endowment that restrict the purchase of securities in companies in specific industries. These guidelines would not be met by an investment in a mutual fund or other commingled vehicle designed for unrestricted investors.

Investors may also prefer having greater control over their investments, independent of the manager. A separate account gives them the flexibility of keeping the assets in the same account even if they change managers. There may also be fee advantages. However, it is not clear whether separate accounts are safer. This would depend on the credit quality of the custodian holding the assets. Some investors believe separate accounts receive more attention from an investment manager than do commingled funds; this depends on the organization of the investment manager's operations.

From a regulatory perspective, mutual funds have been closely monitored by the SEC, which has been interested in protecting small investors who purchase mutual fund shares. Recently the SEC has become interested in monitoring limited partnership investment vehicles as well even though their investors are wealthy or considered sophisticated. The Department of Labor (DOL) and bank regulators are responsible for enforcing laws regarding commingled pools. The DOL enforces ERISA laws, which define prudent management standards for pension assets. Separate account management is typically overseen either by the SEC or bank regulators.

7.6   Implementing the Equity Mix

Sample Equity Mixes

Once a target mix of equities has been determined, an easy way to implement this mix is to use index funds in the form of exchange traded funds (ETFs), mutual funds, separate accounts, or commingled pools. This can be an efficient (low fee) and effective (small risk of return varying significantly from the index) way to ensure that the intended return behavior is realized. The key determinants for selecting a passive investment manager include fees, forecast tracking error, and liquidity. For taxable investors, turnover, the level of unrealized gains, and the tax treatment of gains are also key variables. Tax considerations are covered in more detail in Chapter 12. Active management may be attractive for investors seeking to earn returns higher than the indexes. Unfortunately this comes with two risks—identifying an appropriate benchmark to ensure effective implementation of your equity portfolio and underperformance versus the benchmark. Investors may choose a mix of active and indexed investments or a portable alpha strategy as well, adopting active portfolios for styles that seem to offer the best opportunity for value added.

At the implementation stage it is important to consider the structure of the proposed portfolios. Building a diversified mix of equity managers includes art as well as science. Consider each potential manager's investment process. Although it may be easy to classify them into growth and value, large and small, try to classify their philosophies too. For example, consider whether a manager follows a momentum or a contrarian approach. Does their analysis begin at the stock level? Do they take a top-down macro view or a strictly bottom-up, company-by-company and stock-by-stock

EXHIBIT 7.13
Comparing Portfolio Characteristics

		SMG Equity Fund	S&P 600 Small-Cap
Size	Asset-Weighted Market Capitalization	$2,741 million	$1,403 million
	Median Market Capitalization	$1,012 million	$805 million
	Allocation to:		
	Over US$2 billion	39%	22%
	US$0.5–2 billion	43%	71%
	Under US$0.5 billion	16%	8%
	Cash	2%	0%
Valuation	Projected EPS Growth (3–5 years)	17.7%	15.1%
	Projected P/E (2 years)	17.1x	15.1x
	Current Ratios:		
	Price/Book	1.5x	2.3x
	Price/Sales	1.0x	1.0x
	Price/Book	1.5x	2.3x
	Price/Earnings	13.3x	17.0x
	Dividend Yield	1.5%	0.9%

view? This approach will improve your forecasting ability as a supplement to your historical modeling.

The statistical approach may also be supplemented by a characteristics approach, reflecting a collection of portfolio value, growth, and market capitalization measures. Weighted mean and median values are helpful, but a better understanding may be accomplished by studying the distribution of exposures. Exhibit 7.13 reports the characteristics for a single portfolio and its benchmark. Similar analysis should be conducted for an entire mix of equity portfolios and the combined equity benchmark. Although the SMG Fund selects from a small-cap universe, there are some distinct differences with the S&P 600 small-cap index. The fund holds larger stocks on average but the distribution of market capitalization is broader, with greater exposure to stocks with capitalizations less than $500 million. The fund also seems to follow a GARP strategy with higher projected EPS growth than the index but with lower current price multiples.

As an example of setting a mix of equity mutual funds, consider the collection of active funds utilized for the Fidelity Freedom 2030 Fund, a mutual **fund of funds** providing diversification among both asset classes and equity styles. The weights of equity styles and funds are listed in Exhibit 7.14 for comparison with the capitalization-weighted and M–V optimized mixes presented in Exhibit 7.8. The Freedom Fund includes individual funds combining both value and growth stocks. Adjusting for these blended funds, the Freedom Fund equity allocation is 70.9 percent in large-cap stocks—similar to the 70 percent capitalization-weighted portfolio, but growth appears to be more heavily weighted than value within both the large-cap and mid-cap funds. The fund does not allocate to dedicated small-cap funds. The international allocation falls between the M–V optimized portfolios; using inputs based on historical estimates, the M–V had no allocation to international equities while using the JS estimates resulted in an allocation over 35 percent for both risk aversion parameters. From an investment point of view, the absence of small-cap exposure and the modest tilt toward growth is inconsistent with historical trends. This may be

EXHIBIT 7.14 Sample Equity Mix: Mutual Fund

Fidelity Freedom 2030 Fund				
Fund Name	**Style***	**Assets ($ millions)**	**% Portfolio**	**% Style**
Fidelity Blue Chip Growth	Large growth	473	12.1%	
Fidelity Growth Company Fund	Large growth	286	7.3	19.5%
Fidelity Equity Income Fund	Large value	516	13.2	13.2
Fidelity Disciplined Equity Fund	Large blend	500	12.8	
Fidelity Fund	Large blend	495	12.7	
Fidelity Growth & Income Fund	Large Blend	493	12.6	38.2
Fidelity Mid-Cap Stock Fund	Mid-cap growth	287	7.4	
Fidelity OTC Portfolio	Large-cap growth	215	5.5	12.9
Fidelity Diversified International Fund	International	162	4.2	
Fidelity Europe Fund	International	233	6.0	
Fidelity Japan Fund	International	57	1.5	
Fidelity Overseas Fund	International	150	3.8	
Fidelity Southeast Asia Fund	International	32	0.8	16.3
Total		3,899		100.0%

*Style definition of domestic funds provided by Morningstar, Inc.
Note: Data as of September 2004.

EXHIBIT 7.15 Sample Equity Mix: Institutional Fund

The State of Hawaii Pension Plan			
Equity Style	**Number of Managers**	**Assets ($ millions)**	**% Weight**
Large-cap growth	4	902	16.2%
Large-cap value	2	1,222	21.9
Large-cap core	2	1,062	19.0
Mid-cap equity	3	424	7.6
Small-cap equity	2	463	8.3
International	5	1,507	27.0
Total	18	5,580	100.0%

Note: As of June 2004.

due to the managers believing in a growth investment philosophy. Lastly, the absence of index portfolios in the fund suggests an investment philosophy supporting active management.

While the Freedom Fund is composed of only Fidelity funds, other investors may have broad discretion and may select from all available equity managers in the form of mutual funds, separate accounts, or commingled pools. As an example, consider the equity allocation of the pension plan managed for employees of the state of Hawaii, summarized in Exhibit 7.15.

Compared to the Freedom Fund, the Hawaii pension plan is tilted toward value, consistent with an M–V optimization approach based on historical trends. The international allocation is more aggressive than either the M–V mix, using expectations based on historical estimates, or the Freedom allocation. As noted earlier, global equity market capitalizations would suggest a 50 percent allocation to international stocks; however, this may not be appropriate for U.S.-based investors.

Although not reported in Exhibit 7.15, 29 percent of the equity investment is allocated to index managers: 60 percent of the large-cap international equity investments (40 percent of the overall international allocation) and 94 percent of the large-cap core exposure. The remaining managers follow active processes. These weightings suggest that the plan sponsor believes active management has a higher chance of success in narrow style strategies or with small-cap stocks. In addition, as a means of diversifying manager risk, no single investment manager is represented in more than one equity style. The state of Hawaii's investment mix is publicly available on the Internet, but the investment vehicles are not listed. Although the plan's asset size would give it the flexibility to choose any structure, it is not reported whether the allocations are in the form of separate accounts or commingled pools.

Equity Portfolio Performance[5]

Once the equity mix has been determined, individual equity managers need to be selected. As discussed in Chapter 6, a good investment manager should be able to articulate his or her investment process, including how securities are selected and weighted. Although there is a fair amount of luck in the investment business, resources can improve a manager's odds of success. On the equity side, these include investment research and analysis, a trading facility, market and fundamental data, and computer systems. People resources are paramount. Investment managers who are bright, well-educated, and seasoned (experienced, honest, and humble) also improve the odds of success.

Retail investors do not have the same access to investment managers available to large, institutional investors. Individuals may hire a financial advisor or use the Internet or traditional media to collect information about prospective managers. As we will see later in the book, simply selecting managers based on returns or rankings is not an effective technique. An investor must carefully study performance, its consistency and correlation with other investments, and the manager's investment process. Like buying a stock, finding a good investment manager requires some guesswork, but it does not have to be a roll of the dice.

As an illustration of how a diversified mix of active equity managers can be constructed to closely reflect and outperform a passive benchmark, consider the performance of broad averages of mutual funds defined by the Lipper indexes. Lipper compiles groups of mutual funds based on their prospectus guidelines and management styles. Historically this led to groupings such as "equity income," focused on growing dividend income, and "capital appreciation," ignoring dividends in search of price growth. In the last few years Lipper developed new categorizations based on historical return behavior, reflecting popular designations such as large-cap growth, mid-cap value, and small-cap core.

We can use the Lipper indexes to explore the behavior of a sample equity mix. Consider proportional allocations to five Lipper categories: 35 percent each to large-cap growth and value, 10 percent each to small-cap growth and value, and 10 percent to international. This construction is equivalent to selecting an equally weighted basket of many active mutual fund managers for each category. At the beginning of each month, the portfolio is rebalanced to the target 35/35/10/10/10 weights. Net of fees, the Lipper mix returned 7.6 percent per annum versus 8.0 percent for the index mix. Exhibit 7.16 charts the performance of the mutual fund mix relative to investing in the underlying equity style indexes. The results suggest that the two annual return series are highly correlated. This makes sense because the allocations within each equity

---

[5] Chapter 16 revisits the manager selection process, providing additional discussion and detail.

EXHIBIT 7.16   Sample Investment Mix of Active Mutual Funds

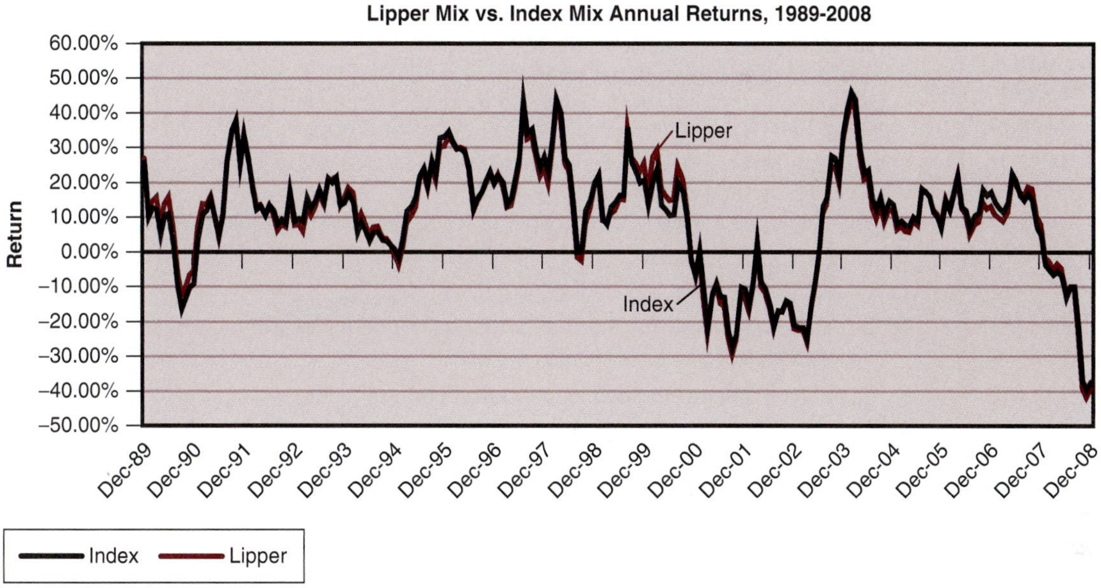

Lipper Mix vs. Index Mix Annual Returns, 1989-2008

style are highly diversified, limiting the influence of any particular manager. Despite this diversification, there will be times when the return difference is large. In particular, the Lipper portfolio outperformed the indexes by over 6 percent for the 12 months ending in February 2000.

7.7   Equity Portfolio Investment Objectives

Overview of Manager Guidelines

Many investors hiring an equity manager prepare a formal document detailing investment objectives and guidelines. This is common for institutional investors such as pension plans for their separate accounts and is also a key part of commingled pool trust agreements, mutual fund prospectuses, and limited partnership agreements. The primary reason for defining investment objectives is to clarify the manager's investment process, articulate any constraints on the process, and provide performance targets and risk expectations.

From the manager's point of view, investment guidelines should clearly spell out what the manager is hired to do. Does the portfolio to be managed use a passive or active process? If passive, is it a sampling or full replication strategy? If active, what is the method for creating added value? If it is a structured active strategy, what risks are being taken, and what risks are managed and to what extent? For all strategies, what are the performance objectives, both for active return and return volatility?

At a minimum, equity investment guidelines should include the following key elements. Note that some objectives may specify a performance target versus a peer group, not an index.

1. Specific benchmark(s), such as the S&P 500 total return index or specific universe peer group quartile ranking.
2. Target excess return, such as 200 basis points per annum or a peer ranking target.
3. Investment process, including investment universe—such as a flow chart illustrating the steps for security selection and portfolio construction.

EXHIBIT 7.17
Sample Abbreviated Investment Guidelines Active Growth Manager

- XYZ is hired to manage an active growth style U.S. equity portfolio.
- Investment process is a bottom-up approach focusing on individual stock selection.
- Manager seeks to outperform the Russell 1000 Growth index by 2 percent over any three- to five-year period, net of fees.
- Manager seeks to underperform by no more than 5 percent over any four-quarter period.
- Predicted beta will be between 1.2 and 0.8, measured using BARRA, versus the Russell 1000 Growth index.
- Cash will be maintained at less than 5 percent; there are no liquidity requirements.

4. Target risk constraints, such as worst-case underperformance over a three-year period.
5. Cash level constraint, such as no more than 5 percent.
6. Security or market restrictions, such as no stocks with market cap less than $100 million, or maximum active weight for a security, industry, or market-cap range.
7. Time horizon for performance or risk, such as a three- to five-year period.
8. Reporting requirements, such as performance attribution provided quarterly.
9. Trading restrictions, such as at least 20 percent of trading with discount brokers.
10. Derivative restrictions, such as futures contracts acceptable but no leverage.
11. Liquidity, tax, legal, and unique issues or constraints.

A short but thorough sample guideline for an active growth manager is presented in Exhibit 7.17.

Note that the guidelines specify objectives, not guarantees. This informs the investor and protects the manager. In addition to written guidelines, a process chart, such as Exhibit 7.18, is useful in articulating the manager's strategy. By its inclusion in the manager's quarterly report, it helps remind the investor what the particular manager is doing.

Sample Manager Guidelines

Mutual fund prospectuses are designed to provide sufficient information to potential small investors about the risks of the investment. Prospectus requirements are developed and enforced by the SEC, but there still remains a lot of leeway for the manager. From the manager's point of view, the prospectus should provide enough information for the investor to feel informed, but not impose restrictive guidelines that limit the flexibility of the management company. As an extreme example, managers may avoid identifying an explicit performance benchmark in their investment objective. The

EXHIBIT 7.18
Sample Process Chart

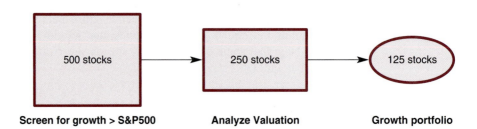

| Screen for growth > S&P500 | Analyze Valuation | Growth portfolio |
| 500 stocks | 250 stocks | 125 stocks |

EXHIBIT 7.19   **Sample Mutual Fund Prospectus Investment Guideline: Wellington Fund**

Investment Objective

The fund seeks to conserve capital and to provide moderate long-term growth in capital and income.

Primary Investment Strategies

The fund invests 60 percent to 70 percent of its assets in dividend-paying and, to a lesser extent, non-dividend-paying common stocks of established, medium-size and large companies. In choosing these companies, the advisor seeks those that appear to be undervalued but to have prospects for improvement. These stocks are commonly referred to as value stocks. The remaining 30 percent to 40 percent of the fund assets are invested mainly in investment-grade corporate bonds, with some exposure to U.S. Treasury and government agency bonds, as well as mortgage-backed securities.

Primary Risks

An investment in the fund could lose money over short or even long periods. You should expect the fund's share price and total return to fluctuate within a wide range, like the fluctuations of the overall stock and bond markets. The fund's performance could be hurt by

- *Stock market risk,* which is . . .
- *Investment style risk,* which is the chance that returns from mid- and large-capitalization value stocks will trail . . .
- *Interest rate risk,* which is . . .
- *Credit risk,* which is . . .
- *Manager risk,* which is the chance that poor security selection . . .

Vanguard Company's Wellington Fund prospectus is a good example (Exhibit 7.19)—articulating risks but not specifying a performance benchmark.

The prospectus goes on to explain these risks in further detail, provide expense information, and list historical performance summaries.

An institutional investor's investment guidelines need not be as general and vague as those in a mutual fund prospectus. In this case the investor has the flexibility to make the guidelines as detailed as desired. A good example (Exhibit 7.20) is the active large-cap equity guidelines prepared by the Montana Board of Investments. Note that a performance benchmark is specified, but no level of excess return is defined, providing flexibility to plan management. Of course this may lead to future misunderstandings between the client and manager. A reasonable excess return objective may be preferred.

Except for the lack of a specific target excess return over a specific time horizon, the Montana document includes comprehensive investment guidelines. One could make the case that excess returns and market cycles are too hard to forecast, making it unrealistic to explicitly state a target level; but listing target excess returns does make it clear what both the manager and investor seek as goals. However, from the manager's perspective it is better to have the guideline be general (or perhaps even better, very low), such as outperforming the S&P 500 over a market cycle, rather than the more specific exceeding the S&P 500 by 2 percent. Even if the manager's mean excess return is 2 percent, the client may be unhappy half of the time. Moreover, listing a peer ranking target in addition to a strict benchmark-relative target will provide even clearer expectations. However, the investor must not expect the manager to exceed all these benchmarks all the time.

There are both common and conflicting goals between investor and manager in defining equity portfolio objectives. As an illustration of this point, consider the special case when a manager is competing for new business. Though it is a good

War Story *Massachusetts PRIM Board*

Pension consultants can be helpful to plan sponsors seeking to replace an investment manager. They can provide performance data, share personal experience with prospective managers, and suggest a short list of managers for consideration. In practice, if a manager does not produce good performance after three years, he or she will be replaced. This could lead to one-third of managers being replaced every year. To illustrate this, consider the hiring decisions of the Massachusetts PRIM board. Public investments include equity managers, and in 2000, 33 percent of the outstanding stable of managers had been added that year.

MA PRIM Board
Managers Hired, 2000

	Number	% Outstanding
Public investments	6	33
Private investments	7	11

Pension consultants follow several steps when assisting a plan searching for a new manager:

1. Select asset allocation target, such as 60 percent U.S. equity.
2. Select equity allocation target, such as 25 percent large-cap growth.
3. Distribute a request for proposal and identify three finalists.
4. Organize presentations.
5. Select the preferred manager.
6. Negotiate fees.
7. Finalize the management contract.
8. Send the wire.

The final presentations (step 4) are sometimes called "beauty contests." If three managers are presenting, each is required to present and entertain questions for 30–60 minutes, frequently one following the other. The investment committee listens and, after some guidance from the consultant, selects their favorite manager.

Most selections are made by thoughtful, sophisticated investors after careful analysis. However, in some cases the process can be rushed, a disturbing situation when hundreds of millions of dollars are at stake. There can also be conflicting guidance during an interview, which the manager must handle diplomatically.

Consider one case from the late 1990s when a manager was asked to present a risk-controlled active U.S. equity strategy to a U.K. investor. The award was to be $500 million, and the search required competing managers to make a formal presentation in London. As the portfolio manager waited in the lobby, he was informed that the investment meeting was running late and his presentation would need to be no more than 25 minutes, including questions, instead of the planned 45 minutes! Moreover, during the presentation, the consultant stated that the investment objectives included a 1 percent excess return target, a 3 percent tracking error standard deviation guideline, *and* a requirement that the portfolio could not underperform the S&P 500 by more than 3 percent in *any* 12-month period. Any student of statistics knows that these standards are contradictory; assuming normality, there is a significant chance of 3 percent or more underperformance in any given 12-month period and a very high chance that over a period of several years, there would be at least one 12-month period when performance would fail to meet this criteria. The manager complimented the consultant's decision to include specific statistical guidelines, tactfully explained the high level of strictness the downside target provided, and stressed how his strategy would meet these guidelines perfectly. Following the 25-minute presentation, he was awarded the $500 million account.

idea for a manager to clearly state her or his investment process, objectives, and guidelines to sell the strategy, it is tempting to overpromise in order to win the business. However, it is important to manage expectations appropriately so that once a client decides to hire the manager there are no unrealistic expectations that will be hard to meet.

EXHIBIT 7.20 **Investment Guidelines: Active Large-Cap Equity Investment, State of Montana**

OBJECTIVES

Return requirement: The investment objective of the MTCP is to provide an acceptable total rate of return on invested funds. Capital appreciation is the primary objective with current income considered as a secondary objective. Attainment of the investment objective is characterized by achieving an annualized, time-weighted total rate of return that exceeds the Standard & Poor's 500 index (S&P 500 index) return over a five-year rolling period.

Risk tolerance: MTCP is a highly diversified stock pool, which assumes market risk subject to the following:

- Maximum tracking error of 400 basis points compared to the S&P 500 index as calculated by Barra or similar products.
- A minimum of 100 issues will be held within the portfolio.
- No issue shall constitute more than 10 percent of the total market value of the portfolio.
- Stock holdings of MTCP are restricted to issues on the approved stock list. The approved stock list is composed of all the S&P 500 index issues plus issues approved by the chief investment officer. Staff will submit. . .
- MTCP assets will be fully invested, defined as invested 95 percent in common stocks, preferred stocks, securities convertible into common or preferred stocks, or equity derivatives. MTCP may invest in the American Depository Receipts (ADRs) or comparable securities of large-capitalization foreign firms.
- MTCP may hold up to 5 percent of its assets in a stock performance index futures fund (SPIFF) or in STIP.

CONSTRAINTS

Liquidity: Liquidity needs are minimal. MTCP will maintain a minimum of $4,000,000 in the stock performance index futures fund (SPIFF) or in STIP.

Time horizon: Retirement benefit payments are long-term obligations. Therefore, the time horizon of MTCP is long-term in nature. Common stocks, by definition, do not have maturity dates and thus are consistent with the long-term objective of MTCP.

Tax considerations: Taxes are not a consideration because all participants are tax-exempt.

Legal/authorized securities: Legal constraints on the management of investment funds for the state of Montana are defined in the Montana Code Annotated 17-6-201.

Unique circumstances: None.

Summary

Instead of considering broad asset classes, this chapter introduced equity strategies, both active and passive, and focused on the process for allocating assets among these strategies. Equities within styles are more highly correlated than within market cap ranges, and international equities offer lower correlation with domestic categories. Although not perfect, the M–V framework is useful for constructing diversified portfolios based on the expected return, risk, and correlation structure of the equity strategies. The M–V model can be supplemented with an understanding of the investment process of the investment manager and the return characteristics of the strategy. Using market value weights can be a useful starting point for setting the equity mix.

Implementation of target allocations was also discussed, including mutual fund and institutional applications. Several examples were presented. The chapter concluded with a review of sample equity investment objectives and client guidelines.

Problems

1. Define these terms:
   a. Completeness fund.
   b. Quantitative versus fundamental.
2. List
   a. Two key factors for manager selection.
   b. Two key items for investment objectives.
3. Use the Chapter 7 Excel Outbox.xls file to explore active risk calculations:
   a. Calculate the active risk by computing the active returns versus the Russell 2000 Value index. How does the active risk differ in the Russell 2000 Value index versus the S&P 500?
   b. Divide the time period into two. How does the estimated active risk differ in the two periods? Examine the volatility of the index returns. Does the level of active risk seem to be related to market volatility? How would a manager protect herself from violating active risk guidelines because of growing market risk?
4. Calculate the expected return for portfolios with allocations for international, large, and small growth and large and small value strategies. Use the worksheet <Problem 4> in the spreadsheet Chapter 7 Questions.xls.
   a. Target mix of 35/35/10/10/10.
   b. Target mix of 20/20/20/20/20.
5. Design a sample equity strategy:
   a. List your objectives.
   b. Design a sample process chart.
6. Calculate the weights for the M–V optimized portfolio using the historical expected returns, standard deviations, and correlations presented in Exhibit 7.7. Use the M–V optimization spreadsheet developed in Chapter 3. The optimization should maximize utility by changing the weights across the five equity strategies (large-cap growth and value, small-cap growth and value, and international stocks) subject to the full-investment and no-short-sales constraints.
7. Calculate the weights for the M–V optimized portfolio with the JS expected returns presented in Exhibit 7.10 by using the M–V optimization spreadsheet developed in Problem 6. The optimization should maximize utility by changing the weights across the five equity strategies (large-cap growth and value, small-cap growth and value, and international stocks) subject to the full-investment and no-short-sales constraints.

Chapter 8

Equity Portfolio Construction

Chapter Outline

8.1 Introduction

Equity managers buy and sell stocks. They may trade them in bulk or one by one. They may buy them to initiate or add to an existing position, for their potential price appreciation, or for their diversifying characteristics. They may sell them to initiate a short position or reduce an existing position, in anticipation of price depreciation, or to hedge. Although stocks come in different forms, this chapter focuses on managing common stock portfolios; yet its content applies to a broad range of strategies.[1]

Chapter 7 discussed selecting the appropriate mix for a diversified blend of equity funds. This chapter moves to the next level of detail, taking the point of view of the manager of an individual equity portfolio. The objective for this chapter is to guide managers in the most appropriate method for building portfolios, given their objectives, skills, and investment opportunities. It will be useful for the general investor as well. It explains the construction process and, in turn, how individual equity accounts impact the overall profile of the equity exposure.

This chapter builds on terminology, concepts, and applications introduced in Chapter 7. Active and passive strategies are fully developed, and the implications of the

---

[1] As previously noted, preferred stock tends to behave more like fixed-income securities. Convertible bond prices tend to follow the price of the underlying common stock unless the share price has fallen substantially.

active–passive decision for performance objectives and portfolio construction techniques are examined. Active equity portfolio approaches are discussed, beginning with the management of sector allocations and extending to managing both style and sector exposures and finally the use of risk modeling and optimization techniques. The importance of benchmarking and the goal of consistent active performance will be reviewed. The chapter concludes with the presentation of equity portfolio construction examples utilizing Excel-based tools.

As we will discuss in Chapter 10, international equity portfolio construction is similar to domestic equity portfolio management. Although there are some differences in risk factors, trading procedures, transaction cost levels, and data availability, the techniques described in this chapter may be readily applied to overseas equity portfolios.

8.2   Passive versus Active Management

Portfolio managers have traditionally managed portfolios actively by purchasing securities that they believed offered attractive upside and limited downside and selling less desirable securities. Little concern was given to benchmarks; for that matter, little concern was given to relative performance. Clients were simply shown their growth in principal, realized capital gains, and investment income.

This changed in the late 1960s when Michael Jensen[2] completed his PhD dissertation. His research showed that, on average, and in most cases, mutual funds did not earn a fair return given their level of risk, as defined by the CAPM beta. Additional studies followed demonstrating that many, if not a majority of institutional managers, underperformed the S&P 500 index on a gross, let alone risk-adjusted, basis. In 1973 Wells Fargo Bank introduced an alternative for institutional investors—the first index fund—and passive equity management was born. Indexing has been popular and has grown consistently since its introduction. In 1976 the mutual fund firm Vanguard began to offer an S&P 500 index mutual fund to individual investors. By 1997 the Vanguard 500 Index Fund was the single largest mutual fund. Assets exceeded $70 billion in 2009, and the fund continues to be one of the largest offered in the United States. Even traditional active management shops like Fidelity Investments began offering index mutual funds in 1987.

The Record of Active Management

To set the stage for discussing equity portfolio construction, we should review the performance of active portfolio management relative to the performance of passive index portfolios. One reason is that the flow of assets between active and passive funds is influenced by relative performance. The growth of index fund assets has been especially strong immediately following one- and three-year periods of poor performance by active managers. It is also important to understand the likely sources of return for actively managed portfolios and whether the manager adds value net of the fees charged.

The relative performance of the typical active manager was once coincident with the relative performance of small-cap stocks. This was because active managers tended to exhibit smaller average market caps than the market cap–weighted indexes. Once adjusted for market cap, and net of fees, active managers tended to closely track the equity indexes but underperform on average.

[2] See Jensen (1968)

EXHIBIT 8.1 Performance of Active Large-Cap Value and Growth Mutual Funds versus Large-Cap Value and Growth Indexes, 1988–2008

Three-Year Rolling Returns
Average of Lipper Large-Cap Value and Growth *versus*
Average of Russell 1000 Value and Growth Indexes

Exhibit 8.1 compares the three-year rolling return of actively managed large-cap equity mutual funds and large-cap equity indexes from January 1988 through December 2008. The performance of actively managed funds is measured as the average of the Lipper large-cap growth and large-cap value indexes. The index return is measured as the average of the Russell 1000 growth and value indexes. For the period, the average large-cap mutual fund underperformed the average of the large-cap indexes by 1.00 percent per year. Expense ratios, which average 1–1.5 percent per year, help explain the underperformance. With so many managers trading stocks, the average manager seems to equal the market—before fees.

Some return histories of mutual funds, including some old versions of the Lipper series, have been subject to survivor bias because they include only funds in existence at the end of the time series. Funds that go out of business or are absorbed into other funds tend to exhibit below-average performance. Excluding these funds biases the average return upward.[3] Also note that conclusions about the performance of active management are affected by the data used and the period selected for analysis. For example, over the period 1990–1994, the Lipper data suggest that active managers slightly outperformed net of fees.

Many investors recognize that large companies are actively followed by more security analysts than are small and overseas companies. Typically 15 or more Wall Street

---

[3] As we will discuss in Chapter 11, this bias is pronounced for alternative investment vehicles, many of which have short reported track records.

EXHIBIT 8.2 **Performance of Active Small-Cap Growth and Value Management**

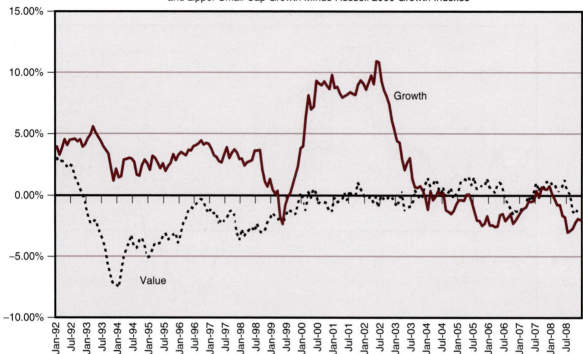

Three-Year Rolling Returns
Lipper Small-Cap Value Minus Russell 2000 Value Indexes
and Lipper Small-Cap Growth Minus Russell 2000 Growth Indexes

analysts follow each of the companies comprising the S&P 500. This compares to four analysts for the typical company within the small-cap Russell 2000.[4] Many consider this observation sufficient support for actively investing in small-cap stocks. At first glance the historical record seems to support this case. From January 1989 to December 2008 the average after-fee return for small-cap value and growth mutual funds was 8.3 percent, whereas the average of the Russell 2000 Value and Growth index returns was 7.6 percent. This is despite higher small-cap management fees due to their smaller size and increased specialization relative to large-cap funds.

However, the excess return is generated solely by the growth managers and may be explained to some extent by strategy differences and survivorship bias. Over the same period, small-cap value funds outperformed growth funds by 1.7 percent. Dividing the funds into growth and value groups demonstrates that active small-cap value funds underperformed their benchmark, on average, and small-cap growth funds outperformed. The growth portfolios outperformed by 2.3 percent per year, and the value portfolios underperformed by 0.8 percent. The pattern of relative performance is charted in Exhibit 8.2. Once combined into one classification, the broad Lipper Small Cap universe trails the Russell 2000 index by 27 basis points (though this is after expenses).

Overall, historical performance suggests a mixed record for actively managed mutual funds. On average, active large-cap managers have underperformed the S&P 500, likely due to fund expenses. Conversely, the typical active small-cap manager has

[4] Median values as of May 2009; source FactSet.

EXHIBIT 8.3
**Number and Asset
Levels of Equity
Mutual Funds
Offered in the U.S.**

Source: *2008 ICI Fact Book.*

Panel A: All Equity Funds		
	Number of Funds	**$ under Management (Billions)**
1970	323	$ 45.1
1985	562	111.3
2000	4,385	3,961.9
2007	4,767	6,521.4

Panel B: Equity Index Funds					
Index Funds			**ETFs**		
	Number of Funds	**$ under Management (Billions)**		**Number of Funds**	**$ under Management (Billions)**
1985	NA	$ 1.2	1985	0	$ 0.0
2000	251	353.4	2000	80	65.6
2007	336	750.6	2007	547	544.7

underperformed the index, though by less than the expense ratio; this is influenced by the outperformance of small-cap growth managers. Moreover, there are caveats to these results. The data used and period analyzed affect the conclusions; as noted, active large-cap managers outperformed the indexes earlier in the sample period. Survivor bias may also influence results.

Growth in Equity Fund Management

Interestingly, in spite of the mixed performance record of active management, active disciplines continue to prosper. The number of active mutual funds has grown exponentially since 1980, following a stagnant decade in the 1970s and just before the beginning of the great bull market in U.S. equities. Exhibit 8.3 reports the number and dollar value of equity mutual funds, including index funds, between 1970 and 2007. The industry grew dramatically in the 1990s in both assets and number of funds. Although the vast majority of these funds are actively managed, the portion invested with passive managers has increased substantially as well, growing to 11 percent of mutual fund assets; over 50 percent is managed versus the S&P 500 index. Growth in index-based exchange traded funds (ETFs) has also been impressive: from one fund with $460 million in assets in 1993 to $545 billion in 547 funds in December 2007.

8.3 Passive Portfolio Construction

Index managers seek to match the performance of a published index more closely and consistently than competitors. In other words, index managers try to *track* the index, and any difference in return is called **tracking error.** The return objective is called **tracking tolerance.** Successful S&P 500 indexes track within a few basis points of the index before management fees, whereas Russell 2000 indexes perform within tens of basis points. The larger tracking error for the Russell 2000 occurs because the index is broader and less liquid and its constituents are less correlated. Small-cap index funds also tend to have higher transaction costs and higher turnover. In July 2009, the median bid-ask spread for the Russell 2000 was eight times the level of the S&P500 median. While the S&P 500 turns over

5 percent per year, the Russell 2000 style indexes have exceeded 30 percent annual turnover.[5]

The competitive peers for an index fund are other index funds. However, as mentioned, asset flows to index funds are driven by their performance relative to actively managed funds. Institutional investors tend to maintain a strategic allocation to passive management with manager selection based on the record of tracking error and the management fee.[6]

Full Replication

The best way to ensure that a portfolio's return matches the index return is to buy every stock (constituent) in the index in the exact weight as in the index. This approach is called **full replication.** Full replication is practical for large asset levels and indexes with few constituents. The S&P 500 index is commonly tracked using full replication for managing mutual funds, commingled pools, or large separate accounts. There are two elements to managing an index portfolio using full replication: constituents and weights calculated from current prices and total shares outstanding. Because the index is market cap–weighted, if there are no asset flows all the manager needs to do is reinvest dividend income and buy and sell stocks when the Standard & Poor's committee announces, typically in advance, changes in the constituents. Except for changes in index constituents (typically due to corporate actions) and shares outstanding (typically due to secondary or rights offerings), weights adjust automatically, in tandem with the index, as prices change. These trades must be done precisely and at low cost, with cash kept to a minimum, to minimize tracking error. It has been joked that a monkey could run an index fund. That may be true for a poorly tracking fund, but precise tracking requires true attention to detail and is especially challenging for portfolios subject to cash flows, as discussed in the accompanying Theory in Practice box.

Sampling

If an index has many constituents, or the portfolio asset level is small, a portfolio manager needs to consider selecting a sample of securities instead of buying the entire index. For example, a sampling approach is preferred for the Russell 2000 index, due in part to the high transaction and maintenance costs required for full replication. Index construction techniques and models of stock behavior can be used to improve upon simple equal weighting for a random sample of stocks. Because larger-cap stocks tend to represent a larger proportion of indexes, it makes sense to ensure a representative sample of the largest stocks. For example, simply buying the largest-weighted names in the S&P 500 can provide a rough index fund, though it may be subject to sector and style (especially market-cap) biases. The correlations within different style groups of equities tend to be higher than within the overall index. It would make sense, then, to ensure a representative sample of each of these groups. A **stratified sample** approach takes advantage of both these observations.

It is recognized in the investment industry that size (market capitalization) and style (growth versus value) are two major factors that influence security returns. As

---

[5] S&P 500 turnover averaged 4.7% over the ten years ending 2008; in 2007, Russell implemented rules to reduce turnover to their indexes following 30% average turnover levels for the 2000 growth and value indexes in 2005 and 2006.

[6] Some index fund management fees are zero. The manager is paid from a portion of the **stock lending** income. Short sellers pay stock owners—frequently index funds—a fee for the privilege of borrowing their stock.

Theory in Practice
Managing Cash Flow in an Index Mutual Fund

Some portfolios experience regular cash flows. In particular, mutual funds are subject to daily or more frequent flows. Inflows must be invested and outflows require liquidity, both leading to transaction costs. Some contributions or withdrawals are known in advance. If not, there is timing risk. Mutual fund portfolio managers, for example, may not know exact cash flow figures by the close of business. If a contribution arrives by 4:00 p.m., it must be given the 4:00 p.m. fund valuation price. Waiting until the following day to invest will lead to tracking error. To the extent that inflows are associated with rising markets, this will lead to performance drag. Index funds are especially sensitive to cash flows, and any transaction costs will be visible in the tracking error. Portfolio managers can address this issue in several ways:

1. One method to protect the performance of a commingled index fund, and its participants, would be to invest inflows outside the fund and then contribute to the fund in kind.* Similarly outflows would be withdrawn from the fund in kind and then liquidated. However, SEC regulations prohibit mutual funds from isolating flows in this manner.

2. Fund companies may institute transaction fees paid out of contributions and withdrawals that go directly to the fund, offsetting the transaction costs. These fees are a constant proportion of flows, and only an estimate of true costs.

3. The portfolio manager may purchase futures contracts at low cost to invest cash and remain 100 percent exposed to the market at all times. The availability of futures trading until 4:15 p.m. provides a little leeway.

4. Last-minute telephone orders can be restricted. Systems may be developed to monitor telephone, mail, and Internet orders and share that information with the portfolio manager. Unfortunately for portfolio managers, many orders are taken by third parties and arrive later in the evening or overnight. In this case forecasting models must be developed.

* Payment in kind involves transferring the security rather than its monetary value in cash.

---

evidence, consider all the size- and style-based indexes produced by Russell (Exhibit 7.1), Wilshire, and Standard & Poor's. Fama and French (1992) studied these relationships, focusing on market capitalization as a measure of size and book/price (B/P) ratio as a simple measure of style exposure.[7] In fact, tests over the period 1963–1990 confirmed that beta was not a statistically significant factor in a three-variable regression including B/P and market-cap. Lakonishok, Schleifer, and Vishny (1994) and Fama and French (1993) confirmed these results, with Fama and French noting that these factors "capture much of the cross section of average stock returns." Earlier work by Barr Rosenberg, beginning in 1973, described these factors, together with other style factors and industry affiliations, as having powerful influences on a stock's relationship with the overall market, thereby determining the stock's beta. His work also discussed the importance of risk unique to a stock, called specific risk, uncorrelated with style and industry characteristics.

This evidence suggests that to control tracking error a portfolio should offer similar P/B, market cap, and industry exposures as the index with small differences in individual security weights. Therefore, stratifying stocks into large and small market

[7] Although Graham and Dodd (1934) are credited with motivating the first style-based strategy, size and P/B as risk factors were examined by Banz (1981) and Statman (1980) respectively. The apparent explanatory power of fundamental valuation ratios is known as the *anomalies literature* and is reviewed in Chapter 15.

cap and high and low P/B stock groups, as well as explicitly selecting securities from within each group, should improve the subset of stocks selected to build the portfolio. The formal portfolio construction process follows:

Create a Stratified Sample

Select	All securities in the index with index weight $> L$.
Sort	All securities into size/style subsamples.
Randomly select	A prespecified number of securities from each subsample.

Optimize the Portfolio

Minimize	Weighted active risk.
By choosing	The weights of the individual securities.
Subject to	A fully invested portfolio.
	Weights greater than or equal to zero.
	Similar factor exposures (F_j) as the index.
	Similar sector exposures (S_j) as the index.

There are several methods for constructing a portfolio designed to closely match an index. Barr Rosenberg's work suggests one technique. His approach involves developing an equity risk model and applying the model within an optimization. This approach is similar to the risk models described in Chapters 3 and 7. However, an equity model does not directly estimate the risk of each security and its correlation with every other security. Instead the model estimates the expected return premiums, risk, and correlations of style and sector factors and calculates the exposure of each security to these factors. Recall the cross-sectional models covered in Section 4.2 of Chapter 4. The models may be implemented using regression techniques on unidentified canonical factors, macro variables, or market factors. Rosenberg's approach is to use fundamental factors (P/B, earnings growth, market cap, and industry allocations) that can be easily identified. This approach provides strong explanatory power—exactly what is needed for an index fund manager.

The advantage of a fundamental risk model is that it quantifies the expected return premium and risk of style, sector, or stock exposures that differ from the benchmark index. An optimization may then be used to select stock weights to minimize the risk of return differences between the portfolio and the index. This difference determines forecast active risk (compared to the realized active risk calculated in Chapter 7). Commercial vendors, including BARRA and Northfield, provide such risk models for portfolio managers. The disadvantage of this process, besides being complicated, is that security and factor risk must be forecast, with error, and the optimization may overweight positions whose risk is underestimated and, conversely, underweight positions whose risk is overestimated. In addition, although this is addressable to some extent, nonlinear relationships can be a challenge for regression estimation techniques. As a result, active volatility may be higher than forecast.

Development and application of a fundamental risk model is beyond the scope of this book. Large databases are required and application requires ongoing updating of the model. However, there is an easy-to-apply (though less effective), alternative to using a complicated risk model, and it provides an illustration of portfolio construction technique within a multi-factor framework. A simple optimization approach may be used within Excel if we assume that the risk of each stock, after controlling for factor and sector risk, is equal and independent. This allows the objective function to be specified as the sum of squared security weight differences between the portfolio and index. Constraints control sector and factor exposures. Note that this simplified approach does not require sector and factor risk to be equal between the portfolio and the benchmark. The individual importance of the factors may be incorporated into the optimization problem by adjusting the tightness of the constraints. The assumption of equal security risk may also be relaxed by incorporating individual security constraints. The optimization problem can now be translated into equations (where n = number of securities in the index, m = total number of securities in the sample, s = number of subsectors, I = index, and P = portfolio):

Create a Stratified Sample

Select	All i, with $\omega_{Ii} > L$, for total of l securities.
Sort	All securities into s subsamples based on factors F_j.
Randomly select	$(m - l)/s$ securities from each subsample.

Optimize the Portfolio

Minimize	$\Sigma_{i=1,n} (\omega_{Ii} - \omega_{Pi})^2$
By choosing	Σ_{Pi}
Subject to	$\Sigma_{i=1,n} \omega_{Pi} = 1$
	$\omega_{Pi} \geq 0$
	$\Sigma_{i=1,n} \omega_{Pi} F_{ij} = F_{Ij}$
	$\Sigma_{i=1,n} \omega_{Pi} S_{ij} = S_{Ij}$

Consider the 500 stocks in the S&P 500. Selecting the largest market-cap stocks before sorting into style groups improves the sampling process by avoiding the possibility of excluding the largest weighted stocks in the index. Exhibit 8.4 plots the

EXHIBIT 8.4   **Weight Distribution of Securities in the S&P 500**

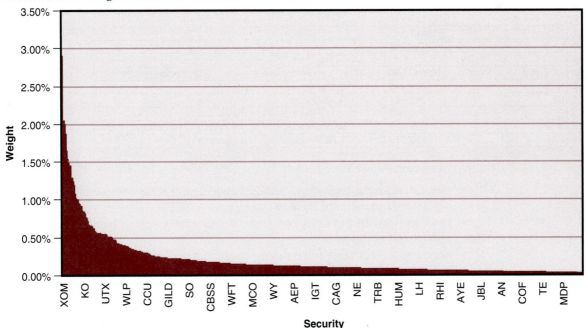

Note: Data as of June 2006.

distribution of security weights, in descending order by market cap from left to right, in the S&P 500. Like many large-cap indexes, the largest stocks represent the majority of the market capitalization of the index; the largest 25 of the 500 companies have individual weights of 0.75 percent or more and together account for close to 35 percent of the index.

Clearly it is important to include the largest market-cap stocks in sample selection to avoid large differences in individual stock positions in the final portfolio.

Sorting all the stocks into four groups based on market cap and P/B and then creating four random samples selected from these groups will lead to a better representation than simply creating a single random sample. It will ensure that the sample is broadly distributed and helps capture nonlinearities in the relationship between style factors and stock returns that might be missed if we select only one sample and ignore the factor subsamples. While less important for indexing the large-cap S&P 500, it is especially important for tracking broad or small-cap indexes.

Excel Outbox
Passive
Management

The spreadsheet Chapter 8 Excel Outboxes.xls demonstrates the application of the stratified sampling and optimization technique for managing an equity index portfolio. The process has three stages: data preparation, sample selection, and optimization.

Data Preparation
In this step we calculate the index portfolio weight; calculate the weighted average factor and sector exposure; and select the *L* largest securities. The constituent names, primary industry affiliations, and market capitalizations for any S&P index are readily available on Standard & Poor's Web site. The necessary data are provided in the <Data-Template> worksheet. The worksheet should appear as follows:

	A	B	C	D	E	F
1	S&P 500 INDEX		effective after the close June 1, 2006			
2						
3	Weighted Average		Market-cap			
4			P/B			
5			Cyclical			
6			Financial			
7			NonCyclical			
8						
9	Ticker	Weight	Market Cap	P/B	Sector Name	S&P Sector_Name
10	XOM		378,448	3.12	Cyclical	Energy
11	GE		346,371	3.26	Cyclical	Industrials
12	C		243,641	2.12	Financial	Financials
13	MSFT		238,198	5.61	Cyclical	Information Technology
14	BAC		223,018	1.68	Financial	Financials

The sectors include the following:

- Cyclicals: industrial, technology, and consumer durable companies whose fortunes are highly correlated with the business cycle.
- Financial: financial and utility companies whose returns tend to be highly correlated with interest rate dynamics.
- Noncyclicals: health care and consumer staple companies whose performance tends to be less correlated with the business cycle or interest rates.

The index portfolio market weights are calculated as the ratio of the stock's market capitalization and the total market capitalization of the index:

- In cell B10 enter =C10/SUM(C$10:C$509). Then copy cell B10 to cells B11 through B509.

The weighted factor exposures for the index are calculated in row 3:

- In cell D3 enter =SUMPRODUCT($B$10:$B$509,C$10:C$509).
- In cell D4 enter =SUMPRODUCT($B$10:$B$509,D$10:D$509).
- In cell D5 enter =SUMPRODUCT($B$10:$B$509,INT(E$10:E$509=C5)), and then copy cell D5 to cells D6:D7.

The function INT creates a dummy variable that equals 1 if the condition is met and 0 otherwise.

The resulting worksheet should look like this:

	A	B	C	D	E	F
1	S&P 500 INDEX		effective after the close June 1, 2006			
2						
3	Weighted Average		Market-cap	87,644		
4			P/B	3.87		
5			Cyclical	52.78%		
6			Financial	24.16%		
7			NonCyclical	23.06%		
8						
9	Ticker	Weight	Market Cap	P/B	Sector Name	S&P Sector_Name
10	XOM	3.17%	378,448	3.12	Cyclical	Energy
11	GE	2.90%	346,371	3.26	Cyclical	Industrials
12	C	2.04%	243,641	2.12	Financial	Financials

Security Selection

This involves two criteria: selecting securities with index weights greater than the specified threshold value and random selection of securities from the size/style groups. Organize the securities into four groups:

- Step 1: Sort by index weight—select <Data-Template>.

The template should appear as follows:

	A	B	C	D	E	F
1	Step 1: Sort by Index Weight					
2						
3						
4						
5	#	Ticker	Index Weight	Market Cap	P/B	Sector_Name
6	1					
7	2					

- Copy and paste-special-value cells A10:E509 from worksheet <Data-Template> to cells B6:F505 to worksheet <Sample-Template>.
- Sort cells B6:F505 based on index weight (column C) from largest to smallest (descending).

(continued)

(continued)   The result should look like this:

	A	B	C	D	E	F
1	**Step 1: Sort by Index Weight**					
2						
3						
4						
5	#	Ticker	Index Weight	Market Cap	P/B	Sector_Name
6	1	XOM	3.17%	378,448	3.120	Energy
7	2	GE	2.90%	346,371	3.260	Industrials
8	3	C	2.04%	243,641	2.210	Financials

- Step 2: Sort by P/B.

  The template should appear as follows:

	H	I	J	K	L	M
1	**Step 2: Sort P/B**					
2						
3						
4						
5		Ticker	Index Weight	Market Cap	P/B	Sector_Name
6	1					
7	2					

- Copy and paste B6:F505 to I6:M505.
- Sort cells I6:M255 based on P/B (column L) from largest to smallest (descending, no header row).
- Sort cells I256:M505 based on P/B (column L) from largest to smallest.
- This divides the securities into four groups: larger with higher P/B, larger with lower P/B, smaller with higher P/B, and smaller with lower P/B. The order of the rankings is important only in that it places the larger stocks at the top, making it easier to screen on the index weight threshold. Otherwise it would not matter because the correlation between the size and style factors is nearly zero, −0.07. It is important to check the correlation between factors because a high correlation may result in a sample bias, meaning that further randomization of the sample selection is required.

  The result should look like this:

	H	I	J	K	L	M
1	**Step 2: Sort by P/B**					
2						
3						
4						
5		Ticker	Index Weight	Market Cap	P/B	Sector_Name
6	1	Q	0.13%	15,559	–	Telecommunication Services
7	2	TXU	0.23%	27,544	55.200	Utilities
8	3	AMZN	0.13%	15,507	47.200	Consumer Discretionary

- Step 3: Selection.

The template should appear as follows:

	O	P	Q	R	S	T	U	V	W	X
1	Step 3: Selection									
2		Weight:								
3		Rnd								
4		Total:								
5	Random Number	Saved Random Number	Indicator	Indicator	Group	Ticker	Index Weight	Market Cap	P/B	Sector_Name
6										
7										

- Excel contains a function for generating random numbers from a uniform distribution over the range [0.1]. In cell O6 enter =RAND() and then copy to cells O7:N505.
- The function regenerates a new set of random numbers whenever the spreadsheet recalculates—that is, every time the <ENTER> key is pressed if auto-calc is on. To provide a single set of numbers to work with, copy and paste-special-value cells O6:O505 to cells P5:P505.
- In cell Q6 enter =IF(OR(J6>=Q\$2,P6>=Q\$3),1,0). This function indicates whether the security meets either the market capitalization or random number criteria for inclusion in the sample.
- In cell Q2 enter 0.0075. One rule of thumb is to use the weight of the stock defining the fifth percentile of the sample. The threshold for large-cap indexes may be larger than that for smaller-cap indexes because mid-cap and small-cap indexes tend to have more uniform index weights. Without a risk model, trial and error (and simulation) are required to determine the correct threshold. Higher thresholds will allow more flexibility in selecting stocks beyond the largest-weighted industries, but they will reduce the portfolio's exposure to the largest individually weighted names. Another rule of thumb is to include all stocks with index weights greater than 25 basis points or 10 basis points. This will impact the required sample size.
- Some adjustment of the threshold for the random number will be required. Because the ultimate desired sample size in this example is 100 (or 20 percent (1 − 80 percent) of the total universe), enter 0.80 in cell Q3. Some trial and error are required in this step to reach the correct sample size in practice.
- In cell Q4 enter =SUM(Q6:Q505). If the random series is the same as this example, the initial results should show a sample size of 127. To reduce this to 100 a threshold of 0.866 was needed. Select a value in cell Q3 to reach a value of 100 in cell Q4.
- In cell Q6 enter =IF(OR(J6>=Q\$2,P6>=Q\$3),1,0). This is the selection criteria formula, including the stock if either condition of a large enough weight Q\$2 or large enough random value Q\$3 holds.
- Copy Q6:Q505 and then paste-special-value to cells R6:R505 to preserve the values for later sorting. Copy the paste-special-value I6:M505 to T6:X505. Sort R6:X505 by the indicator (column R, descending), then by index weight (column U, descending), and then P/B (column W, descending).
- The top 100 names represent the sample constituents that will be optimized to form the index tracking portfolio.

Although your sample will differ, it will look something like the following:

	O	P	Q	R	S	T	U	V	W	X
1	Step 3: Selection									
2		Weight:	0.75%							
3		Rnd	0.866							
4		Total:	100							
5	Random Number	Saved Random Number	Indicator	Indicator	Group	Ticker	Index Weight	Market Cap	P/B	Sector_Name
6	0.4598	0.3986	0	1	1	XOM	3.17%	378,448	3.120	Energy
7	0.7353	0.4330	0	1	1	GE	2.90%	346,371	3.260	Industrials
8	0.2168	0.4924	0	1	2	C	2.04%	243,641	2.120	Financials

(continued)

(continued)

Optimization

The next step is to select optimal security weights for the 100 stocks. The worksheet <Opt Index-Template> should appear as follows:

	A	B	C	D	E	F	G	H	I	J
1	Objective		Min							
2										
3		Constraints	Target	Range	Wtd Avg					
4		Market Cap								
5		P/B								
6		Cyclical								
7		Financial								
8		Non-Cyclical								
9		Weight								
10										
11										
12										
13		Ticker	Index Weight	Market Cap	P/B	Sector	Major Sector	Weight	Active Weight, bp	$(\omega_\Pi - \omega_I)^2$
14	1									
15	2									

- The data from the Step 3 template must be copied to the worksheet. Copy T6:X105 to B13:F114.
- Objective: The objective is to minimize the sum of squared differences in weights between the portfolio and the index active weights.
  - In cell J14 enter =(H14-C14)^2 and then copy to cells J15:J113.
  - In cell D1 enter =SUM(J14:J113). This is the sum of the squared weight differences that will be the objective to minimize in Solver.
  - In cell I14 enter =(H14-C14)*10000 and copy down to row 113. This is the active weight in basis points.
- By changing: The portfolio weights are contained in cells H14:H113. Start by entering equal weights of 0.01 in each cell to seed the optimization.
- Constraints: The constraints will be entered as ranges rather than equalities. The constraints will set weighted-average market cap and P/B within ±10 percent of the index values and limit sectors to +10 percent of the index weights. Note that the tighter the constraints, the less stable the solution. As the index changes through time, a more tightly constrained portfolio will generate higher turnover levels. This is discussed further in Chapter 12.
  - Market cap:
    - Target: In cell C4 enter =Data!$D$3.
    - Range: In cell D4 enter 0.10.
    - Wtd Avg: In cell E4 enter =SUMPRODUCT(D14:D516,H14:H516).
    - Solver: There will be two constraints—the upper bound, E4 ≤ (1+D4)*C4, and the lower bound, E4 ≥ (1 − D4)*C4.
  - P/B:
    - Target: In cell C5 enter =Data!$D$4.
    - Range: In cell D5 enter 0.10.
    - Wtd Avg: In cell E5 enter =SUMPRODUCT(E14:E516,H14:H516).
    - Solver: There will be two constraints—the upper bound, E5 ≤ (1+D5)*C5, and the lower bound, E5 ≥ (1−D5)*C5.
  - Sector constraints require only an upper bound because the weights are additive. To make the optimization more tractable, the sectors will be reduced to only three major sectors: cyclicals, noncyclicals, and financials. A mapping is provided in the template in N14:O23.
    - In cell G14 enter =OFFSET(O$13,MATCH(F14,N$14:N$23,0),0) and then copy to cells G15:G113.

- Target: In cell C6 enter =Data!$D5 and then copy to cells C7:C8.
- Range: In cells D6:D8 enter 0.10.
- Wtd Avg: In cell E6 enter =SUMPRODUCT(H$14:H$113,INT(G$14:G$113=B6)) and then copy to cells E7:E8.
  - Solver: There are three constraints—each sector's upper bound, such as E6 ≤ (1+D6)*C6. Note that a lower bound may be added if desired.
- Budget: The weights need to total to 100 percent:
  - Target: In cell C9 enter 100%.
  - Sum of weights under Wtd Avg: In cell E9 enter =SUM(H14:H113).
  - Solver: There is one constraint: C9 = E9.
- Nonnegative weight constraint:
  - Solver: H14:H113 ≥ 0.
- Note that maximum weights or maximum active weights may be added to the constraints.
- Solver is now ready to be run. The Solver Parameters window should look like the following:

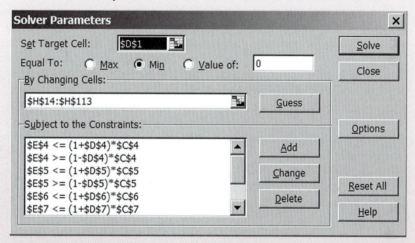

Additional constraints are shown here:

- The solution should look something like the following, with optimal weights in column H:

	A	B	C	D	E	F	G	H	I	J
1	Objective		Min	0.0175						
2										
3		Constraints	Target	Range	Wtd Avg					
4		Market Cap	87,644	10%	96,409					
5		P/B	3.87	10%	3.73					
6		Cyclical	53%	10%	58%					
7		Financial	24%	10%	26%					
8		Non-Cyclical	23%	10%	16%					
9		Weight	100%		100%					
10										
11										
12										
13		Ticker	Index Weight	Market Cap	P/B	Sector	Major Sector	Weight	Active Weight, bp	$(\omega_\Pi - \omega_I)^2$
14	1	XOM	3.17%	378447.8	3.12	Energy	Cyclical	5.95%	278.3	0.00
15	2	GE	2.90%	346370.6	3.26	Industrials	Cyclical	3.40%	49.9	0.00

(continued)

| (concluded) | This S&P 500 example is used to illustrate sampling and optimization techniques. Using commercial vendor* tracking risk forecasts, the optimization results are superior to simply cap weighting the initial sample of 24 stocks whose index weights were greater than 75 basis points. However, the optimized 100-stock sample reflects equivalent tracking risk to simply cap weighting the 100-stock sample. An improvement in tracking risk (over cap weighting) depends on index characteristics, minimum index weight parameters, and constraint settings.

* Provided by BARRA. |

8.4 Goals for Active Management

Active managers are paid to deliver value, typically defined as additional return over and above peer and index benchmarks. These return targets are well specified for institutional managers, such as public mutual funds, pension accounts, and foundations. As discussed in Chapter 7, the period over which outperformance is measured varies. Some institutional investors measure performance over a market cycle, which is typically interpreted as three to five years. Heisler, Knittel, Neumann, and Stewart (2007) found evidence suggesting that investors focus on three- and five-year periods but may also fire a manager with very poor one-year results.

Some managers, such as personal trust officers, are not closely monitored by clients using benchmarks. In addition, the many constraints on trust accounts, such as unique tax situations or required trade approval by the client, can impact the management of the account. In such cases the manager may be paid a salary for simply maintaining and perhaps growing the account relationship.

Managers often state that "you can't eat relative performance" and that total performance is what matters. Total performance is important: Higher performance will always allow you to eat better than lower performance. Moreover, assets flow to the most successful managers. Academic and industry studies show that individual investor contributions go to the highest-ranked mutual funds. As a result, the goal for mutual fund managers, and many institutional money managers, is to outperform their peers. Studies have found clear evidence that pension and other institutional assets flow to managers who have outperformed indexes over one-, three-, and five-year periods. For these clients consistency is as important as relative performance.

Many investors, both individual and corporate, are taxed. As a result, performance after taxes is important. However, postponing gain realization can conflict with seeking the best pretax performance. A manager needs to balance the cost of realizing gains early with the potential drag from maintaining an unattractive holding. Mutual fund ranking groups now publish both before- and after-tax returns of funds, and many tax-managed mutual funds are now available.

With increased client sophistication, there has been a demand for performance consistency relative to specific benchmarks. Many institutional investors seek to limit the level of underperformance, setting beta and tracking risk guidelines. To satisfy these guidelines, managers need to construct their portfolios carefully and continually monitor their portfolios' risk profiles.

Investment Processes

Portfolio managers come in all shapes and sizes, and so do their processes. The reality of the investment management business is that someone is always underperforming, giving others the opportunity to gather assets. As the market cycles, one style

EXHIBIT 8.5   **Lipper's Equity Mutual Fund Classifications**

Source: Lipper: A Reuters Company Copyright 2001 ©Reuters.

Balanced	General Equity	Large-Cap Core	Pacific Region
Balanced Target Maturity	Global Flexible Port	Large-Cap Growth	Real Estate
Canadian	Global	Large-Cap Value	S+P 500 Index
Capital Appreciation	Global Small-Cap	Latin American	Science + Technology
China Region	Gold Oriented	Mid-Cap Core	Small-Cap
Convertible Securities	Health/Biotechnology	Mid-Cap Growth	Small-Cap Core
Emerging Markets	Income	Mid-Cap Value	Small-Cap Growth
Equity Income	International	Multi-Cap Core	Small-Cap Value
European Region	International Income	Multi-Cap Growth	Specialty Equity
Financial Services	International Small-Cap	Multi-Cap Value	Specialty/Miscellaneous
Flexible Income	Japanese	Natural Resources	Telecommunication
Flexible Portfolio	Large-Cap	Pacific Ex Japan	Utility

or approach is on top, leading to asset flows and perhaps new strategies. We have discussed the many approaches to active equity management; Lipper has 48 classifications of equity funds, defined by universe and by investment style, which are displayed in Exhibit 8.5.

Active equity disciplines may be defined by growth and value philosophies, using fundamental or quantitative techniques, and implemented in either long-only or long/short portfolios. Benchmark relative, long-only portfolios may be considered similar to long/short portfolios, except that their ability to underweight is limited by the benchmark weight. Portfolio guidelines define the portfolio's universe, risk levels, and benchmark. Effective portfolio construction processes deliver the desired portfolio active bets, cash positions, characteristics, style exposures, industry weights, beta, and tracking risk.

Fundamental techniques involve individual analysts and managers carefully reading through 10-K forms, annual reports, and trade journals, seeking to understand how companies best make money in a particular industry. This includes an understanding of industry key trends, how an industry is valued relative to the overall market, and how individual stocks are valued within the industry. This information is used for ranking either the attractiveness of the industry or the stocks within the industry or both. Valuation approaches include simple relative multiples, discounted cash flow models, or detailed return on invested capital techniques. Recommendations come in the form of stocks and industries and perhaps commodity and cash exposures. Portfolios may have either a constant style bias or a changing bias based on momentum and valuations. The size of the universe from which to select securities depends on the size of the research team and the thoroughness of its approach. Fundamental managers may use simple quantitative tools to narrow their focus or expand their coverage. Momentum managers may look at the 52-week winners for ideas, whereas deep value managers may look at the 52-week losers list.

Quantitative techniques involve collecting fundamental data, Street research estimates, and technical measures and studying their relationships to valuations or returns. Typical variables include P/S, ROE, earnings variability, quality of earnings, profitability measures, uses of capital, consensus earnings changes, and price trends. Similar to fundamental managers, the objective is to forecast returns. The distinction is that quantitative managers rely to a greater extent on computer models, rather than qualitative judgment, to forecast. In fact, many believe the models allow them to exploit the opportunities created by the behavioral tendencies of other traders. They may use simple regression techniques or highly sophisticated statistical models. Recommendations come in the form of stocks but may also be in the form of industries or style factors. Stock recommendations may be ranked within the overall universe or within industries or sectors. The breadth of the selection universe depends on the size of the historical database, and it frequently exceeds the research coverage of fundamental managers.

The most successful active processes generate value consistently relative to indexes and peers. Investors seek out the most consistent managers and direct their assets to them; inconsistent managers risk clients becoming disillusioned and firing them. Consistent performance depends on several factors, as explored in Stewart (1998): the number, alpha, and correlation of the bets, where a *bet* is defined as any active weight the manager makes relative to the benchmark. The greater the number of bets, their value added, and their independence, the higher the probability that a portfolio will outperform over a given period. This does not mean a concentrated strategy will not be consistent. It simply means that a concentrated strategy needs to deliver more value added if it seeks to deliver the same level of consistency as a more broadly diversified portfolio. In addition, if there are many bets, but they are correlated even by a modest amount, they will not provide a level of consistency equal to that provided by a highly diversifying process. Ideally an active process generates a lot of high-value, unique investment ideas.

Whether the equity recommendations are generated by fundamental or quantitative techniques, they come in the form of stock, industry/sector, or style factor bets. Stock recommendations may be in one of several contexts—total return, market relative, or industry/sector relative. The simplest to consider is industry relative. In this context, the process ranks stocks within an industry or sector, regardless of the overall forecast for the industry's or market's performance.

8.5 Sector Management

Sector management is a common technique for constructing an active equity portfolio. Consider a ranking of stocks, each within a particular industry or sector. The portfolio manager seeks to hold, and more heavily weight, the highest-ranked stocks and exclude the lowest-ranked stocks. The portfolio will be fully invested with no cash and no sector skew. A sample algorithm can be outlined to illustrate this approach:

1. Rank the stocks within the sector.
2. Include the top stocks in the portfolio.
3. Double the weight of the top half of that group.
4. Neutrally weight each sector.

Implementing this approach is equivalent to selecting the stocks for inclusion in each sector, assigning a weight of two-thirds to the half of the selected stocks and one-third to the bottom half of selected stocks, normalizing the weights to 100 percent within each sector, and multiplying each stock weight by the sector weight within the universe. Other weightings that favor the more highly ranked stocks can also be applied. Exhibit 8.6 considers the example of a sector that represents 25 percent of the benchmark and contains 10 stocks. The top-ranked stocks receive a final weight of 5.6 percent in the portfolio and the sector weight is neutral, equaling the benchmark.

This approach effectively captures analyst or model stock rankings within each sector, and the sector exposure neutralization provides one form of risk control. This approach is

EXHIBIT 8.6
Sample Weighting
Algorithm for a 25
Percent Weighted
Sector

Rank	Initial	Normalized	Final
1	66.7%	22.2%	5.6%
2	66.7	22.2	5.6
3	66.7	22.2	5.6
4	33.3	11.1	2.8
5	33.3	11.1	2.8
6	33.3	11.1	2.8
7	0.0	0.0	0.0
8	0.0	0.0	0.0
9	0.0	0.0	0.0
10	0.0	0.0	0.0
	300.0%	100.0%	25.0%

similar to the Passive Management Excel Outbox index optimization if it ignored index weights and excluded constraints on market cap and P/B. As a result, there may still be unintended style bets. For example, the portfolio may have a smaller market cap and lower P/B than the benchmark. And if the benchmark is an index, the portfolio's active security weights relative to the index may not accurately reflect the rankings. That is, highly ranked stocks with large index weights may actually be underweighted in the active portfolio.

As an illustration of these points, consider the following mutual fund that "seeks to reduce the impact of industry weightings on the performance of the fund relative to the Standard & Poor's Index (S&P 500)."[8] Although sector weights are closely managed relative to the benchmark, style factors are not as closely aligned, as illustrated in Exhibit 8.7. These characteristics are consistent with a portfolio that is managed to incorporate modest style bets while limiting sector risk. However, if the manager seeks

[8] Fidelity Disciplined Equity Fund, 9/30/06.

EXHIBIT 8.7
Portfolio Sector and
Style Exposures

Source: Fidelity.com.

Panel A: Sector Weights			
	Fund	Index	Active
Consumer discretionary	10.1%	9.9%	0.2%
Consumer staples	7.8	9.4	−1.6
Energy	10.7	9.1	1.6
Financials	20.9	21.8	−0.9
Health care	11.2	12.4	−1.2
Industrials	12.0	10.7	1.3
Information technology	14.0	14.9	−0.9
Materials	4.4	2.8	1.6
Telecommunication services	3.8	3.4	0.4
Utilities	2.4	3.3	−0.9

Panel B: Style Characteristics		
	Fund	Index
Dividend yield	1.4%	1.9%
Price/book	2.9	2.8
Price/earnings (IBES one-year forecast)	13.2	14.6
Price/sales	1.3	1.6
One-year EPS growth (IBES forecast)	16.7%	15.2%
Weighted average Market cap ($ billions)	$77.60	$94.60

Note: Fidelity Disciplined Equity Fund, 9/30/06.

to manage total active risk, there are ways to build a portfolio that balances both sector and style exposures and controls the weights of individual stocks.

8.6 Style and Sector Management

As we have discussed, controlling only the sector exposures may generate unintended biases in the other factor exposures of a portfolio. Some managers may be comfortable with some factor exposures but do not want them to dominate portfolio risk because a high correlation in individual bets may lead to low performance consistency. A common factor theme may create what is essentially a single (style) bet in the portfolio.

An alternative approach is to manage both style and sector exposures, together with individual security weights relative to the benchmark. The technique developed for passive management in Section 8.3 may be modified and effectively applied to active management. Recall that the goal was to randomly select a subset of the index and minimize the sum of squared weight differences. For active management, both the subset selection and objective function need to be modified:

Create a Stratified Sample

Select	All i, with $\omega_{Ii} > L$, for total of l securities.
Sort	Securities into s subsamples based on factors F_j.
Select	Highly ranked securities from each subsample.

Optimize the Portfolio

Maximize	$\Sigma_{i=1,n} \omega_{Pi}\alpha_i - \lambda\Sigma_{i=1,n}(\omega_{Ii} - \omega_{Pi})^2$
By choosing	ω_{Pi}
Subject to	$\Sigma_{i=1,n} \omega_{Pi} = 1$
	$\omega_{Pi} \geq 0$
	$\Sigma_{i=1,n} \omega_{Pi} F_{ij} = F_{Ij}$
	$\Sigma_{i=1,n} \omega_{Pi} S_{ij} = S_{Ij}$

The objective function is designed to maximize the portfolio's expected value added with a penalty for taking active risk, where alpha (α)[9] is defined as the risk-adjusted expected active return on a security, and active risk is measured as the squared weight differences between the portfolio and the index. Ideally the alphas are explicit excess return forecasts, but in practice a relative ranking factor may be used. As a result, the optimization process seeks to deliver the greatest exposure to stock alphas while managing the size of individual stock weights and factor exposures. In practice, lambda (λ) may need to be adjusted to allow feasible portfolios. This optimization model is similar to the program developed in Chapters 3 and 7, where the goal was to maximize utility using total portfolio return and risk (or relative return and risk for asset-liability problems). Here the objective is to maximize utility based on *active* return and *active* risk. Within the Excel Outbox, risk is assumed to depend on factor exposures and individual stock weights.

---

[9] Note that alpha, α, has a different meaning here than it did in Chapters 3–5.

Excel Outbox
Active
Management

The construction of an active portfolio is illustrated in the <Opt Active-Template> in the spreadsheet Chapter 08 Excel Outboxes. For ease of demonstration, the portfolio is constructed from the same subset of 100 stocks used to construct the sample index portfolio. Using the same samples for both the index and active optimizations makes it easy to see the impact of the active stock rankings on the final portfolio. However, in this case, alphas are also assigned. For simplicity, the alpha rankings are assumed to be relative to other stocks within the four style subsets. In practice, the weight of the subsets may be affected by sector and style rankings or influenced by alphas determined relative to the overall index.

The worksheet <Opt Active-Template> should appear as follows:

	A	B	C	D	E	F	G	H	I	J
1	Objective		Min							
2										
3		Constraints	Target	Range	Wtd Avg					
4		Market Cap								
5		P/B								
6		Cyclical								
7		Financial								
8		Non-Cyclical								
9		Weight								
10										
11										
12										
13		Ticker	Index Weight	Market Cap	P/B	Sector	Major Sector	Weight	Active Weight, bp	$(\omega_\Pi - \omega_I)^2$
14	1									
15	2									

The example assumes the alphas are given. In practice the alphas would be generated from an active fundamental or quantitative process. The Excel example assigns higher alphas to the stocks with higher random numbers, making them more likely to be included in the final portfolio—a convenience to ensure that the same names are in both the index and active final portfolios.

- Copy the data in cells in B14:J113 from the worksheet <Opt Index-Template> to cells B14:J113 in the worksheet <Opt Active-Template>.
- In cell K14 enter =Sample!P6*0.1−0.05 and copy to row 113.* These are the alphas, assumed to be uniformly distributed between approximately ±5 percent with an average of approximately 0 percent. The actual values in the worksheet will depend on the random series.
- Objective: The objective is to minimize $\Sigma_i\, \omega_{Pi}\alpha_i - \lambda\, \Sigma_i\, (\omega_{Pi} - \omega_{Ii})^2$.
  - In cell D1 enter =SUMPRODUCT(K14:K113,H14:H113)-D2*SUM(J14:J113).
  - In cell E10 enter =SUM(I14:I113).
  - In cell D2 enter 0.25 for λ. Feel free to experiment with this value.
- By changing: The portfolio weights are contained in cells H14:H113. Start with equal weights of 0.01.
- Constraints: The constraints will be entered as ranges rather than equalities. The constraints will be weighted average market cap and P/B within ±10 percent of index values, and sector limits to +10 percent of the index. Note that the tighter the constraints, the less stable the solution.
  - Market cap:
    - Target: In cell C4 enter =Data!$D$3. This is the value for the benchmark.
    - Range: In cell D4 enter 0.10.
    - Wtd Avg: In cell E4 enter =SUMPRODUCT(D14:D516,H14:H516).

(continued)

(continued)

- Solver: There will be two constraints—the upper bound, $E4 \leq (1+D4)*C4$, and the lower bound, $E4 \geq (1-D4)*C4$.
- P/B:
  - Target: In cell C5 enter =Data!$D$4.
  - Range: In cell D5 enter 0.10.
  - Wtd Avg: In cell E5 enter =SUMPRODUCT(E14:E516,H14:H516).
  - Solver: There will be two constraints: the upper bound, $E5 \leq (1+D5)*C5$, and the lower bound, $E5 \geq (1-D5)*C5$.
- Sector constraints will include only an upper bound.
  - Target: In cell C6 enter =Data!$D5 and then copy to cells C7:C8
  - Range: In cells D6:D8 enter 0.10.
  - Wtd Avg: In cell E6 enter =SUMPRODUCT(H$14:H$113,INT(G$14:G$113 = B6)) and then copy to cells E7:E8.
  - Solver: For each sector the constraint is the upper bound, such as $E6 \leq (1+D6)*C6$.
- Budget: The weights must total to 100 percent.
  - Target: In cell C9 enter 100%.
  - Wgt Avg: In cell E9 enter =SUM(H14:H113).
  - Solver: C9 = E9.
- Nonzero weights:
  - Solver: H14:H113 $\geq$ 0.

The Solver Parameters window should look as follows:

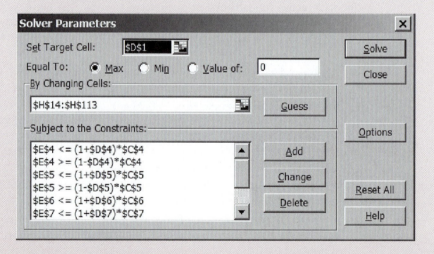

The other constraints are listed here:

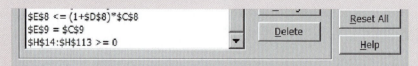

Click <Solve>. The template should look like the following, though the actual weights and stocks will differ due to the different "random" series:

	A	B	C	D	E	F	G	H	I	J	K
1	Objective		Min	0.03							
2			λ	0.25							
3		Constraints	Target	Range	Wtd Avg						
4		Market Cap	87,644	10%	96,409	10%					
5		P/B	3.87	10%	3.49	−10%					
6		Cyclical	53%	10%	48%	−5%					
7		Financial	24%	10%	27%	2%					
8		Non-Cyclical	23%	10%	25%	2%					
9		Weight	100%		100%	0%					
10		Active			5,711						
11											
12											
13		Ticker	Index Weight	Market Cap	P/B	Sector	Major Sector	Portfolio Weight	Active Weight, bp	$(\omega_\Pi - \omega_I)^2$	Alpha
14	1	XOM	3.17%	378447.8	3.12	Energy	Cyclical	4.02%	85.21	0.0001	−1%
15	2	GE	2.90%	346370.6	3.26	Industrials	Cyclical	3.90%	99.56	0.0001	−1%

If the alphas are influencing the final portfolio, the active portfolio characteristics should differ from the index fund's characteristics. There should be clear differences in the individual weights of the stocks, as reflected by the sum of squares and the weights on the 10 largest stocks in the benchmark. In one initial run, illustrated below, the market cap and P/B exposures are similar by design—the stocks were selected from all four exposure groups to ensure a broadly diversified portfolio. Note that the weight of XOM is lower in the active portfolio than in the index portfolio, due to the negative alpha. If the selection process is correlated with style, it may be difficult to eliminate a style bias within the active portfolio. Also note that adding a risk model to the optimization would allow explicit risk comparison of stock, sector, and style exposures. Currently this needs to be controlled by setting style and sector constraints and sum of squares targets using rules of thumb or adjustment following multiple runs.

Constraints	Target	Index	Active
Market Cap	87,644	96,409	96,409
P/B	3.87	3.73	3.49
Cyclical	53%	58%	48%
Financial	24%	26%	27%
Non-Cyclical	23%	16%	25%
Weight	100%	100%	100%
Sum of Squares	-	0.0175	0.0339

Security	Target	Index	Active	Alpha
1 XOM	3.17%	5.95%	4.02%	−1%
2 GE	2.90%	3.40%	3.90%	−1%
3 C	2.04%	2.56%	0.18%	0%
4 MSFT	1.99%	2.52%	0.00%	−2%
5 BAC	1.87%	2.40%	6.81%	4%
6 WMT	1.64%	1.67%	0.00%	−3%
7 PG	1.54%	1.57%	0.00%	−4%
8 JNJ	1.49%	1.52%	7.17%	5%
9 PFE	1.45%	1.49%	0.00%	−2%
10 AIG	1.29%	1.84%	2.49%	2%

* In this example the security alphas are simply a linear function of the random variables used to select the index sample, facilitating an easy comparison with the index optimization.

8.7   Identifying Style

Consider a situation in which a manager develops an investment strategy that seems to outperform the S&P 500. There are two possible explanations: The manager is generating real alpha or the alpha is an artifact of comparison to the wrong benchmark. How do you determine the appropriate benchmark for a strategy—one that reflects the style or type of stock the portfolio typically holds? This is a common problem for investors who want to confirm their manager's style in order to effectively classify, evaluate, and allocate to that manager.

Although investors frequently interview managers about their investment approaches, portfolio characteristics also provide important clues to a manager's style. The price/book ratio, for example, is a good measure of a portfolio's tendency toward value; a low P/B ratio reflects a relatively low market price compared to the book value of the assets held by a company. Other price multiples have similar interpretations. The price/earnings (P/E) ratio identifies the price investors are paying for a current or forecast dollar of earnings. The price/sales (P/S) ratio reflects the price investors are willing to pay for a dollar of sales revenue. P/S may be useful for a portfolio of technology stocks that have revenue but virtually no earnings or book value.[10] Portfolio dividend yield is also useful for characterizing a portfolio's style exposure.

Some investors seek to calculate P/E divided by earnings growth to represent how much investors are paying for current earnings and future earnings growth. Earnings or sales growth reflects the change in profitability or revenue for the company. Earnings, sales, and growth levels can be calculated using trailing, one-year, or three-year periods—or forward numbers based on analyst projections.

Beyond style, size exposure can be examined. The size of the average company in the portfolio can be calculated using market capitalization. Portfolio market cap can be computed as a weighted average using portfolio weights, or using medians or weighted medians, to reflect the nonlinear relationship between market cap and portfolio risk.

Beyond summary statistics, another technique for measuring style is to regress the portfolio returns against one or more market indexes. The regression coefficients and *R*-squared identify the average linear relationship and explanatory power of the market index returns for the return of the portfolio. Readers may recall the "market model" technique for estimating portfolio beta. The regression approach for estimating style using one benchmark is virtually identical to the market model technique.

Consider the following example of a portfolio reflecting small-cap stocks managed with a valuation discipline. When compared to the S&P 500, we would expect the strategy to show a smaller average market capitalization and lower price ratios. As shown in Exhibit 8.8, these expectations are borne out. The portfolio reflects a value bias in the valuation criteria (lower P/E, P/B, P/S, and PE/G and higher dividend yield), a similar growth profile, and smaller company size. The large number of stocks is unusual for an active portfolio; but if the asset size is large, the manager may need to buy a lot of names to put all the money to work. One consideration is the influence of a single stock, with extreme characteristics, on the portfolio averages. Consider the impact on the portfolio's average market capitalization of adding a 3 percent position in General Electric stock, whose market cap is over $100 billion. This illustrates the importance of reviewing the distribution of style characteristics, not simply the average.

---

[10] Note that sales revenue accrues to the entire company, so enterprise value (equity plus net debt) may be a more appropriate numerator.

EXHIBIT 8.8

Sample Portfolio Descriptive Statistics

	Portfolio	S&P 500
P/E	18.4	29.0
P/B	1.9	3.7
P/S	0.9	1.8
PE/G	1.4	2.4
Div yield	0.5	1.4
Forecast earnings growth, 1 year	15.2	14.3
Forecast sales growth, 1 year	15.9	15.1
Forecast earnings growth, 3–5 years	15.8	14.7
Wtd med cap ($B)	1.0	61.4
Mean cap ($B)	0.9	20.9
Number securities	788	500

Note: Data as of 12/31/2001.

To determine a historical return relationship between a portfolio and style indexes, a multivariate regression model may be estimated. Define R_t as the portfolio's return in period t and b_{Style} as the regression coefficient for the style benchmarks: large-cap value, large-cap growth, small-cap value, and small-cap growth . The regression equation becomes the following:

$$R_{Portfolio,t} = a + b_{LargeValue} R_{LargeValue,t} + b_{LargeGrowth} R_{LargeGrowth,t} + b_{SmallValue} R_{SmallValue,t} + b_{SmallGrowth} R_{SmallGrowth,t} + e_t$$

The regression results using monthly returns over a five-year period are reported in Exhibit 8.9. The results indicate that the portfolio return series is largely explained by the index returns, with an adjusted R-squared of 91 percent, and most highly correlated with the small-cap value index, with a coefficient of 1.093 and a t-statistic greater than 4.5. Interestingly, the coefficient for large-cap value is negative, but it is not statistically significant. While such a result may be in part spurious, it is also

EXHIBIT 8.9

Style Fitting from Monthly Data

Panel A: Regression Statistics		
	Coefficient	t-Stat
Russell 1000 Value	−0.788	−1.546
Russell 1000 Growth	0.070	1.558
Russell 2000 Value	1.093	4.733
Russell 2000 Growth	0.452	1.543
Sum	0.826	

Panel B: Quadratic Optimization Results	
	Coefficient
Russell 1000 Value	0.000
Russell 1000 Growth	0.126
Russell 2000 Value	0.874
Russell 2000 Growth	0.000
Sum	1.000

Note: Period covers 2/1997–1/2002.

informative. The target portfolio's security weights will not necessarily reflect a linear average of the style indexes' stocks. Large returns in a few highly weighted securities, exaggerated in the portfolio, may be short-term and not necessarily reflective of the portfolio's average style exposure. Therefore, coefficients less than 0.0 or greater than 1.0 are not surprising. As a result, large coefficients, or coefficients of unexpected sign, may accurately reflect the portfolio's style, noise, or most probably both.

The selection of indexes parallels the 2×2 style and size matrices published by vendors like Morningstar. They present coefficients estimated over rolling periods and may plot their movement across time. In these cases, coefficients that are negative or greater than 1 are problematic to explain. However, Sharpe (1992) proposed a simple method that addresses this problem. The technique involves an optimization that solves for coefficients in the regression equation that minimize the variance of the error term, subject to the constraint that the individual coefficients that are positive sum to 1.0. Sample results of this approach are shown in Panel B of Exhibit 8.9. In this example the optimized coefficients tell a similar style story as the regression estimates but avoid the hard-to-explain negative coefficients.

Although helpful, both the characteristic and regression techniques are subject to error, and conclusions based on them should be taken with a grain of salt. There is a lot of noise in the data, and the resulting coefficients vary through time and by technique. For example, historical returns tell us the average exposure over time, but not current exposures. The securities in the benchmark indexes are market capitalization–weighted, and the portfolios are typically not. Moreover, the index composition may change, with such reconstitutions affecting the results for both techniques. It is best to take away a general understanding of manager tendencies, rather than assume high confidence in the specific values or trends of the estimates.

Excel Outbox
Identifying Style

This outbox demonstrates two techniques for identifying the style of, or appropriate benchmark for, an active equity strategy. The monthly returns for the active strategy (Equity Fund) and the four style indexes are contained in cells B4:F63 of worksheet <Identify-Template> in spreadsheet Chapter 08 Excel Outboxes. The template should appear as follows:

	A	B	C	D	E	F	G
2							e
3	Date	Equity Fund	Russell 1000 Value	Russell 1000 Growth	Russell 2000 Value	Russell 2000 Growth	
4	Feb-97	1.16	−2.43	−0.68	0.95	−6.04	
5	Mar-97	−1.83	−4.72	−5.41	−2.68	−7.06	

Regression
The first approach will be to regress the fund returns against the style indexes. These are the results presented in Panel A of Exhibit 8.9. We will use the =LINEST(known *y*'s, known *x*'s,const,stats) function. This is a range array formula that calculates the coefficients and statistics for multiple regression. Here are the formula inputs:

- Known *y*'s are the dependent variable—the equity fund returns.
- Known *x*'s are the independent variables—the style index returns.

- const is an indicator, if "TRUE" the intercept is estimated.
- stats is an indicator, if "TRUE" the regression statistics are reported.

The range in the template should appear as follows:

	I	J	K	L	M	N
2						
3						
4	Regression	R2000G	R2000V	R1000G	R1000V	Intercept
5	b					
6	SE					
7						
8	F					
9	SS					
10	t-stat					
11	R2					
12	R2-Adj					
13						
14						
15	Optimization					
16	Objective	Min	$\sigma^2(e) =$			
17		R1000V	R1000G	R2000V	R2000G	Total
18	b					

- Highlight cells J5:N9 and type =LINEST(B4:B63,C4:F63,TRUE,TRUE) and then<CTRL> <SHIFT><ENTER>. LINEST is a range array formula that calculates the coefficients and statistics for multiple regression.
- In cell J10 enter =J5/J6 and then copy to cells K10:N10. This calculates the coefficient *t*-stat as the ratio of the coefficient and its standard error.
- In cell J11 enter =J9/(J9+K9). This calculates the R^2 as the ratio of the sum of squared regression (SSR) over the total sum of squared error.
- In cell J12 enter =1−((1-J11)*(60−1)/(60−4−1)). This calculates the adjusted R^2.

The result should look like this:

	A	I	J	K	L	M	N
2							
3	Date						
4	Feb-97	Regression	R2000G	R2000V	R1000G	R1000V	Intercept
5	Mar-97	b	0.45167	1.09274	0.06956	−0.78784	0.49104
6	Apr-97	SE	0.29268	0.23086	0.04464	0.50952	0.16580
7	May-97		0.91697	1.21104			
8	Jun-97	F	151.86181	55.00000			
9	Jul-97	SS	890.89240	80.66393			
10	Aug-97	t-stat	1.5432	4.7333	1.5582	−1.5462	2.9615
11	Sep-97	R2	0.91697				
12	Oct-97	R2-Adj	0.91094				

(continued)

(concluded)

Optimization

The second approach uses a constrained optimization to estimate the coefficients. These are the results presented in Panel B of Exhibit 8.9. The technique minimizes the variance of the estimation errors.

The template should appear as follows:

	I	J	K	L	M	N
15	Optimization					
16	Objective	Min	$\sigma^2(e) =$			
17		R1000V	R1000G	R2000V	R2000G	Total
18	b					

- In cell G4 enter =B4-SUMPRODUCT(C4:F4,J$18:M$18) and then copy to cells G5:G63.
- In cell J18:M18 enter 0.25 to provide a starting point for the optimization.
- In cell N18 enter =SUM(J18:M18).
- In cell L16 enter =VAR(G4:G63).

In Solver:

- Set target cell: L16.
- Equal to: Min.
- By changing: J18:M18.
- Subject to the constraints:
  - J18:M18 ≥ 0.
  - N18 = 1.

The Solver Parameters window should look like this:

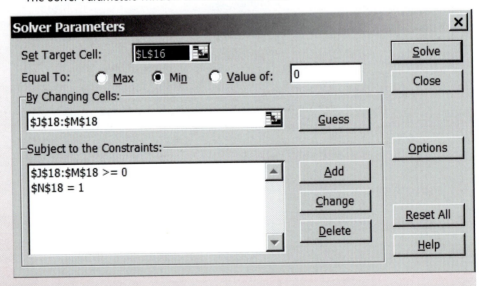

The results should look like this:

	Min	$\sigma^2(e) =$			
Optimization					
Objective	Min	$\sigma^2(e) =$	1.85142		
	R1000V	R1000G	R2000V	R2000G	Total
b	0.00000	0.12625	0.87375	0.00000	1.00

8.8   Sample Active Portfolio

Boston University (BU) offers its students an opportunity to work on a live equity portfolio. Students are allocated to one of five sectors, from which they choose narrower industries to study. Stocks are assigned buy, hold, or sell recommendations, and 12-month target prices (the expected future prices) are forecast. The selection universe includes all stocks smaller than $1 billion in market cap and those included in the S&P 600 small-cap index, the portfolio's benchmark; of course student analysts follow only a small subset of this universe. Students are rewarded with course grade points for successful stock picks relative to their S&P 600 sectors, both as individual analysts and as members of sector teams. Sector evaluation is based on the active performance of the sector within the live portfolio constructed from the student analyst stock picks.

Investment Philosophy

To succeed, the students' active equity strategy clearly needs an effective stock selection process. In this case, the covered stocks are followed by only a few Street analysts, the student analysts spend three months studying their industries before making recommendations, and the students have real skin in the game.[11] It is conceivable, therefore, that their recommendations could add value. In fact, since initiation of the fund, they have. So the key to investment success is to develop an effective portfolio construction process to capture this value added.

The BU portfolio construction process captures the stock selection within industries, and industry selection within sectors. Because there is no style component in the active selection process, style, as well as sector exposure, is neutralized as much as possible while preserving stock and industry bets.

Portfolio Construction

Preparation of the final trade list involves several steps. First an algorithm is used to prepare an initial portfolio. The algorithm assigns the highest overweights relative to the index to buy recommendations with large alphas; sell recommendations, with low alphas, receive zero weights or large underweights. Negative weights are allowed because short selling is permitted. Stocks without analyst coverage receive hold recommendations, zero alphas, and initial slight underweights. As a result, stocks that are heavily weighted in the benchmark are automatically in the first-step portfolio. The alphas are the analyst's forecast active return calculated for each stock from the target and market prices, net of a constant assumed 10 percent market return, and adjusted for the stock's volatility. A partial listing of the portfolio at this stage is shown in Exhibit 8.10.

The second step is to analyze the sector and style exposures of the portfolio. This is conducted within a portfolio risk analysis system that provides an understanding of the portfolio's active risk relative to its benchmark, and the source of the risk. If total portfolio risk, industry weights, sector weights, or style characteristics are out of tolerance, individual holdings are adjusted. This is not an optimization approach; it is a pro forma approach that is easy to implement with a small number of securities. In the BU case, total holdings are approximately 50 securities.

The third step is a qualitative review by student analysts of proposed sector, industry, and individual stock weights to ensure that the proposed portfolio accurately reflects the student analyst forecasts and recommendations. Any proposed adjustments

---

[11] In the form of grade points, not dollars.

EXHIBIT 8.10 **Sample Portfolio Listing: First Step**

Sector	Ticker	Recom	Alpha	Buy/Sell	Total Risk	Benchmark Weight	alpha/sd	Target Wt
TECH	ZIGO	SELL	−23.1%	−1	60%	0.00%	−0.385283	−1.0%
INDUS	NSH	SELL	−7.3%	−1	55%	0.00%	−0.132012	0.0%
CONSUMER	SRR	SELL	2.1%	−1	36%	0.09%	0.057356	0.1%
CONSUMER	PYX	HOLD	−9.8%	0	38%	0.00%	−0.257437	0.0%
FINL	CGI	HOLD	8.2%	0	23%	0.00%	0.354753	0.5%
CONSUMER	MW	HOLD	16.9%	0	48%	0.29%	0.352083	0.8%
CONSUMER	SWB	BUY	30.0%	1	76%	0.00%	0.395352	1.6%
FINL	ICH	BUY	52.7%	1	49%	0.00%	1.076366	2.5%
HEALTH	LIFE	BUY	4.3%	1	35%	0.00%	0.122044	1.2%
NotCov	NVR	HOLD	−5.0%	0	33%	0.88%	−0.151515	0.9%
NotCov	SWN	HOLD	−5.0%	0	44%	0.78%	−0.113636	0.8%
NotCov	MEE	HOLD	−5.0%	0	45%	0.72%	−0.111111	0.7%

EXHIBIT 8.11
Final Portfolio Descriptive Statistics

Panel A: Portfolio Characteristics

	Portfolio	S&P 600
Earnings growth est	17.4%	14.9%
P/E forward est	16.8x	15.6x
Market cap (wtd med)	$1,200 m	$881 m
Holdings	48	600

Panel B: Active Sector Weights

Note: As of spring 2006.

are reviewed in the portfolio analysis system before a target portfolio is prepared and compared to the current portfolio. Through time, the portfolio is adjusted immediately if student recommendations change. Sample characteristics of the fund are illustrated in Exhibit 8.11. The portfolio displays slightly higher earnings growth, valuation multiple, and market cap than the benchmark. All sector weights differ by less than 5 percent, with industrials representing the largest difference of nearly 5 percent. The risk analysis system forecasts a beta of 1.1, and an active return standard deviation of

8.4 percent, for the fund. Although style and industry exposures generate similar levels of active risk, the largest source of active risk in the fund is due to individual stock positions. The high level of risk specific to the individual companies is a direct result of the small number of issues held.

Summary

This chapter has introduced the topic of equity portfolio construction, reviewing techniques for constructing and analyzing passive and active strategies. The first index fund was introduced in 1973; indexing has been popular and has grown consistently since then. As of December 2007 the assets invested in index mutual funds had increased to over $750 billion, while exchange traded funds (ETF) had grown to over $500 billion. The goal of an active manager is to add value—that is, increase portfolio return without simply adding risk. The objective for passive managers is to closely match the performance of a published index more consistently than competitors. The chapter reviewed two methods for meeting this objective: full replication and stratified sampling. Full replication, used when fund assets are large or there are few stocks in the index, involves holding all the constituents in the index in the same weights as the index. Stratified sampling is used when fund assets are limited or the number of stocks in the index is large; this is an optimization technique that allows selection of a subset of stock that is expected to closely match the risk exposures of the index.

Historically, the performance record for actively managed mutual funds is mixed; on average, active large-cap mutual fund managers have underperformed the S&P 500, likely due to fund expenses, whereas the average active small-cap manager has performed similarly to small-cap indexes. Despite this mixed performance record of active management, active disciplines continue to prosper. The number of active mutual funds has grown exponentially since 1980—just before the beginning of the great bull market in U.S. equities. As of December 2007 there were $6.5 trillion dollars invested in 4,767 equity mutual funds, the vast majority of these being actively managed. The techniques used to construct a passive portfolio can be modified for the construction and management of an active portfolio to manage either sector or style exposure.

Tips were provided to help identify the style of an equity portfolio process using holdings and return series. Finally, a sample portfolio process was reviewed, illustrating an algorithm used as a tool for constructing a preliminary portfolio, which was finalized following risk analysis and qualitative review.

Problems

1. Define these terms:
   a. Survivorship bias.
   b. Tracking tolerance.
2. Compare these alternative portfolio construction processes:
   a. Sampling versus full replication.
   b. Sector management versus full optimization.
3. Find an active equity strategy on the Internet.
   a. List the strategy's investment objectives.
   b. Identify the portfolio construction process.
   c. List the strengths and weaknesses of the process.

4. Review the records of separate account equity managers and compare with mutual fund results reported in Exhibits 8.1 and 8.2. How do large-cap active and small-cap active compare?

5. Construct an index portfolio without a capitalization constraint using the spreadsheet provided in the Passive Management Excel Outbox. How do the risk exposures change?

6. Reconstruct the index portfolio from Problem 5 with only 50 stocks. How do the risk exposures compare to the index portfolio constructed with 100 stocks?

7. Update the <Identify-Template> spreadsheet using returns for the Fidelity Low Price Stock Fund. How do the coefficients and explanatory power (R^2) change? b_{Style}

Chapter 9

Fixed-Income Management

9.1   Introduction

Chapters 7 and 8 discussed the management of equity portfolios. More precisely, they dealt with portfolios consisting of a single type of instrument: common stock. This chapter is devoted to bonds, or more generally, fixed-income portfolios.

It is only a slight exaggeration to say that the term *fixed income* encompasses almost all public securities that are not common stocks. Not long ago, say 40 years, the world of financial instruments was fairly simple. Common stocks represented ownership of corporations, entitling holders to a pro rata share of the profits once the company met all its obligations. Bonds entitled their holders to a stream of fixed periodic interest payments and a final repayment of principal at maturity. Preferred stock also promised periodic payments that had to be made before corporate earnings could be divided among common stock holders. Unlike bonds, however, preferred stocks were usually perpetual obligations—that is, they did not have a finite maturity. Because they promised fixed, periodic payments, bonds and preferred stock were called *fixed income.*

With the advent of loan securitization, such as mortgage-backed securities (MBS) and derivatives-based structured products, the variety of fixed-income instruments available to investors has exploded over the last 40 years. Periodic payments may be fixed, floating, or contingent on market developments or the decisions of other economic agents. Payments may be in cash or in-kind, in one or multiple currencies, secured or unsecured, linked to inflation, and so on. In short, the fixed-income market has moved far beyond fixed-rate bonds with repayment of principal at maturity. Nonetheless, the vast majority of the market is composed of fairly standard structures that can be analyzed with a common set of tools. These tools give the portfolio manager a set of risk and return measures upon which to base investment decisions.

In the preceding chapters it was not necessary to delve into the methods of analyzing specific stocks in order to understand the issues involved in managing a stock portfolio. Similarly, in the present chapter we need not dwell on the details of specific fixed-income instruments or on the methods required to model, analyze, and value them.[1] The focus is on portfolio strategies to meet client objectives.

The next section briefly reviews the basic concepts from fixed-income analysis that we will need in this chapter, provides some perspective on the composition of the fixed income universe, and examines some important characteristics of fixed income versus equity returns that affect their respective roles in client portfolios. Section 9.3 discusses the three main types of fixed-income portfolio mandates: passive, active, and structured. The final three sections examine these mandates in more detail.

9.2 Fixed-Income Markets, Instruments, and Concepts

Analysis of fixed-income instruments can be quite complex. The complexity arises from a combination of two factors. First, fixed-income instruments promise the holder specific payments, at specific times, under specific conditions. In some respects this makes the fixed-income analyst's job easier. Unlike corporate earnings, which are the foundation of equity analysis and valuation, the cash flows on fixed-income instruments are prescribed by rules known to all interested parties. Therefore the focus of fixed income analysis is primarily on valuation of known (albeit often contingent) cash flows. This places a high premium on mathematically precise analysis. The second source of complexity is the heterogeneity of the instruments themselves. In principle, virtually any set of cash flow rules could be turned into a fixed-income security with its own challenges for modeling and valuation.

For present purposes, however, we need not be concerned with the details of valuing specific fixed-income instruments. Rather, we will take for granted that we know how to analyze and value the instruments and instead focus on managing a bond portfolio to meet client objectives. For this we need only a few key concepts and results. These will be reviewed soon, but first let us look at the universe of available securities and the markets in which they trade.

The U.S. Bond Market

While many customized instruments are created to fit the specific needs of an issuer and an investor, standardized instruments dominate the public bond market. Exhibit 9.1 breaks down the taxable U.S. bond market, represented by the Barclays Universal index, into its major components.

Almost a third of the U.S. taxable bond market consists of Treasury (23 percent) and government agency (9 percent) obligations. The bulk of these issues are traditional fixed-rate bonds with semiannual coupon payments. Although most agency bonds do not carry the full faith and credit of the U.S. government, bond investors have traditionally viewed these bonds as virtually free of default risk—that is, virtually certain to make all the promised payments when due and in full. In 2008, however, market confidence in agency obligations was shaken by the near collapse of the

---

[1] A detailed treatment of these issues can be found in Fabozzi (2007).

Even in the best of times, U.S. government agency debt trades at a yield spread over comparable-maturity Treasury notes and bonds. Part of the spread is due to liquidity differences: Treasuries are among the world's most liquid securities. In the case of FNMA and FHLMC debt, however, the spread also reflects the fact that they are hybrid public–private entities that do not have the full faith and credit backing of the U.S. government. At best their debt has an implicit guarantee.

Despite the absence of explicit government backing, accounting and executive compensation scandals, and mounting concern over its massively leveraged exposure to mortgage defaults, the spread on FNMA's five-year notes ranged between 23 and 42 basis points from January 2006 through June 2007. The spread widened sharply in early 2008, however, as the mortgage crisis deepened and its severity became apparent. When Bears Stearns collapsed on March 14, 2008, the spread stood at 117 basis points. When the federal government seized control and effective majority ownership of both FNMA and FHLMC over the weekend of September 5–8, 2008, the spread tightened from 95 bp to 65 bp. The government did not, however, extend explicit backing to their debt, and the spread widened sharply again as major financial institutions (Lehman, AIG, Washington Mutual, Wachovia, and Merrill Lynch to name just a few) failed and the global financial system teetered on the brink of collapse. By November 20, 2008, as the Big Three automakers begged for massive government assistance, the spread had moved to 164 basis points—nearly five times the average level in the January 2006–June 2007 period.

In the months following the fateful weekend of September 12–15, 2008, when Lehman collapsed and Merrill Lynch sold itself to Bank of America to avoid a similar fate, the Federal Reserve and the Treasury committed trillions of dollars to providing liquidity to the financial system, supporting specific companies, and cushioning the decline in economic activity. By late May 2009 the spread on five-year FNMA notes had fallen to around 50 basis points—not too far above its precrisis level. Broader market conditions were not back to normal, however. The Fed was still a major buyer of Treasuries and MBS. The Fed funds rate was still near zero, and investors still demanded only a few basis points of interest to hold one-month Treasury bills. But at least the T-bill rate was positive. At the height of the crisis T-bills traded at negative interest. Yes, as in the height of the Great Depression, investors paid for the privilege of simply getting their money back!

Source: Detailed chronologies of events during the 2007–2009 credit crisis can be found on various Internet sites. Spreads cited here reflect Bloomberg generic series.

two largest issuers—the mortgage giants known as Fannie Mae (FNMA) and Freddie Mac (FHLMC)—and the government's decision not to directly back their bonds. Nonetheless, the government provided massive support to these agencies, and as confidence in the global financial system is restored, U.S. agency bonds are regaining their quasi-government status. Therefore, absent a perpetual threat of global collapse, roughly one-third of the U.S. taxable bond market consists of bonds whose cash flows are, for practical purposes, known with certainty. The key issue with respect to these bonds is the value today of $1 to be received at each future date. Changes in the market's assessment of these values translate into gains or losses for the bondholders.

Residential mortgage-backed securities (MBS), at roughly 36 percent, are the largest component of the U.S. market. These securities represent claims on the monthly principal and interest payments made by home owners on their mortgages. All of the MBS contained in the Universal index are backed by one of the three government

EXHIBIT 9.1
Composition of the U.S. Taxable Bond Market

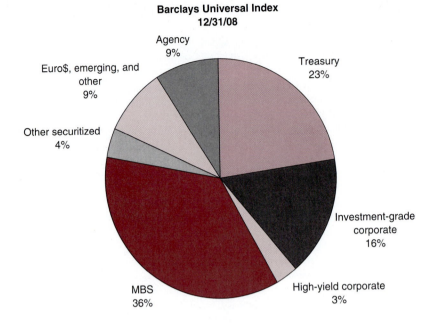

Barclays Universal Index
12/31/08

Agency 9%

Treasury 23%

Euro$, emerging, and other 9%

Other securitized 4%

Investment-grade corporate 16%

MBS 36%

High-yield corporate 3%

mortgage agencies:[2] FNMA (51 percent), FHLMC (37 percent), and Ginnie Mae (GNMA, 12 percent). GNMA obligations carry the full faith and credit of the U.S. Treasury. Although the FNMA and FHLMC obligations are subject to the same concerns as their bonds, default risk is a secondary consideration for agency-guaranteed MBS. The primary concern for (agency) MBS investors is home owners' right to prepay all or a portion of their loans at any time. Typically home owners choose to refinance when they can do so at lower interest rates. Conversely, they often make only the minimum required payments if a new mortgage would carry a higher rate. Therefore, MBS investors must recognize that they are likely to be repaid slowly when reinvestment opportunities are attractive for them (that is, when interest rates are high) and quickly when reinvestment opportunities are unattractive (when interest rates are low). Assessing and valuing this prepayment risk is the key consideration for MBS investors.

Bonds issued by corporations make up nearly 20 percent of the taxable bond market. The vast majority, about 85 percent, are termed *investment-grade* because they carry one of the top four credit ratings from Standard & Poor's, Moody's, or Fitch. The remainder, roughly 15 percent, are mostly deemed *high-yield* or (pejoratively) *junk* because they are rated below investment-grade. Although special structures are not uncommon, especially within high-yield bonds, most corporate bonds pay fixed, semi-annual coupons with full repayment of principal at maturity—just like Treasuries. The difference, of course, is that corporations sometimes default on their promised payments. Corporate bondholders face at least two types of credit risk. First, there is the risk of actual default. Second, there are gains and losses induced by changes in either the market's assessment of the issuer's ability to meet its obligations or the market's general willingness to bear credit risk.

[2] A small amount of nonagency MBS is classified as home equity securities and included in the asset-backed securities component of the index.

Mortgage loans that qualify for securitization within agency-guaranteed MBS are called *conforming loans*. Nonconforming loans generally fail to qualify for one or more of the following reasons:

- Loan principal that exceeds the program limit.
- Nonstandard principal and interest payment provisions.
- Insufficient documentation of borrower income and assets.
- Poor credit quality or excessive loan-to-value ratio.

Loans that are too large for agency programs are called *jumbo* loans, and loans with poor credit quality are labeled *subprime*. High-quality loans with less than full documentation are called *Alt-A* loans. More generally, loans with limited documentation of borrower financials are sometimes called *low-doc, no-doc,* or simply *liar loans*. Loans with complex or nonstandard structures exist in a variety of configurations. One particularly pernicious structure, called an *option ARM,* allows the borrower to decide among various payment options each month—including some that fail to cover the interest due, resulting in a rising loan balance. Combining this negative amortization option with a low teaser rate that jumps to the market level after the introductory period creates a trap for unwary borrowers stretching to qualify for larger loans.

According to Lehman Brothers data, agency MBS accounted for $4.25 trillion of the roughly $9.0 trillion total MBS outstanding as of September 2007. Of the nonagency MBS, $2.35 trillion were backed by jumbo prime loans, $1.2 trillion by Alt-A loans, and $1.2 trillion by subprime loans. Because it is difficult to get consistent, reliable pricing for nonagency MBS, Barclays does not include them in its index. Collateralized mortgage obligations (CMOs) that repackage MBS cash flows into new securities are also not included.

Default risk has become a much bigger issue for private-label MBS, especially those based on mortgages originated with lower underwriting standards or troublesome structures. Holders of these securities must assess both the risk of being repaid too quickly or too slowly (prepayment risk) and the risk of not being paid in full (default risk). The aggregate credit risk inherent in these securities became evident when, starting in 2007, escalating defaults on low-quality mortgages set off a chain reaction that brought the global financial system to the brink of collapse in the fall of 2008.

The remainder of the Barclays Universal index is composed of U.S. dollar bonds issued by foreign entities ("Euro$, emerging, and other"), commercial mortgage-backed securities (CMBS), and asset-backed and other structured securities. Asset-backed securities (ABS) are similar to MBS in that they are created by pooling payments on underlying loans. For example, there are ABS based on credit card balances, auto loans, and home equity loans. Because the underlying loans are almost never guaranteed, a typical ABS issue has several "tranches" with various levels of credit risk depending on specific rules for allocating credit losses.

From a trading perspective, the bond market is quite different from the equity market. Whereas most equity trading occurs on organized exchanges (physical and electronic) with brokers earning commissions for handling execution, bond trading is almost exclusively done over-the-counter with an institutional investor contacting bond dealers directly to find the best price. No commission is paid. Instead the dealer makes a profit from the difference between the buying and selling prices (the bid–ask spread) and from the return on the dealer's inventory of bonds less the cost of financing that inventory.

The size of the typical trade is also different in the bond market. In the equity market even very large trades are usually broken into reasonably small pieces for execution. Retail orders of only a few hundred shares are easily accommodated and in fact are welcome because they provide liquidity for large institutional trades. In contrast, bonds trade in increments of $1 million to facilitate movement of institutional holdings in an over-the-counter market. Retail investors are thus effectively shut out of direct participation in the same market as institutional investors.[3]

While so-called initial public offerings of stock generate excitement in the equity market, new stock issuance accounts for a very small fraction of equity trading. In fact U.S. corporations often buy back more outstanding stock than they issue in a given year; that is, aggregate net equity issuance is negative.[4] Therefore, the stock market is mainly a **secondary market**—a market in which investors trade existing securities. In contrast, the bond market is a **primary market** that revolves around new issuance. On any given day almost all bond trading occurs in new issues (if any) plus a relatively few liquid securities, including the most recently issued Treasuries at key maturities (the so-called **on-the-run** issues), a few recently issued corporate bonds, and generic MBS securities priced near par (referred to as the *current coupon* issues). Therefore, for most bonds, especially corporate bonds, active trading ceases a few days or weeks after issuance.

Why is there such an emphasis on new issuance in the bond market? One simple reason stems from the finite maturity of bonds. Most borrowers need to refinance their debt when it matures. So a significant portion of the new issuance is in fact refinancing. In addition, as the economy grows, there is an ongoing need to raise capital. Equity capital can be obtained either by issuing stock or by retaining earnings. As just noted, in the aggregate public corporations raise relatively little new equity capital by issuing stock. Net new equity capital is raised primarily through retained earnings. On the debt side, however, new capital must be raised through new issuance. The structure of the bond market also encourages emphasis on new issues. It would be very expensive for bond dealers to maintain an inventory of hundreds or thousands of different issues to facilitate secondary trading. Instead they concentrate on new issues for which they earn hefty underwriting fees from the issuers and hold a few large, liquid issues for secondary trading. Most inventory of less liquid issues resides in client portfolios. Dealers buy and sell these less liquid bonds mostly to accommodate their clients and to make room in client portfolios for the latest new issues. As part of this process, dealers often recommend trades based on holdings lists submitted by clients. In so doing, the dealer hopes not only to earn a spread but also to keep track of who owns which bonds—information that facilitates subsequent trades.

---

[3] Retail investors can and do trade bonds. Indeed they are significant holders, especially of tax-exempt debt issued by state and local governments. However, retail investors typically trade through brokers at a substantial markup over the pricing available to institutional players trading directly with market makers (dealers). In recent years, some brokerage firms have begun to offer retail investors online access to their bond inventory. In addition, some corporate bonds trade on the NY Bond Exchange, although the trading volume is quite low.

[4] On the basis of Federal Reserve Flow of Funds data, from 1952 through 2005, U.S. corporations bought back roughly $450 billion more stock than they issued. In contrast, net issuance of corporate bonds was roughly $3.0 trillion. Net equity issuance was negative in 25 of the 54 years, with 20 years of negative net issuance occurring from 1980 onward. Even in the 29 years of positive net equity issuance, corporate bonds always accounted for more than 80 percent of the combined net issuance.

A Review of Key Fixed-Income Concepts

Virtually every valuation concept in fixed income relates to some measure of *yield* or *yield spread.* There are various measures of yield, but all of them attempt to answer essentially the same question: If nothing else happened, what rate of return would be earned simply due to the passage of time? **Yield-to-maturity,** the most commonly used measure, is simply the discount rate that equates the present value of a bond's promised cash flows to its market price. It turns out that an investor will earn a return equal to the yield-to-maturity if (1) the bond is held to maturity and (2) all of the coupons are reinvested at that same yield-to-maturity until the maturity date. Assuming no default, the first condition eliminates the possibility of capital gains or losses because the bond will be worth par at maturity. The second condition ensures that reinvested coupons earn the same rate as the initial investment.

Suppose we drop the second condition (reinvestment at the original yield-to-maturity) but continue to assume the bond is held to maturity. If the coupons are reinvested at a higher rate, the investor's return will also be higher. Conversely, reinvesting the coupons at a lower rate implies a lower return. The longer the investment horizon, the larger the impact of the reinvestment rate on the realized return.

Now suppose the bond will be held for only a brief period—say a few weeks. Then the key determinant of the realized return is the price at which it is sold. Standard present value analysis implies that if the bond's yield rises, the price of the bond declines and vice versa. The relationship between price changes and yield changes can be approximated as[5]

$$\Delta P / P \approx -D \, \Delta Y + \tfrac{1}{2} C (\Delta Y)^2 \qquad \textbf{(9.1)}$$

where ΔP and ΔY denote change in price and yield respectively, D is called modified duration (or simply **duration**), and C is called **convexity.** Equation (9.1) says that the percentage change in price is approximately equal to minus the bond's duration times the change in yield plus one-half the bond's convexity times the change in yield squared. For example, for a bond with duration = 5 and convexity = 20, a 1 percentage point increase in yield ($\Delta Y = .01$) reduces the value of the bond by .049 or 4.9 percent.

For standard fixed-coupon bonds there are messy, but straightforward, equations for duration and convexity. For instruments whose cash flows are contingent on future events, like MBS, there are no easy formulas. Instead we calculate duration and convexity by valuing the instrument at different yields and observing the change in price. To be more precise, suppose we value the instrument at yield levels Y, $(Y - \delta)$, and $(Y + \delta)$ and obtain prices P, P^-, and P^+ respectively from our valuation model. Then the instrument's duration and convexity are[6]

$$D = \frac{P^- - P^+}{2\delta P} \qquad \textbf{(9.2)}$$

$$C = \frac{P^- - 2P + P^+}{\delta^2 P}$$

Because this method works for virtually any instrument, we will treat Equation (9.2) as the definition of duration and convexity. Note that duration is defined such that it will be positive except in rare cases.

---

[5] The symbol "$\approx$" is used to indicate that this relationship is only an approximation, not a true equality.

[6] Readers who are familiar with calculus may recognize that duration and convexity, as defined in Equation (9.2), reflect discrete approximations of the first and second derivatives of price with respect to yield.

According to Equation (9.2), duration is simply the percentage change in price arising from a change in yield of magnitude 2δ. If we graph price as a function of yield, duration is the slope of a line connecting P^- and P^+, divided by P. Convexity measures how the slope of the price–yield relationship changes around P. If the slope is the same on either side of P, then $(P^- - P) = (P - P^+)$ because these reflect yield changes of $\pm\delta$. Convexity would be zero in this case because the numerator in Equation (9.2) is simply the difference between these two quantities. Convexity is positive if price increases at an increasing rate as the yield declines $[(P^- - P) > (P - P^+)]$. Negative convexity implies that price increases more slowly as yield declines. Although the mathematical correspondence is not exact, it is often useful to think of convexity as the change in duration as yield declines—positive if duration increases and negative if duration decreases.

Equation (9.1) may now be interpreted as follows. For very small yield changes, duration alone provides a close approximation. For larger yield changes, we need to adjust for changes in duration by adding the convexity term. If convexity is positive, as it is for most instruments, the adjustment reduces the price impact of yield increases and accentuates the impact of decreases in yield. Therefore, if convexity is positive bondholders gain more or lose less than duration alone would imply. Not all instruments have positive convexity, however. In particular, MBS tend to display significantly negative convexity due to the home owners' option to prepay their loans. Similarly, callable bonds are negatively convex. For these instruments, duration alone understates losses and overstates gains due to yield movements. All else the same, investors prefer instruments with positive convexity and demand a higher expected return to compensate for negative convexity.

To help develop some intuition, note that duration may be loosely interpreted as a weighted average of the time until each cash flow will be received with the weights based on the present value of each cash flow.[7] Using this interpretation, we can deduce that longer-maturity bonds have higher duration. Similarly, bonds with lower coupons have higher duration because the final repayment of principal at maturity accounts for a bigger portion of the total value. In fact, for zero-coupon bonds duration is essentially equal to their maturity.

Exhibit 9.2 shows key statistics as of 6/29/2007, just before the credit crisis began in earnest, for the Barclays Aggregate index and some of its components plus the Barclays High-Yield index. Together the Aggregate and High-Yield indexes make up nearly the entire Barclays Universal index shown in Exhibit 9.1. The first two columns show the average coupon and average maturity of each index or subindex. The next column shows the average yield-to-maturity. The **nominal spread** is the average difference, in basis points, between each bond's yield-to-maturity and the yield-to-maturity on a similar-maturity Treasury bond. The concept of option-adjusted spread is explained below. The last two columns show the average (option-adjusted) duration and convexity of each index.

The relationships among the statistics in Exhibit 9.2 reflect typical market conditions. Longer-term bonds offer higher yields. Longer-term corporate bonds (the "credit" indexes) offer higher spreads—both nominal and option-adjusted—than shorter-term credit instruments. High-yield—that is, lower-quality—bonds offer a much higher spread than investment-grade bonds. Note that duration is less than maturity and that

---

[7] This interpretation is exact for a different definition of duration known as *Macaulay duration* (see Equation (9.3) in Section 9.6). However, this measure is useful only for instruments with known cash flows.

EXHIBIT 9.2   Bond Market Statistics: Barclays Aggregate and High Yield, 6/29/2007

	Coupon	Maturity	Yield-to-Maturity	Nominal Spread (bp)	Option-Adjusted Spread (bp)	Duration	Convexity/100
Aggregate	5.40	7.27	5.69	70	53	4.70	−0.16
Government	5.05	6.37	5.17	16	11	4.48	0.28
1-3 Year	4.49	1.87	5.04	12	10	1.67	−0.07
Intermediate	4.77	4.11	5.14	15	11	3.32	0.05
Long	6.65	17.83	5.29	21	7	10.40	1.47
Credit	5.91	9.94	5.93	94	89	6.03	0.70
1-3 Year	5.32	2.02	5.45	53	51	1.86	0.05
Intermediate	5.68	5.24	5.76	81	78	4.28	0.26
Long	6.62	24.23	6.45	134	124	11.38	2.03
MBS	5.42	6.78	5.99	102	65	4.13	−1.14
High Yield	7.92	7.84	8.22	314	292	4.57	0.07

the difference is especially pronounced for longer-maturity bonds. Therefore, maturity is at best a rough guide to the interest rate sensitivity of bond prices. Convexity rises much faster than duration as maturity increases. This fact becomes particularly important when we consider different portfolios with the same duration. Also note that the home owner's option to prepay results in strong negative convexity for the MBS. Indeed this effect is so strong, and MBS are such a large portion of the market, that the whole investment-grade universe (the Barclays Aggregate) also has negative convexity.

Having introduced the concept of duration, we can address a key question for portfolio managers: Do I win or lose if rates rise or fall? The answer depends on the relationship between the investment horizon and the duration of the portfolio. If rates rise, the portfolio will suffer an immediate capital loss, but subsequent cash flows can be reinvested at a higher rate. Over very short horizons the capital loss will clearly outweigh any benefit from reinvestment. Over extremely long horizons reinvestment opportunities dominate. Logic suggests that these two factors balance out over some horizon, leaving the realized return equal to the initial yield. It turns out that this balance occurs if the investment horizon is equal to the duration of the portfolio. Strictly speaking, this is just a rule of thumb; it is only precisely true under some simplifying assumptions. Nonetheless this is a fact that every bond portfolio manager must know. As we will see, it is especially important in managing structured portfolios.

Although yield-to-maturity and nominal yield spreads are useful for summarizing and comparing bond pricing, we need to delve a little deeper. A bond's yield-to-maturity is actually a complex average of the rates, known as **spot rates,** that apply to each of its cash flows. In general the market assigns a different rate to each future date. The pattern of spot rates is the term structure of interest rates (or simply the **term structure**). The term structure is usually, but not always, upward-sloping because investors generally demand higher rates for longer-term investments.

Why do we care about the term structure? There are at least two reasons. First, the term structure reflects the time value of money over different horizons and is therefore fundamental to correct valuation of fixed-income instruments. If a (default-free) bond's price is not consistent with the prevailing term structure, then it is mispriced. That is why sophisticated models used to value instruments with embedded options, such as MBS, are always calibrated so that they value zero-coupon bonds in accordance with the observed term structure. Second, movements of the term structure are undoubtedly the biggest driver of overall fixed-income returns.

Empirical research has shown that term structure movements can be broken into three main components. The first component, known as *shift,* corresponds to an equal increase or decrease in rates at all maturities. Empirically this accounts for roughly 90 percent of the volatility of interest rates. The second most important component, accounting for roughly 5 percent of interest rate volatility, is called *twist.* This corresponds to a rotation of the term structure creating a steeper or flatter curve. The third component, *butterfly,* accounting for perhaps 2 percent of volatility, reflects changes in the curvature of the term structure with middle maturity rates rising or falling relative to the short and long maturities.

Excel Outbox *Term Structure* *Movements*	This box builds a simple term structure incorporating the three primary types of movements: shift, twist, and butterfly. Subsequent Excel applications link to this underlying term structure. Use the worksheet <Term Structure – Template> in the spreadsheet Chapter 09 Excel Outboxes.xls. The inputs are in the shaded fields. B3 sets the level of rates. B4 allows for parallel shifts. B5 allows for steepening or flattening the curve (twists). B6 allows for curvature—a kink occurs at the maturity entered in C6 with the spot rate at that maturity changing by the amount entered. The other spot rates adjust proportionately on each side, like butterfly wings, around the specified maturity.

- In cell B3 enter 0.03.
- In cells B4:B6 enter 0.
- In cell C6 enter 1.92.
- In cell C12 enter =$B$3+$B$4+$B$5*C10+$B$6*(1−ABS(C10−$C$6)/$C$6).
- Copy cell C12 to cells D12:H12.
- In cell B10 enter 0.
- In cell C10 enter*=DAYS360($B9,C9)/360, and then copy to cells D10:H10.

Row 11 shows differences from this date.

- In cell C11 enter =$G10−C10, and then copy to cells D11:H11.

The remainder of the table calculates implied forward rates—that is, rates implied by the relationship between spot rates of different maturities. These are used as reinvestment rates in later Excel applications. The diagonal values form a sequence of single-period rates linking the spot rates of all maturities.

- In cell D13 enter =((1+D$12)^D$10/(1+$C$12)^$C$10)^(1/(D$10−$C$10))−1.
- Copy cell D13 to cells E13:H13.
- Copy cell D13 to cell E14. Replace "C" with "D". Then copy cell E14 to cells F14:H14.
- Copy cell E14 to cell F15. Replace "D" with "E". Then copy cell F15 to cells G15:H15.
- Copy cell F15 to cell G16. Replace "E" with "F". Then copy cell G16 to cell H16.
- Copy cell G16 to cell H17. Replace "F" with "G".

The completed table should look like this:

	A	B	C	D	E	F	G	H
1	**Term Structure**							
2	Changes to spot rates							
3	Level:	3.00%						
4	Shift:	0.00%						
5	Twist:	0.00%						
6	Butterfly:	0.00%	1.92					
7								
8						Spot		
9	Date	15-Sep-08	15-Feb-09	15-Aug-09	15-Feb-10	15-Aug-10	15-Feb-11	15-Aug-11
10	Time	0.00	0.42	0.92	1.42	1.92	2.42	2.92
11	T-t		2.00	1.50	1.00	0.50	0.00	−0.50
12	15-Dec-08	0.00	3.00%	3.00%	3.00%	3.00%	3.00%	3.00%
13	15-Feb-09	0.42		3.00%	3.00%	3.00%	3.00%	3.00%
14	15-Aug-09	0.92			3.00%	3.00%	3.00%	3.00%
15	15-Feb-10	1.42				3.00%	3.00%	3.00%
16	15-Aug-10	1.92					3.00%	3.00%
17	15-Feb-11	2.42						3.00%

Changes to the Term Structure

Shift: Enter 0.01 in cell B4. The chart should show a parallel shift in the yield curve to 4 percent:

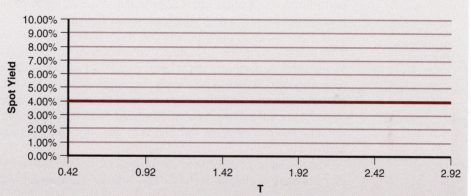

Twist: Enter 0.01 in cell B5. The chart should show an upward-sloping yield curve:

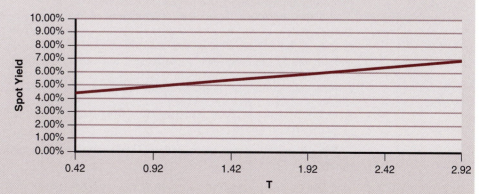

(continued)

(concluded)

Butterfly: Enter 0.01 in cell B6. The yield curve should show a kink at 1.92:

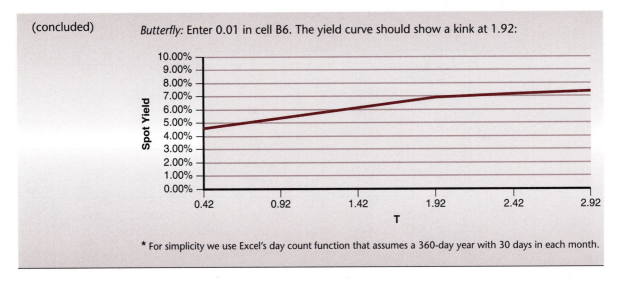

* For simplicity we use Excel's day count function that assumes a 360-day year with 30 days in each month.

Armed with this brief introduction to the term structure, we can consider two important issues. First, how can we generalize our duration, convexity, and spread concepts to cover instruments with uncertain cash flows? Second, how might we position our portfolio in anticipation of changes in the shape of the term structure? In particular, how can we take advantage of steepening or flattening of the curve?

In Equation (9.2) duration and convexity were defined in terms of yield changes. This will not work for instruments with uncertain cash flows, like MBS, because a yield cannot be computed in the usual way. What we can do, however, is shift the entire term structure up and down, apply our sophisticated valuation model, and measure the price changes. Equation (9.2) still applies, but we now interpret a change in yield as adding or subtracting a common spread at each point on the term structure. When duration and convexity are calculated in this way, they are usually labeled as *option-adjusted* or *effective* duration and convexity.

The notion of a yield spread can be generalized in essentially the same way. Instead of computing a yield-to-maturity and subtracting a similar-maturity Treasury yield,

Excel Outbox
Duration,
Convexity, and
Approximate
Bond Returns

This application links duration and convexity to shifts in the term structure and explores the return approximation given in Equation (9.1).

Use the worksheet <Duration – Template> in the spreadsheet Chapter 09 Excel Outboxes.xls.

Cells B2:B4 indicate that we are using the August 2011 Treasury note with 5 percent coupon and $1,000 face value. It matures on the 15th of the month.

Cells B6:H8 reference the <Term Structure> worksheet.

[In setting up the main table, use "Paste Special-Formulas" to avoid overwriting formats.]

- In cell B7 enter = 'Term Structure'!B10. Then copy to cells C7:H7. Then copy cells B7:H7 to cells B8:H8.

Rows 9 and 11 contain the cash flows, while rows 12 – 14 compute PV and Macaulay duration.

- In cell C9 enter =($B4*$B3)*(C7−B7). Copy to cells D9:H9.
- In cell H10 enter = B4.
- In cell C11 enter = SUM(C9:C10).
- In cell C12 enter = C$11*(1 + 'Term Structure'!C$12)^−C$7.

- In cell C13 enter = C12/$B12.
- In cell C14 enter = C$13*C$7.
- Copy cells C11:C14 to cells H11:H14.
- In cell B12 enter = SUM(C12:H12).
- In cell B13 enter = SUM(C13:H13). [Check that B13 = 1.00.]
- In cell B14 enter = SUM(C14:H14).

The completed table should look like this:

	A	B	C	D	E	F	G	H
1	**Duration**							
2	T:	Aug 2011n						
3	C:	5.00%						
4	F:	1000.00						
5								
6	Date	15-Sep-08	15-Feb-09	15-Aug-09	15-Feb-10	15-Aug-10	15-Feb-11	15-Aug-11
7	Time	0.00	0.42	0.92	1.42	1.92	2.42	2.92
8	T-t	0	2.00	1.50	1.00	0.50	0.00	−0.50
9	Coupon		20.83	25.00	25.00	25.00	25.00	25.00
10	Face							1000.00
11	Total		20.83	25.00	25.00	25.00	25.00	1025.00
12	PV	1056.12	20.58	24.33	23.97	23.62	23.28	940.33
13	X:	1.00	0.019	0.023	0.023	0.022	0.022	0.890
14	D:	2.754	0.008	0.021	0.032	0.043	0.053	2.597

The duration calculated in cell B14 is Macaulay's duration as defined later in Equation (9.3).

To calculate the modified duration and convexity (see Equation (9.2)):

- Copy the bond price from B12 to C19. [Use "Paste Special – Values".]
- Enter −0.0010 in cell B4 on the Term Structure tab. Copy the bond price from B12 to B19.
- Enter 0.0010 in cell B4 on the Term Structure tab. Copy the bond price from B12 to D19.
- In cell B20 enter = (B19/$C19−1). Copy to cell D20.
- In cell B21 enter = (B19−D19)/(2*D18*C19).
- In cell B22 enter = (B19−2*C19+D19)/(B18*B18*C19).
- In cell B23 enter = −B21*B18+0.5*B22*B18*B18.

The result should look like this:

	A	B	C	D
18	δ:	−0.10%	0.00%	+0.10%
19	P	1058.95	1056.12	1053.30
20		0.2679%		−0.2669%
21	D:	2.674		
22	C:	10.00		
23	ΔP/P	0.2679%		

Note that for a 10 basis point decline in yields, the percentage price change approximated using duration and convexity (B23) is virtually identical to the actual percentage price change in B20.

Next consider larger yield changes:

- In cell A32 enter ='Term Structure'!B3.
- In cell A26 enter = A$32+B26. Copy to cells A27:A31 and then to A33:A38.
- In cell B26 enter = −A32.
- In cell B27 enter = B26+(A$32/6). Then copy to B28:B38.
- In cell C26 enter = (C$11*(1 + $A26)^ −C$25). Copy to D26:H26. Copy C26:H26 to C27:H38.

(continued)

(concluded)

- In cell I26 enter = SUM(C26:H26). Copy to I27:I38.
- In cell J26 enter = I26/I\$32−1, and then copy to J27:J38.
- In cell K26 enter = (1 −\$B\$21∗B26)∗I\$32, and then copy to K27:K38.
- In cell L26 enter = (1 −\$B\$21∗B26+0.5∗\$B\$22∗B26∗B26)∗I\$32, and then copy to L27:L38.

The resulting table should look like this:

	A	B	C	D	E	F	G	H	I	J	K	L
25	Y	δ	0.42	0.92	1.42	1.92	2.42	2.92	P	ΔP/P	D	D+C
26	0.00%	−3.0%	20.8	25.0	25.0	25.0	25.0	1,025.0	1,145.8	8.49%	1,140.8	1,145.6
27	0.50%	−2.5%	20.8	24.9	24.8	24.8	24.7	1,010.2	1,130.2	7.01%	1,126.7	1,130.0
28	1.00%	−2.0%	20.7	24.8	24.7	24.5	24.4	995.7	1,114.8	5.55%	1,112.6	1,114.7
29	1.50%	−1.5%	20.7	24.7	24.5	24.3	24.1	981.4	1,099.7	4.13%	1,098.5	1,099.7
30	2.00%	−1.0%	20.7	24.6	24.3	24.1	23.8	967.5	1,084.9	2.73%	1,084.4	1,084.9
31	2.50%	−0.5%	20.6	24.4	24.1	23.8	23.6	953.8	1,070.4	1.35%	1,070.2	1,070.4
32	3.00%	0.0%	20.6	24.3	24.0	23.6	23.3	940.3	1,056.1	0.00%	1,056.1	1,056.1
33	3.50%	0.5%	20.5	24.2	23.8	23.4	23.0	927.1	1,042.1	−1.32%	1,042.0	1,042.1
34	4.00%	1.0%	20.5	24.1	23.6	23.2	22.7	914.2	1,028.4	−2.62%	1,027.9	1,028.4
35	4.50%	1.5%	20.5	24.0	23.5	23.0	22.5	901.5	1,014.9	−3.90%	1,013.8	1,014.9
36	5.00%	2.0%	20.4	23.9	23.3	22.8	22.2	889.0	1,001.7	−5.15%	999.6	1,001.7
37	5.50%	2.5%	20.4	23.8	23.2	22.6	22.0	876.8	988.7	−6.38%	985.5	988.8
38	6.00%	3.0%	20.3	23.7	23.0	22.4	21.7	864.8	975.9	−7.59%	971.4	976.1

Note that the approximate prices based on duration only (column K) and based on duration and convexity (column L) are very close to the true prices in column I.

The table and chart at the bottom of the worksheet examine the approximation in terms of percentage price changes. The formulas for columns A through D were already in the template.

- In cell E42 enter = C42 − \$B42. Copy to F42.
- Copy E42:F42 to E43:F54.

The chart should look like this:

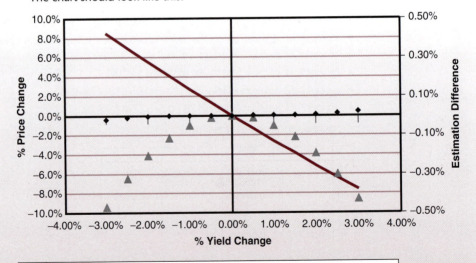

The downward-sloping line is the actual percentage price change (on the left axis) corresponding to the yield change on the *x*-axis. The triangles and diamonds show the errors (on the right axis) using only duration and using duration and convexity. The error using duration alone is significant for large yield changes. When both duration and convexity are used the error is quite small. Because the Tnote has positive convexity, the true percentage price change is always greater than the estimate based on duration alone; that is, the approximation overestimates losses and underestimates gains.

Theory in Practice
The Swap Curve and Swap Spreads

Option-adjusted spreads are usually defined and measured relative to a default-free term structure derived from Treasury securities. The same methodology can be applied using rates derived from other benchmark instruments. In particular, it is increasingly common to quote spreads relative to the spot rates embedded in interest rate swaps.

A standard interest rate swap entails the exchange of periodic interest payments between two counterparties. One side pays a fixed rate, say 6 percent, while the other side pays based on an index of floating interest rates. The most common index is the London Interbank Offer Rate (LIBOR) corresponding to the frequency of the swap payments. Thus a swap with semiannual payments would typically entail floating-rate payments based on the six-month LIBOR reset on each payment date. The swap curve is the set of fixed rates that the market demands in exchange for floating-rate payments at LIBOR on swaps of various maturities. These rates imply a set of spot rates that, like spot rates derived from Treasury securities, can be used to discount future cash flows. If a bond is quoted at "LIBOR +25," it means that its price reflects rates 25 basis points higher than those embedded in the swap curve.

Quoting spreads relative to the swap curve is particularly useful for investors and issuers in the corporate bond market. The swap curve reflects the borrowing costs of high-quality banks. Better credits trade at "LIBOR minus" whereas worse credits trade at "LIBOR plus." Because swaps are liquid derivative instruments, both investors and corporations can take either side of the trade. Therefore, the swap curve reflects both borrowing and lending opportunities for market participants who are not free of default risk.

we shift the entire term structure until we find a level such that our valuation model assigns a price equal to the price of the instrument in the market. The amount by which we need to shift the term structure is called the **option-adjusted spread (OAS)**[8] because the underlying valuation model takes into account (adjusts for) any cash flow uncertainty due to options embedded in the security.[9] Exhibit 9.2 showed the OAS for various indexes. Note that in every case the OAS was less than the nominal spread. This is because the nominal spread does *not* explicitly account for embedded options, and the options embedded in most instruments favor the issuer rather than investor. Therefore, the nominal spread generally overstates the attractiveness of the bond.

Suppose we anticipate that the term structure will flatten without a change in the overall level of rates. Specifically, assume short-term rates will increase and long-term rates will decrease by the same amount while middle maturities remain unchanged. How can we take advantage of this view? To keep things simple, consider two strategies: (1) Buy an intermediate-maturity bond or (2) buy a combination of a short-maturity

---

[8] The precise definition of the OAS may vary depending on how it is incorporated into the underlying valuation model. In particular, in many models a given OAS does not translate into exactly the same shift at all points on the term structure. However, the differences are minor. For present purposes we can simply define OAS in terms of an equal shift in spot rates at all maturities.

[9] We should note a subtle point regarding the cash flows. Depending on the instrument, option exercise and therefore cash flows may depend on the original term structure or on the shifted term structure. MBS prepayments are typically assumed to depend on the underlying (unshifted) Treasury term structure. Under this assumption, the OAS affects valuation of the MBS only through the discount rates applied to the cash flows. For callable corporate bonds, however, the OAS affects the decision to exercise the option because the firm will call the bond only when/if it can replace the debt with cheaper funding. The shifted term structure (inclusive of the OAS) indicates the spread the market demands on the firm's obligations. All else the same, a higher OAS today implies more expensive current and future refinancing opportunities for the firm. Thus, for a callable corporate bond, the OAS affects both the timing of cash flows (that is, option exercise) and the discount rates applied to the flows.

bond and a long-maturity bond such that the value-weighted average of their durations equals the duration of the intermediate bond. The first strategy is called a **bullet** because it is concentrated on a single maturity. The second strategy is called a **barbell.** Because the two strategies have the same duration, you might think their returns would be the same. However, if we are correct about the flattening of the term structure, the barbell will usually have a higher return. By construction, the value of the bullet position is unchanged. The short-maturity position within the barbell will lose money while the long-maturity position will gain. However, the weights within the barbell must be such that what happens to the long end of the curve generally dominates.[10] As a result, when the curve flattens, a barbell usually outperforms a bullet of the same duration. Conversely, when the term structure steepens, the bullet does better. Positioning for changes in the slope of the term structure is one of the bread-and-butter strategies of active fixed-income managers.

Equation (9.1) helps explain why the yield on a bullet maturity bond is virtually always higher than the weighted average yield of a duration-matched barbell position. Suppose all yields rise or fall by the same amount. To a first approximation, the bullet and the barbell will have the same return because they have the same duration. In terms of Equation (9.1), this means that the term involving duration is the same. As noted earlier, however, convexity increases more rapidly than duration as we extend maturity. Therefore, the weighted average convexity of the barbell will exceed the convexity of the duration-matched bullet. According to Equation (9.1), higher convexity implies a higher return regardless of the direction of the yield shift. To avoid being dominated by the barbell, the intermediate-maturity bullet bond must offer a higher yield. How much higher depends primarily on the volatility of interest rates. Higher volatility implies a bigger advantage to the more convex position (the barbell) and requires a larger yield premium for the bullet maturity. Therefore, we see that changes in interest rate volatility give rise to butterfly changes in the shape of the yield curve with the wings of the curve moving opposite to the body of the curve. Active bond managers generally want to shift into barbell positions in anticipation of higher volatility. Conversely, when they anticipate declining volatility active managers want to shift into more intermediate bullet positions.

---

[10] An exception to this rule occurs if the short-maturity leg of the barbell has a duration very close to that of the bullet and the long-maturity leg has a very long duration. In that case the weight on the long-maturity leg is so small that the change in the short-maturity yield determines the return on the barbell. A similar result could also occur if the short-maturity yield moves much more than the long-maturity yield. However, that entails a change in the shape, not just the slope, of the yield curve.

Excel Outbox	This outbox examines the impact of yield changes on the horizon return of a buy-and-hold position in the 5 percent August 2011 Treasury Note. The holding period horizon is February 15, 2011.
Buy and Hold	

Use the worksheet <Buy&Hold–Template> in the spreadsheet Chapter 09 Excel Outboxes.xls.

Rows 6–12 are identical to the duration outbox. Copy and paste those formulas. Note that the Macaulay duration of the note (2.75) is only slightly longer than the holding period (2.42). Therefore, we should expect to observe relatively small changes in the future value (FV) of the bond for small parallel changes in yield.

- In cell C13 enter =C$11*(1 + 'Term Structure'!$G13)^C$8.
- In cell D13 enter =D$11*(1 + 'Term Structure'!$G14)^D$8.
- In cell E13 enter =E$11*(1 + 'Term Structure'!$G15)^E$8.

- In cell F13 enter =F$11*(1 + 'Term Structure'!$G16)^F$8.
- In cell G13 enter =G$11*(1 + 'Term Structure'!$G17)^G$8.
- In cell H13 enter =H$11*(1 + 'Term Structure'!$H17)^H$8.
- In cell B13 enter =SUM(C13:H13).

Note that the future values in row 13 are calculated using implied forward rates from the Term Structure tab as the reinvestment rates for cash flows occurring before the horizon and to discount later cash flows back to the horizon date.

The following table shows the effect of yield changes on the expected value of the bond on February 15, 2011:

- In cell B23 enter = B13.
- In cell C23 enter =SUM(C13:F13).
- In cell D23 enter =H13.
- In cell E17 enter =B17–B$23, and then copy to E18:E29.
- In cell F17 enter =C17–C$23, and then copy to F18:F29.
- In cell G17 enter =D17–D$23, and then copy to G18:G29.
- Enter −0.03 in cell B4 of the Term Structure tab, and then copy and paste values from B23:D23 to B17:D17.
- Repeat for indicated shifts from −0.02 to 0.03.
- Reset B4 on the Term Structure tab to 0.

	A	B	C	D	E	F	G
16	δ:	FV	CF<T	CF>T	Total	CF<T	CF>T
17	−3.00%	1,145.83	95.83	1,025.00	11.5	(3.5)	15.0
18	−2.00%	1,141.92	97.00	1,019.91	7.6	(2.4)	10.0
19	−1.00%	1,138.08	98.18	1,014.90	3.8	(1.2)	4.9
20	−0.50%	1,136.19	98.77	1,012.42	1.9	(0.6)	2.5
21	−0.20%	1,135.07	99.12	1,010.94	0.7	(0.2)	1.0
22	−0.01%	1,134.36	99.35	1,010.01	0.0	(0.0)	0.0
23	0.00%	1,134.32	99.36	1,009.96	−	−	−
24	0.01%	1,134.28	99.37	1,009.91	(0.0)	0.0	(0.0)
25	0.20%	1,133.58	99.59	1,008.98	(0.7)	0.2	(1.0)
26	0.50%	1,132.47	99.95	1,007.52	(1.9)	0.6	(2.4)
27	1.00%	1,130.64	100.54	1,005.10	(3.7)	1.2	(4.9)
28	2.00%	1,127.03	101.73	1,000.30	(7.3)	2.4	(9.7)
29	3.00%	1,123.50	102.93	995.57	(10.8)	3.6	(14.4)

The following plot shows the total change in FV at the target date (line), the offset between changes due to CF received, and reinvested, prior to the target date (darker bars), and changes due to CF to be received after the target date (lighter bars). Notice that because $D_A^M > t_H (2.76 > 2.42)$, the capital gains impact (CF > T) dominates, resulting in a net surplus when the yield decreases and a net shortfall when the yield increases.

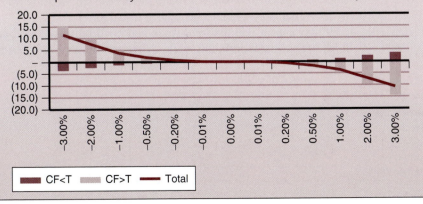

Empirical Properties of Stock and Bond Returns

Exhibits 5.4 through 5.7 of Chapter 5 examined the properties of stock and bond returns over various horizons based on a vector autoregression (VAR) model of market dynamics. Here we revisit this topic by looking at simple statistics calculated directly from the data. There are advantages to both of these approaches. By imposing some structure in the form of estimated parameters, the VAR model allowed us to examine the properties of returns at virtually any horizon. This is especially useful for very long horizon properties because we simply do not have enough nonoverlapping sample periods at long horizons to draw reliable conclusions from sample statistics. On the other hand, a model may oversimplify reality. Therefore, it is also useful to look directly at the data. Exhibits 9.3 through 9.5 address three questions: What is the correlation between stock and bond returns? How do stock and bond returns relate to inflation? Do the markets display mean-reverting behavior? The analysis reflects monthly logarithmic returns for the S&P 500 index and for a Treasury note with roughly five years to maturity at the beginning of each month—that is, a "constant-maturity" Treasury note.

Exhibit 9.3 shows that on average monthly returns on stocks and bonds were positively correlated from January 1970 through the end of 2008. Dividing the sample based on whether stock returns for the month were positive or negative shows that stocks and bonds were positively correlated in "up" markets and weakly negatively correlated in "down" markets. Looking only at months in which the stock market fell by more than 5 percent, however, indicates a strong negative correlation. Taking these results at face value implies that bonds offer significant diversification potential and that they are especially effective just when diversification is needed most—when stocks do poorly.

Exhibit 9.4 examines the correlation of stock and bond returns with realized inflation for all five-year periods from January 1930 through December 2008. Nominal returns for both stocks and bonds display positive correlation with realized inflation. For stocks, the correlation arises solely from capital gains and losses. For bonds, the income component of return has a strong positive correlation with inflation while capital gains and losses exhibit negative correlation with inflation. This is exactly what we should expect. When inflation is unexpectedly high (low), interest rates and bond yields rise (fall), inducing capital losses (gains) that are offset by the opportunity to reinvest at higher (lower) rates. Because these five-year maturity bonds have duration less than five years, the reinvestment component dominates over our five-year horizon. Therefore, the total bond return has positive correlation with realized inflation. This effect is not, however, strong enough to fully hedge against inflation. The real return on bonds shows a strong negative correlation with realized inflation. In contrast, real stock returns are almost uncorrelated with realized inflation. Therefore, stocks appear to be a reasonably good hedge against inflation.

It may appear odd that *real* stock and bond returns exhibit very different correlations with realized inflation while the correlations of *nominal* returns with inflation

EXHIBIT 9.3

Correlation of Stocks and Bonds: Monthly Log Returns, January 1970–December 2008

All months	.12
Stocks up	.23
Stocks down	−.12
Stocks < −5%	−.32

EXHIBIT 9.4
Stock and Bond
Correlations with
Realized Inflation:
All Five-Year Periods,
January 1930–
December 2008

	Bonds	Stocks
Nominal return	.19	.31
Income	.43	.01
Capital gain/loss	−.34	.30
Real return	−.61	−.06

are fairly similar. The key lies in the overall volatility of asset returns. Stock returns are much more volatile than either inflation or bond returns. Even a modest positive correlation with inflation is sufficient to imply that nominal stock returns tend to rise enough to fully offset unexpectedly high inflation (and vice versa), leaving real stock returns nearly uncorrelated with inflation. Nominal bond returns are much less volatile. For bonds, the direct impact of higher or lower inflation dominates and results in strong negative correlation of real bond returns with inflation.

Exhibit 9.5 shows the serial correlation of returns over periods ranging from one month to 10 years. A negative correlation indicates that high returns tend to be followed by low returns in the subsequent period and vice versa. As discussed in Chapters 4 and 5, this type of mean-reverting behavior dampens volatility over longer horizons. As shown in Chapter 5, risk-averse investors find this pattern of returns particularly attractive and tend to hold more of such assets the longer their investment horizon. Conversely, a positive correlation of returns over time is indicative of trending and implies an especially pronounced increase in wealth volatility over longer horizons. All else the same, such assets become less attractive to risk-averse investors as the investment horizon increases.

The exhibit indicates that both real and nominal stock returns exhibit mean reversion over horizons greater than three years. Bond returns seem to trend. Therefore, the data appear to support the notion of investing more heavily in stocks over long horizons. This result must be interpreted with care, however. First, there are few non-overlapping periods in the sample for the longer horizons. Second, these correlations are unconditional statistics. As discussed in Chapter 4, if investment opportunities change over time, investment decisions should be based on *conditional* rather than unconditional measures of risk and return. That is, we want to take into account all information that could improve our estimates of future returns. If the serial correlation reflected in Exhibit 9.5 arose from relationships that could have been predicted based on information known at the start of each period (such as valuation measures), then the unpredictable portion of returns—that is, the true investment risk—might not exhibit such strong serial correlation.

EXHIBIT 9.5
Serial Correlation
of Returns: January
1926–December 2008

	Stocks		Bonds	
	Nominal Return	Real Return	Nominal Return	Real Return
1 month	.08	.09	.15	.23
1 year	.01	−.02	.21	.30
3 years	−.26	−.26	.50	.29
5 years	−.14	−.11	.60	.33
10 years	−.04	−.16	.58	−.02

9.3 Fixed-Income Mandates

As discussed in Chapter 8, equity portfolio managers are typically assigned to either replicate (passive management) or beat (active management) a benchmark market index. Implicit in these mandates is a focus on the portfolio's total return over an indefinite horizon. While many fixed income mandates share this perspective, the inherent properties of fixed-income instruments make them well suited for addressing other types of objectives as well. In particular, fixed income is especially useful whenever cash flow requirements or specific investment horizons are important considerations. More broadly, fixed income is usually the primary investment vehicle whenever a reasonably well-defined liability must be satisfied with a high degree of certainty.

In a sense, every fixed-income portfolio mandate is intended to address the client's need to fund a liability—that is, a spending requirement. The important question from the portfolio manager's perspective is whether the manager is required to address the liability explicitly. If not, the manager effectively has a **total return mandate.** As in the equity arena, the assignment will typically entail matching or beating the return on a standard benchmark subject to a set of investment guidelines. Although the manager may have input into the choice of benchmark and the guidelines, the client or the client's advisor is responsible for ensuring that the benchmark is consistent with meeting the client's underlying objectives. In a **structured mandate** the manager must customize the portfolio to the specific characteristics of the client's liabilities. Therefore, a structured mandate is an exercise in **asset–liability management.**

At the risk of oversimplifying, we can think of total return mandates as being generic in the sense that many different clients might hire the manager to manage a similar portfolio. Mutual funds are a classic example in which many clients (the shareholders) hire the manager with a common mandate. In contrast, structured mandates are clearly unique to the particular client and liability structure.

Note that tailoring a portfolio to ensure coverage of a specific liability usually entails giving up some opportunities to enhance total return. That is, attaining a high degree of downside protection almost always requires sacrificing most, if not all, of the potential to grow the assets relative to the liabilities. Therefore, structured mandates are costly. They become even more costly if they need frequent adjustment to reflect changing liabilities.

When is a client likely to opt for a structured mandate? First, it must be possible to specify the liability concretely with respect to the size and timing of required payments. Otherwise there is little point in tailoring the portfolio to reflect anything beyond the broad characteristics of the liability, and a total return mandate with an appropriate benchmark, or perhaps a combination of such mandates, is likely to be more cost-effective. As an example, a defined benefit pension plan might opt for a structured portfolio to address the portion of its liabilities owed to retirees but might address the less certain liabilities arising from the active workforce with total return mandates. Second, it must be important that the fixed-income portfolio fully fund the liability. If the client can easily cover potential shortfalls from other sources, there is little reason to incur the opportunity cost of a structured portfolio. Third, the mandate should encompass virtually all of the fixed-income assets allocated against these specific liabilities. Otherwise the effort put into constructing a customized solution will be vitiated when it is combined with other mandates.

Although institutional clients hire outside managers for relatively straightforward structured mandates, institutions with complex, mission-critical liability funding situations tend to bring their fixed-income portfolio management expertise in-house. In particular, insurance companies and other financial institutions usually manage both the asset and liability sides of their businesses in-house. For these firms, profitability—indeed solvency—depends on carefully managing the return differential between financial assets and liabilities. In addition, the details of the firm's balance sheet are proprietary information. The upshot is that many of the most interesting asset–liability management mandates (that is, structured mandates) are not entrusted to outside managers. Most fixed-income managers who manage money for outside clients have a total return mandate.

Fixed-income portfolios have not always been managed for total return. In the 1950s and 1960s it was standard practice to adopt a buy-and-hold approach focused on generating high current income with little attempt to capture interim capital gains or avoid capital losses. Rates were low and stable in that era. Mortgage-backed and other structured securities did not exist, and secondary trading in bonds was limited. Thus it made sense to focus on "reaching for yield" to enhance return. The focus shifted to total return in the 1970s as both the level and volatility of rates increased sharply. Liquidity improved as managers sought to trade more actively. Perhaps even more importantly, the introduction of fixed-income derivatives, such as interest rate futures, facilitated more active trading. The explosion of new fixed-income instruments and the introduction of new types of derivatives, like interest rate swaps, in the 1980s and 1990s expanded the opportunities to add value through active trading and reinforced the focus on total return. Today the total return perspective is entrenched.[11]

If interest rate volatility increases substantially, the most likely driver will be a return to higher and more volatile inflation. As discussed in the previous section, traditional bonds are poor hedges against inflation. By construction, however, inflation-protected bonds offer the investor a stream of income that compensates for realized inflation. At this point inflation-linked bonds represent a small portion of the fixed-income market. For most managers they are simply one of many relative value alternatives within an actively managed portfolio. However, heightened awareness of potential inflation risks, especially among those in or near retirement, is leading to increased interest in a relatively new type of fixed-income mandate: real return.

9.4   Passive Management

Construction of a passive equity portfolio was described in some detail in Chapter 8. Although broadly similar, the bond index manager's problem is somewhat more complex than the equity index manager's assignment. The added complexity arises from the heterogeneity of fixed-income instruments, time-varying risk characteristics, and the virtual absence of a secondary market for many issues included in standard fixed-income benchmarks.

Consider creating a portfolio to track the Barclays Aggregate index. Basic characteristics for this broad, investment-grade index and its main subcomponents were shown in Exhibit 9.2. As of December 2008 the "Agg" (as it is commonly known) contained roughly 9,100 issues: 1,400 government, 3,100 corporate, and 4,600 securitized.[12] It is clearly impractical to hold all these issues according to market value weights.

[11] Ironically, however, hunger for yield in an environment of low rates, tightening spreads, and seemingly unlimited liquidity played a major role in the weakening of credit standards and the explosion of leverage that culminated in the credit crisis of 2007–2009.

[12] In September 2005 there were roughly 6,200 issues in the Aggregate index, of which 2,500 (40 percent) were securitized. Securitization of loans, mostly mortgages, accounted for about 72 percent (2,100 of 2,900) of the net increase between September 2005 and December 2008.

An equity manager faces this same situation with broad indexes like the Russell 2000. However, at least in principle, the equity manager can select virtually any subset of the index to include in a portfolio and adjust the portfolio with relative ease. In contrast, the bond manager must recognize that relatively few bond issues trade actively and that today's liquid new issue will be tomorrow's illiquid legacy. As a result, a bond index manager does not have the luxury of picking bonds randomly or of eschewing illiquid instruments.

Liquidity is not the only characteristic that changes as a bond ages and market conditions change. Even for bonds without embedded options, basic risk–return characteristics such as duration and convexity change over time as maturity shortens and the bond price moves relative to par, reflecting the evolution of market conditions. Similarly, a bond's sensitivities to changes in the yield curve and credit spreads change over time. Embedded options, like the prepayment option in MBS, imply even less stable characteristics. The upshot is that to create a portfolio that tracks an index closely without frequent and costly rebalancing, a manager must match the structure of the index across several dimensions—maturities, coupons, credit qualities, sectors, individual credit exposures—in addition to the broad requirement of matching the index's duration.

Note that "passive" does not mean "static." Due to new issues and elimination of issues that no longer meet the requirements for inclusion, indexes evolve over time and will not be tracked well by a fire-and-forget static portfolio. As a result, well-constructed passive portfolios require careful monitoring and regular trading. To put this another way, passive portfolios require ongoing management.

The fraction of a portfolio allocated to each category, subcategory, or individual issuer does not adequately capture the impact on portfolio performance. Suppose for example that utility bonds compose 2 percent of the index and that long-maturity bonds account for most of that market value. Investing 2 percent in short-maturity utility bonds would match the market value weight of the utility sector in the index. Because longer bonds have higher durations, however, the portfolio would not be as sensitive to the yield spread of the utility sector. If utilities outperform—that is, if their spread tightens—the portfolio will not keep pace with the index. Therefore, in addition to matching the portfolio weight, the manager should match the **contribution to duration** —defined as portfolio weight times duration—of the holdings in each category to that of the index. The same is true for individual credits.

Instruments with embedded options need special attention in the construction of a passive portfolio. These instruments fall into two main groups: MBS and callable bonds. As noted earlier, the risk characteristics of these instruments are especially sensitive to changing market conditions. This has two implications. First, the MBS and callable bond subindexes have a disproportionate impact on the ability to track the overall index. Second, the portfolio may track the index poorly if bonds with and without embedded options are freely substituted in the process of satisfying overall portfolio composition (such as coupon or quality) constraints. The practical solution to both of these concerns is to impose explicit matching requirements for the callable bond and MBS subindexes in addition to conditions for the overall index.

Within the MBS subindex, we need to distinguish securities along at least four dimensions: coupon, age/seasoning, issuer/guarantor, and original maturity. Each of these factors has a significant impact on underlying loan prepayments. Higher coupons prepay faster. All else the same, prepayments ramp up and then plateau as loans age. However, prepayments on older loans may be "burned out" if the borrowers have already passed on attractive opportunities to prepay. Due to differences in underwriting standards and

Theory in Practice   *Tracking MBS*

The MBS component of the Barclays Aggregate Index consists of "index generics" or "annual aggregates" defined by three attributes: the agency program, the coupon, and the origination year of the underlying mortgages—for example, 2008 5 percent FNMA 30-year. Each generic is a composite of thousands of tradable MBS securities ("pools") sharing those three characteristics. However, the generics themselves are not tradable; so how do we create a manageable portfolio of tradable securities to track the MBS?

Agency MBS trade in two ways. The heaviest volume occurs in TBA ("to-be-announced") contracts for MBS specified by program and coupon but not by origination year. Subject to certain rules, the seller can deliver any MBS pool(s) in that program with that coupon. In general, the seller will choose to deliver recently created pools (current or recent "production") because those usually have the least favorable prepayment characteristics. TBAs settle monthly. If the buyer and seller can agree on a price adjustment (the "drop"), a TBA contract can be rolled from month to month allowing delivery to be postponed—in principle indefinitely. MBS also trade on a specified pool basis. Due to the seller's TBA delivery option, buyers looking for specific pools almost always pay a premium over the corresponding TBA price.

There are essentially two problems for the index manager. Individual MBS pools may not be representative of the corresponding index generic. This is especially true for older, seasoned origination years or coupons far from current market levels. Therefore, taking delivery on TBA contracts may not result in a sufficiently representative sampling of pools. Indeed, due to the seller's delivery option, regularly taking TBA delivery is almost certain to result in a portfolio of pools with adverse characteristics. On the other hand, it can be difficult to find sufficient quantities of representative, seasoned, or off-market pools. And buying such pools on a specified basis is more expensive.

Dynkin and colleagues (2001) outline two relatively simple strategies to address these issues:

1. *Rolling current-coupon TBA contracts:* By rolling TBAs rather than taking delivery, the manager effectively obtains generic exposure to the current/recent production portion of the index while avoiding the idiosyncratic tracking risk of individual pools. The drawback is that current-coupon TBA contracts generally do not provide close tracking of the seasoned and off-market portions of the index.

2. *Buy large pools from current production and allow them to season in the portfolio:* Larger pools tend to be more representative of their index generics. Buying them while they are still current/recent production should entail little, if any, premium over TBA pricing. Retaining seasoned and off-market pools improves tracking of these components of the index.

Of course these two strategies are not mutually exclusive. Combining them provides the opportunity to trade off the lower cost and reduced idiosyncratic risk of TBA rolls against improved matching of the seasoned and off-market portions of the MBS index.

Source: See Dynkin et al. (2001) for a detailed discussion.

---

securitization practices, MBS issued by the major agencies—GNMA, FNMA, and FHLMC—prepay at different rates. Similarly prepayment depends on whether the underlying loans originated as standard 15-year or 30-year amortizing loans or if they have a specialized maturity structure such as a balloon repayment of principal. Due to the complexity of the prepayment option, the passive bond manager should match the index weights within each cell of a four-dimensional grid defined by these factors.

Duration, and therefore contribution to duration, captures the impact of parallel shifts in the term structure of interest rates. Although shifts of this nature are by far the most important source of overall interest rate movements, significant steepening or flattening of the yield curve occurs too. When the term structure steepens (flattens), the present value of near-term cash flows rises (falls), the present value of distant cash flows falls (rises), and the present value of intermediate cash flows is roughly unchanged. To guard against the impact of these movements, the cash flow pattern of the passive portfolio should match that of the index. Note that with adequate matching of cash flows it should not be necessary to impose an explicit constraint on convexity.

To match the cash flow pattern of an index, it is usually sufficient to select a reasonably small set of discrete horizons. For example, the set {0, .5, 1, 2, 3, 4, 5, 10, 15, 20, 30 years} might be chosen. The cash flows of the bonds are then mapped into these maturities by prorating them between adjacent nodes. For example, a cash flow that occurs in 8 years is treated as if 40 percent occurs in 5 years and 60 percent in 10 years.

Not surprisingly, callable bonds and especially MBS pose a potential problem for cash flow matching. Due to the embedded options, the cash flows on these instruments are uncertain.

However, the sophisticated models needed to value these instruments can also generate an expected (that is, probability-weighted) stream of cash flows. These expected flows should be used in the cash matching process.

Exhibit 9.6 brings all these considerations together and adds a final element: the objective of minimizing cost. With this objective, the key steps in constructing a passive

EXHIBIT 9.6　Key Steps in Passive Portfolio Construction

- Establish a grid of characteristics to be used in defining "cells":
  - Broad categories, such as government, corporate, MBS, other structured.
  - Sectors:
    - Corporate, such as financial, industrial, utilities.
    - MBS, such as two-dimensional breakdown of programs {GNMA, FNMA, FHLMC} × {15-year, 30-year, balloon}.
  - Credit quality: AAA, AA, A, BAA, etc.
  - Embedded options, such as none, callable, or putable.
  - MBS coupons, such as increments of 0.5%.
  - MBS seasoning, such as < 1 yr, 1–3years, >3years.
  - Cash flow horizons, such as {0, .5, 1, 2, 3, 4, 5, 10, 15, 20, 30}.
- Obtain or calculate the following information for each security in the index:
  - Issuer.
  - Characteristics as defined above .
  - Percentage weight in index.
  - Expected cash flows allocated to specified set of horizons.
  - Duration.
- Determine the tradable subset of index securities and obtain the following:
  - Bid and ask prices for securities already owned.
  - Ask prices for securities not already owned.
- Match broad index characteristics:
  - Duration.
  - Percentage of expected cash flow at each specified horizon.
- Match cell magnitudes:
  - Percentage of portfolio—that is, portfolio weight.
  - Contribution to duration [= sum of (duration × weight) across securities in cell].
- Constrain contribution to duration by issuer.
- Optimize: Select the par amount of securities to buy and sell to minimize the cost of the portfolio, including the impact of bid–ask spreads, subject to the matching constraints.

portfolio define a linear programming (LP) problem because both the objective (the cost) and the constraints (the matching conditions) are linear in the decision variables (the buy/sell amounts). Virtually any optimization package, including the Excel Solver add-in, has an algorithm for solving linear programming problems. Importantly, many of these algorithms can handle large LP problems involving many variables (securities) and many constraints.

Excel Outbox
Bond Index
Construction

The bond index portfolio will be constructed from a universe of 544 bonds using the spreadsheet Chapter 09 Excel Outboxes. Due to the limit Solver places on the number of decision variables (maximum of 200), the set of bonds used to construct the index is sampled from this larger universe. The <Index-Universe> worksheet provides the set of available bonds. The <Data> worksheet samples from the universe to satisfy the Solver limit. The worksheet should appear as follows:

	A	B	C	D	E	F	G	H	I
1		Sample:			6.01%		5.36%	7.68	
2		Universe:			5.88%		5.29%	6.80	
3		Issuer	Ask	Maturity	Coupon	Sector	YTM	Duration	Rating
4	4	140							
5	1	GNMA 30-yr Fixed 4.500	99.75	26-Dec-38	4.50% Mortgage		4.55%	16.257	AAA
6	2	GNMA 30-yr Fixed 5.000	103.09	26-Dec-38	5.00% Mortgage		4.34%	16.129	AAA

A number entered into cells A5:A152 will select that bond from the universe. Specific bonds can be selected. For example, all of the mortgages, the first 15 bonds in the universe, will be included in the sample. The remainder of the sample is selected by stratified sampling. The Treasury notes and bonds in the universe are sorted by coupon and maturity. The corporate bonds are sorted by sector and then by rating. This clusters the bonds in a manner similar to the size and style groups used to construct the equity index. Bonds selected at equal intervals through the universe should create a reasonably representative sample. The approach provided starts with the bond indicated in cell A20 and then samples at intervals set by cell A4. The average coupon, YTM, and duration of the sample and universe, reported in cells E1:H2, suggest the sample is representative of the universe. To provide some guidance if bonds are selected manually, the table in cells K4:P16 reports the range of identification numbers assigned to bonds in each sector, the number of bonds within the sector, and the percentage this represents of the universe.

	K	L	M	N	O	P
4		Sector	Bonds Numbered		#	%
5	Mortgage		1	15	15	2.8%
6	Treasury	T-NOTE	16	101	86	15.8%
7		T-BOND	102	141	40	7.4%
8	Corporate	Basic Materials	142	162	21	3.9%
9		Communications	163	217	55	10.1%
10		Consumer, Cyclical	218	237	20	3.7%
11		Consumer, Non-Cyclical	238	297	60	11.0%
12		Energy	298	342	45	8.3%
13		Financial	343	449	107	19.7%
14		Industrial	450	487	38	7.0%
15		Technology	488	498	11	2.0%
16		Utilities	499	544	46	8.5%

With our limited sample of 148 bonds, it is not possible to impose all of the conditions outlined in Exhibit 9.6. To keep the problem tractable, the objective will be to create a portfolio that minimizes the weighted average price of the portfolio while matching the weighted average duration and maintaining similar sector and rating exposures as the

(continued)

(continued) index. Thus only a few of the basic conditions from Exhibit 9.6 are imposed. The program template should appear as follows:

	A	B	C	D	E	F	G	H	I	J	K
1	Bond Index Construction										
2											
3											
4	Program	Objective	Min	ΣP_i			=				w
5											
6											
7											
8		Constraints			**Target**	**Range**		**Value**			
9											
10			Σw_i		1.0000						
11		Portfolio	ΣD_i		6.0000						
12			ΣC_i		5.08%						
13			wi								
14			Treasury		38.54%						
15			Mortgage		38.33%						
16			Energy		1.76%						
17			Financial		11.30%						
18			Consumer, Cyclical		1.23%						
19		Sector	Industrial		0.76%						
20			Consumer, Non-Cyclical		2.61%						
21			Utilities		1.50%						
22			Basic Materials		0.73%						
23			Technology		0.43%						
24			Communications		2.82%						
25			AAA		80.20%						
26			AA		5.00%						
27		Rating	A		7.90%						
28			BBB		6.88%						
29			< BBB		0.02%						

The target value:

- In cell H4 enter =SUMPRODUCT(K$5:K$152,Data!C$5:C$152)/100.
- In cell J5 enter =Data!B5 and then copy to cells J6:J152.
- In cells K5:K152 enter 0.01 to provide a starting point for optimization.

The portfolio values:

- In cell H10 enter =SUM(K$5:K$152).
- In cell H11 enter =SUMPRODUCT(K$5:K$152,Data!H$5:H$152).
- In cell H12 enter =SUMPRODUCT(K$5:K$152,Data!E$5:E$152).
- In cell F13 enter 0, and in cell G13 enter 0.03.
- In cell H14 enter =SUMPRODUCT(K$5:K$152,INT(Data!F$5:F$152 = C14)) and then copy to cells H15:H24. Use copy-paste-formula to avoid writing over the formatting.
- In cell H25 enter =SUMPRODUCT(K$5:K$152,INT(Data!I$5:I$152 = C25)) and then copy to cells H26:H29.

The portfolio values will be constrained within a range:

- Start with a 10 percent band around the index value: In cells F9 and G9 enter 0.10.
- In cell F12 enter =(1 − F$9)*E12 and then copy to cells F14:F29.
- In cell G12 enter =(1 + G$9)*E12 and then copy to cells G14:G29.

In Solver:

- Set target cell: H4.
- Equal to: min.
- By changing cells: K5:K152.

- Subject to these constraints:
  - Fully invested: H10 = E10.
  - Portfolio duration equal to target: H11 = E11.
  - Portfolio coupon within ±10 percent of the target: H12 ≤ G12; H12 ≥ F12.
  - Sector and ratings exposure within ±10 percent of the target: H14 ≤ G14 ... H29 ≤ G29 and H14 ≥ F14 ... H29 ≥ F29.
  - Long-only: K5:K152 ≥ F13.
  - Maximum 3 percent individual position weight: K5:K152 ≤ G13.
- Open the Options box:
  - Set Iterations to 500.
  - Check the "Assume Linear Model" box.

The results should appear as follows:

	A	B	C	D	E	F	G	H
1	Bond Index Construction							
2								
3								
4	Program	Objective	Min	ΣP_i			=	1.0276
5								
6								
7								
8		Constraints			Target	Range		Value
9						10%	10%	
10		Portfolio	Σw_i		1.0000			1.0000
11			ΣD_i		6.0000			6.0000
12			ΣC_i		5.08%	4.57%	5.59%	5.10%
13			wi			0.00%	3.00%	
14		Sector	Treasury		38.54%	34.69%	42.39%	41.36%
15			Mortgage		38.33%	34.50%	42.16%	34.50%
16			Energy		1.76%	1.58%	1.94%	1.58%
17			Financial		11.30%	10.17%	12.43%	12.43%
18			Consumer, Cyclical		1.23%	1.11%	1.35%	1.11%
19			Industrial		0.76%	0.68%	0.84%	0.84%
20			Consumer, Non-Cyclical		2.61%	2.35%	2.87%	2.87%
21			Utilities		1.50%	1.35%	1.65%	1.65%
22			Basic Materials		0.73%	0.66%	0.80%	0.66%
23			Technology		0.43%	0.39%	0.47%	0.47%
24			Communications		2.82%	2.54%	3.10%	2.54%
25		Rating	AAA		80.20%	72.18%	88.22%	81.14%
26			AA		5.00%	4.50%	5.50%	2.87%
27			A		7.90%	7.11%	8.69%	8.42%
28			BBB		6.88%	6.19%	7.57%	7.57%
29			< BBB		0.02%	0.00%	0.02%	0.00%

9.5 Active Management

Managers of passive portfolios would ideally like to track the benchmark index perfectly. In contrast, active managers deliberately deviate from the benchmark in an effort to enhance return. Those that are allowed only modest tracking risk focus on small tilts in sector, coupon, maturity, credit quality, or issuer weightings while retaining the requirement that the portfolio match more aggregated characteristics of the benchmark. Such mandates are often described as enhanced indexes. As the tolerance for mismatches expands to include duration bets or significant investment in off-benchmark instruments, such as high-yield bonds in a portfolio benchmarked against the Barclays Aggregate, we move into fully active management.

A Sample Active Mandate

As of March 9, 2006, the Teachers Retirement System of Texas (TRS) had established the fixed-income portfolio guidelines summarized in Exhibit 9.7. The stated objectives make it clear that this is a total return mandate intended to provide diversification and deflation protection to the overall retirement fund. The composition of the plan's benchmark, the Barclays Universal index, was shown in Exhibit 9.1.

The guidelines allow the manager to vary the duration of the fund by plus or minus two years relative to the benchmark.[13] To put this latitude in perspective, according to Equation (9.1) a duration differential of two years translates into roughly a 2 percent difference in return if yields increase or decrease by 1 percent (100 basis points). Therefore, there is considerable scope for enhancing return if the manager can anticipate changes in the overall level of interest rates. Conversely, poorly timed duration

---

[13] Recall that duration is commonly ascribed a time dimension, such as years, because for instruments with known cash flows it is proportional to the value-weighted average of the time until each dollar is received.

EXHIBIT 9.7

Sample Fixed Income Mandate: Teachers Retirement System of Texas

Source: TRS Web site. TRS Investment Policy Statement adopted March 9, 2006.

Objectives of fixed income portfolio	Long-term return in excess of benchmark. Diversification of retirement fund. Diversified exposure within fixed income. Deflation hedge for retirement fund.
Benchmark	Barclays Universal Index.
Broad risk limits:	
Duration	Benchmark ± 2 years.
Tracking error	0.75% per month.
Composition limits:	
Governments (including agencies)	No limit.
Securitized (MBS,CMBS,ABS)	Up to max(index weight, 70%).
Nonagency MBS	Max(index weight,10%).
Nonagency CMBS	Max(index weight, 8%).
ABS	Max(index weight,10%).
Credit	Up to max(index weight, 50%).
Minimum rating	B.
Non–investment grade	15% including high-yield funds. 10% excluding high-yield funds.
Unrated securities	2%.
Single issuer	3%.
Nondollar	10%.
Prohibitions	No leverage. No short sales. No futures or swaps.

bets could seriously undermine performance. The overall tracking error risk of this portfolio is limited to 0.75 percent per month. Applying the common approximation that standard deviations scale with the square root of the time horizon, this would correspond to 2.6 percent annual tracking error.[14] As a rule of thumb, generating excess return equal to one-half the tracking error risk is solid performance. Hence we can infer that the portfolio is expected to beat its benchmark by, say, 1.00–1.25 percent per year (before fees) over a three- to five-year horizon. If TRS expects substantially more (or less) than this, the risk budget or other parameters probably need reconsideration.

The next section of the exhibit lays out the limitations on the broad categories of securities—governments, structured, and credit—and some key subcomponents of those groups. There is no limit on government securities because these securities are deemed safe subject to the overall limit on interest rate risk imposed by the duration constraint and the tracking error budget. Comparison with Exhibit 9.1 indicates that the overall limits on credit (50 percent) and structured securities (70 percent) are substantially above the benchmark weights for these broad categories. As a result, the manager has wide latitude to overweight or underweight credit and structured securities.

The structured securities category includes residential mortgage-backed securities (MBS), commercial mortgage-backed securities (CMBS), and asset-backed securities (ABS). The key limitation imposed by the TRS guidelines concerns the use of instruments that are not standardized and guaranteed by a government agency: nonagency MBS and CMBS and the entire ABS market. These securities entail credit exposure to both the underlying borrowers and the institutions that securitize the loans. In addition, the underlying loans and structured securities may be more heterogeneous and therefore more difficult to analyze. On the plus side, the investor usually earns a higher return in exchange for these additional risks. The TRS guidelines allow the manager to exploit opportunities in these areas, but the combined limits are less than half of the maximum overall exposure to structured securities.

The limitations on credit deal primarily with the high-yield market. While permitting a small allocation to unrated securities, the client has imposed a general minimum credit rating of B and an overall 15 percent limit on non–investment-grade securities. The 15 percent limit on high yield, far above the benchmark weight, is consistent with the general theme of allowing ample flexibility. The single B minimum rating appears somewhat restrictive because it means that the portfolio can invest only in the higher-quality segment of the high-yield market. However, this restriction applies only to direct investment in high-yield securities. Lower-quality securities may be used through investment in high-yield mutual funds or other pooled vehicles explicitly approved by the board of trustees.

The Barclays Universal index includes only securities denominated in U.S. dollars. The 10 percent limitation on nondollar securities is therefore an explicit statement that the manager is allowed to make this type of off-benchmark investment. The guidelines allow purchase and sale of foreign currencies in order to affect trading in foreign-denominated securities. Interestingly, however, the guidelines do not seem to address the issue of whether the manager can use currency hedging transactions to reduce currency exposure without having to sell the underlying

---

[14] The impact of time horizon on risk and return was discussed in detail in Chapters 3–5. Recall that the "square root of *T*" result is based on independent and identically distributed logarithmic returns. Appendix 1 of Chapter 3 gives a better approximation for adjusting the standard deviation of gross returns (that is, arithmetic returns). However, that formula requires the mean as an input as well.

bond. In the absence of that authority, the manager cannot separate the bond and currency decisions. The next chapter discusses why it can be important to separate these decisions.

The last portion of Exhibit 9.7 lists the three main prohibitions imposed on this portfolio. First, the portfolio cannot use leverage; that is, it cannot borrow. This is a standard provision that, loosely speaking, differentiates a traditional portfolio mandate from a hedge fund. Second, the manager cannot sell securities short. Third, the manager cannot use interest rate swaps or financial futures. Although other types of instruments, like options and forwards, are not explicitly mentioned, the prohibition appears to apply to all derivative instruments. Together the second and third prohibitions are rather restrictive. They eliminate the possibility of explicit arbitrage trades: long one instrument and short another similar instrument. More generally, they limit the manager's ability to express the view that a security is expensive versus a generic or specific alternative. In addition, the prohibition on derivatives keeps the manager from efficiently adjusting the portfolio's risk exposures using these liquid, generic instruments. Derivatives have become so ingrained into the fixed income markets that this complete prohibition is somewhat unusual in a fully active total return mandate.

It is worthwhile to emphasize that the portfolio manager will be judged based on the portfolio's performance versus the specified benchmark. The choice of the benchmark and the role of this portfolio within the overall pension plan (such as its contribution to asset diversification and asset–liability risk control) are beyond the scope of the fixed income manager's mandate.

Universes and Benchmarks

Active portfolio mandates are usually benchmarked against a market index such as the Barclays Universal. The index represents the passive alternative. Fail to beat the index, and the client may conclude that it is not worth paying active management fees. Often the portfolio is also implicitly or explicitly benchmarked against active alternatives in the form of a universe of other, similar managers' portfolios. Fail to beat most of the competition, and the client may take the portfolio elsewhere even if the manager has beaten the index. Therefore, the manager must watch both the benchmark index and the competition.

In general, the index is somewhat more important for managers with institutional clients than it is for mutual fund managers. Institutional clients view their portfolios as filling a specific role within their overall plans and choose benchmark indexes to fulfill that role. The active manager's job is to enhance performance while preserving the broad risk–return properties that the client needs within the asset allocation. Therefore, institutional clients are not usually quick to replace a manager in whom they have confidence. On the other hand, mutual fund investors and their financial advisors are notorious for chasing the latest hot fund. Mutual fund managers are therefore under constant pressure to beat the competition—whomever that turns out to be this week, month, quarter, or year.[15]

Having one's performance judged against a universe can be an especially harsh experience in fixed income. Two types of universes are particularly frustrating. The first is a homogeneous but narrowly defined universe such as one composed of portfolios that invest in only agency MBS. Because the correlation among these securities

---

[15] See Chapter 15 for further discussion of this issue.

tends to be extremely high, there may be little difference between top and bottom quartile performance in this universe. As a result, these managers face the possibility that even a minor mistake could blow the whole year in terms of competitive performance. The other extremely frustrating type of universe lies at the other end of the spectrum: a heterogeneous catchall universe. In the late 1990s all mutual funds investing heavily in foreign bonds were included in a single Lipper category even though their mandates varied widely. Some invested only in emerging markets while others used only developed markets. Some invested in both. Some had to hedge the currency risk, some could not hedge, and some could actively manage the currency exposure. Given this heterogeneity and the high volatility of currencies and emerging markets, funds with extreme mandates tended to dominate both the top and the bottom quartiles. The managers of these funds had no place to hide when the market thrashed their mandated exposures. Managers with more flexible mandates faced a different problem. They were doomed to the middle of the pack unless they took aggressive bets versus their benchmarks. The point, of course, is that poorly selected benchmark indexes and universes may convey conflicting incentives to the manager.

Active Strategies and Tactics

How can active bond managers add value? There are, of course, many approaches. However, most strategies are variations on a few common themes that fall into the following categories:

- Interest rate anticipation.
- Yield curve positioning.
- Relative value or spread bets.
- Structure bets.

Interest rate anticipation is perhaps the most basic of fixed income strategies. It is deceptively simple: Extend duration when rates are likely to decline and shorten duration when rates are likely to rise. The trick, of course, is correctly calling the direction of interest rates. Virtually every fixed income manager watches the macroeconomy and the key central banks, like the U.S. Federal Reserve, to assess the prospects for rising or falling rates. It is easy to understand why. The level of interest rates is by far the biggest driver of fixed-income returns. Few other bets have as much potential to enhance portfolio return as getting a significant duration bet right. The temptation to bet on rates is therefore difficult to resist. Nevertheless, calling the direction of rates has proven notoriously difficult, especially in the short run. As a result, many managers eschew duration bets altogether or limit themselves to small deviations from the benchmark—much smaller than the $\pm$ 2-year range allowed in the TRS mandate just discussed.

The basic yield curve positioning strategy—barbells versus bullets—was described in Section 9.2. There are two primary considerations: the slope of the yield curve and the trade-off between yield and convexity. A barbell of long and short maturities will generally outperform an equal-duration, intermediate-maturity bullet bond if the yield curve flattens. The converse is true if the curve steepens. Therefore, the manager wants to shift between these two types of positions in anticipation of significant changes in the slope of the yield curve. Typically the curve flattens (steepens) as rates in general rise (fall), so managers frequently combine a barbell position with shortening duration and a bulleted posture with extending duration.

Excel Outbox
Active Strategies

Some active strategies try to benefit from expected changes in the yield curve. The question is this: What portfolio should be held to best take advantage of an active view? The worksheet <Active – Template> in the spreadsheet Chapter 09 Excel Outboxes.xls examines the returns to different strategies for various changes in the yield curve. The four strategies considered are these:

- Bullet 1: A portfolio that is 100 percent long an August 2009 Treasury note with duration 0.91.
- Bullet 2: A portfolio that is 100 percent long an August 2010 Treasury note with duration 1.85.
- Bullet 3: A portfolio that is 100 percent long an August 2011 Treasury note with duration 2.75.
- Barbell: A portfolio that is 50 percent long the August 2009 note and 50 percent long the August 2011 note. The duration of the portfolio is 1.85—the same as the August 2010 note.

The template for cash flows and present values should appear as follows:

	A	B	C	D	E	F	G	H	I
8	Date		15-Sep-08	15-Feb-09	15-Aug-09	15-Feb-10	15-Aug-10	15-Feb-11	15-Aug-11
9	Time								
10	T-t								
11									
12	Barbell	CF							
13									
14		PV							
15	Bullet 1	CF							
16		PV							
17	Bullet 2	CF							
18		PV							
19	Bullet 3	CF							
20		PV							

- In cell C9 enter ='Term Structure'!B10 and then copy to cells C9:I10.
- In cell D11 enter = .5*D15 and then copy to cell E11.
- In cell D12 enter = .5*D19 and then copy to cells E12:I12.
- In cell D13 enter = sum(D11:D12) and then copy to cells E13:I13.
- In cell D14 enter =D$13*(1 + 'Term Structure'!C$12)^−D$9 and then copy to cells E14:I14.
- In cell D15 enter =(E$4/2)*E$6, and in cell E15 enter =E6 + (E4/2)*E6.
- In cell D16 enter =D$15*(1 + 'Term Structure'!C$12)^−D$9 and then copy to cell E16.
- In cell D17 enter =($F4/2)*$F6 and then copy to cells E17:F17; in cell G17 enter =F6 + (F4/2)*F6.
- In cell D18 enter =D$17*(1 + 'Term Structure'!C$12)^−D$9 and then copy to cells E18:G18.
- In cell D19 enter =($G4/2)*$G6 and then copy to cells E19:H19; in cell I19 enter =G6 + (G4/2)*G6.
- In cell D20 enter =D$19*(1 + 'Term Structure'!C$12)^−D$9 and then copy to cells E20:I20.
- In cell C14 enter =SUM(D14:I14) and then copy to cells C16, C18, and C20.

The completed table should appear as follows:

	A	B	C	D	E	F	G	H	I
8	Date		15-Sep-08	15-Feb-09	15-Aug-09	15-Feb-10	15-Aug-10	15-Feb-11	15-Aug-11
9	Time		0.00	0.42	0.92	1.42	1.92	2.42	2.92
10	T-t		0.00	2.00	1.50	1.00	0.50	0.00	−0.50
11				12.50	512.50				
12	Barbell	CF		12.50	12.50	12.50	12.50	12.50	512.50
13				25.00	525.00	12.50	12.50	12.50	512.50
14		PV	1041.26	24.69	510.97	11.99	11.81	11.64	470.17
15	Bullet 1	CF		25.00	1025.00				
16		PV	1022.29	24.69	997.60				
17	Bullet 2	CF		25.00	25.00	25.00	1025.00		
18		PV	1041.54	24.69	24.33	23.97	968.54		
19	Bullet 3	CF		25.00	25.00	25.00	25.00	25.00	1025.00
20		PV	1060.23	24.69	24.33	23.97	23.62	23.28	940.33

The shaded cells are the price of the bond/portfolio for the given term structure. Paste-special-value these cells to cells B25:E25. These provide the base price for examining the return to each strategy for given changes to the term structure. The approach will be to shift the yield curve by changing cells B4:B6 in the <Term Structure> worksheet developed earlier, recording the new prices in cells B26:E31, and calculating the return in cells F26:I31. To make the process easier, the strategy values to be copied also appear below the table in the range B33:E33.

The template should appear as follows:

	A	B	C	D	E	F	G	H	I
24		Barbell	Bullet 1	Bullet 2	Bullet 3	Barbell	Bullet 1	Bullet 2	Bullet 3
25	Price								
26	Shift (−)								
27	Shift (+)								
28	Twist (−)								
29	Twist (+)								
30	Butterfly (−)								
31	Butterfly (+)								

- In cell F26 enter =B26/B$25−1 and then copy to cells F26:I26.

  We will consider six scenarios:

- *Shift (−):* A −1 percent shift of all spot rates—that is, a downward shift in the yield curve
- *Shift (+):* A +1 percent shift of all spot rates—that is, an upward shift in the yield curve.
- *Twist (−):* A −1 percent shift in the August 2011 spot rate—that is, a flattening yield curve.
- *Twist (+):* A +1 percent shift in the August 2011 spot rate—that is, a steepening yield curve.
- *Butterfly (−):* A −1 percent shift in the August 2010 spot rate—that is, a downward kink in the yield curve.
- *Butterfly (+):* A +1 percent shift in the August 2010 spot rate—that is, an upward kink in the yield curve.

  To populate the table:

- In cell B4 on worksheet <Term Structure> enter −0.01.
- Paste-special-value cells B33:E33 into cells B26:E26 .
- Repeat for a +1 percent shift, a ± 1 percent twist, and a ± 1 percent butterfly.

(continued)

(concluded)   The completed table and chart should appear as follows:

	A	B	C	D	E	F	G	H	I
24		Barbell	Bullet 1	Bullet 2	Bullet 3	Barbell	Bullet 1	Bullet 2	Bullet 3
25	Price	1,041.3	1,022.3	1,041.5	1,060.2				
26	Shift (−)	1,060.2	1,031.4	1,060.5	1,089.0	1.82%	0.89%	1.82%	2.72%
27	Shift (+)	1,022.9	1,013.4	1,023.1	1,032.5	−1.76%	−0.87%	−1.77%	−2.62%
28	Twist (−)	1,088.0	1,030.5	1,077.8	1,145.4	4.48%	0.81%	3.48%	8.03%
29	Twist (+)	999.0	1,014.2	1,007.2	983.9	−4.06%	−0.79%	−3.30%	−7.20%
30	Butterfly (−)	1,050.4	1,026.6	1,060.2	1,074.3	0.88%	0.42%	1.79%	1.33%
31	Butterfly (+)	1,032.2	1,018.0	1,023.4	1,046.4	−0.87%	−0.42%	−1.74%	−1.30%

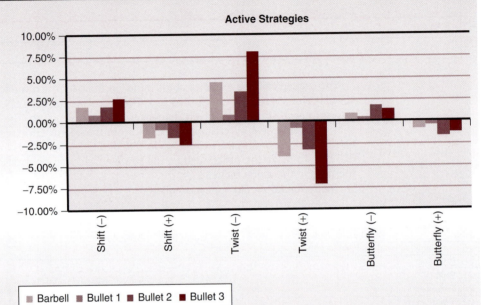

Active Strategies

Legend: Barbell · Bullet 1 · Bullet 2 · Bullet 3

As we would expect, the longest-duration bullet bond has the highest return when the yield curve shifts downward, whereas the shortest-duration bond is best when the curve shifts upward. Therefore, if we anticipate declining (rising) rates, we should extend (shorten) duration.

The barbell outperforms the bullet with the same duration when the curve flattens (negative twist) but underperforms the bullet with a steepening curve (positive twist). These moves actually reflect "bull flattening" and "bear steepening" because in our Term Structure spreadsheet "twist" induces a nonparallel increase/decrease in all spot rates. In anticipation of these moves, the manager would want to combine the barbell with extending overall duration (bull flattening) or the bullet with shortening overall duration (bear steepening).

Bullet 2 is the most sensitive to the butterfly movements because its maturity coincides with the kink in the yield curve: Yields at longer and shorter maturities move less. The barbell with the same duration as Bullet 2 outperforms that bond when the curve flexes upward and underperforms when the curve flexes downward.

A barbell position is more convex than an equal-duration bullet bond. Any fluctuation in rates will tend to cause the barbell to outperform the bullet. To avoid domination, the bullet must offer a higher yield. The required yield advantage rises or falls with the volatility of interest rates. If a manager believes a bullet's yield more than compensates for the likely volatility of rates, the manager should hold the bullet to collect the extra income and to capture the benefit of a reduction in the yield premium when the market comes around to the manager's view. Conversely, the barbell is appropriate when the bullet offers little extra yield or the market is underestimating the likely volatility of rates.[16]

The yield curve is usually upward-sloping. Therefore, bonds "roll down" the curve over time as their remaining maturities decline. A strategy known as "riding the yield curve" entails selecting the steepest portion of the yield curve and buying bonds with maturities at the longer end of that range. The implicit alternative is to hold a barbell of bonds with maturities in the flatter segments of the curve on each side. The idea is that the yield on the chosen bond will decline more rapidly as it rolls down the steep portion of the curve. What could go wrong? Managers typically employ this strategy at the shorter end of the yield curve because the curve is generally steepest there. Therefore, the path of short-term rates is critical to its success. In effect, riding the yield curve is a bet that the slope of the curve overstates the extent to which short-term rates will rise during the holding period. If not, the curve will flatten, mitigating or even eliminating the expected roll-down effect.

A similar strategy entails buying less liquid bonds that will roll into a more liquid portion of the curve. Recall that most secondary market trading occurs in a relatively few liquid issues. Liquidity in the Treasury market is concentrated in the maturities that the government includes in its regular auctions. As a reflection of their liquidity, these maturities, such as two years, five years, and ten years, trade at slightly lower yields than somewhat longer and shorter bonds. This lets active managers systematically buy slightly longer maturities and sell them when they have shortened to more liquid maturities. They will still not be as liquid as the bonds most recently issued at that maturity—the so-called "on-the-run" bonds—but potential arbitrage among virtually identical bonds with the same maturity allows the strategy to benefit as the bond rolls into the more liquid maturity. Of course the bond must be sold before it shortens even further and once again loses the liquidity premium.

It generally pays to take credit risk. That is, a portfolio of corporate bonds is highly likely to outperform an otherwise identical portfolio of Treasury securities over a sufficiently long horizon. This does *not* mean that corporate bonds are consistently underpriced in the market. Rather, it means that corporate bonds offer a risk premium over and above the amount needed to compensate for the actuarially expected value of credit losses. Just as stocks earn a risk premium, corporate bonds earn a credit risk premium. Many, and perhaps most, active fixed income managers take advantage of this premium by overweighting credit within their portfolios most of the time.

Exhibit 9.8 shows the extra return earned by the Barclays Credit index and three maturity-based subindexes relative to the corresponding Treasury indexes over various

---

[16] Of course options are the instrument of choice if one is looking for a pure play on volatility. For example, a straddle (that is, long a put and call with the same strike price) expresses no view on the direction of the market (or the shape of the yield curve) but benefits from high volatility.

EXHIBIT 9.8
Log Excess Returns on Barclays Credit Indexes versus Treasuries: Periods Ending 12/30/2007

	1–3 Years*	Intermediate	Long-Term	All Maturities
5 years	0.74%	0.88%	0.43%	0.70%
10 years	0.60%	0.54%	−0.52%	0.13%
15 years	0.66%	0.78%	−0.45%	0.43%
20 years		0.76%	−0.26%	0.55%
30 years		0.51%	−0.01%	0.21%
35 years		0.56%	0.03%	0.18%

* One- to three-year Treasury return series begins in 1992.

horizons ending 12/30/2007 (before the full credit crisis hit in 2008). The last five years of the sample were very favorable for credit instruments of all maturities. The longer periods, however, indicate that there has been little, if any, compensation for credit risk at the long end of the curve. As a result, managers tend to take credit risk primarily in short to intermediate maturities.

It is unclear why the credit risk premium tends to be especially attractive at short maturities. Nonetheless, these bonds generally offer disproportionately high yield spreads per unit of volatility. Combining this fact with the generally poor risk premium offered by long-term credit instruments leads to a **credit barbell** strategy: combining short-maturity corporate bonds with long-maturity government bonds.

So-called **crossover credits** (bonds rated just below investment grade by one rating agency and barely investment grade by another) also offer particularly attractive opportunities. Many fixed income mandates allow only investment-grade bonds. Consequently, those who can invest in bonds of only slightly lower quality tend to find attractive opportunities. Holders of these bonds can earn additional yield disproportionate to the incremental credit risk. In addition, the potential impact of an upgrade to an investment-grade rating makes crossover credits an especially fertile ground for managers who focus on analysis of individual credits.

The extra risk premium offered by crossover credits is an example of a more general proposition: Noneconomic barriers to the free flow of capital distort valuations, creating market segments offering exceptional risk–return trade-offs. Such opportunities are increasingly rare and fleeting, however, because levered investors with few restrictions, like hedge funds, can apply significant amounts of capital to exploiting and eliminating them.

Spread bets (also called relative value bets) are predicated on the notion that yield spreads tend to converge toward cross-sectional averages at any point in time, and these cross-sectional averages mean-revert over time. Thus outliers among similar securities will tend to converge toward a common spread. Similarly, the spread for, say, BAA bonds over Treasuries will revert toward an average level over time.

Exhibit 9.9 illustrates the spread trading opportunities arising from mean reversion in credit spreads. The exhibit shows the spread between the Barclays Intermediate Credit index and the Barclays Intermediate Treasury index, a trend line reflecting

EXHIBIT 9.9
Intermediate Credit Spread Trading Opportunities: Barclays Intermediate Credit versus Intermediate Treasury

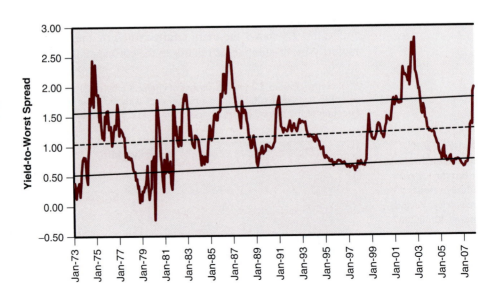

a gradual increase in the credit spread, and bands indicating ± 1 standard deviation around the trend line. Ideally we should use option-adjusted spreads (OAS) to correct for the impact of embedded options in the bonds underlying each index. However, OAS data extend back only a few years. Instead the exhibit reflects an older, cruder measure known as **yield-to-worst** (YTW). For each bond, the yield-to-worst is simply the yield-to-maturity calculated as if exercise of the embedded option(s) will occur at the worst possible time from the investor's perspective. Over the 35-year sample period of 1973–2007, the Intermediate Treasury index returned 7.86 percent annually while the Intermediate Credit index earned 8.44 percent. Switching between Treasuries and credit whenever the spread reached one standard deviation above or below the trend line would have boosted the return to 8.85 percent.

Interpretation of Exhibit 9.9, and the trading strategy it suggests, requires some care because it reflects an "in-sample" or ex post experiment. The trend line and standard deviation of the spread over the whole period were not known at the time each monthly investment decision would have been made. The exhibit therefore overstates the reliability of the trading signal provided by the yield spread. On the other hand, the trading strategy does not incorporate other information that would have been available to investors, such as economic indicators and corporate sector financial ratios. Combining such information with the yield spread might have provided an even more powerful trading strategy. Nonetheless, decisions always look easier with hindsight. Indeed, what the chart does not show is what happened in the next 12 months. After breaching the upper band in November 2007, the spread blew out to nearly 600 basis points in November 2008—roughly nine standard deviations above the trend and more than double the widest spread in the sample!

In most of the strategies we have discussed, selection of specific securities is a secondary consideration. The primary focus is on broader, more thematic sources of performance. In contrast, credit analysis is about selecting individual issuers and securities. For many managers who systematically overweight credit and eschew duration bets, bottom-up security selection is the primary source of potential value added.

Credit analysis has much in common with fundamental equity analysis. Both entail intensive scrutiny of a company's business, strategy, and financial position. However, credit analysts and equity analysts have different perspectives and emphasize different aspects of the firm's prospects. Indeed, because the interests of bondholders and shareholders often conflict, credit analysts and equity analysts may reach entirely different investment conclusions about the same firm.

For bondholders the key question is whether a borrower will make promised payments on time and in full. With rare exceptions, bondholders will not receive more than was promised. Ultimately the borrower must have cash to meet its obligations. Whereas equity analysts traditionally focus heavily on a company's earnings (that is, the income statement), credit analysts are usually more interested in the firm's statement of cash flow. Over time, of course, there should be a strong correspondence between earnings and cash flows, but the timing of revenue and cost recognition in the income statement can differ substantially from the timing of cash receipts and disbursements in the cash flow statement.

To illustrate this point, consider two firms. The first firm has announced it will undertake a substantial capital expenditure program to expand capacity over the next five years. The second firm, its competitor, will expand capacity by leasing rather than building and owning the new facilities. To a first approximation, the earnings implications of the two strategies are the same. An equity analyst might therefore be indifferent between the two announcements. The cash flow implications are quite different, however. The

Theory in Practice   *Chrysler's Secured Debt*

In principle, holders of secured debt must be paid in full before unsecured creditors receive anything. Reality is far less cut-and-dried, especially if the government gets involved.

There are two basic forms of corporate bankruptcy. A Chapter 7 filing implies that the firm is no longer a viable business and its assets will be liquidated to satisfy at least some of its obligations. A Chapter 11 filing means that the firm *may* be worth more as a going concern—if it can restructure its business and its liabilities. Successful reorganization means a larger pie divided among the claimants. Because each class of creditors (not every individual creditor) must approve the plan, senior claimants must often cede value to junior claimants to get the deal done. Depending on how the votes line up, small holders may be powerless, or they may wield disproportionate power as a blocking coalition. Therefore, bargaining power may be as important as priority of claim.

When Chrysler filed for bankruptcy on April 30, 2009, the U.S. government forced the 46 secured bondholders to accept roughly 29¢ on the dollar for $6.9 billion in debt. The secured debt holders received no ownership of the new entity that "bought" Chrysler's assets; but an unsecured creditor, the United Auto Workers union, received 55 percent ownership. The government was able to dictate terms to the secured bondholders because it was the only potential source of "debtor in possession" financing sufficient to allow Chrysler to avoid liquidation, and it made a credible threat to withhold that financing. The fact that the biggest holders of Chrysler secured debt had received government loans under the Troubled Asset Relief Program (TARP) might have been a factor as well.

How could the most senior claimants be treated so harshly? The bondholders had legal priority, but they did not have the bargaining power to enforce it. As one administration official observed, "You don't need banks and bondholders to make cars." Other observers thought the real issue was not making cars—it was winning elections.

Source: *The Wall Street Journal,* "U.S. Played Rough with Chrysler's Creditors," May 11, 2009, provides a blow-by-blow description of the battle.

---

first firm will have large cash outflows over the next five years, no subsequent cash outlays, and (noncash) depreciation charges against (cash) revenues for the life of the project. The second firm will make a steady stream of lease payments against (cash) revenues over the life of the project. At the time of the announcements, a credit analyst is likely to look more favorably on the second firm's bonds due to its steady cash flow pattern. The first firm's bondholders face much more uncertainty regarding the firm's ability to meet its obligations over the next five years.

Credit analysts also tend to focus more on a firm's balance sheet than do their equity analyst brethren. Of course both shareholders and bondholders care about the firm's overall debt-to-equity ratio. Beyond that, however, bondholders have a much keener interest in the details of the firm's liabilities because where a particular bond fits within the spectrum of obligations can make the difference between receiving full, timely payments and fighting for scraps on the creditors' committee. In general, it is better to get your payments earlier than the other creditors, so shorter maturities are usually safer. Similarly, it is better to have an explicit claim on specific assets, so secured bonds are safer than unsecured debt.

At the time of issuance, the rights of the bondholders and the obligations of the issuer are specified in detail in an **indenture** document. The indenture typically includes things that the issuer must do, known as **positive covenants,** and things the issuer cannot do unless certain conditions are satisfied; the latter are called **negative covenants.** One of the most important negative covenants pertains to the issuer's ability to borrow additional funds while the bonds remain outstanding. In general, subsequent borrowing tends to impair the position of existing bondholders, especially if the subsequent debt can have higher priority—that is, if it can be senior to the outstanding bonds. All else the same, therefore, bondholders want to place stringent conditions on subsequent borrowing.

As noted, the interests of bondholders and shareholders conflict. Indeed, once the bonds are outstanding their interests diverge. Of course both bondholders and shareholders generally benefit if a firm is successful. But beyond the point at which default is unlikely, most of the benefit accrues to the shareholders. The shareholders get all of the upside provided the bondholders receive their promised payments. If the bondholders are not paid in full, then at least in principle, the equity is worth nothing. Therefore, shareholders effectively own a call option on the value of the firm. Standard option theory implies that shareholders have an incentive to exploit the bondholders by increasing the volatility of the firm's outcomes. This can be done by increasing leverage (additional borrowing) or by taking more risk in the business. The only way bondholders can protect themselves is to have strong covenants in the indenture. Therefore, in addition to dissecting a firm's current financial statements, the credit analyst must assess how changes in financial structure might subsequently affect the holders of each bond issue.

Another type of bottom-up, relative value bet focuses on the structure of individual securities. There are three primary considerations: embedded options, the fixed or floating nature of interest payments, and the rules for sharing collateral cash flows among the tranches of securitized deals.

Traditionally borrowers issued fixed-coupon bonds with and without embedded call options based on their needs and their assessment of current market opportunities. That is, they sought to exploit the fact that investors, attracted by the higher coupons on callable bonds, sometimes charged too little for the call provision. Savvy investors could play the same game in the secondary market, trading between callable and noncallable bonds. Similarly, issuers would choose between fixed and floating coupons in an effort to minimize their ultimate financing costs. Typically they would issue fixed-coupon bonds when they expected rates to rise and floating paper if they expected lower rates. Investors, of course, wanted to buy the opposite: fixed-coupon bonds if rates were going to decline and floating-rate bonds in a rising rate scenario. Again, lack of clarity in the relative valuation of different structures provided opportunities for well-informed issuers and investors.

Two developments have taken much of the potential value added out of these traditional structural bets. First, the widespread use of option-adjusted valuation models has largely leveled the playing field with respect to valuation of embedded options. These models also assess the relative valuation of fixed versus floating coupons. As a result, few opportunities remain from gross errors in the valuation of standard structures. Second, the rapid growth and maturation of the interest rate swap market has provided a relatively liquid market in which issuers and investors can actively trade interest rate options as well as fixed versus floating rates. Therefore, structure bets now trade explicitly and independently of underlying bond issues. Both sides of the market, as well as dealers, can easily act upon and arbitrage away valuation discrepancies. The upshot is that the market is more efficient, and adding significant value through structural bets now requires a greater quotient of superior foresight.

The explosive growth of securitization has shifted the focus of structure bets to analysis of these more complex instruments. Whereas investment-grade bond issuers usually exercise embedded options rationally, there is overwhelming evidence that home owners and consumers do not make economically efficient use of their rights

Theory in Practice
Credit Default Swaps and Counterparty Risk

Credit default swaps (CDS) provide a mechanism for transferring default risk. The buyer of credit protection makes periodic payments to the seller in exchange for the promise of compensation if a specified issuer defaults on its debt during the term of the CDS. As shown in the following table, the cost of five-year credit protection on major U.S. banks increased dramatically during the 2008–2009 credit crisis.*

	June 6, 2008	April 3, 2009
Citigroup	118 basis points	640 basis points
Bank of America	86	354
JP Morgan	86	190

Before the crisis hit with full force, an investor could buy five-year credit protection on $1 million of Citigroup debt for $11,800 per year. At that time Bank of America and JP Morgan were priced as comparable credits. By April 3, 2009, with the market awaiting the outcome of the government's stress tests, the cost of five-year protection on $1 million of Citigroup debt had jumped to $64,000 per year, and protection on Bank of America was almost twice as expensive as on JP Morgan.

CDS are like insurance policies for holders of the underlying bonds. However, CDS buyers need not hold the underlying bonds, or indeed have any claim on the issuer. Thus, unlike true insurance policies, CDS do not require the buyers of protection to have an "insurable interest." In addition, the CDS market is unregulated, so sellers of credit protection are not subject to the kind of supervision and capital requirements faced by regulated insurance companies.

The unregulated nature of the CDS market was a major contributor to the near collapse of the global financial system in the fall of 2008. The volume of CDS outstanding dwarfed the underlying corporate credit market. That alone was a troubling sign because it suggested that the CDS market had grown far beyond facilitating risk transfer and had become an arena for speculation. In September 2008, coincident with the failure of Lehman Brothers, an unregulated unit of the giant insurer AIG was unable to meet mounting collateral calls on its massive short CDS positions. If it could not cover its obligations, the counterparties—many of the world's largest financial institutions—would be left exposed to potentially crippling losses. On September 16, in what proved to be only the first round of emergency financing for AIG, the U.S. government provided an $85 billion loan in exchange for nearly 80 percent ownership of the firm. With the collapse and rescue of AIG and the bankruptcy of Lehman Brothers in the same week, counterparty risk moved into the spotlight, and the credit crisis struck with a vengeance.

* Indicative pricing from Bloomberg.

with respect to loan payments. Similarly, institutional borrowers with poor credit or complex loan agreements may not be able to refinance efficiently. Sophisticated market participants may therefore place significantly different values on the same pool of loans based on differing assessments of borrower behavior. These differences cannot be arbitraged away. Slicing and dicing the cash flows from a pool of loans into various tranches compounds the potential for differential valuation by investors and magnifies the potential value added from superior analysis. Complex structures and unique or heterogeneous types of collateral increase the stakes. Investors in deals backed by so-called subprime mortgages found that out the hard way beginning in the first half of 2007.

9.6   Structured Portfolios

The hallmark of a structured portfolio is its one-to-one correspondence with a specific liability. The client dedicates a pool of assets to fund the liability and tasks the portfolio manager with customizing a portfolio to meet those obligations with a high degree of certainty. Because the liability is unique to the client's situation, so is the portfolio. Although institutional clients sometimes hire outside managers for relatively straightforward structured mandates, institutions with complex, mission-critical liability funding situations usually manage the fixed-income portfolio in-house.

The prototypical structured mandate involves funding a stream of known future cash flows. In practice, of course, some uncertainty surrounds the magnitude and timing of required payments.[17] Nonetheless, most of the discussion here maintains the assumption of a known liability stream. Two considerations help to justify this abstraction. First, the liability stream is usually highly predictable even if it is uncertain; if not, a structured portfolio mandate is probably inappropriate. Second, modest uncertainty with respect to the liabilities does not alter the essentials of the asset–liability problem.

Cash Matching

Suppose we need to fund a stream of future liability payments denoted by L_i at dates denoted by t_i. The obvious solution would be to create a portfolio with cash flows exactly matching these required payments—no more and no less. Unfortunately it is rarely possible to create such an ideal portfolio. Nonetheless, the logic of the approach is compelling. It is therefore useful to consider its practical limitations.

Implicit in the notion of cash flow matching is the requirement that enough cash must be available on or before the due date for each liability payment. That is, assets will not be sold to cover required payments, so the asset cash flows must occur earlier than the corresponding liability flows. Receiving cash earlier is, of course, more expensive. Therefore, a cash-matched portfolio generally costs more than the present value of the liability stream.

The potential to earn interest on cash balances somewhat mitigates the extra cost of the cash-matched portfolio. The interest earned on cash means that the cash flow from other assets can be slightly smaller and therefore less expensive. The offset is small, however, because prudence dictates a conservative assumption for the future interest rate on cash—generally well below the yield on longer-term bonds.

The cash flow pattern of a typical bond—small regular coupon payments with a large payment of principal at maturity—reinforces the cost implications of the cash-in-advance requirement. This pattern does not necessarily correspond well with the pattern of liability flows. Consider, for example, liability flows that are equal in magnitude. Matching such flows one-for-one with bond principal payments would waste the cost of the bond coupons. On the other hand, trying to fund a significant portion of each liability flow with coupons would tend to generate principal payments on some dates far in excess of the cash needed for those dates. Therefore, the cash-matched portfolio will represent a compromise between accumulating coupons to allow purchasing smaller principal amounts and buying large principal amounts on some dates to generate a significant flow of coupons at earlier dates. The upshot is that significant cash balances are likely to arise.

[17] See, for example, the discussion of DB plan liabilities in Chapter 2.

By its nature, a cash-matched portfolio is a conservative solution to the asset–liability problem. There is little point in imposing a cash-in-advance requirement without also limiting consideration to instruments entailing little, if any, uncertainty regarding the timing and magnitude of cash flows. Therefore, investment is limited to very high-quality bonds with known cash flows. Conceptually, zero-coupon Treasury securities are nearly ideal. They entail no credit risk, and there are no coupons to complicate targeting specific liability flows. Quarterly maturities are available out to 30 years. But their nature—default-free, liquid, and horizon-targeted—causes these securities to be expensive. Again, the practical problem with cash matching is the cost.

Immunization

The appeal of a perfectly cash-matched portfolio is that it will exactly fund the liability stream regardless of subsequent changes in interest rates. The idea underlying **immunization** is to fund the liability at lower cost with minimal risk of falling short due to interest rate movements. To attain a lower cost, the cash-in-advance requirement must be relaxed. That is, immunization allows asset sales as needed to cover required flows. The key question, of course, is how to control the interest rate risk.

Consider the simple case of a single liability payment, L_H, to be made on horizon date t_H. Recall from Section 9.2 that changes in the general level of interest rates have two opposing effects on a portfolio's return over a given horizon. An increase in rates reduces the horizon value of the portfolio because all subsequent cash flows are discounted more heavily. On the other hand, cash flows occurring before the horizon can be reinvested at a higher rate. The net effect depends on the relationship between the investment horizon and the portfolio duration.

Unfortunately we cannot make unambiguous statements about the balance between the capital gain and reinvestment effects of interest rate changes without some simplifying assumptions. The following proposition summarizes a key result:

Proposition: Define the **Macaulay duration** of a portfolio as

$$D_A^M \equiv \left(\frac{1}{PV} \right) \sum_i PV(A_i)\, t_i \tag{9.3}$$

where A_i denotes the cash flow at horizon t_i, $PV(A_i)$ denotes the present value of A_i, and PV is the total portfolio value—that is, the sum of the present values.

For portfolios with known cash flows, the Macaulay duration equals the modified duration as defined in Equation (9.2) times 1 plus the portfolio yield-to-maturity (y). That is,

$$D_A^M = (1 + y)D$$

Note that because yields are positive, the Macaulay duration exceeds the modified duration. Therefore, the Macaulay duration slightly overstates the sensitivity of a bond's price to changes in its yield (see the first term in Equation (9.1)).

If the term structure of interest rates is flat and there is a single, immediate parallel shift in the level of rates, then

- The portfolio return over horizon t_H is unchanged if $D_A^M = t_H$.
- The capital gain impact dominates if $D_A^M > t_H$.
- The reinvestment impact dominates if $D_A^M < t_H$.

This proposition has three important implications. First, to guard against parallel shifts in the yield curve, the Macaulay duration of an immunized portfolio must match the investment horizon. More generally, it needs to match the Macaulay duration of the liability stream. Second, matching duration protects against only parallel shifts in the term structure of interest rates. Third, because durations change with the passage of time and with each change in rates, an immunized portfolio requires monitoring and adjustment to maintain protection against subsequent rate movements.

Equation (9.3) indicates that the Macaulay duration is simply a weighted average of the times until receipt of each cash flow. The Macaulay duration of a zero-coupon bond is therefore equal to its remaining maturity. Therefore, the ideal immunized portfolio for a single-date liability is a zero-coupon bond with maturity matching the liability horizon. Because this is an exactly cash-matched portfolio, we know that in this special case matching Macaulay duration protects the portfolio from all interest rate risk—not just one-time parallel shifts.

Now suppose there is no zero-coupon bond with exactly the right maturity. To balance the risk of having to reinvest at low rates against the risk of having to sell securities at high rates, both longer and shorter maturities need to be incorporated so that the Macaulay duration remains equal to the liability horizon. Now, however, changes in the slope of the yield curve will affect the return. If the curve gets steeper, the horizon value of the longer cash flows will decline while reinvestment of the earlier flows will occur at reduced rates. Both effects imply that the portfolio will not generate enough value to cover the liability at the horizon. Of course the reverse occurs if the curve becomes flatter rather than steeper: The portfolio will generate more than enough to cover the liability.

It should be apparent that concentrating the asset cash flows as close to the liability horizon as possible mitigates the risk arising from changes in the slope of the yield curve. By doing so, the earlier cash flows will not be reinvested for long, so their accumulated value at the horizon will be relatively insensitive to the reinvestment rate. Similarly, the value of the remaining, longer cash flows as of the horizon date will not be very sensitive to the rates prevailing at that time.

A measure called **dispersion,** denoted by I_A and defined as

$$I_A \equiv \left(\frac{1}{PV}\right) \sum_i PV(A_i)(t_i - D_A^M)^2 \qquad (9.4)$$

quantifies the concentration of cash flows. Note that dispersion is analogous to a variance. The Macaulay duration takes the place of the mean. The fractions of total asset value contributed by each cash flow, $[PV(A_i)/PV]$, take the place of probabilities.

The foregoing discussion suggests that the immunized portfolio should have three properties. First, its cost should be equal to the present value of the liability stream so that the liability is fully, but not overly, funded. Second, it should have a Macaulay duration equal to the liability horizon. Third, among portfolios satisfying the first two criteria, it should have the lowest possible dispersion.

Now consider the more general case in which liability payments are due at multiple horizons. As it turns out, this requires only a slight modification of the preceding analysis. The cost of the immunized portfolio should still equal the present value of the liability stream. The duration criterion generalizes straightforwardly to require equating the Macaulay duration of the portfolio with that of the liability stream. But a complication arises with respect to the dispersion of asset cash flows versus the dispersion of liability cash flows. The prior discussion suggests that it would be a good idea to match the dispersion of the liability payments. However, if that is not feasible, should the asset flows be more dispersed or less dispersed than the liability payments?

To answer this question, we need to consider the second-order effects of interest rate changes on the value of the assets and the liabilities. Recall from the discussion accompanying Equation (9.1) that duration captures only the impact of small yield changes. For larger movements, the convexity term of that equation becomes important. For equal duration, higher convexity leads to a better return irrespective of the direction of rates. Therefore, the immunized portfolio needs to be at least as convex as the liability stream. It turns out that with equal durations and present values, this is exactly equivalent to requiring that the portfolio cash flows be more dispersed than the liability payments. Given this fact, the problem of selecting an immunized portfolio becomes:

$$\text{Minimize } I_A \quad \text{subject to} \quad PV(A) = PV(L) \qquad \textbf{(9.5)}$$

$$D_A^M = D_L^M$$

$$I_A \geq I_L$$

The Solver in Excel can handle this problem quite easily. The only required inputs are the cash flows and discount rates for both the liability and the potential bond investments. Ideally, a complete term structure of spot rates should be used to discount the cash flows. The decision variables are the par amounts (or equivalently the portfolio weights) to invest in each bond.

Excel Outbox

Immunization

with Multiple

Liability Flows

This Excel exercise examines immunization of multiple liability flows and the impact of both shifts and twists on the immunization.

Use the worksheet <Immunization–Template> in the spreadsheet Chapter 09 Excel Outboxes.xls.

In setting up the main table, use "Paste Special-Formulas" to avoid overwriting formats. Cells B7:H9 reference the <Term Structure> worksheet.

- In cell B7 enter = 'Term Structure'!B9. Copy to cells C7:H7. Then copy cells C7:H7 to cells C8:H9.
- In cell B13 enter =SUM(C13:H13).
- In cell B14 enter =SUM(C14:H14).
- In cell B15 enter =SUM(C15:H15).
- In cell B16 enter =SUM(C16:H16).
- Copy B13:B16 to B21:B24 .

Rows 10 and 11 contain two liability cash flow streams, and row 12 totals the liability flows.

- In cell D10 enter 12000, and in cell G11 enter 13000.
- In cell C12 enter = sum(C10:C11). Copy to cells D12:H12.

Rows 13–16 compute the PV, duration, and dispersion of the liabilities. Rows 21–24 compute the PV, duration, and dispersion of the asset portfolio.

- In cell C13 enter = C12*(1 + 'Term Structure'!C$12)^−C$8.
- In cell C14 enter = C13/$B13.
- In cell C15 enter = C14*C$8.

- In cell C16 enter = C14*(C$8−$B15)^2.
- Copy cells C13:C16 to cells D13:H16.
- Copy cells C13:C16 to cells C21:C24, and then copy cells C21:C24 to cells D21:H24.

Rows 17–20 set up the cash flows of the three bonds listed at the top of the template.

- In cell C17 enter = ($B$4/2)*$B$5.
- In cell C18 enter = ($C$4/2)*$C$5, and then copy to cells D18:E18.
- In cell C19 enter = ($D$4/2)*$D$5, and then copy to cells D19:G19.
- In cell D17 enter = $B$5 + ($B$4/2)*$B$5.
- In cell F18 enter = $C$5 + ($C$4/2)*$C$5.
- In cell H19 enter = $D$5 + ($D$4/2)*$D$5.
- In cell C20 enter = $B$3*C17 + $C$3*C18 + $D$3*C19, and then copy to cells D20:H20.

Row 25 computes the FV of the surplus (assets−liabilities) as of the final liability cash flow.

- In cell C25 enter = (C$20−C$12)*(1 + 'Term Structure'!G$13)^C$9.
- In cell D25 enter = (D$20−D$12)*(1 + 'Term Structure'!$G14)^D$9.
- In cell E25 enter = (E$20−E$12)*(1 + 'Term Structure'!$G15)^E$9.
- In cell F25 enter = (F$20−F$12)*(1 + 'Term Structure'!$G16)^F$9.
- In cell G25 enter = (G$20−G$12)*(1 + 'Term Structure'!$G17)^G$9.
- In cell H25 enter = (H$20−H$12)*(1 + 'Term Structure'!$H17)^H$9.
- In cell B25 enter =SUM(C25:H25).

To determine the immunized portfolio:

- In Solver
  - Minimize B24.
  - By changing B3:D3.
  - Subject to B21 = B13; B23 = B15; B24 ≥ B16.
  - Solve.

The results should look like this:

	A	B	C	D	E	F	G	H
1	**Multi-Liability Immunization**							
2	Bond	Aug 2009n	Aug 2010n	Aug 2011n				
3	#:	8.94	9.73	4.69				
4	C:	5.00%	4.00%	3.00%				
5	F:	1,000	1,000	1,000				
6								
7	Date	15-Sep-08	15-Feb-09	15-Aug-09	15-Feb-10	15-Aug-10	15-Feb-11	15-Aug-11
8	Time		0.42	0.92	1.42	1.92	2.42	2.92
9	T-t		2.00	1.50	1.00	0.50	0.00	−0.50
10	Liability 1			12,000				
11	Liability 2						13,000	
12	CF		−	12,000	−	−	13,000	−
13	PV	23,783	−	11,679	−	−	12,104	−
14	X:	1.00	0.00	0.49	0.00	0.00	0.51	0.00
15	D	1.68	0.00	0.45	0.00	0.00	1.23	0.00
16	Dispersion	0.56	0.00	0.29	0.00	0.00	0.28	0.00
17	Aug 2009n		25.00	1025.00				
18	Aug 2010n		20.00	20.00	20.00	1020.00		
19	Aug 2011n		15.00	15.00	15.00	15.00	15.00	1015.00
20	CF		488.31	9426.80	264.85	9991.46	70.32	4758.27
21	PV	23783	482.34	9174.81	253.99	9441.14	65.47	4365.23
22	X:	1.00	0.02	0.39	0.01	0.40	0.00	0.18
23	D:	1.68	0.01	0.35	0.02	0.76	0.01	0.54
24	Dispersion	0.56	0.03	0.22	0.00	0.02	0.00	0.28
25	FV of Surplus	(0)	518	(2,690)	273	10,140	(12,930)	4,688

(continued)

(continued)

Note that the negative cash flows and FVs for August 2009 and February 2011 imply that assets will have to be sold to cover liability payments.

The next tables explore the impact of term structure movements:

- In cell B36 enter = $B$25.
- In cell C36 enter = SUM($C$25:$F$25).
- In cell D36 enter = $H$25.
- In cell E30 enter = B30−B$36, and then copy to E31:E42.
- In cell F30 enter = C30−C$36, and then copy to F31:F42.
- In cell G30 enter =D30-D$36, and then copy to G31:G42.
- Copy cells B30:G42 to cells C47:H59.
- In cells F47:H59, replace all occurrences of "$36" with $53.

For term structure shifts:

- Enter −0.03 in cell B4 of the Term Structure tab, and then copy and paste values from B36:D36 to B30:D30.
- Repeat for the indicated shifts from −0.02 to 0.03.
- Reset B4 on the Term Structure tab to 0.

The chart should look like this:

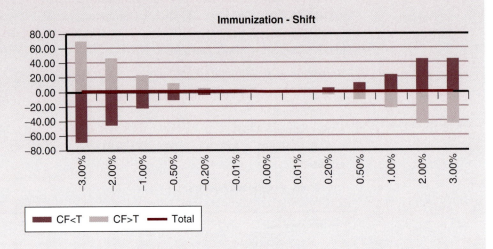

The total FV of the surplus is virtually unaffected by parallel shifts because the FVs of net cash flows before and after the horizon change by offsetting amounts. Increases in yield imply higher reinvestment income on early net cash flows but lower value as of the horizon date for net cash flows to be received beyond that date. The opposite is true when the term structure shifts downward.

We will examine twists around the 1.92 horizon—that is, the yield at a maturity of 1.92 will stay (approximately) constant. Due to the way the <Term Structure> sheet is constructed, this will require entering a shift as well as the twist.

- Enter −0.0075 in cell B5 and +0.0144 in cell B4 of the Term Structure tab, and then copy and paste values from C53:E53 to C47:E47.
- Repeat for the twists indicated in column A and the corresponding shifts in column B.
- Reset B4 and B5 on the Term Structure tab to 0.

The resulting graph should look like this:

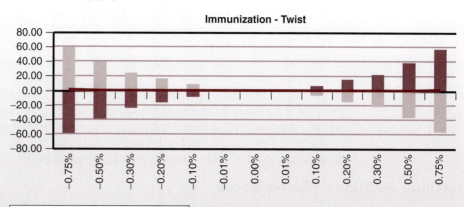

Because we matched the dispersion of the liability stream, the surplus at the horizon date is insensitive to changes in the slope of the term structure. Steepening of the curve reduces the value of the cash flow to be received after the horizon date because it is discounted more heavily. The FV of the cash flows received and reinvested before the horizon increases because a steeper curve implies higher forward rates.* To see this, examine what happens to cells G13:G16 in the <Term Structure> worksheet. These forward rates were used as the reinvestment rates for the cash flows received before the horizon date (look at cells C25:F25 in this worksheet). Flattening the curve has the opposite effect: The value of the distant cash flow increases while the FV of the early cash flows declines.

Note that there is no guarantee that the implicit reinvestment rates in this analysis will be realized. For example, in the twist = +.0075 scenario, the implied reinvestment rate for the one-year period from February 2010 to February 2011 is 4.44 percent (look at cell G15 in the <Term Structure> worksheet). But after the specified twist/shift combination, the 0.92-year spot rate is 2.25 percent. Therefore, the forward rate builds in an increase in the one-year spot rate of roughly 219 basis points by the time the February 2010 cash flow is reinvested. If, however, market rates have not changed by that time, the reinvestment will have to be made at 2.25 percent—a much less favorable outcome. This is the outcome that was implicitly assumed in the text when it was stated that a steeper curve meant less attractive reinvestment opportunities.

* Recall that forward rates are the implicit interest rates linking spot rates of different maturities. For example, if the three-year spot rate is 5 percent and the two-year spot rate is 4.5 percent, then the implicit one-year rate two years forward is 6.01 percent because $(1.05)^3 = (1.045)^2 * (1.0601)$.

Contingent Immunization

Suppose a pension fund or other entity with well-defined liabilities has more than enough assets to create an immunized portfolio; that is, it has a surplus. One appealing strategy would be to establish the immunized portfolio—effectively a customized riskless asset—and invest the surplus funds in a more aggressive, total return portfolio. If the risky portfolio performs well, the surplus will grow. If not, the potential damage is limited because the immunized portfolio is there to cover the liabilities.

Contingent immunization carries this idea a giant step further. Unless the assets drop to a level just sufficient to immunize the liabilities, there would seem to be no reason to fund the more conservative, immunized portfolio. Instead invest all the assets in the more aggressive, total return portfolio in an effort to increase the surplus more rapidly. Only if the surplus evaporates is the immunized portfolio actually established. At that point, of course, it will require all the available assets.

This strategy is similar to the constant proportional portfolio insurance (CPPI) strategy discussed in Chapter 5. Each attempts to benefit from the higher expected return on the risky portfolio without giving up the downside protection of the riskless portfolio. CPPI uses a gradual adjustment mechanism that shifts between the two portfolios in response to changes in the surplus. Contingent immunization involves a one-time movement of all assets between the two portfolios if and only if the surplus falls to zero. The Achilles heel of both strategies is the danger of failing to complete the transition into the riskless portfolio at the critical time.

Matching Additional Risk Measures

The discussion up to this point has assumed that the required liability payments are fixed. More generally, there is no predictable relationship between the timing or magnitude of the payments and market movements. In many instances, however, choices available to either the payer or the receiver link the liabilities—implicitly or explicitly—to market movements. In that case matching the broadest characteristics of the liability stream (duration, dispersion or convexity, and market value) may not ensure adequate risk control.

As a simple example, consider an annuity contract calling for fixed monthly payments for 30 years based on 5 percent market rates; that is, the scheduled payments are identical to a 30-year mortgage at 5 percent. Suppose, however, that the owner of the annuity can cancel it after five years and receive a refund of the remaining principal. In effect, the owner of the annuity has a put option, which changes the nature of the liability significantly. Effective duration will decrease substantially as rates rise because potential cancellation limits the decline in liability value. On the other hand, lower rates will still increase the value. Therefore, effective convexity is increased by the cancellation feature. Standard option pricing arguments imply that duration, convexity, and the liability's value will now depend on interest rate volatility. They will also be sensitive to the slope of the yield curve because a steep curve implies rising rates and higher likelihood of contract cancellation.

The challenge of matching a liability involving complex embedded options was encountered earlier in the context of passive management. There the relevant liabilities were the subindexes composed of mortgage-backed securities (MBS) and callable bonds. The problem is that risk measures such as duration and convexity are snapshots. Simply matching these statistics at one point in time does not ensure that they will remain matched over time as market conditions change, especially when there are embedded options. In the context of passive management, we can address this problem by stratifying the subindex based on characteristics relevant to exercise of the specific embedded options, such as coupon, seasoning, and program for MBS. While imperfect, the stratification helps limit the degree to which the portfolio's characteristics drift relative to the index.

Stratification works well for index replication because the liability is simply a portfolio of existing securities. In the case of a unique liability stream, the stratification approach is not so straightforward because the liability does not necessarily correspond to any portfolio of standard securities. The alternative is greater emphasis on matching risk measures.

In the presence of embedded options, calculating accurate risk measures requires a valuation model that reflects the dynamics of term structure movements. The general idea is the same as we described in Section 9.2 for calculating effective duration and convexity. After calibrating the model to current market parameters, such as the term structure and interest rate volatility, the parameters are perturbed—individually or in combination. The resulting price changes are divided by the size of the parameter shifts to obtain standardized sensitivities. Similarly, measures reflecting the pattern of cash flows, such as dispersion, use the model to determine *expected* cash flows reflecting the implied probabilities of interest rate movements.

The cancellable annuity example suggests the type of additional sensitivities that are likely to be most relevant. First, as with any situation involving options, changes in volatility are important. Second, changes in the shape of the yield curve imply changes in the probabilities of future interest rate movements; hence it is important to measure the impact of standardized changes in the slope and shape of the curve. And third, concentration of potential option exercise at specific horizons may make the value and risk characteristics of the liabilities particularly sensitive to rates at specific points on the yield curve. Such sensitivity is captured by so-called **key rate durations.** These are calculated by dividing the term structure into segments, each centered on a key maturity, and measuring the price impact of shifting each segment in isolation. In effect, the key rate durations are a decomposition of the total duration into the portions due to each maturity range.

It may be possible to enhance the effectiveness of matching risk measures by identifying important components of the liability structure and, using derivatives, creating synthetic securities approximating that structure. The idea is essentially the same as for stratification: The risk characteristics of the portfolio are much more likely to *stay* matched to those of the liabilities if the assets share as much of the underlying structure as possible.

As an example, suppose our cancellable fixed annuity describes at least a portion of the liabilities reasonably well. We might create an asset that pays a fixed amount for 30 years but terminates with return of principal if long-term rates are above 5 percent in 5 years. To do so, combine the following three positions:[18]

- Buy a 5-year floating-rate note paying the London Interbank Offer Rate (LIBOR).
- Enter a 30-year interest rate swap agreeing to make floating-rate interest payments at LIBOR in exchange for *receiving* fixed-rate payments at 5 percent.
- Buy a "swaption" conferring the right to enter a 25-year swap at the end of 5 years, *paying* 5 percent and receiving LIBOR.

At the end of five years, if rates are above 5 percent, exercising the swaption offsets the original swap, and the floating-rate note matures. The position effectively terminates with return of the principal. If rates are below 5 percent, the swaption is worthless and the original swap remains in effect. The floating-rate note can be rolled over into a sequence of short-term notes paying LIBOR. Because the interest on the floating-rate note covers the required floating-rate payments on the swap, the position generates a sequence of fixed cash flows at 5 percent.

[18] For a brief description of interest rate swaps, see the Theory in Practice: The Swap Curve and Swap Spreads box in Section 9.2. A "swaption" is simply an option to enter into a specified swap position in the future.

Summary

Fixed-income instruments promise the holder specific payments, at specific times, under specific conditions. Therefore, the focus of fixed-income analysis is primarily on valuation of known (albeit often contingent) cash flows. The essential challenge for the fixed-income portfolio manager is to buy cash flows at the lowest possible price. In this sense, fixed-income investing is always about the income.

Equity portfolio managers are typically assigned to either replicate (passive management) or beat (active management) a benchmark market index. Implicit in these mandates is a focus on total return over an indefinite horizon. Although many fixed-income mandates share this perspective, the inherent properties of fixed-income instruments make them especially useful whenever cash flow requirements or specific investment horizons are important considerations. More broadly, fixed income is usually the primary investment vehicle whenever a well-defined liability must be satisfied with a high degree of certainty.

After a review of key bond market characteristics and concepts, this chapter addressed essential considerations in managing passive, active, and structured fixed-income portfolios. The discussion of passive portfolio management illustrated much of the detail involved in this heterogeneous, complex asset class. The treatment of active management highlighted some of the value-added strategies that every fixed-income portfolio manager should know. The classic structured portfolio techniques of cash matching, immunization, and contingent immunization were developed in an intuitive and logical progression. The chapter concluded by considering the complexities arising from uncertain liabilities.

Problems

1. What innovations account for the rapid growth in the variety of fixed-income instruments over the last 40 years?

2. Aside from changes in the general level of interest rates, what is the primary source of risk faced by holders of mortgage-backed securities (MBS)? How does this affect the duration and convexity of these securities?

3. How does trading in the bond market differ from trading in the equity market?

4. Distinguish between a primary market and a secondary market. Which best characterizes the stock market? The bond market? Why?

5. What conditions are sufficient to ensure that the return on a standard fixed-coupon bond is equal to its yield-to-maturity? What are the implications of dropping each of these conditions?

6. Over what horizon do the capital gain and reinvestment impacts of yield changes (approximately) balance out? Which dominates over shorter horizons? Over longer horizons?

7. A fixed-income instrument is currently priced at 100.25. Your valuation model indicates a price of 102.30 at a yield 50 basis points (0.5 percent) lower and a price of 96.70 at a yield 50 basis points higher. What is the effective duration of the instrument? What is its effective convexity? Is it likely that the instrument involves any embedded options? If so, are the options more likely to favor the investor or the issuer? Based on that view, would you expect the option-adjusted spread on this instrument to be greater than, equal to, or less than its nominal yield spread?

8. Why is the term structure of interest rates central to fixed-income analysis and portfolio management? What is a spot rate? All else the same, should a bond manager focus on the risk of shifts, twists, or butterflies?

9. Which will typically provide a higher return when the term structure steepens—a bullet or an equal-duration barbell position? What if the term structure flattens? Which usually offers a higher (weighted-average) yield-to-maturity? Why is a yield differential sustainable?

10. What do the empirical data suggest about the potential diversification benefits of combining stocks and bonds? Do the data support the notion that stocks are a good hedge against inflation? What about the notion that stocks are less risky in the long run?

11. Suppose the standard deviations of nominal stock returns, nominal bond returns, and unexpected inflation are 20 percent, 5 percent, and 3 percent respectively and that the correlation of nominal stock and bond returns with unexpected inflation are each 0.30. Compute the correlation of real stock and bond returns with unexpected inflation. [Recall that real return = nominal return − inflation.]

12. From the perspective of a portfolio manager, what is the fundamental distinction between a total return mandate and a structured mandate? Under what circumstances is a client likely to choose a structured mandate?

13. Explain the rationale for each of the following in managing a passive bond portfolio:

    a. Matching duration.

    b. Matching the distribution of cash flows.

    c. Stratifying the index on multiple dimensions.

    d. Matching contribution to duration by sector and issuer.

    e. Separate consideration of securities with and without embedded options.

14. Explain the rationale underlying (a) a credit barbell strategy, (b) an emphasis on crossover credits, and (c) rolling down the curve.

15. What is the key assumption underlying yield–spread trading strategies? Why might they be less profitable in real time than they appear in hindsight? Is the growth of hedge funds likely to make these trades more or less reliable as a source of active returns? Did it work for Long-Term Capital Management (LTCM)?

16. XYZ Corporation is coming with a large new issue of corporate debt. Your colleague informs you that your firm's equity analysts know the firm well and have given it their highest rating. He says you can rely on their recommendation and buy the new bonds for your fixed-income portfolios. How should you respond?

17. It could be argued that creating structured instruments and trading them profitably is all about making things too complicated for most people to understand or value. What developments have mitigated this effect with respect to traditional structures such as embedded options? What role did this notion play in the credit crisis of 2008–2009? Why might it make the 2008–2009 crisis more difficult to solve than the LTCM crisis in 1998? [*Note:* This requires some research into each of these crises.]

18. Explain the pros and cons of cash matching versus immunization for funding a liability stream.

19. Explain why each of the following conditions is important for an immunized portfolio: (a) equating the value of the assets to the value of the liabilities, (b) equating

the Macaulay duration of the assets and liabilities, and (c) requiring that the cash flows of the assets be at least as dispersed as the liabilities. Suppose the available assets exceed the present value of the liabilities; that is, there is a surplus. Would it still be a good idea to match the duration of the liabilities?

20. In practice, liability streams are rarely known with absolute certainty. Which is likely to be more problematic for portfolio management—uncertainty arising from the deliberate choices of other agents, such as redemptions, or uncertainty arising from involuntary events, such as mortality and accidents? Why?

21. Repeat the analysis in the "Immunization with Multiple Liability Flows" Excel Outbox requiring the dispersion of the asset flows to be positive but not necessarily greater than the dispersion of the liabilities. Do not allow short positions. How does this change the results?

Chapter 10

Global Investing

10.1 Introduction

Up to this point, we have not needed to distinguish between domestic and foreign investments when introducing general portfolio management techniques. All the discussion in the prior chapters applies to both domestic and international investment perspectives. However, international investing introduces additional considerations for portfolio management. The most significant of these arise from the need to manage currency exposure. Hence much of this chapter focuses on the impact of currency on portfolio decisions.

Expanding to a global investment perspective typically requires some changes for both the client and the portfolio manager. For the client, the changes entail a new or modified investment policy statement. To implement the new mandate, the portfolio manager must revamp some aspects of the investment process. The next section discusses the necessary changes in each of these areas.

If foreign markets simply offered "more of the same," the benefits of international investing would be somewhat limited. As we show in Section 10.3, however, this is not the case. In particular, U.S. and non-U.S. markets differ in both composition and risk–return characteristics. Thus international equities and bonds offer investors expanded opportunities.

Although both foreign stocks and bonds entail currency exposure, currency management is a more important consideration for bond investors. Currency exposure substantially increases both the risk and the potential return of unhedged foreign bonds. On the other hand, currency-hedged bond returns are quite similar and highly correlated across markets. Hence passively eliminating currency exposure diminishes the potential value added from international bonds. In contrast, hedging or not hedging currency exposure has only a modest impact on the risk–return characteristics of international equity markets. Therefore equity managers often treat currency as "noise," whereas bond managers actively manage the exposure.

Currency management decisions are considered in detail in Section 10.4. We first develop the fundamental *covered interest parity* relationship linking interest rates and currencies. Building on this relationship, we examine four basic strategies: no currency hedging, direct hedging, cross-hedging, and proxy hedging. Our analysis shows that currency decisions and underlying asset decisions can be made independently. The final portion of Section 10.4 explicitly incorporates uncertainty about underlying asset returns. With uncertain asset returns, standard "static" hedges do not eliminate currency risk. Achieving a complete hedge requires a dynamic trading strategy involving both the currency-hedging instrument and the underlying asset.

Does international investing deliver on the promise of diversification? It is now widely recognized that correlations among markets tend to be higher during periods of high volatility or falling markets. The implication would seem to be that international investing fails to deliver diversification just when it would be most beneficial. As we discuss in Section 10.5, this simple logic fails to account for the impact of ex post conditioning on extreme outcomes. Unfortunately, more sophisticated statistical analysis supports the notion that international diversification is less effective than average correlation levels suggest. To make matters worse, the common practice of using active managers to fulfill an asset allocation may further compromise diversification if these managers systematically tilt toward more highly correlated markets.

What are the implications of economic and financial integration for global investing? Global capital mobility raises a fundamental question for bond investors: What makes foreign bonds different? To answer this question, Section 10.6 examines the conditions under which two markets share a common yield curve. It turns out that this is really about the currency. For equity investors, globalization raises the issue of whether industry-specific factors or country-specific factors are now more important drivers of stock returns. Section 10.6 reviews recent evidence in the industry-versus-country debate and the implications for the global investment process.

Some clients hire a currency overlay manager to manage their aggregate currency exposure, leaving their various asset managers free to focus on selecting stocks and bonds. Similarly, it is often advantageous to assign responsibility for currency and asset decisions to specialists within a portfolio management team. However, separating asset and currency decisions may lead to suboptimal decisions unless the mandates assigned to each manager are incentive-compatible. Section 10.7 shows how to set up incentive-compatible mandates.

10.2 Investing with a Global Perspective

Is international investing really different? The answer depends on whether we are looking at "the forest" from a high altitude or we are on the ground surrounded by "the trees." From ground level, the differences among markets are often quite apparent. Laws, regulations, and economic policies are different. Accounting standards are different. Market conventions, business practices, and available resources are different. Wealth and income distributions, production technologies, spending patterns, and social norms are different . . . and so on. Together these differences imply that global investing offers not merely more choices, but truly differentiated opportunities to enhance return and reduce risk.

In 1776 a Bostonian might have considered an investment in, say, South Carolina to be foreign. Other than being subjects of the same distant king, Massachusetts and South Carolina had little in common. The available modes of transportation and communication made them geographically distant and economically distinct. One had an agrarian economy based on slave labor; the other had a commercial and industrial economy based on trade, manufacturing, and services. Each had its own government, customs, culture, resources and currency.* These factors would have contributed to both the risk and the potential reward of a "foreign" investment in South Carolina. These same factors—laws and regulations, government policies, resources and industrial composition, technology, currencies and financial systems, customs and cultures—differentiate foreign and domestic investment opportunities today.

* A brief history of currencies in the colonies can be found at www.coins.nd.edu/ColCurrency.

From a higher-level perspective, however, many of these differences fade into the background. Although they are important for assessing the attractiveness of particular investments, they do not introduce fundamentally new considerations for portfolio management. Therefore, we will not delve deeply into the details of specific markets and instruments.

International investing does introduce one key consideration for portfolio management: currency. In a global portfolio, we must manage both the underlying assets and the currency exposures arising from those assets. Much of this chapter will therefore deal with the impact of currency on portfolio decisions. The remainder of this section addresses incorporating a global perspective into the investment policy statement and the operational changes that are typically required to accommodate international investment.

The Investment Policy Statement Revisited

The investment policy statement (IPS) translates the client's needs into an understandable investment plan. Suppose a client has an IPS in place but wants to shift to a global investment perspective. What changes would this require in the IPS?

Recall from Chapter 2 that the most vital sections of the IPS are the objectives and the constraints. Here we briefly outline the likely changes to each of these sections:

- Objectives
  - Return
  - Risk

Although the client's overall risk and return objectives may not be affected by shifting to a global perspective, protection of purchasing power may play a more prominent, or at least a more explicit, role. Exposure to foreign currencies can help hedge against sustained erosion in the purchasing power of the client's home currency. On the other hand, substantial currency exposure tends to increase shorter-term volatility. Thus both the risk and return objectives need to address the expected benefits and risks of currency exposure.

Explicit risk and return expectations need to reflect the expanded opportunity set. Extra care may be required to ensure that expectations reflect realistic assessments of future opportunities rather than extrapolations of prior results. Investors are often attracted to foreign markets following strong performance relative to their domestic market, but there may be little reason to expect this relative performance to persist in the future. Extrapolating past currency trends is a particularly seductive, but dangerous, trap for the unwary.

If risk and return objectives are stated relative to a benchmark, a new benchmark must be selected reflecting the expanded investment opportunity set. Even if relative risk–return objectives are not specified, an appropriate benchmark is needed for performance analysis.

- Constraints
  - Time horizon

Shifting to a global perspective should not alter the client's investment horizons, but the time horizon may impose constraints on foreign exposures, especially with respect to currency. Because currencies tend to be volatile over short horizons, investors with relatively short horizons may need to limit overall currency exposure. The same would be true for higher-risk international assets such as emerging markets.

  - Liquidity

Investors with high liquidity needs will want to maintain that liquidity in the currency (or currencies) in which they anticipate critical disbursements. Other investors may need to allow for the fact that various foreign markets, especially emerging markets, are generally somewhat less liquid than U.S. markets. However, for most investors liquidity considerations should not impede investment in publicly traded foreign securities.

  - Taxes

Many foreign securities are subject to withholding taxes on interest and dividend payments. Tax treaties between countries usually allow investors to reclaim some or all of these taxes. The IPS may need to address these taxes, especially if full recovery may not be possible for some investments.

  - Legal

Foreign investments should not raise special legal considerations for most investors. However, clients with complex tax or legal situations may need to address this issue explicitly. Less developed markets may sometimes institute restrictions on capital movement, so special attention should be given to legal guidelines for investing in emerging markets.

  - Unique

By definition, unique constraints are idiosyncratic to the client. These considerations may, for example, imply limitations on specific countries or instruments. If so, these limits would be addressed here.

Operational Considerations for International Investing

With the help of modern communication technology it is easier than ever to manage a global portfolio from one central location, such as New York. But there is no way to get around the fact that various markets operate in different time zones and are subject to local rules about trading and settlement. Even if a security trades "after hours" in another market center, the home market is almost always deeper and more liquid. The upshot is that geography still matters, at least for trading and for the operational aspects of international investing.

To illustrate this point, consider a Boston fund manager investing in Japanese securities. Depending on daylight savings time, Tokyo is 13 or 14 hours ahead of Boston. The Tokyo market is closed during the normal Boston workday and vice versa. Delivery of Japanese securities must occur in Tokyo time in accordance with local market procedures, and settlement will of course be in yen. To handle delivery and settlement, the Boston investor needs a custodian bank operating in the Tokyo market. Of course the manager will need similar services in other markets too. Thus the manager typically uses one of the giant custodial banks, like Citibank, to maintain custody operations in all the major financial centers. The main custodian bank arranges for subcustodians in markets it does not service directly. Similarly, to access the depth and liquidity of local markets, the manager may need to staff the trading desk around the clock or even have a desk in each major time zone.

Geography may be important in investment decision making as well. At one end of the spectrum, a global index fund manager has relatively little need for continuous access to specialized local knowledge and analysis. On the other hand, a manager who takes concentrated positions in small-cap companies may need to devote significant resources to maintaining investment personnel in the local market. The latter also has a greater need to maintain relationships with local broker–dealers and other financial institutions that are plugged into the flow of information via their local clientele.

Time zone differences also create pricing issues for global portfolios. U.S. mutual funds strike their net asset values (NAVs) at 4:00 New York time. At that point "today's" prices for Japanese securities are already 13–14 hours old, but the market in Tokyo has not yet opened for "tomorrow." Using stale prices to set NAVs would enable investors to buy and sell fund shares based on knowledge of subsequent news. To eliminate, or at least mitigate, this opportunity, funds have adopted so-called fair value pricing methods that may update prices at 4:00 ET based on models of cross-market security correlations.

10.3   Global Investment Opportunities

It is axiomatic that expanding the investment opportunity set beyond the domestic market cannot make investors worse off. But if foreign markets offered the same opportunities as domestic ones, the benefit might be rather limited, especially for investors whose domestic market already offers a broad and deep menu of liquid investments. In this section we briefly examine the composition and performance of global stock and bond markets.

Global Equity Opportunities

Exhibits 10.1–10.3 reflect the composition of the MSCI World index, an index of 23 developed markets, as of December 31, 2007. Financial stocks constituted the largest fraction of market value (22.5 percent), followed by consumer noncyclical stocks (17.3 percent), industrials (11.5 percent), and energy (11 percent). The broad sectors shown in Exhibit 10.1 are broken into 70 industry groups in Exhibit 10.2. The exhibit also shows an index of concentration across countries, with and without the United States, for each sector.

The Herfindahl concentration index measures how evenly market shares are distributed. Its most common application is to assess market power among firms within an industry. Here we use it to measure how evenly each sector's total market value is spread among the 23 markets in the MSCI World index. The index computation squares each country's share within the sector and sums across markets. If market value within a sector were spread evenly across countries, the concentration ratio would be $1/N$, where N is the number of countries. With the United States included, this would be $1/23 = .0435$. A more uneven distribution results in a higher index value, with 1.0 indicating that one country accounts for all the market value within

EXHIBIT 10.1
Sector Breakdown of the MSCI World Index: December 31, 2007

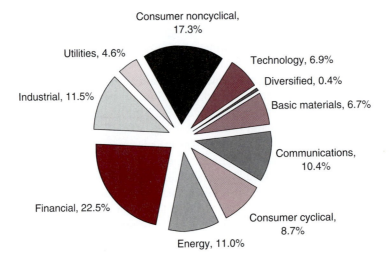

the sector. A value less than, say, 0.10 (equivalent to being evenly distributed among 10 countries) indicates a reasonably even distribution, whereas a value above 0.20 (equivalent to being spread evenly among only 5 markets) clearly reflects substantial concentration.

With or without the United States, almost all the sectors show evidence of market value concentration. The only exception is the financial sector. Excluding the United States, the market value of financial stocks is spread fairly evenly across markets. This is consistent with the fact that financials are the largest sector in 14 of the 22 non-U.S. markets and among the largest three sectors in all markets but Norway, Finland, and New Zealand. Comparing the concentration ratios with and without the United States confirms that developed market equity capitalization is heavily concentrated in the United States. In particular, the United States has a disproportionately large share of the market capitalization in technology, energy, communications, and consumer non-cyclicals. Although the U.S. share of the other sectors is large in absolute terms, those sectors are underrepresented in the U.S. market.

Whereas Exhibit 10.2 examined the concentration across markets within each sector, Exhibit 10.3 considers concentration across the 70 industry groups within each country. The vertical bars (left axis) show concentration ratios, while the line (right axis) reflects the market share of the largest industry within that market. The markets are arranged from left to right in ascending order of concentration. Japan and the United States are the least concentrated by industry, slightly less than the MSCI World index itself, with their largest industries representing less than 10 percent. In contrast, Finland and Greece are highly concentrated. Their largest industries, communications and banking respectively, represent more than 60 percent of their market capitalization. Banking is the largest single industry in 11 of the 23 markets, whereas oil and gas is the largest sector in 5 markets. The largest industries in the remaining countries are pharmaceuticals (2), telecommunications (2), electric utilities (1), real estate (1), and insurance (1). In 18 of the 23 countries, the largest industry accounts for at least 20 percent of total market capitalization.

It should be clear that investment opportunities are not distributed evenly throughout the global equity markets. Making investment decisions based on geography, such as by investing in local market indexes, often entails significant, albeit implicit, industry bets. Conversely, selecting industries, or individual stocks within industries, as if

EXHIBIT 10.2   Sector Composition: Industry Groups and Concentration across Markets—MSCI World Index, December 31, 2007

Sector	Industry Groups		Index of Concentration across Markets	
			All Markets	Excluding United States
Basic materials	Chemicals Forest products and paper	Iron/steel Mining	0.142	0.146
Communications	Advertising Internet	Media Telecommunications	0.298	0.117
Consumer cyclical	Airlines Apparel Auto manufacturers Auto parts and equipment Distribution/wholesale Entertainment Food service Home builders Home furnishings	Housewares Leisure time Lodging Office furnishings Retail Storage/warehousing Textiles Toys/games/hobbies	0.262	0.289
Consumer noncyclical	Agriculture Beverages Biotechnology Commercial services Cosmetics/personal care	Food Health care products Health care services Household products Pharmaceuticals	0.344	0.177
Diversified	Holding companies		0.230	0.257
Energy	Coal Energy—alternative sources Oil and gas	Oil and gas services Pipelines	0.350	0.248
Financial	Banks Diversified financial Services Insurance Investment companies	REITS Real estate Savings and loans Venture capital	0.167	0.090
Industrial	Aerospace/defense Building materials Electrical components and equipment Electronics Engineering and construction Environmental control Hand/machine tools	Machinery—construction and mining Machinery—diversified Metal fabricate/hardware Manufacturing— misc. Packaging and containers Shipbuilding Transportation	0.274	0.164
Technology	Computers Office/business equipment	Semiconductors Software	0.692	0.230
Utilities	Electric Gas	Water	0.195	0.151

they all operate in the same environment ignores differences among local economies and markets. Section 10.6 examines this issue in the context of the ongoing "country effects versus industry effects" debate.

EXHIBIT 10.3 **Industry Concentration of Developed Equity Markets: December 31, 2007**

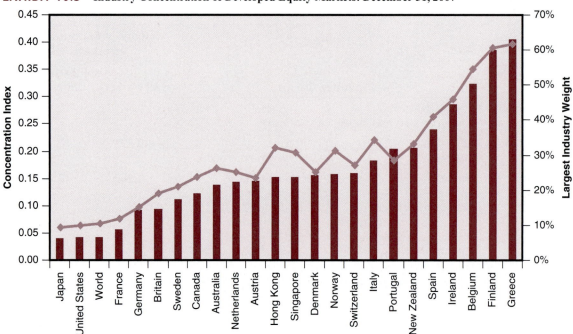

Exhibit 10.4 shows risk and return statistics for the broader MSCI All-Country World index and the markets that have been included in that index since at least October 1996. We must of course keep in mind that such statistics, especially mean returns, are always specific to a particular period. Nonetheless, the exhibit illustrates some important points. First, currency movements may or may not have a significant impact on longer-term average returns. For most of the markets, the mean returns in local currency and U.S. dollars are similar. For the index as a whole the difference is only a few basis points. However, for a few emerging markets, such as Argentina, Columbia, and Turkey, the currency impact has been dramatic. Second, currency movements do not necessarily increase the volatility of returns. The U.S. dollar returns of the Danish and German stock markets were actually less volatile than the local currency returns. More generally, for most markets the volatility of U.S. dollar returns was only modestly higher than the local volatility. This helps explain why most equity managers do not attempt to hedge currency movements—at least within the major developed markets. Third, local currency and U.S. dollar returns have very similar correlations with the U.S. market. Again, this helps explain why many equity managers treat currency as noise in making investment decisions. The exhibit also illustrates a surprising fact: A portfolio of foreign markets can be more highly correlated with the domestic market than are *any* of its constituent markets. In this example, individual market correlations with the United States range from 0.06 for Pakistan to 0.78 for Canada with an average correlation of 0.50. The market-value-weighted average correlation is 0.61. Nonetheless, the non-U.S. portfolio has a 0.81 correlation with the U.S. market. The upshot is that combining a broadly diversified international index with a domestic market may offer less potential diversification than investing in a few selected foreign markets. To understand why, we need to consider correlations among the foreign markets themselves.

EXHIBIT 10.4   Global Equity Markets: October 1996–April 2006

	Cap Weight: April 2006	Mean Return		Volatility		Correlation with United States	
		Local	U.S.$	Local	U.S.$	Local	U.S.$
AC World		8.97	8.84	14.75	15.00	0.95	0.94
x-US*		10.92	11.18	14.80	15.77	0.83	0.81
Argentina	0.1%	30.58	19.08	42.27	41.76	0.30	0.33
Australia	2.3	13.16	13.61	11.82	17.85	0.61	0.62
Austria	0.2	16.15	16.20	17.88	19.24	0.43	0.34
Belgium	0.5	12.93	12.94	17.74	18.98	0.65	0.54
Brazil	0.8	28.25	24.60	31.70	42.12	0.60	0.59
Canada	3.3	13.45	16.15	17.21	20.53	0.79	0.78
Chile	0.1	11.37	9.90	20.63	24.29	0.52	0.57
China	0.6	5.67	5.66	40.50	40.48	0.44	0.44
Colombia	0.0	35.46	27.24	33.50	35.27	0.14	0.21
Czech Republic	0.1	20.21	22.90	27.42	30.25	0.27	0.24
Denmark	0.3	16.53	16.26	19.34	18.52	0.65	0.61
Finland	0.7	25.74	24.98	38.39	37.27	0.64	0.63
France	4.2	13.24	12.98	19.90	19.08	0.75	0.72
Germany	3.1	12.03	11.63	24.35	23.55	0.76	0.73
Greece	0.3	19.69	18.45	32.29	31.75	0.39	0.37
Hong Kong	0.7	8.85	8.83	27.97	27.99	0.56	0.56
Hungary	0.1	29.60	26.99	32.41	33.81	0.55	0.51
India	0.5	20.45	18.37	27.70	28.91	0.29	0.29
Ireland	0.4	10.17	10.07	19.14	18.65	0.67	0.64
Israel	0.2	17.42	15.15	24.74	26.75	0.57	0.56
Italy	1.6	14.65	14.48	21.76	21.37	0.59	0.56
Japan	11.0	3.11	3.52	16.82	20.55	0.44	0.44
Jordan	0.0	16.60	16.63	18.20	18.27	0.06	0.06
Korea	1.3	20.29	22.34	39.75	48.37	0.44	0.43
Mexico	0.4	24.21	21.38	25.17	29.29	0.67	0.68
Netherlands	1.5	10.51	10.10	20.41	19.57	0.74	0.71
New Zealand	0.1	8.53	8.49	17.15	21.95	0.45	0.45
Norway	0.4	15.81	16.77	21.83	23.66	0.65	0.58
Pakistan	0.0	28.79	24.14	40.80	42.18	0.11	0.13
Peru	0.0	18.18	15.89	26.82	27.70	0.27	0.26
Philippines	0.0	0.30	−5.09	29.90	35.27	0.44	0.40
Poland	0.1	13.78	14.45	30.46	35.12	0.48	0.47
Portugal	0.1	12.43	12.27	20.98	21.50	0.53	0.46
Singapore Free	0.4	5.50	5.18	26.70	29.93	0.58	0.57
South Africa	0.7	16.85	15.21	23.40	28.49	0.51	0.48
Spain	1.6	17.47	17.07	22.42	22.05	0.71	0.67
Sweden	1.1	16.96	16.09	26.28	27.25	0.69	0.69
Switzerland	3.0	11.54	11.49	17.50	16.88	0.70	0.59
Taiwan	1.0	5.99	5.17	28.87	31.37	0.49	0.50
Turkey	0.2	61.82	35.35	59.67	61.10	0.44	0.48
United Kingdom	10.4	8.26	9.83	13.89	13.89	0.78	0.75
United States	45.4	9.54	9.54	15.95	15.95	1.00	1.00
Venezuela	0.0	32.83	17.06	43.93	47.31	0.26	0.31

* x-US is a weighted average of markets shown using April 2006 weights.

EXHIBIT 10.5   **International Diversification: Impact of Correlation between Foreign Markets**

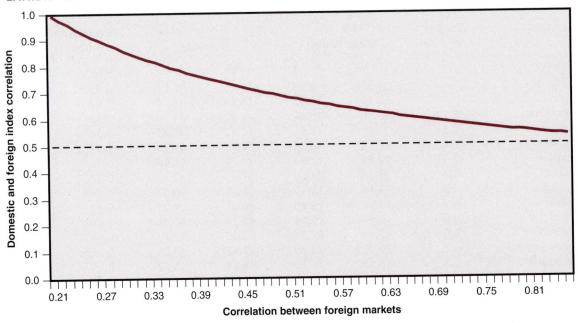

Exhibit 10.5 graphs the correlation of a hypothetical foreign index with the domestic market. All foreign markets have the same 0.50 correlation with the domestic market. The level of correlation between any two foreign markets is shown on the horizontal axis. When the correlation between foreign markets is low, the foreign index is almost perfectly correlated with the domestic market. In essence, diversification among the foreign markets eliminates fluctuations that are not driven by their common correlation with the domestic market (much as beta is more statistically powerful for explaining the risk of a portfolio than the risk of an individual stock). As the correlation among foreign markets increases, the correlation between the foreign index and the domestic market declines toward 0.50—the correlation of each individual foreign market with the domestic market. All else the same, of course, higher correlation among the foreign markets also means the foreign index will be more volatile. If we are adding only a modest amount of international exposure to our portfolio, correlation with the domestic market is generally the more important consideration. At higher levels of international exposure, the volatility of the international portfolio itself becomes increasingly important.

Global Bond Opportunities

Although non-U.S. issuance of corporate bonds, especially lower-quality bonds, and structured or collateralized instruments has grown significantly since the late 1990s, the vast majority of corporate bonds are still found in the U.S. market. In part, this is due to historically heavy reliance on bank financing rather than public debt issuance outside the United States. In addition, the recent explosion of mortgage-backed security (MBS) issuance in the United States (think "subprime crisis") has maintained the relative concentration of such vehicles in the United States.

EXHIBIT 10.6
Citigroup World
Broad Investment
Grade Index:
January 2008

	World	U.S.	Non-U.S.
By type:			
Government-sponsored	65.0	35.5	84.7
Credit/corporate	12.7	25.0	4.5
Collateralized	22.3	39.6	10.8
By maturity (excluding MBS):			
1–3 years	27.2	27.6	27.0
3–7 years	34.0	32.2	35.1
7–10 years	18.0	18.6	17.6
> 10 years	20.8	21.6	20.3
By quality:			
AAA/AA	83.7	81.1	85.4
A	12.3	9.3	14.2
BBB	4.1	9.7	0.3
By currency:			
USD	39.9	100.0	0.0
EUR	36.6		60.9
JPY	15.4		25.6
GBP	4.9		8.1
Other	3.3		5.4

Exhibit 10.6 breaks down the Citigroup World Broad Investment Grade index (the "World BIG") and its U.S. and non-U.S. components along four dimensions: type of issue/issuer, maturity, credit quality, and currency. Whereas the U.S. market is roughly evenly split among government, credit/corporate, and collateralized issues, the non-U.S. markets are heavily concentrated in government and government-sponsored bonds. There is little difference in the maturity structure of the markets, but the non-U.S. markets are skewed somewhat toward higher quality. The big differentiating factor is, of course, currency denomination. The upshot is that relative yield curve movements and currencies remain the primary focus of global fixed-income investing.

Whereas global equity investors often treat currency as noise, currency management is a key component of global bond investing. As we will discuss in the next section, the cost of hedging currency exposure is a function of interest rate differentials. In addition, many of the same macroeconomic factors drive currency movements and bond yields. Perhaps the most significant consideration, however, is simply that currency movements are large and volatile relative to the underlying bond returns.

Exhibit 10.7 illustrates the impact of currency on global government bond returns. Over the January 2000–December 2007 period, depreciation of the U.S. dollar roughly doubled the return on 11 of the 12 nondollar markets in the JPMorgan Global Government Bond index (GBI). The 12th market, Japan, did so poorly that its large weight sharply reduced the overall index return. On the other hand, currency-hedged returns were quite similar to the local currency returns. Again the exception was Japan, where there was a substantial 3.36 percent pickup on the hedge. Turning to volatilities, for the individual markets unhedged returns were roughly three times as volatile as local returns or hedged returns. Contrary to what we saw for global equities, currency exposure dramatically increases the risk of global bonds. As shown in the last set of columns, it also substantially reduces correlation with the domestic market.

EXHIBIT 10.7 **Global Government Bond Markets: January 2000–December 2007**

	Mean			Volatility			Correlation with United States		
	Local	Hedged	USD	Local	Hedged	USD	Local	Hedged	USD
GBI traded		5.66	6.70		2.88	6.77		0.93	0.64
Australia	5.90	4.10	10.14	3.53	3.60	11.06	0.73	0.73	0.26
Belgium	5.14	5.64	10.36	3.18	3.14	10.29	0.82	0.83	0.48
Canada	6.74	6.73	11.87	3.76	3.75	8.28	0.85	0.85	0.39
Denmark	5.06	5.38	10.23	2.89	2.85	10.06	0.82	0.83	0.46
France	4.94	5.42	10.14	3.16	3.13	10.24	0.82	0.83	0.48
Germany	4.90	5.39	10.11	3.14	3.12	10.24	0.80	0.81	0.48
Italy	5.22	5.70	10.42	3.28	3.25	10.23	0.82	0.83	0.48
Japan	1.71	5.07	1.00	2.05	2.17	9.11	0.24	0.25	0.34
Netherlands	5.01	5.50	10.23	3.07	3.04	10.26	0.82	0.83	0.47
Spain	5.18	5.67	10.39	3.20	3.16	10.24	0.81	0.83	0.48
Sweden	5.25	5.74	9.32	3.09	3.06	11.13	0.74	0.75	0.36
U.K.	5.35	4.27	8.31	4.15	4.15	8.89	0.75	0.75	0.50
U.S.			6.61			4.94			1.00
EMBI +			11.99			7.87			0.20

10.4 The Impact of Currency

Because most foreign securities entail currency exposure, global investing requires a firm understanding of the impact of currency on investment returns. In this section we examine the implications of four basic currency management decisions. The four alternatives are (1) unhedged returns, (2) direct hedging into the domestic currency, (3) cross-hedging into a third currency, and (4) proxy hedging into the domestic currency using a third currency.[1]

First we need to define some notation. Let

r_i = The log return on an asset denominated in currency i.
y_i = The log risk-free rate in currency i.
S_{ij} = The spot exchange rate—units of currency i per unit of currency j.
F_{ij} = The forward exchange rate—units of currency i per unit of currency j.
s_{ij}, f_{ij} = The log of spot and forward exchange rates.
Δs_{ij} = The change in the log spot exchange rate = log FX return.

A subscript d will denote our domestic currency, which is the base currency of the portfolio. That is, we are interested in investment performance measured in this currency. For ease of exposition, we will refer to this currency as the dollar. Note that the spot exchange rate, S_{ij}, is the price for immediate delivery of one currency versus another whereas the forward exchange rate, F_{ij}, is the price set today for delivery of one currency versus the other on a future date.

Before considering asset returns combined with the four alternative currency decisions, we need to develop the relationship between spot exchange rates and forward

[1] Readers who are not already familiar with currency hedging may find this material challenging to digest on the first pass. Working through the Excel Outbox as you read the material should help clarify the mechanics and impact of the alternative currency strategies.

exchange rates. Suppose we invest $1 at the dollar-denominated riskless rate, y_d. At the end of the period we will have $\exp(y_d)$ dollars. Alternatively, suppose we convert $1 into currency i at the spot rate (S_{di}), invest for one period at the currency i–denominated riskless rate (y_i), and convert the proceeds back to dollars at the forward exchange rate (F_{di}). At the end of the period we would have $[\exp(y_i)\,(F_{di}/S_{di})]$ dollars under this strategy. Because both of these investments are risk-free, they must provide the same return. Thus we have the **covered interest parity** relationship:

$$\exp(y_d) = \exp(y_i)\left(\frac{F_{di}}{S_{di}}\right) \tag{10.1}$$

Equivalently, in terms of logs,

$$f_{di} - s_{di} = y_d - y_i \tag{10.2}$$

According to this equation, if the domestic currency has a higher interest rate, currency i must be more expensive in the forward market than it is in the spot market by exactly the interest rate differential. In this case currency i trades at a **forward premium.** Of course, if the foreign market has a higher interest rate, its currency will trade at a **forward discount**—that is, it will be less expensive for future delivery than for immediate delivery. Again, the forward exchange rate differential is equal to the difference in interest rates.

Unhedged Returns

Now suppose we buy an asset denominated in currency i and do not hedge the currency exposure. The dollar value of this position is simply its price in currency i multiplied by the spot exchange rate, S_{di}. The logarithmic dollar-denominated return is simply the difference between the log of this value at the beginning and at the end of the investment period. Because the log of a product is the sum of the logs, it is straightforward to see that the dollar-denominated log return has two components: the currency i log return on the security, r_i, and the change in the log of the spot exchange rate, Δs_{di}. This is shown in the first line of Equation (10.3) below. The second and third lines of the equation use the covered interest parity relationship in Equation (10.2) to decompose the unhedged return into four parts. The first part is the dollar-denominated risk-free rate. The second part is the local currency excess return on the security—that is, the return in excess of the currency i riskless rate, $(r_i - y_i)$. As we will see, the hedged return on the asset equals the sum of these two terms. The third term is the change in the spot exchange rate. The final term subtracts the forward premium or discount.

$$
\begin{aligned}
R &= r_i + \Delta s_{di} \tag{10.3}\\
&= y_d + (r_i - y_i) + (y_i - y_d) + \Delta s_{di}\\
&= y_d + (r_i - y_i) + \Delta s_{di} - (f_{di} - s_{di})
\end{aligned}
$$

The third and fourth components of the return highlight the relationship between the appreciation or depreciation of the spot exchange rate (Δs_{di}) and the forward premium or discount ($f_{di} - s_{di}$). Suppose the foreign currency trades at a forward premium so that $(f_{di} - s_{di}) > 0$. Then the net impact of leaving the currency unhedged is positive if and only if the foreign currency appreciates by more than the forward premium.

If the foreign currency appreciates by less (or perhaps even depreciates), a greater return could have been achieved by hedging the currency exposure. Similarly, if the foreign currency is at a forward discount $[(f_{di} - s_{di}) < 0]$, the spot exchange rate needs to depreciate by less than the discount.

Hedged Returns

If we do not want to bear the risk of currency fluctuations, we can hedge it by selling the future value of the investment at the forward exchange rate. We will assume for now that the terminal value of the investment is known so that all currency risk can be eliminated. Later we will consider the problem of hedging an unknown future asset value. By hedging the currency the investor earns the forward premium or discount on the foreign currency $(f_{di} - s_{di})$ but forgoes the appreciation or depreciation of the spot exchange rate over the period, Δs_{di}. Hence the last two terms in Equation (10.3) drop out. The hedged return is therefore equal to

$$R = y_d + (r_i - y_i) \qquad (10.4)$$

As shown in Equation (10.4), the hedged return is equal to the domestic currency risk-free rate plus the local currency (currency i) excess return on the security. By rearranging the equation it is easy to see that the hedged return is also equal to the local currency security return, r_i, plus the interest rate differential between the two markets $(y_d - y_i)$. When the interest rate differential favors the domestic currency, the investor is said to "pick up" yield on the hedge.

Cross-Hedging

In general there is no reason to restrict consideration to two currencies—the security's local currency (currency i) and our domestic currency (the dollar). Exposure to a different currency—call it currency j—can be introduced by cross-hedging. Cross-hedging can be viewed as a two-step process. First, eliminate exposure to currency i by hedging back into the dollar. Second, create exposure to currency j by hedging the dollar into that currency. The first step takes us from Equation (10.3) to Equation (10.4). The second step adds back the currency terms but with currency j rather than currency i. Thus the cross-hedged return is

$$R = y_d + (r_i - y_i) + \Delta s_j - (f_{dj} - s_{dj}) \qquad (10.5)$$

In practice, implementation of a cross-hedge does not require two steps. Instead the investor simply sells the terminal value of the investment into currency j at the forward exchange rate between currencies i and j, which is $F_{ij} = F_{dj}/F_{di}$.

Proxy Hedging

Cross-hedging deliberately introduces full exposure to a third currency while eliminating exposure to the security's native currency. Proxy hedging seeks to eliminate most of the currency risk but on better terms than are available with a direct hedge. Instead of selling currency i into dollars at the forward rate, F_{di}, the investor sells currency j into dollars at the forward rate, F_{dj}. Thus currency j is used as a proxy for currency i. Provided currencies i and j are highly correlated, like the euro and the Swiss franc, the hedge will be effective in eliminating most, but not all, of the currency risk. The investor is "long" currency i through the underlying security and "short" currency j due to the hedge. Thus the investor is exposed to the relative movements of these two currencies.

The investor benefits if the security's native currency appreciates more than the proxy currency—that is, if $\Delta s_{di} > \Delta s_{dj}$. As with the direct hedge, however, the full currency impact must include the forward premium or discount. In this case the relevant premium or discount is between currencies i and j. All else the same, it is more profitable to hedge using the currency that trades at the highest forward premium or, equivalently, the currency with the lower interest rate. Thus the proxy hedge will be more profitable with a greater forward premium of currency j versus currency i $(f_{ij} - s_{ij})$. Bringing these two currency components together, the proxy-hedged return is

$$R = y_d + (r_i - y_i) + \Delta s_{di} - \Delta s_{dj} + (f_{ij} - s_{ij}) \qquad \textbf{(10.6)}$$

Exhibit 10.8 illustrates the impact of alternative currency decisions. The top portion reflects market conditions as of February 2008. The euro was trading at around $1.48 in the spot market. Short-term USD interest rates were well below EUR rates but still above Swiss rates. As a result, the Euro traded at a forward discount versus the dollar while the Swiss franc (CHF) was at a forward premium versus both the dollar and the euro. The bottom portion of the exhibit shows the currency return for a euro-denominated asset under alternative strategies assuming the euro and Swiss franc appreciate by 2.0 percent and 1.0 percent respectively versus the dollar.

A decision not to hedge the euro exposure results in a 2.70 percent higher return composed of 2.0 percent spot appreciation plus the 0.70% percent forward discount avoided by not hedging. Replacing the euro exposure with Swiss franc exposure by cross-hedging boosts the return by only 0.78 percent because "paying away" the 0.22 percent forward

EXHIBIT 10.8
Returns with Alternative Currency Strategies

Market Parameters			
	Spot Exchange Rate (USD per)	Six-Month Forward Exchange Rate (USD per)	Log Six-Month Interest Rate (Per Annum)
Euro (EUR)	1.4800	1.4696	4.27
Swiss franc (CHF)	0.9180	0.9200	2.42
U.S. dollar (USD)			2.86

Returns for Euro-Denominated Asset				
	Unhedged	Direct Hedge	Cross-Hedge to CHF	Proxy Hedge with CHF
USD risk-free rate	1.43	1.43	1.43	1.43
Asset: local excess return	0.87	0.87	0.87	0.87
Hedged return	2.30	2.30	2.30	2.30
EUR spot change	2.00			2.00
CHF spot change			1.00	−1.00
Forward premium/ discount earned or paid				
USD back into EUR	0.70			
USD into CHF			−0.22	
CHF into EUR				0.92
Currency return	2.70	0.00	0.78	1.92
Total USD return	5.00	2.30	3.08	4.22

premium on the franc to create the CHF exposure partially offsets the 1 percent appreciation of the CHF. Using the CHF as a proxy hedge improves the return by 1.92 percent
relative to the direct hedge. With this strategy the investor gets the 2 percent appreciation
on the euro, loses the 1 percent appreciation on the CHF, and picks up the 0.92 percent
forward premium on the CHF versus the EUR. In this example, the unhedged return is
best, followed by the proxy hedge and the cross-hedge. All three are better than the direct
hedge. Note that this is an ex post result driven primarily by the assumed spot appreciation of the EUR and CHF. If we instead assumed these currencies each depreciated by 1
percent versus the dollar, the currency return for both the unhedged and the cross-hedged
strategies would be negative. The proxy-hedged currency return would still be positive,
however, due to the 92 basis point forward premium on the CHF versus the EUR.

Asset versus Currency Decisions

Equations (10.3) through (10.6) make it clear that the currency and underlying asset
decisions can be, and ideally should be, independent. Examining these equations
shows that achieving the highest expected return entails two decisions. With respect to
assets, select the one with the highest expected hedged return regardless of its native
currency. That is, compare assets across markets based on Equation (10.4). Then select
the most attractive currency exposure by comparing unhedged, hedged, cross-hedged,
and proxy-hedged returns utilizing all available currencies. Note that the best currency
decision will be the same regardless of the underlying asset. Any other combination of
asset and currency decisions will have a lower expected return.

There are two important caveats to this general prescription. First, risk considerations prevent us from investing based solely on expected return. Hence we need to
consider volatilities and correlations among the hedged assets and the currency returns
inclusive of forward premiums or discounts. Second, in practice investment policy
restrictions may force a joint decision by limiting the use of hedging instruments or
prohibiting currency exposures that do not arise from an underlying asset position.

Excel Outbox
Currency
Strategies

This Excel box implements the four basic currency strategies: unhedged, direct hedge,
cross-hedge, and proxy hedge.

Use the worksheet <CurrencyStrategy–Template> in the spreadsheet Chapter 10 Excel
Outboxes.xls.

The market parameters for three currencies (USD, EUR, and CHF) are at the top of the
template. Start by converting the interest rates to their continuously compounded (log)
equivalents:

- In cell E6 enter = 100∗LN(1+D6/100), and then copy to cells E7:E8.

The FX rates given for EUR and CHF are quoted versus USD. To get spot and forward
rates between the EUR and CHF (quoted as EUR per CHF):

- In cell B12 enter = B7/B6, and then copy to cell C12.

The forward premiums or discounts are calculated in two ways: directly from the quoted
FX rates and, based on the interest rate parity relationship, using interest rate differentials:

- In cell B15 enter = 100∗LN(C6/B6).
- In cell C15 enter = 0.5∗(E$8−E6). [Note that the six-month period requires the 0.5.]
- Copy cells B15:C15 to cells B16:C16.
- In cell B17 enter = 100∗LN(C12/B12).
- In cell C17 enter = 0.5∗(E6−E7).

Note that the two methods give the same result. Any small differences are due to the fact that the quoted forward FX rates were truncated at four decimal places. The table should look like this:

Returns with Alternative Currency Strategies				
		Market Parameters		
	Spot Exchange Rate (USD per)	Six-Month Forward Exchange Rate (USD per)	Six-Month Interest Rate (% Per annum)	Log Six-Month Interest Rate (% Per Annum)
Euro (EUR)	1.4800	1.4696	4.36	4.27
Swiss Franc (CHF)	0.9180	0.9200	2.45	2.42
US Dollar (USD)			2.90	2.86

Calculated Parameters			Return Assumptions (% Log)	
	Spot	Forward		
Cross FX Rates: EUR per CHF	0.6203	0.6260	Asset (EUR)	3.00
Fwd Prem(+)/Disc(−) (% Log)	Direct Calculation	Int. Rate Diff	EUR Spot Chg	2.00
EUR vs USD	−0.705	−0.704	CHF Spot Chg	1.00
CHF vs USD	0.218	0.219		
CHF vs EUR	0.923	0.924		

To calculate returns using the four basic currency strategies:

- In cell B22 enter = 0.5*$E$8, and then copy to cells C22:E22.
- In cell B23 enter = $E$12 − (0.5*$E$6), and then copy to cells C23:E23.
- In cell B25 enter = B22 + B23, and then copy to cells C25:E25.
- In cell B27 enter = $E14, and then copy to E27.
- In cell D28 enter = E15.
- In cell E28 enter = −E15.
- In cell B30 enter = −C15.
- In cell D31 enter = −C16.
- In cell E32 enter = C17.
- In cell B34 enter = sum(B27:B32), and then copy to cells C34:E34.
- In cell B36 enter = B25 + B34, and then copy to cells C36:E36.

The bottom part of the table should now look like the bottom of Exhibit 10.8.

Hedging Uncertain Returns

The hedged return formulas given so far assume we know the future local currency value of the foreign asset and are therefore able to sell precisely the right amount of foreign currency in the forward market. This is rarely true in practice, of course, so we need to consider the interaction of uncertainty with respect to both the future asset price and the exchange rate.

To keep the exposition simple, we consider an example in which there are only three possible outcomes for the asset price and exchange rate. In addition, we assume that the initial exchange rate is 1.00 and that the risk-free rate is the same in both

EXHIBIT 10.9

Hedging a Risky Asset

	Initial Value	Outcome 1	Outcome 2	Outcome 3
Foreign currency values:				
Foreign risky asset	100	120.07	105.00	86.14
Foreign deposit	100	105.00	105.00	105.00
Domestic currency values:				
Foreign currency (one unit)				
Spot	1	0.9331	1.2365	1.0298
Sold forward		0.0669	−0.2365	−0.0298
Foreign deposit				
Unhedged	100	97.97	129.84	108.13
Hedged	100	105.00	105.00	105.00
Foreign risky asset				
Unhedged	100	112.03	129.84	88.71
Hedged	100	119.06	105.00	85.58

markets. Thus the two currencies initially exchange one-for-one in both the spot and forward markets.

The top portion of Exhibit 10.9 shows the potential foreign currency outcomes for the foreign risky asset and for a foreign deposit. The bottom section of the table shows hedged and unhedged domestic currency values for these assets along with the value of the foreign currency (that is, the spot exchange rate) and the payoffs from selling one unit of the foreign currency forward. The hedged returns reflect selling 105 units of the foreign currency at the forward rate. That is, for hedging purposes we assume that the foreign asset earns the foreign risk-free rate over the period.

The hedged domestic currency value of the foreign deposit is the same as its foreign currency value in each possible outcome. Thus it is perfectly hedged. For the risky foreign asset the hedge is exact only for the second outcome. Under this outcome the final value of the asset assumed for hedging purposes (105) turns out to be correct, and the investor has sold exactly the right amount of the foreign currency. Under the first outcome the terminal value of the risky asset is much higher than was assumed in the hedge (120.07 versus.105). The investor must therefore sell the extra 15.07 units of foreign currency at the ending spot exchange rate (0.9331) rather than at the forward rate (1.0000). The result is a loss of 1.01 (120.07 − 119.06) relative to a perfect hedge. Under the third outcome, the asset drops in value (from 100 to 85.58) while the exchange rate appreciates (from 1.0000 to 1.0298). The investor sold too much foreign currency forward and must buy 19.42 units of the currency at the higher spot rate to make full delivery on the forward. This generates a loss of 0.56 (86.14 − 85.58) relative to the perfect hedge.

Note that the hedge failed because the underlying asset value and the exchange rate moved in opposite directions. Such divergent moves result in a loss relative to a perfect hedge. Whether the asset price rises or falls, the investor ends up buying or selling a residual amount of the foreign currency at an exchange rate that is less favorable than the forward. Conversely, positive correlation between the asset price and the exchange rate would generate a gain relative to the perfect hedge. In that case, the investor buys or sells the excess currency at an exchange rate that is more advantageous than the forward.

In theory, it is possible to create a perfectly hedged version of the foreign asset. Such an instrument, called a **quanto,** embodies converting a variable *quantity* of foreign currency at a predetermined exchange rate on a specific future date. To create the quanto we must dynamically adjust our positions in *both* the underlying asset and the forward exchange contract in response to changes in the underlying asset price, changes in the forward exchange rate, and the passage of time.

If the local currency price of the asset, P_i, and the spot exchange rate have a joint lognormal distribution, then the domestic currency value of one quanto share is[2]

$$\text{Value of quanto share} = (S_{di} P_i)\left(\frac{Q}{F_{di}}\right) \exp(-\rho\sigma_i\sigma_s\tau) \quad \textbf{(10.7)}$$

where Q is the exchange rate locked in by the quanto, ρ is the correlation between the asset price and the exchange rate, σ denotes standard deviation, and τ is the time remaining to the hedge horizon. There are three components to this value. The first is simply the domestic currency value of the foreign asset $(S_{di} P_i)$. The second component is the ratio of the quanto exchange rate to the currently prevailing forward rate (Q/F_{di}). If this ratio is greater (less) than 1, the quanto locks in a more (less) favorable currency conversion than is currently available in the market. The last component is an adjustment for the correlation impact already discussed. The term is greater than or less than 1 depending on the sign of the correlation, ρ. As we saw, if the asset price and the exchange rate are negatively correlated, then hedging based on a fixed quantity of foreign currency tends to generate a loss relative to the perfect (quantity-adjusting) hedge. Thus, all else the same, a quanto share will be worth more than one unhedged share of the foreign asset. If the correlation is positive, however, the quanto is worth less than one unhedged share. In this case, the quanto forgoes the opportunity to sell additional foreign currency when both the asset price and exchange rate are high and buy back foreign currency when both the asset price and exchange rate are low.

From Equation (10.7) we can see that a perfectly hedged share corresponds to owning

$$N = \left(\frac{Q}{F_{di}}\right) \exp\left(-\rho\sigma_i\sigma_s\tau\right) \quad \textbf{(10.8)}$$

shares of the unhedged foreign security. To hedge the currency exposure we must sell the future value of these shares in the forward market. Obviously we do not know the future value. It turns out, however, that we may treat the foreign security as if it is risk-free. We simply scale up the current value of the shares using the foreign currency risk-free interest rate as the expected return. Thus we sell

$$N P_i \exp(y_i\tau) \quad \textbf{(10.9)}$$

units of the foreign currency at the forward rate.

As might be expected, when the local currency price of the security increases/decreases, we must increase/decrease the hedge in the forward market to reflect more/fewer units of the foreign currency. Because the asset price does not appear in Equation (10.8), we do not need to buy or sell shares when the asset price changes. A change in the forward exchange rate requires adjustment of both the number of shares held and the hedge. When the forward rate increases (decreases), the quanto is equivalent to fewer (more) underlying shares and we must therefore sell (buy) shares. The currency hedge must be adjusted accordingly.

---

[2] The value of the quanto and the required dynamic trading strategy are derived in Piros (1998).

Excel Outbox
Creating
Quantos

This outbox illustrates replication and valuation of quanto assets and call options using a single-period framework with three potential future values for the foreign risky asset and the spot exchange rate.

Use the worksheet <Quanto–Template> in the spreadsheet Chapter 10 Excel Outboxes.xls.

The template contains current and potential future values for the foreign risky asset, foreign deposit, domestic deposit, and spot exchange rate. Start by filling in the corresponding domestic currency values:

- In cell E10 enter = 1−E9, and then copy to cells F10:G10.
- In cell E13 enter = E9*E6, and then copy to cells F13:G13.
- In cell E14 enter = E13+E$6*E$10, and then copy to cells F14:G14. [Note that $E$6 is used to capture the foreign interest rate.]
- Copy cells E14:G14 to cells E18:G18.
- In cell E17 enter = E5*E9, and then copy to cells F17:G17.

The table should now look like this:

	A	B	C	D	E	F	G
1			CREATING QUANTOs				
2			Replication	Current	Possible Future Values		
3			Yes/No	Price/Cost	1	2	3
4	**Foreign Currency Values**						
5	Foreign Risky Asset			100.00	120.07	105.00	86.14
6	Foreign Deposit			100.00	105.00	105.00	105.00
7	**Domestic Currency Values**						
8	Foreign Currency (1 Unit)						
9	Spot			1.0000	0.9331	1.2365	1.0298
10	Sold Forward		Yes	0.0000	0.0669	−0.2365	−0.0298
11							
12	Foreign Deposit						
13	Unhedged		No	100.00	97.97	129.84	108.13
14	Hedged				105.00	105.00	105.00
15							
16	Foreign Risky Asset						
17	Unhedged		Yes	100.00	112.03	129.84	88.71
18	Hedged				119.06	105.00	85.58
19							
20	Domestic Deposit		Yes	100.00	105.00	105.00	105.00
21							

To define the quanto:

- In cell E23 enter = Max(E$5−$C23,0)*$B23, and then copy to cells F23:G23.

Note that this is the payoff to a call option on the foreign risky asset with the strike price given in cell C23. Owning the risky asset itself is equivalent to setting the strike price to 0. The foreign currency value of the option is converted to domestic currency at the fixed exchange rate in cell B23. This is the quanto feature. Now set up the replicating portfolio:

- In cell D13 enter = D9*D6.
- In cell D17 enter = D5*D9.
- In cell D25 enter = D17.
- In cell D26 enter = D13.
- In cell D27 enter = D20.
- In cell D28 enter = D10.

- In cell E25 enter = E17*$B25.
- In cell E26 enter = E13*$B26.
- In cell E27 enter = E20*$B27.
- In cell E28 enter = E10*$B28.
- Copy cells E25:E28 to cells F25:G28.
- In cell E30 enter = SUM(E25:E28), and then copy to cells F30:G30.
- In cell D30 enter = MMULT(TRANSPOSE(B25:B28),D25:D28) [This is an array formula, so use <CTRL><SHIFT><ENTER>.]

In Solver:

- Set Target Cell: D30.
- Select MIN.
- By changing cells: C25:C28.
- Subject to the constraints: E30:G30 = E23:G23.
- Solve.

The results should look like this:

	A	B	C	D	E	F	G
22	**Quanto**	Fixed FX	Strike				
23		1.0000	0		120.0685	105.0000	86.1419
24	**Replicating Portfolio**	Position		Unit Cost			
25	Foreign Asset	1.0043		100.00	112.5107	130.3921	89.0928
26	Foreign Deposit	0.0000		100.00	0.0000	0.0000	0.0000
27	Domestic Deposit	0.0028		100.00	0.2901	0.2901	0.2901
28	Sold Fwd	108.5747		0.0000	7.2678	-25.6822	-3.2409
29							
30				100.7041	120.0685	105.0000	86.1419

Note that the possible *domestic currency* values for the quanto are exactly the same as the possible *foreign currency* values of the risky asset. That is, the quanto is a perfectly hedged version of the foreign risky asset. The replicating portfolio requires buying slightly more than one share of the foreign risky asset, putting a small amount into a domestic deposit, and selling 108.5747 units of the foreign currency in the forward FX market. The total cost, 100.7041, exceeds the domestic currency cost of buying one share of the foreign risky asset (100). The difference is the value of the perfect currency hedge.

An alternative replicating portfolio can be obtained by borrowing at the foreign interest rate instead of selling the foreign currency in the forward market:

- In cell C10 put "No".
- In cell C13 put "Yes".
- In cell C26 (within the shaded box) put 0. Do *not* overwrite cell B26.
- Solve.

The result should look like this:

	A	B	C	D	E	F	G
22	**Quanto**	Fixed FX	Strike				
23		1.0000	0		120.0685	105.0000	86.1419
24	**Replicating Portfolio**	Position		Unit Cost			
25	Foreign Asset	1.0043		100.00	112.5107	130.3921	89.0928
26	Foreign Deposit	-1.0340		100.00	-101.3069	-134.2569	-111.8156
27	Domestic Deposit	1.0368		100.00	108.8647	108.8647	108.8647
28	Sold Fwd	0.0000		0.0000	0.0000	0.0000	0.0000
29							
30				100.7041	120.0685	105.0000	86.1419

(continued)

(concluded)   The cost of this alternative replicating portfolio is exactly the same as before. Indeed, due to the interest parity relationship between interest rates and spot/forward exchange rates, this portfolio is exactly equivalent to the first portfolio. It is just a different way to implement the strategy. In practice, however, implicit borrowing through the forward exchange market is much more cost-effective and efficient than explicit borrowing.

To create a quanto call option, simply put in a positive strike price, say 100. To see the impact of being able to sell the foreign currency at a forward exchange rate above the current market rate, put a value greater than 1.0000 in cell B23.

Note: The keen observer will no doubt wonder why no dynamic adjustments are required in this example. With only three possible outcomes for the foreign asset price and the exchange rate there are also just three outcomes for the Quanto. We can create the Quanto by combining the right amounts of three instruments. In essence we are just solving a problem with "three equations and three unknowns." The dynamic adjustments discussed above are required when there are many possible outcomes for the asset price and exchange rate.

10.5　International Diversification: Failure to Deliver?

The Correlation Conundrum

One of the primary arguments in favor of international investment has always been the diversification potential of investing in economically and politically distinct markets. As the discussion in Section 10.3 showed, however, a diversified portfolio of international markets may be much more highly correlated with the domestic market than any of the foreign markets are individually. As a result, international diversification can be much less powerful than we would expect from pairwise correlations.

To our knowledge, the potentially deceptive nature of pairwise correlations for overall diversification has not been fully appreciated in the investment literature. On the other hand, another issue with respect to international correlation continues to cause considerable angst: Correlations seem to be higher during periods of high volatility or falling markets. That is, international diversification seems to fail just when it would be most valuable.

The evidence suggesting failure of international diversification tends to take two forms. First, when we look back at specific market crises, such as October 1987, most markets seem to have suffered simultaneously. Second, if we compute market volatility through time and estimate correlations in high- and low-volatility periods, higher volatility tends to coincide with higher correlations.[3]

To assess the investment implications of this evidence, we must distinguish between *conditional* and *unconditional* correlations. In Chapter 4 we saw how time-varying investment opportunities give rise to the distinction between conditional and unconditional statistics, such as means and variances. Recall that if two random variables X and Y are related, then the distribution of X conditional on knowing the value of Y differs from the distribution of X with no information about Y. The latter is the unconditional distribution of X.

[3] See Bookstaber (1997) for examples of market movements during specific crises. Solnik, Boucrelle, and Le Fur (1996) illustrate analysis of volatility and correlation over time.

EXHIBIT 10.10

Conditional Correlation of Extreme Returns: Two Assets, 500 draws from Bivariate Normal Distribution

Unconditional correlation	
True value	.500
Sample correlation	.499
Conditional correlations, sorted by absolute value of asset 1	
Largest half	.528
Smallest half	.224
Largest 20%	.492
Smallest 20%	.014

Note: Mean = 10%, standard deviation = 15%.

It makes no mathematical sense to consider the correlation between X and Y conditional on Y taking a specific value. But what if we condition on Y lying within a certain range? Then Y is still uncertain, and it makes sense to think about the conditional correlation of X and Y.

Exhibit 10.10 illustrates the importance of distinguishing between conditional and unconditional correlations in the current context. It shows the outcome of generating 500 random returns for each of two assets that have a bivariate normal distribution with means of 10 percent, standard deviations of 15 percent, and true unconditional correlation of one-half. The top part of the table shows that the sample correlation is 0.499—almost exactly the true unconditional value. Suppose we sort the sample based on the absolute value of the first asset's return and then compute the correlation for the largest and smallest halves of the sample. The correlation for the larger moves is 0.528 (slightly higher than the unconditional correlation) while the correlation for the smaller moves is substantially lower at only 0.224. If we condition on even more extreme moves—the biggest 20 percent and smallest 20 percent of the returns—the difference is even starker. The two assets appear virtually uncorrelated (0.014) for small moves, while the correlation conditioned on the largest returns for the first asset is again roughly one-half.

Note that the different correlations obtained in this example do not arise from a changing relationship between the two assets. Instead it is conditioning on the magnitude of one asset's return that affects the measured correlation. Thus, referring back to the evidence on international correlations, we should not be surprised that ex post selection of crisis periods or high-volatility periods tends to show higher correlation among markets. This is simply due to the presence of nonzero unconditional correlation.

Recognizing that variation in measured correlations over time may simply reflect conditional dependence on ex post realized volatility, Forbes and Rigobon (2002) tested whether *unconditional* correlations are higher in crisis periods. The authors found no evidence to support such "contagion." Instead they found that removing the conditional impact of realized volatility revealed persistently higher levels of unconditional correlation. This suggests that the problem is not failure of diversification in key periods but rather that empirical correlations systematically overstate the underlying diversification potential of international markets.

Whereas Forbes and Rigobon focused on getting better estimates of the underlying interdependence of markets embodied in unconditional correlations, Longin and Solnik (2001) attempted to differentiate between correlations conditional on extreme negative returns and conditional on extreme positive returns. They found a powerful asymmetry: much stronger correlation in the lower tail but little influence on correlation for the

EXHIBIT 10.11
Diversification
Benefits of
International
Equities:
Structured versus
Traditional Active
Management,
Quarterly 1986–1995

		Type of International Management		
		EAFE Indexed	Active Core	Fully Active
Correlation with S&P 500		.58	.60	.68
	S&P 500	**Blend: 65% U.S., 35% International**		
Mean return	14.8	14.9	15.3	14.7
Standard deviation	14.8	14.8	15.4	13.9
Frequency of losses (%)	20.0	17.5	17.5	20.0

upper tail. Hence they concluded that bear markets (rather than simply volatility) are internationally contagious.

What are the implications for international investing? Unfortunately, the more rigorous statistical analysis just cited supports the conclusion of simpler, casual observation. International diversification offers less protection than average correlations would suggest, and it is most likely to fail when we need it. Ironically, this may be largely attributable to investor behavior. When the going gets tough, investors tend to bail out of all risky assets even if objective evaluation of the fundamentals would warrant a more selective response.

International Diversification with Active Managers

As discussed in Chapter 5, asset allocation decisions typically assume index performance and index characteristics for each asset class, but active managers are often hired to fulfill at least some of the asset classes. This practice raises the possibility that these active managers may not deliver the risk–return benefits envisioned for their asset classes. Obviously active managers may fail to produce higher return (alpha); but just as importantly, their active strategies may alter the risk characteristics of their asset classes and undermine their contribution to overall portfolio diversification.

Exhibit 10.11 illustrates this problem. In the late 1980s and early 1990s traditional, active international equity managers tended to systematically overweight European stocks and underweight Japanese stocks relative to the MSCI EAFE index.[4] The top row of the exhibit shows that this resulted in a higher correlation with the U.S. market reflecting the typically higher correlations of the European markets. In contrast, structured "active core" portfolios designed to eschew major tilts had only a slightly higher correlation than a pure index portfolio.

The lower part of the exhibit shows risk–return characteristics for the U.S. market as well as 65/35 percent combinations of the U.S. stocks with each type of international management. During this period, blending the S&P 500 with the EAFE index had little impact on mean return and volatility. However, it reduced the frequency of negative returns. Introducing modest active bets without major tilts (the active core blend) increased both mean return and standard deviation and preserved the benefit of less frequent losses. In contrast, fully active international management reduced risk as measured by standard deviation but did not reduce the frequency of losses.

10.6 Implications of Globalization

Economic globalization has increased dramatically since the 1980s. In the late 1980s the collapse of the Soviet Union and removal of the Berlin Wall started the process of reintegrating former Soviet bloc countries into the global market economy after nearly a

---

[4] See Hernandez and Stewart (1996) for a full discussion.

Theory in Practice
Global Secular Forces in the Early 21st Century

Around the turn of the 21st century the global economy experienced two powerful supply shocks. First, the effective supply of labor essentially doubled as the world's two most populous nations, China and India, integrated more fully with the rest of the world. Second, the revolution in computer and communications technology made it possible to separate the locus of production from the locus of consumption of goods and services to an extent never before possible. Both of these shocks were positive in that they allowed faster real growth with lower prices and inflation. Hence the global economy experienced a deflationary boom in the early years of this century.

In a simple textbook economy the adjustment to these shocks would have been quick and smooth, but not painless. Wages around the world would have converged. Capital and production would have moved instantaneously to the most cost-efficient locations. Labor's share of world income would have fallen relative to capital's share, reflecting the new abundance of labor. Incomes and relative prices (including exchange rates) would have adjusted to maintain full employment of all resources. On net, former low-wage/labor-intensive countries would gain at the expense of former high-wage/capital-intensive countries.

These adjustments are indeed occurring, but it is an ongoing, secular process rather than a discrete event. While less than fully flexible prices, exchange rates, and especially wages prolong the adjustment, the need to move physical capital around the world is an even more significant factor. Global migration of productive capital takes time. New capital must be deployed in cost-efficient locations while the old capital in inefficient locations is depreciated and/or scrapped. In the meantime, the return on investment capital is higher in the new markets.

Before the global credit crisis of 2007–2009 it appeared that the convergence implied by these secular forces would occur via very rapid growth in the "new" markets rather than a reduction in living standards in the "old" high-cost markets. In the wake of the crisis, however, this benign scenario is less certain. The crisis induced massive wealth destruction—in effect an immediate write-off of capital in the old high-cost economies. In addition, extraordinary government deficits are likely to leave U.S. taxpayers with a permanently higher tax burden to cover the debt service, much of which is owed to China. Thus it has become more likely that a period of diminished living standards for the United States and other old economies will be part of the convergence process.

Source: These themes were discussed more fully in "A Global Economic View," Prudential Investments LLC, October 2005.

half-century behind the Iron Curtain. The early 1990s brought the North American Free Trade Agreement (NAFTA) among the United States, Canada, and Mexico. The dream of the European Economic and Monetary Union (EMU) was realized on January 1, 1999, when a single currency, the euro, replaced those of 11 member nations. China officially entered the World Trade Organization in December 2001. More generally, there has been a strong trend toward freer trade and capital movements among the world's markets.

It should be clear that the process of globalization can have important ramifications for the relative attractiveness of specific investments across markets and over time. Our current focus, however, is on how globalization alters the way we should think about international investing. Does capital mobility lead to convergence of (default-risk-free) interest rates and hence imply that investing in foreign bonds is redundant? On the equity side, does a firm's home market still matter or just its position within a global industry? We will look at the fixed income and equity situations in turn.

Interest Rate Convergence: When They Do and Why They Don't

When will two markets share a common yield curve? That is, under what conditions will interest rates of all maturities converge across markets? From the discussion of currency hedging in Section 10.4, it should be clear that (default-free) interest rate differentials reflect the relative price of currencies. Indeed Equation (10.2) shows that there is a one-to-one correspondence between the interest rate differential for a given maturity and the forward discount or premium between the two currencies. Absence of an interest rate differential implies absence of a forward exchange rate premium or discount and vice versa.

Equality of interest rates at a specific maturity is not particularly meaningful here. It simply means that the two term structures cross at that maturity. Similarly, even if two markets happen to share a common yield curve at a particular time, the curves may later diverge. In either case, it should be clear that the markets still offer distinct investment opportunities.

Two conditions are necessary and sufficient to ensure that default-free interest rates of *all* maturities will *always* coincide. First, there must be perfect capital mobility between the markets; this ensures equalization of risk-adjusted expected returns. Second, there must be a credibly fixed exchange rate between the two currencies. If investors are convinced that the exchange rate will not change over a given horizon, then there can be no forward premium or discount over that horizon and hence no interest rate differential. Otherwise, uncertainty over the sustainability of the exchange rate will induce uncertainty about future interest rate differentials. Such uncertainty implies different risk–return characteristics for bonds denominated in the two currencies and hence distinct investment opportunities.

Note that capital mobility alone is *not* sufficient to enforce interest rate convergence and hence not sufficient to make foreign (default-free) bonds redundant. Reducing impediments to capital mobility will of course tend to eliminate inefficiencies across markets. But globalization of fixed-income markets does not equalize interest rates.

Even if *nominal* interest rates converge, *real* interest rates may not. Indeed persistent real interest rate differentials are a primary reason why fixed exchange rate regimes fail. Suppose two countries have a fixed exchange rate and nominal interest rates have converged, but inflation is persistently higher in one market. Higher inflation means a lower real interest rate and, according to basic economic theory, stronger aggregate demand for goods and services. With the exchange rate fixed, the central bank cannot tighten policy (raise rates) to fight inflation. Therefore, domestic sectors of the economy, especially rate-sensitive sectors such as real estate, are likely to overheat and fuel even higher inflation. In the meantime, with higher inflation and a fixed exchange rate, the export sector becomes increasingly uncompetitive. Eventually there is intense pressure to adjust the exchange rate or even to float the currency. At that point the fixed exchange rate has lost credibility, and nominal interest rates will diverge, especially at longer maturities.

Intuition might suggest that the cost of goods and services should be the same regardless of location or currency denomination. International economists refer to this notion as **purchasing power parity** (PPP). If PPP always held, an inflation differential would always lead to an exactly offsetting change in the exchange rate, and a given nominal return would imply the same real return for investors regardless of their home market or currency. Similarly, a fixed exchange rate would eliminate inflation differentials. The failure of PPP is what allows real interest rates to diverge.

Why does PPP fail? If all goods and services were freely traded among economies, the answer would simply be rigidities such as regulations, local preferences, costs, and taxes that inhibit full exploitation of price differentials across markets. That is, the so-called *law of one price* fails. This is certainly part of the story. A more important

Throughout the 1990s global fixed income managers placed bets on the formation of the European Economic and Monetary Union (EMU) as the potential member nations struggled to engineer sufficient convergence among their macroeconomies. Successful adoption of the common currency implied that (nominal) interest rates would converge; failure implied that convergence would not be sustained. A correct bet on convergence offered significant profit because the "peripheral" markets would tighten by hundreds of basis points relative to the "the core" (Germany and France). Italy, for example, traded 600 basis points over Germany in the early going. Of course the consequences of ultimate failure rose as convergence progressed: Spreads would undoubtedly "blow out" again, bringing large losses on convergence trades.

With the adoption of the single currency on January 1, 1999, the yield curves of participating countries traded in a tight band. The peripheral markets still offered a small spread versus benchmark German bonds; this was due in part to liquidity. More importantly, it also reflected concern over the sustainability of the monetary union.

The peripheral countries, Spain and Italy in particular, had higher pre-EMU interest rates because historically they had higher inflation and weaker fiscal discipline and, especially in the case of Italy, used periodic currency devaluation to restore competitiveness. Although the EMU imposed some discipline, these markets still warranted somewhat tighter monetary policy than the core economies. Under the one-size-fits-all monetary policy of the European Central Bank, these economies became increasingly uncompetitive and dependent on capital inflows. Meanwhile Spain experienced a massive real estate bubble. In early 2008 the worsening global credit crisis curtailed capital flows and pushed yield spreads to levels last seen when formation of the EMU was likely but not a certainty.

---

factor is that many products, especially services, are inherently local and hence not traded across markets. The prices of these products respond to domestic economic conditions and can differ significantly across markets. Domestic conditions can also indirectly affect prices of traded products because the traded and nontraded sectors must compete for local factors of production, such as labor and land.

Thus global fixed income markets remain distinct despite increasing globalization. Interest rates, both nominal and real, will tend to converge if countries follow policies that are consistent with stable exchange rates and similar inflation rates. In the absence of fully credible fixed exchange rates and purchasing power parity, however, each market can and will respond to its domestic economy.

Are Hedged Bonds Redundant?

Given the close relationship between interest rate differentials and currency forwards, it is natural to ask whether hedged foreign bonds are equivalent to domestic bonds. The answer is yes provided that each foreign cash flow is hedged to its specific due date.

Suppose a foreign bond will generate a sequence of cash flows denoted by C_t, each cash flow has been hedged back to our domestic currency at forward rates denoted by F_t^*, and under current market conditions new hedges could be established at rates F_t. Using the notation of Section 10.4, the domestic currency value of this bond plus the associated hedges is given by

$$S \sum_t \exp(-y_{lt}\, t)\, C_t \;+\; \sum_t \exp(-y_{dt}\, t)\, C_t \,(F_t^* - F_t)$$

Note that we have added maturity subscripts where needed but, for simplicity, have omitted currency subscripts on the exchange rates. The first term is the foreign price of the bond (the discounted present value of the cash flows), converted at the spot exchange rate *S*. The second component is the domestic currency value of the hedges. Each term in the summation will be positive (negative) if the hedge was put on at a forward rate that is more (less) favorable than current market forward rates. Using Equation (10.1) and rearranging, it is straightforward to show that this expression reduces to

$$\sum \exp(-y_{dt}\, t) C_t F_t^*$$

This is exactly equivalent to a domestic currency bond with cash flows $(C_t F_t^*)$.

In practice, global fixed income managers do not hedge each cash flow individually. Instead they hedge primarily with relatively short-maturity forward contracts, typically three months or less. Foreign bonds hedged in this manner are not equivalent to domestic bonds. To see why, consider 10-year zero-coupon bonds hedged with three-month currency forward contracts. From Section 10.4 we know that the interest rate exposure inherent in the forward contract is equivalent to being long a three-month zero-coupon note in the domestic currency and short a three-month zero-coupon note in the foreign currency (see the derivation of Equation 10.1). Recall from the previous chapter that the duration of a zero-coupon bond is approximately equal to its maturity. If foreign yields decline by 1 percent relative to domestic yields, a foreign 10-year zero-coupon bond will outperform a similar domestic bond by 10 percent while a three-month currency hedge loses 0.25 percent. The currency-hedged foreign bond outperforms the similar domestic bond by 9.75 percent in this example. Note that the hedged foreign bond will perform even better if the foreign yield curve flattens relative to the domestic yield curve.

Global Equities: Country versus Industry Effects

Which is more important—the fact that ExxonMobil and Total are both integrated oil companies or the fact that one is American and one is French? Does it matter that shares of both companies trade on a U.S. exchange? These questions have important implications for the way we approach global equity investing.

Traditionally the shares of firms domiciled in various countries have been viewed as inherently different, even for firms in essentially the same business. Implicit in this perspective is an assumption that factors specific to each local economy and market are among the most significant drivers of equity returns. Under this assumption, correlations among country-specific stock indexes should be low enough that simply investing across national markets (via country indexes) provides substantial diversification. On the other hand, if global economies and markets are fully integrated, national markets with similar industry compositions should be fairly highly correlated. In that case investing geographically is likely to offer only modest risk reduction.

In contrast, global integration should enhance the importance of industry factors driving the performance of similar firms throughout the global market. However, economic integration would not necessarily increase the correlation between inherently different businesses. Thus diversification across global industries should remain a potent source of risk reduction even in a globally integrated market.

The degree of market integration and relative importance of country effects and industry effects affect not only how we want to construct a portfolio (that is, how we control risk) but also how we organize the investment research process. Highly segmented markets with strong country-specific factors put a premium on understanding local conditions. In large measure this implies a heavier emphasis on top-down analysis of the local macroeconomy, policies, and politics as well as frequent interaction with local market participants. With modern communications technology much of this can be accomplished remotely from a central investment headquarters. Nonetheless, the premium on local knowledge suggests the need for country and regional specialists residing in the markets they cover and perhaps covering the full range of companies within those markets. At the other end of the spectrum, highly integrated markets with predominant industry factors lend themselves to an emphasis on bottom-up analysis of similar businesses regardless of location. Here the premium is on thoroughly understanding the industry and the competitive positions of the individual firms. This suggests organizing the research effort along industry lines, as is typically done for purely domestic, fundamental equity processes. Of course these perspectives are not mutually exclusive. It might, for example, make sense to divide the equity market into two groups: stocks that represent global competitors and are valued similarly, and others that either do not compete globally or are not valued in the same fashion.

Despite a growing empirical literature, there is no real consensus on whether globalization has changed the relative importance of country effects versus industry effects or even whether it has reduced the diversification available to global investors. Unfortunately, but not surprisingly, the results vary depending on the sample period, the markets studied, and the statistical methodology employed. To illustrate the issues and the sometimes conflicting results, we will briefly summarize three essentially contemporaneous studies, each utilizing a broad array of markets and a long sample that extends beyond the late-1990s technology bubble.

Note that there are two complementary, but distinct, notions of *importance* here. The first is how well *industry* and *country* describe the cross-sectional characteristics, such as correlations, of global equity returns. Clearly a factor that better explains the cross-sectional risk structure is important because it is a more reliable guide for diversification. The second notion of *importance* pertains to the magnitude of diversification. Low correlation among portfolios differentiated on the basis of a particular factor, such as country or industry, implies strong diversification potential and hence that the factor is an important consideration in portfolio construction.

Bekaert, Hodrick, and Zhang (2005) used various linear factor models containing both global and local factors to study the correlation structure of weekly returns for country/industry portfolios spanning 23 countries and 26 industries from 1980 through 2003. One of the models, originated by Heston and Rouwenhorst (1994), separates each country/industry portfolio return into the sum of three components: a country return common to all portfolios from that country, a global industry return common to all portfolios from that industry, and an unexplained residual return. The authors found that this simple "country plus industry" model explained the cross-sectional correlation structure as well as more general models with only global factors, but not as well as models incorporating both global and local factors. Within the HR model, using only country effects explained the correlation structure somewhat better than using only industry effects. From this perspective, country effects appear more important than industry effects. The fact that the average correlation between country portfolios (0.37) was well below the average correlation between industry portfolios (.62) reinforces this conclusion.

To assess whether industry effects are becoming more important over time, BHZ subdivided their sample into six-month intervals and tested for a linear trend in average portfolio correlations over the full sample. They found no trend in average industry correlation and no significant upward trend in average country correlation except within Europe. There was also no trend in country correlation relative to industry correlation over the full sample. However, there was a sharp decline in industry correlation relative to country correlation within the 1990–2000 subperiod used in several prior studies. Excluding the technology–media–telecom sector did not eliminate this sub-period trend. Thus the rising importance of industry effects relative to country effects reported in earlier papers appears to have been temporary but not entirely attributable to the late-1990s technology bubble.

Carrieri, Errunza, and Sarkissian (2006) reached quite different conclusions based on a narrower data set (17 countries, 10 industries) and a slightly longer period (1976–2003). They found that cross-country correlations have trended upward both in absolute terms and relative to cross-industry correlations. Furthermore, the increased importance of industry diversification was not specific to the 1990s. In addition, the increased cross-country correlation appears to reflect correspondingly higher correlations of industrial production and increased alignment of industrial structure across countries.

What accounts for these different conclusions? The BHZ and CES studies actually asked slightly different questions. The BHZ study focused on the *unconditional* correlation structure of returns, whereas the CES analysis examined the correlation structure *conditional* on a set of information variables.[5] In addition, CES imposed an explicit model of how (conditional) correlations evolve through time, whereas BHZ simply examined correlations from various subperiods. Both approaches offer insights, but neither provides a definitive answer.

Lewis (2006) provided yet another perspective on the issue of country correlations and shed light on whether foreign company shares traded on a U.S. exchange offer the same diversification as shares traded abroad. Whereas the CES study assumed continuous evolution of risk parameters, the Lewis study identified discrete breakpoints in each market's relationship to other markets. For most markets, only one or two break-points were found within the 1970–2004 sample: one in the early 1990s and one in the late 1990s. In general, correlations among markets increased. Foreign stocks that also trade in the United States became significantly more correlated with the U.S. market even after accounting for increased correlation between their home markets and the United States. Thus foreign stocks traded in the United States are not an adequate substitute for investing directly in foreign markets.

What conclusions can we draw from the mixture of evidence? First, both global and local factors are important. Global integration remains an ongoing process. Second, both country and industry are important. Chapter 8 illustrated the importance of managing both style and sector/industry risks in a domestic portfolio. In a global portfolio, we need to consider country risk as well.

10.7　Currency Overlays: Incentive-Compatible Performance Evaluation

As discussed in Section 10.4, forward contracts let us separate decisions with respect to currency exposure from the selection of underlying assets. Carrying this logic a step further, it may be advantageous to assign responsibility for currency and asset decisions to specialists within the portfolio management team. Similarly, some clients hire a **currency overlay** manager to manage their aggregate currency exposure, leaving their various asset managers free to focus on selecting stocks and bonds. Whether the separation occurs within a portfolio management team or across management firms, manager mandates and the associated performance evaluations should be structured carefully to ensure compatible incentives.

---

[5] The distinction between conditional and unconditional risk and return parameters was discussed in Chapter 4.

To highlight the issues as clearly as possible, the following discussion assumes that an overall portfolio mandate will be managed by an asset specialist and a currency specialist. Neither will be individually responsible for overall performance. Instead each will be evaluated (and compensated) based on his or her individual benchmark. The individual benchmarks must of course add up to the client's overall benchmark. The question is how to give both incentive-compatible mandates to ensure that their decisions will be consistent with the best overall performance.

A good incentive structure should adhere to the following three principles:

- *Fairness:* Each manager's performance should reflect only decisions within his or her authority.
- *Invariance:* Economically equivalent exposures should result in the same measured performance.
- *No conflict of interest:* The "invisible hand" of self-interest should induce decisions that result in the best overall portfolio performance. That is, neither manager should need to choose between the good of the client and his or her own performance.

In the current context, the fairness principle rules out measuring the asset manager's performance based on unhedged returns. Unhedged returns reflect both asset and currency movements, but the asset manager does not have authority over the final currency exposures. On the other hand, because the currency manager cannot control the choice of assets, the cost or benefit of hedging the associated currency exposure should not be included in his or her performance. Fairness therefore requires that the asset manager bear the cost or reap the benefit of hedging the currency exposures arising from his or her decisions. The fairness principle also implies that a currency overlay structure is inappropriate if the investment policy restricts currency decisions based on asset positions—such as if exposure to a currency is allowed only if it arises from an underlying asset position.

It is sometimes suggested that each manager's performance should be measured based on the trades he or she initiates rather than on portfolio exposures. Exhibit 10.12 illustrates that the invariance principle rules out this approach. Two scenarios are considered. In the first scenario the asset manager buys a U.K. government bond (a "gilt"). The currency manager wants exposure to the British pound (GBP) and therefore takes no action in this scenario. The portfolio is therefore long both the gilt and the currency. In the second scenario the asset manager creates exposure to gilts by combining U.S. cash with a gilt futures contract. The gilt futures contract is economically equivalent to borrowing GBP cash to buy a gilt, and hence it entails no net currency exposure. To get exposure to GBP in this scenario, the currency manager must go long GBP versus the U.S. dollar in the forward market. As in the first scenario, the portfolio is long gilts and long the currency. Therefore the measured performance of each manager should be the same in either case. This will not be the case if performance is measured based on each manager's trades rather than on the exposures arising from his or her decisions.

EXHIBIT 10.12
The Principle of Invariance— Equivalent Positions (Each Manager's Trades in Bold)

	Scenario 1	Scenario 2
Asset manager	**Long U.K. gilt**	**Long gilt futures + U.S. cash**
Currency manager	No trade (keep GBP exposure)	**Long GBP via forward**
Portfolio	Long gilt and long GBP	Long gilt and long GBP

EXHIBIT 10.13   **Conflict of Interest Example**

Market and Return Assumptions

Country	Local Currency Asset Return	Local Deposit Rate	Spot FX Change versus USD	Asset Return (USD) Unhedged	Asset Return (USD) Hedged	FX Return: Spot Change+Forward Premium or Discount
Germany	7.00	5.00	1.00	8.00	9.50	−1.50
U.K.	10.50	11.25	−3.00	7.50	6.75	0.75
Japan	9.50	9.00	−1.00	8.50	8.00	0.50
U.S.	8.40	7.50		8.40	8.40	

Decisions under Alternative Performance Criteria

		Asset Performance Criteria		
		Local Returns	**Unhedged Returns**	**Hedged Returns**
Currency Performance Criteria	Spot FX change	UK asset EUR	Japanese asset EUR	German asset EUR
	FX return including forward premium or discount	UK asset GBP	Japanese asset GBP	German asset GBP

Asset/Currency Combinations and Optimal Decisions

		Currency Decision			
		EUR	**GBP**	**JPY**	**USD**
Asset Decision	Germany	8.00	**10.25**	10.00	9.50
	U.K.	5.25	7.50	7.25	6.75
	Japan	6.50	8.75	8.50	8.00
	U.S.	6.90	9.15	8.90	8.40

Exhibit 10.13 shows the incentive effects induced by different ways of measuring bond and currency performance. The top portion of the exhibit contains performance expectations for four asset markets and their associated currencies. The U.K. asset has the highest expected return in local currency but the lowest expected return in U.S. dollars with or without hedging. The German asset has the lowest local currency return but the highest return hedged into U.S. dollars. The euro (EUR) is expected to appreciate against the dollar, but not by as much as its forward premium. Hence purchasing EUR in the forward market entails an expected loss. The British pound and Japanese yen are expected to depreciate against the dollar, but not by as much as their forward discounts. Purchasing these currencies in the forward market is therefore expected to generate a net gain.

The center portion of the exhibit shows the decisions that would be in each manager's own interest depending on how her or his performance is measured. The asset manager's choice is shown in the upper right corner of each cell and the currency manager's choice in the lower left corner. The asset manager would select the U.K.

asset if he or she will be measured on local currency returns, the Japanese asset based on unhedged dollar returns, and the German asset based on hedged dollar returns. The currency manager would choose exposure to the euro based on spot currency performance but would prefer exposure to the pound if his or her performance will be measured inclusive of forward premiums and discounts.

The bottom portion of the exhibit shows the expected returns available from each pair of asset and currency decisions. Looking across each row, the highest expected return is achieved by combining that asset with exposure to GBP. Similarly, looking at each column, the highest expected return is achieved by combining that currency exposure with the German asset. Returning to the middle section of the exhibit, we see that the managers will select the German asset hedged into GBP if and only if the asset manager is measured on the basis of hedged returns and the currency manager is measured on currency performance inclusive of forward premium or discount. So that is the incentive-compatible performance evaluation structure.

To illustrate how this works in practice, consider a portfolio managed against the unhedged JPMorgan Global Government Bond index (GBI). Based on our discussion, the bond manager would be judged against the hedged GBI. The currency manager's benchmark would be the difference between the overall portfolio benchmark (the unhedged GBI here) and the hedged benchmark. As shown earlier in Exhibit 10.7, the GBI returned 6.70 percent/year unhedged and 5.66 percent/year hedged for 2000–2007. Suppose the active portfolio returned 7.70 percent and that with full currency hedging it would have earned 6.06 percent. Based on this information, the bond manager added 0.40 percent/year [6.06 − 5.66] versus the hedged index. The currency manager's contribution to overall return was 1.64 percent [7.70 − 6.06], whereas passive currency exposure would have generated only 1.04 percent [6.70 − 5.66]. Thus the currency manager added 0.60 percent/year. By construction, the two managers account for the 1.00 percent value added of the overall portfolio.

Excel Outbox	This outbox demonstrates the separation of asset and currency decisions from the perspective of investors with different base currencies.
Separating Asset and Currency Decisions	Use the worksheet <Asset&Currency–Template> in the spreadsheet Chapter 10 Excel Outboxes.xls.

The template contains (expected) local currency asset returns, local currency deposit rates, and expected spot exchange rate changes versus the dollar for four countries and currencies: Germany/EUR, UK/GBP, Japan/JPY, and the United States/USD. Start by computing the forward premiums or discounts versus USD and the unhedged asset returns expected by a U.S. investor:

- In cell E5 enter = C$8 − C5, and then copy to cells E6:E8.
- In cell F5 enter = B5 + D5, and then copy to cells F6:F8.

To compute the hedged return for each asset from the perspective of each investor's home currency (be careful with "$" here):

- In cell C13 enter = $B5 + $E5 − $E$5.
- Copy to cells C13:F16.
- In cells D13:D16 REPLACE $E$5 with $E$6.
- In cells E13:E16 REPLACE $E$5 with $E$7.
- In cells F13:F16 REPLACE $E$5 with $E$8.

(continued)

(concluded)

To compute the potential currency return available to each investor from hedging into each of the currencies (be careful with "$" here):

- In cell C22 enter = ($D5 − $E5) − ($D$5 − $E$5). Copy to cells C22:F25.
- In cells D22:D25 REPLACE ($D$5-$E$5) with ($D$6-$E$6).
- In cells E22:E25 REPLACE ($D$5-$E$5) with ($D$7-$E$7).
- In cells F22:F25 REPLACE ($D$5-$E$5) with ($D$8-$E$8).

The results should now look like this:

Hedged Returns

Asset	Investor's Home Currency			
	EUR	GBP	JPY	USD
Germany	7	13.25	11	9.5
UK	4.25	10.5	8.25	6.75
Japan	5.5	11.75	9.5	8
US	5.9	12.15	9.9	8.4

Currency Returns

Hedge Into	Investor's Home Currency			
	EUR	GBP	JPY	USD
EUR	0	−2.25	−2	−1.5
GBP	2.25	0	0.25	0.75
JPY	2	−0.25	0	0.5
USD	1.5	−0.75	−0.5	0

Note that regardless of the investor's home country or currency, the expected hedged return is highest for the German asset. Similarly, regardless of the home currency, each investor obtains the highest currency return in GBP. Thus for each investor the most attractive strategy is the German asset hedged into GBP.

Summary

A multitude of factors—laws and regulations, government policies, resources and industrial composition, technology, currencies and financial systems, customs and cultures—differentiate foreign and domestic markets. As long as these differences persist, global investing should offer opportunities to enhance return and reduce risk.

The discussion in prior chapters still applies when we adopt a global investment perspective. However, international investing introduces additional considerations for portfolio management. The most significant of these arise from the need to manage currency exposure. As a result, much of this chapter focused on the impact of currency on portfolio decisions. We also examine the investment implications of increased globalization and the vexing question of whether international investing fails to deliver diversification when it would be most beneficial.

Problems

1. Suppose you have daily local returns for various global markets. In Chapter 4 it was shown that more frequent sampling, such as daily rather than monthly data, usually results in more precise risk measures. Why might this not be the case for cross-market correlations?

2. Match each of the 23 developed country markets in the MSCI World index with its largest industry (by market value) as of 12/31/2007. What was the largest single firm in that country and industry?

3. Which of the sectors and industry groups shown in Exhibit 10.2 would you expect to be most exposed to global competition? Least exposed? What are the implications for the country versus industry effects debate?

4. Show that the correlation between an equally weighted index of N foreign markets and the domestic market is

$$\frac{\rho\sqrt{N}}{\sqrt{1 + (N - 1)\phi}}$$

where ρ is the correlation of each foreign market with the domestic market and ϕ is the correlation between each pair of foreign markets. What restriction must be placed on the relationship between ρ and ϕ to ensure that this is a valid correlation coefficient? Assuming positive correlations, what effect does greater diversification (larger N) have on the correlation between the foreign index and the domestic market?

5. Starting with the unhedged return in Equation (10.3), show that selling the investment proceeds into currency j at the forward rate between currencies i and j yields the cross-hedged return in Equation (10.5).

6. Using the market information in the top portion of Exhibit 10.8, reconsider the four currency strategies in the bottom portion of the exhibit from the perspective of a Swiss investor and a euro-based investor. Will they end up with exposure to the same currency as the U.S. investor? Why or why not?

7. Explain why the value of a quanto depends on the correlation between the local currency asset price and the exchange rate. What does this imply for the slippage inherent in a static currency hedge?

8. Japanese government bond yields are substantially below those on U.S. Treasury securities. Does a U.S. investor pick up or give up yield by hedging JGBs into dollars?

9. The U.S. Treasury is usually considered the world's best credit. Yet the Treasury pays substantially higher interest rates than the Japanese government. How can this situation persist?

10. Your portfolio management team delegates currency decisions and asset decisions to specialists whose personal compensation depends heavily on performance relative to their individual benchmarks. The benchmark for the overall portfolio is a 50 percent hedged version of the XYZ Global index. Three published versions of the XYZ index are available: unhedged, hedged, and local currency. How would you calculate the benchmark for the overall portfolio? What should the benchmark be for the asset manager? For the currency manager?

Chapter 11

Alternative Investment Classes

11.1 Introduction

Up until this chapter, the discussion has focused on managing portfolios of well-defined asset classes. Pricing data on equities, investment-grade bonds, and cash instruments in developed markets are readily available and not subject to significant pricing problems or survivorship bias. Passive investment in these asset classes is readily accomplished through separate accounts, mutual funds, or ETFs. This is not the case with alternative investment classes, which require a new approach to evaluating the risk–return profile. Note that we are careful to avoid the term *alternative asset classes*. As Erb and Harvey (2006) note, these investments are more like asset "strategies" due to the general lack of effective passive alternatives or the unavailability of market capitalization–weighting schemes.

If alternative investments offer an opportunity to expand the efficient set, then merely investing in familiar assets—stocks, bonds, and cash—will be suboptimal. Commodities, real estate, and new business ventures are all considered alternative investments. Hedge funds, which frequently invest in publicly traded stocks and bonds, are also considered alternative investments due to the leverage, hedging, and derivatives often used in their portfolio construction, resulting in returns that are either higher or uncorrelated with long positions in common asset classes. Investors tend to believe alternative investments offer opportunities for further portfolio diversification but may be too volatile to justify large allocations. This view is beginning to change. University endowments, with long-term horizons, have significantly increased their investment

EXHIBIT 11.1
Asset Totals for Common and Alternative Investments

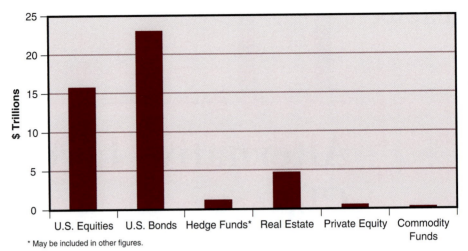

* May be included in other figures.

Note: As of December 2005. Sources: hedge funds, HFRI; real estate, RREEF Deutsche Bank; private equity, Thomson Venture Economics; and commodity funds. Morgan Stanley.

in alternatives over the last 10 years. While allocations to alternatives remain smaller than allocations to U.S. equities and bonds for most investors, their size has grown to substantial levels, as illustrated in Exhibit 11.1.

Moreover, portfolios diversified into alternatives performed well during the market downturn in 2001–2002, leading to increased visibility and interest in alternative investments. However, it is important to note that published returns for hedge funds, private equity, venture capital, and real estate may not reflect the returns realized by investors,[1] and the resulting bias may overstate returns and understate volatility and correlation with other asset classes. Hedge fund data are composed of returns voluntarily reported by the managers, leading to potential biases. Capital invested in commodities does not generate income and efficiency trends suggest commodity prices may not increase in the long term. Published private equity returns are not marked to market. As a result of all these issues, simply loading historical returns, volatilities, and correlations from published data into the asset allocation models developed in earlier chapters may not provide true optimal allocations. Further, because market capitalization data are not meaningful for all investment classes, it is not easy to create market-weighted investment class portfolios when alternative investments are included. Lastly, alternative investments typically exhibit nonnormal distributions. Given these considerations, techniques beyond M–V optimization should be explored.

Many hedge funds invest in publicly traded equities and bonds, the subject of previous chapters, so this chapter begins with a discussion of hedge funds in Sections 11.2 and 11.3. Venture capital investing focuses on start-up companies that have not yet made it to the public marketplace, and private equity funds invest in established companies that are not publicly traded. These strategies are reviewed in Section 11.4. Real estate investing is discussed in Section 11.5, and commodities are reviewed in Section 11.6. The last section in the chapter describes techniques to set optimal asset allocation mixes, relying on historical behavior of asset classes but without requiring the assumption of well-behaved return distributions.

---

[1] In late 2008 Harvard Management was reported to have shopped $1.5 billion in private equity investments, typically carried on the books at cost or appraisal value, and received bids for only 60 cents on the dollar.

Finally, here are some words of caution from Robert Lovell, Jr., who defined an alternative investment as "one that has outperformed, is outperforming and you fear will continue to outperform something you now own." As they would with stocks or bonds, investors in alternatives should be careful to invest on valuation and diversification, not fashion.

11.2   Hedge Funds

There are at least two reasons why hedge funds are considered alternative investments. First, as a group, their return behavior is different than stocks or bonds. Second, individually they reflect very different strategies and may invest in different asset classes than long-only publicly traded equities or bonds. In the 1970s and 1980s the typical hedge fund, such as those run by Robertson and Soros, were global macro funds, betting on currencies and investing across markets. Today's hedge funds span the range of possible strategies, and those in familiar strategies offer different portfolio construction. For example, equity hedge funds may go short as well as long, use derivatives, and leverage their portfolios.

Definition of a Hedge Fund

Hedge funds have experienced explosive growth as a category, and implosions as individual products. As reported in Exhibit 11.2, the number of hedge funds has grown from 200 with $38 billion in assets under management (AUM) in 1990 to over 6,000 funds managing $1.4 trillion by 2008. The creation of the first hedge fund is credited to Alfred Winslow Jones in 1949, and it had all the essential elements that typify a hedge fund: The market risk of long stock positions was hedged with short positions, and leverage was used to enhance returns. In 1952 his general partnership was changed to a limited partnership and included a 20 percent incentive fee, and Jones's entire net worth was invested in the fund. His investment approach was made public in 1966, and by 1968 there were approximately 20 funds, including those formed by Soros, Steinhardt, and Buffett.[2]

[2] Gabelli (2005) offers a concise historical overview. Warren Buffett has argued that Benjamin Graham predated Jones, advocating a long/short approach to portfolio construction.

EXHIBIT 11.2
Number and AUM of Hedge Funds (1990–2008)

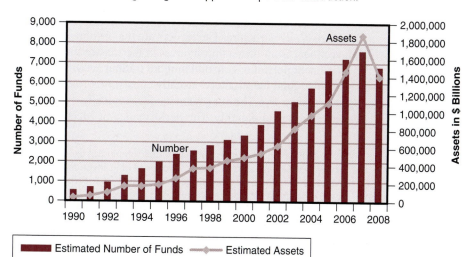

Wall Street veteran Richard Bookstaber (2003) asks this question: What is a hedge fund? His answer is that there is no such thing as a hedge fund. He argues that the vast diversity of styles and strategies defies classification by current schemes; "The proper study of hedge funds cannot be differentiated from a general study of investments." As a result, alternative investments are a description of what an investment fund is *not* rather than what it is. So rather than defining alternatives as not traditional, he defines traditional assets as not alternative.

Hedged equity funds, Jones's successors, experienced the most rapid growth of any strategy during the 1990s and were a key factor in attracting flows to hedge funds in general due largely to their stable performance relative to the equity markets in bull markets and positive returns in bear markets. In fact hedge funds are frequently described as *absolute return strategies*. Equity hedge funds are relatively easy to establish, with low entry costs, and are highly scalable due to deep and liquid equity markets. As a result, the demand for hedge funds was met by a large supply of buy-side analysts and portfolio managers attracted by the higher compensation and lower investment restrictions available at hedge funds.

How a Hedge Fund Works

In most cases and similar to mutual funds, hedge funds are structured as limited partnerships (LPs) or limited liability companies (LLCs) that hire advisors to manage securities held in the fund. While still bound by securities law, hedge funds historically did not register as investment companies under the Investment Companies Act of 1940 (see the War Story: Hedge Fund Regulation box). In consequence, there are restrictions on the investments hedge funds can accept.[3] In addition, hedge funds cannot solicit investments from, or offer their services to, the public. They rely instead on previously established relationships, third-party marketing firms, and consultants to locate investors. Further, instead of a prospectus, a hedge fund produces a *private offering memorandum* outlining the fund's strategies, risks, conflicts of interest, liquidity terms, and fee structure.

To manage investments for both U.S. and non-U.S. investors and ensure preferable tax treatment for each group, managers typically create a domestic onshore fund for U.S. investors and an offshore fund for non-U.S. investors, connected through a *master–feeder* structure. The feeders are the onshore and offshore funds, and their only investment is an ownership interest in the master fund. The master fund is the actual investment portfolio, consolidating all trading activities.

Hedge fund fee structures usually consist of a fixed management fee and a variable performance fee. The management fee, typically 1–2 percent of assets under management, is paid monthly. The performance or **incentive fee,** typically 20 percent, is

---

[3] As of 2009, a fund that does not make public offerings is exempt from SEC registration if the fund has or fewer 100 investors (a 3(c)(1) fund) or all of its investors are *qualified purchasers* (a 3(c)(7) fund). However, there are "look through" provisions to prevent the pyramiding of 3(c)(1) funds, and 3(c)(7) funds must register if assets exceed $10 million and there are 500 or more investors. Both *accredited investors* and qualified purchasers invest in Section 3(c)(1) hedge funds. Accredited investors are generally institutions or corporations meeting Regulation D requirements and individuals with total net worth in excess of $1 million or annual income in excess of $200,000 (or joint income of $300,000). Qualified purchasers are generally individuals with liquid net worth of $5 million, institutions with net worth of $25 million, or trusts with total assets in excess of $5 million.

charged on returns above a specified hurdle rate and above a high-water mark. The **hurdle rate** is a prespecified minimum rate of return below which the fund does not charge an incentive fee. The **high-water mark** is the highest cumulative return attained by the fund, net of fees. The incentive fee is not received unless the fund return exceeds both of these criteria. Note that the management fee is earned even if performance does not exceed the hurdle rate or high-water mark. The calculation of fees is illustrated in the Theory in Practice: Fee Calculation box.

Unlike mutual funds or closed-end funds, hedge funds usually do not offer daily liquidity; rather investors are required to invest their money for longer periods. There are four features of hedge fund liquidity: redemption frequency, notification period, lock-up, and gating. The **redemption frequency** indicates when, or how often, investors can sell their holdings. The **notification period** indicates how far in advance investors must indicate their intention to redeem from the fund. The **lock-up** is the initial period over which the investor cannot redeem holdings, whereas a **gate** limits the amount of fund assets, or investor assets, that can be redeemed at any one time. Consider a fund that offers quarterly redemptions with 90 days notification, has a 25 percent fund level gate, and a one-year hard lock. The lock means investors would have to wait at least one year after investing before they could redeem. The investors would then be able to redeem from the fund four times a year, such as at the end of each calendar quarter, and would be required to notify the fund 90 days in advance. The gate means that the total amount that could be redeemed by all investors in any quarter could not exceed 25 percent of the fund's AUM. If requests for more than 25 percent of the fund's AUM were made, the 25 percent would be redeemed and pro-rated to investors who submitted redemption requests. The requested redemptions in excess of 25 percent would be rolled to the next available redemption date—that is, the next quarter end. The rationale behind restricting liquidity is to allow the fund time to unwind positions without adversely affecting the fund's other investors. While this is particularly important for funds that engage in strategies involving complex, longer-dated, or illiquid positions, liquidity is a concern for all funds.

Liquidity terms vary across strategies, but quarterly redemptions are the most typical. Prior to 2008, the trend was toward less liquidity, partially driven by the short-lived SEC registration requirements and the fact that successful funds could demand less liquid terms from investors. Although most investors must accept the liquidity and fee structure, larger investors, such as institutions and funds of funds (FoF), can often negotiate more attractive terms in a *side letter*. The impact of 2008 on liquidity terms has yet to be seen.

These preferential terms are a source of value added for FoF. In addition to liquidity, side letters may specify special fees, transparency, or other benefits to a shareholder. In fact a prospective investor may want to ask a hedge fund manager what special arrangements exist with other investors.

Consider a fund fee structure with a 1.5 percent management fee and a 20 percent incentive fee with a high-water mark (HWM). Define the *gross* return as the return earned by the fund's investments, the *net gross* return as the gross return less the management fee only and the *net net* return as the gross return less both the management and incentive fees. Assume that in month 1 the gross return was 0.500 percent and in month 2 the gross return was −1.000 percent. The fee calculations for month 2 are:

$$\text{Net gross return} = \text{Gross return} - \text{Management fee}$$
$$= -1\% - (1.5\%/12) = -1.125\%$$
$$\text{Cumulative return} = (1 + \text{Previous cumulative return}) \times (1 + \text{Net gross return}) - 1$$
$$= (1 + 0.375\%) \times (1 - 1.125\%) - 1 = -0.754\%$$
$$\text{HWM} = \text{Maximum cumulative return through the previous month}$$
$$= 0.375\%$$
$$\text{Incentive fee} = \text{Incentive fee} \times \max[0, (1 + \text{Cumulative return})/(1 + \text{HWM}) - 1]$$
$$= 20\% \times \max(0, (1 - 0.754\%)/(1 + 0.375\%) - 1]$$
$$= 0\% \text{ because the cumulative return} < \text{HWM}$$
$$\text{Net net return} = \text{Net gross return} - \text{Incentive fee}$$
$$= -1.125\% - 0.000\% = -1.125\%$$

To see how the high-water mark works, assume that in month 3 the gross return is 2 percent. This is high enough to bring the cumulative return up to 1.107 percent, above the 0.375 percent high-water mark (notice that the high-water mark remains at 0.375 percent because the net gross return in month 2 was negative). The incentive fee is charged only on the return above the high-water mark to avoid double-charging ($=0.20 \times ((1.01107)/(1.00375) - 1) = 0.00146$). Typically the incentive fee is accrued monthly but paid quarterly or at the end of the year. This is illustrated in the following table:

Month	1	2	3	4	5	6
Gross return	0.500%	−1.000%	2.000%	−1.500%	1.000%	2.000%
Management fee	0.125	0.125	0.125	0.125	0.125	0.125
Net gross return	0.375	−1.125	1.875	−1.625	0.875	1.875
Cumulative return	0.375	−0.754	1.107	−0.536	0.334	2.215
High-water mark	0.000	0.375	0.375	1.107	1.107	1.107
Incentive fee	0.075	0.000	0.146	0.000	0.000	0.219
Net net return	0.300	−1.125	1.729	−1.625	0.875	1.656

Hedge Fund Styles and Returns

A hedge fund style is a broad categorization that groups strategies based on the assets traded and the investment process. Exhibit 11.3 shows one scheme for organizing hedge fund strategies into styles. Exhibit 11.4 summarizes historical returns using this classification scheme.

In examining hedge fund (and other alternative investment) returns, one should consider whether they

1. Offer the ability to extend the efficient frontier. This includes whether the low correlation to traditional assets is stable through time, including during financial crises.
2. Are sufficiently lognormal to allow the use of M–V portfolio allocation.

War Story *Liquidity*

In 2005 investor redemptions following weak performance triggered a run on the London-based Bailey Coates' Cromwell Fund. This created a liquidity spiral as selling, in anticipation of the fund having to liquidate positions, drove down share prices of underlying holdings, which in turn forced the fund to sell more shares to meet redemptions. To protect remaining shareholders, the fund was liquidated in April 2005.

EXHIBIT 11.3 **Hedge Fund Styles and Strategies**

Style		
Relative value		**Strategies that seek to exploit perceived mispricings between equivalent securities.**
	Convertible arbitrage	Price relationship between convertible bonds and the underlying common stock.
	Options arbitrage	Volatility trading strategies typically through listed options on stock or equity indexes.
	Mortgage-backed securities	Focuses on mortgage-backed securities (MBS) and collateralized mortgage obligations (CMO).
	Long/short credit	Price relationship between corporate bonds along the credit curve (from high-yield to investment-grade).
	Credit arbitrage	Price relationship between equity, debt, options, and credit instruments of the same issuer.
	Asset-backed securities	Focus on bond or debt securities collateralized by the cash flows from a pool of securities.
	Fixed-income arbitrage	Price relationship between fixed-income securities and derivatives.
Event-driven		**Strategies that seek to exploit perceived mispricings created by identifiable market events.**
	Merger arbitrage	Invest in companies that are being acquired or are involved in a merger.
	Distressed securities	Invest in securities of firms that have filed for bankruptcy protection or are negotiating with creditors to avoid bankruptcy.
	Asset-based lending	Provide loans to small and medium-sized companies, secured by their assets.
	Capital structure arbitrage	Price relationships between securities across the full corporate capital structure of the same issuer.
	Private placement arbitrage	Invest in privately negotiated securities in public companies.
Hedged equities		**Strategies that seek to exploit perceived mispricings between equity securities.**
	Quantitative MN market neutral equity	Construction of portfolios with minimal market exposure using quantitative selection techniques.
	Fundamental market neutral equity	Construction of portfolios with minimal market exposure using fundamental selection techniques.
	Long/short equity	The classic hedge fund strategy. Buy undervalued and sell overvalued stocks, but not necessarily market neutral.
	Event-driven equity	Long/short equity strategy based on identifiable events and catalysts.
Trading		**Strategies that seek to exploit expected price movements using fundamental and technical analysis methods.**
	Macro strategies	Longer-term directional positions across markets based on expected shifts in macroeconomic conditions.
	Futures strategies	Wide range of strategies that are implemented through various futures instruments.

EXHIBIT 11.4 **Hedge Fund Monthly Return Summary Statistics, 1990–2008**

	US Equities (S&P 500)	US Bonds (Lehman/ Barclays Agg)	Hedged Equity (HFRI Equity Hedge Total)	Event Driven (HFRI Event Driven Total)	Macro Trading (HFRI Macro Total)	Relative Value (HFRI Relative Value Total)	Emerging Markets (HFRI Emerging Markets Total)	Fund of Funds (HFRI Fund of Funds Composite)
				Gross Returns				
Standard Deviation	4.2%	1.1%	2.7%	2.0%	2.3%	1.3%	4.2%	1.7%
Skewness	−0.68	−0.28	−0.23	−1.40	0.41	−2.38	−0.91	−0.72
Excess Kurtosis	−1.46	−2.33	−0.95	1.43	−2.20	12.23	0.72	0.99
				Log Returns				
Standard Deviation	4.3%	1.1%	2.6%	2.0%	2.2%	1.3%	4.3%	1.7%
Skewness	−0.89	−0.32	−0.39	−1.54	0.32	−2.60	−1.25	−0.87
Excess Kurtosis	−0.86	−2.29	−0.81	2.07	−2.20	13.65	2.21	1.39

Note: Passow (2005) provides results for the period January 1990 to April 2004.

One way to examine the return distribution of hedge fund strategies is by creating portfolios of randomly selected funds from within a strategy designation using the Hedge Fund Research Inc. (HFR) database. The results of such an approach, presented in Exhibit 11.4, indicate:

1. The return distributions of hedge funds appear to extend the efficient frontier of traditional assets.
2. All but emerging markets strategies exhibit lower volatility than U.S. equities. Strategies such as event-driven and relative value display greater skew and higher excess kurtosis than U.S. equities and fixed income. These strategies display a high probability of small positive returns and a small (though larger than a normal distribution would suggest) probability of a large loss. This was particularly evident during the 1994 bond and 1998 Russian/LTCM crises.
3. Individual hedge funds can display highly non-normal and non-lognormal return distributions. Hedge funds are often intentionally exposed to tail risk (kurtosis), with the result that a M–V optimized portfolio of hedge funds may be riskier than expected. An alternative allocation method is needed to perfectly capture these higher moments.

Data Issues

It is argued that the published performance of hedge funds is overstated due to data issues that arise from the voluntary reporting of hedge fund performance. Funds report when they are alive and seeking capital. If they cease to exist or are closed to new investments, they generally do not report. This leads to several potential biases in forming expectations about return and risk from available databases:

- *End-of-life reporting bias:* If a fund stops reporting during the last months prior to its liquidation due to poor performance, or after closing to new business following good performance, this creates a net bias in the return series. Academic research estimates a net bias of up to +6 percent.
- *Survivorship bias:* If the database includes only currently existing funds and removes funds that have closed or no longer report, this is likely to leave more successful funds in the database, creating an upward return bias. Estimates range between 0.6 percent and 3.7 percent.
- *Back-fill bias:* When a fund is added to a database, its return history is also typically included, or backfilled. To the extent that funds with successful operating performance are more likely to be added to a database, the return is biased upward. A fund that has posted poor returns does not report, and its unsuccessful history is not added to the database. In total, estimates suggest this generates a bias of between 1.4 percent and 5.0 percent.

Bonafede, Foresti and Toth (2004) study estimated that the published hedge fund databases are in total upwardly biased by 3.5–5 percent per year. However, Fung and Hsieh (2009) have found that half the funds removed from one database may have either elected not to report or elected to report to a different database.[4] This suggests that estimates of survivor and end-of-life reporting bias may be overstated. A review of the HFR database indicates that between 1990 and 2006 the average fund of funds return, which is not subject to the mentioned biases but includes an additional layer of fees, was 4.2 percent lower per annum than the average hedge fund return. Regardless, it is important to adjust for potential sample biases when developing return forecasts and allocating assets.

11.3 Manager Selection

Sources of Alpha

Investors hire active portfolio managers to generate alpha (excess returns over a passive alternative). For managers to consistently generate alpha, they must be able to consistently exploit market inefficiencies. Although luck can be a source of alpha, by definition a fund should not be able to consistently generate luck. Sources of alpha include *informational asymmetries, behavioral patterns, market segmentation,* and *disintermediation.* These sources may be categorized into *behavioral* and *structural* groups. Behavioral sources include pricing opportunities arising from informational asymmetries or self-imposed constraints by investors. Structural sources arise from imposed constraints linked to regulatory or market segmentation.

Constraints on Standard Investment Products

The investment processes of mutual funds and other institutional portfolios are commonly constrained by guidelines, rules, and regulations. In contrast, hedge fund managers have the freedom to go short, lever, implement custom derivative positions, purchase illiquid issues, invest in nonstandard markets and instruments, and take large,

---

[4] William Fung and David Hsieh, "Measurement Biases in Hedge Fund Performance Data: An Update," *Financial Analysts Journal* 65, no. 3 (2009), pp. 36–38.

A principal–agent relationship exists when an intermediary is hired to act for an individual or entity. This can create a conflict of interest for the intermediary between personal profit and fiduciary responsibility to the investor. That is, even if the agent can generate alpha, the agent might want to extract this alpha through fees and other benefits. In the case of hedge funds there are two principal–agent relationships: between the hedge fund and the issuers of the securities held (in practice firm management) and between the hedge fund and its investors. It has been argued that the combination of a flexible fee structure and compensation linked to performance helps align the interests of investors and hedge fund (intermediary) managers, thus mitigating principal–agent conflicts.

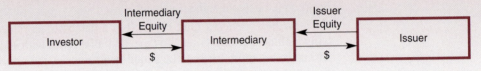

undiversified bets within highly concentrated portfolios. This freedom lets hedge funds concentrate on identified opportunities in their areas of expertise without being tied to a benchmark, improving the odds for generating alpha.

The business of hedge funds also creates an advantage over traditional management organizations: the ability to attract professionals with stronger analytical capabilities and broader experience due to their generous compensation schemes. In addition, smaller firms with only one business may allow more time to focus on pure investing. This combination of broad skills and investment flexibility allows hedge funds to (1) implement unique, more efficient, or sophisticated strategies, (2) operate in markets that require complex and sophisticated strategies, and (3) implement more effective strategic risk taking. Their investment activity also supports more efficient movement of capital in the marketplace, promoting prices that more accurately reflect full information.

Behavioral Sources

Behavioral patterns are created by the decisions of investors or the constraints they impose on their actions, as opposed to structural constraints imposed by business policy or regulation. Examples include *performance chasing, investing in familiar assets* (avoiding small or illiquid securities), *benchmarking,* and the mistaken belief of possessing an informational advantage. *Informational asymmetries* are the classic source of market inefficiency; to consistently add alpha you need to either act on information before the market or have a unique way of using the information available. However, with *Regulation FD* requiring simultaneous distribution of material company information to all U.S. investors, it has become difficult to receive information before others, requiring more sophisticated analysis of the information to generate alpha.

Although benchmarking has the positive effect of separating alpha from beta, it may produce incentives to lower risk, including locking in a bonus or not investing in ideas (such as if the payoff is beyond the bonus deadline) that benefit the fund manager (agent) over the investor (principal). It can also reduce risk taking if senior management continually asks why such big bets are being taken—instead of why bigger bets are not being taken. The absolute return focus of hedge fund compensation attempts to mitigate these problems by paying incentive fees for incremental return above the high-water mark.

Benchmarking also restricts the flexibility of strategies. When mutual funds attempted more flexible investment strategies in the 1990s, they were accused of *style drift* by academics, consultants, and customers. The result in many cases was portfolio managers keeping close to narrowly defined benchmarks and remaining fully invested. Although this helped performance in the late 1990s, it contributed to their poor performance between 2000 and 2002. Ironically, it has been suggested that this link to benchmarks and the subsequent poor performance put pressure on fees, helping to spark the movement to hedge funds by managers and investors.

Structural Sources

Market segmentation impedes investment in some areas, preventing capital from moving freely and limiting the ability of investors to compete away inefficiencies. Segmentation results from institutional, contractual, or regulatory restrictions placed on asset managers. Funds that are not restricted can exploit these opportunities. Examples include short sale restrictions, the use of derivatives, and leverage, all offering a competitive advantage to hedge funds at the expense of institutions prevented from holding particular assets or gaining large exposure to an asset.

Disintermediation occurs when an intermediary is replaced by another market participant who can fulfill the role less expensively, offering part of the premium as return to investors. Examples include the emergence of hedge funds in the secured lending and securitization markets and other hedge funds engaging in private equity strategies.

The Due Diligence Process

Any management firm's investment process should be studied before an investor hires the firm. The flexible structure of hedge funds can make it difficult to clearly and cleanly define their investment process. The cost of less regulation is a lack of transparency and the increased due diligence necessary when investing in hedge funds compared to traditional investment managers. This higher cost can be realized by building in-house expertise, hiring a consultant, or investing through funds of funds. The growth of hedge fund assets has led to concerns that inefficiencies, and in turn alpha, will shrink as the industry grows. This erosion can take the form of skill dilution or saturation. Skill *dilution* occurs when new funds are less talented than established funds. This implies that while the market may remain inefficient, the alpha is captured by established funds. If so, fund selection becomes a critical component of expected returns. Skill *saturation* occurs in two forms. Manager saturation occurs when a manager's assets grow to the point that transaction costs erode the fund's alpha. Asset class saturation occurs when the market becomes more efficient due to competition and, as a result, all funds experience lower alpha. In response, managers can either increase leverage or enter other markets. If they increase leverage, even more assets are chasing diminishing opportunities, increasing risk and possibly further diluting alpha. Moving to new markets may mean drifting from the core strategy of the fund and accepting less expertise. Both cases put an additional premium on due diligence and the ability of funds to continue to find new markets or strategies.

Qualitative and Quantitative Considerations

Similar to evaluating a company and its stock, due diligence for alternative investments, including hedge funds, is both qualitative and quantitative. Qualitative techniques include reviewing the *investment philosophy, process,* and *management*—that is, the abilities of management and the competitive environment:

- Can the manager identify and articulate a credible alpha opportunity?
- Does the manager's investment process make sense for the alpha opportunity?

- Is the manager capable and experienced in this market?
- How much capacity is available within the strategy? How much capacity can the manager handle?

It is also important to understand *business risk.* This is an evaluation of the risk that the fund fails and of the liquidity costs if it does. Although this is related to the liquidity of the positions held by the fund, it is also concerned with the liquidity available to investors should they want to redeem. Issues for review include:

- Below a certain level of assets, the fund is unable to meet its operating costs and may experience cash flow issues, potentially impacting the fund's ability to implement its strategy, perhaps leading to redemptions and liquidity issues. Above a certain level, the concern is alpha erosion.
- The investor base and its concentration can also impact business risk. A high concentration by a single investor or investor type increases the risk that an investor crisis, and subsequent redemptions, may force the fund to liquidate positions. This is particularly relevant if large investors have side letters giving them preferential terms.

Quantitative considerations include the performance measurement and attribution techniques discussed in Chapters 8 and 13. Because there are numerous hedge fund strategies, the key is to understand the important risks for the particular strategy:

- *Market risks:* Equity, interest rate, credit, volatility, and currency.
- *Jump to default:* The risk to the portfolio given the default of a particular position.
- *Liquidity and leverage:* What is the risk of a liquidity squeeze if the manager is forced to liquidate? How much of the portfolio could be liquidated in a certain number of days assuming the fund represents a particular percentage of the average trading volume and if other market participants are selling?

There are at least two approaches to measuring the risk exposures of a portfolio. The *top-down* approach examines the returns generated by the portfolio to estimate the implied exposures to various risk sources. The advantage of this approach is that it requires little transparency on fund holdings. The disadvantage is that the factor exposures are estimates that represent the average of the fund over the analysis period and do not necessarily represent the exposures of the fund on a given day. The *bottom-up* approach requires full position transparency. The exposures of the fund can then be calculated from the individual position exposures. However, transparency is frequently not available from hedge funds, this approach requires a comprehensive risk model, and it is not straightforward to calculate the risk exposures for exotic instruments.

A third alternative is to ask the fund manager to report portfolio exposures. This has a self-policing aspect. It is a red flag if the manager cannot or will not accurately report portfolio exposures—potentially signaling fund risk management or operational issues. This approach also overcomes the inaccuracies of analyzing returns and avoids the cost of collecting and analyzing position-level information.

Operational Considerations

One estimate is that 50 percent of hedge fund failures have been due to operational, not investment, issues. The operational areas to examine include portfolio monitoring, trading procedures, cash control, portfolio pricing, NAV calculation, and compliance policy. A thorough review of company policies, custodial relationships, and client relations is key. Some investors even hire private detectives to check the backgrounds of firm principals.

As an illustration of the potential problems faulty hedge fund operations may cause, consider the case of the Bayou Fund. The fund immediately began to lose money after its founding in 1996. Rather than admit to poor performance, the fateful decision was made to hide the initial losses because of confidence they would be recovered. Bayou traded through Bayou Securities and in 1997, according to the SEC, transferred commissions back to the fund to cover losses. In 1998, as losses continued, it created a sham accounting firm to produce false audits for the next six years. These actions meant there was no independent way for investors to verify the positions traded and the value of the fund, hiding the extent of the losses from current and prospective investors.

In a last desperate attempt to attract capital the original Bayou Fund was liquidated in January 2003 and four successor funds were created. The hope was that the new money could be traded to recoup prior losses. In one sense the strategy worked: Inflows peaked at $125 million in 2003, but performance did not improve. The Superfund took in a net $90 million in 2003 but lost $35 million through trading. In its annual statement, Bayou Management reported that its Superfund had earned more than $25 million. In all, the Bayou Funds lost $49 million in 2003.

When the losses became too large to hide (prosecutors claim over $350 million), the firm was closed. At this point there was little left for investors. Principals Israel and Marino subsequently pleaded guilty to fraud and conspiracy charges. In addition to jail time (Israel faces up to 30 years and Marino 50 years), each count carries a possible fine of $250,000 plus possible restitution. Of course this failure pales in comparison to the Madoff scandal of 2008.

Fund of Funds

A fund of funds (FoF) is a hedge fund that invests in other hedge funds. They are structured similarly to hedge funds (as limited partnerships) and have similar fee structures. FoFs fall into four basic risk and strategy styles:

- *Conservative* funds attempt to generate consistent absolute returns over the medium term with low volatility and correlation to major stock and fixed-income market indexes. They allocate primarily to relative value strategies with modest allocations to event-driven and hedged equities and possibly small allocations to trading strategies.
- *Diversified* funds attempt to protect capital over the medium to long term during down equity markets and outperform during up markets by holding a diversified portfolio allocated across the relative value, event-driven, hedged equities, and trading strategies.
- *Growth* funds seek to outperform the broad equity indexes over a market cycle with moderate correlation to the equity markets. They primarily allocated to directional strategies within the hedged equities style.
- *Global trading* funds attempt to generate high returns over the long term with low correlation to major equity and fixed-income market indexes. Returns are expected to be highly volatile. They allocate across strategies within the trading style.

The same issues that differentiate hedge funds from traditional assets differentiate FoFs from hedge funds; they are designed to deal with the challenges of direct investment while adding another principal-agent level. They provide access, due diligence, manager selection, diversification, liquidity, and lower minimum investment levels. As a side benefit to the industry, FoFs are viewed as providing an accurate view of the return and risk of investing in hedge funds including the experience of investing

EXHIBIT 11.5
Proportion of Hedge Funds by Category (1990–2008)

Source: Hedge Fund Research, Inc.

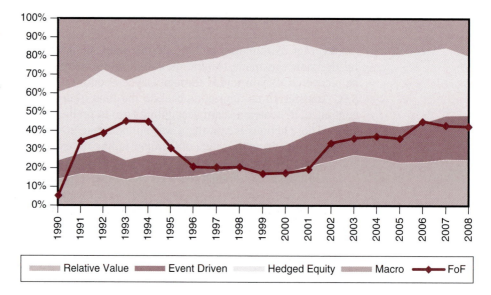

in failed funds, mitigating data issues. As a result, returns to hedge funds as an investment class may be best viewed in the HFRI Fund of Funds Composite index.

The main drawback of investing in FoFs is the added principal agent relationship and layer of fees. FoF managers generally charge a 1–2 percent management fee and a 10–15 percent performance fee. The number of fund of hedge funds has increased dramatically. As of December 2008 there were approximately 2,350 FoFs, suggesting that many investors see them as a cost-effective means to invest in hedge funds. Exhibit 11.5 illustrates the proportion of assets invested through time in different hedge fund styles, and the proportion of total assets invested through FoFs.

11.4 Venture Capital and Private Equity

Venture capitalists invest in start-up or early-stage companies that need capital and perhaps management expertise. Venture capital firms review numerous business proposals and capital needs and seek to invest in the most promising ideas. Returns are realized when the companies go public or are sold to another company or investor. Much like hedge funds, venture capital (VC) and private equity (PE) funds are typically limited partnerships (LPs) or limited liability companies (LLCs) offered to institutional or high net worth investors. VC funds are managed by professionals experienced in identifying attractive business concepts, providing expert business oversight, and selling businesses that have gained traction. VC firms tend to concentrate expertise in specific industries, such as telecom or computer hardware. They also tend to specialize in stages of financing, including seed, early, and later stages. Their officers have business management (executive or start-up) and financing (investment banking or corporate finance) backgrounds. The goal of VC firms is to identify enough big winners and avoid enough losers to generate an overall attractive return. One rule of thumb is to have the goal of at least one big winner for every nine losers.

Private equity shops specialize in leveraged buyouts of existing companies, some of which are publicly listed. Companies are purchased in part with borrowed money, and the funds are usually leveraged up to three times assets. Their goal is to restructure the companies and improve their profitability and thereby values (typically based on EBITDA multiples) before selling them back to the public or other management organizations. Private equity firms may be separated into different styles by size (small to mega) and financing (buyouts, recapitalizations, and short-term mezzanine financing). Professionals at private equity firms include analysts (frequently with management consulting experience), who collect detailed information about potential investments, and partners, who confirm the value, negotiate the price and financing of the deals, and direct the restructurings. Firms frequently partner with operating specialists who implement the new business strategy.

Much like hedge funds, there is no way to accurately gain passive exposure to venture capital and private equity funds. Because their investments are private, outsiders cannot gain access to the underlying investments unless they are an investor in the fund, though multiple funds may invest in the same underlying companies and the basics of large deals are reported in the press. Management fees and account minimums can be high. Many firms charge a base fee of 2–3 percent combined with a sharing fee of 20–30 percent of profits. Investors (called limited partners) contribute capital over time when called by the manager (general partner). Capital, including capital gains, is returned when the underlying investments are liquidated. Whereas public equity funds frequently invest in over 100 stocks and turn over 100 percent per year, private equity funds invest in 20–25 companies and do not reinvest the proceeds of sales. Investors are committed to contributing specific funding over time and cannot easily redeem their contributions. A typical fund invests over five years and then divests for five or more years. New funds are introduced regularly by a single firm. A sample of large individual funds is listed in Exhibit 11.6. Fund names include the name of the management firm plus a number, designating the fund's placement in order of funding.

Performance Record of Venture Capital and Private Equity

As mentioned earlier, alternatives have been especially popular following their strong performance relative to the public equity markets of 2000–2002. Although weaker than hedge funds, VC and PE funds performed substantially better than the stock indexes. In fact they seemed to avoid the steep equity market declines. But how could that be the case, if they too invest in equities and in many cases are leveraged? VC and PE firms report their performance based on the IRR of cash distributions and appraisals of ongoing projects. Formal appraisals are done for subsequent financings of the

EXHIBIT 11.6
Listing of Top Private Equity Funds

Source: *BusinessWeek,* Sept. 17, 2007.

Name of Fund	Vintage Year	Amount Raised ($ billion)
Blackstone Capital Partners V	2005	21.7
KKR 2006 Fund Private Investors	2006	15.7
TPG Partners V	2006	14.0
GS Capital Partners VI	2006	12.2
Permira Europe IV	2006	12.1
Providence Equity Partners VI	2006	12.0
Apollo Investment Fund VI	2005	10.1
GS Capital Partners V	2005	8.5
Hellman & Friedman Capital Partners VI	2006	8.4
The Fourth Cinven Fund	2006	8.3
Clayton, Dubilier & Rice Fund VII	2004	4.1

underlying companies. Performance is not based on true market values. As a result, their reported performance is influenced by cash drag, pricing estimates, and results earned over multiyear periods. The lack of market liquidity in 2001–2003 also resulted in fewer cash valuations and more stale valuation estimates. Because there are more liquidity events in a given fund over time, extending the return measurement period provides a better measure of risk and return. Consider Exhibit 11.7, which compares standard deviations of quarterly and annual return data. VC published returns are compared with returns of the Russell 2000 index; PE is compared with the S&P 500. The VC annual standard deviations are dramatically higher than the quarterly estimates, reflecting the impact of limited intermediate valuations of investments resulting in positive serial correlation. Recall the discussion in Chapter 4 about the impact of time frames on the level of serial correlation and the impact of serial correlation on volatility over different horizons. The annualized standard deviations of the equity indexes are more similar to their quarterly figures, reflecting low serial correlation in underlying valuations.

A better way to measure the true behavior of PE and VC investing for comparison to other investments is to convert published data into data that reflect market valuations of the underlying investments. In other words, calculate returns based on prices that might be realized if the VC or PE fund were liquidated at the end of each quarter.

One technique for estimating market returns of VC and PE, proposed by Woodward and Hall (2004), is to calculate regression coefficients on lagged returns of market indexes and then combine the multiple lagged coefficients to provide a single coefficient that may be applied to the current period return of the market index. This is illustrated in the regression equation:

$$R_{VC,t} = a + b_0 R_{M,t} + b_1 R_{M,t-1} + \dots b_N R_{M,t-N} + e_t$$

Using quarterly data, an eight-quarter lag, and returns for the Thompson VC index and the NASDAQ market index provided the results shown in Exhibit 11.8.

Note that all coefficients are positive and that seven of the nine are significant at the 10 percent level. The adjusted R-square is 0.603, and the F-statistic is 17.4. Although not shown here, pre- and post-1995 results are similar.

The sum of the coefficients is 1.658. This means we may use that coefficient times the NASDAQ monthly return to estimate a monthly series. Applying the 1.658 coefficient to monthly NASDAQ returns yields a 20-year cumulative return several percentages lower than the Thompson VC series. A constant may be added to the monthly returns to yield the same cumulative return (if we assume there are no reporting biases in the data). The resulting standard deviation of annual returns is slightly higher than

EXHIBIT 11.7

Comparison of PE and VC Return Standard Deviations by Period

Annualized Standard Deviations of Alternative Investments (Based on Quarterly & Annual Returns, 1981–2005)		
	Quarterly	Annual
Venture Capital	21.7%	43.4%
Russell 2000	21.7%	18.3%
Private Equity	14.3%	20.2%
S&P 500	15.1%	15.7%

EXHIBIT 11.8
Estimate of Relationship between VC and NASDAQ Returns

Source: These results are from Stewart and Stewart (2007).

Regression Results Using Quarterly Obs. Lagged Nasdaq vs VC	Coeff.	Significance
(Constant)	−0.015	0.116
N	0.544	0.000
N-1	0.221	0.000
N-2	0.251	0.000
N-3	0.173	0.001
N-4	0.157	0.004
N-5	0.097	0.068
N-6	0.045	0.398
N-7	0.148	0.006
N-8	0.023	0.671
F-test	17.371	0.000
R-Square	0.603	
Sum of Coefficients	1.658	

Note: 1988–2005.

EXHIBIT 11.9
Return and Volatility Results of Modeled VC Data, 1986–2005

Series	Period	Return	Standard Deviation (Annual)
VC Data	20-Year	15.5%	46.2%
Modeled	20-Year	12.8	54.8
Modeled + 0.2%/month	20-Year	15.5	54.8

the annual VC series. These observations are illustrated in Exhibit 11.9. These results, compared with Exhibit 11.7, make it clear: VC offers attractive returns, but the true risk is much higher than suggested using published return data.

Excel Outbox
Modeling Market Value Venture Capital Returns

Modeling market value returns for venture capital investing is a straightforward application of multiple regression techniques. Within Excel, the key is to copy multiple columns of market return data, each offset by one period to facilitate the running of a lagged model, from which multiple coefficients will be combined into a single market factor. This summed factor will then be multiplied times the market return series to prepare a modeled market value venture capital return series.

Go to the <Template> worksheet in the Chapter 11 Excel Outboxes.xls file. It will look like the following:

	A	B	C	D	E	F	G	H	I	J	K	L	M
1													
2	Period	All VC	NASDAQ	Lag 1	Lag 2	Lag 3	Modeled VC		Beta Estimates				Sum of Betas
3									t	t-1	t-2	t-3	
4	Mar-96	8.90%	4.50%										
5	Jun-96	16.80%	7.76%										

To lag the NASDAQ return series:

- In cell D5 enter =C4, then copy D5 to cells D6:D43
- In cell E6 enter =C4, then copy E6 to cells E7:E43
- In cell F7 enter =C4, then copy F7 to cells F8:F43

(continued)

(concluded) As described in Chapter 8, use the =LINEST (known *y*'s, known *x*'s,const,stats) function. This is a range array formula that calculates the coefficients and statistics for multiple regression where the formula inputs are:

- Known *y*'s are the dependent variable, the venture returns.
- Known *x*'s are the independent variables, the market index returns.
- const is an indicator; if "TRUE" the intercept is estimated.
- stats is an indicator; if "TRUE" the regression statistics are reported.
- Highlight cells I4:L4 and enter =LINEST(B7:B43,C7:F43,TRUE,FALSE) and then<CTRL><SHIFT><ENTER>.
- Sum the coefficients in M4 by entering =SUM(I4:L4).
- Apply this coefficient to model the venture quarterly returns by entering =$M$4*C7 in cell G7 and then copying cell G7 to cells G8:G43.

The results should look like the following:

	A	B	C	D	E	F	G	H	I	J	K	L	M
1													
2	Period	All VC	NASDAQ	Lag 1	Lag 2	Lag 3	Modeled VC				Beta Estimates		Sum of Betas
3									t	t-1	t-2	t-3	
4	Mar-96	8.90%	4.50%						0.1968	0.2237	0.2308	0.5616	1.2129
5	Jun-96	16.80%	7.76%	4.50%									
6	Sep-96	4.30%	3.18%	7.76%	4.50%								
7	Dec-96	7.10%	4.57%	3.18%	7.76%	4.50%	5.54%						
8	Mar-97	1.40%	−5.49%	4.57%	3.18%	7.76%	−6.65%						

The results for market-value PE returns are similar, though not as dramatic. Using the Russell MidCap index, we can also estimate lagged regression coefficients over eight lagged quarters, which total to 1.24 and may be used to generate a time series for PE market-value returns using the monthly MidCap index returns. Cumulative modeled returns are slightly lower than the VC data with substantially lower volatility (25 percent versus VC's 55 percent). The lower volatility makes sense. PE funds invest in well-established companies that actually produce earnings—less risky companies than the recipients of VC financing. Historically PE funds looked like they provided a better risk–return trade-off than VC funds. Using these two new time series, we may create a comprehensive asset allocation model, which will be discussed in Section 11.7.

11.5 Real Estate

Introduction to Real Estate

Almost everyone is exposed to real estate. We either live in our own home or rent it from someone else who owns it. As real estate prices rise, we either benefit from the appreciation or suffer from the increase in rent.

Investing in real estate is a very old profession. Consider the purchase of the island of Manhattan by Peter Minuit from the Lenape Indians in 1626. New York City and the value of its real estate grew dramatically with growth in industry, finance, and immigration throughout the 1800s and 1900s. Currently there are many vehicles to gain exposure to real estate, in many investment strategies. The goal is to benefit from appreciation due to commodity inflation (lumber forests for example), restructuring (remodeling and new management), development (converting open land to other uses), and economic growth. All investments will benefit from the latter. As a point of reference, RREEF, a research division of Deutsche Bank, has estimated the stock of real estate in the United States to be $9.5 trillion in 2006, of which $4.7 trillion is owned by professional investors. The United States represents over a third of the world's investment real estate.

Prices for real estate were relatively low in the early 1990s following a 1980s building boom, the late 1980s S&L crisis, and the 1990–1992 economic recession. Vacancy rates were high due to economic conditions; supply was high as the government auctioned off properties from failed S&Ls; and even amateur real estate investors were buying up properties at half the replacement rates (the cost of rebuilding the property). By the mid 2000s valuation multiples for stable cash flow, low-vacancy properties had grown to all-time highs, and cash flow yields were close to mortgage rates. New construction costs rose to all-time highs as well, impacted by growing prices for steel and wood. The only way to generate value in this environment was to identify poorly managed properties, purchase them, and then reposition them. The strategy of simply buying dramatically undervalued properties and waiting for the national market to improve had passed by 2006. The next property recession began in 2007 and picked up steam in 2008, providing the beginnings of a new cycle in real estate values. Opportunities for regional or local turnarounds remain, however. Silicon Valley property values were depressed following the dot-com boom, and there are occasional turnaround opportunities on a given street. Interest in overseas investing by U.S. investors has grown, as have their valuations in recent years. The European market offers an opportunity due to the presence of less sophisticated players, but this has been changing. Asia is a tougher environment due to legal uncertainties.

As an example of a real estate deal, consider a portfolio of office properties. A real estate firm will seek investors in a limited partnership or LLC, much like a hedge, venture, or private equity fund. Once assets are committed, the firm may seek properties that reflect high vacancies and offer opportunities for remodeling but do not yet reflect that in their price. Acquisition prices are quoted per square foot, and benchmarks include replacement cost and cash flow valuations at assumed vacancy rates. Purchases and renovations are financed with a combination of the fund's assets plus debt, resulting in two to three times leverage. Following investments in tenant improvements, owners seek to reduce vacancies and charge higher lease rates. Special care is taken to evaluate the local business climate before buying in an effort to capture strengthening demand for office space. Once vacancy rates improve, the owners will explore selling the property at a higher valuation. Many real estate LPs focus on one type, such as office space, but will diversify between specific types and geographic regions. They may also diversify between strategies, including development and repositioning.

More aggressive forms of real estate investing can generate higher returns. Consider brownfield investing,[5] in which the fund manager identifies contaminated properties, arranges insurance protection, manages government and public relations, and directs cleanup of the property. The initial costs of these properties tend to be close to zero, allowing the corporate owners to shed their liability. Frequently a deal is arranged to sell to or partner with developers before the cleanup has begun.

Real estate investment trusts (REIT) let individual investors gain exposure to real estate through publicly listed equity. REIT securities trade on stock exchanges and provide ready liquidity for investors. The underlying trust company raises capital (IPO and

---

[5] One example is Renova Partners of Massachusetts, which focuses on converting contaminated industrial sites into commercial and residential developments.

debt financing), purchases and manages real estate, charges a fee, and distributes (at least) 90 percent of after-tax income in the form of dividends. Debt is typically 50 percent or more of the capital structure. The growth of REITs was phenomenal but ended with a sharp decline in market values in 2008, as illustrated in Exhibit 11.10. REITs concentrate in owning office, residential, and retail property or providing mortgages.

Performance Record of Real Estate

Real estate values are affected by many factors. These include the supply of new properties (building rate), demand (by institutional and individual investors), economic factors (demand for office space or rental properties), interest rates (financing costs and cash flow valuation), and replacement cost (building materials). Like private equity and venture capital, there are problems in using historical pricing data for real estate. NCREIF is an institutional real estate organization that collects and distributes a quarterly return index based on valuations of individual properties, weighted by their valuation. Partnership management fees are excluded, and properties are reported on an unleveraged basis. The Property Index (NPI) includes only income-producing properties and concentrates on apartment, industrial, office, and retail properties. The key problem with the index is that property appraisals tend to be stale measures of current valuation, even if the appraisals are fresh. This is because appraisals are based on past transactions. Like private equity data, the NPI is subject to serial correlation, and volatility measures based on these data are unrealistically low. Fortunately, there are REIT indexes priced daily by the public market. These index returns provide standard deviation levels more in line with equities. A comparison of standard deviations calculated using the two series is presented in Exhibit 11.11. Note that part of the difference may be the result of leverage in underlying REIT operations—the NPI index seeks to remove the impact of leverage within LPs.

EXHIBIT 11.10
Growth of REITs: Market Capitalization through Time

Source: National Association of REIT, Composite Index.

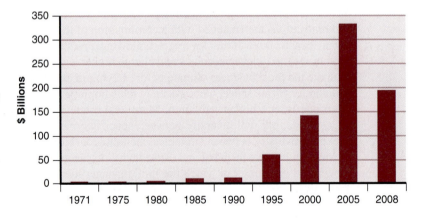

EXHIBIT 11.11
Comparison of Real Estate Return Standard Deviations

NPI Index		REIT Index	
Quarterly	Annual	Quarterly	Annual
3.2%	5.9%	13.8%	16.0%

Note: 1978–2007, NACREIF NPI index versus NAREIT index.

11.6   Commodities

Commodities include metals (basic and precious), energy, agriculture, animal products, and building materials. A sample list of commodities is provided in Exhibit 11.12. These items are things we eat or use to heat our schools or supply our factories. They make up a large portion of the CPI (food represents 18 percent, transportation 17 percent, and housing 42 percent) and therefore provide a tool to roughly hedge inflation. Their price behavior tends to be related to the business cycle, though in a different way than stocks. Commodities tend to be uncorrelated with each other and historically exhibit negative serial correlation. Some commodities exhibit pricing seasonality and others display unique behavior, providing opportunities for diversification. Commodity futures contracts have generated long-term performance consistent with the equity markets, offering a potentially attractive opportunity for returns.

There are two ways for a portfolio manager to gain exposure to commodities: Purchase them directly on the *spot market* and store them or buy *futures contracts* tied to the spot prices and roll the contracts before expiration to avoid taking delivery. Interestingly, returns to these two strategies differ markedly. Real returns to physical commodities have been close to zero over the long term, whereas returns to portfolios of futures have generated risk and return similar to the U.S. equity markets. The reason behind the difference continues to be a subject of study.

Commodity Prices and Returns

Why would real returns to the average commodity be zero? If they represent a large portion of inflation, then as a group, depending on the weighting, they should exhibit a real return of zero. They do not represent a use of capital like equities, which offer opportunities for cash flow generation—they represent an input to industry. Over time, demand for commodities changes. Rapid economic growth in general or in a particular sector will raise demand for specific commodities. However, price increases will lead to increased supply (think of the oil industry expanding capacity in the late 1970s). Striving for efficiency reduces cost and demand (think of the auto industry following the 1970s), pressuring commodity prices downward. Of course there are ongoing concerns about scarcity of particular commodities. For example, 2008 saw growing concern that production of oil was peaking at a time of increased demand by developing markets, leading to a price spike. Over the last three decades, commodities performed strongly in the inflationary 1970s, poorly in the low-inflation 1990s, and strongly again in the 2000s. The empirical record suggests that a buy-and-hold return of physical commodities is 3.5 percent on an annual basis versus inflation of 4.1 percent over the 1959–2004 period, ignoring storage costs (see Gorton and Rouwenhorst, 2006). Different weighting and rebalancing schemes generate different returns, some higher than inflation.

Why would an investment in commodity futures generate significantly higher returns than commodities? A *forward contract* is a legal agreement to purchase an asset at a prespecified time and price (the forward price). A *futures contract* standardizes the

EXHIBIT 11.12
Sample List of Commodities, Traded on U.S. Futures Exchanges

Commodity Class	Sample Commodities		
Metals	Gold	Copper	Silver
Agriculture	Corn	Cotton	Orange Juice
	Live Cattle	Milk	Lumber
Energy	Crude Oil	Natural Gas	Gasoline

definition of the asset and requires daily marking to market, or cash flow equal to the change in the futures price, resetting the contract value (not the futures price) to zero each day. Collateral in the form of cash or Treasury bills is required to purchase or sell a futures contract. A futures price may be approximated by a forward price.[6]

Consider two alternatives: purchasing 100 ounces of gold and holding them for three months, or going long a futures contract for delivery of 100 ounces of gold in three months and investing the present value of the futures price in T-bills. Note that both scenarios end in the same result—100 ounces of gold in three months. If there are no storage or transaction costs, arbitrage requires the following relationship.

$$\text{Futures price} \approx \text{Spot price}(1 + \text{T-bill period rate})$$

The spot price is set by supply and demand for the commodity, and the futures price is set, through arbitrage, by the spot price and short-term interest rates. Gold futures are similar to financial futures (like stock index futures) because gold has no seasonality and low storage costs (online providers charge 12 basis points per annum for storage and insurance). However, other commodities have transportation and storage costs and seasonality, requiring costly storage of the commodity in bulk in the off-season. As a result, storage costs and *convenience yields* (the marginal benefit of having a commodity now instead of months from now) are important in determining the futures price for most commodities. In this case, the return from holding a futures contract for a few months

$$\text{Futures price} \approx \text{Spot price}(1 + \text{T-bill period rate}) + \text{Storage} - \text{Convenience}$$

depends on the convenience yield relative to the storage cost. As storage costs and convenience yields change, the *basis* (the difference between the spot and futures prices) changes. Over time, most of the variation in futures prices is determined by the spot price. Holding a futures contract for a few months, letting the basis shrink as maturity approaches, is called the *roll return*. For many commodities, rolling the futures and holding T-bills generates a positive return over the spot return. Evidence suggests that the commodities that have generated high roll returns in the past tend to be expensive to store (see Erb and Harvey, 2006) or may be difficult to provide for just-in-time inventory management, suggesting they reflect convenience yields in excess of storage costs.

This pricing discussion is called the *theory of storage.* An alternative theory of futures pricing includes a return premium for holding futures by providing a risk transfer service to commodity producers or consumers who want to hedge the position they are forced to take for doing business. This theory is related to Keynes's (1930) theory of *normal backwardation* and is called the *hedging pressure hypothesis.* The return for maintaining a (long or short) futures exposure will be higher than that from exposure to the spot due to a risk premium paid for taking that risk. Note that the forecast premium is equal to the difference between the discounted expected future spot price and the futures price. Also note that the hedging pressure theory can cut either way. Keynes's theory of normal backwardation assumes that the net pressure is from producers hedging their future sales so that buyers (that is, long futures positions) earn the risk premium. On average the futures varies with the spot but may offer a different average return due to the risk premium. Just as convenience yields are unobservable in the theory of storage, the expected future spot price is unobservable in the premium theory.

---

[6] Theoretical values differ due to the marking to market feature.

EXHIBIT 11.13
Performance
Characteristics of
Commodity Futures

Source: Gorton & Rouwenhorst
(2006)

Annualized Returns over T-Bills, 1959–2004			
	Commodity Futures	Stocks	Corporate Bonds
Return	5.2	5.7	2.2
Standard Deviation	12.1	14.9	8.5
Correlation with Commodities	—	−0.1	−0.3

Indexes: Equal-weighted Futures, S&P500 and Ibbotson Corporate Bond

Performance Record of Commodities

Due to the realities of futures pricing and the historical presence of a positive average risk premium, a long position in fully collateralized commodity futures has generated average returns similar to, yet uncorrelated with, U.S. equities even though some commodity futures have displayed negative premiums over time. Because individual commodities behave uniquely, the level and behavior of the portfolio return depends on how the individual commodities are weighted and rebalanced. For example, the Goldman Sachs Commodity index is weighted according to the five-year average world production level of each commodity underlying the futures contracts. As illustrated in Exhibit 11.13, annual return correlations of an equally weighted index are negative with both stocks and bonds (0.05 and −0.14 for monthly) and reflect an annual return standard deviation in between stocks and bonds. Not shown in the exhibit, but important, is the tendency for commodity returns to be more positively skewed than equities and positively correlated with inflation (stocks and bonds are negatively correlated over monthly periods). Gorton and Rouwenhorst (2006) suggest, and provide supporting evidence, that low correlations are due to the commodities performing strongly later in the business cycle than do stocks and bonds.

11.7 Allocating Assets Including Alternatives

Issues for Implementing Investments in Alternatives

Alternative investments differ from, and behave differently than, standard bonds, equities, and cash instruments, providing opportunities for both return and diversification. Investing in alternative investments is also different, most cannot be invested in passively, but require the selection and hiring of investment managers. ETFs representing commodity futures, or an index of REITS can provide ready-made broad diversification for commodities and real estate. A fund of funds investment in hedge funds can provide diversification, but style bias and sample selection noise as well as additional fees impact its efficiency. Investing in a diversified mix of venture or private equity funds is the most challenging. Each fund will be diversified across a few projects, but full diversification (sufficient to accurately reflect the behavior of the investment class) requires multiple funds. Consider the investments by the Massachusetts PRIM Board as illustrated in Exhibit 11.14. While private equity represents 6.3 percent of its portfolio, it represents 65 percent of the individual managers.

Implementation issues aside, the opportunities for diversification from alternatives are summarized in Exhibit 11.15, displaying a correlation matrix of the major common and alternative investment classes. In particular, the low, and in some cases

EXHIBIT 11.14
Massachusetts PRIM Board Investments

	% Allocation	Number of Managers
US Equities	44.7	9
US Fixed Income	25.7	8
International Equity	18.2	4
Private Equity	6.3	68
Real Estate	5.1	6
Total	100.0	95

Note: $31.4 billion as of December 2000.

EXHIBIT 11.15 **Return Correlations of Common and Alternative Asset Classes, 1970–2006**

	Large Equity	Bonds	Cash	Small Equity	International	Emerging Markets	Venture Capital	Private Equity	Hedge Funds	Real Estate	Commodities
Large Equity	1.0000										
Bonds	0.2631	1.0000									
Cash	−0.0178	0.0852	1.0000								
Small Equity	0.6402	0.1520	−0.0522	1.0000							
International	0.3645	0.1317	−0.0735	0.4768	1.0000						
Emerging Markets	0.3170	−0.0089	−0.0996	0.4772	0.5147	1.0000					
Venture	0.5833	0.1610	−0.0607	0.8827	0.4997	0.4731	1.0000				
Private Equity	0.6972	0.2151	−0.0514	0.9474	0.5301	0.5037	0.9064	1.0000			
Hedge Funds	0.3991	0.1402	−0.0022	0.7548	0.4041	0.4547	0.7000	0.7235	1.0000		
Real Estate	0.4655	0.2404	−0.0621	0.6600	0.3547	0.4420	0.4959	0.6335	0.4625	1.0000	
Commodities	−0.0720	−0.0523	−0.0279	0.0445	0.0086	−0.0489	0.0092	0.0154	0.1297	−0.0200	1.0000

negative, correlation between commodities and all other asset classes seems especially attractive for diversification—the futures premium has provided an attractive return over the last 35 years.

Section 11.2 reported that hedge fund returns do not appear normally or lognormally distributed. It is important to note that returns from many alternative investments are non-normal. This is illustrated in Exhibit 11.16, which shows skewness and excess kurtosis levels substantially different from normality, that is, values different from zero. Positive skewness means there are more frequent returns greater than the mean (right tail) than there are in a symmetric distribution. Positive excess kurtosis indicates a more acute peak than a normal distribution and a greater chance for extreme values (fat tails). Domestic and international equities, including VC and PE, are skewed to the left. Commodities, cash, and bonds display return distributions skewed to the right.[7] The investment classes with the most symmetric return distributions are real estate and developed international equities while commodities are the most symmetric in log return space. International equity exhibits the flattest return (and log return) distribution. Standard mean–variance statistics may not be effective in evaluating the risk of alternative asset allocations. As a result, we need to consider nonparametric techniques for evaluating risk. A straightforward and effective method is to explore historical return frequencies of varying asset allocations compared to a common benchmark such as a 60/40 equity/bond allocation. This is similar to the stress testing discussed in Chapter 6. Key frequency levels include downside measures, such as the proportion of monthly, quarterly, and annual periods below meaningful levels. For example, it is intuitively appealing to explore the frequency of periods with returns below −1 percent, −5 percent, and −10 percent. Similarly, it

[7] Note that the statistics displayed in Exhibit 11.4 may differ due to varying time periods.

EXHIBIT 11.16 **Sample Statistics of Monthly Returns on Common and Alternative Asset Classes, Based on Reported and Modeled Return Series, 1970–2006**

	S&P500 Index	TBond	TBill	Russell 2000 Index	EAFE	Emerging Markets	Venture Capital	Private Equity	Fund-of-Funds	Real Estate	Commodities
					Gross Returns						
Mean	0.918%	0.677%	0.495%	1.145%	0.816%	1.470%	1.590%	1.321%	0.839%	0.913%	1.116%
Standard Deviation	4.426%	2.968%	0.233%	6.189%	4.770%	8.274%	10.798%	6.379%	1.360%	4.247%	5.407%
Excess Kurtosis	−1.0964	−0.4076	−1.5530	0.2363	−2.2186	3.1782	−1.3921	−0.7046	1.8159	4.4325	−0.7190
Skewness	−0.3493	0.4700	0.8861	−0.3541	−0.1632	0.3701	−0.4133	−0.4521	−0.3128	0.1387	0.4734
					Log Returns						
Mean	0.816%	0.632%	0.494%	0.946%	0.700%	1.125%	0.980%	1.109%	0.827%	0.820%	0.969%
Standard Deviation	4.438%	2.934%	0.232%	6.253%	4.767%	8.245%	11.150%	6.449%	1.353%	4.228%	5.313%
Excess Kurtosis	−0.3151	−0.7515	−1.5754	1.6694	−2.1092	3.6857	0.6327	0.7753	2.2390	3.0563	−1.2524
Skewness	−0.6175	0.2846	0.8769	−0.8662	−0.3588	−0.6009	−1.0697	−0.8885	−0.4516	−0.3920	0.1693

is helpful to explore worst-case scenarios, including identifying what happened in the worst 10 percent, 5 percent, and 1 percent of periods. Transforming the data to help visualize these results in terms of *value at risk* (VaR), or the dollar equivalent of these return situations, is also helpful.

Such a table may be developed in Excel, and macros may be defined to simplify multiple scenario analysis. Care must be taken in specifying the routines to calculate frequency levels. While standard deviations, skewness, and kurtosis are easily calculated in Excel formulas, as shown in Stewart and Stewart (2007), sorting routines are needed to compute downside frequencies based on historical results.

Risk Analysis of Investment Allocation

As a sample analysis, begin with the asset allocation of Yale University's endowment. Yale has been known to make aggressive allocations to alternative investments and earn strong performance from that bet. The allocations are very different from the old rule of thumb of 60 percent stocks and 40 percent bonds, as illustrated in Exhibit 11.17. To fully understand the risk taken by this allocation, it is important to view more than beta and standard deviation.

EXHIBIT 11.17
Yale University Endowment Asset Allocation

	Portfolio (% allocation)	Benchmark (% allocation)
Cash	0%	0%
Bonds	5%	40%
Large US Equity	10%	60%
Small US Equity	4%	0%
International Equity	10%	0%
Emering Markets	4%	0%
Venture Capital	7%	0%
Private Equity	10%	0%
Hedge Funds	25%	0%
Real Estate	13%	0%
Commodities	13%	0%
Total	100%	100%

Note: As of 2006.

EXHIBIT 11.18   **Return Risk Analysis of Yale Endowment Allocation**

Source: Stewart and Stewart (2007).

| | | | | Monthly | | | |
| | | | | % Frequency of Return | | | |
	Beta	Actual Standard Deviation	Standard Deviation	<−1%	<−3%	<−5%	Minimum
Portfolio	0.65	2.6%	3.1%	20.8%	8.9%	2.3%	−15.2%
Benchmark	1.00	0.0	3.2	25.6	8.9	3.7	−10.4
Difference	−0.35	2.6	−0.1	−4.8	0.0	−1.4	−4.7

| | | | | Quarterly | | | |
| | | | | % Frequency of Return | | | |
	Beta	Actual Standard Deviation	Standard Deviation	<−1%	<−5%	<−10%	Minimum
Portfolio	0.78	4.2%	6.2%	19.1%	8.7%	2.5%	−18.1%
Benchmark	1.00	0.0	6.1	26.0	7.6	1.6	−17.1
Difference	−0.22	4.2	0.1	−6.9	1.1	0.9	−1.0

| | | | | Annually | | | |
| | | | | % Frequency of Return | | | |
	Beta	Actual Standard Deviation	Standard Deviation	<−5%	<−10%	<−25%	Minimum
Portfolio	0.67	9.6%	12.3%	8.7%	2.8%	0.2%	−25.3%
Benchmark	1.00	0.0	13.0	9.9	3.3	0.2	−26.9
Difference	−0.33	9.6	−0.7	−1.2	−0.5	0.0	1.6

Traditional risk characteristics are calculated for the portfolio relative to the 60/40 benchmark using returns data between 1970 and 2006. Returns data sources include published market equity and bond indexes, adjusted venture and private equity time series, a FoF series for hedge funds, REITs for real estate, and a production-weighted commodity futures index.[8] Two portfolios are created and rebalanced monthly. Beta, standard deviation, and active standard deviation are calculated from the monthly and independent quarterly and annual portfolio returns. (By *independent* we mean no overlapping periods.) Portfolio returns are sorted from smallest to largest, and the frequency of portfolio returns below several target levels are computed. VaR calculations are also tabulated assuming a $1,000,000 portfolio, illustrating the typical dollar values lost in extreme situations. These are illustrated in Exhibit 11.18.

Looking at beta, the portfolio appears to be much more conservative than the traditional 60/40 mix. The beta measure is significantly lower than 1.0, with levels ranging from 0.65 to 0.79 depending on the return period employed. However, the return standard deviations and frequency of negative returns tend to be similar to the benchmark for all three return periods. VaR results provided in Exhibit 11.19 illustrate that the portfolio is riskier by at least one measure, with modestly lower worst-case scenarios for most monthly, quarterly, and annual periods. For example, the worst 1 percent of

[8] Full data details are listed in the chapter appendix.

EXHIBIT 11.19   Value at Risk Analysis of Yale Endowment Allocation, Average Loss ($000)

Source: Stewart and Stewart (2007).

Assumed Total Asset Value (000) = $1,000

Monthly

Value at Risk Analysis of Yale Endowment Allocation, Average Loss ($000)

	Worst 1%	Worst 2.5%	Worst 5%	Worst 10%	Worst 25%	Worst
Portfolio	−109	−83	−64	−48	−28	−152
Benchmark	−82	−71	−61	−48	−30	−104
Difference	−26	−11	−3	0	2	−47

Quarterly

Value at Risk Analysis of Yale Endowment Allocation, Average Loss ($000)

	Worst 1%	Worst 2.5%	Worst 5%	Worst 10%	Worst 25%	Worst
Portfolio	−148	−125	−105	−80	−41	−181
Benchmark	−137	−112	−93	−73	−44	−171
Difference	−11	−13	−12	−7	2	−10

Annually

Value at Risk Analysis of Yale Endowment Allocation, Average Loss ($000)

	Worst 1%	Worst 2.5%	Worst 5%	Worst 10%	Worst 25%	Worst
Portfolio	−200	−160	−128	−93	−31	−253
Benchmark	−189	−152	−127	−99	−47	−269
Difference	−11	−8	−1	6	15	16

monthly periods result in an average loss of $109,000 for the portfolio compared to $82,000 for the benchmark. Note that the worst period may not be the same for the portfolio and the benchmark.

The sample statistics displayed in Exhibit 11.19 illustrate that beta or even standard deviations are insufficient risk measures. The 2006 Yale allocation is slightly more, not significantly less, risky than the standard 60/40 mix based on historical frequencies. Note that mean returns were higher over the 1970–2006 period for the Yale allocation (12.9 percent versus 11.2 percent per annum), due to the lower bond and higher private equity and commodity allocations, and perhaps due to the additional risk taken. In practice, with live performance, there may be additional sources of return such as tactical allocation between the asset classes and the selection of individual managers, which may generate higher (or lower) returns than the scenario assuming a fixed allocation to passive indexes and manager averages.

Computing Optimal Allocations

What is the best approach for selecting portfolio allocations between both common and alternative assets? There are several challenges, many of which have been discussed earlier. Historical returns are interesting, and provide some guidance for future long-term behavior, but are not accurate mean return forecasts for the future. Techniques such as James–Stein estimates suggest that long-term mean returns for different assets are truly closer than the historical sample means suggest. Higher moments may be more stable, but relationships between asset classes tend to change under extreme situations—remember how correlations of risky assets increase in severe down markets?[9]

[9] See Chapters 8 and 9.

Assuming we are reasonably comfortable forecasting from sample statistics, we still have the problem of dealing with returns not being normally or lognormally distributed. Four-moment optimization techniques that allow targeting levels of skewness and kurtosis in addition to mean and variance are available. However, it is not clear what levels of these parameters to target within constraints or what weights to apply within an objective function. There is another approach, discussed in Chapter 5, that does not rely on mean–variance. The mean–lower partial moment (LPM) approach considers downside risk but may be easily solved in Excel with Solver. Review of the full downside frequency of optimal solutions, such as illustrated in Exhibits 11.18 and 11.19, may be combined with the LPM approach to ensure a full understanding of the behavior of any optimal allocation prior to its implemention.

Standard variance is defined as the sum of the squares of all deviations from the expected return. Recall that LPM incorporates as a measure of risk only squared deviations below a threshold return, such as zero.[10] Constraints on skewness and kurtosis may be added, but as we just mentioned, target levels are not obvious. One approach is to set target levels similar to those for a benchmark portfolio.

As an example of applying LPM, consider an objective function equal to expected portfolio return less the partial sum of squared differences from zero, multiplied by a risk aversion parameter set at 0.5. Expected returns are computed using James–Stein estimates based on log returns between 1970 and 2006. Mean estimates for most asset classes are similar, though lower for bonds and especially cash investments. Constraints are set to ensure that weights are all nonnegative, total to 100 percent, and are individually no more than 25 percent. Summary statistics for the optimal, Yale Endowment, and 60/40 benchmark portfolios are listed in Exhibit 11.20.

Coincidentally, asset weights of the optimal and Yale portfolios are not dramatically different. They both have large allocations to hedge funds, real estate, and international equities. However, the optimal portfolio does not have allocations to private equity and

[10] An appendix to Chapter 13 gives the details of LPM and other risk measures.

EXHIBIT 11.20
LPM Optimal Portfolio versus Yale Portfolio

	Percent of Portfolio (%) Optimal Portfolio	Percent of Portfolio (%) Yale Portfolio	Percent of Portfolio (%) 60/40 Benchmark
Cash	7%	0%	0%
Bonds	25%	5%	40%
Lg US	3%	10%	60%
Sm US	0%	4%	0%
Int. Dev.	0%	10%	0%
Em. Mkts	15%	4%	0%
VC	0%	7%	0%
PE	0%	10%	0%
Hedge Funds	25%	25%	0%
Real Estate	25%	12.5%	0%
Commodities	0%	13%	0%
Total	100%	100%	100%

Sample Statistics

	—Annualized—				—Monthly—		
	Log Mean	James–Stein Mean	Total Standard Deviation	Active Standard Deviation	Skewness	Kurtosis	Partial Square Differences
Optimal Portfolio	10.1%	9.4%	10.8%	9.8%	−0.001	5.896	0.048
Yale Portfolio	11.0	9.7	12.3	9.6	−0.784	3.501	0.067
60/40 Benchmark	9.4	9.5	13.0	0.0	−0.067	0.872	0.064

Return Risk Analysis

Annually

% Frequency of Return

	Beta	Actual Standard Deviation	Standard Deviation	<−5%	<−10%	<−25%	Min
Optimal Portfolio	0.56	9.8%	10.8%	4.9%	2.6%	0.0%	−24.7%
Yale Portfolio	0.67	9.6	12.3	8.7	2.8	0.2	−25.3
60/40 Benchmark	1.00	0.0	13.0	9.9	3.3	0.2	−26.9

Value at Risk Analysis

Assumed Total Asset Value (000) = $1,000

$ Average Loss ($000)

	Worst 1%	Worst 2.5%	Worst 5%	Worst 10%	Worst 25%	Worst
Optimal Portfolio	−211	−161	−118	−67	−2	−247
Yale Portfolio	−200	−160	−128	−93	−31	−253
60/40 Benchmark	−189	−152	−127	−99	−47	−269

venture capital and has a much larger allocation to bonds. Using raw, low volatility, PE and VC return series would have led to higher allocations for those investment classes.

In terms of risk, the optimal portfolio exhibits lower beta, standard deviation, and partial standard deviation. Historical skewness for the optimal portfolio is neutral compared with the negatively skewed Yale portfolio returns. Both portfolios exhibit positive kurtosis. Using James–Stein estimates, the two portfolios' return forecasts are similar; historical returns for the Yale portfolio are higher. Frequencies of large negative returns are for the most part lower for the optimal portfolio.

Many alternatives are considered uncorrelated with the equity markets and are expected to hold their value even when stocks decline. This was the experience in 2000–2002, providing evidence supporting the decision to raise allocations in the mid-2000s. The 2008 market environment tested this thesis.

A discussed in this chapter, alternatives do not offer the liquidity provided by direct investment in the public markets, and published returns for alternatives may be subject to biases. Reported performance figures must be adjusted to fully understand what happened in the market decline in 2008; they are reported in Exhibit 11.21.

EXHIBIT 11.21   2008 Reported and Modeled Returns

US Stocks	US Bonds	International Equities	Hedge Funds	Private Equity	Venture Capital	Real Estate	Commodities
S&P 500	Lehman Agg	EAFE	Fund of Funds	Modeled	Modeled	NAREIT	GSCI
−38.5%	5.1%	−45.1%	−21.3%	−46.3%	−66.3%	−37.3%	−46.50%

Some points of reference may be helpful. The common stock of Blackrock, a large money manager of private equity and other investments, declined over 45 percent for the year, and Cogent Partners, a valuation firm, was quoted as noting that late 2008 bids for private equity in the secondary market were coming in at 50–60 percent of net asset value.

Based on the weights in Exhibit 11.20, both the optimal and 60/40 mixes would have experienced declines of just over 20 percent while the Yale mix would have declined well over 30 percent. Long-term performance from alternatives investing has been strong, but 2008 made it clear there was a downside. Although better than the worst case predicted in Exhibits 11.19 and 11.20 for the 60/40 and optimal mixes, the results were worse than anticipated for the Yale mix.

For investors with large allocations to alternatives, and liquidity needs, 2008 posed two challenges. Many hedge fund managers imposed redemption restrictions, reducing investors' access to their funds. And while it became difficult to redeem from the hedge funds, private equity and real estate firms continued their capital calls, increasing investors' need for cash. Cash requirements had to be satisfied by selling publicly traded securities, which were under severe stress, requiring liquidation at low prices.

These were more than mere paper losses: The decline in asset values had a real impact. Performance and liquidity challenges forced many big investors such as Harvard University to enter into a policy of financial constraint. In fact it was reported they were budgeting for a 30 percent decrease in the endowment's value for the June-to-June fiscal year. Another big alternatives investor, CalPERS, was forced to develop plans to increase employer dollar contributions by 15–30 percent to meet pension commitments.

Summary

Up to this chapter, discussions focused on the behavior and use of common asset classes such as stocks and bonds. So-called alternative investments were added to the mix in this chapter, with hedge funds accorded special focus due to their size and rapid growth. The hedge fund section included a discussion of fund selection, which also applies to active management selection problems for other investment classes. Alternative investments offer opportunities for diversification and return, but they exhibit different characteristics. Implementing an investment in alternatives requires specialized vehicles, and several require hiring active managers because passive investment strategies do not exist. Published return data do not reflect true market returns and must be modified before their behavior can be understood. Returns are also not lognormally distributed, requiring an expanded set of techniques for both portfolio construction and risk analysis.

Problems

1. Consider the James–Stein mean estimates used in the optimization problem in Section 11.7 and illustrated here, compared with sample means. How might the optimal portfolio weights change if historical sample means were used?

James–Stein Mean Estimates

	Large Equities	Bonds	Cash	Small Equities	International Equities	Emerging Markets	Venture Capital	Private Equity	FoF	Real Estate	Commodities
Orig Mean	0.0934	0.0869	0.0627	0.1027	0.0680	0.1144	0.1042	0.1212	0.1003	0.0889	0.1152
JS Mean Est	0.0962	0.0934	0.0628	0.0962	0.0962	0.0962	0.0962	0.0962	0.0997	0.0962	0.0962

2. Consider the objective function used in the optimization problem in Section 11.7. How might the optimal weights change if the objective function included active risk relative to the benchmark for the following benchmarks?
   a. The Yale portfolio.
   b. A defined benefit plan liability.

3. Consider the objective function used in the optimization problem in Section 11.7.
   a. How might the optimal solution change if constraints were used to target skewness and kurtosis of the benchmark? Review Exhibit 11.16 before answering.
   b. Discuss the role of intuition in seeking optimal solutions with and without these moment constraints.

Appendix

Sources for Return Series

Cash = 30-day Tbills
Bonds = 20-year Tbonds
Large US Equity = S&P 500 Index
Small US Equity = Russell 2000 Index
International Equity = MSCI EAFE Index
Emerging Markets = MSCI Emerging Market Index (1988–2006), MSCI Singapore Index (1970–1987)
Venture Capital = Estimated Market Value Model (lagged returns) relative to NASDAQ
Private Equity = Estimated Market Value Model (lagged returns) relative to Russell Midcap Index (1979–2006), NASDAQ, Average of Russell 2000 and S&P 500 (1970–1978)
Hedge Funds = HFRI Composite Fund-of-Funds Index (1990–2006), Estimated returns using the Russell 2000 Index and Tbills (1970–1989)
Real Estate = NAREIT Index (1973–2006), Estimated returns using the S&P 500 Index and Tbonds (1970–1972)
Commodities = GSCI Production Weighted Commodity Futures Index

Chapter 12

Portfolio Management through Time: Taxes and Transaction Costs

Chapter Outline

12.1   Introduction

Portfolio management is an inherently dynamic process. In Chapter 5 we saw that changing investment opportunities induce dynamic adjustments in our desired, or target, portfolio. For investors with finite lives, the mere passage of time will induce portfolio adjustments due to shortening investment horizons. At an even more basic level, market movements require us to *rebalance* portfolios to avoid drifting away from our desired positions.

This chapter focuses on two sources of friction—transaction costs and taxes—that affect our ability to keep an actual portfolio aligned with our ideal, target portfolio over time. These factors have both direct and indirect effects on performance. The direct impact is, of course, the drain on assets when the costs are incurred. One indirect impact arises because frictions inhibit fully capturing the potential value added of the ideal portfolio. Another indirect impact is especially important in the case of taxes. Because taxes alter the relative risk–return characteristics of available assets, tax avoidance may induce managers to select portfolios that would be suboptimal on a pretax basis.

This chapter begins with a discussion of the nature and causes of *performance shortfall*—the tendency for strategy simulations to overstate the potential performance of a live portfolio. Section 12.3 discusses rebalancing a portfolio in the absence of taxes and transaction costs. The nature and impact of trading costs are covered in Section 12.4. Sections 12.5–12.7 are devoted to taxes. The first of these sections summarizes taxation of investment returns in the United States. The second considers tax-driven portfolio positioning for individual investors. The third examines the tax and performance implications of gain or loss realization and turnover.

Taxes and transaction costs introduce an inherently high level of complexity into portfolio decisions. There are no simple, universal best strategies for contending with these factors in the real world. However, some strategies are clearly better than others; this chapter points the way toward effective management of taxes and trading costs.

12.2   Performance Shortfall

Investment strategies are frequently back-tested on paper[1] before they are traded live, or tested live in-house on a small scale before being offered to clients. These hypothetical results show what procedures are necessary to implement the strategy and help form performance expectations before the strategy is scaled up. These expectations are important because they indicate whether the strategy will be attractive to investors (does it meet their return and risk objectives?) and to the portfolio manager (will the strategy be profitable?). These expectations also provide the inputs for portfolio optimization to determine whether (and in what allocation) the strategy is included in an overall portfolio. Consider an ideal portfolio, one that is based on fresh information regardless of any trading issues. An ideal portfolio is the one you would create fresh, from cash, every day without regard to transaction costs, liquidity, or taxes. This portfolio tends to have high levels of turnover because there are no restrictions on trading.

The simplest back test calculates performance of this ideal portfolio without any adjustment for transaction costs. We can call this the *back-test ideal paper portfolio.* The back-test ideal portfolio is a series of holdings back in time and may be subject to data mining or look-back biases if the developer is not careful. A portfolio that recognizes the presence of transaction costs and other real-world challenges will be different than the ideal portfolio even if it is maintained on paper. We can call this the *practical portfolio,* and it may be maintained historically within a simulation or from live management.

In practice, the hypothetical results from a back test always seem to be superior to results from a portfolio using the same strategy when traded live. This difference between expected returns from the back-test ideal portfolio and live portfolio results is referred to as a *performance shortfall.* If the manager runs an ideal portfolio on paper alongside the live portfolio, the difference between paper ideal and live portfolio returns may be called the *implementation shortfall*—a term coined by André Perold in 1988. Exhibit 12.1 illustrates the performance of three hypothetical portfolios, the first two on paper and the third truly invested.

As suggested by the name, the implementation shortfall is typically negative, at least on an expected basis. Portfolio managers may also measure another shortfall between live and paper practical portfolios. As discussed in Chapter 6, these differences should be monitored on an ongoing basis and analyzed for feedback to improve the strategy.

---

[1] The results from the paper portfolio are often called "pro forma returns." *Pro forma* comes from the Latin meaning "as a matter of form." The use of this term in finance likely parallels its use in accounting for projected financial statements. Unfortunately *pro forma* can also mean a token effort to satisfy the minimum requirements.

EXHIBIT 12.1
Sample Performance Records

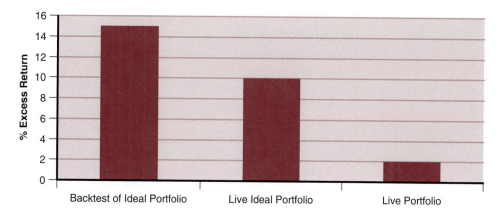

EXHIBIT 12.2
Sources of Performance Shortfall

1. Look-back bias
2. Implementation costs
   – Transaction costs
   – Opportunity costs
3. Signal capture/implementation lag
4. Execution performance and errors

The goal of this section is to introduce the sources of performance and implementation shortfalls and methods for limiting them. Later sections will discuss sources in detail and provide guidance for effectively managing live portfolios. Although the analysis of implementation shortfall is often narrowed to just measurement and attribution of transaction costs, there are several sources of shortfall. As listed in Exhibit 12.2, in addition to transaction costs, we consider the effects of look-back bias, opportunity costs, signal capture problems, and poor execution. Note that look-back bias impacts the component of performance shortfall between back test and live (paper or real) portfolios.

Look-Back Bias

By necessity, back testing a strategy typically entails applying the investment discipline to the observed history of market information and prices. Although there are an infinite number of possible histories, there is only one realized history. However, there is a problem with using history to forecast the behavior of an investment strategy. To paraphrase Mark Twain, while history may rhyme it rarely repeats. In particular, past data may be skewed by events that do not occur in the future,[2] or the future may hold events that have not been observed in the past.[3] Even if the past is a good model for the future, there is always the risk of data mining—that is, overfitting an investment strategy to spurious correlations and noise.

As illustrated in Exhibit 12.1, look-back bias can create a large difference between the back test and the live portfolio. The best protection against look-back bias is to address a few simple questions. First, are the data used to test the model

---

[2] An example is scenario analysis, in which prior events are used to test the robustness of a strategy. This form of stress test is useful as a measure of how the strategy reacts to shocks but is not a perfect forecast unless all aspects of the event repeat.

[3] Unexpected, or Black Swan events, are discussed at length by Taleb (2007).

representative of the current underlying financial markets involved? This question has two aspects:

- Has the structure of the market changed? For example, investors have learned the hard way that high-yield bond default rates estimated from "fallen angel[4]" bonds are not necessarily representative of default rates on original issue junk and that default rates of mortgages originated to be held on a bank's balance sheet may not represent default rates of mortgages originated for securitization.
- If the market structure has not changed, is the period selected to test the strategy representative of longer-term relationships in the market? In other words, does the sample represent at least a full market cycle or simply a particularly favorable environment? The strategy may fail as the markets move into a different part of the cycle, or a secular change, over which the strategy was not tested.

A simple method for checking for look-back bias is to test the model *out-of-sample.* This can be done by splitting the sample period into subperiods, developing and fitting the model over the earlier periods, and testing it on the later periods. Note that repeating a back test multiple times, with adjustments based on what the researcher has learned from earlier runs, is not a test, but instead data mining—simply choosing a strategy you know worked in the past. Similarly, one must be careful selecting the best live test portfolio among many based on a single test period.

Another check for look-back bias is to question whether the decision factors used in the strategy make economic sense. If not, the strategy may be using spurious factors. The general rule should be to keep the model as simple as possible. It is better to be approximately right than precisely wrong.[5]

Implementation Costs

Before a portfolio goes live with significant assets, the manager needs to decide what changes should be made to the ideal portfolio. Does the manager trade whenever desired, adjusting weights, even by a small amount, for minor improvements in the portfolio? This might be the case if, as modern portfolio theory typically assumes, each trader is *atomistic* and her or his actions do not affect market prices.[6] However, practitioners know this is not always the case and recognize that transaction costs and liquidity reduce their flexibility. Transaction costs are a function of market liquidity with the cost increasing with trade size, volatility, and the potential information content of the trade.

There are three transaction cost components to trading, all of which are described in detail in Section 12.4:

- *Commission:* the explicit per-share or per-trade costs of trading that are known and easily modeled.
- *Bid–ask spread:* the difference between the buy and sell price quotes for a small quantity, quoted by a single market maker or from the best buy and sell prices of market participants. This level varies through time.
- *Market impact:* the impact of quote changes as trade quantities increase. The level changes with trade size and varies through time.

[4] A fallen angel is a low quality bond which was originally issued as an investment grade security
[5] This is in the spirit of Bookstaber's (2007) concept of using coarse measures for risk management—that is, rules that intentionally trade off being suboptimal with respect to observed risks in order to be robust to unobserved risks.
[6] The presence of an investment strategy in the market is not effectively captured in a back-test. The greater the percentage of volume represented by the strategy, the more this assumption is violated.

A separate *opportunity cost* may also be considered, defined as the cost of nonexecution—that is, the impact on the strategy return of not trading. Opportunity cost is present whenever a live portfolio experiences lower turnover levels than the unconstrained ideal portfolio. The cost may be in returns, such as forgone alpha, or risk, such as higher tracking volatility. This may be estimated by comparing the performance of a paper portfolio managed assuming zero transaction costs with one limited by turn-over controls. Portfolio managers must decide how to balance the costs of trading with the missed opportunity for value added. As an example, recall the War Story: A Struc-tured Active Small-Cap Equity Product box in Chapter 6. Holding limits based on the trading volume of individual issues were incorporated into both the paper portfolio utilized in the back test and the live management.

There is also a trade-off between trading quickly and being patient. Executing a full trade quickly lowers opportunity costs but increases potential market impact costs. Even if the trade contains no information and is simply executed to implement a hedge or reduce tracking error, the trade can result in market impact. Slower execution lowers market impact but increases opportunity cost because the full order may not be exe-cuted or the trade may be filled later at a disadvantageous (average) price. Opportunity costs from patient trading depend on the character of the value-added process—for example, they may be small if alphas are realized over a long time.

Accurately modeling transaction costs in a back test is challenging. It is virtually impossible to account for every eventuality. Still, it is worth exploring. Running multiple back tests assuming different turnover levels will help a manager better understand the balance between transaction and opportunity costs. Approaches to esti-mating the performance impact of transaction costs include live testing, exaggerating cost assumptions, and applying a haircut to performance estimates on the assumption that the designer will miss something. As the strategy ages, the transaction costs may be more easily understood.

Signal Capture and Implementation Lags

Chapter 6 introduced the idea of an investment signal and whether it may be captured with investment instruments. The concept of signal capture as a component of performance shortfall explores whether the trade was really ever executable. That is, was the information used to generate the trade signal in the back-test portfolio truly available when the live strategy required it? Moreover, was sufficient liquidity truly available in the marketplace to execute the trade? A good example of this is Chapter 6's "War Story: The Danger of Not Thinking through the Investment Signal" box, illustrating the mistaken use of revised economic data in a back test, effectively assuming it was available before the revision's release. The prescription for signal capture is careful attention to details when developing the investment strategy.

The concept of *implementation lag* recognizes that a delay may exist between confirmation of an investment signal and the final execution, such as the lag between a portfolio manager's trade order and the trader's completion of the order. In contrast, the concept of opportunity cost assumes that a trade was identified but not executed either completely or at all. Failure to promptly execute a trade means the loss of potential profit.

Opportunity cost and implementation lag are trading issues pertaining to execution of a trade to capture a signal—more precisely the loss of expected profit from not trading at the assumed model price. Signal capture is a modeling issue reflecting the cost of not generating a signal in time to trade. This usually occurs because the signals are based on information that is not actually available when the trade signal needs to be generated. The arrival and accuracy of information and the impact on a trading strategy can sometimes be subtle. As a result, most firms test their new strategies live in-house before offering them to the public.

Poor Execution, Trade Errors, and Fraud

Even if all else goes right—the model is not overfit, it is developed over a representative sample period, transaction costs are completely and well modeled, and signals are captured in time to trade—implementation surprises can occur. These surprises can be broadly categorized as either mistakes or fraud; the essential difference is the presence or absence of intent.

Poor execution and trade errors are unintentional deviations from strategy. Poor execution is defined as costs higher than justified by market conditions and simply results in reduced performance. Lack of training or ineffective incentives are common sources of poor execution. Trade errors can be both positive and negative.[7] The good news for investor clients is they usually get to keep gains from the good errors and typically get compensated for the bad errors.[8] Fraud is intentional deviation from strategy. The typical motivation is to hide poor performance or to increase the personal gain of a trader or manager. Unfortunately fraud is never a positive surprise, may be difficult to control, and in some cases can be devastating.

These operational considerations are important and have been responsible for a number of large and high-profile losses. A study of hedge funds found that 56 percent of hedge fund collapses—funds that ceased operations—were directly related to

---

[7] An example is the dreaded "fat finger" error of hitting the wrong key when executing a trade.

[8] Some hedge fund management agreements state that the fund itself accepts the impact of trade errors.

EXHIBIT 12.3   **Historic Trading Losses**

Firm/Fund	Loss ($ billion)	Issue
MGRM (1993)	1.3	Declining oil prices and poaching by other traders led to large liquidity demands and mark to market losses in futures hedge.
Orange County (1994)	1.6	Poor risk oversight resulted in highly levered positions in floating-rate notes, which generated large losses as interest rates rose.
Barings (1995)	1.3	Nick Leeson made unauthorized speculative trades. After initial success, he hid mounting losses in the bank error account. An attempt to recoup losses proved catastrophic when the Kobe earthquake led to a large sell-off.
Daiwa (1995)	1.1	Unauthorized bond trades.
Sumitomo (1996)	2.3	The chief copper trader executed off-the-book and false trades for more than 10 years. Before collapsing, the trades were profitable as they drove up the price of copper.
LTCM (1998)	4.0	High leverage and expansion into trades outside core strategy generated large losses as bond price differences did not converge and Russia defaulted.
Bayou (2006)	0.4	To cover trading losses in 1998, Bayou created its own auditing firm. Losses grew, and the fund closed in 2006.
Amaranth (2006)	9.0	Poor risk oversight allowed large natural gas positions, which generated large profits followed by larger losses as price differences did not increase.

operational issues.[9] Exhibit 12.3, showing some high-profile losses, confirms that execution issues matter.

The constants in these episodes have been the absence of enforcement for best risk management practices and a trading culture that made it difficult to constrain apparently profitable operations. The prescription for preventing mistakes is attention to both investment and operational risks, checks on strategy execution, and compliance with risk limits. For a potential investor in a fund, due diligence involves a review of not only the strategy but also the personnel executing the strategy. Consider whether they are experienced across market cycles and if they have successfully implemented similar strategies. Background checks and references are important. A review of the back and middle office and pricing policy is also a good idea. This should be done by a disinterested third party such as an outside auditor. Ultimately a haircut can be applied to performance expectations, time must be devoted to exploring what could go wrong and the investor should diversify (and fingers should be crossed for good luck) to account for the unknown. As an outside investor, if results seem too good to be true (consider the Madoff case in 2008), be cautious.

12.3   Portfolio Adjustments without Taxes or Costs

Taxes and transaction costs introduce friction into the portfolio adjustment process. This friction implies that our actual portfolio will deviate from our ideal target (or paper) portfolio. With taxes and trading costs it is simply not worthwhile to respond to every change in the investment environment. In the absence of these frictions, however,

---

[9] Capco Research Working Paper, "Understanding and Mitigating Operational Risk in Hedge Fund Investments," 2002.

EXHIBIT 12.4
**Prototypical
Rebalancing
Strategies**

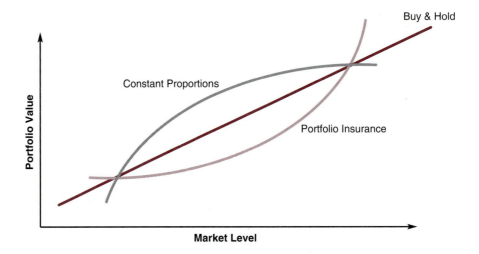

we can adjust completely and immediately to ensure that the portfolio always reflects our preferences and our view of market opportunities.

Although the term *rebalancing* is often used imprecisely, it generally connotes the process of adjusting portfolio weights in response to market movements. The goal is to be more effectively positioned for future market changes. In this section we ignore taxes and trading costs to focus on three prototypical rebalancing strategies for the target portfolio: *buy and hold, constant proportions,* and *portfolio insurance.* Exhibit 12.4 illustrates the relationship between portfolio value and market level for these three strategies. The chart can represent either the value of an individual asset position within the portfolio in relation to its price or the value of the whole portfolio in relation to the overall market.

Buy and hold is essentially a "do-nothing" strategy: The portfolio manager neither buys nor sells in response to changes in market value. The position increases or decreases in value linearly with the market. All else the same, this implies that we are willing to increase or decrease the portfolio weight in a rising or falling market. Using this strategy with respect to overall equity (risky) exposure means taking on more risk as wealth increases and vice versa. This could reflect risk tolerance that increases or decreases with wealth. Alternatively, this strategy could be justified by extrapolating price trends so that perceived compensation for risk rises or falls with the market. From the perspective of an individual security position within a diversified portfolio, allowing the portfolio weight to rise or fall with the price must reflect perceived compensation for the security's risk because the impact on overall risk tolerance would be negligible.

Maintaining constant portfolio weights (a constant proportions strategy) requires systematically selling winners and buying losers. As shown in Exhibit 12.4, the process of selling high and buying low creates a concave relationship between portfolio value and market prices. The strategy underperforms the buy-and-hold strategy if the market moves strongly in either direction, but the trades boost return in a market with frequent reversals but little net movement. In the parlance of the options market, this strategy is "short volatility."

As we saw in Chapter 3, an investor whose risk tolerance is independent of wealth and who faces the same investment opportunities in every period should select the same portfolio in every period. Therefore, the constant proportions strategy may be viewed as the canonically neutral strategy. It does not rely on expectations of either trending or mean-reverting prices. Similarly, it is not based on a changing attitude toward risk.

Although mean reversion is not required to justify selling winners and buying losers, it certainly would reinforce the benefit of doing so. All else the same, investors who expect prices to mean revert want to go beyond maintaining constant portfolio weights to a strategy of sharply reducing exposure after a rally and buying dips aggressively.

Investors whose relative risk tolerance increases rapidly with wealth, or who expect strongly trending markets, want to buy winners and sell losers. As discussed in Section 5.6, this behavior is the essence of portfolio insurance. This strategy generates a convex relationship between portfolio value and the market. It outperforms the buy-and-hold strategy in trending markets, but it does poorly in trendless markets with frequent reversals. In options parlance, it is "long volatility."

12.4   Transaction Costs

Cost Components

In 2006 Bank of America began offering zero brokerage trading fees for retail customers with $25,000 or more in assets. These offers sound like a great deal until you realize that there are more than commissions in total trading costs. As noted, investment professionals typically describe the existence of three types of trading costs. In addition to commissions, there are the **bid–ask spread** and **market impact** costs. The bid–ask spread is the cost one needs to pay to trade immediately. It represents the fee charged by a **market maker** (either a *dealer* or an exchange *specialist*) to maintain a risky inventory[10] and offer you direct access to either shares or liquidity. It is equal to the difference between the ask or offer (the price the investor needs to pay to buy) and the bid (the price the investor receives from selling).

Market impact is similar to the bid–ask spread, but it reflects the fact that the market maker will need to charge a higher fee (higher ask or lower bid) for larger orders to compensate for greater risk in her or his book. Bid–ask spreads are typically quoted for 1,000 or so shares for the typical stock. Prior to 1999, minimum spreads on the NYSE were 1/8 of a dollar. Since the switch to a decimal system, some spreads have declined to a penny, but the order size for which the spread is valid may have also decreased.

Differing commission structures suggest different trading strategies. For example, the traditional constant *cents-per-share* commission schedule indicates that higher-priced securities would incur a lower percentage commission cost. This would favor trading higher-priced stocks more frequently than lower-priced stocks. *Per trade* commissions, such as an $8.95 fee no matter the number of shares, favor larger trades and suggest the imposition of a minimum trade size. The percentage cost declines as the dollar size of the trade increases. Of course the commission may represent only a small portion of the total trade cost.

Bid–ask spreads and market impact tend to increase with a decrease in volume or an increase in dealer inventory risk. Consider a used car dealer who already has several unpopular autos of the same make on the lot. The next time someone tries to sell the same model, the dealer will bid a much lower price than for another, easier-to-sell

---

[10] In practice, brokers may or may not actually have the security in inventory. They may take a long or short position on the security and manage the risk of their overall book composed of positions in many potentially diversifying individual securities and not worry too much about an individual position. Of course they will need to borrow a security to go short and may seek to offset some of the risk through hedging techniques.

EXHIBIT 12.5
Representative
Volume, Bid–Ask
Spread, and Market
Impact Data: Stock
(SPY) and Bond
(AGG) ETFs

	Daily Dollar Volume in 000's	$ Trade Size in 000's	Quoted Bid—Ask Spread for $ Trade
SPY	$7,221,806		
Best		$ 202	0.01%
Second best		9,158	0.02
Third best		14,710	0.04
Total		24,070	0.03%
AGG	22,061		
Best		1,480	0.31%
Second best		1,460	0.33
Third best		101	0.87
Total		3,040	0.34%

Note: INET Electronic Market, January, 24 2006.

model that is not currently on the lot. In 1971 Jack Treynor[11] published a paper called "The Only Game in Town" and listed key factors determining the cost of trading. He explained that there are two types of investors: those who truly have valuable information or insights, and those who do not (even though they may think they do). The securities dealer loses trading against the first group and wins trading against the second. The higher the price volatility, the greater the risk the dealer assumes in maintaining an inventory; the lower the volume (especially of the second group), the lower the profit for maintaining a book.[12] As a result,

1. High-volume, low-volatility securities will reflect lower total transaction costs than low-volume, high-volatility issues.
2. Transaction costs increase with trade size, urgency, and perceived information content of the trade.

As an example, consider the data in Exhibit 12.5 illustrating costs for trading ETFs. "Best" reflects the trade size and spread between the lowest ask and the highest bid quoted in the market. Trading volume is shown for two securities, one significantly higher-volume than the other. The data show the higher bid–ask spread and market impact costs of the lower-volume security. The exhibit also shows growing published bid–ask spreads as the order size grows. This reflects aggregate traders' *order books,* or lists of bids and offers for each additional order. The traders are willing to take on a bigger long inventory, or a bigger short position, only if they are compensated with a lower price to buy shares from the investors or a higher price to sell. As investors increase their orders, the costs of executing the orders increase more and faster for the lower-volume security than the higher-volume security because it will be harder for the trader to offset the new position in the lower-volume security. Total costs, including commissions, are listed in Exhibit 12.6, which illustrates that high cents-per-share

[11] Published under the pseudonym Walter Bagehot while he was editor of the *Financial Analysts Journal,* this is a classic in the study of **market microstructure.** Market microstructure concentrates on the economics of trading and recognizes that quantity of supply and demand, *per unit of time,* is what determines prices in the marketplace.

[12] In addition to compensation for maintaining an undiversified inventory of securities and to accept the risk of being on the wrong side of an information-based trade, market makers also need to be compensated to cover basic processing costs.

EXHIBIT 12.6
Representative Transaction Cost Data, SPY and ETF Sample Trades

Sample $10 Million Trade in SPY, Price of $125			
	Alternative Brokerage Commissions		
	$10/Trade	**1 Cent per Share**	**5 Cents per Share**
Bid-ask spread	0.010%	0.010%	0.010%
Market impact	0.030	0.030	0.030
SEC tax	0.002	0.002	0.002
Brokerage commission	0.000	0.008	0.040
Total	0.042%	0.050%	0.082%

commission structures can nearly double the total transaction costs for low market-impact securities. AGG's low volatility suggests that the security's cost to transact should be low, but this effect is overwhelmed by its low market volume. Small-cap stocks with both low volume and high volatility would reflect even higher spreads—their market impact costs would represent the majority of total transaction costs.

This discussion encourages the investor to consider adjusting positions gradually, allowing the dealer to sell off or hedge some inventory before putting in the next order. It also encourages the investor to evaluate the timeliness of information or insights and compare that with the additional cost of executing quickly. Of course there is a game going on here, with the investor seeking to hide his or her true intentions from the trader, who wants to know the true size of the order.

Historical transaction costs incurred by an investment firm may be measured (with some error) and used to help evaluate the quality of trader execution and to model future costs for strategy design and implementation. Forecast costs will depend on the expected order size, volume, and volatility. The cost relationship is typically nonlinear, with percentage cost increasing with trade size (unless it is a block trade arranged off the exchange floor). Other than commissions, basic cost functions for equities may be described as follows:

$$\text{Bid–ask spread} = f_1 \text{ (Share volume, Price volatility)}$$

$$\text{Market impact} = f_2 \text{ (Trade size relative to Share volume, Share volume, Price volatility)}$$

The first step in measuring historical transaction costs is to collect execution prices during the day and compare them to a benchmark. The benchmark price can be one of several options:

- Prior night's close.
- Open bid–ask average or transaction.
- Volume-weighted price (VWAP).
- Posttrade.

Volume-weighted price (VWAP) is a measure approximating prices at which a trader should have been able to execute in a given day. Unfortunately, as a benchmark[13]

---

[13] Stewart (1985) demonstrates that the average of bid and ask prices may not necessarily be a better measure of true price (market maker inventory neutral) than the latest transaction price. It depends on how specialists/market makers set their spreads to encourage buy or sell orders due to inventory positions. Empirical evidence suggests that for large-cap stocks, both are equally good measures; for small-cap stocks, the average of the bid and ask is better.

this measure can be gamed because a trader knows its value during the day and can hold back some buy order volume until the next day if prices are rising. Although it may reflect low volume, the opening is typically the preferred measure since it incorporates information released overnight. An examination of post-trade price levels may also provide insight. A subsequent price decline suggests the trader may be forcing too much volume through the market. If tick-by-tick trade data are available, the prior trade price may also be used as a measure. For accuracy, the benchmark should remain the same for any leftover orders executed on subsequent days.

As discussed, it is important to recognize the total drag on a portfolio from trading. The difference between open and execution prices represents a large portion of the cost. Collecting timestamps and measuring the change in prices following order transmission could be used to calculate any impacts from the time lag between when a portfolio manager decides to buy or sell and when that information is made available to the trader and in turn to the marketplace. One way to easily estimate total implementation cost is to compare the realized portfolio return to the return of a buy-and-hold paper portfolio. This buy-and-hold portfolio is updated at the beginning of each period but not during the period and is readily available in accounting databases. Any difference between live and paper portfolio returns reflects the total implementation cost, net of the benefits from making trades before the end of the day or month. If there is value from trading during the period instead of at the end, this estimate is a lower bound of transaction costs.

Both historical results and forecast estimates can help us understand strategy implementation costs to design a better strategy, simulate performance, and estimate product capacity. They can also help us understand individual security costs so we can compare individual security alphas before deciding to trade and decide how quickly to trade.

Excel Outbox
Estimating
Transaction
Costs from
Portfolio Returns

Although many investment operations may not have the resources to build a transaction cost estimation system, there are ways to estimate these costs with readily available data, providing information to improve the investment process. The first example involves an active small-cap equity strategy. Both live market value–based and paper buy-and-hold performance data are available. The difference between the two series provides an estimate of transaction costs. <Template 1> in Chapter 12 Excel Outbox.xls looks like the following:

	A	B	C	D	E	F	G
1							
2	date	live performance	benchmark	active return		buy & hold return	Transaction Cost Estimate
3							
4	Mar-09	8.93	8.07			9.26	
5	Feb-09	−9.56	−11.82			−9.25	
6	Jan-09	−7.51	−12.49			−7.34	
7	Dec-08	4.91	6.1			4.78	
8	Nov-08	−10.05	−11.74			−10	
9	Oct-08	−15.20	−19.71			−15.05	
10	Sep-08	−7.04	−6.75			−7.39	
11							
12	Average						

To calculate the monthly active return, in cell D4 enter +B4-C4 and copy to rows 5 through 10. In cell D12 enter = AVERAGE(D4:D10). This is the monthly average active return.

Calculate the difference between live and buy-and-hold performance to estimate transaction costs. In cell G4 enter +B4-F4. Copy to cells G5:G10. In cell G12 enter =AVERAGE(G4:G10). This represents an estimate of the monthly average transaction cost. The updated worksheet should look like this:

	A	B	C	D	E	F	G
		A	B	C	D	E	F	G
1							
2	date	live performance	benchmark	active return		buy & hold return	Transaction Cost Estimate
3							
4	Mar-09	8.93	8.07	0.86		9.26	−0.33
5	Feb-09	−9.56	−11.82	2.26		−9.25	−0.31
6	Jan-09	−7.51	−12.49	4.98		−7.34	−0.17
7	Dec-08	4.91	6.1	−1.19		4.78	0.13
8	Nov-08	−10.05	−11.74	1.69		−10	−0.05
9	Oct-08	−15.20	−19.71	4.51		−15.05	−0.15
10	Sep-08	−7.04	−6.75	−0.29		−7.39	0.35
11							
12	Average			1.83			−0.08

The results indicate that the portfolio is experiencing an average trading drag of 8 basis points per month. If turnover is 10 percent a month, this represents an 80 basis points realized transaction cost per roundtrip dollar traded (assuming there's no value-added from trading before month-end)—not too large for a small-cap portfolio. Note that the monthly estimates are not always a detractor (see Dec-08 and Sep-08). There is sufficient noise (some trades will make money despite commissions, bid–ask spreads, and so on) in the estimate to cause this. In practice, a longer series would be used to provide a higher-confidence estimate. The PM can use this information in her or his investment process, trading off expected alpha with forecast trading cost.

Consider a second example: a sample-based, tax-managed passive portfolio targeted to track the Russell 3000 index while minimizing capital gains realization. The portfolio has experienced significant cash flows.* In this case the available data are monthly performance and turnover levels. The idea is to compare tracking with turnover to determine the size of transaction costs. <Template 2> looks like the following:

	A	B	C	D	E
1	End of Month	Portfolio	Benchmark		Total
2	Date	Return	Return	Tracking Error	Turnover %
3	31-Mar-02	3.72%	4.11%		33.34%
4	30-Sep-02	−10.41%	−10.74%		29.07%
5	30-Jun-02	−6.81%	−7.38		23.30%
6	31-Aug-02	−0.07%	0.52%		20.04%

(continued)

(concluded)

Enter +B3-C3 in cell D3 and copy down to row 29. In cell D31 enter =AVERAGE(D3: D29). This is the average tracking error. In cell E31 enter =AVERAGE(E3:E29). This is the average turnover. The result should look like this:

	A	B	C	D	E
28	31-Mar-05	−1.78%	−1.69%	−0.09%	3.05%
29	31-Mar-06	1.83%	1.73%	0.11%	0.91%
30					
31				−0.03%	**10.03%**

The results suggest that the trading drag is 3 basis points per month at 10.03 percent turnover, indicating a 0.003/.1003 or 31 basis points transaction cost per roundtrip dollar traded. The embedded chart illustrates the relationship between turnover and tracking error:

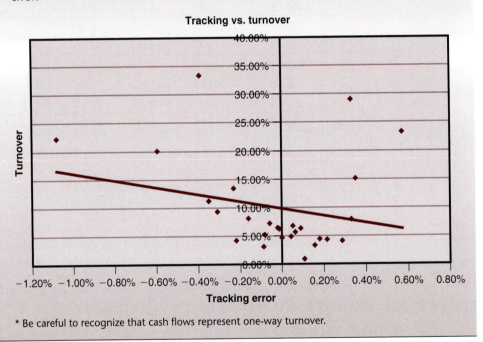

Tracking vs. turnover

* Be careful to recognize that cash flows represent one-way turnover.

Rebalancing with Transaction Costs

When transactions are costly, reallocating a portfolio entails a trade-off. On one hand, holding a suboptimal portfolio imposes a less attractive risk–reward profile. This is the opportunity cost of not trading, defined in Section 12.2, and within the context of portfolio optimization, may be called a "suboptimality" cost. On the other hand, there is the explicit cost involved in trading, including commissions, bid-ask spreads and market impact. There is a third consideration as well: Our current trading decisions affect the costs—both suboptimality costs and trading costs—that we expect to bear in future periods. Therefore, at any point in time our objective is to minimize the sum of three costs:

$$\text{Total cost} = \text{Suboptimality cost of position after current trades}$$

$$+ \text{Trading costs of current trades}$$

$$+ \text{Expected future costs}$$

The trade-off between current and future costs implies that we should ideally treat rebalancing as a dynamic programming problem—similar to our treatment of changing investment opportunities in Chapter 5. In the current context, the problem can be formalized as

$$J(\omega_t, \omega^*) = \min_v \left[S(\omega_t + v_t, \omega^*) + T(v_t) + \xi(J(\omega_{t+1}, \omega^*)) \right]$$

where $J()$ is the optimized cost as a function of the current portfolio weights, ω_t, and the target portfolio weights, ω^*. For simplicity, the target weights are assumed to be constant throughout this discussion. $S()$ represents the suboptimality cost of trading to $(\omega_t + v_t)$ rather than to ω^*. $T(v_t)$ reflects the transaction costs of our current trades, v_t. The final term is the expected value of the optimized cost *next* period conditional on our current trading decisions. The formal solution of this problem is beyond the scope of this book. Nonetheless it provides the framework for understanding the impact of transaction costs on trading and portfolio positioning.

Recall from Chapter 3 (see Exhibit 3.5) that a risk-averse investor will be indifferent between a risky portfolio and some certainty equivalent level of wealth. Higher certainty equivalents correspond to more attractive risky portfolios. Hence the suboptimality cost, $S()$, may be interpreted as the reduction in certainty equivalent wealth due to holding a portfolio other than ω^*. In general this cost will be small for portfolios near the target, but it will grow at an increasing rate as we move further away. The bottom curve in Exhibit 12.7 reflects this pattern. Intuitively we would expect the optimized cost function, $J()$, to have this general shape as well. For present purposes, therefore, we will subsume future costs into the suboptimality cost and focus on the impact of specific transaction cost structures.

Fixed Costs

Transaction costs usually entail some fixed costs, such as processing charges imposed by a custodian bank or a discount broker's flat commission per trade. Even if these explicit fixed charges are absent, the time required to handle each trade imposes an implicit minimum cost per trade.

Exhibit 12.7 shows the trading impact of purely fixed transaction costs. Moving leftward from the target portfolio, ω^*, the suboptimality cost is initially well below the fixed cost of trading.[14] At ω_0 the suboptimality cost of not trading equals the cost of trading. Thus for any initial portfolio in the "no-trade region" (ω_0, ω^*), it is not worthwhile to trade. A similar argument would show that the no-trade region extends to the right of the target. The upper curve labeled "total cost" combines the suboptimality cost curve and the fixed cost of trading. For any initial portfolio to the left of ω_0 the total cost obtained by trading all the way to the target portfolio, ω^*, is less than the suboptimality cost of the initial portfolio. Hence it is optimal to trade to the target from these positions. To summarize, with fixed costs the optimal policy is to trade only if the portfolio is sufficiently far from the target portfolio and then to trade all the way to the target allocation.

Proportional Costs

Whereas fixed trading costs make it inefficient to break larger trades into pieces, proportional costs imply that there is neither an advantage nor a disadvantage to piecemeal

---

[14] For simplicity, the discussion focuses on a single risky asset subject to transaction costs. Therefore, in Exhibit 12.7 the horizontal axis refers to the weight, ω, of this asset in the portfolio. The remainder of the portfolio is implicitly held in cash.

EXHIBIT 12.7
Trading with Fixed Transaction Costs

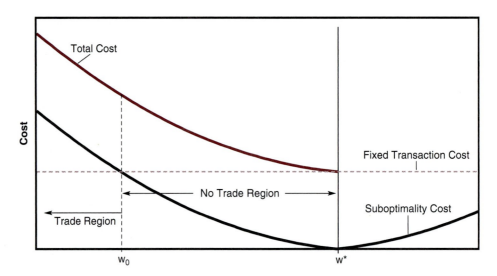

execution. As we will see, this lets us take advantage of the fact that subsequent market movements may reduce or eliminate the need to trade.

Starting at portfolio ω_0 in Exhibit 12.8, the optimal policy is to trade to portfolio ω_1 rather than trade all the way to the target, ω^*. At ω_1 the marginal reduction in suboptimality cost (the downward-sloping curve) is just offset by the marginal increase in transaction costs. Beyond that point, the total cost (upper curve) increases. Having reached ω_1, should we trade again? No: The marginal cost of trading is still equal to the marginal reduction in suboptimality cost, so there is no net benefit to trading. Starting at any point in the interval (ω_1, ω^*), the total cost curve is upward-sloping. Hence ω_1 defines the boundary of a no-trade region. Of course a similar argument would show that the no-trade region extends to the right of target.

Why trade only to the boundary of the no-trade region? If we trade into the interior of the region, we incur higher transaction costs with certainty. By stopping at the boundary, we allow for the fact that subsequent market movements may move us closer to the target without having to incur additional trading costs. Of course, if the market

EXHIBIT 12.8
Trading with Proportional Transaction Costs

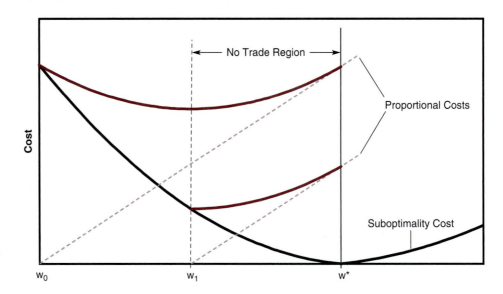

moves us further away we incur additional costs to get back to the boundary. With a proportional cost structure, however, these additional costs are the same as we would incur to move an equal distance into the no-trade region. Trading only to the boundary just balances the expected savings from favorable price movements that move us toward the target against the expected cost of offsetting adverse price movements that move us further away.

Up to this point, our discussion has ignored the fact that in general we will not trade all assets in a portfolio at the same time. Exhibit 12.9 shows the no-trade region when there are two assets with proportional costs (plus a cash account). Equivalently, this graph may be interpreted as a two-dimensional slice of the no-trade region when there are many assets. From any point outside the region, the optimal policy entails trading to the nearest boundary of the region along the shortest path.

The size of the no-trade region is determined primarily by the level of costs and by the investor's risk aversion.[15] Not surprisingly, the more costly it is to trade, the larger the no-trade region. Because more risk-averse investors are more sensitive to deviations from the target, higher risk aversion (lower risk tolerance) results in a smaller no-trade region.

The no-trade region in Exhibit 12.9 is skewed to the right; that is, the southwest-to-northeast diagonal is longer than the northwest-to-southeast diagonal. This reflects a negative correlation between the two assets. With negative correlation, market movements are more likely to push the two portfolio weights in opposite directions than in the same direction. Deviations from the target toward the northeast or southwest are therefore likely to be self-correcting, and relatively large deviations in these directions can be tolerated without trading. Conversely, deviations toward the northwest or southeast are likely to be reinforced by subsequent market movements and hence require relatively prompt correction. Of course the no-trade region would be skewed to the left for positively correlated assets.

Increasing Costs

While the explicit costs of trading tend to be fixed and/or (roughly) proportional to the trade, market impact costs generally increase as we attempt to execute more shares per unit of time. Thus, there is an incentive to break large trades into smaller pieces

---

[15] Donohue and Yip (2003) studied the effects of various parameters on the no-trade region.

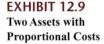

EXHIBIT 12.9
**Two Assets with
Proportional Costs**

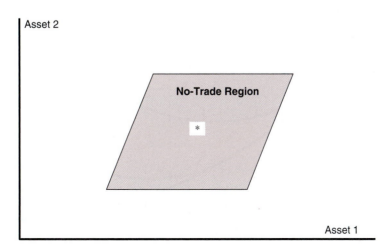

executed gradually over time. Unfortunately, trading too slowly may entail large, persistent deviations from the target portfolio and hence substantial suboptimality costs.

The impact of increasing costs is illustrated in Exhibit 12.10. Starting at portfolio ω_0, the first trade takes us to ω_1, where the marginal reduction in suboptimality cost is just offset by the marginal increase in current transaction costs. Trading beyond that point in the first period entails sharply rising total costs and therefore is not worthwhile. However, having reached ω_1 in the first period, we trade to ω_2 in the second period. With increasing transaction costs, this second trade costs less than the incremental cost of a correspondingly bigger trade in the first period. It is worth incurring this cost to reduce the suboptimality cost further. A third, albeit smaller, trade will also be worthwhile followed by another, and so on. Thus an increasing cost structure leads to a sequence of progressively smaller trades toward the target.

Transaction Costs and Target Portfolios

In the foregoing discussion we took the target portfolio, ω^*, as given to focus on the trading implications of transaction costs. Implicitly we assumed the target portfolio to be the portfolio that would be selected in the absence of transaction costs. It turns out that this is true for purely fixed or proportional costs. In general, however, increasing costs affect the target portfolio.[16]

The optimal trading strategy with *fixed costs* implies that we should trade to our target portfolio immediately whenever we are sufficiently far away. In essence, we will never spend time outside the no-trade region surrounding the target. The no-trade region embodies the trade-off between the suboptimality costs of being away from the target and the fixed transaction costs. Therefore, there is no reason to select a target portfolio that would be suboptimal in the absence of transaction costs.

The situation is essentially the same with *proportional* transaction costs. Although we do not trade all the way to the target, the optimal policy ensures that we will not spend time outside the no-trade region. Again, the no-trade region accounts for the balance between suboptimality and trading costs, and there is no reason to select a target portfolio that would be suboptimal in the absence of costs.

[16] To our knowledge, Piros (1983) was the first to address this issue.

EXHIBIT 12.10
Trading with Increasing Transaction Costs

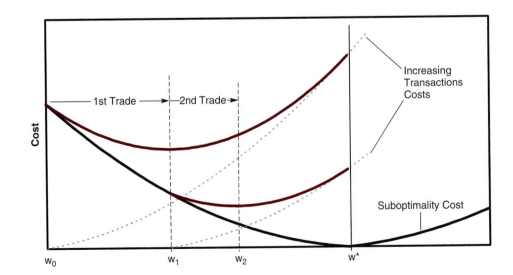

With *increasing* costs it is prohibitively expensive to trade immediately to our target portfolio. To avoid the potential cost of large adjustments, we need to make frequent small trades in an effort to keep the actual portfolio close to the target. The expected cost of this trading will in general alter our choice of target portfolio. That is, the target portfolio will not be the same as it would in the absence of increasing transaction costs. We will select different optimal weights to recognize that some securities will involve different cost structures.

A simple example should help make this clear. Consider two assets that differ only in that one provides most of its expected return in cash while the other generates only an expected capital gain. Setting aside tax issues, there would be no reason to favor one asset or the other in the absence of transaction costs. All else the same, however, the second asset is likely to require more active trading to keep its weight in the portfolio close to the target. Hence market impact costs would tend to tip the scale in favor of the asset that pays most of its return in cash.

Turnover versus Value Added

Because trading is costly, it is natural to ask whether we can reduce turnover without sacrificing value added. Of course the simple answer is no. We cannot expect to reduce turnover without also reducing value added. The real question is how much value added can be retained while substantially reducing turnover.

Grinold and Kahn (2000) suggest a useful rule of thumb for this issue: We can capture 75 percent of an active strategy's potential value added with only 50 percent of the turnover. This guideline assumes we simply cut each trade in half; therefore it is somewhat conservative. Prioritizing trades based on value added and identifying differential transaction costs across securities will generally enable us to preserve even more value added.

12.5 Taxation of Investment Returns in the United States[17]

Benjamin Franklin observed that nothing is certain except death and taxes. Although some taxes on investment returns may be postponed, and in a few exceptional cases avoided, most investment income is taxed, creating the incentive to customize investment strategies to maximize after-tax returns. Because U.S. federal and state taxes are typically assessed based on receipt or realization of income, investment returns are taxed when interest and dividends are received or when securities are sold. However, many institutions, including pension plans, endowments, and foundations, are not (or virtually not) subject to taxes. Defined contribution accounts are not subject to taxes, but with the exception of **Roth IRA** accounts, their eventual distributions are taxed at ordinary income rates. Similarly, investment returns within deferred annuity contracts and life insurance policies are not subject to income tax. Other than death benefits, however, distributions from these contracts are taxed as ordinary income.

Current U.S. tax law treats various transactions and instruments differently. Interest on corporate and federal government bonds is taxed as ordinary income. For individuals, this can result in a 40 percent or higher effective tax rate. On the other hand, interest on municipal bonds is tax-exempt at the federal level. States also treat interest as ordinary income, though they exclude Treasury bond interest from income taxes.

[17] The U.S. tax code is extremely complex and is subject to frequent revisions. This section provides only a broad overview of the most essential elements pertaining to investment decisions. See IRS Publication 550, *Investment Income and Expenses,* for details about federal taxation.

Traditionally dividend income was also treated as ordinary income. In 2003, however, it was formally recognized that this double taxation (taxed first at the corporate level and again at the individual level) was inappropriate. Since then the maximum individual tax rate on **qualified dividend** income has been 15 percent—the same as the top rate on long-term capital gains and well below the top ordinary income tax rate of 36 percent. Under current law, this more favorable treatment ends in 2011. To qualify for the lower rate the dividend must be paid by a U.S. corporation or a qualified foreign corporation, and the investor must satisfy a 61-day holding period requirement. Preferred stock dividends qualify provided the preferred stock does not qualify as debt for corporate taxation (that is, the dividends are not deductible as interest expense). However, most dividends from real estate investment trusts (REITs) are treated as ordinary income because they represent rental income that is not taxed at the corporate level as long as the REIT pays out at least 90 percent of such income. To mitigate the impact of double taxation, corporations that receive dividends from other publicly traded corporations can exclude 70 percent of those dividends from taxable income. Combining this rule with the 34 percent top corporate tax rate implies that U.S. corporations pay a top federal rate of 10.2 percent on dividends received.

Until 2003 it made sense for companies to transfer cash to investors by buying back stock rather than paying dividends. This allowed taxable investors to pay a capital gains tax rather than the higher rate on ordinary income. The federal capital gains tax rate is 15 percent[18] if the investment is held for more than one year. Most state tax laws follow a similar rule at a lower rate.[19] Investments held for less than one year are taxed at ordinary income rates. The legislative idea is to encourage long-term investment and discourage short-term trading. Capital losses may be used to offset other gains and up to $3,000 of ordinary income. Long-term losses must first be netted against long-term gains before offsetting short-term gains or ordinary income. Excess losses may be carried over to the next year's tax period. Interestingly, any gains from short sales, including those earned from positions maintained for more than one year, are treated as short-term gains for tax purposes.

Some investments may not generate any cash flows, but the tax authorities still tax the investment return on an **accrual basis.** For example, zero-coupon bonds are assumed to accrue interest, and that accrual is taxed each period as if it were received in cash. The market discount on low-coupon bonds must also be accrued as interest. Similarly, Treasury Inflation-Protected Securities (TIPS) reflect increasing principal at the rate of the CPI, which is taxed as ordinary income.

As if the regular tax code were not sufficiently complex, individual investors are also subject to the alternative minimum tax (AMT) and to phased-out deductibility of investment expenses. Each of these can alter the effective tax rate paid on investment returns.

The AMT was designed to ensure that high-income individuals pay at least a minimum tax rate based on an alternative measure of taxable income. The AMT calculation limits or disallows some deductions, such as state and local taxes paid, and adds income that is not taxable under the basic tax code, like interest on some municipal

---

[18] Investors with taxable income below a certain threshold currently pay no tax on long-term capital gains and qualified dividends. In general, the specific rates and provisions mentioned in the text are those that apply to investors with significant investment income or who are in the top tax bracket.

[19] A few states, such as New Jersey, treat capital gains as ordinary income regardless of holding period.

Theory in Practice
Carried Interest—Your Capital, My Gain?

Asset management firms usually charge fees stated in terms of basis points on assets under management (AUM); for example, a firm charging 50 basis points on AUM of $1 billion would collect $5 million in fees each year. Because these fees represent payment for professional services, they are treated as ordinary income for tax purposes.

The situation becomes less clear, indeed quite controversial, when a manager also collects a performance fee in the form of a "carried interest" in the fund being managed. This arrangement is common in private equity and other alternative asset classes. Carried interest is essentially a profit-sharing arrangement designed to take advantage of partnership accounting and tax laws to transform fees into capital gains. Rather than take a performance fee in cash as it is earned, the manager leaves it in the fund as carried interest. In effect, the manager then owns part of the fund even if she or he did not put up any of the original capital. Later, often when underlying portfolio investments are liquidated and the proceeds are distributed to investors, the manager will receive this carried interest as a profit-sharing distribution labeled as a capital gain. Thus the partners of the management firm pay the 15 percent capital gains tax rate on these fees rather than the much higher ordinary income tax rate paid by other high-income professionals.

Is this really a capital gain? Well, some of it may be. Until it is paid out, the manager's profit share is at risk alongside the investors' original capital. Hence at least part of the eventual distribution to the manager is likely to represent investment gains and losses. But what about the ownership stake the manager accrues in lieu of cash fees—the carried interest itself? That, as they say, is in the eye of the beholder.

bonds. The investor must calculate tax liability under both the regular code and the AMT and pay the higher bill.

Many tax code provisions apply only to taxpayers above or below certain thresholds of adjusted gross income (AGI). The AMT is an important example; phase-outs of deductions are another. Increases in AGI above the threshold increase taxable income more than dollar-for-dollar because allowable deductions are decreased by a fraction of the excess AGI above the threshold. This implies a higher effective marginal tax rate. Interestingly, this can affect the relative attractiveness of mutual funds and separate accounts. Mutual fund expenses are netted against income within the fund, so the investor pays taxes only on the net income. With a separate account, however, the investor must pay tax on the account's gross income but may be able to deduct only part of the management fee and other expenses.

In addition to taxing investment income each year, the federal government and most states impose an estate tax on wealth at the time of an individual's death.[20] Large estates are taxed at very high rates on assets over a specific size. In 2008 estates over $2,000,000 were taxed at 45 percent. Due to a quirk in prevailing law, the rate will drop to 0 percent in 2010 but increase sharply to 55 percent on estates exceeding $1,000,000 in 2011. The cost basis for calculating subsequent gains on bequeathed investments is *stepped up* at the date of death, so the inheritor starts with a zero capital gain.

[20] Until 2001 state estate taxes paid were credited against the federal estate tax liability. In effect states got a portion of the federal estate tax revenue. The credit was phased out and finally eliminated in 2005. Most states now impose a distinct estate tax over and above the federal tax. The thresholds and rates in the text refer to the federal estate tax.

12.6 Strategies to Reduce Individual Investor Taxes

It's not what you make, it's what you keep; but you cannot take it with you. Virtually every individual investor is concerned with accumulating enough wealth for his or her own needs. Many are also interested in preserving and transferring wealth to future generations or charitable causes. In this section we outline strategies for mitigating the impact of taxes on each of these objectives. The focus is mainly on broader asset allocation decisions. Tax considerations within a security-level portfolio are the focus of the next section.

Enhancing After-Tax Returns

As noted in the previous section, interest payments on bonds issued by municipal governments are tax-exempt at the federal level. The idea is for the federal government to reduce the borrowing costs for state, county, and other local governments. Most states also exempt interest on municipal bonds issued within that state.[21] As should be expected, this tax advantage is reflected in lower municipal bond yields. In general, very short-term municipal yields embody the top tax rate, but longer-term yields reflect a lower implicit tax rate. Therefore, investors in the highest tax brackets usually find it advantageous to use municipal bonds for their fixed-income allocations.

Municipal bond investors should be aware that despite their generally exempt status these bonds can still generate a tax liability. First, interest paid on municipal bonds issued to support private activities is subject to the alternative minimum tax. Second, only the actual coupon payments are tax-exempt. The accrual of the market discount on a low-coupon bond is taxable. Therefore, a bond selling at par and a bond selling at a discount have different tax consequences. Third, capital gains on bonds sold before maturity are taxable.

The differential taxation of long-term and short-term capital gains and losses creates an incentive to postpone realization of gains at least until they qualify for long-term treatment but to realize losses as short-term whenever possible. Consistent application of this strategy leads to an accumulation of unrealized long-term gains and a carryforward of realized, but unused, short-term losses. Realization of losses is complicated by the **wash sale rule,** which disallows a loss for tax purposes if the same security is repurchased within 30 days. Thus the tax benefit of realizing the loss must be weighed against the opportunity cost of exiting the position for at least 31 days. Postponing gains without harvesting losses, however, leads to a phenomenon known as *lock-in:* a strong disincentive to sell appreciated securities due to the tax consequences as the market rises over time.

Postponement of gains, even without routine loss harvesting, is an effective strategy for individual investors. Consider the tax impact of actively managed mutual funds compared to index and tax-managed funds. Exhibit 12.11 shows that both a moderate turnover (50 percent/year) equity fund and an index fund incur significant tax costs over long periods. Terminal wealth is 18 percent higher for 5 percent turnover versus 50 percent turnover after 30 years. As a result, active fund managers must overcome both higher management fees and higher tax costs.

Whereas the search for pretax performance often leads investors to allocate assets to various specialized funds or managers, tax considerations generally point toward fewer, broader tax-managed portfolios within which capital gains and losses can more easily be offset. For example, a single all-cap core fund is likely to be more tax-efficient than a collection of size- and style-specific funds. The single broader portfolio

---

[21] In *Department of Revenue v. Davis* (2008) the U.S. Supreme Court upheld Kentucky's law exempting municipal bonds issued within that state but taxing municipal issues from other states.

EXHIBIT 12.11   **After-Tax Returns of Funds with Different Turnover Levels:**
Total Return of 10% with 2% Dividend Yield

Horizon (Years)	0% Turnover		5% Turnover Index Fund		50% Turnover Active Fund	
	After Liquidation	Before Liquidation	After Liquidation	Before Liquidation	After Liquidation	Before Liquidation
1	8.0	9.6	8.0	9.5	8.0	8.8
10	8.5	9.6	8.4	9.3	8.1	8.2
30	9.0	9.6	8.7	9.1	8.1	8.2
50	9.2	9.6	8.8	9.1	8.1	8.1

20% capital gains tax, 20% dividend tax based on 15% federal rates, and assumed 5% state rates.
Note: See Stewart (1992) for the techniques to develop Exhibit 12.11.

facilitates offsetting gains and losses across cap sizes and styles. In addition, it avoids the turnover that arises in a collection of narrower mandates when securities migrate between cap size and style boxes. Nonetheless, many tax-managed value, growth, and small-cap funds are offered in the marketplace.

The desire to combine tax efficiency with the expertise of multiple managers has led several investment platform providers to offer a new service, overlay management, for their **separately managed account** (SMA) clients. In the traditional SMA program each manager executes her or his own trades without considering the combined tax impact on the client. Therefore, for example, the client's overall portfolio may experience wash sales due to the uncoordinated actions of different managers. In an overlay management framework, each of the client's managers submits a model portfolio to the overlay manager, who then consolidates the positions, minimizes the overall tax impact of trading, and executes only selected trades. Importantly, the client's actual portfolio will not generally reflect all of the underlying managers' ideas.

Equalization of the top federal tax rate on qualified dividends and long-term capital gains has greatly reduced a long-standing incentive for individual investors to favor low-dividend/high-capital gain stocks. This incentive remains, however, due to the ability to postpone realization and taxation of capital gains. On the other hand, for corporations the dividend exclusion encourages investment in high-yielding stocks. This benefit can be so large that an actively managed equity portfolio tilted toward high-yielding stocks and incurring transaction costs and taxes on realized gains can still outperform a simple index fund.[22]

ETFs have grown in popularity in the last few years. They are generally more tax efficient than similar mutual funds because the share creation and redemption process allows ETFs to systematically replace low-cost **tax lots** with higher-cost lots. Unlike open-end mutual funds, ETFs accept subscriptions and meet redemptions only in shares of the underlying portfolio securities, such as the 500 stocks composing the S&P 500. When new ETF shares are issued, the fund receives the underlying securities at current market values. When ETF shares are redeemed, the fund can deliver any shares it owns. Tax efficiency dictates delivering the lowest-cost shares. Therefore, the subscription or redemption process tends to minimize potential capital gain realization within the ETF. Before selecting an ETF over a mutual fund, however, it is important to weigh the tax advantage against the likely transaction costs of trading. The cost of frequent trades may outweigh the enhanced tax efficiency.

[22] See Stewart (1992) for further details.

Nuclear power plants have a limited life. After 40 years or so of operation they need to be shut down, and their sites must be cleaned up. Not surprisingly, this can represent a significant cost in the billions of dollars. Utility companies put money aside every year of a plant's operation to prepare for this large expense. Federal law facilitates the creation of a trust account to hold the dedicated assets. Similar to a defined benefit plan trust, these assets are invested for the long term. Unlike a pension plan, the proceeds are distributed over a few years, and the income and gains are taxable. Because corporations are allowed a deduction on 70 percent of dividend income, it typically makes sense to seek returns in the form of dividend income rather than capital gains. The specific benefit and strategy depend on the time horizon, but it is usually preferable for equities to be invested in a portfolio of high-dividend-yielding stocks as long as diversification can be managed.

Funds with high-turnover strategies, like some hedge funds, are a very inefficient vehicle for taxable investors. High turnover implies a high volume of predominantly short-term realized gains. In addition, gains on short positions are treated as short-term regardless of the actual holding period. Like fully active equity and high-yield mutual funds, hedge funds are better placed within tax-deferred vehicles like a 401(k) or IRA.

Most individual investors have both taxable and tax-deferred accounts. Therefore, wealth accumulation is affected by both what they own and where they own it. The former decision is asset allocation; the latter is often called **asset location.** In general, investments that generate ordinary income (bonds and REITs), short-term gains (hedge funds), or high turnover (active equity) should be placed in tax-deferred accounts. Low-turnover strategies and tax-exempt securities belong in a taxable account.

The tax code allows life insurance companies to do something that no other financial institution can do: Create and sell tax-deferred investment vehicles.[23] **Variable annuities** are essentially mutual funds with an **annuity wrapper.** The wrapper provides the tax-deferred accumulation privilege, a death benefit, and a sequence of periodic distributions following the accumulation period. As might be expected in a monopolistic market, annuity fees are generally quite high.[24] Hence it is often said that annuities are "sold not bought." In addition, annuity distributions are generally taxed as ordinary income. Thus these vehicles tend to turn capital appreciation into ordinary income—the exact opposite of what many investors, especially very high net worth investors, seek.

Wealth Preservation and Transfer

Individuals may deduct from income any donations made to charitable organizations. In fact individuals may deduct, at market value, appreciated securities without paying capital gains taxes. Therefore, appreciated securities are an ideal vehicle for charitable giving.

Individuals may also give assets to others (in 2009 to a maximum of $13,000 per year per recipient) without incurring taxes. However, gifts in excess of this amount are

[23] Many financial institutions can administer and manage tax-deferred retirement plans, like IRAs, but insurance companies are the only private institutions that can confer tax-deferred status on their own obligations.

[24] No-load, lower-cost alternatives are becoming more readily available, providing competition for traditional providers.

subject to a gift tax, paid by the giver, which is essentially equivalent to paying an estate tax. A program of systematic giving is an effective method of transferring assets without paying estate taxes. Due to the annual limitation, however, transferring significant amounts in this way requires a long horizon.

Giving or selling assets to a **trust** for the benefit of succeeding generations or a charitable organization can remove those assets from the taxable estate while the grantor retains, through the terms of the trust, some control over how and when the assets are utilized. Trusts can be structured in myriad ways depending on the needs and objectives of the grantor and the tax status of the beneficiaries. Often the objective is to freeze the value of certain assets, transferring subsequent appreciation to the beneficiaries. A **grantor retained annuity trust (GRAT)** is essentially a private fixed-rate annuity vehicle. The grantor transfers assets to the GRAT; the trust promises to return the assets in installments with interest at the lowest rate allowed by the IRS at the time the GRAT is established. If structured properly, the transfer to the trust is free of gift and estate taxes regardless of its size. If the trust assets earn more than the required interest rate, the excess goes to the beneficiaries. For example, assuming the assets earn 10 percent/year more than the required rate, a $10 million GRAT would transfer $1 million per year to the beneficiaries without gift or estate taxes.

Whereas a GRAT is designed to transfer assets to the beneficiaries gradually over time, a life insurance trust is designed to generate a lump sum to offset some or all of the estate taxes that will be due upon the grantor's death. Suppose, for simplicity, a taxable estate of $5 million and a 50 percent estate tax rate; that is, when the individual dies there will be a $2.5 million tax bill and $2.5 million preserved for the heirs. Suppose a $2.5 million life insurance policy can be purchased. The individual can give the annual premium to the trust. The trust buys and owns the life insurance policy so that the policy is not part of the individual's taxable estate. Upon the individual's death, the trust receives the $2.5 million death benefit tax-free, and the taxable estate generates $2.5 million net of tax. Therefore the beneficiaries receive the full $5 million. Note that a $5 million insurance policy would have been required if the insured individual owned the policy rather than putting it in a trust—because life insurance death benefits are included in the estate if the *owner* of the policy dies. This distinction between the insured party and the owner of the policy is crucial.

General Recommendations

Although tax rules and minimization strategies are complicated, Exhibit 12.12 lists a few simple, general recommendations that can significantly improve after-tax performance.

EXHIBIT 12.12 Basic Tax-Related Recommendations for Individual Investment Policy

- Fully utilize 401(k), IRA, 529, and variable annuity tax deferral options.
- Place high-interest and high-short-term gain investments in tax-deferred accounts.
- Place low-turnover and tax-exempt investments in taxable accounts.
- Postpone realization of capital gains.
- Avoid realizing short-term gains. Harvest capital losses when available.
- Do not hire a low-turnover active manager for a taxable account. Instead combine index funds and high-turnover active manager(s).
- Use broad mandate tax-managed funds. Avoid narrow tax-managed mandates.
- Give to the maximum.
- Donate appreciated assets rather than cash to charities.
- Exploit ways to freeze asset values and transfer subsequent appreciation.

War Story   *Biotech Tax-Managed Fund**

As time goes on, deferrals of capital gains realization lead to a growing lock-in of security positions. The manager would like to diversify a portfolio, but with fewer and fewer options this becomes difficult, leading to a portfolio with unintentional biases.

Consider the idea of a portfolio of biotech stocks for providing a tax-efficient equity investment. Many early stage biotech companies fail, providing some nice capital losses for the investor. The few stocks of companies that are successful over the long term have huge price appreciation, but they create no capital gain realizations if the manager doesn't sell the positions. Of course the problem becomes obvious after 10 or 20 years—who wants all their equity exposure concentrated in only two or three successful biotech companies?

* As observed by William Hayes, portfolio manager of the Fidelity Health Care Fund between 1981 and 1989.

12.7   Tax Managing a Portfolio of Securities

There are a lot of moving parts when we seek to maximize the after-tax return of an equity portfolio. We have already discussed the two main considerations: (1) postponing gains while harvesting losses and (2) balancing the tax impact of capital gains versus dividends. If there were no transaction costs, wash sale rules, or alpha considerations, the portfolio manager should realize losses immediately and avoid realization of short-term gains. Under older tax laws that taxed dividends more heavily than long-term gains, it was advantageous to sell just before rather than after a significant dividend, provided the sale would generate a long-term gain. The position could then be reestablished at the lower ex-dividend price. If the sale would entail a short-term gain, however, there was no benefit to avoiding the dividend. Under current law, the situation is reversed. Receiving a (qualified) dividend is more tax efficient than realizing a short-term gain and no worse than realizing a long-term gain. Therefore current law is actually tilted in favor of dividends.

Due to the tax impact of even low levels of turnover, the portfolio manager needs to keep a close watch on the details. In particular, a time/date stamp and trade price must be tracked for each tax lot of each security in the portfolio. Tax efficiency dictates careful selection of the tax lot(s) to be delivered whenever a security is sold. Any lots that will generate short-term losses should be delivered first, followed by long-term losses, long-term gains, and finally short-term gains. In general, this ordering is consistent with delivering the highest-cost lots first.

Unfortunately, a tax-efficient delivery policy reinforces the lock-in effect described in the previous section. As the market moves higher over time, the manager has less and less flexibility to minimize taxes while maintaining portfolio diversification and incorporating fresh value-added ideas. Eventually the manager must strike a balance between taxes, risk, and value-added return.

The lock-in effect is particularly acute for individuals, such as corporate executives, who have a large portion of their net worth concentrated in a single stock with a low cost basis. One solution to this problem is to participate in an **exchange fund**—a mutual fund vehicle designed to provide diversification without the need to sell a concentrated position. Brokers solicit a group of investors, who each swap a large quantity of shares in one security for shares in a newly created mutual fund, composed of a more diversified portfolio of the investors' collective positions (and some real estate shares, as required by the IRS ruling allowing exchange funds). Although not perfectly diversified, and offering little opportunity for management, this is much better than the investors' original concentrated positions.

The process of gains realization can be thought of as an option. The manager can realize the gains now or defer them to be realized in the future. Deferral entails risk and a potentially higher future cost if the tax treatment becomes less favorable. Only if the investment will be held to death or used for gifts will there be no future cost. As a result, in most cases the cost of realizing capital gains sooner rather than later is early payment of taxes.[25] In other words, the cost is the time value of the tax payment, not the payment itself. For a passive portfolio, the time value of money can be significant because the positions are held for a very long time (20 years for a 5 percent turnover portfolio). For an active portfolio with 50 percent turnover, it is only two years on average. This assumes that the alpha will last on average two years.

Consider a stock that earns 10 percent total return each year in capital gains in a world of 20 percent gains tax. If the stock is sold at the end of each year, the two-year return is 16.6 percent after tax. If the stock is held for the full two years before selling, the return is 16.8 percent. The difference of 20 basis points is the cost of paying the tax early. At any point in time, the cost of paying the current tax and reinvesting the proceeds in a different security may be compared with the alternative of holding the security for a longer period. One practical approach involves assuming the alternative holding period is five years and adding the after-tax return difference to the total of other transaction costs when comparing the result with the potential alpha pickup (the difference in expected excess returns between the current and potential holding) before deciding whether to swap the positions.

For active, value-style equity fund managers, tax implications can be especially frustrating because they tend to sell their winners and perhaps buy more of their losers. In contrast, momentum managers may be less constricted by tax implications unless their strategy generates more short-term rather than long-term realized gains.

As noted, early realization can be treated as a transaction cost. A potential trade may then be evaluated for its diversification and alpha benefits and its commission, bid–ask spread, market impact, and tax-related costs.[26] Of course the tax cost will differ for each tax lot. With the added complexity of tax lots, optimizers are frequently modified to include **integer programming** techniques. These advanced optimizers treat each lot as a discrete bundle of shares to be bought, held, or sold.

Summary

Portfolio management is an inherently dynamic process. Market movements, fundamental developments, and changing investor circumstances all require ongoing monitoring and at least periodic adjustment of portfolios. Taxes and transaction costs introduce significant friction into the process.

Failure to adequately account for potential trading costs is a main reason why real portfolios often fail to live up to the potential suggested by back tests of the strategy. In particular, ignoring or underestimating market impact costs will almost surely result in an implementation shortfall. Trading costs are not the only factor, however. Some

---

[25] As long as both realizations are treated as long- or short-term.

[26] The equity portfolio construction examples provided in the Excel outboxes in Chapter 8 may be extended to cover simplified transaction and tax costs by adding trading cost terms to the objective functions.

trades may simply not get executed. Other trades may be partially executed or may be delayed. Similarly, the back testing may implicitly or explicitly utilize information that would not have been available for real-time trading. Operational errors compound the potential slippage.

In the absence of taxes and transaction costs, portfolio adjustments reflect changes in the desired target portfolio. Buy and hold, constant proportions, and portfolio insurance are prototypical strategies. Buy and hold is essentially a "do-nothing" strategy: We neither buy nor sell in response to changes in market value. Using this strategy with respect to overall equity (risky) exposure means taking on more risk as wealth increases and vice versa. It requires that risk tolerance increases with wealth or that one's perceived compensation for risk rises or falls with the market.

A constant proportions strategy requires systematically selling winners and buying losers. This strategy underperforms a buy-and-hold strategy if the market moves strongly in either direction, but the trades boost return in a market with frequent reversals but little net movement. As we saw in Chapter 3, an investor whose risk tolerance is independent of wealth and who faces the same investment opportunities in every period should select the same portfolio proportions in every period. Thus the constant proportions strategy may be viewed as the canonically neutral strategy. It does not rely on expectations of either trending or mean-reverting prices and is not based on a changing attitude toward risk.

Investors whose relative risk tolerance increases rapidly with wealth, or who expect strongly trending markets, want to buy winners and sell losers. This behavior is the essence of portfolio insurance. This strategy outperforms the buy-and-hold strategy in trending markets, but does poorly in trendless markets with frequent reversals.

There are three basic varieties of transaction costs: fixed, proportional, and increasing. Most brokers charge either a fixed amount per trade or a fee per share executed. Similarly, custodian banks typically charge a fixed processing fee per trade. Hence the explicit costs of trading are either fixed or proportional to the size of the trade. For small trades, the bid–ask spread is essentially a proportional cost as well. As we increase the size of our trade, however, the effective bid–ask spread widens. That is, we have to pay more or accept less to trade more shares within the same time frame. Therefore, market impact costs are increasing in the size of the trade.

Fixed and proportional transaction costs make it inefficient to trade as long as we are sufficiently close to our ideal target portfolio weights. Thus there is a no-trade region around the target allocations. When market movements push the actual allocation outside the region, we want to trade back to the no-trade region. If fixed costs are significant, we want to move inside the region—all the way to the target if there are no proportional costs. With proportional costs but not fixed costs, we trade only to the nearest point on the boundary of the region.

The fixed and proportional components of cost are especially relevant for small positions and for maintaining established positions. Increasing costs arising from market impact are key factors when we seek to establish new or large positions. Increasing costs imply that we should trade gradually toward our desired position. In general, this will entail a sequence of progressively smaller trades because the opportunity cost of not holding our ideal portfolio declines with each trade.

While U.S. taxation of investment returns is extremely complex, many of the most important investment implications arise from its most basic provisions. Long-term capital gains and qualified dividends are taxed at lower rates than interest and short-term gains. Long-term gains are the most favored because taxation is deferred until the gain is realized. Indeed, unrealized gains remaining in one's estate at death are never taxed. Although the ability to offset ordinary income with realized investment losses is limited, losses can be carried forward indefinitely to offset future gains. The tax code also allows individuals to establish tax-exempt or tax-deferred retirement accounts.

These provisions imply two effective tax management strategies. First, realize any significant losses immediately but postpone realization of gains at least until they qualify as long-term. Second, hold instruments that generate interest or nonqualified dividends in tax-deferred or tax-exempt accounts.

Unfortunately, postponing realization of capital gains tends to create a lock-in effect that makes it progressively difficult to capture potential value added without incurring a tax drag on performance. Refreshing the portfolio with new ideas requires turnover, but turnover entails realizing gains. This problem is especially acute for value-oriented managers because their style leads them to buy low and sell winners. Research suggests that it is better to combine an index fund with a high-turnover active manager than to select an active manager with only moderate turnover.

Problems

1. Your firm runs all its client portfolios using the same strategy. The individual portfolios have similar characteristics and many of the same securities, but they are not identical. Should you bring them into alignment? What bearing do transaction costs have on this decision? Does the nature of the trading costs (fixed, proportional, or increasing) influence your decision?

2. Consider two index funds. ABC is equally weighted whereas XYZ is market value–weighted. Which is likely to incur greater trading costs? Which is likely to make larger capital gains distributions to shareholders?

3. What are the main sources of implementation shortfall? How might each be mitigated in designing strategy back tests?

4. Indicate how each of the following strategies relates to (a) changes in risk aversion, (b) expected price trends or reversals, and (c) buying or selling volatility:
   i.   Constant proportions.
   ii. Buy and hold.
   iii. Portfolio insurance.

5. You seek to maximize after-tax return by investing your client's bond allocation in municipal bonds. What are the risks of this type of investing? Under what economic situation would this not be advisable?

6. The duration of your alpha process declines from two years to one year. How will this affect your portfolio's turnover, transaction costs, and tax liability? How might it affect your portfolio's number of holdings?

Chapter 13

Performance Measurement and Attribution

Chapter Outline

13.1   Introduction

Performance measurement, attribution, and appraisal are vital elements in the investment management process. Though often not given the same attention as asset allocation or security selection, they are the essential feedback loop in this dynamic process. Portfolio evaluation has three steps:

1. **Performance measurement** is the process of calculating portfolio returns and risk over the evaluation period. It attempts to answer the question of how well the portfolio performed. This is the input to performance attribution.

2. **Performance attribution** attempts to identify the source of portfolio returns. This is an attempt to identify the risk factors that best explain performance and, by inference, the impact on performance of the manager's investment decisions.

3. **Performance appraisal** is the subjective evaluation of performance results and analysis to determine if the manager has demonstrated skill. That is, were returns due to greater market risk or to the asset class and security selection skills of the portfolio manager?

Performance measurement, attribution, and appraisal allow investors, PMs, and chief investment officers (CIOs) to

- *Evaluate decisions:* Investors want to evaluate the success of their own financial decisions or the decisions made on their behalf by managers. This evaluation helps them determine (1) whether they are on track to reach their investment goals and (2) the impact of their, or the PMs', investment decisions. The results provide an assessment of whether the portfolio is behaving as desired. It is not enough that excess returns are positive; the returns should also arise from expected sources. PMs and CIOs have similar concerns. PMs are acting on behalf of investors. To manage the portfolio effectively, they need to know whether and how their decisions are adding value. CIOs are responsible for understanding these issues at the firm level. Are the investment strategies generating good returns from the expected sources? Are the PMs doing their jobs effectively? If not, the process requires examination.

There are also the issues of industry standards and perception. The CFA Institute has produced standards for accurate measurement and reporting of performance. These standards represent best practices within the industry. They were designed to provide clear, comparable, and unbiased information so investors can assess the extent to which managers add value through their decisions—and, just as importantly, whether managers are acting in their clients' best interests. Compliance with these standards has therefore become an important signal of good faith within the industry.

- *Determine compensation:* Investors want to pay for, and managers deserve to get paid for, only skill, not luck. Therefore, it is important to assess whether observed performance was generated simply by exposing the portfolio to higher risk. Investors can easily increase risk themselves, such as with leverage, and they should not pay a premium to a manager for returns that merely reflect compensation for risk. However, the investor should be willing to pay a premium for incremental return, net of the manager's fee, beyond the risk assumed.

- *Identify skill:* The common thread here is the desire to identify skill; this is linked to compensation. Investors who pay fees for active portfolio management want to make sure they are getting their money's worth—that is, the fee should not be larger than the alpha. Portfolio managers want to make sure they are being fairly compensated for their efforts, and the CIO wants to retain and pay skilled managers. The meritocracy of financial markets requires assessment of skill. Bear in mind, however, that performance attribution analysis alone cannot identify investment skill that is likely to persist into the future.

The objective of this chapter is to outline the basic steps, introduce the basic tools, and highlight important issues in performance measurement and attribution. As in many areas of finance, there are multiple ways to accomplish the same objective. The goal is to use a simple framework consistent with the theory introduced in earlier chapters. As you become more comfortable with the methodology, you can expand to frameworks that are more complex, develop your own techniques, and adopt methods tailored to specific situations.

The reliability of performance measurement, attribution, and assessment depends on the quality of the inputs, such as the data and assumptions going into the analysis. As we will demonstrate here, even the seemingly straightforward task of calculating raw returns can be fraught with errors. Filtering those returns through a particular risk model largely determines the attribution of performance between skill and compensation for risk. The upshot, of course, is that performance analysis should be done carefully and the results interpreted just as carefully.

The chapter follows the three steps of portfolio evaluation. Meaningful attribution begins with accurate performance measurement. There are three components to performance measurement: price data, flows, and the calculation of return and risk. Section 13.2 reviews the basics of security valuation: return and risk measures. A brief examination of

In September 2003 Eliot Spitzer, then New York State Attorney General, charged major mutual fund groups with facilitating market timing trading for favored clients. One academic study estimated that buy-and-hold mutual fund investors lost up to $5 billion per year because of market timing trading.*

Market timing is the practice of actively trading mutual funds to profit from anticipated short-term market movements. In particular, the idea is to take advantage of the time zone differences among international stock markets through time zone arbitrage. The potential for arbitrage arises if mutual funds are priced using NYSE closing prices for U.S. securities while foreign securities are priced earlier in the day. This means that the NAV for mutual funds that do not adjust for this timing difference will be struck based on stale prices.

Ethical issues surrounding trading practices are discussed in Chapter 14.

* Zitzewitz (2003).

the impact of flows and errors on the calculation of portfolio return illustrates the point just made: Interpret results carefully. Section 13.3 discusses performance attribution. It begins with a discussion of benchmarking. Because attribution involves comparison to benchmarks, selection of appropriate benchmarks is a key to generating meaningful results. The remainder of the section focuses on the two main approaches to attribution: returns-based and holdings-based. The principles of effective performance appraisal are considered in Section 13.4.

13.2   Performance Measurement

Meaningful attribution begins with accurate performance measurement. Inaccurate price data lead to inaccurate performance measurement, to incorrect attribution, and potentially to poor portfolio allocation decisions, or as it's often put, garbage in, garbage out. There are three components to performance measurement: price data (purchases, sales, and valuations), flows (income and contributions), and the return calculation.

Security Valuation

Performance measurement begins with security valuation. The goal is to value assets at the best available price. This means prices that are accurate, consistent, and timely. However, prices may be measured with error. Two important sources of error are illiquidity and timing.

There are essentially two methods for valuing securities. **Mark-to-market** valuation sets the asset value equal to the market price. For publicly traded assets, when the market is liquid and the asset trades actively, this provides the best price. That is, this valuation accurately reflects the price at which you can buy and sell the asset in a timely manner. The closing trade price is most commonly used for pricing exchange-traded equities, and the average of the bid and ask prices is typically used for unlisted issues. These prices are consistent assuming the price series has been properly adjusted for splits, stock dividends, and coupon payments.

One issue for market prices is timing. This is an important issue when an asset trades on multiple markets that close at different times. For stocks listed on multiple exchanges, a so-called composite price may be published. However, U.S. mutual funds need to strike a net asset value (NAV) by 4:00 p.m. Eastern time. As a result, they

Short-term investments are frequently invested in money market instruments such as commercial paper, Treasury bills, and repurchase agreements, exhibiting 30-day average maturities. These instruments are highly liquid and offer short maturities, but they tend to generate low returns relative to even slightly longer maturities. One product designed to offer higher returns without a lot of interest rate risk would invest in old corporate notes and bonds with less than one year left to maturity. These instruments are illiquid in the marketplace and offer relatively high yields if a trader can find them. Pricing these instruments, even on a monthly basis, for fund valuation is one of the key challenges to offering this type of fund. A typical solution is to call three brokers for quotes and use the average. However, brokers who did not sell the illiquid bond to the client will not want to spend the time necessary to provide this information. To get multiple quotes, the portfolio manager may have to get involved; that is where a conflict of interest may arise. The portfolio manager may seek high quotes, especially at year-end, to support a higher return (in the short term) and thereby improve the PMs bonus. Of course pricing may reverse in the following month, but there is still an incentive to manipulate the prices. In fact there is one example in the business where a PM was scheduled to go on vacation the last week of December and collected December 31 quotes one week before the end of the year! Although this may be cumbersome in some instances, it is important that professionals who are separate from the portfolio management process handle pricing.

typically use the closing NYSE price for listed companies. This creates a problem of stale prices because some securities do not trade at 4:00 p.m. In particular, trading in foreign stocks ends earlier in the day.

Liquidity is another issue. If the market is illiquid or the asset does not trade actively, the observed market price can be stale or distorted by market impact when actually buying and selling the asset. A restricted stock received from an IPO is an extreme example. Although market prices are available, such stocks may be valued at a discount to the market price of unrestricted shares to reflect the additional costs of immunizing the portfolio against the risk of being unable to sell the restricted shares. Similarly, most corporate bonds are not traded on exchanges, and dealers may be reluctant to report trade prices to a central location. Institutional investors therefore rely on pricing services that use models to price most bonds based on market prices for a small sample of actively traded issues.

As the name implies, a **mark-to-model** price is based on a valuation model. The idea is to infer a fair value—an estimate of the most likely price at which the security could be traded in the market. This approach is used when a security is not publicly traded or is illiquid and does not trade actively. If the model is applied consistently, it should produce a consistent price. It also addresses the issue of timely pricing for securities that do not trade actively. However, the problem is accuracy: The implied price is only as good as the model. Even if the model is applied diligently and in good faith, model prices can differ significantly from realized market prices. The only way to know for certain, of course, is to execute a trade in the security.

Real estate values are usually assigned by a professional appraiser. Typically the appraiser bases his valuation on the value of comparable properties in conjunction with a hedonic model—essentially a regression that factors in market conditions and characteristics of the property. As discussed in Chapter 11, a significant body of literature indicates that even freshly appraised pricing tends to reflect stale valuations. This

War Story *The Viaducto*

In the late 1970s the Mexico City government repainted the lines of the *Viaducto* from a four-lane highway to a six-lane highway, increasing the number of lanes by 50 percent. The unfortunate result of this effort to reduce congestion was an increase in fatal accidents. In response, the *Viaducto* was repainted back to four lanes, decreasing the number of lanes by 33 percent. Eager to report evidence of social progress, the government reported a net capacity increase of 17 percent, simply subtracting the 33 percent decrease from the 50 percent increase.

Source: *The Economist*, "The Perils of Percentages," April 16, 1998.

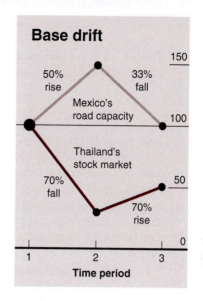

Base drift

is not surprising because the primary inputs (transaction prices and appraised values for comparable properties) are virtually never contemporaneous.

Return Measures

An asset's return is the percentage change in its value over a defined period. The inputs are the asset's end-of-period price, beginning-of-period price, and any cash flows. Suppose we have a sequence of asset prices, V_t, measured without error and associated cash flows, CF_t, where $t = 0, 1, \ldots, N$. These prices and cash flows translate into familiar single-period arithmetic returns given by

$$R_t = \text{Total proceeds/Initial investment} = (V_t - V_{t-1} + CF_t)/V_{t-1} \quad \textbf{(13.1)}$$

As an example, assume an asset starts with a price of 100.00, has no cash flow, and ends the period with a price of 103.95. The single-period return is

$$R_1 = (103.95 + 0 - 100.00)/100.00 = 3.95\%$$

Things become more complicated as we move to calculating returns over multiple periods. Two issues in particular need to be addressed: base drift and net flows into the portfolio. Base drift arises due to changes in the denominator of the return calculation. The effect is not material when the denominator changes by only a small amount, as is usually the case when we work with frequently sampled data. However, as the changes become large the impact becomes material.

Beyond creative accounting, the *Viaducto* example in the War Story: The *Viaducto* box highlights a potential for error when dealing with percentage changes. In any (arithmetic) return calculation, percentage increases and decreases are not symmetrical because the denominator changes. In this example, because the base shift was large, the impact of the asymmetry is quite noticeable—the 33 percent decrease cancels out the 50 percent increase. Repainting the highway from four to six lanes and back to four lanes should produce no change in capacity:

$$\text{Total return} = (4 - 4)/4 = 0\%$$

Clearly, simply subtracting the returns is wrong. The common practice of averaging returns also produces a misleading result:

$$\text{Average return} = (50\% - 33\%)/2 = 8.3\%$$

The chart in the same War Story box shows that the same problem arises if a decrease is followed by an increase. Share prices in Thailand fell by 70 percent in dollar terms between July 1997 and mid-January 1998 and subsequently rose by 70 percent. Although investors may have thought that the losses had been recovered, it would actually have required a 233 percent increase in the market to make up for the 70 percent drop!

So how should we calculate return to account for base shift? To calculate a return from a sequence of subperiod returns, the single-period returns should be linked by compounding. For the *Viaducto* example this gives

$$\text{Compounded total return} = (1 + R_2)(1 + R_3) - 1 \qquad \textbf{(13.2)}$$
$$= (1 + 0.50)(1 - 0.33) - 1$$
$$= 0\%$$

Alternatively, we can use log returns.[1] As in previous chapters we will use a lowercase r to denote a log return. For the *Viaducto* the log return is

$$\text{Log return} = \ln(1 + R_2) + \ln(1 + R_3) = r_2 + r_3$$
$$= \ln(6/4) + \ln(4/6) = 40.55\% - 40.55\% = 0\%$$

Log returns are generally preferred for performance measurement because we can simply add returns to obtain returns over longer periods. In addition, the use of log returns facilitates statistical analysis of performance because the assumption of normally distributed errors is more reasonable in the context of log returns.

The Impact of Flows and Errors

One objective of performance measurement is to identify manager skill. However, portfolio flows and pricing errors can distort performance measurement. To demonstrate the importance of accounting for contributions, Exhibit 13.1 considers the case of two investors holding identical portfolios. These investors add and withdraw identical amounts from their portfolios at the end of periods 1 and 2. The only difference is the timing of the withdrawals versus the contributions. Investor A adds and then withdraws whereas investor B withdraws and then adds.

The total return to the underlying securities is

$$\text{Total return(securities)} = (1 + 0.10)(1 + 0.05)(1 - 0.10) - 1 = 3.95\%$$

Because both investors are invested in the same portfolio, they should realize the same return. However, investor A times the flows well, adding before a positive return and

---

[1] See Appendix I of Chapter 3 for a discussion of continuous compounding and log returns.

EXHIBIT 13.1
The Impact of Flows

Period	Return	Investor A BB	EB	Flow	Investor B BB	EB	Flow
1	10.0%	100.00	110.00	20.00	100.00	110.00	−20
2	5.0%	130.00	136.50	−20.00	90.00	94.50	20
3	−10.0%	116.50	104.85		114.50	103.05	

withdrawing before a negative return. The result is a total return of 4.85 percent instead of 3.95 percent.

$$\text{Total return(investor } A) = 104.85/100 - 1 = 4.85\%$$

If the flows are not accounted for properly, investor A will incorrectly attribute the 0.90 percent return contribution of the cash flows to the manager. The investor is likely to believe the manager has more skill than the security returns warrant and may overcompensate the portfolio manager.

In the case of investor B, the manager does not want the investor's timing included in performance measure. The adverse timing of the cash flows resulted in a 0.90 percent reduction in the total return to only 3.05 percent.

$$\text{Total return(investor } B) = 103.50/100 - 1 = 3.05\%$$

It should be clear that separating the impact of flows from the impact of investment decisions benefits both the manager and the investor. The manager is evaluated only on the decisions under her or his control. For the investor it provides a better measure of manager skill and more closely ties the manager's compensation to skill in managing the portfolio. The War Story box about the Beardstown Ladies illustrates how performance distorted by inflows can lead to embarrassing consequences.

Removing the influence of cash flows requires valuing a portfolio every time a contribution or withdrawal occurs. Given those valuations, calculation of so-called **time-weighted returns** is simply an application of Equations (13.1) and (13.2). The only complication arises from the need to adjust the beginning-of-period portfolio value, V_{t-1}, in Equation (13.1) to reflect the contribution or withdrawal. The ending value in each period should not include the impact of the next contribution or withdrawal. Note that the cash flow $CF(t)$ shown in Equation (13.1) represents part of the investment return (that is, coupons and dividends) rather than contributions or withdrawals The subperiod returns are then compounded as in Equation (13.2) to determine the return over the full period. For example, for investor A,

Period 1: $R(1) = 110.00/100.00 - 1 = 10.0\%$
Period 2: $R(2) = 136.50/130.00 - 1 = 5.0\%$
Period 3: $R(3) = 104.85/116.50 - 1 = -10.0\%$

Total return(investor A) $= (1 + 0.10)(1 + 0.05)(1 - 0.10) - 1 = 3.95$

Notice that the calculated returns now agree with the security returns for each subperiod and for the full period.

An alternative technique that includes the impact of inflows and outflows is **dollar-weighted returns.** This is an internal rate of return (IRR) calculation for the portfolio. For investor A the result is

$$104.85 = 100(1 + R)^3 + 20(1 + R)^2 - 20(1 + R)^1$$

The left side of this equation is the final value of the portfolio. The right side reflects each contribution and withdrawal, a common rate of return R, and the number of periods since each cash flow occurred. For investor A the dollar-weighted return (per period) is $R = 1.49\%$. This is similar to the return per period calculated from the total return: $(1.0485)^{1/3} - 1 = 1.59\%$. The 0.10 percent by which total return per period exceeds the IRR is due to the favorable timing of the contributions and withdrawals. Conversely, for investor B, the IRR is 1.08 percent versus 1.01 percent calculated from the total return. The difference in this case reflects adverse timing of flows.

There are advantages and disadvantages to both techniques. Time-weighted returns are not sensitive to the timing and amount of contributions or redemptions. Because most managers have little or no control over these flows, this method more accurately measures a manager's value added. However, the need to value the entire portfolio on every cash flow date increases both the administrative costs and the likelihood of pricing error, particularly if there are illiquid assets in the portfolio. Dollar-weighted returns are sensitive to the timing and amount of flows in and out of the portfolio. If the manager controls the cash flows, it is appropriate to include this impact. Dollar-weighted returns also have the advantage that valuations are required only at the beginning and end of the evaluation period. However, if there are both contributions and withdrawals during the evaluation period, the IRR calculation does not have a unique solution. That is, more than one rate of return will equate the present and future values of the cash flows, and mathematically all these solutions are equally valid. Therefore, it may not be clear which to use for evaluating performance. Nonetheless, in many instances there will be only one relevant choice after discarding extreme or otherwise unreasonable results.

There is yet another wrinkle. Even with cash flows accounted for, pricing errors can lead to distortions. Suppose an asset is priced with error at the end of the first period, but it is properly priced at the end of the second period. If a cash flow occurs when the asset is mispriced, this distortion will carry forward even if the mispricing is subsequently corrected.[2] Formally,

$$R(1) = V(1)(1+e)/V(0) - 1$$
$$R(2) = V(2)(1+c)/V(1)(1+e+c) - 1$$
$$R\text{ total} = (1+R(1))(1+R(2)) - 1 = V(2)/V(0)((1+c)(1+e))/(1+c+e) - 1$$

where e is the proportional mispricing of the asset and c is the proportional cash flow occurring at the end of the first period. The total return calculation consists of the

---

[2] Stewart (1987) showed that contribution activity biases returns even if errors average to zero over time.

There is extensive evidence that mutual fund investors fare significantly worse than the mutual funds in which they invest. How can this be the case? The answer lies in the timing of flows in and out of the funds. The performance of the fund itself is calculated using the daily net asset value (NAV) and reflects the return earned on a share held for the entire evaluation period. By construction, it does not reflect subscriptions and redemptions of fund shares.

The investment performance experienced by individual fund investors, however, does reflect the timing of their fund share purchases and redemptions. Unfortunately individual investors tend to chase recent performance. Money pours into the funds with the highest recent returns and pours out of the funds with the worst recent performance. Because extremes of performance tend to reverse over time, individual investors tend to buy into funds just before good performance fades and sell funds just before performance improves. The adverse timing implied by this behavior means that typical mutual fund investors underperform the funds in which they invest. As discussed in Chapter 15, institutional investors display similar behavior, though to a lesser extent.

standard $V(2)/V(0)$ term—but with an adjustment that is zero if either $c=0$ or $e=0$ and is nonzero if both $c \neq 0$ and $e \neq 0$.

As a numerical example, consider investor A from the previous example but with the portfolio mispriced by 1 percent at the end of the first period. Exhibit 13.2 shows the case in which contributions are positive. The columns reflect no pricing error ($e = 0$), positive pricing error ($e > 0$), and negative pricing error ($e < 0$) respectively.

In the case of a positive pricing error, the end of period 1 value of the portfolio is now

$$EB(1) = 100.00(1 + 0.10 + 0.01) = 111.10$$

This implies a first period return of 11.10 percent. The pricing error is reversed (that is, eliminated) in the second period. The final portfolio value is 136.50, implying a return of 4.12 percent in the second period. The total return is calculated as $(1.111)(1.0412)-1=15.68\%$, which is higher than the true 15.5 percent return on the portfolio. This distortion results from the changing portfolio value. The overstated asset base at the end of the first period means that the subsequent price correction has a smaller proportional impact than the initial error. Base shift strikes again. The result is that the portfolio return will be slightly overstated with a positive error and slightly understated with a negative pricing error.

EXHIBIT 13.2   **The Impact of Pricing Errors and Positive Flows**

Period	Return	$c > 0, e = 0$ BB	EB	Flow	$c > 0, e > 0$ BB	EB	Flow	$c > 0, e < 0$ BB	EB	Flow
1	10.0%	100.00	110.00	20	100.00	111.10	20	100.00	108.90	20
2	5.0%	130.00	136.50		131.10	136.50		128.90	136.50	
Period 1			10.00%			11.10%			8.90%	
Period 2			5.00%			4.12%			5.90%	
Total	15.50%		15.50%			15.68%			15.32%	
Distortion						1.0114			0.9884	

EXHIBIT 13.3 The Impact of Pricing Errors and Negative Flows

Period	Return	c < 0,e = 0 BB	EB	Flow	c < 0,e > 0 BB	EB	Flow	c < 0,e > 0 BB	EB	
1	10.0%	100.00	110.00	−20	100.00	111.10	−20	100.00	108.90	−20
2	5.0%	90.00	94.50		91.10	94.50		88.90	94.50	
Period 1			10.00%			11.10%			8.90%	
Period 2			5.00%			3.73%			6.30%	
Total	15.50%		15.50%			15.25%			15.76%	
Distortion						0.9836			1.0168	

The opposite occurs when the portfolio experiences outflows. The outflows lower the portfolio value at the beginning of the second period. The correction of the pricing error in the second period is therefore a larger percentage of the portfolio value than the original error. As Exhibit 13.3 shows, in this case the portfolio return will be slightly understated with a positive pricing error and overstated with a negative pricing error.

To minimize the impact of potential pricing errors on measured performance, fund managers should seek to invest contributions close to the time of day when the valuations are determined. This is particularly true for large contributions.

Risk Measures[3]

The most frequently used risk measures can be categorized along two dimensions: (1) whether they capture total risk or only so-called systematic risk and (2) whether both upside and downside return variations are considered risk (symmetric measures) or only downside variations are deemed to be risk (asymmetric measures).[4] The symmetric, total risk category is virtually synonymous with standard deviation. The symmetric, systematic risk category is synonymous with beta. There are various asymmetric total risk measures, all designed to capture some aspect of downside risk. Although distinct upside and downside beta values are sometimes calculated for active portfolios, the downside component is rarely considered in isolation and virtually never used as a general risk measure. Therefore, the asymmetric, systematic risk category is essentially empty.

Standard deviation measures the total variation around the expected value of a random variable and is undoubtedly the most heavily used measure of dispersion in statistics. It is also the most heavily used measure of investment risk. In the context of investment returns, standard deviation measures total risk; that is, it encompasses both systematic and nonsystematic risk components. It is a symmetric risk measure in the sense that it treats both upside and downside deviations as risk. If returns are normally distributed, the standard deviation embodies all there is to know about the dispersion of returns. For other probability distributions, the standard deviation is a useful but incomplete measure of dispersion.

Beta measures the sensitivity of an asset's return to a benchmark portfolio. For example, beta = 1.2 implies that, on average, the asset's return increases or decreases

---

[3] See the chapter appendix for a more formal exposition of the risk measures discussed in this section.
[4] Note that symmetry of the risk measure and symmetry of the probability distribution are distinct issues. We may use a symmetric risk measure, such as standard deviation, even though the distribution of returns is not symmetric—and vice versa.

by 1.2 percent for each 1 percent increase or decrease in the benchmark return. As with standard deviation, beta is a symmetric risk measure. It derives its usefulness as a risk measure from the capital asset pricing model (CAPM). According to the CAPM, risk that is not associated with the benchmark (that is, the market) portfolio can be eliminated through diversification. Hence, assuming the portfolio being analyzed is sufficiently diversified, we need only consider the so-called systematic risk measured by beta.

The main limitation of these measures is that they assume investors have a symmetric notion of risk; in other words, upside variation in returns is viewed the same as downside variation. Academic research and practitioner observation both indicate that investors are more concerned with downside risk than upside risk. Losing money is considered a risk; making extra money is not. This asymmetry in the perception of risk becomes even more important in conjunction with the fact that realized returns are not normally distributed. There are too many observations in the tails, and the distribution may be skewed.[5]

Asymmetric total return measures are specifically designed to capture tail and downside risk. One such measure, shortfall probability, was introduced in Chapter 3 and used extensively in Chapter 5. The **lower partial moment** was also used in Chapters 5 and 11. Recall that the LPM is analogous to the variance except that derivations are calculated relative to a threshold return that need not equal the mean,[6] and only variation below the threshold return is considered. **Value at risk** (VaR) is a related measure that focuses exclusively on the lower tail of the distribution. The VaR is the *minimum* dollar loss that should occur with a given frequency or probability over a specified period. For example, if an investment would be expected to lose *at least* $1 million on 1 out of every 20 days (5 percent of the time), then its daily VaR at the 5 percent level would be −$1,000,000. Note that VaR is the *minimum* loss (not the *maximum* loss) occurring with 5 percent probability. Some of the losses actually experienced are almost certain to be much larger than the VaR. Some investors who misunderstood the meaning of VaR were no doubt shocked by the losses they sustained in 2008.

The main advantage of downside risk measures is that they are more in line with the way individuals think of risk. A major disadvantage is that the mathematics of portfolio allocation is far more complex. There are simple formulas relating both portfolio variance (equivalently standard deviation) and portfolio beta to the variance–covariance matrix of the individual securities. There is no such simple relationship between downside risk measures for individual securities and downside risk measures for a portfolio of securities. Hence, while we can examine historical downside risk statistics for a specific portfolio given its historical returns, it is much more difficult to assess the downside risk characteristics of alternative or prospective portfolio compositions. Typically this requires simulating individual security and portfolio returns.[7]

Interestingly, although historical returns for both individual securities and portfolios exhibit non-normality, the most commonly used downside risk measures appear to be somewhat insensitive to these deviations from normality. That is, the downside risk values are similar to those that would arise from a normal distribution with the same central tendency (mean) and dispersion (standard deviation). Intuitively, this is because the departures from normality are modest: The distribution of returns is "only

[5] Non-normality of returns was discussed in Chapters 5, 6, and 11.
[6] Setting the threshold equal to the mean gives the semivariance.
[7] See Section 5.4 of Chapter 5 for a discussion of using simulation in asset allocation decisions.

a little bit" skewed and the tails are "only a little too fat." The upshot is that for many purposes we need not explicitly consider the non-normality of returns.

Under the assumption of normality, the mean and standard deviation completely characterize the return distribution. Mathematically our downside risk measures can tell us nothing more. Nonetheless, by virtue of their closer correspondence with the way people perceive risk, they may still be useful as alternative or additional perspectives on risk. In some of our M–V asset allocation analysis (see Chapters 3 and 5), for example, we incorporated the intuitive notion of shortfall risk even though (given normality) the shortfall risk simply reflected the relationship between the portfolio mean and standard deviation. That is, stating our constraints in terms of shortfall risk was mathematically redundant but intuitively more meaningful.

13.3 Performance Attribution

Performance attribution attempts to identify the sources of returns. To identify alpha, we need to measure what portion of a fund's returns are generated by systematic risk exposures. This is important because active managers should be compensated based on their ability to generate alpha—that is, to add return that is not due to simply increasing risk. The goal of this section is to outline the basic tools used to attribute return to risk and to managers' decisions.

There are two primary ways to approach the performance attribution problem. The choice of approach usually boils down to the availability of data. **Returns-based attribution** is a top-down approach that requires only returns data for the portfolio and for asset class indexes. As the name implies, **holdings-based attribution** requires the history of security-level holdings for both the portfolio and the benchmark index as well as returns data for all the securities in either the portfolio or the benchmark. Clearly this bottom-up approach requires substantially more data than the returns-based approach. The advantage is that holdings-based attribution can provide much more insight into the sources of return. Both approaches can answer the basic questions of whether the manager is adding value and, if so, how much. But the holdings-based approach says more about what types of decisions are adding and subtracting value.

Benchmarks

Alpha (the return added beyond compensation for risk) is measured relative to a benchmark. The benchmark portfolio is therefore a critical element in performance attribution. The benchmark represents the passive alternative to the active strategy being examined. To make the comparison meaningful, it is important to set an appropriate benchmark.

A well-designed and well-selected benchmark should have the following characteristics:

1. *Identifiable:* The constituents, and their weights, within the benchmark are clearly defined.
2. *Prespecified:* The benchmark and its composition are known before the active portfolio is invested.
3. *Investable:* The benchmark contains only securities in which the portfolio manager could actually invest at reasonable cost and in amounts commensurate with the size of the managed portfolio.
4. *Representative:* The benchmark captures the investment universe and overall strategy of the portfolio being evaluated.

Exposure-based attribution relies on the systematic risk exposures reported by the fund. This approach is particularly useful for evaluating hedge fund performance where transparency and the dynamic strategies sometimes used limit the effectiveness of returns and holding-based analysis. This approach has the additional benefit of signaling whether a manager has risk management processes and infrastructure to accurately capture the portfolio risks.

To illustrate the importance of these criteria, consider some benchmarks that would not satisfy them. The median manager in a universe is a classic benchmark that is neither identifiable nor prespecified. The manager being evaluated cannot know in advance and most likely will not even know ex post what was in the median manager's portfolio. Although the situation has improved, some indexes still include securities or significant blocks of shares that are virtually unavailable to the market because they are locked away in the hands of strategic holders, such as governments and corporate affiliates. These indexes are clearly not investable benchmarks. Investability may also be impaired by factors such as market capitalization, liquidity, and transaction costs. The issue is not whether every constituent security is accessible at low cost, but whether those that can be accessed allow the PM to track the index closely. Finally, a large-cap value index would not have been a representative benchmark for an Internet stock portfolio in the late 1990s because Internet stocks were mainly small-cap growth companies. Even Internet stocks that compared poorly to other Internet stocks looked like stars compared to a benchmark like the S&P Large-Cap Value index.

The appropriate weighting scheme is an additional consideration in selecting a benchmark. Equally weighted benchmarks accentuate the importance of smaller capitalization stocks relative to large-cap stocks, while large-cap issues dominate market value–weighted indexes. Active equity managers tend to weight stocks somewhere between equal and market cap weights. Therefore, a reasonable argument can be made for either weighting scheme. Nonetheless, the vast majority of active portfolios are benchmarked against market value–weighted benchmarks. An equally weighted portfolio requires constant rebalancing as relative security valuations change. By construction, a market value–weighted portfolio requires no rebalancing simply due to market movements. Market value–weighted benchmarks are therefore more consistent with the benchmark's role as the passive portfolio alternative to the active portfolio.[8]

Returns-Based Analysis

Returns-based analysis infers performance attribution by examining the actual returns of a portfolio. Assuming the returns accurately reflect the true performance of the portfolio, this method provides attribution based on the actual, albeit unobserved, decisions of the manager. As noted earlier, the key advantage of this approach is that it requires only returns data; the disadvantage is that it is an imprecise tool. Although the active portfolio may evolve throughout the evaluation period, returns-based analysis effectively attributes performance to an unchanging average portfolio. This has two important implications. First, the analysis cannot identify the impact of dynamic decisions.

[8] Note that *any* weighting scheme other than market value weighting requires constant rebalancing due to market movements. Thus the recently developed notion of *fundamental weighting* based on factors such as employment, sales, or book value also implies frequent trading to maintain the specified weights.

In *A Random Walk Down Wall Street,* Burton Malkiel suggested that "a blindfolded monkey throwing darts at a newspaper's financial pages could select a portfolio that would do just as well as one carefully selected by experts."

In 1988 *The Wall Street Journal* began a contest based on this premise. Each month the performance of a random portfolio was compared to a portfolio selected by professional analysts. The random portfolio was selected by WSJ staff members throwing darts at the WSJ stock tables. The professionals selected one stock (long or short). At the end of six months, the price appreciation for the professionals' stocks and the dartboard stocks were compared (dividends were not included). The winner was the equally weighted portfolio with the highest return. The two best-performing professionals were invited back for the next contest, and two new professionals were added.

Although this was an amusing experiment in efficient market theory, the construction of the contest was flawed: There was no control for risk. Liang (1999) found that the beta of the professionals' selections was 60 percent higher than the beta of the dartboard portfolio. Therefore, simply comparing the two portfolio returns was inappropriate. The professionals' portfolio would have a higher expected return simply from its greater market risk.

Second, the averaging out of portfolio changes may distort any decomposition across sources of valued added. In addition, the performance may not reflect the current portfolio and may not be indicative of return and risk going forward.

Direct Comparison

The simplest approach to returns analysis directly compares the return of the portfolio to other funds professing to manage to the same style. This approach is naïve: It makes no attempt to control for strategy. More importantly, it makes no attempt to control for the risk factors that might be driving returns. The famous *Wall Street Journal* dartboard portfolio contest illustrates this basic point (see the related Theory in Practice box).

Peer Comparison

Peer comparisons attempt to overcome these shortcomings by comparing portfolio returns to peers selected to be similar in strategy and presumably risk. Peer comparison is popular, intuitive, and appealing because it directly compares a portfolio to alternative investments. What could be more representative and investable? The methodology is straightforward: Identify a peer group of alternative investments with the same stated investment process or universe, such as large-cap growth funds. Then rank order the funds based on the evaluation period returns. The median fund becomes the threshold of over- and underperformance. If the peers have been selected carefully, this should satisfy most of the benchmark criteria. The funds are identifiable. The funds are representative, although careful attention is needed to ensure that the peer funds are investing as stated; this is particularly true for the types and levels of risk taken. Even funds that follow the same investment process may vary widely in the amount of market and style risk taken. Selecting peers based on stated investment process assumes that the peers are comparable in risk and style. Unfortunately this is not necessarily true in practice. The main problem, however, is the one identified earlier: The median fund and its composition are not known in advance. Therefore, this benchmark is not prespecified or investable. Survivor bias is also an issue. As fund sponsors close or merge underperforming funds, the average return of the remaining funds in the peer group will rise. This will overstate the peer group return, understate the risk, and more important, for the manager, make it more difficult to outperform the median.

Market Index Comparison

Although business considerations make it difficult to eschew peer comparisons altogether, well-known and widely available market indexes are generally better performance benchmarks. The most widely used indexes are investable, identifiable, and prespecified.[9] The key consideration is selecting an index that is representative of the opportunities available to the manager and at least the broad characteristics of the manager's strategy. For example, for a domestic equity portfolio the benchmark should generally reflect the style (growth/value/blend) and capitalization (large/mid/small) that predominate within the active portfolio. Given the plethora of indexes available, it should not be too difficult to find an appropriate benchmark for a portfolio. However, in some instances, such as an active manager with a pronounced strategy bias, it may be desirable to create a custom benchmark (sometimes called a *normal portfolio*) designed to replicate the manager's style but not tactical bets.

Risk-Adjusted Returns

Having selected a benchmark, we can now examine methods for risk-adjusting portfolio returns to make portfolio comparisons more meaningful and improve evaluation of manager skill. A portfolio's alpha is the return generated over and above the compensation for taking risk. All active managers seek to generate alpha, and those who can do so consistently deserve to be well paid.

To measure alpha we need to know what risk and return combinations are achievable simply by combining the riskless asset with the benchmark portfolio. Suppose we invest a fraction β_i in the benchmark portfolio and a fraction $(1-\beta_i)$ in the riskless asset. With the use of the M–V tools developed in Chapter 3, it is straightforward to show that the expected return of this portfolio is

$$E[R_i] = R_f + \beta_i(R_M - R_f) \tag{13.3}$$

where R_f denotes the riskless rate and R_M denotes the expected return on the benchmark. The standard deviation of this portfolio is $[\beta_i \sigma_M]$.

Taking the riskless rate and the expected return on the benchmark as given, Equation (13.3) defines a line, called the **security market line (SML),** relating portfolio expected return to the portfolio's beta. That is, it shows the expected return commensurate with any level of systematic risk. **Jensen's alpha**[10] can then be defined as follows:

$$\alpha_i = R_i - E[R_i] = R_i - \{R_f + \beta_i(R_M - R_f)\}$$

As an example (Exhibit 13.4), consider two assets. Asset 1 has return of 20 percent and beta of 1.20, whereas asset 2 has a return of 5 percent and beta of 0.10. The risk-free rate is 3 percent, and the index return is 12 percent. The alphas for the two assets are

$$\alpha_1 = 0.20 - \{0.03 + 1.2(0.12 - 0.03)\} = 6.2\%$$
$$\alpha_2 = 0.05 - \{0.03 + 0.1(0.12 - 0.03)\} = 1.1\%$$

[9] Small-cap, corporate bond, and emerging market indexes suffer from liquidity issues. In addition, changes in the composition of indexes are not always predictable. Nonetheless, portfolio managers can know the composition of the benchmark when they make their investment decisions provided index changes are announced before they become effective.

[10] See Jensen (1968, 1969).

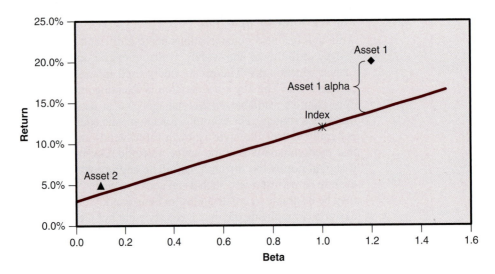

EXHIBIT 13.4

The Security Market Line and Jensen's Alpha

Because, by definition, the alpha of the index is 0, both portfolios produced a higher risk-adjusted return than the index. Asset 1 has a greater alpha than asset 2 and would be ranked higher based on this criterion.

In our development of the SML, beta (β) was the fraction of a simple two-asset portfolio that was invested in the benchmark portfolio. To make the SML and Jensen's alpha useful for performance analysis, we need to be able to determine the beta of any asset or portfolio. It turns out that we can estimate alpha and beta simultaneously using regression analysis. Given data on excess returns over the riskless rate, we regress the excess return of the portfolio on the excess return of the benchmark allowing for a nonzero intercept. The coefficient on the benchmark excess return is our estimate of the portfolio's beta. The estimated intercept is our estimate of the portfolio's alpha. A statistically significant and positive alpha is consistent with a skilled manager. The R^2 of the regression equals the fraction of the portfolio's variance explained by the benchmark—that is, the fraction that reflects systematic risk. The remaining volatility is unsystematic risk that could be diversified away by making the portfolio conform more closely to the benchmark. Therefore, R^2 is also a measure of diversification.

Risk Ratios

Although Jensen's alpha adjusts for risk through the SML, it does not indicate how efficient a portfolio is in generating its risk-adjusted return. Two portfolios might have the same alpha but quite different levels of risk. All else the same, investors presumably prefer the lower-risk portfolio. This logic leads to consideration of risk ratios.

Risk ratios divide the return premium (the return minus the risk-free rate) by risk. This normalizes the excess return and allows for direct comparison and ranking of the ratios for different assets or portfolios. Mathematically, these ratios measure the slope of a line drawn from the risk-free asset through the asset being measured. The asset with the highest slope has the highest incremental return per unit of risk.

The **Treynor ratio**[11] is given by

$$TR_i = (R_i - R_f)/\beta_i$$

[11] See Treynor (1965).

Although in principle the SML applies to all asset classes, it is customarily associated with equities. A similar relationship can be developed specifically for bonds using the concept of duration. As discussed in Chapter 9, duration measures the change in bond price for a small change in yield. Also recall that parallel shifts in the yield curve account for a very large portion of overall interest rate risk. With this in mind, we can approximate the return on a bond portfolio as the sum of three components: the riskless rate, a risk premium proportional to duration, and the impact of changing yield. That is,

$$R \cong R_F + D\delta - D\Delta Y$$

This implies that $[(R - R_F)/D] = (\delta - Y)$ for any bond portfolio. Equating this ratio for an arbitrary portfolio P with the ratio for a benchmark bond index, M and arranging gives a "bond market line":

$$R_P = R_F + (D_P/D_M)(R_M - R_F)$$

Using the bond market line, the alpha of a portfolio I is

$$\text{Alpha} = R_I - \{R_F + (D_I/D_M)(R_M - R_F)\}$$

Returning to the earlier example, the Treynor ratio of asset 1 is $= (0.20 - 0.03)/1.2 = 0.14$ whereas the Treynor ratio of asset 2 is 0.20. The index has a Treynor ratio of 0.09. As before, both assets are more attractive than the index. Despite its much lower overall return and its lower alpha, asset 2 would be preferred to asset 1 based on the Treynor ratio. The key is the difference in betas. The return on asset 2 is only a quarter of asset 1's return, but its beta is *12 times* lower.

A positive Jensen's alpha coincides with a Treynor ratio greater than the index. As this example shows, however, rankings based on alpha and on Treynor ratios do not have to be the same. In theory, the asset with the higher Treynor ratio should be preferred because we can always adjust the absolute level of risk and return by borrowing or lending at the risk-free rate. The broken lines in Exhibit 13.5 indicate expected return and beta combinations that could be achieved using asset 1 (dotted line) or asset 2 (dashed line) and the risk-free asset. The slope of each line is the Treynor ratio for the associated asset. Note that by levering asset 2 we could match asset 1's 20 percent expected return but with much lower beta. Therefore, asset 2 would be preferred.

This approach has limits, however. In practice, the availability and cost of financing do not remain unchanged as leverage increases. Instead it becomes increasingly difficult and costly to arrange larger credit lines. Given the practical limitations on leverage, many managers and individuals would prefer asset 1 to asset 2.

The **Sharpe ratio,**[12] defined as

$$SR_i = (R_i - R_f)/\sigma_i$$

uses standard deviation rather than beta as the risk measure. As with the Treynor ratio, the presumption is that investors can use leverage to adjust the absolute level of risk and therefore are looking for the highest excess return per unit of risk.

Jensen's alpha and the Treynor ratio assume that beta is a sufficient measure of risk; that is, nonsystematic risk is insignificant. If this is true, the Treynor and Sharpe ratios

[12] See Sharpe (1966).

Theory in Practice M^2

M^2 was first proposed by Graham and Harvey and later popularized by Leah and Franco Modigliani.* Like the Sharpe ratio, M^2 is based on total risk; however, M^2 is not a ratio. Like Jensen's alpha, M^2 measures an absolute level of risk-adjusted return. Formally,

$$M^2 = \{R_f + \sigma_M((R_i - R_f)/\sigma_i)\} - R_M$$

The expression in brackets is the expected return on a combination of portfolio i and the risk-free asset that has the same standard deviation (that is, total risk) as the benchmark. M^2 measures the difference between this return and the actual return on the benchmark. A positive M^2 means that the portfolio has a higher Sharpe ratio than the benchmark.

Inspection of the formula shows that rankings based on M^2 will always be the same as those based on the Sharpe ratio.

* See Graham and Harvey (1997) and Modigliani and Modigliani (1997).

EXHIBIT 13.5

The Security Market Line and the Treynor Ratio

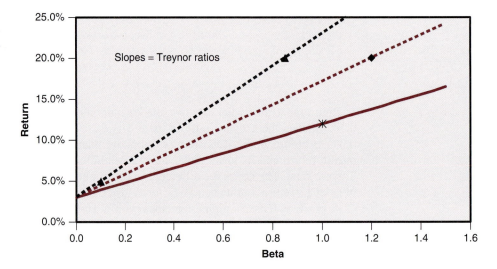

should be similar. If nonsystematic risk is significant, however, the two ratios may rank portfolios quite differently. In this case, the Treynor ratio may not be appropriate because it will understate (perhaps substantially) total portfolio risk. Thus the Sharpe ratio is generally more reliable.

The Treynor ratio is still useful. Comparison of the Sharpe and Treynor ratios provides a simple way to gauge the level of diversification within the portfolio. Similarly, differences between portfolio rankings based on the two ratios are an indicator of relative diversification among portfolios. More (less) diversified portfolios will tend to rank higher using the Sharpe (Treynor) ratio. The Treynor ratio may also be useful in evaluating assets or funds that will be only a small part of a larger overall portfolio. In that case, diversification *within the fund* may not be important because nonsystematic risk may be diversified away within the broader portfolio.

The **Sortino**[13] **ratio** is a variation on the Sharpe ratio. There are two differences between these two ratios. First, the Sortino ratio considers downside risk rather than

---

[13] See Sortino and Price (1994).

440

total risk; that is, it measures risk as downside volatility rather than standard deviation. Second, the Sortino ratio measures excess return relative to a target or required return rather than relative to the riskless rate. The Sortino ratio is given by

$$\text{Sortino ratio}_i = (R_i - T)/DR$$

where R_i is the asset or portfolio return, T is the target or required rate of return for the investment strategy under consideration, and DR is the square root of the lower partial moment (LPM).[14] The threshold return used in calculating the LPM need not equal T. For example, the LPM could reflect only potential losses (a threshold return of zero), while the target return T is positive.

The Sortino ratio is particularly useful in two situations. First, when the return distribution is inherently non-normal, such as when there is a significant optionlike component to the portfolio strategy, the downside risk measure may result in substantially different portfolio rankings. As noted in the previous section, however, for many portfolios non-normality may not be serious enough to warrant the additional complexity inherent in calculating downside risk. Second, because the downside risk threshold and target return can take any desired value, the Sortino ratio has an advantage whenever the investment objective is sensitive to specific return levels. For example, in absolute return applications, such as hedge funds, the downside risk threshold and the target return might both be set at zero. The Sharpe ratio does not provide this flexibility.

The **information ratio (IR)** is defined as the portfolio's active return relative to a benchmark divided by its tracking error risk:

$$IR_i = (R_i - R_B)/\sigma_{SR}$$

Tracking error risk is the standard deviation of the active return—the difference between the portfolio and the benchmark return. The higher the information ratio, the higher the excess return of the fund, given the amount of risk involved, and the better the fund manager. The IR is particularly useful in enhanced index applications, where the objective is to match the risk of the index but generate higher return. The information ratio differs from the Sharpe and Treynor ratios in that it compares the performance of the portfolio to the benchmark rather than to the risk-free asset. Therefore, the sign of the IR may differ from the sign of the Sharpe and Treynor ratios.[15]

Note that all these ratios are simple tools for evaluating past performance. They are not necessarily valuable for forecasting superior risk-adjusted performance.

Style Analysis

We have already seen an example of style analysis in Chapter 8 (Section 8.8). The question there was whether the S&P 500 was the appropriate benchmark for a given portfolio. We can extend this type of analysis to identify what proportion of portfolio returns is due to style exposure and what proportion is alpha. Therefore, it allows effective classification of a manager and assessment of her or his skill.

---

[14] See the chapter appendix for the formal definition of the lower partial moment and the downside risk measure used in the Sortino ratio.

[15] For a full discussion of information ratios and the factors determining their level, see Grinold and Kahn (2000).

EXHIBIT 13.6
Unconstrained Style Analysis

Returns-Based Style Analysis: Unconstrained with Stock Classes Only		
	Coefficient	*t*-statistic
Intercept	0.491	2.962
Russell 1000 Value	−0.788	−1.546
Russell 1000 Growth	0.070	1.558
Russell 2000 Value	1.093	4.733
Russell 2000 Growth	0.452	1.543
Sum of size/style coefficients	0.826	
R-squared	.917	

To review briefly, the strategy examined in Chapter 8 was a small-cap value portfolio constructed by selecting low P/E stocks from the small-cap universe. To determine the relationship between the portfolio and the style indexes, a regression model was estimated:

$$R = a + b_{1000V}R(1000V) + b_{1000G}R(1000G) + b_{2000V}R(2000V) + b_{2000G}R(2000G)$$

The regression results are shown in Exhibit 13.6. The results indicate that the model explains the returns well. The R^2 shows that variations in the four size/style indexes explain 92 percent of the variation in the strategy's return. Conversely, only 8 percent of the variation in the portfolio returns is unique to the strategy. The strategy is highly correlated to the Russell 2000 Value index. This is consistent with the claim that the manager is implementing a small-cap value strategy. The coefficients on the other size/style indexes are not statistically different from zero even at a 10 percent level of significance. The positive and statistically significant alpha (intercept) estimate suggests that the manager has skill.

How do we interpret these results? The answer depends on what we are trying to assess. If our aim is to assign the portfolio to one of the familiar style quadrants, then small-cap value is clearly the best category. We can also conclude that the manager exhibits skill. If, on the other hand, we are interested in assessing the likely return on this portfolio, we need to be more careful. Strictly speaking, we should use all the coefficients for this purpose, not just the statistically significant ones. Note in particular that the large-cap value and small-cap growth coefficients are large in absolute value. Thus these components are important in describing the return even though they are not statistically significant. Our best forecast of the monthly return on this strategy would therefore be

0.491% + (1.093 × Russell 2000 Value return)

+ (0.452 × Russell 2000 Growth return)

+ (0.070 × Russell 1000 Growth return)

− (0.788 × Russell 1000 Value return)

Aside from the 49 basis points of alpha, this is the same return as would arise from a portfolio that is long 109.3 percent small-cap value, long 45.2 percent small-cap growth, long 7 percent large-cap growth, and short 78.8 percent large-cap value. These coefficients suggest that this strategy has an especially strong small-cap tilt (note the sizable short in large-cap value) and a tilt toward growth, at least relative to a pure

EXHIBIT 13.7
**Constrained Style
Analysis**

Returns-Based Style Analysis: Constrained Portfolios including T-Bills		
	Shorting and Leverage Allowed	**No Shorting**
Intercept	0.422	0.387
T-Bills	0.173	0.145
Russell 1000 Value	−0.779	0.000
Russell 1000 Growth	0.070	0.108
Russell 2000 Value	1.089	0.745
Russell 2000 Growth	0.447	0.002
Sum of size/style coefficients	0.827	0.855
R-squared	.920	.917

small-cap value portfolio. Therefore, we might expect this manager to do relatively well within a small-cap value universe when smaller caps and growth stocks are outperforming the broader market.

There are at least two potential issues with respect to this unconstrained regression. First, although the regression accounts for almost all the variation in the portfolio returns (92 percent), it does not account for all the *assets*. The coefficients on the size/style indexes sum to only 0.826; that is, they account for only 82.6 percent of the portfolio. If we are sure that all relevant asset classes have been included, we might ascribe the other 17.4 percent of the portfolio to active positions. We might instead interpret it as reflecting a fully invested but relatively low-beta portfolio. Alternatively, we might constrain the coefficients to sum to 1. Doing so may help address the second potential issue: overfitting the data. Due to noisy data or sample period–specific events, the regression model may find relationships that do not reflect the true underlying strategy. Constraining the coefficients helps to alleviate this problem by imposing a minimal level of structure on the implied portfolio. In addition to constraining the sum of the coefficients, we might require that all the asset class coefficients be nonnegative.

When we impose constraints we are effectively incorporating prior information or beliefs in an attempt to improve our estimate of the underlying relationship. If the data are reasonably consistent with these assumptions, the resulting model should explain the portfolio returns almost as well as the unconstrained regression but provide a more parsimonious picture of the strategy. This approach was developed by Sharpe (1992).

Exhibit 13.7 shows two constrained models for our sample strategy. Both models allow investment in T-bills in addition to the four size/style indexes. For the model in the middle column the portfolio weights must sum to unity, but short positions are allowed in any asset including T-bills. The results are virtually identical to the previous regression except that the missing 17.3 percent of assets is now accounted for by T-bills. The slightly lower alpha is due to the small return contribution that is now attributed to T-bills. The model in the right column prohibits short positions in the four equity indexes but still allows leverage. The R^2 indicates that this model fits just as well as the unconstrained regression. But the short position in large-cap value is gone, and the coefficient on small-cap growth is virtually zero too. Apparently these were an artifact of overfitting the sample data. There is still a growth tilt relative to the primary small-cap value nature of the strategy, but the tilt is much smaller than it appeared in the unconstrained regression. The alpha is a few basis points lower, but it still appears that the manager has skill.

Holdings-Based Attribution

The alternative to returns-based analysis is to estimate returns and performance factors from the individual portfolio holdings. This bottom-up approach has the advantage of being fully transparent. The pricing and the actual risk of the portfolio are directly measured. The data requirements are one obvious drawback of this approach. In addition, detailed data do not automatically translate into greater clarity. Converting the portfolio into meaningful risk and return measures requires an understanding of the underlying strategy. Due to the heterogeneity of fixed-income instruments and the ubiquity of derivatives in fixed-income portfolios, this is typically easier for equities than for fixed-income strategies.

Allocation Effect and Selection Effect

We start by decomposing the weight of each security within the portfolio into three components: the weight of its asset class in the portfolio, the weight of its sector within its asset class, and its weight within its sector.[16] Let

$$C_i = \text{portfolio weight of asset class } i$$

$$S_{ij} = \text{weight of sector } j \text{ within asset class } i$$

$$A_{ijk} = \text{weight of security } k \text{ within sector } j \text{ of class } i$$

Then the portfolio weight on security k is given by $W_k = C_i S_{ij} A_{ijk}$. For example, if a portfolio is allocated 60 percent to equities in the form of the S&P 500 SPDR ($C_i = 0.6$), the technology sector represents approximately 20 percent of the SPDR ($S_{ij} = 0.20$), and Microsoft represents roughly 10 percent of the technology sector, then Microsoft has a weight within the portfolio of $0.6 \times 0.2 \times 0.1 = 1.2\%$.

The portfolio return is given by

$$R_P = \Sigma_k W_k R_k$$

Substituting for W_k, we can decompose the portfolio return as

$$R_P = \Sigma_k W_k R_k = \Sigma_k \Sigma_j \Sigma_i C_i S_{ij} A_{ijk} R_k$$

That is, the portfolio return can be viewed as a function of each security's return and its weight within each group. This general decomposition allows us to view the portfolio at either the sector level

$$R_P = \Sigma_k W_k R_k = \Sigma_j \Sigma_i C_i S_{ij} [\Sigma_k A_{ijk} R_k] = \Sigma_j \Sigma_i C_i S_{ij} rs_j$$

where $rs_j = \Sigma_k A_{ijk} R_k$ is the sector j return, or at the asset class level

$$R_P = \Sigma_k W_k R_k = \Sigma_i C_i [\Sigma_j S_{ij} rs_j] = \Sigma_i C_i rc_i$$

where $rc_i = \Sigma_j S_{ij} rs_j$ is the asset class i return.

In this framework, managers can attempt to add value at three levels. First, they can deviate from the asset class weightings within the benchmark. Second, they can

---

[16] The portfolio could be subdivided even more finely by adding subcategory layers. Whether this is useful may depend on the strategy and the types of decisions being assessed. Similarly, country or regional categories would be needed for global portfolios.

deviate from the benchmark sector composition within the asset classes. Third, they can change the weightings of specific securities—including omitting some altogether or holding securities that are not in the benchmark. The first and second decision levels give rise to **allocation effects,** whereas the impact of the third level is the **selection effect.** Keep in mind that being *able* to calculate a particular effect does not necessarily make it meaningful to do so. For example, measuring a sector allocation effect may or may not provide useful information if the manager is a "pure stock picker" for whom sector weights are an afterthought. On the one hand, unintentional sectors bets might explain the ex post performance but would imply little about skill. On the other hand, such unintentional sector bets might raise questions about the manager's risk control.

To demonstrate the process, we can start with the decomposition at the level of the asset class. Consider a portfolio that holds only stocks and bonds. The total impact of changing the weights and securities is the active return:

$$AR = R_P - R_B$$
$$= \Sigma_i C_{Pi} rc_{Pi} - \Sigma_i C_{Bi} rc_{Bi}$$
$$= (C_{Ps} rc_{Ps} + C_{Pb} rc_{Pb}) - (C_{Bs} rc_{Bs} + C_{Bb} rc_{Bb})$$

where C_{Pi} is the weight of the asset class $i(=s$ (stocks), b (bonds)) within portfolio P and rc_{Pi} is the return to asset class i within portfolio P. C_{Bi} and rc_{Bi} are similarly defined for the benchmark. The active return can be decomposed into the allocation effect:

$$AA_{AE} = (C_{Ps} - C_{Bs})(rc_{Bs} - R_B) + (C_{Pb} - C_{Bb})(rc_{Bb} - R_B)$$
$$= \Sigma_i \{(C_{Pi} - C_{Bi})(rc_{Bi} - R_B)\}$$

The $(C_{Pi} - C_{Bi})$ terms capture the manager's allocation choices—the weight differences from the benchmark. These are scaled by the $(rc_{Bi} - R_B)$ terms, which capture the incremental return contribution of the asset class relative to the benchmark. Note that in calculating the allocation effect we use returns for the benchmark and its components, not the portfolio's returns. The sector allocation effect can be measured analogously with sector instead of asset class weights and returns. The selection effect

$$AA_{SE} = C_{Ps}(rc_{Ps} - rc_{Bs}) + C_{Pb}(rc_{Pb} - rc_{Bb})$$
$$= \Sigma_i \{C_{Pi}(rc_{Pi} - rc_{Bi})\}$$

captures the return difference between the securities in the benchmark and those in the portfolio weighted by the *portfolio's* allocations. By construction, the sum of the allocation and selection effects equals the total active return for the portfolio.

This decomposition is intuitive and simple, but it is not the only possible way to decompose active returns. It also has some inherent limitations. Because the weights are assumed to be fixed over the measurement period, the performance impact of dynamic allocation and security selection decisions are not captured. This could be mitigated within a multiperiod context by judicious selection of periods. However, the need to compound the allocation and selection effects through time makes multiperiod attribution more complex (see the next section).

In the decomposition just discussed, the allocation and selection effects have different reference points. The allocation effect measures the impact of weight differences using benchmark returns, whereas the selection effect measures the impact of return differentials using the weights in the active portfolio. An alternative decomposition developed by Brinson and Fachler (1985) uses the benchmark as the reference point for both the allocation and the selection effects:

$$\text{Brinson}_{AE} = \Sigma_i (C_{Pi} - C_{Bi}) rc_{Bi}$$

$$\text{Brinson}_{SE} = \Sigma_i C_{Bi} (rc_{Pi} - rc_{Bi})$$

$$\text{Interaction effect} = \Sigma_i (C_{Pi} - C_{Bi})(rc_{Pi} - rc_{Bi})$$

Unfortunately the common reference point for the allocation and selection effects comes at a cost. With the Brinson decomposition, the allocation and selection effects do not sum to the total active return of the portfolio. The missing piece, called the **interaction effect,** is essentially a residual required to account for the total active return. The Excel Outbox discussing the Brinson model illustrates this approach.

Excel Outbox
The Brinson Model

Use the \<Single-Period Brinson-Template\> worksheet in the Chapter 13 Excel Outboxes .xls spreadsheet. The portfolio and benchmark are constructed from three sectors with the following returns and weights within the portfolios:

	A	B	C	D	E	F	G	H	I	J
		Benchmark		Portfolio			Allocation	Selection	Interaction	Total
		Allocation	Return	Allocation	Return		Effect	Effect		
1										
2										
3	Sector 1	20%	2%	10%	2%					
4	Sector 2	30%	3%	30%	4%					
5	Sector 3	50%	4%	60%	9%					
6	Total									

- The portfolio and benchmark returns can be calculated using the portfolio return formula developed earlier. In cell B6 enter =SUM(B3:B5), and in cell C6 enter the formula =SUMPRODUCT(B3:B5,C3:C5). These formulas can then be copied and pasted into cells D6 and E6.
- *Allocation effect:* To calculate the allocation effect for sector 1, enter =(D3−B3)*C3 in cell G3. This formula can then be copied (using special paste formula to retain the formatting) to cells G4 and G5. The total allocation effect is calculated by entering =SUM(G3:G5) in cell G6.
- *Selection effect:* To calculate the selection effect for sector 1, enter =B3*(E3−C3) in cell H3. This formula can then be copied to cells H4 and H5. The total selection effect is calculated by entering =SUM(H3:H5) in cell H6.
- *Interaction effect:* To calculate the interaction effect for sector 1, enter =(D3−B3)*(E3−C3) in cell I3. This formula can then be copied to cells I4 and I5. The total interaction effect is calculated by entering =SUM(I3:I5) in cell I6.
- *Total effect:* The total effect can be calculated directly or by summing the allocation, selection, and interaction effects. The direct calculation for sector 1 is =(D3*E3)−(B3*C3) entered in cell J3. As a check, this should equal =SUM(G3:I3). Copy cell J3 to cells J4:J5 and enter =SUM(J3:J5) in cell J6.

	A	B	C	D	E	F	G	H	I	J
		Benchmark		Portfolio			Allocation	Selection	Interaction	Total
		Allocation	Return	Allocation	Return		Effect	Effect		
1										
2										
3	Sector 1	20%	2%	10%	2%		−0.20%	0.00%	0.00%	−0.20%
4	Sector 2	30%	3%	30%	4%		0.00%	0.30%	0.00%	0.30%
5	Sector 3	50%	4%	60%	9%		0.40%	2.50%	0.50%	3.40%
6	Total	100%	3.30%	100%	6.80%		0.20%	2.80%	0.50%	3.50%

What do the results indicate? The active return was 3.50 percent. Examining the individual effects, we see that most of this came from selection. Examining the sectors shows that most of the active return was generated in sector 3. The value added from that sector arose from correctly overweighting the sector as a whole and from selecting securities within the sector.

The bottom portion of the template provides an alternative "four portfolio" calculation method that will be useful in extending the framework to multiple periods.

- In cell D11, enter = SUMPRODUCT(B3:B5,C3:C5).
- In cell D12, enter = SUMPRODUCT(D3:D5,C3:C5).
- In cell D13, enter = SUMPRODUCT(B3:B5,E3:E5).
- In cell D14, enter = SUMPRODUCT(D3:D5,E3:E5).
- In cell D16, enter = D12 − D11.
- In cell D17, enter = D13 − D11.
- In cell D18, enter = D14 − D13 − D12 + D11.
- In cell D19, enter = D14 − D11.

The table should look like this:

	A	B	C	D
9	**Alternate "Four Portfolio" Calculation**			
10			Portfolio	
11	1	R(B)		3.30%
12	2	R(2)		3.50%
13	3	R(3)		6.10%
14	4	R(P)		6.80%
15			Effects	
16	Allocation	R(2) − R(B)		0.20%
17	Selection	R(3) − B(B)		2.80%
18	Interaction	R(P) − R(3) − R(2) + R(B)		0.50%
19	Total	R(P) − B(B)		3.50%

Multiperiod Attribution

As noted previously, multiperiod attribution enables us to take into account the evolution of portfolio positions. The question, of course, is how to combine the attribution results from each individual period into meaningful results for the entire evaluation period. The basic idea is to compound the single-period results. However, the cumulative results will depend on the order of arithmetic operations: which items are multiplied, which are added or subtracted, and in what order.

The Brinson decomposition can be restated in terms of the return on four portfolios: the benchmark, the active portfolio, and two hypothetical portfolios. One hypothetical portfolio (labeled portfolio 2) has the same asset class weights as the actual portfolio but the same asset class returns as the benchmark. The other hypothetical portfolio (labeled portfolio 3) has the same asset class weights as the benchmark but the same asset class returns as the actual portfolio. Therefore, the four returns in each period are

$$R_B = \Sigma_i \, C_{Bi} \, rc_{Bi}$$

$$R_2 = \Sigma_i \, C_{Pi} \, rc_{Bi}$$

$$R_3 = \Sigma_i \, C_{Bi} \, rc_{Pi}$$

$$R_P = \Sigma_i \, C_{Pi} \, rc_{Pi}$$

In terms of these four returns, we can restate the Brinson decomposition as

$$\text{Brinson}_{AE} = R_2 - R_B$$
$$\text{Brinson}_{SE} = R_3 - R_B$$
$$\text{Interaction effect} = R_P - R_3 - R_2 + R_B$$

To extend this model to multiple periods, we can simply compound the return on each of these four portfolios to obtain the corresponding cumulative returns and then compute the allocation, selection, and interaction effects for the full evaluation period as above (see the Excel Outbox discussing the extended Brinson model). Note that this is not equivalent to directly linking the period-by-period attribution results.

Excel Outbox
The Extended
Brinson Model

Use the <Extended Brinson-Template> worksheet in the Chapter 13 Excel Outboxes.xls spreadsheet. The portfolio and benchmark are constructed from three sectors with the following returns and weights over three periods:

	A	B	C	D	E
1		Benchmark		Portfolio	
2	**Period 1**	Allocation	Return	Allocation	Return
3	**Sector 1**	20%	2%	10%	2%
4	**Sector 2**	30%	3%	30%	4%
5	**Sector 3**	50%	4%	60%	9%
6	**Total**				
7					
8					
9	**Period 2**	Allocation	Return	Allocation	Return
10	**Sector 1**	20%	−5%	10%	0%
11	**Sector 2**	30%	−2%	20%	1%
12	**Sector 3**	50%	−3%	70%	3%
13	**Total**				
14					
15					
16	**Period 3**	Allocation	Return	Allocation	Return
17	**Sector 1**	20%	−5%	25%	−4%
18	**Sector 2**	20%	−3%	65%	−4%
19	**Sector 3**	60%	−7%	10%	−1%
20	**Total**				
21					
22					
23	**Compounded**		Return		Return
24	**Sector 1**				
25	**Sector 2**				
26	**Sector 3**				
27	**Total**				

The benchmark and portfolio returns for each period are calculated using the same formulas as the single-period Brinson outbox:

- In cell B6 enter =SUM(B3:B5).
- In cell C6 enter =SUMPRODUCT(B3:B5,C3:C5).
- Copy these formulas to cells D6:E6, B13:C13, D13:E13, B20:C20, and D20:E20.
- In cell C24 enter =(1+c3)*(1+C10*(1+C17)−1, and then copy to cells C25:C27 and to cells E24:E27.

The completed template should appear as follows:

	A	B	C	D	E
		Benchmark		Portfolio	
1					
2	**Period 1**	Allocation	Return	Allocation	Return
3	**Sector 1**	20%	2%	10%	2%
4	**Sector 2**	30%	3%	30%	4%
5	**Sector 3**	50%	4%	60%	9%
6	**Total**	100%	3.30%	100%	6.80%
7					
8					
9	**Period 2**	Allocation	Return	Allocation	Return
10	**Sector 1**	20%	−5%	10%	0%
11	**Sector 2**	30%	−2%	20%	1%
12	**Sector 3**	50%	−3%	70%	3%
13	**Total**	100%	−3.10%	100%	2.30%
14					
15					
16	**Period 3**	Allocation	Return	Allocation	Return
17	**Sector 1**	20%	−5%	25%	−4%
18	**Sector 2**	20%	−3%	65%	−4%
19	**Sector 3**	60%	−7%	10%	−1%
20	**Total**	100%	−5.80%	100%	−3.70%
21					
22					
23	**Compounded**		Return		Return
24	**Sector 1**		−8%		−2%
25	**Sector 2**		−2%		1%
26	**Sector 3**		−6%		11%
27	**Total**		−5.71%		5.21%

The extended Brinson attribution uses the "four portfolios" method introduced in the single-period outbox. The template should appear as follows:

(continued)

(continued)

	G	H	I	J	K	L	M
1		Four Portfolios				Asset Allocation	
2		Period	Cumulative			Period	Cumulative
3	R(B)				AA$_{AE}$		
4	R(2)				AA$_{SE}$		
5	R(3)				AA$_{IE}$		
6	R(P)				AA$_{TE}$		
7							
8							
9		Period	Cumulative			Period	Cumulative
10	R(B)				AA$_{AE}$		
11	R(2)				AA$_{SE}$		
12	R(3)				AA$_{IE}$		
13	R(P)				AA$_{TE}$		
14							
15							
16		Period	Cumulative			Period	Cumulative
17	R(B)				AA$_{AE}$		
18	R(2)				AA$_{SE}$		
19	R(3)				AA$_{IE}$		
20	R(P)				AA$_{TE}$		
21							
22							
23			Cumulative				Cumulative
24	R(B)				AA$_{AE}$		
25	R(2)				AA$_{SE}$		
26	R(3)				AA$_{IE}$		
27	R(P)				AA$_{TE}$		

- In cell H3 enter =SUMPRODUCT(B3:B5, C3:C5).
- In cell H4 enter =SUMPRODUCT(D3:D5, C3:C5).
- In cell H5 enter =SUMPRODUCT(B3:B5, E3:E5).
- In cell H6 enter =SUMPRODUCT(D3:D5, E3:E5).
- Copy cells H3:H6 to cells H10:H13 and H17:H20. Use paste special formula to avoid overwriting the cell formatting.
- In cell I3 enter = H3, and then copy to cells I4:I6.
- In cell I10 enter =(1+I3)*(1+H10)−1, and then copy to cells I11:I13 and I17:I20.
- In cell I24 enter I17, and then copy to cells I25:I27.

To calculate the active allocation effects,

- In cell L3, enter =H4−H3.
- In cell L4 enter = H5−H3.
- In cell L5 enter =H6−H5−H4+H3.
- In cell L6 enter =H6−H3.
- Copy cells L3:L6 to cells L10:L13 and L17:L20.
- In cell M24 enter =I25−I24.
- In cell M25 enter =I26−I24.
- In cell M26 enter =I27−I26−I25+I24.

- In cell M27 enter =I27−I24.
- In cell M3 enter =L3, and then copy to cells M4:M6.
- In cell M10 enter =(1+L10)*(1+M3)−1, and then copy to cells M11:M13 and M17:M20.

The final table should appear as follows:

	G	H	I	J	K	L	M
		Four Portfolios				Asset Allocation	
1							
2		Period	Cumulative			Period	Cumulative
3	R(B)	3.30%	3.30%		AA$_{AE}$	0.20%	0.20%
4	R(2)	3.50%	3.50%		AA$_{SE}$	2.80%	2.80%
5	R(3)	6.10%	6.10%		AA$_{IE}$	0.50%	0.50%
6	R(P)	6.80%	6.80%		AA$_{TE}$	3.50%	3.50%
7							
8							
9		Period	Cumulative			Period	Cumulative
10	R(B)	−3.30%	0.10%		AA$_{AE}$	0.10%	0.30%
11	R(2)	−3.00%	0.39%		AA$_{SE}$	4.90%	7.84%
12	R(3)	1.80%	8.01%		AA$_{IE}$	0.40%	0.90%
13	R(P)	2.30%	9.26%		AA$_{TE}$	5.40%	9.09%
14							
15							
16		Period	Cumulative			Period	Cumulative
17	R(B)	−5.80%	−5.71%		AA$_{AE}$	1.90%	2.21%
18	R(2)	−3.90%	−3.52%		AA$_{SE}$	3.60%	11.72%
19	R(3)	−2.20%	5.63%		AA$_{IE}$	−3.40%	−2.53%
20	R(P)	−3.70%	5.21%		AA$_{TE}$	2.10%	11.38%
21							
22							
23			Cumulative				Cumulative
24	R(B)		−5.71%		AA$_{AE}$		2.19%
25	R(2)		−3.52%		AA$_{SE}$		11.34%
26	R(3)		5.63%		AA$_{IE}$		−2.61%
27	R(P)		5.21%		AA$_{TE}$		10.92%

13.4 Performance Appraisal

Investment performance is an important determinant of compensation and career advancement for portfolio managers. In some instances, such as a formula translating basis points over the benchmark into cash at bonus time, the link is explicit and well defined. In other instances, such as the opportunity to manage a new, bigger, or more visible portfolio, the link may be more indirect or qualitative. Whatever the mechanism, the assessment of performance clearly has important implications for a manager's career and personal financial success. With this in mind, it should be clear that performance evaluation can have strong incentive effects.

Chapter 14 will directly address incentives and ethical issues that arise from and surround various practices within the investment business. Although some of the issues discussed there have an impact on either measured performance or management of company profits, in most instances they do not directly alter underlying investment decisions. The focus in this section is on three broad principles that help to ensure that the performance evaluation process itself does not induce poor investment decisions.

The first principle underlying effective performance evaluation is **fairness.** The method of measuring and attributing performance should accurately reflect those decisions, and only those decisions, over which the manager has control. If, as is typically the case, the manager cannot control flows in and out of the portfolio, then it is unfair to reward or punish the manager for the performance impact of such flows. In most situations the use of dollar-weighted rather than time-weighted returns would be unfair. On the other hand, managers usually have discretion over the level of cash held *within* the portfolios they manage. Fairness therefore implies that managers should not be evaluated based only on the invested portion of their funds.

The second principle requires that performance evaluation should be **invariant** to the implementation of economically equivalent positions. This issue arises whenever various instruments or combinations of instruments provide essentially the same risk–return opportunities. Almost by definition, it arises in any portfolio that uses complex securities, structured products, or derivative contracts. Chapter 10 invoked the invariance principle to explain why accounting for trading decisions rather than risk exposure decisions is not a good basis for performance evaluation.[17] In that example, we showed that focusing on trading decisions distorts the measured performance of a currency overlay manager versus the manager of the underlying asset portfolio.

The third, and arguably the most important, principle of effective performance evaluation requires that there should be **no conflict of interest** between the manager and the client (or management firm). What is good for the client must be good for the manager and vice versa. In some situations, such as an ERISA client, the manager is legally obligated to put the interests of the client ahead of his or her own. In other instances, it is a matter of ethical conduct or, even more simply, just good business. Nonetheless, it is important that the performance evaluation process align the manager's interests with those of the client so that pecuniary and nonpecuniary incentives are not in conflict.

Summary

Performance measurement, attribution, and appraisal are significant elements in the investment management process. Though rarely accorded the same attention as the investment strategy, they are the essential feedback loop in this dynamic process. In particular, they enable investors, managers, and CIOs to evaluate decisions, identify skill, and determine compensation.

This chapter outlined the basic steps and introduced the primary tools of performance measurement and attribution. In the process, we highlighted some practical pitfalls and ambiguities. As with the M–V model in asset allocation, despite their imperfections, the tools discussed in this chapter are the workhorses of performance analysis in the industry. With these tools as a foundation, you should be able to extend the ideas to more complex frameworks (such as multifactor risk models), develop your own techniques, and adopt methods tailored to specific situations.

[17] See Exhibit 10.12 and the related discussion.

Problems

*After studying this chapter, students should be equipped to complete the "Third Deliverable" assignment for each of the cases in this book's appendix.

1. Bob had $130,000 in the BFT Growth Fund when he retired at the end of 1993. At the end of 1994 he redeemed $10,500. Each year from 1995 through 2005 his redemption increased by 5 percent. Sam receives his annual bonus at year-end. He invested $10,000 in the BFT Growth Fund at the end of 1993. Each year-end from 1994 through 2005 he bought shares worth 5 percent more than he had added the previous year. The annual returns for the BFT Growth Fund follow:

1994	4.85	1999	51.29	2004	3.74
1995	38.65	2000	− 24.53	2005	2.88
1996	25.57	2001	− 20.48	2006	8.56
1997	33.73	2002	− 30.26		
1998	45.09	2003	26.63		

   a. What was the value of Bob's account at the end of 2006? Sam's account?

   b. What was the annualized return on the fund over the entire 13-year period?

   c. What annual return did Bob earn on his holdings of the fund? How about Sam?

2. Use the returns in the \<Data\> tab of the Chapter 13 Excel Outboxes.xls spreadsheet to compute the following measures for each of the three portfolios: mean, standard deviation, beta, shortfall probability, expected shortfall, lower partial moment of degree 2, downside risk, VaR at the 5 percent level, alpha, Treynor ratio, Sharpe ratio, Sortino ratio, and *M*-squared. The riskless rate is 5 percent. For all measures that require a threshold or target level of return, set that level at 0 percent.

3. Use the regression function in Excel's Data Analysis Toolpack and the data in Problem 2 to estimate alpha and beta for each of the active portfolios. [*Note:* The estimates may be slightly different than those computed directly in Problem 2 due to the degrees of freedom adjustment in the regression function.] Are the alphas statistically significant at the 95 percent confidence level? Are the betas of the two portfolios statistically different from 1 at the 95 percent confidence level? Are they statistically different from each other?

4. What do the results in Problem 2 suggest about the level of diversification in each of the active portfolios? How might this affect the appropriate role of each fund in an overall investment strategy?

5. Compute the tracking error and information ratio for each of the active portfolios in Problem 2. What do these results imply about the skill of each manager? What do they imply about using each of these funds within an asset allocation based on benchmark indexes?

6. Consider the returns-based style analysis results in the following table. Does this manager have skill? The manager claims to adhere to a strict style discipline. Do these results suggest that this is the case? If so, what is the manager's style?

	Intercept	T-Bills	Large Value	Large Growth	Small Value	Small Growth	*R*-Squared
Allow leverage	0.158	−0.092	0.372	0.137	0.000	0.583	0.864
No leverage	0.225	0.000	0.169	0.093	0.000	0.738	0.863
T-bills and SCG only	0.296	0.073	0.000	0.000	0.000	0.927	0.859
T-bills and LCV only	0.059	0.000	1.000	0.000	0.000	0.000	0.799

---

7. Suppose that rotation among styles and capitalizations is an important component of a manager's strategy. How could you adapt the regression-based style analysis to assess whether this rotation is successful?

8. The formulas shown for the allocation and selection effects do not involve portfolio weights and returns at the security level. Is this detailed data really necessary for holdings-based performance analysis? If not, why not? If so, how does it enter the analysis?

9. Using the data in the following table, calculate the allocation and selection effects:

	A	B	C	D	E
		Benchmark		Portfolio	
1		Allocation	Return	Allocation	Return
3	Sector 1	20%	3%	30%	5%
4	Sector 2	30%	4%	10%	2%
5	Sector 3	50%	2%	60%	3%
6	Total	100%	2.80%	100%	3.50%

Appendix

Calculation of Risk Measures

Let $R(i)$, $i = 1, \ldots, N$ represent returns on an asset or portfolio and $P(i)$ the associated probabilities. The $P(i)$ may reflect any valid probability distribution. For historical samples $P(i)=(1/N)$. Without loss of generality we can arrange these returns in ascending order so that $R(i) < R(i + 1)$.

For two assets we let $P(i,j)$ represent the probability that the return on the first asset is $R(i)$ while the return on the second asset is $R(j)$. For notational simplicity, we use the same set of possible returns for both assets.

1. The variance of return is

$$\sigma^2 = \sum_1^N P(i)(R(i) - \mu)^2$$

where[18]

$$\mu = \sum_1^N P(i)R(i)$$

is the mean return. The standard deviation is the square root of the variance.

2. The beta of portfolio A with respect to benchmark portfolio B is

$$\beta = \frac{\sigma_{AB}}{\sigma_B^2}$$

[18] Note that the symbol μ is used here somewhat differently than in Chapters 3–5. In those chapters, μ represented the logarithm of the mean gross return. In terms of the current notation, that would correspond to $\ln(\sum_1^N P(i)(1+R(i)))$.

where

$$\sigma_{AB} = \sum_{i=1}^{N} \sum_{j=1}^{N} P(i, j)(R(i) - \mu_A)(R(j) - \mu_B)$$

is the covariance of A and B.

3. Let θ represent a threshold return such that returns below this level are considered risky while returns above this level are not. Recall that the returns are arranged in ascending order. Letting K denote the largest integer such that $R(K) \leq \theta$, the shortfall probability is given by

$$\text{Shortfall probability} = \sum_{1}^{K} P(i)$$

The expected shortfall is

$$\text{Expected shortfall} = \sum_{1}^{N} P(i) \max(0, \theta - R(i)) = \sum_{1}^{K} P(i)(\theta - R(i))$$

4. The lower partial moment of degree n with threshold return θ is

$$\text{LPM}(n) = \sum_{1}^{N} P(i)[\max(0, \theta - R(i))]^n = \sum_{1}^{K} P(i)(\theta - R(i))^n$$

The LPM of degree 2 is the most commonly used member of this family. Throughout this book, whenever the lower partial moment is referenced without specifying the degree, it should be understood that $n = 2$. If the threshold θ is set equal to the expected return, the LPM(2) is also known as the semivariance.
The downside risk measure in the denominator of the Sortino ratio is the square root of LPM(2).

5. Let $CP(k) = \sum_{1}^{k} P(i)$ be the cumulative probability for the k lowest return values.

Let L be the largest value of k such that $CP(L) \leq 1$. For an investment of $\$X$ and tail probability of λ the value at risk equals $(X * R(L))$. That is,

$$\text{VaR}(X, \lambda) = X * R(L) \ L \text{ such that } CP(\text{L}) \leq \lambda$$

Clearly the VaR is meaningful only if λ is chosen so that $R(L) < 0$ (that is, a loss). Typically $\lambda = .05$, implying that a loss of *at least* the VaR occurs 5 percent of the time.

The definitions here are based on using all possible return values and their true probabilities. In the language of statistics, these formulas represent population statistics. Sample statistics adjust for the fact that a given historical sample will not contain all the possible values in precisely the right proportions. The sample variance scales up the variance formula given here by a factor of $[N/(N-1)]$. Similarly, the covariance formula here is scaled up by $[N/(N-2)]$ to obtain the sample covariance. Intuitively, these adjustments reflect the notion that the effective sample size is reduced by the necessity of estimating the mean(s) before calculating the variance or covariance. Although it does not appear to be standard practice, similar adjustments could be made for the other risk measures.

Chapter

14

Incentives, Ethics, and Policy

Chapter Outline

14.1   Introduction

A successful investment management business requires thoughtful business policies as well as effective portfolio management. Chapters 1 through 13 of this book have described techniques to manage investment portfolios. Risk and performance goals were defined, and strategies were proposed to attain those goals. It was generally assumed the portfolio manager would set goals and act in the best interest of the client. This chapter takes a different tack. It examines the motivation and implications of portfolio managers acting in their own best interest. This chapter discusses the business incentives for portfolio managers who are hired by investment clients. These clients may include institutional investors such as pension plans, endowments and foundations, or individual clients including mutual fund, high net worth, and 401(k) investors. The rewards for success in the investment business can be large, and as a result, the incentives are strong for growing assets under management. Each of these client groups has unique goals, but they all seek strong investment performance. Assets will flow to managers who can generate that performance. Assets will quickly flow out from investment managers who deliver subpar performance or treat their clients poorly. Unrealistic claims, corrupt sales tactics, and misuse of client assets will all quickly destroy clients' trust in a manager—and in turn, the manager's business. To avoid making a fateful mistake, most investment firms define and enforce business ethics policies.

Interests of the Portfolio Manager and the Client

As discussed in Chapter 11, investors expect portfolio managers to apply their expertise and act in the investors' best interests. However, the incentives between these two groups are usually closely but imperfectly aligned. This can lead to inappropriate, and even unethical, behavior by portfolio managers. Inappropriate behavior may include deceptive sales practices, promotion of products that do not offer true value, or outright theft.

Unethical behavior on the part of portfolio managers harms the reputation of all investment professionals. As a result, the investment management industry, together with the federal government, has defined standards of conduct. The SEC, the U.S. Department of Labor, the National Association of Security Dealers (NASD), and the CFA Institute have all worked to establish laws and guidelines for best practices.

In addition to business goals, there are also individual manager goals. Portfolio managers seek large compensation and the opportunity to influence company policy. For example, portfolio managers have personal interests in resource levels, defined responsibilities, and workload. Controlling large asset levels, driven in large part by their investment performance and the visibility of their investment approach, leads to managers receiving both high compensation and influence over business decisions. Rewarding strong performance utilizing clear compensation systems helps in the retention of investment talent. Including rewards for meeting investment guidelines, as well as performance-related objectives, in compensation systems helps reduce conflicts of interest between manager and client. Strong leadership and well-defined, enforced company policies help protect the fortunes of the business.

Revenues in an investment company are driven by management fees, typically computed based on a percentage of assets under management. Index managers tend to charge very low, single-basis-point annual fees, while aggressive hedge fund managers typically charge a 1–2 percent management fee plus a 10–30 percent performance sharing arrangement. Although it may be tempting to promise high performance or introduce untried strategies, clients can become quickly disappointed and firm reputations can be tainted, harming long-term prospects for individuals and companies. Individuals may also be held personally responsible for unethical behavior, including jail time. Many questionable activities in the financial services industry are considered unethical by the layperson. However, many activities that may appear questionable are not, and many that may not readily appear unethical actually are, based on either industry practice or securities law. This chapter provides a summary of investment industry practice as well as business incentives and policy.

Outline of Chapter

Understanding business incentives is important for setting appropriate policies for managing a successful investment operation. Incentives are reviewed in Section 14.2 of this chapter. Ethical standards are important for defining effective operating guidelines. Those are discussed in Sections 14.3 through 14.5. A list of proposed policies is provided in Section 14.6, and a discussion of the special issue of manager compensation is included in Section 14.7.

14.2   The Investment Company Business Model

Variables Influencing Firm Profits

To motivate this review, we start with a discussion of the business model of an investment company. Asset management company profits are determined by several factors, each of which is influenced by several variables. These are described formally as

1. Assets under management (AUM).

$$AUM = f_{AUM} \text{ (level and consistency of return versus peers, client}$$
$$\text{relationships)}$$

2. Proportional fee levels (F).

$$F = f_{fee} \text{ (level of total and active return, capacity)}$$

3. Salaries and other costs (S).

$$S = f_s \text{ (personnel experience and track record, rent, sales costs, IT).}$$

We can combine these factors into a single profit equation:

$$\text{Earnings} = f_{AUM} \, f_{fee} - f_s$$

An investment company earns its revenue as a percentage fee on assets under management (factors 1 and 2). The fee is typically stated in basis points. Institutional commingled or separate accounts are typically billed quarterly, in arrears. Mutual fund fees are withheld daily. Hedge fund and private equity partnership fees are calculated monthly or quarterly and withdrawn from the accounts monthly, quarterly, or annually. Performance, or incentive-based, fees are common in the alternatives arena but may also be found in mutual funds and institutional accounts. These are paid in addition to a fixed base fee and are calculated as a portion of total return, or of excess return over a benchmark. They are usually billed quarterly or annually. These arrangements typically include a high-water mark, discussed in Chapter 11, that ensures a manager must earn back any subsequent underperformance before sharing in future outperformance.

Management fee levels depend on three things: the investment vehicle, the level of potential active return, and the capacity of the discipline. For example, a small-cap equity manager with a strong track record will command a substantially higher fee than an enhanced-index bond portfolio. Mutual fund vehicles tend to offer less aggressive sharing arrangements than institutional accounts. Data provided by the Investment Company Institute in 2003 indicated that the average performance fee impact on 46 large equity mutual funds was quite modest, fluctuating from −3 to +2 basis points on an average total expense ratio of 70 basis points.

Fidelity's Advisor Aggressive Growth equity mutual fund charges 0.02 percent for each percentage point above or below the return of the index up to a maximum performance fee charge of 0.20 percent. This performance fee is calculated over a rolling 36-month period and added to the base fee of approximately 75 basis points. Hedge funds typically charge a 2 percent management fee plus 20 percent of total returns with a high-water mark. Private equity funds frequently charge 30 percent of total returns. Clearly these performance-based fees encourage managers to work hard for good performance. However, they can also encourage taking large risks in hopes of earning large returns.

Soft dollars—some were more aggressive than others, but virtually everyone used them in some form to support their investment business. Although they are still legal, their use is now in question, and several investment firms have committed to paying for research in cash.

This is not a change in the law; it is a change in community standards of ethical behavior. Before "everyone did it"; now its broad use is becoming frowned upon.

In general, portfolio managers do not go to jail for past practices that were legal and accepted but are now frowned upon; but they may get dragged through the mud and lose business to those who never did it.

This raises key questions. How do you draw the line when it may be difficult or impossible to compete with those who are pushing the boundaries of legal and ethical practices? How do you make sure your firm is an early adopter of new standards? Here is a case in point: Mortgage brokers who said in 2009 that they had to originate risky loans for borrowers with little chance of making the payments because otherwise someone else would have done it, and they would be out of business. These firms, and their employees, suffered significant financial and reputational harm and contributed to serious damage to the global economy.

The costs of a management firm include salaries of investment professionals and support staff, technology (IT) expenses, office rent, and sales costs. Until recently, research costs (beyond salaries) were heavily subsidized by **soft dollar** arrangements. This subsidy involves partial or full payment for research services by brokerage firms out of commissions paid for trading portfolios. As ethical standards have changed, soft dollars are becoming a thing of the past; as a result, research costs are a growing expense for investment management firms. Sales costs can include paying salespeople's compensation and expenses, advertising costs, and fees to distributors. Note that sales costs tend to vary but are tied to gross sales. Net sales depend on both new and lost business.

Relative Importance of Variables

As an illustration of the relative size of profit levels, consider revenue, expense, and earnings results from the publicly traded T Rowe Price Group's 2005 annual report. Compensation clearly dominates expenses, totaling 61 percent of total expenses for 2005. Facilities, including depreciation, total only 14 percent. Other expenses include distribution fees to third-party financial advisors who sell the funds, which will be higher for a firm that concentrates on advisor-sold (compared with individual direct

EXHIBIT 14.1

Revenue and Expense Comparison, T Rowe Price Group, 2005

	2005	Percentage of Total
Advisory revenues	$1,235.4	82%
Total revenues	$1,512.1	100
Compensation	$ 522.3	61
Advertising	$ 86.0	10
PPE depreciation	$ 42.3	5
Facilities	$ 74.4	9
Other	$ 131.9	15
Total expenses	$ 857.1	100%
		Margin
Operating profit	$ 655.0	43%
Net income	$ 430.9	28%

sale) products. Note that revenues from 12b-1 fees (distribution costs charged to a mutual fund) offset this expense. Interestingly, costs for information services, listed under other expenses, increased by $7.3 million from 2004 due to the company's decision to reduce soft dollar activity. T Rowe offers funds under its own label but also manages funds for distributors. T Rowe funds generated $1,235 million in advisory fees on $156 billion in average assets, for an average fee of 79 basis points.

An investment company's level and consistency of performance and the strength of its client relationships determine AUM, the key driver of firm profit. Academic research in 2007 by Heisler, Knittel, Neumann, and Stewart (HKN&S) confirmed the expected. Strong relative performance versus peers and benchmarks over multiple trailing time periods, for an extended time, is a key determinant of account and asset growth. Their evidence also indicates that an investment product with some traction will continue to gain assets as long as its performance is good. In other words, a good track record over several years, combined with an effective story that is well publicized, leads to growth. Strong relationships, built with effective communication and responsive service, help retain assets but are eventually dominated by performance results, as demonstrated in 2005 survey work by Karim and Stewart (K&S).

As a further illustration of these observations, consider the two asset management firms T-Rowe Price Group and Janus Capital, Inc. Over the last few years, both fund companies have performed well (as shown in Exhibit 14.2), beating a majority of their peers; but T-Rowe has performed significantly better, resulting in higher asset growth and profit margins. In this case, performance is measured relative to other similar style funds as a percentage of peers beaten. Note that Janus's business also suffered from a bias toward growth funds and a settlement in the mutual fund scandal of 2003 (see the War Story box about this topic).

Employee Compensation

Individual compensation is tied to firm profitability. Many investment firms are employee-owned, and many employees share directly in company profits. In fact a 2004 survey study by Farnsworth and Taylor (F&T) suggests that close to half of the total compensation of investment professionals is in the form of a bonus, and firm profitability represents the largest influence on these bonuses, more important than investment performance. Anecdotal evidence suggests that annual bonus pools are related to recent company profitability and individual payouts are related to individual portfolio manager asset growth as well as performance. Not surprisingly, F&T's evidence suggests that investment performance heavily influences the hiring and firing of managers—perhaps a more important incentive than simple bonus payouts. Many firms employ specific formulas for setting bonus levels and payouts, including benchmark-relative returns, peer rankings, and assets under management relative to other managers in the relevant discipline. In those cases, bonuses are largely independent, at least in the short term, of firm profitability. However, the F&T study suggests these formal compensation systems are in the minority.

EXHIBIT 14.2
Profit and Investment Performance Comparison, 12/31/06

	AUM ($ Billion)	Growth in AUM	Profit Margin	Percentage of Funds Beating Peers
T-Rowe	$334.5	24%	28.0%	80%*
Janus	$167.7	13%	14.3%	68%†

* Five years ending 12/06.
† Three years ending 12/06.

14.3 Incentives for Businesspeople and Portfolio Managers

Short-Term Incentives for the Individual or Small Firm

Consistently strong performance and good visibility will lead to high AUM, high fees, and in turn generous profits and compensation. If management is patient and takes care of its clients, with more than a little luck, assets and profits will come. Individual compensation will benefit, depending on firm and individual asset growth and investment results.

Time is an important factor in success because the window to establish a track record and reputation can vary considerably. As we saw in Chapter 7, institutional investors typically have three- to five-year investment horizons. Standard & Poor's reported in 2006 that the average tenure for a portfolio manager of an equity mutual fund is 5.6 years. Private equity funds have an 8- to 12-year life span. Malkiel and Saha (2005) show that on average 15–20 percent of hedge funds go out of business each year—many in their first year of operation.

Reconsider the investment firm business model. To grow assets quickly, based on results from HKN&S and K&S, and supported by anecdotal evidence, an active equity manager ideally needs the qualities described in Exhibit 14.3. Strong performance numbers will also provide pricing power, allowing the firm to charge higher management fees that will in turn increase profits. Without some historical traction of asset flows, it will take time to build the business unless the firm takes some shortcuts to grow assets.

There are three potential shortcuts to grow an investment business quickly. The first is to hire an experienced team of portfolio managers with the hope that their past record can be replicated in a new operation. These are called *liftouts* in the business and are frequently financed by large financial institutions such as American Express or smaller investment buyout firms such as Rosemont Partners. Liftouts may include capturing established accounts in addition to personnel. The second shortcut, sometimes restricted by management contracts, is to offer cut-rate fees to prospective clients. This benefit may be openly offered to initial clients when getting a business or product off the ground. As discussed in Chapter 11, fund of funds managers invest client assets with multiple hedge fund managers. Fund of fund (FoF) managers often look to negotiate reduced fees with new hedge funds. The reduced fees increase the net return delivered to the FoF and help offset the higher business risk noted earlier.

EXHIBIT 14.3
Key Ingredients to Attract Assets

1. Good performance:
   a. At least a three-year track record, ideally five or more.
   b. Consistent active returns, ideally positive active over one-, three-, and five-year periods.
   c. Consistent style and risk characteristics.
2. A good organization:
   a. Firm reputation.
   b. Manager reputation.
3. A good sales operation:
   a. Effective communication.
   b. Positive sales momentum.

To protect against other investors getting preferential treatment, many FoF also demand *most favored nation* (MFN) provisions. That is, should the hedge fund offer potentially better terms to another smaller investor, these terms would immediately be offered to all larger investors with MFN provisions. These agreements are also common in the institutional business for traditional separate or commingled accounts. A third approach to raise assets involves using questionable tactics like kickbacks. Rewards may come in the form of providing gifts to individual decision makers (or their advisors) or special support to a client firm or, as described in the War Story: 2003 Mutual Fund Scandal box, giving some investors the opportunity to take advantage of other investors. Gifts may come in the form of cash, trips, or jobs. Benefits may be direct or for friends and family. The strategies described in the third approach are clearly questionable in terms of fairness to clients, and as a result, while potentially effective in the short term, will hurt a firm's reputation in the long term, as described in the following section.

Long-Term and Firm Incentives

Self-interest may motivate individuals to break or bend rules. In the investment business, this incentive does not exist solely for start-ups. Salespeople and portfolio managers all benefit from growing assets, fees, and performance in well-established firms.

Firm profits will increase in the short term from increasing management fees using questionable tactics; but is this truly beneficial for the company? Privately owned Wellington Management has been in operation for close to 80 years; Putnam Investments, private until acquired by publicly traded Marsh & McLennan Companies, has operated for 70; and Fidelity Investments has been in operation for over 60. Wellington and Fidelity continue to operate today as healthy companies. Putnam lost significant assets (and was sold by its owner to a Canadian firm in 2007) due to lapses in business judgment as described in the War Story box. Exhibit 14.3 indicates the importance of firm reputation for winning investment mandates. Findings from K&S suggest that managers who are tainted with scandal will be readily fired if they also display mediocre performance.

What about an individual's total career horizon? K&S results indicate that manager and firm reputation are equally important for gaining clients. Moreover, the investment business truly is a small community, especially at the high end. Hundreds of thousands of professionals work in the business, yet the number of investment professionals (those making the investment decisions) numbers in the thousands. Consider that large investment firms which manage over $1 trillion and employ tens of thousands, typically employ fewer than 1,000 investment professionals. An error in judgment at one firm tends to follow an individual as he or she seeks employment elsewhere. As a result, mistakes in the short term harm individuals' long-term careers as well as their employers. Even without judging personal standards of behavior, short-term activity that suggests even the appearance of impropriety is probably not rational. So in the short term there may be an incentive to engage in bribery or hide a problem. However, in the long term, there is risk to the firm's or individual's reputation, which would make it difficult to be effective in the business. In fact there are countless examples of individuals being forced from the business by federal prosecution of crimes. We could draw on general principles and standards in society to encourage ethical behavior by investment professionals. However, the observations here make it clear that ethical behavior by investment professionals is simply rationally optimal.

War Story   *2003 Mutual Fund Scandal*

A Theory in Practice box in Chapter 13 discussed the pricing issues involved in mutual fund market timing—the not necessarily illegal practice by some active trading investors of taking advantage of stale pricing in some funds. In late 2003 additional illegal fund trading practices were discovered based on a phone call to the office of the attorney general of the state of New York, eventually leading to billions of dollars in legal settlements, the destruction of many individual careers, and the election of Eliot Spitzer to the New York State governor's office. What began with a hedge fund called Canary Capital was later called the mutual fund scandal.

Several strategies were employed to make money trading in and out of mutual funds, two of which are illegal. The first involved trading in mutual funds after 4:00 p.m. but receiving the 4:00 closing price. Because many publicly traded companies release financial results following the market close, trading after the fact can yield a small advantage in a given day that can compound into significant returns over time. This activity is strictly forbidden by federal laws enforced by the SEC.

The second strategy was taking advantage of stale pricing in international equity or small-cap funds, as described in Chapter 13. Although this strategy is not illegal in itself, some mutual fund companies were allowing certain customers to frequently trade in funds that officially prohibited rapid trading. Passive shareholders are hurt when their own investment is diluted by the behavior of active traders capturing some of this appreciation. A special favor to facilitate frequent trading could be considered fraud if it violates statements made in fund prospectuses.

Some mutual fund companies were unaware of this activity in their own funds because shareholder transactions may be handled by outside processors, who are charged with collecting fund orders before the close and transmitting them to the firm after the close. Other firms allowed these exceptions in order to boost assets

and in turn improve profits. Some fund companies allowed certain investors to frequently trade their international funds in exchange for large balances parked in other funds. The impact on fund performance would be in single basis points, but the multiyear revenue impact to a firm from higher asset levels could be in the millions of dollars, helping salespeople meet their asset growth targets.

A third mutual fund trading strategy was virtually identical to the second, but in funds that do not prohibit rapid trading. Although legal and allowed (though not desired) for outside investors, this was done in some firms by their own employees—both senior management and portfolio managers. The thought of a fund manager taking advantage of shareholders is considered repulsive by some, and in fact several managers were either removed from their responsibilities or outright fired.

The impact of these cases has been severe. Tainted firms such as Milwaukee-based Strong and Boston-based Putnam lost tens of billions of dollars in assets, paid tens of millions of dollars in fines, and were finally sold off. Portfolio managers and senior executives lost their jobs, and some were personally fined. The entire industry felt the heat. Funds with clean records communicated with customers to remind them that their fund managers place their shareholders' interests first—fully understanding the financial impact a loss in trust can have on an investment firm. Consider a September 25, 2003, letter from First Eagle Funds: "We treat your investments as if they are our own . . . we recognize the seriousness of managing other people's money and appreciate your trust in us." In an informal survey at Boston University at a December 2003 seminar on the scandal, 67 percent of respondents had lost some trust in the mutual fund industry as a result of news reports about the scandal, and 37 percent felt "a lot" of trust had been lost, when previously all these respondents fully trusted the industry.

14.4   Ethical Situations

Clearly, submitting fictional expense reports, engaging in false advertising, and stealing computer equipment would represent serious problems for any organization. However, the investment business has situations unique to its industry that may be categorized into four groups: artificially boosting performance, giving bribes in one form or another, hiding mistakes, and passing off costs in return for favors. The discussion in this section and the following draws on cases prepared by John P. O'Reilly Jr. (2002).

Artificially Boosting Performance

There are at least two reasons to artificially boost performance. One is to increase fees. Higher returns mean higher performance fees. An improved record also makes it easier to sell the product to new investors, increasing assets and thus augmenting management fees. *Pumping a portfolio* or *marking the close* are two terms for increasing the price of an illiquid security that represents a large weight in a portfolio by placing a relatively large buy order for the security on the last day of the performance period. Of course the price will likely reverse on the following day, making this strategy useful only if a manager plans on retiring the next quarter or is happy mortgaging the future period's performance.

Hypothetically, games can be played with large trade orders for multiple accounts, allocating the final shares to benefit one account over another. In this strategy, trades are bundled for efficient management, yet final *trade allocation* is determined at the close of the day after the day's profits are known. In self-interest, high-profit trades could be allocated to accounts for which the manager seeks to increase returns, either to improve performance fees or perhaps to increase the attractiveness of a small new investment discipline. For extra juice, managers can allocate shares of IPOs in a similar fashion.

Paying Bribes and Other Questionable Sales Techniques

Some may say *bribery* is too strong a word for describing the technique of *pay-to-play,* but this sales tactic does involve a payoff. Although most public pension funds may be well managed, these schemes usually involve public plans.[1] The term refers to investment managers supporting public representatives who have influence over the pension plan or other pool of public assets, in the form of campaign contributions or other political activity, either personally or through the investment company. This public employee in turn looks favorably on the firm when assets are distributed to managers.

While not involving a kickback, some managers may cut deals with individual clients, giving them preferential treatment on fees.[2] Clearly it is the client representative's responsibility to secure a beneficial arrangement for the client organization. However, investment managers are commonly required to offer clients with equal or larger investments similar terms for similar services rendered. This is the most favored nation (MFN) clause discussed in Section 14.3, and may be included in management contracts. Because many investment management agreements are arranged privately, notifying other investors becomes the responsibility of the manager. However, there can be cases where multiple clients may have the same pension consultant or financial advisor who is aware of the fee arrangements, leading to the possibility that any unfair treatment will be discovered.

In addition to fees, some clients seek special treatment on trading. Large investors may receive financial compensation or services from brokerage houses and request their managers to generate *directed commissions* for those brokers. This creates a potential conflict of interest when the manager seeks *best execution* for their trades. The manager may agree to the arrangement to secure the business, but knows that transaction costs may be higher for a portfolio subject to trading restrictions. Moreover, because orders

---

[1] Aides to the New York State comptroller, the sole trustee of the state employee pension plan, were indicted in 2009 for pay-to-play violations.

[2] The use of side letters and MFN provisions by hedge funds was discussed in Chapter 11.

Two recent lawsuits contend that mutual fund investors pay fees that are unfairly high. Shareholders of Riversource mutual funds sued the funds' advisor, Amerprise Financial, for charging higher fees than offered to institutional investors for what the plaintiffs claimed were similar services. A second similar case, to be heard by the Supreme Court, involved Oakmark mutual funds advisor Harris Associates as the defendant.*

Mutual funds offer small investors professional management and full record keeping services on small balances. Institutional relationships reflect larger account sizes and limited record keeping services, though perhaps more individual attention. Although small account sizes may justify a higher-percentage fee, the question is how much higher. Business factors influencing fees include investment performance, profit margins, capacity, and competitor pricing; and fees must be approved by the fund board of directors. Legal issues include whether the firms and boards breached their fiduciary duty in setting differential pricing; whether the board was fully informed of differential pricing; and whether ready access to competing funds is sufficient to enforce fair pricing. This last issue—sufficiency of price competition—begs a fundamental question: If there are significant economies of scale and scope in investment management, do the mutual fund companies extract these as excess profit, or does price competition ensure that these efficiencies accrue to the shareholders? Appealing to industry pricing norms to defend a particular fund's fees presumes that those norms reflect vigorous price competition.

*Reuters (2009) provides a review of these cases.

are usually aggregated across accounts, the orders for directed commissions may be delayed until orders with full discretion are fully executed. Trading later in the same direction tends to lead to inferior execution prices. As noted by Wagner (2000), trading complex orders with less sophisticated brokers may lead to higher transaction costs. Commissions paid may be higher for these arrangements as well.

Hiding Mistakes

People make mistakes, and portfolio managers and traders are no exceptions. An order may be entered as a buy instead of a sell, the ticker may be mistyped, or an extra zero may be added to a share amount. When a mistake is made, it can cost the firm if it chooses to reimburse the client. Traders and portfolio managers may also have their bonuses clipped as a result of a mistake.

Portfolio agreements typically include investment restrictions, which frequently involve specific securities. For example, an endowment for a religious institution may wish to exclude stocks of companies in the defense industries. If the description is vague or the list is checked manually, over time there is a chance a restricted security will be purchased in error. As with a trade error, there is an incentive to hide this mistake.

Based on Murphy's law, trade errors always seem to go against the portfolio manager. The price of a mistaken buy declines before the error is caught and vice versa. It could be in the portfolio manager's self-interest to have the trader hide this error, perhaps requesting a favor from the broker (who of course would expect repayment somehow in the future).[3] Traders may be tempted to let the position ride in hopes of the price reversing, or may seek to hide their own trade errors.

[3] Several brokerage firm traders over the years have attempted to hide a modest mistake only to turn it into a career-ending loss and, in at least two cases, a firm-destroying loss (e.g., Nick Leeson).

Use of Commissions for Manager and Sponsor Benefit

Soft dollars have been around a long time in the investment business. In fact, they have been legal since the Securities and Exchange Act of 1934 provided a safe harbor for investment managers to pay commissions, in part for research services and perhaps higher than other brokers' commissions, if the services are used for the benefit of clients. Note that research services are not restricted to those provided by the particular broker. *Third-party services* include Bloomberg, private research reports, and computer systems. Greenwich Associates estimated that soft dollars exceeded $1 billion in 2003 based on survey data. An SEC study indicated in 1998 that 91 percent of equity managers utilized soft dollar arrangements.

The definitions of appropriate soft dollar research allocations and client benefits are subject to interpretation and can lead to abuse of the safe harbor. Consider travel costs to an investment conference or computer hardware, software, and data needs. There may be an incentive to trade more and pay higher commission and execution costs to increase the availability of soft dollars. Reducing hard costs leads to higher profits and potentially higher individual compensation. Of course this would impact the business through worse performance, but perhaps totaling only single basis points. It is also possible that services could benefit one client more than another. There have been unofficial reports of inappropriate uses in the past of soft dollar payments including sales training for marketing personnel, trading hardware, and back-office expenses.

Many pension plan sponsors, especially public or Taft–Hartley plans, have instituted **commission recapture** programs. These combine directed brokerage and soft dollars to encourage managers to trade with specific brokers, who in turn send a portion of the commissions back to the sponsor to pay for administrative costs. In fact many managers and custodian banks offer this as a packaged service and will provide their institutional clients with cash credits available for unrestricted use by the client. Like directed brokerage, these strategies may lead to higher commissions and worse trade execution in the pursuit of credits. The ultimate beneficiary usually loses.

14.5 Industry Guidelines for Good Business Practices

Several industry organizations and government institutions have studied conflicts of interest and best practices in the investment business. In addition to the Securities and Exchange Act of 1934, the Employee Retirement Investment Retirement Act (ERISA) of 1974 and the Investment Advisers Act (IAA) of 1940 provide U.S. federal legislation outlawing unfair and manipulative practices. The SEC enforces the SEC Act, and the Department of Labor oversees compliance with ERISA. The CFA Institute is an independent organization promoting education, certification, and best practices for investment professionals. Its members must follow a detailed list of ethical guidelines that are regularly reviewed and updated, and members are required to sign off on them annually. All these laws and guidelines may be summarized as follows:

1. They require acting
    a. Solely in the interest of beneficiaries.
    b. For the exclusive purpose of providing benefits to participants.
    c. With care, skill, prudence, and diligence.

2. They prohibit or at least require disclosure of
   a. Self-dealing.
   b. Conflicts of interest.
3. They outlaw
   a. Manipulation of securities prices.
   b. Insider trading.
   c. False or misleading statements.

The CFA Institute's guidelines include these:

1. Act with integrity . . . and in an ethical manner.
2. Practice and encourage others to practice in a professional manner.
3. Strive to maintain and improve competence.
4. Use reasonable care and exercise independent professional judgment.

The remainder of this section reviews each of the ethical issues introduced in Section 14.4 and discusses laws and guidelines designed to ensure fair treatment of clients.

Artificially Boosting Performance

Reconsider the case of artificially pumping a portfolio's value as described in Section 14.4. The client loses by paying higher fees in the short term. Because the performance boost is short-lived, the client does not benefit from the higher return. The client may also incur unnecessarily high transaction costs. Federal law clearly prohibits this activity based on ERISA and IAA regulation enforcing fair treatment of investment clients. Excessive trading for the purpose of creating an artificial price is also a securities law violation. And whenever a manager is hired based on artificially inflated performance, a fraudulent sale could be committed. Of course this behavior also violates guidelines set by the CFA Institute for acting with integrity.

Paying Bribes and Other Questionable Sales Techniques

These types of situations may arise in any business context. Clearly members of the defense industry have gotten in trouble making bribes overseas and providing gifts to government decision makers. In the investment business, one can imagine a situation where an investment advisor is asked to pay to participate in a golf tournament for the benefit of a local charity, which happens to be sponsored by the spouse of a government official who oversees management of a public pension fund. A potential conflict of interest would become apparent when the next investment mandate is put out to bid.

Many states have rules prohibiting such practices and require investment firms to explicitly disclose in detail any contributions made by the firms. Many public institutions and private companies limit gifts, including meals and entertainment, to modest amounts to avoid even the appearance of impropriety. Violating these laws and guidelines may lead to losing current business, precluding the opportunity to bid on future business, and potential civil and criminal penalties for perjury. Again, violating the spirit of the CFA Institute guidelines may damage personal and firm reputations, hurting the prospects for career growth and future business.

In the case of MFN agreements, clients expect their advisor to be proactive. If the firm charges a new client a lower fee for the same service, the firm is expected to advise the original client and adjust its billing accordingly. Client contracts require this, but there is little opportunity for verifying compliance, except for the occasional common consultant relationship or movement of personnel between investors. However, if a breach of contract is discovered, there will be a loss of credibility, potential loss of business, and if publicized, damage to the firm's reputation. Note that the "same service" is subject to interpretation in situations such as multiple accounts, first client discounts, and special guidelines, requiring judgment calls in some cases.

Directed commissions may seem harmless enough, but this can obviously become an ethical issue. Occasionally public plans will request trade allocation to a minority-owned broker–dealer as a matter of social policy. Consider a case where the trading firm may not meet a given investment manager's credit guidelines or provide best execution, but the manager wishes to retain the client account. Requiring special trade allocations places additional burdens on traders seeking best execution, perhaps compromising the trade process. In total, the dollars may represent only a few basis points of the underlying portfolio, but it is the beneficiaries' money—not the advisor's or the public sponsor's.

Hiding Mistakes

As mentioned in Section 14.4, asset management firms seek to minimize errors, but they do occur. A substantial error may significantly impact a trader's or portfolio manager's bonus. In self-interest, those making the mistakes may seek to bury them with the aid of a broker who passes off the cost to another trade. If the client is not reimbursed for a true error, the client loses. If the makeup trade is passed to another client's account, that client will lose.

Although it is tempting to avoid reporting mistakes, a manager runs the risk of the error being discovered later, leading to lost business, financial penalty, and harm to reputation. Deliberately hiding mistakes by transferring wealth from one client to another is subject to criminal prosecution, including fines and potential jail time. Insurance, with a deductible, is available to protect a firm from debilitating losses.

Use of Commissions for Manager and Sponsor Benefit

Section 28(d) of the 1934 Securities and Exchange Act provides safe harbor for an investment manager who directs and uses a portion of client account commission dollars to pay for research and services. Without the safe harbor, this would clearly be a breach of fiduciary duty. Note that the law expressly states the money must be used to benefit the client's portfolio. Some perceive this practice as subject to abuse even with regulatory oversight. For example, a compliance system supports a client, but does it truly support the investment process? Would the manager be comfortable sharing this business policy with clients? As a result of this potential conflict of interest, there is a current trend to require disclosure of the use of soft dollars and, in fact, to eliminate their use.

Clients may request commission recapture, and many feel that brokerage is an asset of the client; but ERISA makes it clear that pension assets are to be managed solely in the interest of beneficiaries. Accepting higher commissions to generate revenue for the sponsor, or interfering with trade execution, is clearly not in the interest of the plan beneficiaries. The dollars may represent only a few basis points of the underlying portfolio, but this is the beneficiaries' money. This is a widespread and growing practice, yet ERISA guidelines require sponsors to ensure that best total execution prices, including commission costs, are achieved for the beneficiaries.

14.6 Internal Company Policies to Protect the Franchise

General Policy Discussion

Consider the case of a successful investment firm that has grown its business by building a reputation of strong performance and trustworthiness. Further consider that the clients' observations are accurate, reflecting a business culture that truly places the interests of its investors first. How do you protect this franchise from damage by mistakes and lapses in judgment? The key components of an effective ethics program include the following:

1. *Leadership:* Employees follow their boss. The firm's president or CIO sets the standards of conduct. If a boss cuts corners, the employees will see that behavior as acceptable and act accordingly. At both Putnam and Strong, leadership was lacking in setting policy, enforcement of existing policy, or setting a good example. In the case of Strong, reports indicate the owner was actively trading his own firm's funds to make money off his own unsuspecting customers. But these personal trading profits were trivial compared to the losses incurred in fines and damage to the company.

2. *Education:* In many cases employees need to be taught what behavior is unacceptable. The investment business can be complicated with many subtleties. For example, if a new portfolio manager has not experienced a trade error before, she or he may not know the correct course of action (the right action is to immediately reverse the trade and inform the boss).

3. *Oversight:* Investment actions must be monitored and compared with acceptable procedures. Expert computer systems may be developed to catch many trade errors before they happen. For other activity, review procedures, staffing, and committees may be necessary. Clients should be informed of policies and enforcement procedures.

4. *Enforcement:* Once a breach has been discovered, an investigation must be conducted and appropriate consequences imposed. For example, any profits from a personal trading violation must be disgorged. Clients must be made whole. Repeat violations should lead to dismissal. Employees should feel they are treated fairly, and consistent application of policy is a key part of that.

Policies in an investment firm should be carefully laid out and taught to employees. Clear policies, effective education, and efficient monitoring will all reduce the frequency of errors and their financial and reputational impact on the firm.

Specific Policy Discussion

Investment professionals are not usually looking for opportunities to rob their clients. Most errors in judgment are simply honest mistakes. However, it is important to have procedures in place to prevent or catch these errors before they become serious problems, as well as reduce the chance of occurrence. For example, a formal training program, complete with a manual detailing procedures, should be provided to new employees; common sense can go a long way but cannot be relied on exclusively, especially as the firm's size and business complexity grow. Consider the following business ethics policies common to investment management firms. A full list of potential policies is provided in the chapter appendix.

1. *Sales policy:* Salespeople are paid the commissions they have earned on their sales. Individual investment salespeople typically have a list of prospects, defined

by size, type, or geographic region. They meet with prospects, telling them about their firm's products, and facilitate the sales process. In general, they are working for the benefit of their firm; however, self-interest may motivate them to minimize the importance and visibility of potential conflicts between the firm's and the prospective client's needs. To limit problems, including misunderstandings, inappropriate behavior, and the number of poor business opportunities, effective management prepares good business guidelines, checklists, and even new business review committees. Standard fee arrangements, minimum account sizes, and acceptable client type can all be articulated on paper, with an expiration date. Salespeople may be empowered to accept standard business opportunities, but anything out of the ordinary would go through the committee for review or approval of the level of resource support requirements, appropriateness of fee arrangements, and the reputation of the prospective client. The committee can also help manage independently minded salespeople and investigate sourcing of unusual prospects. The company president should be a member of this committee. These procedures will help reduce the frequency of poor practice or acceptance of poor business relationships.

2. *Trade policy:* Trade orders move from the portfolio manager to the trading room, either directly between the PM and trader or their assistants. Orders may be communicated verbally, in written form, or electronically. Small investment firms may rely on verbal communication between the portfolio manager and trader, but many large firms have automated the process, eliminating the chance for miscommunication. Of course keypunch errors can be made by the PM, or transcript errors can occur if the trader breaks the trade up by hand before transmitting to brokers. Expert systems can be developed that check for reasonableness before an order can be transmitted. For example, a computer system can check the size of sell orders against current portfolio holdings and buy orders against restricted securities lists. To give the PM a chance to review the trade, a "review and confirm" step can be added either before the order is sent to the trader or after the trader converts the PM order to a trade order ready to be sent to a broker—and again for the trader as the order is communicated to the broker.[4] Policy should outline steps to follow when an error is discovered. If PMs review their trade lists the following morning, they should catch most errors. Any erroneous trade should be reversed immediately. Business management should be alerted, and the client should be reimbursed for any negative performance impact. A trade allocation process should also be defined. Allocations should be set before execution, not after. In fact it is important to define an allocation algorithm based on order size or assets. This algorithm will be complicated if it reflects subtleties such as short positions and limits manager gaming strategies. Because it may be in the PM's and trader's interests to hide errors, all transactions should be monitored over several days for reversals, which in turn should be investigated. Firms should have an individual or team assigned to these reviews, reporting to senior management. It may be possible to include in management contracts a clause stating that the investment firm will make best efforts to avoid trade errors, such as restriction violations, but will not be liable for them.

3. *Risk management policy:* As reviewed in Chapter 7, investment management contracts frequently specify diversification, tracking error, or cash level guidelines.

---

[4] Note that there is a cost to this: professionals' valuable time and execution efficiency.

Clients may endure a spell of disappointing performance, but they will not hesitate to terminate a manager with poor performance who also violates management guidelines. Fund companies need to avoid violating prospectus requirements. It may be in the self-interest of a PM to ramp up the risk of a portfolio toward the end of the year if performance has been subpar, with the hopes of a reversal. Or a PM might raise cash if she or he is bearish on the markets despite investment objectives to the contrary. To ensure adherence to guidelines, a monitoring process must be put in place. Portfolio holdings must be collected regularly and evaluated. Violations must be communicated to the PM and, if they persist, to senior management.[5]

4. *Personal trading policy:* In light of the mutual fund scandal of 2003, even the appearance of inappropriate behavior can become a public relations issue. In the 1980s many analysts and portfolio managers were allowed, or even encouraged, to trade in their personal accounts as a way to improve their investing skills. However, there can be a personal incentive to first trade for the PM's own account before trading for the client's portfolio, and clients may be sensitive to this potential conflict of interest. Policies that restrict personal trading within a multiday window of portfolio trading, and involve monitoring of all trading by employees and their family members to enforce this restriction, have become common. As time goes on, it becomes more difficult for PMs to trade their personal accounts. This may result in unanticipated consequences; for example, to some extent these systems may encourage investment professionals to preserve ideas for themselves and exclude them from their funds.[6]

5. *Gifts and entertainment policy:* Both entertainment of prospective clients by salespeople and gifts to traders from brokers may lead to the appearance of conflicts of interest. Company policy setting limits and requiring reporting of gifts and entertainment will help manage this risk. Of course its success will depend on effective monitoring, which has limits. And compliance procedures can become cumbersome for employees. Leadership by example is important for setting standards of behavior for employees. So is enforcement, including penalties for violation.

Large financial firms that have investment banking, brokerage, and custody operations, as well as an investment management arm, need to institute even more policies than the basic few just described. For example, investment bankers and investment firm employees need to be separated to avoid sharing inside information about mergers and other corporate activity. If such information is shared, trading policies must be in place to prevent insider trading, which is a criminal offense. Teams responsible for custody of assets must be separate from the group in charge of managing the assets. Trading with the company's brokerage arm also needs to be managed, if it is permitted at all. Documentation verifying equal or better execution needs to be generated and monitored. Reporting lines (including responsibilities for compensation) should be carefully defined, making sure the compliance monitoring team reports to someone higher in the management structure than the head of the group they are responsible for overseeing.

[5] One example of a risk management procedure, recommended by the FDIC, requires bank officers to take two full weeks away from their jobs in hopes of identifying any cases of embezzlement.
[6] Many hedge fund investors want to see a significant amount of the PM's wealth invested in the fund—enough to align the interests of the PM with investors but not so much that the PM treats the portfolio as a personal account to the detriment of investors.

In 1991 Warren Buffett* assumed the interim chairmanship of Salomon Brothers. The assignment was intended to restore confidence in the firm following the unfolding of a scandal involving Salomon traders entering false bids in Treasury auctions. At this time Buffett spoke about the characteristics he sought when hiring managers to run his company's businesses. They included intelligence (no need for brilliance, just basic smarts), energy (the drive to work hard), and honesty. He said having the first two without the third led to trouble.

What is acceptable in business practice is set by industry norms—but also by the man or woman in charge of the individual business. Employees look to their leader to decide how aggressively and evenhandedly they should act.

Buffett is not alone in setting high standards. Consider Lyle Davis, former chief investment officer of what is now called State Street Global Advisors. Davis was known to motivate his employees by expressing full confidence in their ability to meet very high standards of performance. Another example is John Cook, former president of Fidelity Management Trust Company, who would demand excellence of his investment team, yet exceeded their expectations for recognition when they were doing an outstanding job. Giving investment professionals the necessary resources, insulating them from distractions, and offering them transparent financial incentives go a long way toward strong investment performance and powerful business results.

* Mr. Buffett's firm was the largest shareholder at the time.

14.7   Effective Manager and Analyst Compensation Policies

Portfolio Manager Compensation

Portfolio management objectives are well defined. It is also well understood what drives asset growth and firm profits. Fortunately portfolio manager, firm, and client objectives are closely aligned. As discussed in Section 14.3, performance versus indexes or peers over multiple periods, for extended periods, determines asset levels and in turn management fees. As discussed in Section 14.6, portfolio managers help protect the firm's asset base by keeping clients happy through following the agreed-upon investment process, adhering to client guidelines, and avoiding appearances of impropriety. Portfolio managers can also contribute to the firm by supporting the sales and client service process, mentoring analysts, and sharing ideas with other portfolio managers. Each of these items may be transformed into a formulaic compensation system, as summarized in Exhibit 14.4.[7]

Exhibit 14.4 suggests that salary level and bonus range depend on how big a job the manager has, and how long she or he has been doing it. Managers who run a lot of money versus others in the industry should be paid for a tougher job than their peers within and outside their firm. Large assets and lucrative fees increase the importance of fund managers to the firm and should be reflected in their base compensation, bonus potential, and perhaps company ownership. The bonus payout should be a function of the level and consistency of outperformance versus benchmark indexes and other managers in the industry. This structure is aligned with determinants of asset growth for the firm. The dollar size of bonuses will be determined by the dollar assets under management,

---

[7] Compensation systems may be reflected in dollars or as a proportion of the overall available dollars, such as a bonus pool. In all cases, the formulas are subject to change due to changing market conditions.

EXHIBIT 14.4
Portfolio Manager Compensation Components

1. Salary level and bonus range (multiple of salary) depend on
   a. Assets under management and mandate.
   b. Fee structure.
   c. Tenure and track record.
2. Bonus level (0–100%) depends on
   a. Performance versus benchmark:
      i. One-, three-, and five-year periods.
      ii. Index outperformance.
      iii. Peer ranking.
      iv. Risk parameters.
   b. Nonfund:
      i. Input from other fund managers and head of research.
      ii. Input from sales and client service.
      iii. Number of existing and new accounts.
      iv. Asset growth.
      v. Strategy R&D.
3. Profit sharing and/or equity ownership potentially include
   a. Voting shares.
   b. Phantom ownership.
   c. Bonus pools based on multiyear company performance targets.

the difficulty of running that particular level, and the dollar fees (or profit) generated. To reward a manager for sticking to risk guidelines, a portion of the bonus payout should be tied to risk measurement. For example, 10–25 percent of the payout could be determined by meeting tracking error or beta targets generated over one-, three-, and five-year periods. Including a provision for real-time measurement discourages the tendency to take short-term, high-risk bets at the end of a measurement period.

It is tempting to say that nonfund factors are subjective, but that is not necessarily true. Asset growth, number of meetings, and formal internal peer rankings can all be tracked. A manager's level of adherence to policy should also impact this number, but serious violations should be an overriding factor in any bonus. Specific goals for strategy development can be defined and measured.

The investment business is highly competitive, and talented investment professionals are in high demand. Before finalizing a firm's compensation structure, it is important to survey (perhaps with the help of a consultant) compensation ranges for portfolio managers in the industry. Portfolio managers are always at risk of losing their jobs and earn high compensation partly in return for accepting that risk. Although clients like to talk about "market cycles" with three- to five-year horizons, managers can be fired after two consecutive bad years. Hedge funds can lose their business after only six bad months. Investment reputations built over decades, and leading to high expectations, can be tarnished following a short period of poor performance. The investment business provides professionals with a career trade-off: Much like ballplayers, PMs are rewarded primarily for what they've done lately, yet they also may have many times at bat.

Analyst Compensation

Quantitative, technical, and fundamental analysts develop ideas and share them with portfolio managers. Their job is to identify good investment ideas and convince managers to get the best ones into their portfolios. If the raw performance

EXHIBIT 14.5

Analyst
Compensation
Components

1. Salary level and bonus range (multiple of salary) depend on
   a. Assets under management and revenue generated in research assignment.
   b. Experience and track record.
2. Bonus level depends on
   a. Performance versus benchmarks:
      i. One-year periods.
      ii. Active performance of coverage "on paper."
      iii. Contribution to outperformance of coverage in firm portfolios.
      iv. Diversification impact of ideas.
   b. Nonfund:
      i. Input from fund managers
      ii. Input from head of research.
3. Profit sharing and/or equity ownership opportunities.

of their ideas is good, and this positively impacts fund performance, the analysts are doing their jobs and should be well compensated. These factors are listed in Exhibit 14.5.

A larger investment universe has potentially greater impact on investment performance and firm profits. Salary and bonus ranges should be tied to those factors. Greater experience may be related to higher probabilities of adding value, and tenure and track record are closely related to the market value of the analyst in the industry. Note that analysts in higher-volatility sectors (technology, specialty retail, and energy services) tend to be in higher demand by hedge funds and will command higher compensation levels on the market.

Analysts tend to have shorter time horizons than fund managers. They typically have less experience in the business and are frequently looking at 12-month stock price targets or shorter-volatility trades. The value of an analyst should be measured in at least two ways. First, by collecting and calculating the performance of their buy, sell, and hold recommendations, management can compute the raw material of their ideas. For example, for equity analysts, buys should outperform, sells underperform, and holds be in line with index returns for their sector, with sector volatility taken into account for evaluating statistical significance. Note that these statistical calculations must be done carefully; for example, daily rebalancing of stock recommendations to equal weights leads to a significant upward bias, so monthly portfolios should be built and evaluated instead. See Stewart (1984) and Stewart (1987) for a discussion of these issues. All of these measures may be used for hiring and firing decisions as well as compensation.

Second, by calculating the performance of the live portfolios, the value added from individual analysts can be identified. This confirms whether analysts have been successful selling their ideas to the portfolio managers. For example, active performance of sector-based subsets of a portfolio, relative to sector indexes, compared with the raw material active returns, will confirm whether there is effective implementation of an analyst's ideas. Finally, as illustrated in Stewart (1998), consistency in performance is impacted by the diversification of active investment bets. The more diversifying analysts' investment ideas are, the better it is for the firm. Three good independent stock ideas can be more valuable than a single industry call. To reward analysts for unique ideas, performance correlations can be computed and included in analyst bonus calculations.

Other Investment Professional Compensation

Senior management is typically compensated for meeting business targets, such as overall performance, asset growth, and profitability goals. Their time frame may run from one to three years, and their employment will be extended if they continue to meet these targets. In some cases senior managers are given less than two years to turn things around and will be terminated if they fail. If the firm offers products with different fee schedules, it is important to structure rewards for growth in dollar management fees, not simply assets.

Salespeople are charged with bringing in money that sticks. They are paid largely in commission as a percentage of the first-year revenue of an account, with a smaller *trailer* or portion of ongoing fees for a number of years. Some commission rates depend on the profitability of the business. Trailer formulas reflect the salesperson's ongoing client service role. Because multiple accounts with the same client are highly profitable, incentives may be created to pay a salesperson for capturing second and third accounts within the same relationship.

Summary

"Commerce without morality," as observed by Gandhi, eventually leads to violence. People feel strongly about their money—but fortunately the professional investment business is not considered immoral, at least in most people's view. Perhaps the golden rule is the best guideline, with investment managers treating their clients as they wish to be treated.

Ethics "may be defined as acting in accordance with accepted principles of right and wrong," as stated by O'Reilly (2002). His view is that the guiding principles for investment professionals are determined by the mores of a business that manages other people's money. Ethical conduct is the foundation of any business relationship: Clients transact with the firms they consider capable and trustworthy. Clients should ask specific questions and request representations regarding ethical conduct and practices before awarding accounts. Failure to observe ethical practices will cost a firm both opportunities and existing business. Lapses in judgment may result in legal and dollar liability to the firm and the individual responsible. What is the key ground rule? *Put your client's interest before your own.*

Does the investment business need ethical guidelines and regulations? As mentioned earlier, even if people have good intentions, they need to be educated about what is acceptable and what a company's policies are. Kenneth Safian, president of Safian Investment Research and an investment analyst for over 40 years, states, "Historic human behavior shows that we do need limits and laws." His wish is for young people in business to strive "to be idealistic even though it may not be pragmatic." One of his views on the financial markets is that portfolio managers should be "more conservatively invested when ethics are low, excesses are high," especially if investors do not seem concerned about these conditions.

One large investment organization that is especially concerned with developing a positive corporate culture maintains a formal list of 10 key factors for evaluating employee performance, listed in order of importance. The list was prepared using input from internal managers as well as a human resources consulting firm. The top three items include the ability to effectively use insightful judgment, inspire trust, and focus on the customer.

Success in the investment business requires ethical behavior. The investment business is a small community and can be unforgiving to any individual or firm that forgets this. The key factor in protecting a reputation is the personal standards of the individual. Other important factors include regulatory standards and a corporate culture promoting fiduciary responsibility, education, and enforcement.

Problems

1. Consider the 2003 mutual fund scandal in which sales, investment, and senior management of several firms took advantage of their clients' trust and stole value from those clients.

   a. Research one specific company in the scandal.

   b. List specific breaches of fiduciary duty in that case.

   c. Propose policies, including education, monitoring, and enforcement, to virtually eliminate the chance of this occurring in the future. Discuss the cost of implementing these policies.

2. Consider the case of a trader who places a 10,000 buy order for IBM:[8] Later she discovers the order should have been a sell. She calls back the broker to tell him she now needs to sell 20,000 shares. The price is down, and she'll lose money on the mistake. The broker offers to take the original 10,000 shares on his book, eating the loss for the trader, which helps the trader's year-end bonus. Discuss the following:

   a. What system would lead to the discovery of this error?

   b. How should the client be treated?

   c. Who loses if this is not detected?

   d. Describe a system with proper checks and balances to enforce fair treatment of clients.

3. Trade orders for multiple accounts need to be executed in the trading room. Execution may be better managed if all orders are consolidated. If all trades are completed, it is fair for all orders to receive the average price. However, many times the orders are larger than can be executed in a given day.

   a. Propose an allocation system that fairly allocates the proportion executed.

   b. Explain how this system should be implemented. Discuss what should be reported to clients.

4. Consider the case of a bond manager, responsible for a one-year maturity, lower-quality portfolio. The issues do not trade actively, and the portfolio must be priced by calling the brokers who make markets in the issues. The brokers are busy and do not make money by providing quotes.

   a. The brokers respond to portfolio manager requests (not portfolio manager assistants), so the manager is charged with collecting pricing information. Is there a potential conflict of interest with this procedure?

   b. The portfolio manager is going on vacation the last week of December, so he plans to collect bond prices the week before. Is there a problem with this plan?

   c. Propose an effective procedure for pricing this portfolio.

5. Consider the case of a newly promoted portfolio manager. He places a buy order but later discovers the shares were incorrect. After discussing this problem with the trader, who suggests they wait to see if the price reverses, he keeps the information to himself, hoping the market moves in his direction.

   a. Describe a preferable sequence of actions.

   b. Propose an education program for new portfolio managers.

6. Design a compensation program for a hedge fund portfolio manager. Consider a $1 billion firm with a $100 million portfolio. The portfolio is 100 percent small-cap

[8] Example from O'Reilly (2002).

U.S. equity with an expected gross excess performance of 7 percent. The base fee is 1 percent with 20 percent sharing. The total risk is not expected to exceed a 10 percent annualized standard deviation based on monthly returns. The client base is relatively new and includes a fund of funds.

a. List a framework for salary and bonus compensation. Include percentage levels for each component as well as relevant time frames.

b. Explore the impact of fund longevity. Explain how compensation would be structured for a start-up fund versus one that had been in existence for three years.

Appendix

Sample List of Investment Policies

1.1 Code of ethics
1.2 Insider trading policy
1.3 Personal securities trading policy
1.4 Information barrier
1.5 Conflicts of interest
1.6 Gifts and entertainment
1.7 Privacy: protection of client records and information
1.8 Investment guidelines
1.10 Restricted securities
1.13 Broker selection: best execution, directed brokerage, soft dollar arrangements
1.15 Broker approvals
1.18 Trade allocation
1.19 Transactions with affiliated brokers (principal trades, agency trades)
1.23 Interaccount transfers
1.24 Investments in affiliated investment companies
1.25 Errors and corrections
1.26 Investment company requirements
1.27 Marketing materials and communication with media
1.29 Books and records
1.30 Form ADV
1.31 Custody
1.32 Pricing
1.35 Proxy policy
1.37 Business continuity
1.38 Customer complaints
1.39 Large order notification
1.40 Research analyst conflicts of interest

Chapter 15

Investor and Client Behavior

Chapter Outline

15.1 Introduction

15.2 Theory and Observations of Human Behavior

15.3 Implications for Active Management

15.4 Implications for Setting Investment Policy

15.5 Implications for Manager Selection

15.1 Introduction

As a fiduciary, an investment manager is required to do what is best for her or his client.[1] To address clients' needs effectively, the investment advisor must understand not only clients' cash flow requirements but also their motivations and preferences. The theory and models reviewed in earlier chapters reflect specific client motivations and preferences. However, empirical and anecdotal observations of investor behavior suggest that these assumptions can be incomplete; for example, individuals often appear to consider factors beyond risk and return when making decisions. The result is investor behavior that is sometimes at odds with theory. It is not that people are irrational or are not interested in maximizing wealth. Rather, it appears that the decision-making techniques that work well as survival tools in the natural world do not necessarily translate into success in the financial world, and common investor behavior can frequently lead to poor outcomes. An understanding of these differences will help advisors alert clients to potential errors in judgment, even though the mistakes may appear to make sense, may be the conventional wisdom, or may even be considered standard industry practice. Investor behavior is also important to understand as a potential source of opportunities for active management, creating potential openings for skillful investors seeking to sell at high valuations or buy on the cheap.

Section 15.2 introduces alternative models of individual investment behavior and summarizes a few observations of investor decision making, including a discussion

---

[1] In contrast, "advisors" who are actually brokers rather than registered investment advisors are held to a lower "suitability" standard that allows them to put their employer's interests ahead of their client's interests.

of normative and normal behavior.[2] *Normative* behavior is consistent with theories of rational behavior such as wealth maximization. *Normal* behavior refers to how people seem to make decisions in the real world. In particular, people use *heuristics*—simple rules that are handy for making decisions quickly and with limited information. Unfortunately these rules can lead to mistakes when applied to portfolio management. Many theories from both psychology and sociology have been applied to finance. We review these concepts and also review some empirical studies of the behavior of experienced individual and professional investors.

Sections 15.3 and 15.4 discuss the practical implications of investor and client behavior. Understanding basic tendencies and common nonnormative behavior of prospective clients will help a financial advisor anticipate problems and craft effective communications to successfully guide clients through complicated decisions. Helping keep a client focused on the big picture and from overreacting to short-term events will go a long way toward generating investment results that meet cash flow needs. Certain investor behaviors can also lead to short-term (or longer-term) price anomalies in the marketplace, providing opportunities for active managers.

General guidelines for selecting investment managers are provided in Section 15.5. Mutual funds are ranked by fund analysts largely based on performance versus peers. The institutional marketplace includes sophisticated investors who choose managers largely based on consistent performance versus custom benchmarks. The record is not good for either group, requiring alternative methods for effective manager selection.

15.2 Theory and Observations of Human Behavior

Humans have been an extremely successful species. This is partly due to their physical abilities to stand erect, manipulate objects, and speak. In addition, humans have developed strong survival behaviors that allow them to react quickly using limited information. One such behavior is a **fight or flight** response to stressful situations such as physical danger or the loss of wealth. Investors and clients often become angry and take action, such as taking greater risk or firing their investment advisor, when threatened with a significant decrease in asset prices or underperformance of an investment account.

Another key reason for human success is our ability to adapt and learn quickly. People are adept at and prone to seeing patterns even where they do not exist. This can lead to unrealistic *extrapolation* of short-term trends. Consider prehistoric families on their way to the watering hole. Suddenly a saber-toothed tiger snatches and eats one of the children. The survivors extrapolate that single event into a trend and expect to be eaten themselves if they return. To escape the "loss" of being eaten themselves, they learn to avoid that particular watering hole in the future. Importantly, there is little cost to drawing the wrong conclusion in this case (if another source of water is nearby). Not much is lost if the tiger is not at the watering hole the next day, but the cost is potentially terminal if it is. The modern finance equivalent of trend extrapolation is performance chasing, such as buying stocks that have gone up and selling those that have gone down. This approach may seem perfectly reasonable. The problem is that this behavior may be misplaced in the investment arena because there is a cost to being wrong. Panicking in a liquidity crisis and chasing past performance will

---

[2] Denoting this behavior as normal avoids using the term *irrational,* which seems to imply investors do not seek to maximize wealth or learn correctly from the information at hand.

probably result in below-average returns. Moreover, there is a tendency for people to see patterns in a random sequence, perhaps short-term patterns, and perceive them as trends. As an example, consider a streak of heads when flipping a coin. Clearly coin flipping is a random event, but a sequence of four heads or tails, which is not uncommon, suggests the appearance of a trend.

There are many other common behaviors of which we need to be mindful when investing. These include the tendencies to focus on historical costs, single securities instead of a diversified portfolio, and fees instead of net returns. *Overconfidence, crowd behavior,* and *menu effects* are others. This section introduces a few of these behavioral tendencies and discusses their impact on investment policy, active portfolio strategy, and manager selection. This discussion is introduced with definitions of the basic psychological behaviors and concepts observed in the marketplace.

Normative Behavior

The theory of portfolio management developed in earlier chapters is built on assumptions of how people make decisions. These assumptions provide a model of normative behavior or how people *should* invest. The normative model assumes that people maximize expected utility over total wealth and revise their expectations correctly when given new information.[3] The utility function is designed to capture the preferences of a wealth-maximizing investor. This investor is *rational* in the sense of preferring more to less, experiencing marginally less satisfaction from each marginal increase in wealth, and using information correctly. In a world of uncertainty, these assumptions lead to the investor being risk-averse because a loss has a larger impact on utility than a gain of equal magnitude. The level of risk aversion may be customized to fit the individual and added to the optimization routine, providing customized optimal mixes of risky assets. This model is an effective tool for helping set appropriate investment policy.

However, some limitations exist with this model. The economic world introduced in Chapter 3 requires constant, defined risks and assumes participants know this world. On average, investors' expectations are assumed to be rewarded with the appropriate outcomes, defined as **rational expectations.** Either a (log)normal return distribution or an investor who cares about only return mean and standard deviation are also assumed. A regime of **uncertainty,** where participants are aware they do not know the odds of future events, is inconsistent with this world. How different the two worlds are is a matter of argument. As noted in Chapter 7, tail events occur more often than suggested by a normal distribution. It was also noted (in Chapter 10) that correlations between risky assets change through time, dramatically increasing in times of economic stress. Extending the single-period model presented in Chapter 3 to recognize changing preferences and expectations results in highly complex and even unsolvable problems, as discussed in Chapter 5.

Despite these concerns, the basic framework is powerful and flexible. Enhancements were made in Chapters 3, 5, 7, and 11. For example, in Chapter 3, downside probability was utilized as a key measure of risk. Although it does not follow directly

---

[3] This also assumes that people have enough information about the world to interpret new information correctly. An alternative view is that people process information correctly but do not have enough information about the world to necessarily interpret it correctly. This is the idea of *bounded rationality.* Yet another view is the *rational beliefs framework* of Mordecai Kurz (1994). The idea is that people's beliefs or expectations are rational in the sense that they are consistent with all available information or data, but because the world is nonstationary, people can never fully learn the true "model." Thus they can be systematically wrong at times and still rational. This does not require rationality to be bounded.

from the utility function theory, it lets the user assign a personal level of importance to that risk. Fatter tails and alternative probability distributions, utilized through Monte Carlo simulations, may also be applied to extend the mean–variance model and give the investor a better understanding of the potential impact of decisions. However, prophetic intuition about true probability distributions (no easy thing) needs to apply for any model to be perfectly effective. In other words, the world needs to fit the financial modeler's view to avoid surprises in the future.

It is one thing to apply these tools to develop an appropriate investment program; it is another thing to get a client to agree to the advice. Clients differ in sophistication, so they need to be individually educated as well as guided. To maintain the relationship and avoid being fired, expectations need to be managed. The challenge for investment professionals is to develop products that are easy to use, meet the clients' investment goals, and help keep them on track. To educate clients and maintain their trust, it is helpful to begin with a discussion of commonly observed investor behavior, or even more basic human behavior.

Normal Behavior

A general review of human psychology is beyond the scope of this chapter. However, we can identify two key traits that motivate a discussion of the behavior of investors: loss aversion and the tendency to see patterns. These traits explain many behaviors beyond the desire to simply maximize long-term wealth and provide a backdrop for many concepts of **behavioral finance.** These concepts are summarized in Exhibit 15.1.

Loss aversion is best summarized by Boston Celtics great Larry Bird, who said, "Losing hurts more than winning feels good." It is easy to see why loss aversion would develop as a survival technique. When decisions have all-or-nothing outcomes (like surviving or not surviving) it makes sense to avoid downside risk. In finance this translates into an emotional cost—a loss of pride or feelings of regret—in addition to the wealth cost of realizing a loss. Avoiding what feels like a loss appears to be deeply ingrained human behavior.

EXHIBIT 15.1
List of Behavioral Finance Terms

Basic Behaviors from Psychology and Their Application to Investments	
Psychology	**Investments**
Loss aversion	Prospect theory
Pattern recognition	Extrapolation of trends

Common Concepts from Behavioral Finance

Framing
Mental accounting
Anchoring

Evaluation
Representativeness
Crowd effects
Menu problem

Learning
Overconfidence
Illusion of control
Illusion of skill/knowledge
Hindsight bias

One manifestation of loss aversion is the fight-or-flight response to stress. Coined in 1915 by Walter Cannon, *fight or flight* refers to how animals evaluate and react to a threat. In modern humans, stressful situations lead people to become angry or withdrawn.[4] A sharp drop in value of an investor's retirement portfolio is stressful. Investors are frustrated that what they had before is now worth less. They also begin to worry that they may not have enough for their savings goals, such as falling short of what they need to live on in retirement or not achieving a planned retirement date. They would like to avoid this feeling of regret. The initial response is often *inaction,* which may be encouraged by the feeling that mistakes of commission are felt more painfully than mistakes of omission. That is, people would rather regret they did not act than regret that they did.

A great illustration comes from American football. Why do football coaches always seem to punt on fourth down even when it would seem they may be better off trying for a first down? Although punting is not a sure thing, the regret of a potential first down not attempted may be overwhelmed by the regret of a failed attempt.[5] There is also the aspect of the armchair quarterbacking of fans, broadcasters, and sportswriters (the very ones who might have applauded the attempt until it failed). In investments, this loss aversion expresses itself as a tendency to hold losing positions to avoid realizing the loss, and to sell profitable positions that represent gains. Numerous studies, including Shefrin and Statman (1985), have shown that holding losing positions hurts portfolio performance.

As noted, people are prone to seeing patterns even where they may not exist. One result is that investors may extrapolate a short-term trend too far and try to capture a perceived future direction of the market even when the market action is random. Worrying about a continued decline is understandable, but there is a problem if investors fail to assess the risk objectively and overreact simply to make themselves feel as though they are in control. For example, they may become uncomfortable and want to sell all their risky investments and switch to cash. They may do this at the wrong time, such as when asset prices are too low.

The tendency to avoid risk following a bad market experience is another form of trend extrapolation. Trend following exists in most market cycles and is consistent with performance chasing of securities, asset classes, and individual managers, which is observed in both individual and professional investors. Investors find comfort in trends (extrapolation) but become unhappy when the trend inevitably reverses (loss aversion).

Consider the late 1980s, when many investors sold out of equities following the 1987 crash. This preceded the development in the early 1990s of lifestyle mutual funds for 401(k) investors, composed of multiple asset classes that smoothed out the pattern of reported asset values on investor quarterly statements. Blending the asset classes helped hide the risk of individual asset classes, and extreme trends were dampened. As a result, less sophisticated individual investors in these funds tended to be spooked less and to stay the course longer.

---

[4] Interestingly, scientific evidence suggests that men and women react differently to stress, which is consistent with the observation in finance that men and women invest differently.

[5] Zeus, a computer "coach" developed by End Game Technologies, models and predicts the impact of the plays selected on the expected outcomes of football games. In particular, the program tends to be more aggressive in attempting first down conversions because statistically the expected benefit of a first down can be greater than a safer play such as a punt. According to Zeus, excess risk aversion, such as choosing the safe play, is a shortcoming of human coaches. Romer (2006) reaches a similar conclusion—that NFL teams' conservative decisions on fourth downs do not maximize expected payoffs.

Behavioral Finance

Behavioral finance argues that individuals use cognitive rules of thumb called *heuristics* to simplify decision making. Although heuristics often produce reasonable decisions, in many situations they lead to large, systematic errors. Decision making may be viewed as having two parts: a *framing* phase, in which the problem is put into a particular perspective, and a phase of *evaluation* and choice. Humans then learn from their experience for making future decisions.

Framing

Framing denotes the effects of how a question is asked on how the question is answered. In the normative model, framing does not matter; individuals are assumed to answer a question the same way regardless of how information is presented to them. In practice, however, it appears that people use heuristics to make it easier and faster to organize information, with the result that how information is presented seems to matter. Framing is not the failure of individuals to see hidden information or to perceive complex information, or even a lack of intelligence; it is simply the tendency to react differently to what are perceived to be different situations. A clear example of framing effects is illustrated by a study that asked doctors whether they would prefer surgery or radiation if they themselves were to become cancer patients. When informed that surgery killed 10 percent of patients, 50 percent preferred radiation therapy. When informed that 90 percent would survive surgery, only 16 percent preferred radiation therapy.[6]

Two key heuristics in framing investment decisions are *mental accounting* and *anchoring*. **Mental accounting** is the phenomenon of allocating payoffs to different accounts even when the payoffs are highly fungible. Money seems especially susceptible to this framing effect. One form of mental accounting is called the *house money effect*. This term arises from the observation that some gamblers place their winnings in one pocket, or account, and the money they brought with them in another pocket, or second account. When playing from their winnings they are less risk-averse despite the fact that the money is in their pockets and should be considered part of their total wealth. After all, they can easily move the money between their pockets. This is a violation of risk aversion. Other examples include owning separate portfolios with different objectives (such as holding a low-interest savings account while paying a higher interest rate on credit card debt) or spending only dividends but not capital gains. In many cases, mental accounting is useful. The segmented portfolios are a form of precommitment that imposes self-control and encourages saving by matching costs to benefits, thus avoiding debt. However, this behavior may lead to mistakes in managing diversification.

Anchoring refers to the influence of particular values on how a question is framed. The *sunk cost fallacy*—the idea that purchase prices should be ignored (except for tax implications) but frequently are not—is an example of this behavior. Anchoring arises from the tendency to evaluate problems from a reference point. The purchase price of a stock can be an anchor for the question of whether to hold or sell at a loss. This behavior may result in an investor holding onto a security longer than is warranted, potentially leading to mistakes in managing diversification or maximizing performance.

Evaluation

The normative model of choice assumes that people seek to maximize total wealth over some horizon. However, in practice, people tend to focus on interim changes in wealth and incorporate emotional aspects into investment decisions. Examples of

---

[6] Bornrstein and Elmer (2001) review the literature on the decision-making biases of doctors.

these descriptive evaluation methods include *representativeness,* the *crowd effect,* and the *menu effect.*

Representativeness refers to evaluation by stereotype. Representativeness provides a way to form expectations using limited information. It is easier and faster to compare a problem to a set of predetermined templates created from previously perceived patterns than it is to evaluate each situation from a fresh perspective. As noted, the key problem is that humans quickly detect and interpret patterns even where they do not exist. One reason is survival. Seeing a pattern where none exists is not likely to be harmful in nature, whereas not seeing a pattern when there is one can have dire consequences. In addition, there are patterns to detect in nature, so extrapolation (quickly figuring out the next step) is a competitive advantage. Unfortunately financial markets are not natural environments driven by physical forces, so the same rules do not always apply, and extrapolation can be a financial survival disadvantage. Predictions of long-term trends made from small data samples are consistent with the wide evidence of performance chasing by investors.[7] This behavior leads to performance problems when investors buy into trends that eventually reverse.

The **crowd effect** occurs when your decisions are influenced by the decisions of others. People seek approbation, and going with the crowd also helps limit regret.[8] If everyone else is doing it, you may feel that you cannot be criticized and think that you will not feel as bad if it is a mistake. In addition, there is a rational aspect to following the behavior of others. If you think others have done their homework, their actions convey information. However, this is often not the case. Many frauds have been perpetrated and perpetuated based on the false assumption that others' actions were based on knowledge. The investment firm New Age Philanthropy was able to convince universities, churches, and endowments that it could double their money. Like all Ponzi schemes, New Age was able to attract new money by paying out early investors, who provided evidence or testimonials to subsequent investors. New Age conned $100 million from some of the smartest investors in the country: Laurence Rockefeller, William Simon, and Julian Robertson. Following the crowd instead of doing your own due diligence can lead to investment mistakes—and if many are relying on others' decision making, can lead to a market failure. A telling example is the reliance on the ratings agencies in the 2007–2008 subprime mortgage collapse.

The **menu effect** refers to situations in which people are overwhelmed when faced with too many options. Individuals will often fall back on naïve strategies; for example, if the number of options is reasonable, they may allocate equally between available options.[9] If the total number of alternatives gets large, people will often resort to even simpler strategies, such as selecting one option, often the first listed, in each category.[10] Failure to take the time to make well-informed decisions, or to solicit the help of a professional to review the options, can lead to investment selections that do not fit an investor's needs.

---

[7] Neurological research has shown that the brain anticipates repetition after only two stimuli. This is intriguingly similar to recent studies of the hiring and firing of money managers by pension funds, endowments, and foundations. This research found that these sophisticated investors consistently hired firms that were on a three-year hot streak (Goyal and Wahal 2008, and Heisler et al. 2007).

[8] This is similar to the analysts' motto of avoiding "being alone and wrong" on an earnings forecast.

[9] When asked how he allocated his TIAA–CREF account, Harry Markowitz admitted, "I split my contributions 50–50 between bonds and equities" (Zweig 1998). Additional evidence is reported by Benartzi and Thaler (2001) and Barberis and Thaler (2002).

[10] This demonstrates the value of being listed at the top of Internet searches and why Google can charge for the privilege.

Learning

Economic theory assumes that individuals learn in an unbiased way. In reality, of course, our learning can be biased, frequently by what we have recently experienced. Particular examples include the *illusion of control,* the *illusion of knowledge, overconfidence, familiarity,* and *hindsight bias.*

The **illusion of control** is the belief that we affect outcomes to a greater extent than we really do. This is most obvious in games of chance, where people often act as if they can influence the outcome. In one experiment people were given $1 lottery tickets; half had their numbers assigned, and half got to choose their numbers. They were then asked at what price they would sell their tickets. People who chose their lottery numbers requested an average asking price four times higher than people whose numbers were assigned.[11] In investments, a feeling of control makes us more invested in our actions and their consequences. However, a false sense of our abilities can result in an overestimation of return and an underestimation of risk.

The **illusion of knowledge** is a false sense of what we know. This is reinforced by cognitive dissonance that prevents learning: We tend to ignore contrary or negative results. These biased learning techniques can result in and reinforce overconfidence. The illusion of knowledge can also result from the confusion of causality and correlation. Like the illusion of control, the illusion of knowledge may lead investors to gamble rather than invest.

Confidence can be useful, but overconfidence can be dangerous. The world is scary and complicated. Thinking about all possible risks and optimizing behavior over all possible actions can lead to inaction. Confidence is a mechanism to encourage active decision making. Overconfidence is the belief that your information and ability are better than they really are. Research results suggest that overconfident people tend to trade too much and hold underdiversified portfolios. Psychological tests show that men tend to be more overconfident than women, particularly in areas perceived as male domains. Finance is one of those areas. In an examination of discount brokerage accounts, Barber and Odean (2001) found that men trade more than women and earn returns of 1 percent less per year.[12]

We also tend to place too much trust in the familiar. Familiarity is synonymous with safety. Learning requires taking risk, so risk-averse humans may learn too little. Familiarity is built through repetition of an activity that is intrinsically pleasurable. One problem is that many people are most familiar with their employer's stock and therefore tend to overinvest in company stock. A survey of 246 of the largest companies found that 42 percent of total 401(k) plan assets were invested in company stock.[13] Why is this a problem? It not only fails to diversify human capital risk but can be risky by itself. The Enron 401(k) plan held 60 percent in Enron stock while the Global Crossing plan held up to 53 percent in company stock.

Another impediment to effective learning is *hindsight bias*—that is, rewriting history so previously held opinions incorporate newly learned information. We are always smarter after the fact. We find it hard to admit we do not know something, and admitting we were wrong lowers our positive opinions of ourselves. The problem with hindsight bias is that it fools us into thinking we are smarter than we are and that the past

---

[11] See Langer (1975).

[12] It seems that even joint accounts make a difference: While men traded 45 percent more and earned 1 percent less per year than women, single men traded 67 percent more and earned 1.4 percent less per year than single women.

[13] Schultz (1996).

was more predictable than it was, which can result in the view that the future is more predictable than it is. For example, although it seems everyone recognized the Internet bubble and the credit bubble, people somehow lost money.

Prospect Theory

Kahneman and Tversky (1979) proposed **prospect theory** as a model of decision making that is consistent with observed behavior. Individuals are assumed to exhibit mental accounting and to frame decisions in terms of potential gains and losses relative to a reference point. The result is that investments are viewed separately based on their reference point. Gains and losses are then evaluated using an S-shaped value function. The value function has three key features: It is concave for gains, convex for losses, and steeper for losses. This asymmetry captures loss aversion and the observation of risk-averse behavior for gains and risk-seeking behavior for losses.

In particular, prospect theory captures the desire to hold losing positions until they return to the purchase price so the investor can avoid realizing a loss. Shefrin and Statman (1985) examined the round-trip duration of stock trades. Tax considerations imply that more loss realizations should occur right before the short-term tax holding period expires in order to capture the higher tax rate; and more gains realizations should occur once the higher tax rate expires. The evidence showed, however, that the ratio of loss to gain realizations was constant for both periods. They concluded that the pattern of loss realization is a combination of tax considerations and prospect theory–type behavior—in particular, loss realization aversion.

The tendency to hold losers and sell winners is also at direct odds with the conventional wisdom of holding winners and selling losers, which is espoused by many traders. Heisler (1994) examined trader behavior in the Treasury bond futures market, with round-trip trades categorized as gains or losses based on their midpoint profit. The results showed that losses were held longer than gains, with less successful traders (as measured by profit per contract traded) holding losses longer relative to more successful traders. Odean (1998) found similar results in the trades of discount brokerage clients. Winners that were sold generally outperformed comparable stocks by 2.35 percent, whereas losers that were held underperformed by 1.06 percent.

Recommendations

Although these behaviors appear hardwired into our brains, there are ways to mitigate their effects. First, and foremost, realize that these behaviors exist. Second, the tools described in earlier chapters provide a methodology to incorporate large amounts of information in a uniform manner. Lastly, the investor can add investment restrictions and self-control mechanisms, such as diversification and dollar cost averaging, to avoid the tendency to overreact. Diversification is also an important technique to help avoid mistakes due to framing. A full discussion of recommendations is provided in Chapter 16.

Observations of Individual Investor Behavior

Empirical evidence of the returns realized by individual investors is consistent with the behaviors just summarized. Individual investors underperform buy-and-hold strategies. They tend to get out of their investments following a market drop and get back in too late—only after the market, fund, or security level has seemed to recover. This behavior has been observed in many scenarios, including the selection of mutual fund managers, with investors buying the best-performing of all managers and suffering when performance reverses. One study indicates that the average

EXHIBIT 15.2
Return Trend and
Reversal Behavior in
the Stock Market

	Panel A: One-Year Return Trends		
	S&P 500 Total Return, 1976–2008		
Sorted Return Series	**12-Month Return**	**Subsequent One-Month Return**	**Subsequent One-Month Return**
	Mean	Mean	Proportion > 0%
Lowest 25%	−8.7%	0.1%	54.6%
Highest 25%	33.1%	0.8%	60.8%
	Panel B: Three-Year Return Reversals		
	S&P 500 Total Return, 1976–2008		
Sorted Return Series	**36-Month Return**	**Subsequent 12-Month Return**	**Subsequent 12-Month Return**
	Mean	Mean	Proportion > 0%
Lowest 25%	7.2%	13.9%	82.7%
Highest 25%	93.2%	12.8%	69.3%

investor significantly underperforms the average mutual fund due to poor market timing and fund selection.[14] This tendency is also apparent in magazines and ranking services that recommend mutual funds based largely on past performance relative to other managers.

The performance of individual investors is considered so poor by tactical asset allocation portfolio managers that these managers use measures of individual investor sentiment as a contrary indicator. The stock market sentiment of individuals has been measured and found to be significantly correlated with stock market returns. Positive market returns are followed by increases in bullish sentiment. The tendency to extrapolate trends combined with the return-reversing tendency of equities can explain the poor track record of individual investors. The bullish sentiment of newsletter writers is highly correlated with individual sentiment but is also influenced by 6- to 12-month market declines in stocks, suggesting the presence of a valuation or reversal discipline. However, the forecasting power of newsletters is mixed at best and is no better at extreme market levels.[15]

A simple review of historical returns suggests that there are overall stock market tendencies for both trending, in the short term, and reversal, in the longer term and at valuation extremes. This coincides with observations of investor trend following and poor performance from market timing. An examination of the S&P 500 index shows that, on average, periods of top-quartile one-year returns are followed by above-average one-month returns, and periods of top-quartile three-year returns are followed by below-average one-year returns. This is true of both mean returns and the frequency of realized positive returns and is illustrated in Exhibit 15.2. These results are consistent with the experience of newsletter writers just described.[16]

Performance chasing has also been observed at the individual stock level and may be explained in part by representativeness, which leads investors to confuse a good

---

[14] See Dalbar (2005).

[15] See Clarke and Statman (1998).

[16] Note that these results, although typical, may be influenced by the time series and range selected.

Common thinking in coaching is to get the basketball to the player who seems to be making all the points. It seems to make sense that the player with the hot hand should continue a streak of good shooting.

In 1985 psychologists Gilovich, Vallone, and Tversky studied game notes to identify when a player was declared hot, and compared that observation with subsequent shooting success. They found no evidence that there truly were hot streaks that would persist. The patterns that seemed to represent a trend were simply a natural part of a random sequence, similar to a series of heads when flipping a coin. Players mistakenly extrapolated these false trends, much as many investors do with a random sequence of market moves.

company with a good stock.[17] This result may also be applied to fund selection—investors may confuse good historical records with the likelihood that those funds will produce good future returns, before conducting due diligence on the manager.

One key issue faced by individual investors is the presence of underdiversified portfolios. This is due in part to illusions of skill and control, leading to concentrated bets and aggressive turnover—see Barber and Odean (2000, 2001). There is also the previously cited evidence that many individual investors simply equally weight their 401(k) options, regardless of the asset allocation implications.

Observations of Institutional Investor Behavior

Most research about investors has focused on individuals—how they trade stocks and invest in 401(k) plans. Beginning in the 2000s research was published on the selection of investment managers by pension plans, endowments, and foundations. The results document that institutional plan sponsors use a more sophisticated process of manager selection based on factors beyond simply performance and that they use style benchmarks for performance analysis. However, on average, they do tend to chase long-term performance and react quickly to very poor short-term performance. Del Guercio and Tkac (2002) took an initial step in contrasting the retail and institutional asset management markets by examining asset flows using mutual fund and pension fund samples. They found: that simply outperforming the S&P 500 market index was more important to plan sponsors than to individuals, while the magnitude of out-performance mattered more to individuals; tracking error was significant in explaining flows in the pension fund sample, but not in the mutual fund sample; that risk-adjusted returns, measured using Jensen's alpha, were related to flows in both samples[18]; and that quantitative performance factors explained more variation in flows among mutual funds than pension funds. Lastly, they found that the flow-performance relation was more linear and symmetric among pension fund managers.[19] This suggests that institutional investors may be more willing to fire a manager that delivers poor performance than has been found to be the case among mutual fund investors. Heisler, Knittel, Neumann, and Stewart (2007) found that the most important performance determinant for equity manager selection was consistent one-, three-, and five-year excess performance relative to style benchmarks. However,

---

[17] This is discussed in Shefrin and Statman (1995).

[18] The authors suggested that mutual fund investors were probably not using Jensen's alpha to allocate flows, but showed it was correlated to Morningstar ratings, a value potentially more likely to be used by mutual fund investors.

[19] Sirri and Tufano (1998) found a more asymmetric (convex) relationship for the mutual fund market, that is, investors are more willing to hire a manager that performed well than fire a manager that has performed poorly.

if one-year returns were significantly negative, institutional clients would move assets and accounts. Institutions seem to understand the extremeness of style (for example, deep value versus relative value) to only a limited extent. Survey research by Karim and Stewart (2005) confirms that a vast majority (85 percent) of pension plans state that they study past returns before selecting managers but that they consider other information as well, including a manager's ability to communicate effectively.

Research results in Stewart, Neumann, Knittel, and Heisler (2009) indicate that institutional investors destroyed value by their tactical decisions of investing in fixed income and equity products, on average underperforming the alternative of doing nothing by 1–2 percent per year between 1985 and 2007. Further analysis suggests that asset allocation decisions detract in the short term, and style and manager selection detracts value in the short and long terms. These results suggest that even more sophisticated professional investors are prone to similar behavioral biases as individual investors, though generating smaller performance drag. However, Karim and Stewart (2005) suggest that plan sponsors do not fully understand their mistakes.

Academic research has explored the success of Wall Street strategists who make market calls.[20] Unlike individual investors, their sentiment is not correlated with short-term market moves. However, the record of their short-term calls is just as poor. A wealth of research suggests that Wall Street equity analysts are so slow to increase published earnings estimates that significant changes in estimates tend to be followed by future estimate changes. This reflects underreaction to new company information by Wall Street analysts.[21] Prior to 2000 positive estimate revisions were associated with subsequent positive excess stock returns, but after 2000 they presaged negative excess returns; this suggests that investors first underreacted and then overreacted to analyst earnings estimates.[22] Quantitative trading models often try to exploit the price trends created by analyst earnings revisions.

It is also well known that the average professional money manager has difficulty outperforming the market averages. Over most periods, mutual fund universes underperform passive benchmarks and few funds consistently outperform. Institutional separate account managers have mixed records as well, though there are some bright spots. For example, international equity managers outperformed the EAFE index post-1990 when the Japanese market began its 15+-year bear market.

15.3 Implications for Active Management

General Observations

Active investment managers seek to outperform passive benchmarks and their peers. There are at least three types of active managers: those who bet on markets, asset classes, or volatility; those who rotate positions on styles or sectors; and those who select individual securities, including arbitrage trading. Active managers use both quantitative (computer model–based) and fundamental (company profitability and economic trends) techniques to support their processes. In most cases valuation is a key determinant in their decision making. Behavioral finance suggests that valuations may be influenced by extreme pessimism (leading to undervaluation) and overconfidence (leading to overvaluation).

---

[20] See Clarke and Statman (1998).

[21] See Daniel et al. (2002).

[22] See Xu (2008).

Limits to Market Efficiency and Opportunities for Active Management

There are several theories about how liquidity and uninformed traders create and sustain market inefficiencies. They include *overreaction* and *reversion* and rely on *contrarian* strategies to take advantage of these supposed inefficiencies. Over the long term, prices follow fundamentals, such as company earnings, but seem to vary from fundamentals in the short term and perhaps generate greater volatility than the pattern of fundamentals would suggest.

Observers of financial markets have long believed that security prices could diverge from fundamental values. Arrow (1982) stated that "it seem[s] intuitively clear that daily variations in future and securities markets are excessive relative to the daily changes in information." Shiller (1981) proposed that market prices frequently depart from fundamental value based on evidence that stock prices tend to be more volatile than the future stream of discounted dividends would imply.

Contrarian trading rules were articulated years ago to capture such deviations in fair pricing. If prices display excess volatility, then long-horizon returns should be predictable and trading rules can be developed to generate alpha. Such rules were originally proposed by Graham and Dodd (1934) and later by Dreman (1977, 1998). These are value-based strategies that involve buying stocks in companies that are measured to be undervalued along some objective variable.

With the development of CAPM in the mid-1960s came the first tests for market efficiency. These tests found that several factors beyond beta seemed to explain returns; these variables became known as anomalies. The anomalies literature has suggested several possible variables, including size (Banz 1981), P/E ratio (Basu 1983), book-to-market ratio (Stattman 1980), dividend yield (Keim 1985), and leverage (Bhandari 1988).

DeBondt and Thaler (1985, 1987) were the first to test heuristic decision making as an explanation for security returns. They studied the performance of portfolios constructed of long-term "winners" and "losers." The hypothesis was that extreme movements in price would be followed by subsequent moves in the opposite direction—the more extreme the movement, the more extreme the correction. The three-year return difference between winner and loser portfolios was almost 25 percent, and most of the excess returns occurred in January. The findings suggest that it takes about 2.5 years for price reversals to occur. DeBondt and Thaler appeal to representativeness—individuals seem to place too much importance on short-run economic data and underweight random elements and prior base rate data. If losers are considered risky because they have too much perceived downside potential, such stocks will bear excess risk premiums and force prices lower in the short term, only to reverse in the long run, perhaps responding to stabilizing fundamentals.

If investors also overreact to recent earnings trends, then stocks may show subsequent price reversals as exaggerated fears are not borne out. A related idea was explored by Black (1986): If noise in stock prices is cumulative, the farther prices get from fundamental value, the more aggressive information traders become. Therefore prices will move back toward fundamental value. DeLong, Shliefer, Summers, and Waldman (1990) note that if the errors of noise traders are temporary, and given that asset prices respond to noise trading, asset prices will display mean reversion.

Shefrin and Statman (1995) proposed a mechanism for overreaction as a basis for contrarian rules. Representativeness leads individuals and institutions to the erroneous trading rule that good stocks are those of good companies. Good companies have the subjective characteristics, such as good management and good products, typically associated with strong future performance. These subjective characteristics correspond

A number of urban legends are shared by doctoral students in finance. The story of the two professors who ignore the $20 bill lying on the ground (mentioned in Chapter 6) is one of them. Another involves the hesitancy of a group of finance professors to follow their own research recommendations with their own money.

In the early 1980s when behavioral finance was in its infancy, it was learned that stocks that had performed poorly seemed to reverse after that poor performance. A natural conclusion was to prepare a list of the worst-performing stocks over the last year and invest in them, with the hope of earning big returns.

However, when the list was prepared, and the professors reviewed it while enjoying a brown bag lunch in the faculty lounge, they saw a bunch of small-cap loser companies that no one would want to invest in. And they didn't.

to a set of objective characteristics such as large size and low book-to-market. Good companies also tend to be companies whose stock has risen in response to good fundamental performance.

These are the glamour stocks. People extrapolate the current information of past good performance into the future, ignoring the fact that things can change and more importantly that this information may already be incorporated into the stock price. Therefore, subsequent performance is likely to disappoint. Some portfolio managers may prefer glamour stocks because they appear prudent and can be more easily justified to clients because overall poor performance can be attributed to poor market conditions. Investors will mind a loss somewhat less if they can regard the investment as one that other sensible people would make. It also suggests the contrarian investment strategy of holding neglected stocks—those with little to no analyst coverage—versus widely followed stocks with high analyst coverage.

15.4   Implications for Setting Investment Policy

Several implications for setting investment policy are suggested by observed investor behavior. These include recognizing that asset allocation is a multiperiod problem due to changing preferences (requiring the techniques presented in Chapter 5) or changing expected return and risk, providing an opportunity for forecasting and active management as discussed throughout this book. Special care must be taken in developing investment products and communicating investment policy. In general, a lack of investor sophistication suggests an opportunity for providing education and the need to offer simple rules or products due to limitations in educating nonprofessional investors. This will be further discussed in Chapter 16.

15.5   Implications for Manager Selection

The Morningstar service provides summaries of mutual fund products, including historical performance and screening tools to select funds based in part on historical performance and the Morningstar rating. This rating, heavily touted in mutual fund company advertisements, is a star system "based on how well they've performed (after adjusting for risk)." Morningstar notes that the star system should not be

EXHIBIT 15.3
Morningstar Fund Screener

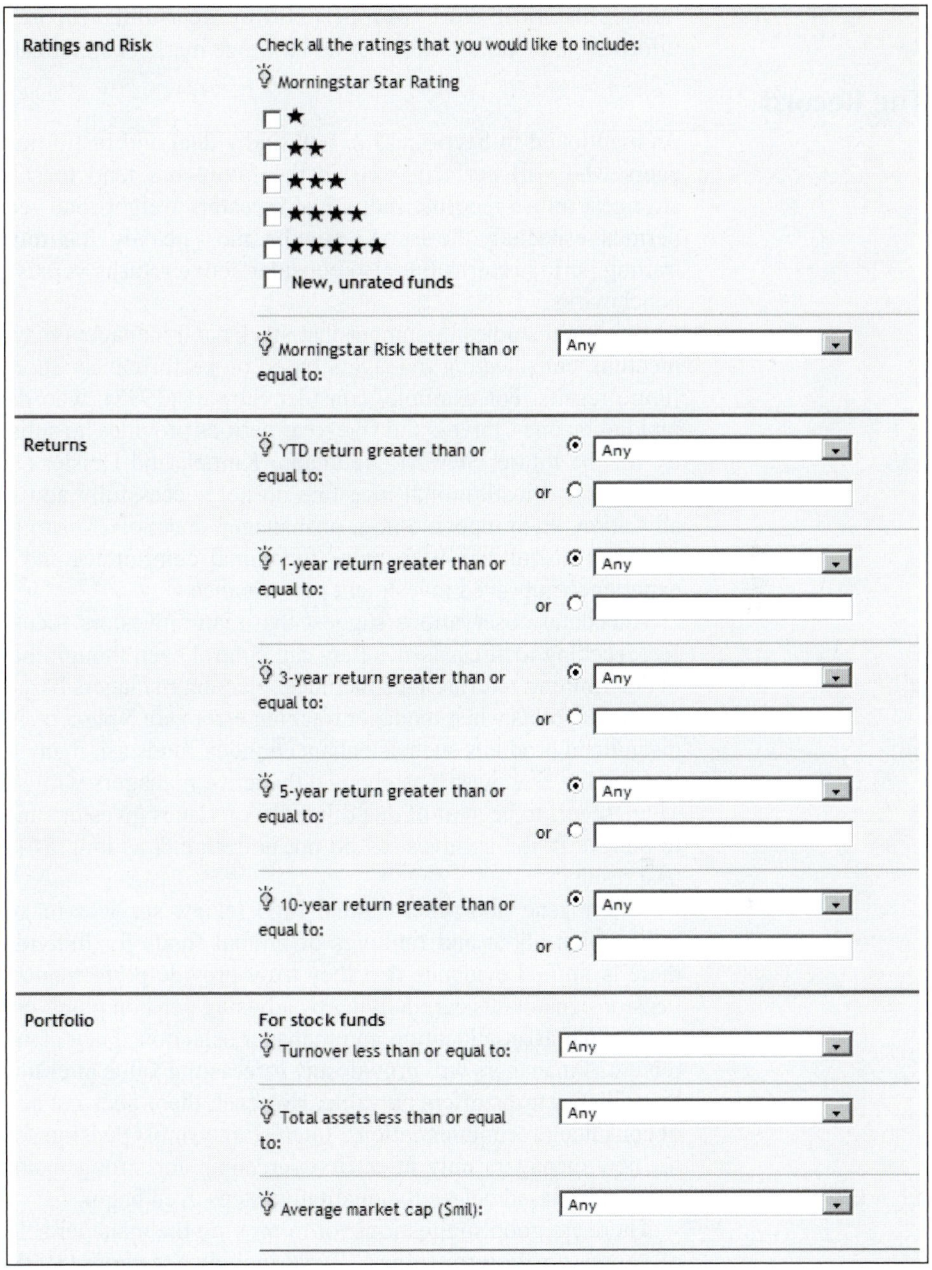

Ratings and Risk	Check all the ratings that you would like to include: 💡 Morningstar Star Rating
	☐ ★
	☐ ★★
	☐ ★★★
	☐ ★★★★
	☐ ★★★★★
	☐ New, unrated funds
	💡 Morningstar Risk better than or equal to: [Any ▾]
Returns	💡 YTD return greater than or equal to: ◉ [Any ▾] or ○ [ ]
	💡 1-year return greater than or equal to: ◉ [Any ▾] or ○ [ ]
	💡 3-year return greater than or equal to: ◉ [Any ▾] or ○ [ ]
	💡 5-year return greater than or equal to: ◉ [Any ▾] or ○ [ ]
	💡 10-year return greater than or equal to: ◉ [Any ▾] or ○ [ ]
Portfolio	For stock funds 💡 Turnover less than or equal to: [Any ▾]
	💡 Total assets less than or equal to: [Any ▾]
	💡 Average market cap ($mil): [Any ▾]

Note: As of July 2008.

considered buy or sell recommendations—just "a tool for identifying funds worthy of further research." Morningstar offers a service selling mutual fund recommendations based on manager philosophy, tenure, and fees, which it suggests has added value over the last five years. Standard Web-based screens, including Morningstar's, include trailing return functions, as illustrated in Exhibit 15.3. This screen shot of the Morningstar Fund Screener includes sorting variables on fund minimums, Morningstar ratings, historical returns over periods from year-to-date up to 10 years, and descriptive information including turnover and average market capitalization.

The Record

As mentioned in Section 15.2, both individual and institutional investors seek managers who will perform well in the future but tend to select managers with the strongest return records. Individual investors weight total return measures over past periods, especially the last 12 months, most heavily. Institutional investors focus on trailing period returns but also consider active returns versus both standard and style benchmarks.

Empirical studies document that stocks and managers may exhibit short-term momentum, but selecting managers based on performance records offers little value for future results. For example, consider Stewart (1998), who demonstrates that simply ranking by one-, three-, and five-year periods provides no subsequent forecasting ability for the future. Stewart, Neumann, Knittel, and Heisler (2009) indicate that even sophisticated institutional investors do not successfully add value by adjusting asset allocation, style repositioning, or manager selection. Karim and Stewart (2005) suggest that institutions with more functional committees and higher turnover do not experience improved investment performance.

Anecdotal observations suggest that many investors focus too much attention on fees, seeking to stress issues they can control even though they may be minor factors in determining returns. This includes selecting managers based on fee differences of a few basis points when manager tracking errors are 5 percent. Many investors in highly disciplined products such as enhanced index funds ask many detailed questions about process but few questions about fully active managers with strong historical records. There seems to be a lot of due diligence on issues investors understand and a tendency to believe in things investors do not understand, as long as they reflect eye-popping past results.

Morningstar and other mutual fund review services make a living by providing information about and rankings of mutual funds for individual investors. However, there is limited evidence that they truly provide performance value for their clients. Pension consultants earn a living by advising pension plans, endowments, and foundations about asset allocation and manager selection. They claim that only a qualitative review of managers will provide any forecasting value after noting that simple ranking by trailing returns offers no value. However, there does not seem to be a public record of consultant recommendations. Interestingly, most pension consultants begin a search for new managers only after first screening for strong historical performance—the process is biased before the qualitative steps even begin.[23]

There are good suggestions for improving the manager selection process—though of course no foolproof ones. These include Stewart's (1998) technique of ranking managers by *consistency* of quarterly outperformance and Treynor's (1990) list of questions to ask prospective active managers. These are discussed in the following chapter.

---

[23] It reminds one of the statement "we're looking for our keys in this corner of the room, not because we think we dropped them there, but because the light is better there."

Summary

Institutional and individual investors are all subject to behaviors that can result in investment errors. These behaviors appear to be the result of deep-seated psychological tendencies that developed as survival skills that allow people to react quickly using limited information. One such behavior is a fight-or-flight reaction to danger. The other is the ability to identify patterns, even where they do not exist. The decision-making techniques that served so well as survival tools in the natural world are not necessarily applicable to survival in the financial world.

Although these behaviors appear to be hardwired into our brains, their effects can be mitigated. Trained investors can apply the models described in earlier chapters to assess and incorporate information consistently. Individual investors can benefit from financial training. Institutional investors should be wary of behavioral tendencies even for experienced investors. For example, only pension officers who had portfolio management experience, or had been burned in the past, appreciated the tendency for pension plans to mistakenly hire managers at the top of their performance cycle.[24] Further academic research, including recent work applying neuroscience, may provide more guidance for understanding investor behavior.

[24] Karim and Stewart (2005)

Problems

1. What is behavioral finance? List four related terms and define them.
2. Why are we concerned about investor behavior? How does it impact the portfolio manager's job in working with clients? How does it influence the opportunity for active management?

Problems 3 through 13 assume that you are participating in psychological evaluations of your decision-making style. Answer the questions, and then check your answers against those listed in the chapter appendix. What did you learn about your personal behavior from each problem? How will you adjust your investment approach now that you are aware of these tendencies?

3. Upon entering a research lab, you are told you have just won $30. You are offered the following options; which do you choose?
   a. A coin flip where you win $9 on heads and lose $9 on tails.
   b. No coin flip.
4. Suppose you plan to attend a baseball game, but on the way you lose $20. The cost of a ticket is $20. Do you buy a ticket and attend the game?
5. You are given the following personality sketch and asked to rank the likelihood that Tom W. is a graduate student in nine fields of specialization:

Tom W. is of high intelligence, although lacking in true creativity. He has a need for order and clarity, for neat and tidy systems in which every detail finds its appropriate place. His writing is rather dull and mechanical, occasionally enlivened by somewhat corny puns and by flashes of imagination of the sci-fi type. He has a strong drive for competence. He seems to have little feeling and sympathy for other people and does not enjoy interacting with others. Self-centered, he nonetheless has a deep moral sense.

Rank the following fields (in the Rank 1 column) from 1 (most likely) to 9 (least likely) that this was Tom W.'s area of specialization in graduate school:

Field	Rank 1	Rank 2
Fine arts		
Business		
Communication		
Computer science		
Education		
Engineering		
Law		
Medicine		
Sociology		

6. Continuing with Problem 5, suppose you are given the following additional information:

   The preceding personality sketch of Tom W. was written during Tom's senior year in high school by a psychologist on the basis of projective tests.

   Using this additional information, rank the fields again, placing your new ratings in the Rank 2 column.

7. Upon entering a research lab, you are offered the following options; which do you choose?

   a. A coin flip where you win $39 on heads and win $21 on tails.

   b. No coin flip, but you win $30 for sure.

8. Upon entering a research lab, you are told you just won $2,000 with the condition that you must choose between the following options. Which do you choose?

   a. A sure loss of $500.

   b. A coin flip that offers a 50 percent chance of losing nothing and a 50 percent chance of losing $1,000.

9. Do you consider your driving skills to be above average, average, or below average?

10. Suppose you hold a diversified portfolio of large-cap domestic and international stocks with some fixed-income securities. Rank the following investments from 1 (riskiest) to 9 (safest) on how they change the risk of the portfolio:

Investment	Rank
Commodities	
Corporate bonds	
High-yield bonds	
Real estate	
Emerging market stocks	
EAFE stocks	
Small-cap stocks	
Small-cap growth stocks	
T-bills	

11. For the following questions, provide an estimate as well as the range within which you feel 90 percent confident the actual answer will lie:

Question	Estimate	Range Low	Range High
Year Washington was first elected president			
Year second European explorer reached the West Indies			
Highest body temperature (°F)			
Boiling point on Mt. Everest (°F)			
Lowest body temperature (°F)			
Freezing point of vodka (°F)			
Number of U.S. states in 1880			
Gestation period of an elephant (months)			
Duration of Mars's orbit around the Sun (days)			

12. Upon entering a research lab, you are told you have just won $1,000 with the condition that you must choose between the following options. Which do you choose?

    a. A sure gain of $500 more.

    b. A gamble that offers a 50 percent chance of winning $1,000 more and a 50 percent chance of no additional gain.

13. Suppose you plan to attend a baseball game, but on the way you lose your ticket for which you paid $20. Do you buy a ticket and attend the game?

As mentioned earlier, your answers to Problems 3–13 should be compared with the answers in the chapter appendix and your observations discussed for each.

14. Revisit the Vanguard questionnaire you first examined in Chapter 3 (Problem 3 at the end of the chapter). Which behavioral biases can you identify in the questions?

15. Look up Morningstar's Web site and explore three topics. Summarize your observations with regard to the following:

    • Frequency of references to historical returns.

    • Disclaimers about use of historical returns and rankings.

    • Discussion of the company's qualitative fund recommendation process.

16. Prepare a questionnaire for investors, asking them what is most important for them regarding their

    • Attitude toward risk.

    • Goals for investing.

    • Past experience with investing.

17. Prepare two 2×2 matrices illustrating a market behavior on one axis and investor behavior on the other, with the first matrix showing how you expect people to behave and the second matrix showing how they should.

18. Create a list of four investor types based on education, experience, and personality; describe each, including what a financial advisor should be sensitive to for each one.

Chapter 16

Managing Client Relations

16.1 Introduction

Chapter 15 outlined a number of behavioral tendencies common to individual and institutional investors. These include loss aversion, extrapolation of trends, representativeness, overconfidence, and crowd behavior. This chapter provides recommendations for addressing the adverse consequences of these behaviors, as well as for effective product design and client retention. The goal is to give investment advisors tools to help manage the client relationship — which may be just as important as managing the underlying investment.

Section 16.2 begins with a list of recommendations to address common investment decision-making errors introduced in Chapter 15. A discussion of the various roles for portfolio managers and the design of effective investment policies for their clients follows in Section 16.3. Sections 16.4 through 16.6 give advice on developing effective sales presentations tailored to specific audiences, as well as guidance for preparing meaningful client reviews. A case study is provided in Section 16.7. In addition, this chapter provides guidance for completing the final reports for the individual, defined contribution, defined benefit, and fund cases that accompany the text.

16.2 General Recommendations for Client Management

Although the behaviors described in Chapter 15 appear to be hardwired into our brains, there are means for mitigating their effects. First, recognize that these behaviors exist. Second, the tools described in earlier chapters provide a methodology to

War Story *Half of a Portfolio Manager's Job*

At times, half of a portfolio manager's job may seem to be explaining poor performance.* Even if portfolio managers generate superior performance more than half of the time, they need to devote themselves to attending to clients and making the case to retain their business when performance is poor. The task may seem overwhelming as clients head for the exit. Moreover, many investment careers end after a period of extended weak results without any opportunity for the manager to experience a rebound, biasing upward the percentage of poor years in a manager's record.

What are the implications of this observation, and how can an investment professional manage this challenge?

1. A portfolio manager must set reasonable return goals to limit both the frequency and magnitude of subpar performance.

2. A portfolio manager should set investment goals beyond simply performance, including risk targets, portfolio characteristics, performance attribution, and cash positions. Even in periods of poor performance, the portfolio manager may be successful in delivering on these other targets, perhaps giving the client some comfort for a few quarters.

3. A portfolio manager must develop effective client relations early on, and in periods of good performance, to build goodwill and reliable communication. A positive relationship will not keep the account during extended periods of negative active returns, but it might buy the manager one or two more quarters. Portfolio managers should also see their clients periodically after the sales presentation.

4. A portfolio manager must understand her or his own discipline—in particular, under what conditions it tends to underperform and how to effectively communicate the investment process. This will help in managing expectations and explaining results. Numerous managers have been fired because they were not able to explain why performance was weak and when it might rebound.

Clearly it is easier to keep a current client than find a new one. It is in the PM's interest to work hard to build and maintain client relationships.

*This statement may be attributed to William Nemerever, partner at Grantham Mayo Van Otterloo (GMO).

incorporate large amounts of information in a uniform manner. Third, investors can adopt new heuristics to help them avoid investing mistakes. For example, investors can add investment restrictions and self-control mechanisms, such as diversification and dollar cost averaging, to avoid the tendency to overreact.

The tendencies to regret losses and to focus on purchase price instead of current price can make it difficult to sell losing positions and look to the future. One helpful technique is to consider, at any point in time, what investors would do if they were allocating a portfolio for the first time from cash, and then move the current portfolio toward that ideal, considering of course the transaction costs required to get there.

Effective investors are not afraid to make investment mistakes, honestly recognize their errors, and learn from them. A first step to remedying faulty learning is to admit we do not know everything. This opens us to evidence that is at odds with our current views, allowing us to evaluate new information frankly. Other steps include avoiding what is beyond our abilities and keeping a record of all trades and their rationale, thereby mitigating hindsight bias by making it difficult to ignore unprofitable trades or incorrect assumptions. Conducting rigorous due diligence, instead of following the crowd and assuming others have done their homework on investment opportunities, should improve the odds for positive investment results and reduce the severity of negative outcomes. Finally, there is diversification. Diversification is an admission that, try as we might, we lack complete knowledge; and an acknowledgment that sometimes we are unlucky and the unexpected happens.

Investors also need to be careful not to let their emotions get the best of them. Some active managers have developed a compensating heuristic that reminds them to be sensitive to their feelings of excitement or dread and explore doing the opposite of what their emotions tell them when evaluating investment opportunities. Contrarian investors cultivate this technique to help them identify opportunities for excess performance and to avoid underestimating risk and overestimating return.[1]

General Implications

Observed market patterns and investor behavior suggest several key considerations for setting investment policy. First, return and risk forecasts, including volatility and correlation, are not fixed. The world changes; investors may be interested in more than maximizing total wealth at a horizon; and individual preferences are likely to change through time, based in part on wealth levels, cost bases, and stages in life. As a result, it may not be appropriate to use a one-period wealth optimization model. Second, recognizing the possibility of return reversals creates an opportunity to model changing expected returns and use them in setting optimal investment policy. Chapter 5 developed techniques to incorporate changing preferences, risks, and returns within an allocation model. Chapters 6, 7, and 11 discussed the benefits of stress testing. In addition, investment managers can develop active strategies that suggest opportunities to revise return, risk, and correlation forecasts for potential inclusion in the portfolio. Chapter 6 provided one example of this approach.

Third, special care must be taken in developing investment products and communicating investment policy. In general, a lack of investor sophistication and constraints in educating nonprofessional investors suggest an opportunity for providing education and the need to offer simple rules or products. To stay on track, an inexperienced investor needs to mitigate the effects of framing issues and feelings of regret. These can be addressed through education and advice from a trusted advisor, by following investment heuristics such as dollar cost averaging, or by investing in products with predetermined asset allocations that do not require rebalancing by the investor. Such simple but effective products encourage staying the course and discourage chasing returns either on the way up or on the way down. These techniques can also boost self-control, which helps reduce the tendency to alter long-term predictions based on short-term results. To help investors avoid diversification errors such as simply distributing assets equally between all options, it is important to give them guidance and clear choices.

16.3   Meeting Client Needs

Portfolio managers differ in their levels of specialization and rigor. As discussed in Chapter 1, portfolio managers come in many forms, from financial advisors who support individual investors, to pension consultants who assist institutional investors, to mutual fund managers who invest assets for individuals, to separate account managers who select securities for institutional clients.

Investment clients may be organized along two dimensions: their sophistication and their responsibilities. Highly sophisticated investors are well informed about investment techniques and the markets and experienced with benchmarking and the ups and downs of the markets. Less experienced investors need more hand-holding.

---

[1] See Graham, Dodd, and Cottle (1962).

Chapter 2 introduced individual and institutional clients with a discussion of needs, responsibilities, and market trends. The section about individual investors noted that psychological needs are as important as tangible goals. Individuals may understandably become angry if their nest eggs decline substantially, requiring them to delay retirement, seek part-time employment during retirement, or significantly reduce their living standards. Chapter 15 introduced evidence that institutional investors are also subject to psychological tendencies, potentially impacting the investment results for their employers. Moreover, institutional investors vary by training and experience; those with less will require more patience on the part of the portfolio manager.

Meeting Individual Investor Needs

The key measure of risk for individuals is the chance of losing money. Managing the fear and regret of these losses plays a large role in working with individual investors. Importantly, defined contribution (DC) plans are now a significant part of retirement planning for individuals. This creates a need for education, which has limits; so products need to be simple enough to understand quickly and without a lot of explanation. Life moves through stages with associated investment needs—buying a home, funding children's education, and saving for retirement. However, life is complicated, and investments cannot be planned with a high degree of confidence early in life.

Consider a common retirement planning strategy: Save as much as possible, invest it conservatively, and spend only income, not principal, in retirement. Combining this strategy with a defined benefit (DB) plan and Social Security, most retirees in the past had enough to live on. However, with the demise of DB plans, the stakes have risen.[2] DC plans offer control and portability, but they shift the performance risk and portfolio construction responsibility to potentially inexperienced investors.

Early in a career, wealth is concentrated in human capital—that is, education and work experience. As people age, they use human capital to accumulate financial wealth, including real estate, which is then spent in retirement. As long as human capital is not highly correlated with the stock market, equities are a diversifying asset; with diversification benefits declining as time goes on and human capital shrinks.[3] Over long periods, inflation-indexed securities are an attractive alternative to nominal fixed-income instruments, and mixing traditional target-based mutual funds with inflation-indexed funds (and insurance products) can be used to tailor investments to individual preferences.[4] Errors in planning for retirement or disappointing market results can be managed by working longer and delaying retirement.[5]

Individual investors have several tax-advantaged methods for saving for their children's education and their own retirement. Returns within 529 college savings plans are not subject to taxes, and IRA and 401(k) retirement plans are subject to taxes only at withdrawal.[6] Individuals should take full advantage of these programs. Yet in practice, retirement savings are too low; the vast majority of retirement investors doesn't maximize the use of their 401(k) plans or rebalance them; and many don't diversify.[7]

[2] DB plans could not be relied on to fully provide for retirement because most did not offer inflation indexing. A $50 monthly check for a 1954 retiree represented only $12.30 in purchasing power by 1985.

[3] See Viceira (2001).

[4] See Campbell et al. (2003).

[5] See Bodie, Merton, and Samuelson (1992).

[6] Chapter 12 outlines the tax implications of these plans.

[7] See Gottlieb (2006).

EXHIBIT 16.1
Summary of Product Offerings to Individual Investor Market

	Business Model	
Business Challenge	**Advice**	**Fund**
Small balances	Questionnaire	Limited offerings
Limited education	Very conservative	Tie to general goals

When designing investment products for the 529, 401(k), and IRA markets, portfolio managers may consider two business models, summarized in Exhibit 16.1. Except for very high net worth investors, the challenge faced by a portfolio manager is the small asset size of the balances and the low level of investment expertise of most investors. Although it is important to ensure that customers understand what they are buying, the small fee revenue generated from small balances makes it difficult to offer customized personal advice.[8]

This challenge is commonly addressed with the use of a questionnaire that categorizes an individual within a limited set of representative investor types and then offers a predetermined asset allocation for the identified representative investor. Sometimes the investor is directed to a diversified mix of mutual funds or ETFs to express the recommended allocation. Mutual fund providers may also offer a premixed fund whose name, such as "aggressive" or "retirement 2020," is tied to the risk, investment goal, and allocation of the fund. The intent is for investors to easily identify a fund that meets their investment goals or styles. Dynamic strategies that are path dependent (influenced by the initial investment date or historical performance) are difficult to implement in this fund format because it requires a growing number of individual funds to meet the needs of new investors—a costly proposition.[9]

The general lack of sophistication in the retail marketplace has led to the development of several techniques to help investors saving for retirement. These include encouraging employees to participate in their employer's DC plan, simple diversification rules such as subtracting your age from 100 to determine your equity allocation, and dollar cost averaging strategies. Economic theory suggests that dollar cost averaging is actually suboptimal in expected return.[10] However, the regret from losses may be so detrimental to future investment behavior and performance that it is a common advisor practice to help avoid having the tactical decisions of when to allocate—and in particular when to implement—the investment policy overwhelm the entire investment strategy.[11]

As noted, loss aversion and regret may be the largest potential sources of unhappiness for individual investors. Gains and losses are typically measured relative to historical nominal cost—usually the original cost, sometimes the highest past market value, and in some cases the opportunity cost of an alternative investment. As a result, advisors may seek to reduce this problem by clearly explaining downside risk and being extra conservative in setting expectations. Fund managers can address this with diversified offerings tied to downside risk, which exhibit lower variability than the underlying individual asset classes.

Of course, customers may not want a product that appears too conservative. Managing downside risk relative to peers may be as important for business success as

---

[8] A 100 basis point fee on the 2005 median 401(k) balance of $55,000 is $550 a year.
[9] Sources suggest that breakeven on a mutual fund is well over $100 million.
[10] See Constantinides (1979).
[11] Eisenhower (1948) offers an excellent discussion of tactics and strategy.

Setting savings and investment policy for retirement is a complicated task, and it is increasingly the responsibility of untrained individuals. How can portfolio managers help individuals set this policy if they do not know them—when balances are so small that it does not pay a financial advisor to work closely with individuals and only a mutual fund will work? Stewart (1992) discusses these issues:

- The growing importance of DC plans for retirement saving.
- The fact that high-return assets are risky—both in the eye of the investor and in true downside risk.
- The apparent ease of setting a savings goal as a percentage of current salary given returns and horizons.
- The important issue of inflation.
- The true complexity of the challenge.

The 2006 Pension Reform Act provided two key tools for improving American retirement savings policy by allowing employers to guide employees free of liability. The first was letting employers offer auto-enrollment; this made 401(k) saving the default option, providing the opportunity to significantly raise participation rates for new employees. The second was allowing employers to assign target date mutual funds (which place a significant yet declining allocation to equities) as a default option (if employees do not make a selection themselves).

What is a good structure for all-in-one mutual funds for retirement investors? Something that is simple, effective, and investable. As discussed in Chapter 15, investors will be unhappy with large decreases in asset values, so short-term downside risk should be managed. Chapter 5 illustrates one dynamic approach for doing so. Bodie and Clowes (2003) propose a safe strategy of investing savings in an immunized real-return portfolio, investing excess savings in long-dated equity call options, and purchasing a real-return annuity at retirement. Although the downside of this approach appears modest, Siegel (2005) suggests that the average return of this strategy may be much lower than buy-and-hold equity strategies.

Because shareholder preferences and retirement plans are not clearly observed by the PM, the decision is ultimately the future retiree's, making transparency, simplicity, and education key factors in successful retirement planning.

managing the total return downside because investors look at total performance and performance versus alternatives. As a result, setting a conservative policy may result in clients being disappointed with returns that are lower than those earned by more aggressive investments.

Handling thousands of customers makes it difficult to communicate with individuals in periods of weak performance; at the same time they have ready access to their balances, benchmark performance, and peer results. The manager can try to reach out to them through e-mail or direct mail, but it can be difficult to gauge their temperature. When investors reach the manager on the phone they may already be angry, or they can simply fire the manager with the click of a mouse. One way to address this is to manage expectations early in the relationship.

Meeting Institutional Investor Needs

Large institutional investors are generally sophisticated—typically well trained and experienced—and are responsible for large asset balances. These characteristics require a different approach to meeting their needs than what has just been described for individual investors. Instead of managing many small investors the portfolio manager never meets, common practice for institutional relationships includes detailed written reports supplemented with face-to-face communication, including annual meetings and quarterly updates. Detailed investment policy statements (IPS) and investment guidelines, as discussed in Chapters 2, 7, and 9, are standard operating procedures.

However, institutional investors are human after all, and they will be disappointed by underperformance even in the short term. As a result, downside probability is still a key measure of risk, yet it is typically calculated relative to a benchmark. In some cases performance relative to peers is important. For example, in the case of fully active international equity funds, a majority of managers have outperformed the EAFE index over the last 10 years. In such an environment merely outperforming the index may not satisfy a client.

It is easier to manage expectations with institutional investors due to their broader, deeper knowledge and experience. The flip side is that they may pay closer attention to results, especially with the aid of a pension consultant. Pension plans, foundations, and endowments are concerned about plan total return and return relative to liabilities and targets, as well as how specific managers contribute to their risk–return profile. Managers who violate guidelines, especially if performance is subpar, may be terminated. Karim and Stewart (2005) document several tendencies of pension plan staffs:

1. Manager selection:
   - Plan staff believe it is important to study past returns for manager selection, yet this should not be the sole criterion.
   - Adjusting return series for risk and investment style is also important.
   - Nonreturn criteria include effectiveness of communication, firm reputation, and manager reputation.
2. Manager performance:
   - Plan staff believe overall manager performance is good.
   - On average, plan staff believe manager performance does not deteriorate once a manager is hired, though more experienced investors believe it does.
   - Plans that tend to chase performance to a greater extent exhibit higher manager turnover.
3. Organization:
   - Plans retaining consultants, or staffed with professionals reflecting higher levels of education, have higher manager turnover.
   - Plans whose committees function more effectively tend to switch managers to a greater extent.
   - Managers who have become "tainted" are terminated more quickly by public plans, especially if performance is poor.

16.4   Manager Selection Process

A key responsibility of investors, or their advisors, is manager selection. Once the asset allocation has been formulated, investors or their advisors must determine how to implement that allocation: One or more portfolio managers must be selected to make and execute security-level decisions. Generalist portfolio managers may hire specialist managers to implement their recommendations. Such layered management is common with pension consultants and with fund of fund structures.

There are many types of investment products:

- Strategic programs, including those offered by a pension consultant or 401(k) provider.
- Tactical asset allocation, which shifts exposure between stocks, bonds, and other categories through cash or derivative markets, seeking to add value over a static allocation.
- Fully active discipline, taking active bets at the security, sector, style, region, and perhaps asset class level, with little concern about benchmarks.
- Structured active discipline, with every bet taken relative to a benchmark, with explicit risk control.
- Passive portfolio, seeking to replicate the performance, sometimes to the basis point, of a benchmark index.

All these products involve hiring someone to manage the money, either in a separate account or in a commingled vehicle such as a mutual fund.

The typical starting point for selecting a manager, typically when replacing a manager who is underperforming, is to begin with a review of his or her track record. On the institutional side, this may involve collecting all managers offering three to five years of live performance in the desired category, selecting those with acceptable records, perhaps reviewing performance attribution analyses or risk-adjusted measurements, interviewing the most attractive candidates, and selecting the one who seems best able to explain her or his investment process and charges reasonable fees. This approach seems common to both institutional and individual investors, but on average both groups lose money using this technique. As has been noted earlier, manager performance tends to trend in the short term and revert in the longer term—and in many cases it seems to reverse just after the manager has been hired. Goyal and Wahal (2008) and Stewart, Neumann, Knittel, and Heisler (2009) confirm this for institutional equity, fixed income, and balanced mandates.

Stewart (1998) finds there is little value in picking managers based on cumulative returns, but determines that the consistency of quarterly value added, and what it suggests about the portfolio structure underlying the performance, is of value. Ranking managers by the frequency of quarterly positive active returns suggests that the value added of consistently performing portfolios is truly robust or well diversified and there is a better than 50–50 chance that the outperformance will persist. Exhibit 16.2 reports the subsequent performance of managers ranked by the level and consistency of active

EXHIBIT 16.2
Subsequent Levels of Consistency and Return Differences between Quintiles Based on Two Ranking Methods: Quintiles Formed from Ranking by Frequency of Positive Active Return, and by Return Average of Four 5-Year Ranking and Measurement Periods, 1981–1996

Ranked by Consistency		Ranked by Return	
Subsequent Difference in Consistency	Subsequent Difference in Return	Subsequent Difference in Consistency	Subsequent Difference in Return
3.8%	1.3%	0.0%	−0.9%

War Story   *What Kind of Car Do You Drive?*

During a due diligence interview, following a discussion of investment process and company philosophy, the final question to a distressed bond portfolio manager was this: "What kind of car do you drive?" The PM hesitated for a few seconds, trying to figure out the question's purpose, and then answered truthfully, "A BMW."

The prospective client responded, "I hope you'll soon be driving a Ferrari." The client was interested in the firm's compensation system and had asked questions to confirm that the PM was well paid and had a strong incentive to make money for the customer. Because previous questions had covered salary, bonus, and firm ownership, this question was also the client's way of saying that the PM was being awarded the business, and the client hoped he would be successful.

returns —that is, the frequency with which the manager generated quarterly positive active returns. The most consistent manager quintile remained marginally more consistent, producing positive active returns 3.8 percent more often and generating greater average subsequent returns that were 1.3 percent higher than the least consistent quintile. In contrast, ranking by the level of active returns resulted in no subsequent difference in consistency, and active returns were 0.9 percent lower. Although the results are statistically significant, they apply to the universe of managers, and to be effective in practice require hiring a broad representative sample of managers.

Beyond studying return behavior, investors may use Treynor's (1990) suggested list of penetrating questions for a portfolio manager during a due diligence interview:

1. Is the process well articulated? Does it include a feedback system?
2. Are the portfolio managers motivated and committed to excellence? What is their incentive structure?
3. Do the managers' answers to questions suggest that she or he is knowledgeable? Does the manager appear slick or thoughtful?

Although not foolproof, the combination of these two methods, and avoiding biasing the list of managers by simply screening trailing returns,[12] may reduce the chance of performance reversals following manager selection.

16.5   Securing New Clients

In order to maintain your investment business, you need to work to grow it.[13] Clients may leave you despite good performance. They may have a change of overall strategy, making your allocation obsolete. They may terminate their pension plan, requiring a liquidation of all assets. Or there may be a change in staff with a new agenda. Of course there is also the chance your performance will be subpar and you will lose assets the old-fashioned way—you earned it. These observations suggest that a firm should ideally offer multiple products to different investors in order to compensate for the inevitable loss of assets by a particular strategy. In practice, and for efficient

[12] Screens are done at the beginning of the process because it can be difficult to secure an investment committee's approval of a manager with an unattractive track record. Although it makes sense to avoid wasting the committee's time, evidence suggests that it would make more sense to educate the committee.

[13] Alexander Webb, III, former chief investment officer at The Boston Co., is known to have said this.

allocation of resources, a successful firm seeking to grow should diversify from its initial product, with either similar products for new markets or new products for the same market.[14]

Individual Investors

Portfolio managers seek to design investment products that meet the wealth targets for education, retirement, and other needs for individual investors. Premixed products are designed for one-stop shopping and may be offered to investors directly, through advisors, or as a recommended investment within a 401(k) plan. Specialized funds are intended as part of a diversified mix selected by the investor. Mutual fund companies use print ads, Web-based marketing, and direct mail to current customers as well as relying on advisors to sell their funds. They also work with DC plan sponsors to help educate employees. On average, retirement investors seem to understand the common advice recommending a higher allocation to equities early in their careers that declines as they approach retirement. They have also increased their use of diversified life cycle funds.

However, there is inexplicably wide dispersion in allocations between retirement investors of the same age; the vast majority of employees don't make maximum use of their 401(k) plans or rebalance their portfolios; many employees retain large allocations of company stock; and when selecting a new investment, individual investors focus on year-to-date or trailing 12-month performance. The return-chasing behavior and the fear of missing out described in Chapter 15 indicate that generating eye-popping returns is one way to gather assets in a given product. This suggests that portfolio managers may want to take high risk with a new fund and hope the markets go in their direction for at least a year.

Research confirms that new assets flow to top-quartile managers and, to some extent, stick there. Goetzmann and Peles (1997) explain this by suggesting that investors hold their losers (they call this *inertia*) due to *cognitive dissonance*—the psychological tendency for humans to adjust their beliefs to make them feel better about past decisions. Their survey data indicate that mutual fund investors maintain upwardly biased recollections about the performance of their funds. This is consistent with studies of institutional investors by O'Barr and Conley (1992) and Karim and Stewart (2005), which indicate that pension plan investors believe their manager selection decisions are appropriate when in fact, on average, institutional investors do not add value from those decisions.

Berk and Green (2004) also explore why individual investors place assets with actively managed mutual funds and keep assets with poorly performing funds, seeking to explain their behavior without assuming investors are acting irrationally. They propose a theoretical model in which skillful managers attract assets after demonstrating strong performance; however, the higher asset level makes it more difficult to implement their strategies and continue to produce competitive returns. This approach is consistent with the economic theory of competition. Mamaysky and Speigel (2002) suggest that investment firms exist because individuals cannot spend the time necessary to monitor the markets. Their theory suggests that differing investor needs require the existence of different firms and different styles. The optimal level of assets for an investment firm is explored by Collins and Mack (1997). They suggest that the target level for a mutual fund complex in 1995 was $20 billion; but this empirical study based its conclusions on expense structures, not the opportunity to generate excess returns. Mutual fund firms Janus and Pilgrim Baxter are two examples of firms generating

---

[14] See Stoltz (1989).

very high returns in a short period in the 1990s, collecting assets quickly before experiencing quick reversals in performance and subsequently asset levels.

Mutual fund products are heavily regulated by the SEC. Fund prospectuses must be distributed before any money can be accepted. Because prospectuses are technical and long, fund companies frequently combine print and online advertising and direct mail with an offer to distribute the prospectus (frequently online). The typical mutual fund advertisement lists performance or Morningstar stars—fund companies know what sells mutual funds.

High net worth investors may buy funds directly or through a financial advisor. Advisors act as gatekeepers and can offer, for higher balances, lower basis point fee institutional products to their clients. Fund companies frequently offer advisors direct access to portfolio managers and in some cases face-to-face visits as is common in the institutional business.

Institutional Investors

The institutional sale is usually face-to-face, commonly following a *request for proposal* (RFP) bidding process. A typical institutional hiring process is summarized in Exhibit 16.3.

EXHIBIT 16.3
Typical Institutional Hiring Process

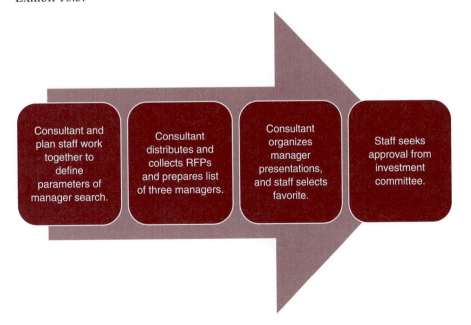

Consultant and plan staff work together to define parameters of manager search.

Consultant distributes and collects RFPs and prepares list of three managers.

Consultant organizes manager presentations, and staff selects favorite.

Staff seeks approval from investment committee.

The hiring process makes it clear that a manager's ability to communicate her or his investment process is important. In addition, potential institutional clients number in the thousands, not tens of millions. This suggests a different business strategy than that pursued in the individual market:

1. Shoot for consistency, not the stars—risk control is an important part of the investment process.
2. Develop a compelling story that can be easily understood by prospective investors. Stick to the story, enhancing it through time to maintain an edge.
3. Treat your clients well—it is a small industry.

Before portfolio managers are invited to make final presentations, they need to establish credibility, a performance record, and name recognition in the marketplace. The firm's sales operation will organize road shows, sometimes for years, to get the word out to pension consultants and prospective clients. This lets the portfolio manager fine-tune the presentation. Another part of the sales process is qualifying prospects—sizing up the business to determine whether it will be profitable enough to pursue. Custom management and dealing with highly demanding clients can require a disproportionately large amount of management time and effort. It may be necessary to accept this sort of client to build a business, but perhaps later this type of clientele can be kept to a minimum.

The goals for a new business presentation include clearly describing the investment process, making sure the listeners know that the presenter understands their needs, convincing the listeners to believe in the strategy's prospects for generating beta or alpha, and managing the prospective clients' expectations for performance. Balancing the need to promise enough to get new business with the need to limit expectations for the future to make it easier to maintain the relationship is a real art, tailored to each prospective client and perfected only after years of experience. Remember, if the business is easy to earn, it will be easy to lose—such clients tend to do little due diligence before making hire, and fire decisions.

The sales presentation may be divided into seven parts, as listed in Exhibit 16.4. The first goal should be to introduce the strategy—what it does and why it should succeed. The presentation will be more effective in gaining a prospective client's approval if the materials are customized to the client's specific needs and are sprinkled with the client's name throughout. Know your audience—are they bankers or tradespeople? Tailoring the delivery to the prospective client's level of sophistication is an important part of getting the message across. Note that some public plans have beneficiaries on the investment board; they may not understand technical terms as readily as others. Some groups are quiet; the presenter may need to spark a two-way conversation by saying something like "prospective clients frequently ask the following during this part of the presentation."

EXHIBIT 16.4
Layout of Sales Presentation

1. Summary of investment product, including thesis suggesting success
2. List of investment objectives
3. Resources
4. Process
5. Performance summary
6. Performance analysis
7. Benefit summary

In the mid 1990s a U.K. pension plan was seeking to place 500 million pounds sterling with a U.S. equity manager. Several firms were selected to present at the consultant's offices in London. More than one challenge faced the manager that day. The first was a reduction in the time scheduled for the presentation. "We're running a little late," said the consultant, "so can you shorten your discussion to 25 minutes?" It can be difficult to adjust the timing and content of a rehearsed presentation, potentially losing opportunities to make key points about the product. Some suggest sticking to originally planned timing to avoid upsetting the delivery at the risk of upsetting the client.* However, someone who is experienced at giving a sales pitch should be able to read the room, cut down the presentation to meet the client's request, and yet still focus on the audience's key concerns.

* See Zenker (1983).

EXHIBIT 16.5
Sample Investment Process Chart

With today's 24-hour, rapid-paced media, one must take care to keep the listeners' attention. Expect to get across one point per slide. Keep slides interesting by blending text with charts, tables, and graphics. An investment process chart is helpful. Exhibit 16.5 provides a simplified example of a chart for a growth equity strategy. Include proof statements; for example, insert a title statement with a supporting bar chart to support the statement. Balance seriousness with fun—show that you have a sense of humor, and the client will look forward to seeing you every quarter. Finally, remember to ask for the business. That simple act shows you will appreciate winning it.

16.6   Retaining Clients

Research has shown that the hiring process is sometimes flawed. Your clients may select you simply because your track record looks good over recent history. If they failed to effectively adjust for the extremeness of your style relative to the benchmark, they may give up on you when short-term performance is poor. In addition to consistently generating strong performance, it is important to know your client and develop effective means of communication. If performance is positive, update the client about any changes in the investment process or personnel, remind them what you are doing for them, and keep them informed about the markets. When relative performance is positive but the markets are down and total performance is negative, there is a need for hand-holding to ensure that the client stays on track. If both total performance and relative performance are negative, your communication must convey your disappointment and convince the client to stay with the strategy.

Communicate frequently. Communicate more if performance weakens. Demonstrate, and explain, why performance is weak and that portfolio characteristics and performance are consistent with the investment process. Demonstrate that active performance tends to reverse with a chart illustrating that strong relative results tend to follow periods of poor active performance.

Communication begins with setting expectations. Chapter 2 discussed the importance of a comprehensive IPS. Expectations are set beginning with the sales process and formalized in the IPS. Portfolio guidelines and side letters are another technique for articulating what is expected of the manager and client. One way to think about expectations mirrors the way many companies manage their earnings outlook: Underpromise and overdeliver. Ojasalo (2001) suggests the following approach for managing customer expectations in professional services:

1. Make fuzzy expectations precise.
2. Make implicit expectations explicit.
3. Make unrealistic expectations realistic.

In the investment business, expectations are focused on performance—the level and the risk of underperforming. There are several ways to make these explicit and more realistic: understating strong historical results and discussing periods of underperformance in the sales process, setting a range instead of a point estimate in the management agreement, and, in a side letter, providing a probability distribution in addition to simple active standard deviation measures.

Ongoing Client Communication

In the investment business, PMs must expect a call at any time. With today's technology, market values, holdings, and returns are available to clients daily, if not tick by tick. Investment reviews are typically done quarterly. In the institutional marketplace, meetings are scheduled annually or more frequently. Mutual fund reports are mailed semiannually but tend to arrive late—in some cases more than three months after the performance period ends. It seems doubtful whether anyone reads such dated material. Exhibit 16.6 provides a sample of the communication materials provided for one popular mutual fund family. The Web site offers return summaries, portfolio characteristics, and top holdings. The prospectus, which must be distributed to the prospective investor, is over 45 pages long, and some may feel much of it looks like the small print in a credit card agreement.

A semi-annual performance report is shown in Exhibit 16.6. These documents tend to summarize the market environment, list fund returns over multiple periods accompanied by a growth chart, and perhaps include a discussion by the portfolio manager. The challenge for the mutual fund company is not just explaining performance but also *reviewing the bidding,* or reminding clients why they first hired the fund manager and convincing them that these reasons are still valid. This can be challenging in face-to-face meetings in the institutional marketplace; but if performance is poor, it is an especially difficult long-distance task. In contrast, reviewing good performance with a client is an opportunity to cross-sell.

Communication in Periods of Poor Performance

Following years of strong performance, and having been recommended in the June 2007 Kiplinger Letter as "the best performer—we note a pattern here," the Loomis Bond Fund suffered from the explosion of credit spreads in 2008.

Theory in Practice   *Concern But Not Alarm*

When an investment strategy is not performing well in the short term, a manager needs to reach out to investors; clients need to know that the investment manager is paying close attention to the portfolio but not panicking. A letter stating, "We are concerned, but not alarmed,"* may be appropriate. Expressing concern confirms that the manager understands the seriousness of the underperformance and of losing money. These words should be followed by a clear discussion of the source of the underperformance and an explanation of why investors should be confident it will reverse. Expressing confidence, with facts to back it up, gives investors hope and supports their decision to stick with the manager.

Extended poor performance, or significant short-term underperformance, requires portfolio managers to go the extra mile. They will need to visit their clients. And before the review booklet is opened, it is imperative a manager express why he or she is there. Clients need to know that the manager shares their pain. In some cases a client will take some time to explain how she or he feels—perhaps an uncomfortable, but deserved, lecture for the manager.

* This wording may be credited to Thomas Cooper, partner at GMO.

EXHIBIT 16.6   **Sample Mutual Fund Communication Materials**

Source: Copyright *American Funds*

Web-site Summary Information

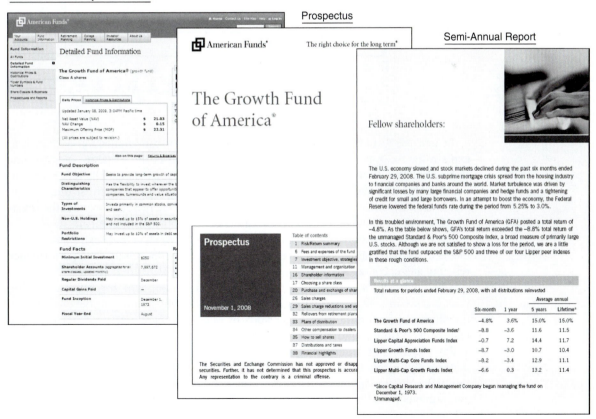

EXHIBIT 16.7 **Sample Communication Materials Regarding Period of Poor Performance**

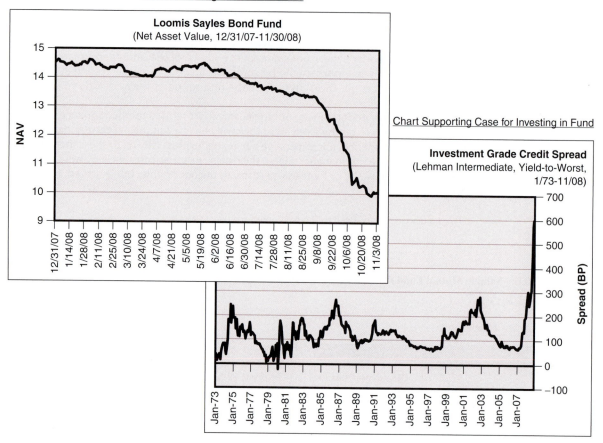

Chart Illustrating Fund Performance

Loomis Sayles Bond Fund
(Net Asset Value, 12/31/07–11/30/08)

Chart Supporting Case for Investing in Fund

Investment Grade Credit Spread
(Lehman Intermediate, Yield-to-Worst, 1/73–11/08)

In late 2008, another Kiplinger[15] report suggested a communication approach to explain the weak performance and express confidence in the strategy—a story line that would have been effective for Loomis's client relations team. The report recommended that now (late 2008) was an unusually attractive time to invest due to high yields and low valuations. It reviews the uniqueness of the period to explain the severity of the performance. The charts in Exhibit 16.7 support this argument.

Even more important, the thesis could be expanded to show how extreme environments in the past subsequently reversed, suggesting the opportunity for a performance rebound and encouraging investors to stay with the fund.

The quarterly or semiannual review is an important tool for communicating with clients in both good and bad times. This is an opportunity to develop a relationship—an important asset in periods of business change or poor performance results. The timing and content are important in building a positive impression. Today's technology facilitates regular virtual or real face-to-face contact. Information shared about mutual funds must meet SEC regulatory standards; institutional communications are not subject to such rules. Exhibit 16.8 lists the key components (and their objectives) of a review document.

[15] Goldberg, 2008.

EXHIBIT 16.8
Key Components of a Portfolio Review and Their Objectives

Section	Objective	Display
Performance	Update client on results and market value, share long-term performance.	Table
Portfolio guidelines	Remind client of goals for account; provide opportunity to discuss needed modifications.	Bullets
Performance attribution	Explain where performance is coming from; demonstrate whether it is consistent with strategy.	Chart
Discussion and outlook	Describe market environment and explain current thinking.	Bullets, charts, etc.
Portfolio characteristics and positions	Demonstrate that portfolio structure is in line with guidelines and stated process; share current bets.	Tables
Free-form	Explanation of strategy improvements, further discussion of performance (especially if weak); update on personnel; opportunity for cross-selling.	Bullets, charts, etc.

16.7   Case Study

Chapter 6 presented a sample tactical asset allocation strategy based on the statistical significance of simple valuation measures. This strategy tends to succeed in market extremes and does not always take active positions. Such a strategy can be hard to sell to investors: Why should they pay a fee if you are not taking an active bet? Sometimes this particular strategy needs years to work. It is not designed to add value on a quarterly basis—it takes only one bet at any time. Clients may become impatient.

This strategy, therefore, is a good example for illustrating the importance of the sales process, developing good relationships with clients, and communicating with them regularly. Perhaps the strategy's best application is as a supplement to an investor's overall investment plan, or as one of several features within a financial advisory service.

In this case, the sales process should turn the strategy's perceived shortcomings into benefits. For example, "Markets tend to reverse at valuation extremes: The larger the extreme, the higher the chance of a reversal and the larger its size. This strategy recognizes this fact and takes positions only at these extremes, where it is most valuable." A chart, such as Exhibit 16.9, may be a helpful illustration of this point showing how valuations, once extended, tend to retract.

EXHIBIT 16.9
Distribution of 12-Month Active Returns and Subsequent Active Returns: Sample TAA strategy from Chapter 6, 1978-2008

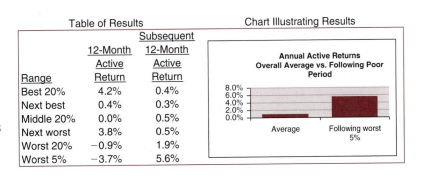

Table of Results

Range	12-Month Active Return	Subsequent 12-Month Active Return
Best 20%	4.2%	0.4%
Next best	0.4%	0.3%
Middle 20%	0.0%	0.5%
Next worst	3.8%	0.5%
Worst 20%	−0.9%	1.9%
Worst 5%	−3.7%	5.6%

Chart Illustrating Results

Annual Active Returns Overall Average vs. Following Poor Period

Average / Following worst 5%

The strategy can also get into trouble—it underperformed in 35 percent of 12-month periods between 1978 and 2008. Market valuation extremes can continue for some time and become even more extreme, only to reverse later. Technology stocks in the late 1990s are a good example. It was easy for clients and senior management to tell portfolio managers in late 1999 to "get with the program" and load up on tech.[16] The hard task was sticking with the discipline.

A chart may be prepared to support this argument, if applicable. For the TAA strategy in Chapter 6, it should show that active performance tends to improve after periods of poor active performance. Exhibit 16.9 offers an example. On average, the strategy generates a 5.6 percent 12-month active return after the worst (bottom 5 percent) 12-month periods.

Enhancing the investment strategy will give clients something to look forward to and help them be patient. Market participants are highly competitive, and ideas travel quickly. The speed of the business increases, and static strategies invariably underperform. It is important that portfolio managers continually upgrade their skills and investment processes to maintain the quality of their investment results.

A plan for improving an investment strategy follows closely the steps outlined in Chapter 6 for developing and managing an investment process. This includes reviewing the philosophy, the source of raw material, and the implementation, including an analysis of transaction costs. The goals of the strategy, as presented in the ISP, should also be reviewed. Implementation of the plan requires a thorough understanding of the strategy process, including any weaknesses revealed since inception, expert thinking about the markets to incorporate current or developing trends, and an effective plan for communicating the planned improvements. This communication includes sharing the plan with senior management and clients. Business managers need to know that performance is being taken seriously and progress is being made to improve it. There is always a limit to patience, but a good plan effectively communicated can buy a few quarters from both clients and the boss. Because investors tend to exit a strategy at the wrong time, sometimes all a portfolio manager needs is one more quarter to save his or her job.

Summary

Sometimes portfolio managers feel that the investment business would be a great one if only they did not have those pesky clients to worry about! Of course the money invested is the clients'—and without them there would be no investment industry. And keeping the clients happy is part of the exciting challenge of the money management business.

This chapter has provided guidance for portfolio managers in supporting the needs of their clients. It began with a list of general recommendations to address the behavioral tendencies common to individual and institutional clients. The manager selection process was reviewed and recommendations made on how to avoid performance chasing and being disappointed by subsequent manager performance. The chapter concluded with a discussion of winning and retaining a client's business. Special attention was paid to retaining clients in times of stress. These topics provide a template with which to build healthy client relationships and help the PM retain the privilege of running money.

This chapter follows 15 prior chapters that discussed the investment industry, presented theoretical foundations and practical tools, illustrated how the tools can be applied, and reviewed the entire investment process through time. Now that you have worked to master this material, we hope it whets your appetite for running money and gives you a strong set of skills to do it effectively.

[16] See the 2001 *Wall Street Journal* article by John Hechinger.

Problems

1. 2008 was a dreadful period for investors. Both the severity and the abruptness of the losses caught investors by surprise and put them in shock. The following letter regarding the 2008 results for a Massachusetts educational foundation was distributed by the investment committee to trustees:

> In 2008 the U.S. financial markets experienced the worst crisis since the 1930s. The S&P 500, down by 38 percent in 2008, displayed its worst year since the Great Depression of 1929–1933. International equities had worse returns in U.S. dollars than U.S. equities. Even investment-grade bonds declined. The only assets earning positive returns in 2008 were money markets and Treasury securities. However, even some money market investments weren't safe from decline.
>
> The CMS portfolio was conservatively invested with approximately 60 percent in stocks, including international stocks. As the markets declined, we chose not to reset this weight, instead allowing the risk exposure to decline. While the CMS portfolio was significantly impacted by the markets, this decision and the bond and cash components helped protect the CMS portfolio, which experienced around a 25 percent decline in 2008. For comparison, many university endowments and pension funds are predicting over 30 percent declines in this period.
>
> The portfolio is now $1.61 million. A 5 percent distribution would total $81,000, and 6 percent would be $97,000. The planned distribution of $28,000 for the second part of the fiscal year 2008–2009, for a 12-month distribution of $88,000, is at the middle of this range. We recommend continuing this $88,000 gifting level for 2009, assuming a stable asset level and anticipating further contributions into the account. Of course we may need to review this decision if the markets deteriorate further or experience a recovery.
>
> Going forward, we plan to slowly move the equity allocation back to 50 percent from the current 45 percent. This allows the plan to buy in at low prices but also protects the account from downside volatility. This will be implemented by investing contributions.
>
> Although it may take years for the markets to fully recover, with the long-term goals of CMS, we believe the portfolio should remain balanced between bond and stock investments. We will continue to monitor the portfolio closely.

   What is the goal of the letter? How do you think the trustees reacted to the letter? How sophisticated do the trustees seem to be? What do you think total and active performance had been over the long term? How could the letter be improved?

2. In general, how weak does performance need to be, and for how long, before the manager must visit the client?

3. What is the pattern of asset and account withdrawals for institutional and individual investors in periods of poor performance in a given year, and over longer periods? What are the implications for business strategy?

4. Explore the asset levels and performance results of the Loomis Bond Fund since 2008. Did performance match expectations? How effective were they in retaining assets? What communication strategies were adopted?

5. A fund review includes the following slide. Where does it belong in the layout of the review? What point is being made? Suggest a discussion to accompany the slide. How would you consolidate this information into a simpler chart? What other information should be provided in the review?

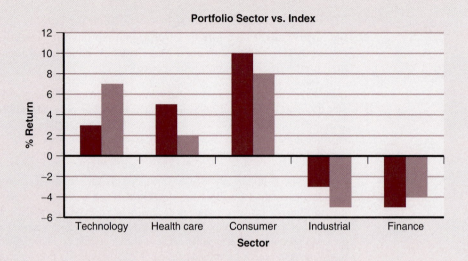

Sample Cases

This appendix contains material for the four cases that we have developed and used in conjunction with *Running Money: Professional Portfolio Management.* The goal in developing these cases was to present realistic situations representative of the types of problems faced by portfolio managers. In fact the first three cases are based on actual business problems. The cases also give students an opportunity to synthesize the material they have learned. By necessity, the book is organized into chapters that cover different aspects of portfolio management. The reality is that investment problems require bringing these different skills together. Here are the four cases:

- John M.: A high net worth individual. The case requires a review of the individual's assets, work plans, and life goals and the development of a custom investment policy that provides real cash flows and is adaptable to future contingencies.
- MSSI: A defined benefit pension plan. The defined benefit case requires analysis of the plan liabilities and development of a custom asset allocation and funding program to maximize return and minimize asset–liability variability.
- McLain Capital: A defined contribution plan. This defined contribution case requires a review of the prospective client's objectives and the design of a comprehensive package of investment products for its employees. This proposal must also consider plan effectiveness as measured by employee adoption and the appropriateness of employee allocations.
- Fairbanks Fund: A small-cap stock fund. The fourth case reflects the essential features of a real money fund run by students under our supervision at Boston University.

In our portfolio management course, case deliverables are broken into parts that allow each case to be divided into four stages. The first is investment objectives; the second is asset allocation; and the third is investment implementation including recommended investment vehicles, transition of assets, and rebalancing. The fourth and final deliverable is a professional, comprehensive presentation including measures of success for both the client and the investment manager. This fourth deliverable may be eliminated if time is limited. We've suggested spacing of the deliverables, and relevant chapters. The specifics of the deliverables differ by case. However, they are all based on the following outline:

1. First deliverable: Client and fund objectives. (Due following coverage of Chapter 2)
   a. Summary of problem.
   b. Objectives (return, risk, and so on).
   c. Key constraints and issues.
2. Second deliverable: Client design of product or solution. (Due following coverage of Chapters 3 and 6; 4 and 5 would be optional)
   a. Proposed product line or investment strategy.
   b. Description of asset allocation.
   c. Description of required explanation and education.
   d. Fund portfolio structure.
      i. Sectors, stocks, style.
      ii. Themes.
      iii. Alphas.

3. Third deliverable: Client implementation and mechanics. (Due following coverage of Chapters 7–12)

   a. Vehicles.

   b. Management issues, such as rebalancing.

   c. Ongoing communication.

   d. Fund performance analysis presentation. (Requires coverage of Chapter 13)

      i. Raw material: individual stocks and total.

      ii. Fund performance attribution.

      iii. Market timing and style.

      iv. Sector and stock selection.

4. Fourth deliverable: Client measures of success (Due following coverage of Chapters 14, 15, and 16)

   a. Client's definition of success

   b. Company's definition

   c. Performance measurement of success

   d. Fund measures of success

      i. Follow-up from earlier presentation

      ii. Analyst stock coverage

      iii. Fund operation review & recommendations

The materials for each case have three components:

- A brief statement of the case.
- The four case-specific deliverable assignments.
- Supporting materials.

John M.

Individual Case: Designing an Investment Plan for John M.

Background

John M. has just sold his business to a larger retail chain for $15 million, resulting in an immediate lump sum after-tax payment of $7 million and residual before-tax cash flows of $1 million in each of the next two years. John will retain the business real estate, which is expected to generate $100,000 (pretax) annually. He will remain with the company for six months without pay to manage the transition.

John is 44 years old and single. He has never had much money and lives modestly. He expects to need $2,000 (after-tax) a week. John has little investment experience having held his financial assets (approximately $100,000 excluding sale of the business) in an interest-bearing checking account for personal and business spending. Although he has received numerous cold call investment solicitations, these have merely resulted in a loss of capital.

The Problem

John has asked Intrepid Investments Inc. to design an investment strategy and investment portfolio. The portfolio should be constructed of broad asset category indexes. John is in the 50 percent tax bracket. He anticipates launching a new venture (after the transition period) for which he wants to hold $1 million in reserve. There are no other regulatory, legal, or personal considerations or restrictions.

The Assignment

You are an associate at Intrepid Investments reporting to Allie Williams. Allie has asked you to handle John's account and keep her informed of your progress. With Allie, you will present your proposed strategy and portfolio to John.

Questions That Immediately Come to Mind

1. What explicit and implicit assumptions (include the necessary values, explanation, or exhibits) do you make to develop your strategy and portfolio?
2. What do you do on the first day?
3. What is the risk of encountering liquidity problems?
4. What is the risk (probability and exposure) that the portfolio's actual performance will depart from expected performance?
5. Suppose John M. decided later to invest 50 percent of his assets (rather than the $1 million) in the new venture. How will this affect the investment strategy and asset allocation going forward?

Outline for First Deliverable: Objectives and Constraints

Individual Investor Case Written Hand-In: 2–3 Pages with Discussion and Bullets

1. Summary of problem:
   a. Income needs.
   b. Spending goals: liability.
   c. Cash flow and time line summary.
   d. Investor profile.
   e. Steps for analysis and proposal.
2. Investment objectives:
   a. Return objective.
   b. Risk measures and objectives.
   c. Time frame.
   d. Liquidity needs: each stage.
3. Constraints and issues:
   a. Regulatory.
   b. Taxes and costs.
   c. Assumptions and follow-up questions.
   d. Potential future changes.
   4. Ongoing performance measurement and monitoring.
5. Plans for adjusting the portfolio.

Outline for Second Deliverable: Product Design and Solution

Individual Investor Case Written Hand-In: 5–10 Pages with Tables and Charts

1. Cash flow analysis.
2. Definition of risk:
   a. Attitude.
   b. Ability.
   c. Inflation.
   d. Liability.

3. Asset allocation analysis:
   a. Utilize key risk measure.
   b. Explore using at least one other risk measure.
   c. Show alternatives within risk–return spectrum: Static or dynamic?
   d. Active or passive allocation: Why?
   e. Recommend allocation (stocks, bonds, duration, cash).
   f. Illustrate historical or forecast behavior, including stress testing.
4. Summary: how to meet goals, objectives, and constraints.

Note to student: This step requires specific percentage allocations. The AA model should include forecast returns (historical variance/covariance matrix OK); the AA analysis must be quantified and include more definitions of risk than simply standard deviation. It would be helpful to offer historical or scenario stress testing of target allocations. Consideration of taxes would also be helpful.

Outline for Third Deliverable: Implementation/Mechanics

Individual Investor Case Written Hand-In: 5–10 Pages Including Time Matrix (Day One and through Time)

1. Cash flow and investment summary, including asset class weights.
2. Vehicles:
   a. How do asset class investments work? Investment strategy, personnel, resources, and so on.
   b. Objectives and guidelines (sample or summary for all classes).
   c. Taxable versus tax-free investing.
3. Matrix (time line—day one and through time; investment steps):
   a. How current money is put to work.
   b. How flows are invested.
   c. How money is raised for expenses.
   d. Where money resides.
4. Management issues:
   a. Key monitoring variables and summary of actions.
   b. Target asset class weights through time.
   c. Mechanics of rebalancing asset class weights to target.
   d. Money/customer moves.
5. Ongoing communication:
   a. What will the client receive?
   b. How will the client and manager work together to direct investments?
   c. Sample/outline report.

Outline for Fourth Deliverable: Measuring Success

Individual Investor Case: 1–2 Pages with Bullets

- Client's definition of success.
- Company's definition of success.
- Performance measurement of success.

Note to student: A formal, bound business presentation document covering all steps is due at this time.

- Multiple tabs.
- Include first three deliverables and measures of success.
- Include appendix of supporting materials.

John completed the firm's standard questionnaire, listed below.

Questionnaire

1. What is your primary investment goal?
   a. _____ Preservation of capital.
   b. _____ Generate income.
   c. _____ Build wealth.
   d. _X_ Other: _____

   I need to generate current income because I'm no longer employed. I also would like to build wealth but I want to preserve my capital as well. So I guess I'd rank them in descending order of importance as shown above. But remember I'm only 44.

2. Investing involves a trade-off between risk and return. Investors who have experienced higher long-term returns have experienced greater fluctuation in value through time with a greater potential for loss versus investors in more conservative investments. Keeping this in mind, how would you finish the following sentence?

   My main investment goal is to

   a. _____ Protect the value of my account. To minimize the chance for loss, I am willing to accept the lower long-term returns provided by conservative investments.
   b. _____ Keep risk to a minimum while trying to achieve slightly higher returns than provided by more conservative investments.
   c. _X_ Balance moderate levels of risk with moderate levels of returns.
   d. _____ Maximize long-term investment returns. Therefore, I am willing to accept large and sometimes dramatic fluctuations in the value of my investments.

3. The following table shows the potential best and worst cases of investing $100,000 for one year in each of four hypothetical portfolios. Portfolios with the greatest gains also have the largest potential losses. In which portfolio would you be most comfortable investing?

Portfolio	Worst Case	Best Case
A _____	$94,000	$117,000
B _X_	$87,000	$129,000
C _____	$82,000	$138,000
D _____	$76,000	$149,000

4. If you invested $100,000 that was performing in line with the market and it lost value, at what point would you sell the investment and move to a more conservative investment rather than waiting for an increase in value?

    a. _____$95,000.
    b. _____$90,000.
    c. _____$85,000.
    d. _____$80,000.
    e. _____$75,000.
    f. _____I would not sell due to the decline.

If in line with the market, I wouldn't sell.

5. Please list any liabilities that add up to a balance of $25,000 or more.

Mortgage = $150,000

6. I am willing to experience potentially large declines in the value of my investment if it will increase the likelihood of achieving high long-term returns.
    a. _____Agree.
    b. _____Somewhat agree.
    c. __X__Somewhat disagree.
    d. _____Disagree.

Somewhat disagree. It's not that I'm not willing to take risk to achieve a good return. But my "high-risk" money will probably go into a new venture. Besides, I feel better taking risk where I have more control.

Notes from Follow-Up Meeting with John M.

After reviewing the initial information provided by John M. and his responses to the questionnaire, you held a follow-up meeting with John to more accurately assess his needs. Here are your notes from that meeting:

- Does John ever plan to get married or have children? If so, is this a possible near-term event or more of a longer-term possibility?

  One never ever knows with these things, though nothing is imminent.

- Does John currently have any philanthropic plans or desires or perhaps the desire to create a charitable foundation?

  Not currently but perhaps further down the road.

- John indicated that he has a relatively modest lifestyle and expense structure. Are there any major expenses that should be planned for, such as a new house, a dream car, a yacht, a private plane, or the like?

  None other than the previously mentioned business venture.

- We have an estimate of rental income of $100,000 per year to work with.
  - How many years does John expect to hold the property?
  - Is the rental income fixed or is there an inflation adjustment?
  - How long is the lease?

- If he plans to sell the property, what is the possible time frame and what is the expected residual value?

  No plans to sell it. The rental income is fixed until the lease expires in five years. The expected lease is to be renewed every five years with the new lease rate adjusted for inflation. However, if the market for retail space is weak there will be no increase in lease rate.

- Does John's sales contract and agreement to remain with the company for six months without pay to help manage the transition preclude John from other employment or preclude John from receiving income from another source?

  No.

- Retirement plans: At what age does John plan to retire and enjoy his "golden years"?

  He considers himself semiretired currently.

- Can John describe the idea for his new business venture? Will it have a similar risk profile to his prior business?

  Plans are not specific yet. Most likely a specialty retail business. Risky. Prior business was mature; this one will obviously be a start-up.

- Is John comfortable with alternative investment strategies?

  Other than a basic, "popular press" understanding, he would need considerable education to get comfortable with the concepts, risks, ...

MSSI

Defined Benefit Plan Case: Designing the Investment Structure for MSSI Corporation's Defined Benefit Plan

Background

MSSI Corporation has a defined benefit plan. You are invited to design and present an investment structure for its pension plan, including an asset liability study and an asset allocation and funding policy, with the anticipation of assuming full investment management responsibility for the plan. To facilitate your work, the board has kindly sent you a copy of its latest actuarial valuation reports as factual bases for your work.

The Problem

The rule of thumb in the pension investment world is the "60/40 rule"—that is, 60% equity and 40% bonds.

1. Can you apply this general 60/40 rule to the plan?
2. What funding levels provide what comfort level of the plan being healthy through time?
3. Can you quantify the risk–return trade-off (in easy-to-understand terms) for the board?

The Assignment

You are an associate portfolio manager at DBSol reporting to Jay. He has asked you to design a program for the pension plan. The program must include the following:

1. An analysis of the current liability. Explore the cost to maintain the plan and the growth of the liability through time.

2. An analysis of the current funding status, including the future of the plan with the current funding and asset allocation strategy. Define key risk measures.

3. Proposed funding and asset allocation strategies.

4. Analysis of these strategies and their potential impact on the funding status of the plan in the future.

Jay suggests starting by looking at the actuarial report and the available spreadsheet. The spreadsheet provides a template for analyzing the liability. Note that you'll need to find and insert (highlighted in yellow) discount rates before the present values make any sense.

Issues Jay would like you to consider

1. How do you quantify the impact of different investment and funding structures?

2. Is the efficient frontier relevant for pensions?

3. How does the current asset allocation compare to an optimal one?

4. You want to find out how well funded the plan is and how healthy it will be in the future. There are at least two determinants. For an ongoing plan, are assets close to 100 percent of the present value of the liability? Second, for a plan that may be frozen, is the plan at least 90 percent funded?

5. Going forward, you want to minimize contributions and pension expense.

Jay has asked you to follow these steps for conducting an analysis:

1. Calculate the duration of the liability

2. Model the liability into the future. How do you expect the present value to change? Use the Excel worksheet (available online) to build this model.

3. What are the annual expenses? Consider long-term horizons when modeling risk and return.

4. Model funding, varying asset allocations, and funding policies.

Here is some guidance from Jay regarding the problem:

---

1. How should we model future liabilities—flatten them out after extrapolating the last few years' trend? Decline them to zero? Any rules of thumb?

   I would keep it level; without an explicit assumption on the company's hiring policy, this is the safest bet.

2. How does the inflation thing work? Are you assuming active lives' benefits grow with inflation and inactive don't?

   Yes. The logic is that active benefits (tied to salaries) rise with inflation, which is some portion of the change in interest rates.

Online Materials

1. Actuarial report.

2. Spreadsheet of benefit projections and valuation tools.

Outline for First Deliverable: Objectives and Constraints

Defined Benefit Plan Case Written Hand-In: 2–3 Pages with Discussion and Bullets

1. Summary of problem:
   a. Assets.
   b. Liabilities (size, definition).
   c. Company profile.
   d. Funding policy.
   e. Steps: analysis, proposal.
2. Objectives:
   a. Income and principal versus total return.
   b. Asset/liability.
   c. Return goals.
   d. Funding requirements.
   e. Risk definition and objectives.
3. Constraints and issues:
   a. Taxes.
   b. Funding.
   c. Inflation.
   d. Company.
   e. Regulatory.
4. Ongoing performance measurement and monitoring.
5. Proposed plan for adjusting.

Outline for Second Deliverable: Product Design and Solution

Defined Benefit Plan Case Written Hand-In: 5–10 Pages with Tables and Charts

1. Funding status:
   a. Summarize, draw conclusions.
   b. Calculate required return and contribution.
2. Asset allocation analysis:
   a. Define risk.
   b. Model liability.
   c. Analyze asset/liability.
      i. Illustrate return.
      ii. Illustrate risk.
      iii. Illustrate trade-off.
   d. Propose percentage funding through time.
3. Recommend:
   a. Allocation (stocks, bonds, duration, cash): static or dynamic?
   b. Illustrate historical or forecast behavior, including stress testing.
   c. Compare with current allocation.
4. Summary: how to meet goals, objectives, and constraints.

Note to student: This step requires specific percentage allocations. The AA model should include forecast returns (historical variance/covariance matrix OK); the AA analysis must be quantified and include more definitions of risk than simply standard deviation. Also needed are specific percentage or dollar funding proposals for the near and long term. Communicate an understanding of the asset–liability problem, including DB funding criteria. It would be nice to have historical or scenario stress testing of the target.

Outline for Third Deliverable: Implementation/Mechanics

Defined Benefit Plan Case Written Hand-In: 5–10 Pages Including Matrix (Day One and through Time)

1. Summarize asset allocation weights.
2. Vehicles:
   a. How do asset class investments work? Investment strategy, personnel, resources, and so on.
   b. Objectives and guidelines (sample or summary for all classes).
3. Matrix (time line—day one and through time; investment steps):
   a. How current money is put to work (trading or the like).
   b. How flows are invested.
4. Management issues:
   a. Key monitoring variables and summary of actions.
   b. Target asset class weights through time.
   c. Mechanics of rebalancing asset class weights to target.
5. Ongoing communication:
   a. What will the client receive?
   b. Sample/outline report.

Outline for Fourth Deliverable: Measuring Success

Defined Benefit Plan Case Written Hand-In: 1–2 Pages with Bullets

- Client's definition of success.
- Company's definition of success.
- Performance measurement of success.

Note to student: A formal presentation booklet with tabs covering all four steps, and an appendix with supporting materials, is required at this stage.

Company Financial Information: Defined Benefit Case, 2008

- Market cap: $350 million, Corporate credit rating: S&P BB
- Total assets: $700 million
- Total liabilities: $350 million
  - Long-term debt: $250 million
  - Other liabilities: $100 million
- Shareholder equity: $350 million

Note to student: While earnings and sales information are not available, an aspiring portfolio manager may want to use market P/E and P/S to estimate them, seeking to match market cap, credit rating, and P/B for finding comparables.

Useful Articles and Sites

The U.S. Department of Labor provides a nice discussion of ERISA, the law that outlines pension management goals, rules for termination, and FASB standards, at www.dol.gov/ebsa/faqs/faq_compliance_pension.html.

There is an interesting *Wall Street Journal* article that is helpful for understanding DB plan issues: Theo Francis, "Pension Plans Take Healthy Turn," *The Wall Street Journal,* January 23, 2007.

Brokerage and investment firms regularly publish papers on DB issues. Here are three good ones:

Andrew Dierdorf, "Managing DB Investment Risk—Are Long Bonds Your Silver Bullet?" *Fidelity Investments Viewpoint* 6, no. 3 (Summer 2005).

M. Moran, A. Cohen, and M. Kim, "Pension Review 2007: High Class Problems," *Goldman Sachs United States Portfolio Strategy,* August 3, 2007.

G. Lather and J. Haugh, "Market Impact of Pension Accounting Reform," *Merrill Lynch Pensions and Investments* 15, October 4, 2006.

McClain Capital

Defined Contribution Plan Case: Designing a Defined Contribution Plan

Background

McLain Capital has been asked to design a 401(k) plan for an institutional client to offer to its employees. The company is a closely held corporation. As a result, it is somewhat paternalistic and wants to make the program easy to use. There are 9,500 eligible employees who know little about investments. This is reflected in the limited options available in the current retirement plan: company stock and guaranteed income contracts (GIC).

The Problem

The company wants a state-of-the-art 401(k) plan tailored to its needs. The client does not want off-the-shelf funds, but rather a custom offering based on commingled pools that already exist. The plan should offer the following benefits:

- Easy to use.
- Effective.
- Multiple offerings.
- Risk-controlled.
- Actively managed.
- No mutual funds.

An effective plan will make it easy for investors to match their retirement goals (such as return, time horizon, and risk aversion) with particular funds. In the short term, the client has asked you to guide investors to move out of GICs and focus on longer-term investments. By diversifying for them across asset classes, it becomes easy for the investors to invest for their own retirement needs. It also dampens return volatility, reduces the tendency to react to short-term results, and provides enough flexibility for investors to customize their investments. The idea is to design investment options that meet their risk–return needs and describe the risk in terms the investors can understand.

The Assignment

You are an associate portfolio manager at McLain Capital reporting to Wally Amundsen. Wally has asked you to design a 401(k) plan that meets these guidelines. McLain Capital offers commingled pools and mutual funds. It has also used other companies' offerings in their own products.

Outline for First Deliverable: Objectives and Constraints

Defined Contribution Plan Case Written Hand-In: 2–3 Pages with Discussion and Bullets

Note to student: The entire product will not be fully designed at this point. Students are free to change things throughout the semester but are required to have a draft plan at this step.

1. Summary of problem:
    a. Company.
    b. Employees.
    c. Responsibilities.
    d. Company and employee requests and requirements.
    e. Participation.
    f. Steps for analysis and proposal.
2. Investment objectives—return, income, liability matching:
    a. Retirement goals. (Can this be quantified?)
    b. Return objectives.
    c. Risk definition, communication, and goals. (Can a liability be defined?)
    d. Ease of use (number of options and so on).
    e. Effectiveness (fit of options with goals and summary).
    f. Products versus advisory service.
    g. Active versus passive.
3. Constraints and issues—liquidity, capacity, horizon:
    a. Costs.
    b. Taxes.
    c. Education, sophistication.
4. Process for ongoing performance measurement and monitoring: market conditions, valuations, investor circumstances.
5. Process for adjustment.

Outline for Second Deliverable: Product Design and Solution

Defined Contribution Plan Case Written Hand-In: 5–10 Pages with Tables and Charts

1. Overall product design summary:
    a. Features.
    b. How to meet goals and objectives.
2. Definition of risk:
    a. How to incorporate into product design.
    b. How to help investors understand.

3. Asset allocation analysis and recommendation:
    a. Use key risk measure: overall versus target.
    b. Explore using at least one other risk measure.
    c. Show product design within risk–return spectrum.
    d. Allocations (stocks, bonds, duration, cash): static or dynamic?
    e. Active or passive allocation: why?
4. Discuss how to meet special needs of investors:
    a. Risk.
    b. Needs.
5. List education requirements.

Note to student: This step requires specific percentage allocations. The AA analysis must be quantified; the AA model should include forecast returns (historical variance/covariance matrix OK). The case also requires a risk measure beyond variance to communicate to non–investment-savvy participants. Interesting extensions to standard lifestyle products include consideration of an employee's postretirement liability stream and historical or scenario stress testing of target allocations.

Outline for Third Deliverable: Implementation/Mechanics

Defined Contribution Plan Case Written Hand-In: 5–10 Pages Including Matrix (Day One and through Time)

Note to student: The requirements include an explanation of procedures used to allocate money on day one and manage it through time, a discussion of the rationale behind selections, and a demonstration that the approach makes sense and can add value.

1. Overall product summary:
    a. Product offerings.
    b. Asset class weights.
2. Vehicles:
    a. How do asset class investments work? Investment strategy, personnel, resources, and so on.
    b. Objectives and guidelines (sample or summary for all classes).
    c. How to select underlying managers, both internal and external.
    d. Track records.
3. Matrix (time line—day one and through time; investment steps):
    a. How current money is put to work (trading and so on).
    b. How flows are invested.
4. Management issues:
    a. Key monitoring variables and summary of actions.
    b. Target asset class weights through time.
    c. Mechanics of rebalancing asset class weights to target.
    d. Money/customer moves.
5. Ongoing communication:
    a. What will the client receive?
    b. How will the participants manage direction of investments?
    c. Sample/outline report.

Outline for Fourth Deliverable: Measuring Success

Defined Contribution Plan Case Written Hand-In: 1–2 Pages with Bullets

- Measures of success:
  - Client's definition of success variables.
  - Company's definition of success.
  - Performance measurement of success.

Note to student: A presentation book with tabs reviewing the first three deliverables and measures of success, plus an appendix of supporting materials, is also required at this time.

Additional Information

The Company

- Most employees are high school, but not college, graduates.
- Employees span all age ranges, with a slightly older average profile than the U.S. working population.
- Employee retention is very high.
- Employees have regular access to computers at work in their offices, in the HR office, or in the employee lounge/break area(s).
- The current plan offers few educational or informational resources.
- Senior management includes many sophisticated finance professionals. The investment committee includes primarily finance people, not HR people.

The Existing Plan

- Current plan participation is 50 percent.
- Contributions are matched at 100 percent up to 4 percent of salary.
- Participating employees contribute from 2.5 percent to 6 percent into the plan.
- The plan vesting schedule is 50 percent after three years and 100 percent after five years.
- The current plan offers company stock and GICs.
- The company pays record keeping costs.
- No actuarial data are available for the plan overall. Standard actuarial tables for individuals would be reasonable proxies.
- The company has a modest DB plan that pays 0.5 percent times the number of years of service times the highest five-year average salary.

McLain Capital

- McLain offers U.S. and developed market overseas products.
- McLain offers several index funds.
- McLain has a 30 percent profit margin target for this business.

General

- Alternative investments are permissible.
- Real estate investments are permissible.
- Commodities investments are permissible.

- The plan sponsor does not want employees closely following fund performance during work hours.
- Selected resources: *Money Market Directory,* Nelson Information, *Institutional Investor, Pensions & Investments,* Employee Benefit Research Institute.

A List of Topics to Explore (Suggested by Wally)

- How do you ensure that the plan is easy to use for all investors?
- What makes a 401(k) plan effective? How should effectiveness be measured? What is the investment goal for the investor?
- At what level should risk be controlled? Do the investment alternatives offer sufficient risk management?
- What type and level of investor communication are necessary to meet the client's requirements?
- What level of education is necessary to meet the client's requirements?
- How do you measure whether the plan is successful for the client?
- How do you ensure that the plan is successful for McLain Capital?

Some Notes from Wally (Prior DC Design Projects)

Identification and Evaluation

It is not clear that the objectives of a 401(k) are significantly different from that of an individual. However, while 401(k) products are targeted for individuals, they must be designed for a representative, rather than specific individual.

- Return requirements: DC participants need to save for retirement. How long is this horizon?
- Income: Consider their goal of saving for retirement. How much will they need? Is there a way to estimate that now?
- Liabilities: Is there a way to estimate the liability for retirement? How accurate can this be?
- Risk metric: Individuals tend to view risk as losing money. Given the (assumed) limited financial experience of the employees, providing comfort and minimizing regret may be necessary.
- Risk tolerance: This will depend on the distribution of employees and is a function of age. Individuals tend to become more risk-averse with age. However, it is possible that the employees are more risk-averse on average (than other populations) due to their lack of experience with equity investments and (potentially) investments in general. This aversion may decrease over time as they become acclimated to equity investments.
- Risk capacity: This will depend on the distribution of employees and is a function of age. Employees closer to retirement have less ability to offset short-term income shortfalls by working more.

Constraints

- Liquidity: Presumably the need for liquidity is low. This money is being invested for retirement. Although participants can borrow from plans under certain circumstances (hardship withdrawals), it is unlikely this will result in large drawdowns (assuming that liquidity shocks of this nature are rare and independent).

- Budget: The ability to make contributions could be limited by budgetary considerations.
- Time horizon: long.
- Taxes: NA.
- Legal: NA.
- Regulatory: 404(c) requires that employers offer a diversity of investment vehicles (at least three options with different risk–return characteristics, with one being a money market); diversification within and among alternatives; changes in investments permitted at least quarterly; participants given adequate information to make informed decisions.

Participant Preferences

- Human capital: Minimize investment in the employer. Employees are already exposed to considerable firm risk.
- Personal: Not applicable for smaller offerings. If a large menu of options is offered, it may be possible to have specialty funds for social issues. Given limited experience (and inability to observe prior experience), no need to be sensitive to investment in assets where employees had previous bad experiences.
- Effort: The firm wants a low-effort offering. It does not want employees spending (office) time actively monitoring or managing their portfolios.
- Minimum investment: Needs to be small enough to handle sum of individual contributions.

The Fairbanks Fund

Fund Case: The Fairbanks Small-Cap U.S. Equity Fund

Note to student: This case is tied to live fund management, and although the description has been generalized, the case was designed around Boston University's student-managed small-cap equity fund.

Background

Whittier Wealth Management, a Boston-based fundamental equity shop, specializes in running small-cap portfolios. Its specialty is a concentrated style with fewer than 50 stocks. It has one core portfolio with an eight-year record with a goal to outperform a small-cap index and other small-cap managers.

Key characteristics of the fund include these:

- S&P 600 is the index benchmark.
- Fully invested U.S. equity fund, with the ability to maintain short positions.
- Selection universe includes small-cap companies, plus the S&P 600 small-cap index.
- Analyst teams are organized into five sectors.

The Problem

The CIO is interested in promoting the fund with the goal of increasing assets from $100,000 to $100 million.

The Assignment

To promote the fund, a document needs to be prepared explaining the objective of the fund, operation of the fund, its current portfolio structure, and performance analysis. In addition, a review of the current operation should be conducted, including realistic suggestions for improving performance. Finally, a review of analyst performance, both individual stock recommendations and actual sector performance, must be conducted. A comparison of the live portfolio performance and paper stock recommendations needs to be completed to estimate the implementation shortfall.

Specifically, the project involves four steps:

1. Documentation of portfolio objectives and operation.
2. Portfolio analysis, including portfolio characteristics and risk model analysis.
3. Performance analysis, including live portfolio returns and analyst raw material.
4. Proposal for improving the fund's operation, increasing its visibility and asset size and participation in university competitions.

Discussion Items

Consider what the manager is being hired for:

1. Active or passive?
2. Investment process?
    a. Portfolio construction.
    b. Balance of risk and return.

Consider the key guidelines:

1. Specific benchmark(s)?
2. Target excess return?
3. Target risk constraints?
4. Cash level constraint?
5. Security/market restrictions?
6. Time horizon?
7. Reporting requirements?
8. Trading restrictions?
9. Derivative restrictions?

Online Materials

1. Portfolio holdings.
2. Stock recommendations.
3. BARRA and FactSet analyses of portfolio and performance.

Outline for First Deliverable: Objectives and Constraints

Fund Case Written Hand-In: 2–3 Pages with Discussion and Bullets

1. Summary of fund operation:
    a. Investment objectives.
    b. Constraints and issues.
    c. Regulatory.

2. Analysis of benchmark and potential peer groups.

3. Plans for next steps.

Outline for Second Deliverable: Product Design and Solution

Fund Case Written Hand-In: 5–10 Pages with Tables, Charts, and Appendix

1. Current fund strategy:
   a. Summary of portfolio structure.
   b. Summary of active bets.
2. Sector and style analysis including interpretation.
   a. Portfolio characteristics and sector weights versus benchmark.
   b. BARRA analysis.
3. Steps for performance analysis.

Outline for Third Deliverable: Implementation/Mechanics

Fund Case Written Hand-In: 5–10 Pages Including Tables and Charts

1. Performance analysis:
   a. Summarize results.
   b. Provide analysis of portfolio versus benchmarks.
   c. Highlight individual names.
   d. Analysis and recommendations.
2. Active performance attribution:
   a. Market timing.
   b. Sector selection.
   c. Stock selection within sectors.
   d. Style influences.
   e. Impact from ETFs (be careful about allocating this).

Outline for Fourth Deliverable: Measuring Success

Fund Case Written Hand-In: 1–2 Pages with Tables or Charts, Bullets, and Summary Page

- Review of paper performance of stock recommendations:
  - By sector.
  - Compared with live fund.
- Summary of portfolio including alpha summary: table.
- Discussion of measuring success:
  - Client's definition of success.
  - Company's definition of success.
  - Performance measurement of success.

Note to student: A formal, bound business presentation document with four tabs is due at this time.

- Multiple tabs including material on first three deliverables.
- Include measures of success.
- Include appendix of supporting materials.

Note to student: Make sure that observations and recommendations are summarized and that the presentation doesn't simply display data.

Whittier Wealth Management: Fairbanks Small-Cap Equity Fund

Portfolio Objectives, Constraints, and Investment Process

Through a dynamic and collaborative process, analysts collectively evaluate and critique investment recommendations prepared from proprietary fundamental research. Portfolio holdings are determined on a consensus basis, with voting led by sector leaders and weightings set by alpha potential and portfolio diversification.

Investment Objectives

The investment objective of the Fairbanks Small-Cap Fund is to maximize growth of assets invested in the fund on a total return basis. Each sector team of research analysts is to be evaluated based on their value added to the portfolio through realized outperformance of their security selections over the relevant S&P 600 sector index. The goals for each analyst include identifying stocks that they expect to outperform or underperform in their sectors over a 6- to 12-month time horizon, and to aid their sector team in achieving the highest realized alpha. In addition, the goal for the fund as a whole is to outperform a benchmark index composed of the S&P 600 Small Stock index. The investment team will manage portfolio risk and minimize loss potential through balancing active risk and potential return. There will be no attempt to time the market or actively rotate investments between sectors.

Investment Constraints

The investment team is limited to a universe of small-capitalization stocks of less than $1 billion, limited coverage by Wall Street (typically fewer than four or five street estimates), and available liquidity ($50,000 per day dollar volume).

Investment Methodology

A pro forma portfolio is created by the CIO utilizing stock recommendations from the analysts. The portfolio is structured to overweight highly recommended stocks with large upside potential as calculated from target prices, adjusted for individual risk and overall portfolio diversification. Sector leaders share the proposed portfolio with their team and make suggestions to the CIO. A final portfolio composed of 25–50 actively selected stocks is supplemented with large-weight index names to meet diversification targets. Total active risk is between 5 and 10 percent, with a majority of the risk from stock selection.

Analysts submit updated research, and an online discussion board is used as an initial discussion forum for critiquing the security analysis. Each member of the investment team poses questions and makes comments about the recommendation. Each analyst proposing the idea performs the necessary research to answer the outstanding questions and is charged with defending her or his investment theses before the collective group in a formal yet brief presentation. The fund is actively rebalanced as investments are added or removed or as the position weightings are altered according to the achievement of the desired alpha.

Sample Portfolio Analyses

Portfolio Composite

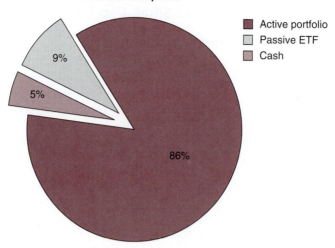

- ■ Active portfolio
- ◻ Passive ETF
- ■ Cash

9%

5%

86%

Investment Characteristics

	Fund	S&P Small-Cap 600	S&P 1500/Broad Market
P/E ratio	14.02	17.03	14.46
Dividend yield	1.61	2.12	3.09
P/B ratio	1.80	1.82	2.96
Median market cap	251M	375M	1,018M

BARRA RISK DECOMPOSITION 9/2/2008

	Risk (% Std Dev)	Contribution (% Active Risk)
Market timing	0.56	0.32
Risk indices	4.45	20.81
Industries	2.58	7.00
Covariance * 2	N/A	3.70
Asset selection	8.05	68.16
Active	9.75	
Total	**20.40**	
Benchmark	**17.37**	

Sector Weighting vs. S&P 600 Benchmark

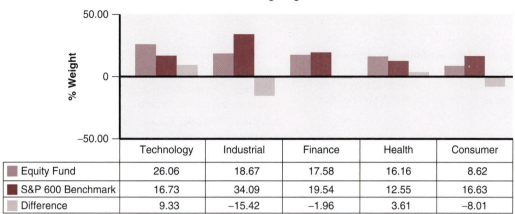

	Technology	Industrial	Finance	Health	Consumer
■ Equity Fund	26.06	18.67	17.58	16.16	8.62
■ S&P 600 Benchmark	16.73	34.09	19.54	12.55	16.63
□ Difference	9.33	−15.42	−1.96	3.61	−8.01

Contribution to Return Comparison

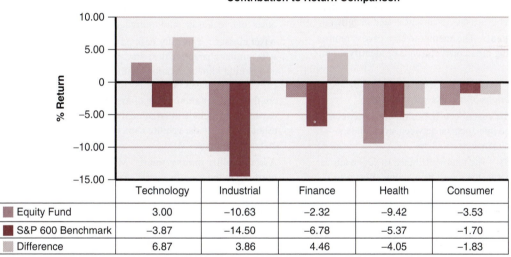

	Technology	Industrial	Finance	Health	Consumer
■ Equity Fund	3.00	−10.63	−2.32	−9.42	−3.53
■ S&P 600 Benchmark	−3.87	−14.50	−6.78	−5.37	−1.70
□ Difference	6.87	3.86	4.46	−4.05	−1.83

Glossary

401(k) plan A qualified plan established by employers into which employees may make salary contributions on an after-tax or pretax basis and directly allocate among investment offerings. Named for the section of IRS tax code that allows tax deferral.

A

Abnormal returns Returns in excess of those predicted by exposure to systematic risk factors.

Accrual basis The most commonly used accounting method. Accrual basis accounting reports income when earned and expenses when incurred. Cash basis accounting reports income when received and expenses when paid.

Accumulated benefit obligation (ABO) Increases in a pension plan's liabilities due to current vested benefits.

Active management The attempt to earn excess returns through forecasting broad market trends or identifying mispriced securities.

Agency bonds Fixed-income securities issued by agencies and organizations of the U.S. government.

Agency cost The cost of conflicts of interest between investors and fund managers or between stockholders, bondholders, and managers.

Allocation effects The return attributed to active allocation decisions, that is, the return from having portfolio weights different from the benchmark.

Alpha Return generated over and above the compensation for taking risk; the return in excess of that predicted by an equilibrium model.

Alternative assets Assets beyond the traditional categories of stocks, bonds, and cash.

American depository receipts (ADR) Shares in foreign stocks that trade domestically.

Anchoring The influence of a particular value on how a question is framed.

Annuity A contract between an individual and an insurance company. The individual makes a lump sum payment or a series of payments. In return, the insurance company makes periodic payments beginning immediately or at some future date. Annuities typically offer tax-deferred growth of earnings and may include a death benefit that will pay beneficiaries a guaranteed minimum amount.

Annuity wrapper The insurance policy attached to the investment portfolio in a variable annuity that allows the investor to earn dividend and capital gain distributions, and realize gains from the sale of shares of the enclosed mutual funds on a tax-deferred basis. The insurance wrapper charge is in addition to those of the investment options within the annuity.

Anomaly A return pattern that contradicts the efficient markets hypothesis.

Arbitrage An investment strategy with zero risk and zero investment but positive returns.

Ask price The price a dealer sets to sell a security.

Asset allocation The set of weights of broad asset classes within a portfolio. There are at least three types of asset allocation: strategic, tactical, and dynamic.

Asset allocation techniques Tools that help professionals set the optimal mix between the broad classes of investments.

Asset-backed security (ABS) A financial security backed by a pool of bank loans, leases, and other assets other than real estate and mortgage-backed securities.

Asset classes Typically defined as groups of securities with similar characteristics. Statistically, their constituents exhibit high correlations within each class, but low correlation between the classes. Stocks, bonds, and cash are the most common forms of asset classes; they may be expanded to include international stocks and bonds, real estate, hedge funds, venture capital, high-yield (junk) bonds and commodities.

Asset–liability management Managing a fixed-income portfolio to the specific characteristics of the client's liabilities.

Asset location The allocation of securities to taxable and nontaxable portfolios.

Assets under management (AUM) The total capital managed by a fund that includes equity and leverage.

B

Backfill bias The distortion to reported returns when funds, and their prior return track records, are added to a database.

Barbell An immunization strategy that employs securities that straddle the duration of the liability.

Base shift The nonsymmetry, in arithmetic return calculations, between percentage increases and decreases due to changes in the denominator.

Basis point 0.01 percent (that is, 1/100 of 1 percent).

Batting average The percentage of profitable trades.

Behavioral finance Models of financial markets that explicitly incorporate observed psychological factors that affect investor decisions.

Benchmark portfolio Portfolio against which an investment strategy is evaluated.

Beta A measure of the systematic risk of a security.

Bid price The price a dealer sets to buy a security.

Bid–ask spread   The difference between a dealer's bid and ask prices. The spread represents the cost to trade immediately.

Bond   The security issued by a borrower. The issuer agrees to pay a fixed amount of interest and repay principal over a specified period.

Bond rating   A subjective assessment of the creditworthiness of a corporation's debt issues.

Book   See *order book.*

Budget constraint   In optimization, the requirement that the portfolio weights sum to unity (1).

Bullet   An immunization strategy that employs securities with durations that are matched to the duration of the liability.

Butterfly shift   A change in the curvature of the yield curve.

Buy and hold   A portfolio rebalancing strategy that is essentially a "do-nothing" strategy: The investor neither buys nor sells in response to changes in market value.

C

Capacity   The amount that can be invested in a trading strategy without markedly reducing expected returns.

Capital asset pricing model (CAPM)   Equilibrium model where expected returns are linear to systematic market risk.

Cash balance plan   A variant of the traditional defined benefit plan. Employees accrue benefit credits based on salary and years of service. The credits are a liability of the employer but represent current cash value rather than future payments. The plan provides portability because the account balance can be rolled over to an IRA or a defined contribution plan if the employee leaves the firm before retirement.

Certainty equivalent   The certain return that equals the expected utility of a risky option.

CFA Institute   An international organization that aims to specify and maintain a high standard for the investment industry.

Closed-end fund   A fund that is traded through brokers at the market price. See *open-end fund.*

Cognitive dissonance   The rationalizing of past mistakes despite contrary evidence in order to make one feel better.

Collateralized mortgage obligation (CMO)   A mortgage-backed security (MBS) in which cash flows are allotted to different classes (see *tranche*) according to prespecified rules.

Commercial mortgage-backed security (CMBS)   A type of mortgage-backed security that is secured by loans on commercial property.

Commercial paper   Short-term unsecured promissory notes issued by large corporations.

Commission   The fee paid to trade.

Commission recapture   A combination of directed brokerage and soft dollars; managers are encouraged to trade with specific brokers, who in turn send a portion of the commissions back to the sponsor to pay for administrative costs.

Commodity Futures Trade Commission (CFTC)   A U.S. federal agency responsible for the open and efficient operation of the futures markets.

Completeness fund   A dynamic portfolio tailored to offset portfolio biases.

Conditional mean   An estimate of the future mean based on currently available information.

Constant proportional portfolio insurance (CPPI)   A dynamic portfolio strategy designed to generate an option-like payoff. The investor sets a floor on the dollar value of the portfolio and then manages the asset allocation depending on the difference between the current portfolio value and the floor value, along with a multiplier that defines the aggressiveness of the strategy.

Constant proportions   A portfolio rebalancing strategy that requires systematically selling winners and buying losers.

Constraints   Restrictions placed on permissible optimization solutions.

Contingent immunization   A fixed-income portfolio that allows for active management until a threshold value is hit. At this point the portfolio switches to an immunization strategy.

Contrarian strategies   An investment approach that attempts to profit from a reversal in identified trends.

Convertible bond   A bond that allows the bondholder to exchange the bond for common stock. The number of shares received is determined by the conversion ratio.

Convexity   The curvature of the bond price–yield equation.

Covered interest parity   A no arbitrage condition that relates interest rates to exchange rates. The return from (1) borrowing in one currency, exchanging it into a second currency, investing in a risk-free security in the second currency, and purchasing a futures contract to convert the second currency back to the first at the end of the holding period; it should offer the same return as (2) holding a risk-free security in the first currency.

Credit barbell   A combination of short-maturity corporate bonds with long-maturity government bonds.

Crossover credit   Bonds rated just below investment grade.

Crowd effect   Decisions being influenced by the decisions of others.

Currency overlay   A portfolio held to manage currency risk. This allows separation of asset allocation decisions from currency issues.

D

Data mining   The process of finding hidden patterns in data.

Defined benefit (DB) plan   A pool of money set aside by a company, government institution. or union to pay retirees a benefit determined by a fixed schedule.

Defined contribution (DC) plan   A pool of money set aside by an individual, and supported by his or her employer, where the benefits in retirement depend on the return to a portfolio managed by the individual.

Dispersion   A measure of the variation in the distribution of returns.

Disposition effect   The observed tendency of investors to sell winners (security whose price has increased) and hold losers (security whose price has decreased).

Diversification   The allocation of a portfolio over multiple assets to avoid excess exposure to any one systematic risk.

Dollar-weighted returns   The internal rate of return (IRR) for an investment that includes the impact of flows.

Duration   The slope of the bond price–yield equation. Duration is a measure of the average maturity of a bond and its sensitivity to parallel shifts in the yield curve.

Dynamic asset allocation   Portfolio allocations driven by changes in risk tolerance, typically induced by cumulative performance relative to goals or an approaching investment horizon.

Dynamic programming (DP)   An optimization process that involves finding the sequentially next best solution until no improvement, within a predetermined tolerance, is possible.

E

EAFE index   The European, Australian, Far East equity index calculated and reported by Morgan Stanley.

Effective duration   The percentage change in a bond's price given a parallel shift in the level of market interest rates.

Effective yield   The annual compounded interest rate of a security.

Efficient frontier   The set of portfolios that maximize (minimize) return (risk) for a given level of risk (return).

Efficient market hypothesis (EMH)   The theory that security prices fully reflect all available information.

Employee Retirement Income Security Act of 1974 (ERISA)   The federal statute that establishes the minimum standards for pension plans in private industry and outlines the federal income tax effects of transactions associated with employee benefit plans.

End-of-life-reporting bias   The distortion to self-reported return caused when funds do not report poor performance before they are closed.

Endowment   A financial institution that provides funding for ongoing educational activities. Endowments are usually associated with a particular college or university.

Equities   Ownership shares (stock) in a firm.

Eurodollars   Dollar-denominated deposits at foreign banks or foreign branches of U.S. banks.

Excess return   Return above the risk-free rate.

Exchange fund   A mutual fund vehicle designed to provide diversification without the need to sell a concentrated position.

Exchange rate   The price of a currency in terms of another country's currency.

Exchange traded funds (ETFs)   Funds that trade as listed securities in a manner similar to stocks.

F

Face value   The value of a bond at maturity.

Factor model   A decomposition of security returns into systematic (exposure to systematic risk sources times exposure) and nonsystematic components.

Fairness   The concept in setting compensation that a managers' performance ratings should reflect only decisions within their authority.

Fat tails   A situation in which more extreme events are observed than expected from a normal distribution.

Federal Home Loan Mortgage Corporation (FHLMC)   A government-sponsored enterprise (GSE), FHLMC is a public corporation. More familiarly known as Freddie Mac, it buys mortgages on the secondary market, then securitizes and sells them as mortgage-backed securities to investors on the open market.

Federal National Mortgage Association (FNMA)   A government-sponsored enterprise, (GSE), FNMA is a public corporation. More familiarly known as Fannie Mae, it purchases and securitizes mortgages.

Feedback loop   A circular process in which part of a system's output is part of the system's input. In financial markets positive feedback can lead to bubbles and crashes.

Fiduciary   Anyone who exercises discretionary authority over a plan's management or assets, including anyone who provides investment advice to the plan.

Fight-or-flight response   A theory that animals react to stress with a general discharge of the sympathetic nervous system, priming the animals for fighting or fleeing.

Fixed annuity   A contract between an individual and an insurance company. The individual makes a lump sum payment or a series of payments. In return, the insurance company makes fixed periodic payments beginning immediately or at some future date.

Fixed cost   A transaction cost that does not change with order size, such as a processing charge imposed by the custodian bank or a discount broker's flat commission per trade. Even if these explicit fixed charges are absent, the time required to handle each trade imposes an implicit minimum cost per trade.

Forward contract   An agreement to deliver a security at a specific time and at a specific price.

Forward discount When a currency is less expensive in the forward market than it is in the spot market.

Forward premium When a currency is more expensive in the forward market than it is in the spot market.

Forward rate A rate of interest for a future period such that investing in sequential forward rates is equivalent to investing in the current spot rate.

Foundation A financial institution that typically provides direct support for charitable activities and/or research grants aimed at finding solutions to significant problems, such as cancer or poverty. In general, foundations disburse their gifts to many unaffiliated recipients.

Framing The effects of how a question is asked on how the question is answered.

Full replication An index construction method that entails holding all constituents of the index in the same weights as the index.

Fund of funds (FoF) A fund that holds other funds in a portfolio.

Fundamental analysis The attempt to earn excess returns by identifying mispriced assets using publicly available information.

G

Gate A limitation on the amount of assets that can be redeemed from a fund in any redemption period.

Gilt A bond issued by the government of the United Kingdom.

Government National Mortgage Association (GNMA) A U.S. government–owned corporation within the Department of Housing and Urban Development (HUD). More familiarly know as Ginnie Mae, it provides guarantees on mortgage-backed securities backed by federally insured or guaranteed loans. Ginnie Mae securities are the only MBS that are guaranteed by the U.S. government.

Grantor retained annuity trust (GRAT) A private, fixed-rate annuity vehicle.

H

Hedge fund A private investment fund available to a limited range of investors that is permitted by regulators to undertake a wider range of activities than other investment funds.

Hedging Allocation to a security to reduce risk.

High-water mark The largest cumulative return realized by a fund in any compensation period. Funds charge incentive fees only on returns above the High-water mark.

Holdback The amount of a final redemption retained by the fund until a final audit is performed. This is to prevent adjustments to paid redemptions due to adjustments to NAV.

Holdings-based attribution Attribution of returns to factors based on the history of security-level holdings and returns for both the portfolio and the benchmark index.

Hurdle rate A minimum return above which the fund manager may charge incentive fees.

I

Illiquidity The inability to transact in a timely manner at or near the current market price.

Illusion of control The psychological tendency to believe one can control, or influence, outcomes over which one clearly has no influence.

Illusion of knowledge The psychological tendency to make stronger inferences than warranted by the data.

Immunization A fixed-income portfolio strategy to mitigate interest rate risk by setting the duration of assets equal to the duration of liabilities.

Implementation shortfall The difference in return between a paper portfolio and live portfolio.

Incentive fee The performance-based compensation to the fund manager.

Increasing costs Transaction costs that increase with order size.

Indenture The contract between the bondholder and bond issuer.

Independently and identically distributed (i.i.d.) When each random variable has the same probability distribution and all of the distributions are mutually independent.

Index ETF An ETF that seeks to replicate the return of a particular market index.

Index fund A fund that seeks to replicate the return of a particular market index.

Individual policy statement (IPS) A summary of the understanding between a client and advisor. The central sections of the IPS define the risk and return objectives as well as important constraints imposed on the portfolio.

Individual retirement account (IRA) A self-directed, tax-deferred investment program available to employees who can make up to a specified maximum annual contribution.

Information ratio The portfolio active return relative to a benchmark divided by its tracking error.

Integer programming An optimization technique for a linear objective function subject to linear constraints where the unknown variables are all required to be integers.

Interaction effect The residual required to account for the total active return in the Brinson model.

Internal rate of return (IRR) The effective compounded rate of return earned on invested capital. For an investment the IRR is the discount rate that makes the net present value of the investment income stream sum to zero.

Invariance The concept in setting compensation that economically equivalent exposures should result in the same measured performance.

Investment grade Bonds that are rated BBB or higher.

J

James–Stein estimators   Variable estimates based on the idea of "shrinking" the individual sample means toward a common value referred to as the "grand mean."

Jensen's alpha   The excess return of an investment measured as the distance between the investment return and the SML.

Junk bonds   Non–investment grade bonds—that is, bonds rated below BBB.

K

Key rate duration   A measure of the sensitivity of a security to interest rates at specific points on the yield curve.

Kurtosis   A measure of the amount of a probability distribution contained in the tails.

L

Life cycle funds   Funds designed so that the asset allocation becomes more conservative as the investor approaches retirement. Also called *target date funds.*

Linear programming (LP)   An optimization technique for a linear objective function subject to linear constraints.

Liquidity   A measure of the ease of trading a particular security or set of securities in different trade sizes. A liquid security can be sold quickly in the desired amount at or near the current market price.

Lock-up   The period over which an investment cannot be redeemed.

London Interbank Offer Rate (LIBOR)   A reference rate based on the interest rates banks charge other banks for unsecured funds in the London wholesale money market.

Long-only constraint   An optimization restriction that requires each weight to be greater than or equal to zero.

Loss aversion   The tendency for people to strongly prefer avoiding losses. Some studies suggest that the pain of a loss is twice as powerful as the pleasure of a comparable gain.

Lower partial moment (LPM)   A measure of probability distributions that considers only outcomes below a particular reference point.

M

Macaulay's duration   A measure of the effective maturity of a bond. See *duration* and *effective duration.*

Management fee   The asset-based compensation to a fund manager.

Marginal utility   The increase or decrease in utility due to a small change in wealth. It is measured as the slope of the utility function.

Market impact   The cost of execution—that is, the impact of price changes caused by trading.

Market maker   An individual or company that is willing to provide liquidity by offering bid and ask quotes.

Market microstructure   The economic analysis of trading where the quantity of supply and demand, per unit of time, is what determines prices in the marketplace.

Market timing   The attempt to generate excess by strategically entering and exiting the market.

Mark-to-market   Setting asset values equal to the market price.

Mark-to-model   Setting asset values based on a valuation model. The idea is to infer a "fair value"—an estimate of the most likely price at which a security could be traded in the market.

Mean reversion   The tendency for asset prices to be pulled toward the trend.

Mean–variance (M-V) framework   A popular model for computing optimal asset allocations.

Mental accounting   The tendency to allocate payoffs to different accounts even when the payoffs are highly fungible.

Menu effect   Describes situations in which people feel overwhelmed by too many options.

Minimum variance portfolio (MVP)   The portfolio with the overall lowest risk (variance) in a mean–variance framework.

Model portfolio   A paper portfolio that is used as a target for creating a trade list.

Modern portfolio theory (MPT)   The principles of how rational investors construct optimal portfolios and the pricing of risky assets. The basic components are the mean–variance framework and the capital asset pricing model.

Mortgage-backed security (MBS)   A bond backed by a pool of mortgages.

Mutual fund   A company that pools and manages investor money.

Myopic strategy   A short-term strategy that does not consider future outcomes when setting allocations today.

N

NASDAQ   The automated quotation system for the over-the-counter stock market.

National Association of Security Dealers (NASD)   A self-regulatory organization responsible for the operation and regulation of the NASDAQ stock market and over-the-counter markets.

Negative covenant   A condition in a bond indenture that precludes certain actions by the bond issuer.

Net asset value (NAV)   The price of a fund share, calculated as fund assets minus liabilities divided by the number of shares.

Nominal spread   The average differential, in basis points, between a bond's yield-to-maturity and the yield-to-maturity of a similar maturity Treasury bond.

Notification period The length of time before a redemption date that an investor is required to indicate his or her intention to place a redemption.

O

Objective function The goal sought in an optimization program.

On-the-run The most recently issued bond for a particular maturity.

Open-end fund A fund that issues and redeems shares at the NAV.

Opportunity cost The cost of nonexecution; that is, the impact on the strategy return of not trading.

Option-adjusted spread (OAS) The spread over the Treasury yield curve that corrects for embedded options. It is the spread required so the present value of a bond's cash flows matches the bond's market price.

Order book (or book) The list of bids and offers available for each additional order. Sometimes simply referred to as the *book*.

Over the counter (OTC) The network of brokers and dealers that buys and sells securities.

P

Par value The face value of a security.

Pension Benefit Guarantee Corporation (PBGC) A self-financing, federally chartered corporation that insures private-sector defined benefit plans.

Pension plan A financial institution that provides income and/or accumulated assets to support employees in retirement.

Performance appraisal The subjective evaluation of performance results/analytics to determine whether a manager has demonstrated skill.

Performance attribution The attempt to identify the source of portfolio returns.

Performance measurement The process of calculating portfolio returns and risk over the evaluation period.

Population moments The unknown underlying return parameters of a distribution.

Portable alpha The investment strategy that combines a beta return with an uncorrelated alpha source.

Portfolio insurance A portfolio rebalancing strategy that requires systematically buying winners and selling losers.

Portfolio manager (PM) Someone who is responsible for delivering investment performance by setting asset and/or security portfolio weights and is held accountable for investment results.

Positive covenant A condition in a bond indenture that requires certain actions by the bond issuer.

Preferred stock An equity that pays a predetermined, fixed or variable dividend.

Primary market The market that deals with the issuance of new securities.

Projected benefit obligation (PBO) Increases in the present value of a pension plan's liabilities due to the vesting of future benefits.

Proportional costs Transaction cost that are a constant percentage of order size.

Prospect theory A model of choice that incorporates observed psychological behaviors of investors.

Prudent expert rule The ERISA standard that requires plan fiduciaries to act with the care, skill, prudence, and diligence of a prudent person *acting in a like capacity.*

Purchasing power parity (PPP) Long-term equilibrium exchange rates equalize the purchasing power of different currencies in their home countries for a given basket of goods.

Q

Qualified dividend A dividend to which capital gains tax rates are applied.

Quanto A derivative in which an underlying security is denominated in one currency, but the derivative settles in a another currency at some fixed rate.

R

Rational expectations The assumption that expectations, set using all relevant information, are on average correct; that is, they are not systematically biased.

Real estate investment trust (REIT) A closed-end fund that invests in various types of real estate and/or real estate mortgages.

Redemption frequency The cycle over which investors can redeem assets from a fund.

Regime A historic period during which conditional expected returns and variances can be estimated as constant parameters.

Relative risk aversion (RRA) A measure of risk aversion defined by the percentage change in marginal utility divided by the percentage change in wealth.

Representativeness Evaluation by stereotype or drawing on previously perceived patterns for decision making.

Resampling The simulation of a large number of randomly generated sample statistics that are used as inputs for M–V analysis. The portfolio weight for each asset is the average from the simulated portfolios.

Returns-based attribution A top-down performance attribution technique that requires only returns data for the portfolio and for asset class indexes.

Risk aversion The willingness to take risk, measured as the curvature of the utility function. One of the most useful measures of risk aversion is the coefficient of relative risk aversion (RRA).

Risk aversion coefficient   The sensitivity parameter in the M–V framework used to measure the degree of risk aversion.

Risk tolerance   The willingness to take risk measured as the inverse of risk aversion.

Roth IRA   A form of IRA to which contributions are not tax deductible.

S

Sample moments   The estimated unknown parameters (mean, variance, and covariance) from a historical sample of returns.

Secondary market   The market where previously issued securities and financial instruments such as stocks, bonds, options, and futures are bought and sold.

Sector rotation   A strategy that actively allocates among different sectors in an attempt to be in the right industry at the right time.

Securities Exchange Commission (SEC)   The regulatory body responsible for protecting investors, maintaining fair, orderly, and efficient markets, and facilitating capital formation.

Securitization   The pooling of securities whose cash flows are allocated to different classes. These classes are then sold and traded.

Security market line (SML)   The relationship between a portfolio's expected return and the portfolio's beta.

Selection effect   The return attributed to active security selection decisions.

Semistrong-form efficiency   Security prices fully reflect all publicly available information.

Separately managed account (SMA)   An individual investment portfolio managed to the individual's preferences where the account manager appoints submanagers.

Sharpe ratio   A measure of relative risk-adjusted performance that compares the portfolio return over the risk-free rate to the total risk (variance) of the portfolio.

Shortfall constraint   An optimization requirement that limits the probability of a return less than or equal to a threshold.

Shortfall risk   The chance of return below a particular threshold over a period of time.

Signal capture   The determination of how to carry out the action based on the trade signal. Signal capture includes specifying the investment instruments used to transform the investment manager's desired bet into a portfolio position.

Signal creation   The conversion of a trading idea into observable potential trades.

Skewness   A measure of the asymmetry of a probability distribution.

Soft dollar commission   A subsidy that involves partial or full payment for research services by brokerage firms out of commissions paid for trading portfolios.

Sortino ratio   A variation on the Sharpe ratio. The Sortino ratio compares returns in excess of a target return to downside risk.

Spot rate   The current interest rate for a given maturity.

S&P Depository Receipts (SPDR)   A family of sector and market ETFs; informally known as *spiders.*

Stein paradox   The phenomenon that when three or more parameters are estimated simultaneously, their combined estimator is more accurate than any method used to estimate the parameters separately.

Stock lending   The lending of stocks from one party to another. The terms of the loan require that the borrower provide the lender with collateral equal to or greater than the lent securities. As payment, the borrower pays a fee quoted as an annualized percentage of the value of the lent securities.

Stop-loss   A sell order that takes effect when a security price falls below a specific level.

Strategic asset allocation   Long-term portfolio allocation.

Strategy philosophy   The basic idea behind a trading strategy.

Stratified sample   An index construction technique in which a limited number of securities are selected from representative groups, such as style groups of equities including small-cap value, large-cap growth, and mid-cap.

Strong-form efficiency   Security prices fully reflect all available information, including inside information.

Structured active   An active equity management approach that is similar to index management but includes modest active bets relative to the benchmark. This style is also known as *index plus* and *risk-controlled active management.*

Structured mandate   The construction of a fixed-income portfolio to the specific characteristics of the client's liabilities.

Style bets   Active exposures to factors associated with either growth or value strategies.

Style neutral   An investment strategy that seeks to take no systematic style exposure.

Survivor bias   The bias in reported returns caused by the removal of closed funds.

T

Tactical asset allocation   Portfolio allocations in response to short-term changes in investment opportunities.

Target portfolio   A desired portfolio allocation.

Tax lot   A record of all transactions and their tax implications involving a particular security in a portfolio.

Term structure   The relationship of yield-to-maturity of Treasury securities.

Tilt   The active risk exposure to a systematic risk factor.

Time-weighted returns   Removing the influence of cash flows requires valuing the portfolio every time a contribution or withdrawal occurs.

Total return mandate   The portfolio objective of matching or beating the return on a standard benchmark subject to a set of investment guidelines.

Tracking error   The return difference between a portfolio and its benchmark.

Tracking tolerance   The return objective for an index fund manager.

Tranche   One of the securities offered as part of a structured note. See *collateralized mortgage obligation*.

Transaction costs   The fees, both fixed and variable, for trading.

Treynor ratio   A measure of risk-adjusted return that compares excess return, security return over the risk-free rate, to the systematic risk of the security, as measured by beta.

Trust company   A financial institution offering banking, investment, and estate administration services.

U

Uncertainty   A situation in which the potential outcomes and probabilities are unknown. In contrast, *risk* is the situation in which estimated probabilities across possible outcomes are known.

Unconditional mean   The mean calculated using all data. This reflects an averaging out of the information contained in the conditional mean.

Unrealized gain   The capital gain on a security that has not been sold.

Utility function   The relationship between satisfaction and total wealth.

V

Value at risk (VaR)   The minimum dollar loss that should occur with a given frequency or probability over a specified period.

Value function   The first step in the DP framework; $V(W_t, x_t, t)$ is equal to the maximized objective at time t.

Value style   An equity strategy that seeks to buy oversold stocks.

Variable annuity   A contract between an individual and an insurance company. The individual makes a lump sum payment (or series of payments) to a portfolio selected from a range of investment options, typically mutual funds. In return, the individual receives periodic payments beginning immediately or at some future date. The value of the payments received will depend on the performance of the selected investment portfolio.

Vector autoregression   An econometric model used to capture the evolution and the interdependencies between multiple time series.

Vesting   The process of gaining the right to a benefit. When a retirement plan is fully vested, the employee has an absolute right to the entire amount of money in the account.

Volume-weighted price (VWAP)   A measure approximating the prices at which a trader should have been able to execute in a given day.

W

Wash sale rule   The disallowing of the tax benefit of realizing a loss if the same security is repurchased within 30 days.

Weak-form efficiency   Security prices fully reflect all market-based information, that is, price and volume data.

Y

Yield-to-maturity   The average return earned on a bond held to maturity.

Yield-to-worst   The lowest average return earned on a bond.

Z

Zero-beta portfolio   The minimum variance portfolio that is uncorrelated to a specific efficient portfolio.

References

Amihud, Yakov, and Haim Mendelson. 1986. "Asset Pricing and the Bid/Ask Spread." *Journal of Financial Economics* 17, pp. 223–49.

Arnott, Robert, and Peter Bernstein. 2002. "What Risk Premium Is 'Normal?'" *Financial Analysts Journal*, March/April, pp. 64–85.

Arrow, Kenneth. 1982. "Risk Perception in Psychology and Economics." *Economic Inquiry* 20, no. 1, pp. 1–9.

Bailard, Thomas, David Biehl, and Ronald Kaiser. 1986. *Personal Money Management*, 5th ed. Chicago: Scientific Research Associates, Inc.

Banz, Rolf. 1981. "The Relationship between Return and Market Value of Common Stocks." *Journal of Financial Economics* 9, no. 1, pp. 3–18.

Barber, Brad, and Terrance Odean. 2001. "Boys Will Be Boys: Gender, Overconfidence, and Common Stock Investment." *Quarterly Journal of Economics* 116, no. 1, pp. 261–92.

Barberis, Nicholas. 2000. "Investing for the Long Run When Returns Are Predictable." *Journal of Finance* LV, no. 1, pp. 225–64.

Barberis, Nicholas, and Richard Thaler. 2002. "A Survey of Behavioral Finance." In *The Handbook of the Economics of Finance*, ed. G. Constantinides, M. Harris, and R. Stulz. Amsterdam: Elsevier B.V.

Basu, Sanjoy. 1983. "The Relationship between Earnings' Yield, Market Value, and Return for NYSE Common Stocks: Further Evidence." *Journal of Financial Economics* 12, no. 1 (June), pp. 129–56.

Bekaert, Geert, Robert J. Hodrick, and Xiaoyan Zhang. 2005. "International Stock Return Comovements." *Journal of Financial Economics* 62 (2001) pp. 327–376

Benartzi, Shlomo, and Richard Thaler. 2001. "Naïve Diversification Strategies in Defined Contribution Saving Plans." *The American Economic Review* 91, no. 1 (March), pp. 79–98.

Berk, Jonathan, and Richard Green. 2004. "Mutual Fund Flows and Performance in Rational Markets." *Journal of Political Economy* 112, no. 6 (December), pp. 1269–95.

Bhandari, Laxmi. 1988. "Debt/Equity Ratio and Expected Common Stock Returns: Empirical Evidence." *Journal of Finance* 43, pp. 507–28.

Black, Fischer. 1972. "Capital Market Equilibrium with Restricted Borrowing." *Journal of Business* 45, pp. 444–54.

Black, Fischer. 1986. "Noise." *Journal of Finance* XXXXI, no. 3, pp. 529–43.

Black, Fischer, and Robert Litterman. 1992. "Global Portfolio Optimization." *Financial Analysts Journal*, September/October, pp. 28–43.

Bloomberg.com. 2008. "Harvard's $36.9 Billion Endowment May Face Losses." November 11.

Bloomberg.com. 2009. "Harvard Sale of Private Equity Said to Be Stymied by Price Drop." January 23.

Bodie, Zvi and Michael Clowes, 2003, Worry-Free Investing: A Safe Approach to Achieving Your Lifetime Financial Goals, Financial Times Management.

Bodie, Zvi, Robert Merton, and William Samuelson. 1992. "Labor Supply, Flexibility, and Portfolio Choice in a Life-Cycle Model." *Journal of Economic Dynamics and Control* 16, no. 3–4 (July–October), pp. 427–49.

Bodie, Zvi, and Victor Rosansky. 1980. "Risk and Return in Commodity Futures." *Financial Analysts Journal*, May/June, pp. 27–39.

Bonafede, Julia, Steven Foresti, and Thomas Toth. 2004. "Alpha: A Right or a Privilege? An Examination of the Challenges and Risks of Hedge Fund Investing." Whilshire Research.

Bookstaber, Richard. 1997. "Global Risk Management: Are We Missing the Point?" *Journal of Portfolio Management*, Spring.

Bookstaber, Richard. 2003. "Hedge Fund Existential." *Financial Analysts Journal*, September/October, pp. 19–23.

Bornstein, Brian, and A. Christine Emler. 2001. "Rationality in Medical Decision Making: A Review of the Literature on Doctors' Decision-Making Biases." *Journal of Evaluation in Clinical Practice* 7, no. 2, pp. 97–107.

Brinson, Gary, and Nimrod Fachler. 1985. "Measuring Non-U.S. Equity Portfolio Performance." *Journal of Portfolio Management*, Spring, pp. 73–76.

Brinson, Gary, Randolph Hood, and Gilbert Beebower. 1986. "Determinants of Portfolio Performance." *Financial Analysts Journal*, July/August.

Brown, Stephen, William Goetzmann, and Bing Liang. 2004. "Fees on Fees in Fund of Funds." *Journal of Investment Management.* February, pp. 76–93.

Burton, Malkiel. 2003. "The Efficient Market Hypothesis and Its Critics." *Journal of Economic Perspectives* 17, no. 1 (Winter), pp. 59–82.

Campbell, John, and Luis Viceira. 2002. *Strategic Asset Allocation Portfolio Choice for Long-Term Investors.* Oxford University Press.

Campbell, John, and Luis Viceira. 2004. "Long-Horizon Mean-Variance Analysis: A User Guide." Harvard University.

Campbell, John, and Luis Viceira. 2005. "The Term Structure of the Risk-Return Trade-Off." *Financial Analysts Journal,* January/February, pp. 34–44.

Campbell, John, Yeung Chan, and Luis Viceira. 2003. "A Multivariate Model of Asset Allocation." *Journal of Financial Economics* 67, pp. 41–80.

Cannon, Walter. 1915. *Bodily Changes in Pain, Hunger, Fear and Rage: An Account of Recent Researches into the Function of Emotional Excitement,* Appleton, New York.

Carrieri, Francesca, Vihang Errunza, and Sergei Sarkissian. 2006. "The Dynamics of Geographic versus Sectoral Diversification: Is There a Link to the Real Economy?" McGill University.

Chaing, Kevin, Ming-Long Lee, and Craig Wisen. 2005. "On the Time Series Properties of Real Estate Investment Trust Betas." *Real Estate Economics* 33, no. 2, pp. 381–96.

Clarke, Roger, and Meir Statman. 1998. "Bullish or Bearish." *Financial Analysts Journal,* May/June, pp. 63–72.

Collins, Sean, and Phillip Mack. 1997. "The Optimal Amount of Assets under Management." *Financial Analysts Journal* 53, no. 5 (September/October), pp. 67–73.

Condon, Bernard, and Nathan Vardi. 2009. "How Harvard's Investing Superstars Crashed." *Forbes,* February 20.

Constantinides, George. 1979. "A Note on the Sub-optimality of Dollar Cost Averaging as an Investment Policy." *Journal of Financial and Quantitative Analysis,* pp. 443–50.

Cowan, Lynn. 2009. "Pensions Further Hammered by December Discount Rate Drop." *Dow Jones Newswires,* January 12.

Cowan, Lynn. 2009. "Pensions See Record Deficit; More Frozen Plans Expected." *Dow Jones Newswires,* January 7.

DALBAR, Inc. 2005. *QAIB 2005: Quantitative Analysis of Investor Behavior.* Boston: DALBAR, Inc.

Daniel, Kent, and Sheridan Titman. 1995. "Evidence on the Characteristics of Cross-Sectional Variation in Stock Returns." *The Journal of Finance* 52, no. 1, pp. 1–33.

Daniel, Kent, David Hirshleifer, and Siew Teoh. 2002. "Investor Psychology in Capital Markets: Evidence and Policy Implications." *Journal of Monetary Economics* 49, pp. 139–209.

De Long, J.B., A. Shleifer, L. Summers, and R. Waldman. 1990. "Noise Traders Risk in Financial Markets." *Journal of Political Economy* 98, no. 4 (August), pp. 703–38.

DeBondt, Werner, and Richard Thaler. 1985. "Does the Stock Market Overreact?" *Journal of Finance* 40, no. 3, pp. 793–808.

Del Guercio, Diane, and Paula Tkac. 2002. "The Determinants of the Flow of Funds of Managed Portfolios: Mutual Funds versus Pension Funds." *Journal of Financial and Quantitative Analysis,* 37, pp. 523–557.

Dornbusch, Rudiger, Stanley Fischer, and Richard Startz. 2001. *Macroeconomics,* 8th ed. New York: McGraw-Hill.

Dremen, David. 1977. *Psychology and the Stock Market: Why the Pros Go Wrong and How to Profit.* New York: Warner Books.

Dremen, David. 1998. *Contrarian Investment Strategies in the Next Generation.* New York: Simon and Schuster.

Dynkin, Lev, Vadin Konstantinovsky, and Bruce Phelps. 2001. "Tradable Proxy Portfolios for the Lehman Brothers MBS Index." Lehman Brothers.

Efron, Bradley, and Carl Morris. 1977. "Stein's Paradox in Statistics." *Scientific American* 236 (May), pp. 119–27.

Eisenhower, Dwight. 1948. *Crusade in Europe.* New York: Doubleday & Company.

Epley, Nicholas, and Thomas Gilovich. 2006. "The Anchoring-and-Adjustment Heuristic. Why the Adjustments Are Insufficient." *Psychological Science* 17, no. 4, pp. 311–18.

Erb, Claude, and Campbell Harvey. 2006. "The Strategic and Tactical Value of Commodity Futures." *Financial Analysts Journal,* March/April, pp. 69–97.

Eric Zitzewitz. 2003. "Who Cares about Shareholders? Arbitrage-Proofing Mutual Funds." *Journal of Law, Economics, and Organization* 19, no. 2.

Fabozzi, Frank J. 2007. *Fixed Income Analysis,* 2nd ed. Hoboken, NJ: John Wiley & Sons.

Fama, Eugene, and Kenneth French. 1987. "Commodity Futures Prices: Some Evidence on Forecast Power, Premiums, and the Theory of Storage." *Journal of Business,* January, pp. 55–73.

Fama, Eugene, and Kenneth French. 1992. "The Cross Section of Expected Stock Return." *Journal of Finance* XLVII, no. 2, pp. 427–465.

Fama, Eugene, and Kenneth French. 1993. "Common Risk Factors in the Returns on Stocks and Bonds." *Journal of Financial Economics* 33, pp. 3–56.

Farnsworth, Heber, and Jonathan Taylor. 2004. "Evidence on the Compensation of Portfolio Managers." Manuscript, March 10.

First Eagle Funds. 2003. Investment letter. September 25. Greenwich Associates. 2003. "Survey of U.S. Equity Soft Dollar Practices."

Forbes, Kristen J., and Roberto Rigobon. 2002. "No Contagion, Only Interdependence: Measuring Stock Market Comovements." *Journal of Finance* LVII, pp. 2223–61.

Forbes. 2009. "Harvard: The Inside Story of Its Financial Meltdown." March 16.

Francis, Theo. 2007. "Pension Plans Take Healthy Turn." *The Wall Street Journal,* January 23.

Gabelli, Mario. 2005. "The History of Hedge Funds— The Millionaire's Club." *www.gabelli.com/news/articles/ mario-hedge_102500.html.*

Gilovich, Thomas, Robert Vallone, and Amos Tversky. 1985. "The Hot Hand in Basketball: On the Misperception of Random Sequences." *Cognitive Psychology* 17, no. 3 (July), pp. 295–314.

Goetzmann, William, and Nadav Peles. 1997. "Cognitive Dissonance and Mutual Fund Investors." *The Journal of Financial Research* XX, no. 2 (Summer), pp. 145–58.

Goldberg, Steven. 2008. "Take a Chance on Loomis Sayles Bond." *Kiplinger.com,* October 28.

Gorton, Gary, and K. Geert Rouwenhorst. 2006. "Facts and Fantasies about Commodity Futures." *Financial Analysts Journal,* March/April, pp. 47–68.

Gottlieb, Jenna. 2006. "Fidelity Exec Outlines the Plan of the Future." *Pensions & Investments,* March 6.

Goyal, Amit, and Sunil Wahal. 2008. "The Selection and Termination of Investment Management Firms by Plan Sponsors." *Journal of Finance* LXIII (August), pp. 1805–47.

Graham, Benjamin, and David Dodd, 1934. *Security Analysis.* New York: McGraw-Hill.

Graham, Benjamin, David Dodd, and Sydney Cottle. 1962. *Security Analysis Principles and Technique.* New York: McGraw-Hill.

Graham, John, and Campbell Harvey. 1997. "Grading the Performance of Market Timing Newsletters." *Financial Analysts Journal,* November/December.

Greer, Robert. 1997. "What Is an Asset Class Anyway?" *JPM,* Winter.

Grinold, Richard, and Ronald Kahn. 2000. *Active Portfolio Management,* 2nd ed. New York: McGraw-Hill.

Grossman, Sanford, and Joseph Stiglitz. 1980. "On the Impossibility of Informationally Efficient Markets." *American Economic Review* 70, no. 3, pp. 393–408.

Hall, Robert and Susan Woodward. 2004. "Benchmarking the Returns to Venture." National Bureau of Economic Research (NBER), January.

Harvard Magazine. 2009. "Endowment Distribution to Be Reduced 8 Percent." March 19.

Hechinger, John. 2001. "All in the Timing: Two Fidelity Funds Suffer after Manager's Exit, Move to Tech Stocks." *The Wall Street Journal,* Dow Jones and Company, Inc., May 14, p. C1.

Heisler, Jeffrey. 1994. "Loss Aversion in a Futures Market: An Empirical Test." *Review of Futures Markets* 13, no. 3, pp. 793–822.

Heisler, Jeffrey, Christopher Knittel, John Neumann, and Scott Stewart. 2007, "Why Do Institutional Plan Sponsors Hire and Fire Their Investment Managers?" *Journal of Business and Economic Studies,* July.

Hernandez, Cesar, and Scott Stewart. 1996. "Active Management of International Equities: Is There a Disconnect between the Asset Allocation Decision and Implementation?" Working Paper.

Heston, S., and K.G. Rouwenhorst. 1994. "Does Industrial Structure Explain the Benefits of International Diversification?" *Journal of Financial Economics* 46, pp. 111–57.

Ibbotson, Roger, and Paul Kaplan. 2000. "Does Asset Allocation Policy Explain 40, 90, or 100 Percent of Performance?" *Financial Analysts Journal,* January/February.

Ibbotson, Roger, and Peng Chen. 2003. "Long Run Stock Returns: Participating in the Real Economy." *Financial Analysts Journal,* January/February, pp. 88–98.

Ineichen, Alexander. 2001. "The Search for Alpha Continues: Do Fund of Hedge Funds Managers Add Value?" *UBS Warburg.*

Intriligator, Michael D. 1971. *Mathematical Optimization and Economic Theory.* Englewood Cliffs, NJ: Prentice-Hall.

Investment Company Institute. 2003. "Performance Fees and Expense Ratios." *Fundamentals* 12, no. 2 (August).

Investment Company Institute. 2008. "Despite Choppy Markets, Workers Keep Saving."

Jensen, Michael. 1968. "The Performance of Mutual Funds in the Period 1945–1964." *Journal of Finance* XXIII, no. 2, pp. 389–416.

Jensen, Michael. 1969. "Risk, the Pricing of Capital Assets, and the Evaluation of Investment Portfolios." *Journal of Business,* 42, no. 2 pp. 167–247.

Jorion, Philippe. 1986. "Bayes-Stein Estimation for Portfolio Analysis." *Journal of Financial and Quantitative Analysis* 21, no. 3, pp. 279–92.

Kahneman, Daniel, and Amos Tversky. 1979. "Prospect Theory: An Analysis of Decision under Risk." *Econometrica* 47, no. 2, pp. 263–91.

Kandel, Shmuel, and Robert F. Stambaugh. 1996. "On the Predictability of Stock Returns: An Asset-Allocation Perspective." *Journal of Finance* LI, no. 2, pp. 385–424.

Karim, Samina, and Scott Stewart. 2005. "Summary of Survey of Decision Making by Public and Corporate Pension Professionals," unpublished manuscript, Boston University.

Karmin, C., J. Scheck, R. Rundle, and J. Levitz. 2008. "CalPERS Looks to Shore Up Assets." *The Wall Street Journal,* October 23.

Kazemi, Hossein, Thomas Schneeweis, and Raj Gupta. 2003. "Omega as a Performance Measure." CISDM Working Paper, June 15.

Keim, Donald B. 1985. "Dividend Yields and Stock Returns—Implications of Abnormal January Results." *Journal of Financial Economics* 14, no. 3, pp. 473–89.

Kendall, Maurice. 1953. "The Analysis of Economic Time Series—Part I: Prices." *Journal of the Royal Statistical Society* 116, no. 1, pp. 11–34.

Khandani, Amir, and Andrew Lo. 2007. "What Happened to the Quants in August 2007?" NBER Working Paper No. 14465

Kim, Tong Suk, and Edward Omberg. 1996. "Dynamic Nonmyopic Portfolio Behavior." *The Review of Financial Studies* 9, no. 1, pp. 141–61.

King, Neil, and Jeffrey McCracken. 2009. "U.S. Played Rough with Chrysler's Creditors." *The Wall Street Journal,* May 11.

Kritzman, Mark. 1991. "What Practitioners Need to Know. . .about Estimating Volatility—Part 2." *Financial Analysts Journal,* September/October, pp. 10–11.

Kurz, Mordecai. 1994. "On Rational Belief Equilibrium." *Economic Theory* 4, pp. 859–76.

Kurz, Mordecai. 1994. "On the Structure and Diversity of Rational Beliefs." *Economic Theory* 4, pp. 877–900.

Lakonishok, Josef, Andrei Schleifer, and Robert Vishny. 1994. "Contrarian Investment, Extrapolation, and Risk." *Journal of Finance* LIX, pp. 541–78.

Langer, Ellen J. 1975. "The Illusion of Control." *Journal of Personality and Social Psychology* 32, no. 2, pp. 311–28.

Leland, Hayne E. 1980. "Who Should Buy Portfolio Insurance." *Journal of Finance* XXXV, no. 2, pp. 581–96.

Lewis, Karen. 2006. "Is the International Diversification Potential Diminishing? Foreign Equity Inside and Outside the U.S." NBER WP#12697.

Liang, Bing. 1999. "Price Pressure: Evidence from the 'Dartboard' Column." *Journal of Business* 72, no. 1, pp. 119–34.

Lo, Andrew. 2003. "Risk Management for Hedge Funds: Introduction and Overview." *Financial Analysts Journal* 57, no. 6, November/December 2001, pp. 16–33.

Loeys, Jan. 2004. "Have Hedge Funds Eroded Market Opportunities?" *JP Morgan Securities Ltd.,* October.

Longin, Francois, and Bruno Solnik. 2001. "Extreme Correlation of International Equity Markets." *Journal of Finance* LVI, pp. 649–75.

Lovell, Robert Jr. 1980. "The Strategic and Tactical Value of Commodity Futures." *Financial Analysts Journal,* May/June, pp. 19–21.

Malkiel, Burton, 2003. *A Random Walk Down Wall Street,* 8th ed. New York: W.W. Norton & Co.

Malkiel, Burton, and Atanu Saha. 2005. "Hedge Funds: Risk and Return." *Financial Analysts Journal* 61, no. 6 (November/December), pp. 80–88.

Mamaysky, Harry, and Matthew Speigel. 2002. "A Theory of Mutual Funds: Optimal Fund Objectives and Industry Organization." Yale School of Management working paper, January.

Markowitz, Harry. 1952. "Portfolio Selection." *The Journal of Finance* 7, no. 1, pp. 77–91.

Michaud, Richard. 1989. "The Markowitz Optimization Enigma: Is Optimized Optimal?" *Financial Analysts Journal* 45, no. 1, pp. 31–42.

Michaud, Richard. 1998. *Efficient Asset Management.* New York: Oxford University Press.

Miles, Mike, Rebel Cole, and David Guilkey. 1990. "A Different Look at Commercial Real Estate Returns." *AREUEA Journal,* Winter, pp. 403–30.

Modigliani, Leah, and Franco Modigliani. 1997. "Risk-Adjusted Performance: How to Measure It and Why." *Journal of Portfolio Management.* 23, no. 2, (Winter) pp. 45–54.

Mood, Alexander M., Franklin A. Graybill, and Duane C. Boes. 1974. *Introduction to the Theory of Statistics,* 3rd ed. New York: McGraw-Hill.

O'Barr, William, and John Conley. 1992. "Pension Fund Management: An Anthropological Study." *Financial Analysts Journal* 48, no. 5 (September/October), pp. 21–27.

O'Reilly, John P. Jr. 2002. "Ethics." Prepared for Boston University School of Management, April 30.

Odean, Terrance. 1998. "Are Investors Reluctant to Realize Their Losses?" *Journal of Finance* LIII, pp. 299–325.

Ojasalo, Jukka. 2001. "Managing Customer Expectations in Professional Services." *Managing Service Quality* 11, no. 3, pp. 200–12.

Passow, Alexander. 2005. "Omega Portfolio Construction with Johnson Distributions." *Risk,* pp. 85–90.

Pension & Investments. 2004. "Hedge Funds, Private Equity Blur Lines." September 6.

Pensions and Investments. 2008, December 22. SEI. 2008. "The Transformation of Wealth Management—Part I."

Piros, Christopher D. 1983. *Transactions Costs and Trading Uncertainty: Implications for Optimal Consumption and Portfolio Management.* PhD thesis, Harvard University.

Piros, Christopher D. 1998. "The Perfect Hedge: To Quanto or Not to Quanto." In *Currency Derivatives: Pricing Theory, Exotic Options, and Hedging Applications,* ed. David F. DeRosa. New York: John Wiley & Sons.

Piros, Christopher D. 2008. "Estimation Error Perturbation: Mean-Variance Optimization for Asset Allocation." Working Paper.

Private Equity Analyst. 2008. *Dow Jones Deal Journal,* November 7.

Quigley, John, and Susan Woodward. 2003. "An Index for Venture Capital." University of California–Berkeley: Institute for Business and Economic Research.

Reuters. 2009. "U.S. Top Court to Decide Case on Mutual Fund Fees." March 9.

Romer, David. 2006. "Do Firms Maximize? Evidence from Professional Football."*Journal of Political Economy* 114, no. 2.

Rosenberg, Barr. 1973. "Random Coefficients Model: The Analysis of a Cross Section of Time Series." *Annals of Economic and Social Measurement* 2, no. 4.

RREEF Research, Deutsche Bank Group. 2007. "The Future Size of the Global Real Estate Market." July.

Sacramento Bee. 2008. "CalPERS Board to Discuss Markets' Impact on the Fund." October 20.

Scherer, Bernd. 2002. "Portfolio Resampling: Review and Critique." *Financial Analysts Journal,* November/ December, pp. 98–109.

Schultz, E. 1996. "Workers Put Too Much in Their Employer's Stock." *The Wall Street Journal,* September 13, p. C1.

Securities and Exchange Commission. 1998. "Inspection Report."

Seigel, Jeremy. 2002. *Stocks for the Long Run: The Definitive Guide to Financial Market Returns and Long-Term Investment.* New York: McGraw-Hill.

Sharpe, William. 1966. "Mutual Fund Performance." *Journal of Business,* January, pp. 119–38.

Sharpe, William. 1967. "Capital Asset Prices: A Theory of Market Equilibrium under Conditions of Risk." *Journal of Finance* XIX, no. 3, pp. 425–42.

Sharpe, William. 1987. "Integrated Asset Allocation." *Financial Analysts Journal* 43, no. 5, pp. 25–32.

Sharpe, William. 1992. "Asset Allocation: Management Style and Performance Measurement." *Journal of Portfolio Management,* Winter, pp. 7–19.

Shefrin, Hersh, and Meir Statman. 1985. "The Disposition to Sell Winners Too Early and Ride Losers Too Long: Theory and Evidence." *Journal of Finance,* July, pp. 777–90.

Shefrin, Hersh, and Meir Statman. 1995. "Making Sense of Beta, Size, and Book-to-Market." *Journal of Portfolio Management* 21, no. 2, pp. 26–35.

Shiller, Robert. 1981. "Do Stock Prices Move Too Much to Be Justified by Subsequent Changes in Dividends?" *American Economic Review* 71 (June), pp. 421–36.

Siegel, Jeremy. 2005. "Perspectives on the Equity Risk Premium." *Financial Analysts Journal Perspectives,* pp. 202–17.

Smith, Peter. 2005. "Deals Highlight New Takeover Hierarchy." *Financial Times,* March 13.

Solnik, Bruno, Cyril Boucrelle, and Yann Le Fur. 1996. "International Market Correlation and Volatility." *Financial Analysts Journal,* September/October.

Sortino, F.A., and L.N. Price. 1994. "Performance Measurement in a Downside Risk Framework." *Journal of Investing* 3, pp. 50–58.

Standard and Poor's. 2006. "Report on Average Large-Cap Equity Mutual Fund PM Tenure."

State Street Corporation. 2006. "State Street Hedge Fund Study." State Street press release, March 29.

Statman, Meir. 1987. "How Many Stocks Make a Diversified Portfolio?" *Journal of Financial and Quantitative Analysis,* September.

Stattman, Dennis. 1980. "Book Value and Stock Returns." *The Chicago MBA: A Journal of Selected Papers* 4, pp. 25–45.

Stewart, John, and Scott Stewart. 2007. "The EMR Model." Project summary of Boston University and Lafayette College joint study, October.

Stewart, Scott, John Neumann, Christopher Knittel, and Jeffrey Heisler. 2009. "Absence of Value: Analysis of the Wealth Impact of Reallocation Decisions by Institutional Plan Sponsors." *Financial Analysts Journal,* 65, no. 6, pp. 34–51.

Stewart, Scott. 1985. "Price Adjustment on the NASDAQ Market." Presented at the Financial Management Association annual meeting, October.

Stewart, Scott. 1987. "Biases in Performance Measurement during Contributions." *Financial Review,* May.

Stewart, Scott. 1992. "A Solution to the Individual Investor's Savings Problem." Working paper, April.

Stewart, Scott. 1995. "The Advantage of High Yielding Equities for Taxable Corporate Investors." In *New Directions in Finance,* ed. D. Gosh and S. Khaksari. London: Routledge Publishing.

Stewart, Scott. 1998. "Is Consistency of Performance a Good Measure of Manager Skill?" *Journal of Portfolio Management,* Spring, pp. 22–32.

Stolz, William. 1989. *Startup: An Entrepreneur's Guide to Launching and Managing a New Venture.* Rochester, NY: Rock Beach Press.

Suri, Anil. 2005. "Introduction to Hedge Funds." Merrill Lynch Global Securities Research & Economics Group, RC#40417303, June.

T Rowe Price Group. 2005. Annual report.

Taleb, Nassim. 2001. *Fooled by Randomness: The Hidden Role of Chance in the Markets and in Life.* New York: Texere.

Taleb, Nassim. 2007. *The Black Swan.* New York: Random House.

The Kiplinger Letter. 2007. June.

The Spectrem Group. 2009. *Affluent Market Insights 2009.*

The VIP Forum. 1998. "Voice of the Millionaire, Volume I."

Theil, Henri. 1971. *Principles of Econometrics.* New York: Wiley.

Tiburon Research. 2005. "Consumer Wealth, Target Markets, and Marketing Strategies."

Trejos, Nancy. 2008. "House Passes Bill to Ease Pension Crunch for Retirees, Companies." *WashingtonPost.com,* December 11.

Treynor, Jack. 1965. "How to Rate Management of Investment Funds." *Harvard Business Review* 43, no. 1, pp. 63–75.

Treynor, Jack. 1971. "The Only Game in Town." *Financial Analysts Journal.*

Treynor, Jack. 1981. "What Does It Take to Win the Trading Game?" *Financial Analysts Journal,* January–February.

Treynor, Jack. 1990. "The Ten Most Important Questions to Ask in Selecting a Money Manager." *Financial Analysts Journal,* May/June, p. 4.

Tritsch, Shane. 1998. "Bull Marketing." *Chicago,* March.

Viceira, Luis. 2001. "Optimal Portfolio Choice for Long-Horizon Investors with Nontradeable Labor Income." *Journal of Finance* LVI, no. 2 (April).

Wagner, Wayne. 2000. "Measuring, Controlling, and Allocating Trading Costs." *AIMR Conference Proceedings—Ethical Issues for Today's Firm,* July, pp. 35–42.

Xu, Peter. 2008. "Why Have Estimate Revision Measures Not Worked in Recent Years?" *Journal of Portfolio Management* 34, no. 3 (Spring).

Zenker, Arnold. 1983. *Mastering the Public Spotlight.* Dodd Mead, January.

Zweig, Jason. 2007. "Your Money & Your Brain." New York: Simon & Schuster.

Index